Lecture Notes in Computer Science 4913

Commenced Publication in 1973
Founding and Former Series Editors:
Gerhard Goos, Juris Hartmanis, and Jan van Leeuwen

Roberto Verdone (Ed.)

Wireless
Sensor Networks

5th European Conference, EWSN 2008
Bologna, Italy, January 30-February 1, 2008
Proceedings

 Springer

Volume Editor

Roberto Verdone
WiLAB: DEIS, Università di Bologna
Via le Risorgimento, 2, 40136 Bologna, Italy
E-mail: roberto.verdone@unibo.it

Library of Congress Control Number: 2007943194

CR Subject Classification (1998): C.2.4, C.2, F.2, D.1.3, D.2, E.1, H.4, C.3

LNCS Sublibrary: SL 5 – Computer Communication Networks and
Telecommunications

ISSN   0302-9743
ISBN 978-3-540-77689-5 Springer Berlin Heidelberg New York

Springer is a part of Springer Science+Business Media

springer.com

© Springer-Verlag Berlin Heidelberg 2008

Typesetting: Camera-ready by author, data conversion by Scientific Publishing Services, Chennai, India
Printed on acid-free paper   SPIN: 12216154   06/3180   5 4 3 2 1 0

Preface

This volume contains the proceedings of EWSN 2008, the fifth European Conference on Wireless Sensor Networks, held in Bologna, Italy, during January 30–31 and February 1, 2008.

Its scope was the creation of a forum where researchers with different experience and background could discuss cross-layer approaches, novel solutions for specific problems and envisage the future development of wireless sensor networks (WSNs).

Out of the 110 papers that were submitted, 23 were selected after a double-blind peer-review process, leading to an acceptance rate of 21%. Six among the accepted papers included authors from North America, three from Asia, all others from Europe with the exception of one from Australia, and one from Brazil: the conference brought together researchers from almost all corners of the world!

Demonstration and poster papers were also presented at the conference, of which separate proceedings were produced, under the supervision of the other TPC Co-chair, Zach Shelby from Sensinode ltd, who managed the reviews of these papers.

The range of topics covered by this conference, including communication protocols, information processing, middleware, operating systems, hardware and field tests, is very wide. This made the vision of a coherent final technical programme more difficult, as few papers cover each of the various topics. But what made such a process even more challenging, is the intrinsic nature of WSNs, which is cross-layer and requires the joint consideration of many aspects when measuring or predicting the performance of a given algorithm, protocol, or technical solution.

As a result, unlike many other conferences and workshops dealing with communication and information technologies, the papers needed to be grouped according to considerations which cross the protocol stack through the various layers; therefore, we put together under the same umbrella and in the same conference session, papers dealing with separate aspects of the same problem.

For this reason this volume, which is organized according to the sequence of sessions proposed in the conference technical programme, does not include chapters devoted to routing, multiple access control, transmission techniques, operating systems. Rather, the papers are grouped according either to the vertical functionality (e.g., localization), the technology investigated (e.g., network coding), or the air interface standard (e.g., Zigbee), etc.

The volume presents a separate block of papers, the best ones, to attract the reader towards works that were judged as the most significant papers submitted to EWSN 2008.

Reading the papers reported in this volume, one very interesting fact emerges. The performance of the technical solutions provided is sometimes predicted through analytical models, or assessed through simulation approaches, as usual for a scientific conference; however, many papers report real measurements performed over test beds where the technical solution, the protocol, and the software developed have been implemented. The possibility offered by existing platforms to customize them and programme the nodes according to the desire of engineers and researchers was fully exploited in this conference, and many papers show performance improvements measured on true prototypes, and platforms.

The editor of this volume, who led the review process for the full papers submitted to the conference, is very thankful to the entire Technical Programme Committee and the external reviewers, the TPC Operational Manager, Chiara Buratti, who was the engine of this process, the Publication Chair, Virginia Corvino, who led the final steps towards this volume, and the Authors of the 110 papers submitted. A special thanks to the Steering Committee, who assisted me in the year before EWSN 2008 took place, in all strategic decisions.

January 2008   Roberto Verdone

Organization

EWSN 2008 was organized under the patronage of Alma Mater Studiorum - Università di Bologna, Italy.

General Co-chairs

Roberto Verdone
Fabio Luigi Bellifemine

Steering Committee

Holger Karl
Koen Langendoen
Roemer Kay Uwe
Thiemo Voigt
Adam Wolisz
Andreas Willig

Publicity Chairs

Paolo Bellavista
Vijay Raghunathan

Technical Programme Committee Co-chairs

Roberto Verdone
Zach Shelby

Technical Programme Committee Operational Manager

Chiara Buratti

Technical Programme Committee Members

Tarek Abdelzaher
Michael Beigl
Fabio Luigi Bellifemine
Jan Beutel
Luciano Bononi
Claudio Borean
Athanassios Boulis

Torsten Braun
Rebecca Braynard
Nirupama Bulusu
Srdjan Capkun
Mun Choon Chan
Julio Concha
Mischa Dohler
Romano Fantacci
Gianluigi Ferrari
Carlo Fischione
Lewis Girod
Cheng Guo
Takahiro Hara
Paul Havinga
Mike Hazas
Wendi Heinzelman
Holger Karl
Bhaskar Krishnamachari
Koen Langendoen
Chenyang Lu
Pedro J. Marron
Gianluca Mazzini
Daniele Miorandi
Amy L. Murphy
Sergio Palazzo
Giovanni Pau
Carlos Pomalaza-Ráez
Mirko Presser
Kay Römer
Christian Rohner
Antonio Ruzzelli
Fortunato Santucci
Andreas Savvides
Maurizio Spirito
John Stankovic
Erik Ström
Leandros Tassiulas
Thiemo Voigt
Klaus Wehrle
Dirk Westhoff
Andreas Willig
Adam Wolisz
Wei Ye
Michele Zorzi

Additional Reviewers

Henoc Agbota
Matthias Andree
Sanjeev Arulampalam
Aline Baggio
Paolo Bellavista
Luca Benini
Sangeeta Bhattacharya
Iacopo Carreras
Octav Chipara
Francesco Chiti
Andrea Conti
David Culler
Francesca Cuomo
Massimiliano D'Angelo
Davide Dardari
Francesco De Pellegrini
Brian Evans
Yu Gu
Gregory Hackmann

Gertjan Halkes
Peter Kootsookos
Sudha Krishnamurthy
Marco Martalò
Paolo Medagliani
Tom Parker
Mats Rydström
Enrica Salbaroli
Thomas Schoellhammer
Aline Senart
Thomas Staub
David Tacconi
Hwee-Xian Tan
Shourui Tian
Sameer Tilak
Qin Xin
Alberto Zanella
Mingze Zhang
Xin Zhang

Publication Chair

Virginia Corvino

Local Arrangements

Enrica Salbaroli
Irene Bortolotti
Silvia Zampese
Vanessa Grotti
Alessandra Marchi

Supporting Institutions: Corporate

Platinum Sponsor
Gold Sponsor
Silver Sponsor

Telecom Italia
Sensinode
SADEL
Thales Italia
X5T

Supporting Institutions: Academia

CNIT - Consorzio Nazionale Interuniversitario per le Telecomunicazioni
DEIS - Dipartimento di Elettronica Informatica e Sistemistica/Università di
Bologna

Table of Contents

Network Coding

Zigbee

Topology

Software

Deployment and Application Development

Clustering-Based Minimum Energy Wireless m-Connected k-Covered Sensor Networks

Habib M. Ammari and Sajal K. Das

Center for Research in Wireless Mobility and Networking (CReWMaN)
Department of Computer Science and Engineering
The University of Texas at Arlington, Arlington, TX 76019, USA
{ammari,das}@cse.uta.edu

Abstract. Duty-cycling is an appealing solution for energy savings in densely deployed, energy-constrained *wireless sensor networks* (WSNs). Indeed, several applications, such as intruder detection and tracking, require the design of k-covered WSNs, which are densely in nature and where each location in a monitored field is *covered* (or *sensed*) by at least k active sensors. With duty-cycling, sensors can be turned *on* or *off* according to a scheduling protocol, thus reducing the number of active sensors required to k-cover a field and helping all sensors deplete their energy slowly and uniformly. In this paper, we propose a duty-cycling framework, called *clustered randomized m-connected k-coverage* ($CRACC_{mk}$), for k-coverage of a sensor field. We present two protocols using $CRACC_{mk}$, namely T-$CRACC_{mk}$ and D-$CRACC_{mk}$, which differ by their degree of granularity of network clustering. We prove that the $CRACC_{mk}$ protocols are minimum energy m-connected k-coverage protocols in that each deploys a minimum number of active sensors to k-cover a sensor field and that k-coverage implies m-connectivity between all active sensors, with m being larger than k. We enhance the practicality of the $CRACC_{mk}$ protocols by relaxing some widely used assumptions for k-coverage. Simulation results show that the $CRACC_{mk}$ protocols outperform existing k-coverage protocols for WSNs.

Keywords: WSNs, Duty-cycling, Clustering, Coverage, Connectivity.

1 Introduction

Coverage and *connectivity* have been jointly addressed in *wireless sensor networks* (WSNs). While coverage is a metric that measures the quality of surveillance provided by a WSN, connectivity provides a means for *source sensors* (or simply *sources*) to report their sensed data to the *sink*. In particular, several real-world applications, such as intruder detection and tracking, require high degree of coverage. Hence, the first challenge is determining the number of active sensors required to achieve a certain degree of coverage requested by an application. Also, for such densely deployed WSNs, where sensors have limited battery power (or *energy*), the second challenge is designing an energy-efficient duty-cycling protocol that turns sensors *on* or *off* during the network operational lifetime. This mechanism helps sensors save energy and extend their lifetime.

R. Verdone (Ed.): EWSN 2008, LNCS 4913, pp. 1–16, 2008.

1.1 Motivations and Problem Statement

In this paper, we focus on m-connected k-coverage in highly dense deployed WSNs, where each location in a sensor field (SF) is *covered* (or *sensed*) by at least k active (or awake) sensors while maintaining m-connectivity between *all* active sensors. For some real-world applications, such as intruder detection and tracking, the design of this type of over-deployed WSN (i.e., m-connected k-covered WSNs) is necessary. Indeed, the limited energy of sensors and the difficulty of replacing and/or recharging their batteries in hostile environments require that sensors be deployed with high density [14] in order to extend the network lifetime. Also, to cope with the problem of sensor failures due to low energy and to achieve high data accuracy, redundant coverage is an effective solution. Moreover, connectivity between sources and sink should also be guaranteed so data originated from the former could reach the latter for further analysis. Thus, coverage and connectivity should be ensured for the correct operation of WSNs. Finally, for such densely and energy-constrained WSNs, it is important that sensors be duty-cycled to save energy. With duty-cycling, sensors are turned *on* or *off* according to a scheduling protocol, thus reducing the number of active sensors required for k-coverage so all sensors deplete their energy slowly and uniformly. Our study is motivated by three main questions:

1. What is a necessary and sufficient condition of the sensor spatial density for complete k-coverage of a SF?
2. What is a relationship between the sensing and communication ranges of sensors to k-cover a SF while ensuring m-connectivity between active sensors?
3. How can we design a duty-cycling protocol for densely deployed WSNs to k-cover a SF with a minimum number of active and m-connected sensors?

1.2 Contributions and Organization

The major contributions of this paper can be summarized as follows:

1. We compute the minimum sensor density required to k-cover a SF. We find that this density depends only on k and the sensing range of sensors.
2. We prove that all active sensors in a k-covered WSN are m-connected if the communication range of sensors is at least equal to their sensing range.
3. We propose a duty-cycling framework, called *clustered randomized m-connected k-coverage* (CRACC$_{mk}$), for k-coverage of a SF while ensuring m-connectivity between all active sensors. Then, we present two minimum-energy configuration protocols using CRACC$_{mk}$, namely T-CRACC$_{mk}$ and D-CRACC$_{mk}$, which differ by their degree of network clustering granularity. Then, we relax some widely used assumptions for coverage in WSNs to enhance the practicality of T-CRACC$_{mk}$ and D-CRACC$_{mk}$. Simulations show that D-CRACC$_{mk}$ outperforms other existing k-coverage protocols for WSNs.

The remainder of this paper is organized as follows. Section 2 presents some assumptions and definitions while Section 3 reviews related work. Section 4 discusses the CRACC$_{mk}$ framework for m-connected k-coverage in dense WSNs and Section 5 describes T-CRACC$_{mk}$ and D-CRACC$_{mk}$ protocols using CRACC$_{mk}$. Section 6 presents simulations of T-CRACC$_{mk}$ and D-CRACC$_{mk}$ while Section 7 concludes the paper.

2 Assumptions and Definitions

In this section, we present our assumptions and key definitions. Relaxation of some widely used assumptions in WSN coverage will be discussed in Section 5.

Assumption 1 (Static and location-aware WSN). *All sensors and a single sink are static and aware of their locations via some localization technique [7].*

Assumption 2 (Sensing and communication disk model). *The sensing range of a sensor s_i is a disk of radius r_i, centered at ξ_i (the location of s_i) and defined by the point set $SD(\xi_i, r_i) = \{\xi \in \mathrm{IR}^2 : |\xi_i - \xi| \le r_i\}$ (also called sensing disk of s_i), where $|\xi_i - \xi|$ is the Euclidean distance between ξ_i and ξ. Also, the communication range of a sensor s_i is a disk of radius R_i, centered at ξ_i and defined by the point set $CD(\xi_i, R_i) = \{\xi \in \mathrm{IR}^2 : |\xi_i - \xi| \le R_i\}$ (also called communication disk of s_i).*

Assumption 3 (Homogeneous sensors). *All sensors have the same sensing range and same communication range.*

Assumption 4 (Random and uniform deployment). *All sensors are randomly and uniformly deployed in a square sensor field.*

Definition 1 (Sensing neighbor set). *The sensing neighbor set of a sensor s_i, denoted by $SN(s_i)$, consists of all sensors in the sensing disk of s_i.*

Definition 2 (Communication neighbor set). *The communication neighbor set of a sensor s_i, denoted by $CN(s_i)$, is a set of all sensors located in the communication disk of s_i.*

Definition 3 (k-Coverage, m-connectivity, and degree of coverage). *A point p in a region A is said to be k-covered if it belongs to the intersection of sensing disks of at least k sensors. A region A is said to be k-covered if every point $p \in A$ is k-covered. A k-covered WSN is a WSN that k-cover a SF. We call degree of coverage provided by a WSN the maximum value of k such that a SF is k-covered. An m-connected WSN is a WSN in which each pair of sensors is connected by at least m paths.*

Definition 4 (Width of a closed convex area). *The width of closed convex area A is the maximum distance between parallel lines that bound A.*

Definition 5 (Largest enclosed disk). *The largest enclosed disk of a closed convex area A is a disk that lays inside A and whose diameter is equal to the minimum distance between any pair of points on A's boundary.*

3   Related Work

Adlakha and Srivastava [1] proposed an exposure-based model to find the sensor density required to achieve full coverage of a desired region based on the physical characteristics of sensors and the properties of the target. Bai et al. [3] proposed an optimal deployment strategy to achieve full coverage and 2-connectivity regardless of the relationship between R and r. Huang et al. [6] studied the relationship between sensing coverage and communication connectivity of WSNs and proposed distributed protocols to guarantee both coverage and connectivity of WSNs. Kumar et al. [8] showed that the minimum number of sensors needed to achieve k-coverage with high probability is approximately the same regardless of whether sensors are deployed deterministically or randomly, if sensors fail or sleep independently with equal probability. Lazos and Poovendran [9] formulated the coverage problem in heterogeneous WSNs as a set intersection problem and derived analytical expressions, which quantify the coverage achieved by stochastic coverage. Li et al. [10] proposed efficient distributed algorithms to optimally solve the best-coverage problem with the least energy consumption. Megerian et al. [12] proposed optimal polynomial time worst and average case algorithm for coverage calculation based on the Voronoi diagram and graph search algorithms. Shakkottai, et al. [13] gave necessary and sufficient conditions for 1-covered, 1-connected wireless sensor grid network. A variety of algorithms have been proposed to maintain connectivity and coverage in large WSNs. Xing et al. [16] proved that if the radius R of the communication range of sensors is at least double the radius r of their sensing range, the network is connected provided that coverage is guaranteed. They also proposed a k-coverage configuration protocol regardless of the relationship between R and r. Zhang and Hou [20] proposed a distributed algorithm, called *Optimal Geographical Density Control*, to keep a small number of active sensors in a WSN regardless of the relationship between sensing and communication ranges. Zhou et al. [21] discussed the problem of selecting a minimum size connected k-cover. They proposed a greedy algorithm to achieve k-coverage with a minimum set of connected sensors. Tian and Georganas [15] improved on the work in [16], [20] by proving that if the original network is connected and the identified active nodes can cover the same region as all the original nodes, then the network formed by the active nodes is connected when the communication range is at least twice the sensing range.

Although all these approaches on coverage and connectivity are promising, none of them provided an exact value on the minimum density of active sensors required to achieve k-coverage. Moreover, all of them were based on the claim that k-coverage implies k-connectivity when the radius of the communication disks of sensors is at least double the radius of their sensing disks [16]. Our work is complementary to these approaches in the two following ways: first, we compute the minimum sensor spatial density necessary for complete k-coverage of a sensor field. Second, we derive a tighter bound on network connectivity of k-covered WSNs, where the radius of the communication disks of sensors only needs to be at least equal to the radius of their sensing disks.

4   Our Framework for m-Connected k-Coverage

In this section, we first model the m-connected k-coverage problem in WSNs. Then, we present our duty-cycling framework, called *clustered randomized m-connected k-coverage* (CRACC$_{mk}$), to k-cover a SF while maintaining m-connectivity between all active sensors.

4.1 m-Connected k-Coverage Problem Modeling

Solving the m-connected k-coverage problem in WSNs requires finding a sensor deployment strategy such that each location in a SF is covered by at least k active sensors while ensuring m-connectivity between all active sensors at any time during the WSN operation. Our approach solution to the k-coverage problem in WSNs consists of decomposing it into two sub-problems, namely *sensor field slicing* and *sensor selection*, and solving them. The *sensor field slicing* problem is to slice a SF into small regions of particular shape (which will be defined later), each of which is guaranteed to be k-covered provided that at least k sensors are randomly deployed in it. The *sensor selection* problem is to select a minimum subset of sensors to remain active such that each location in a SF is guaranteed to be k-covered. Thus, our solution to the k-coverage problem is to find out how to achieve at least k-coverage of a SF and select an appropriate subset of active sensors so that each location in a SF is k-covered. Besides selecting a *minimum* number of active sensors, for energy efficiency, all selected sensors should have the *maximum* remaining energy. Hence, the m-connected k-coverage problem that we deal with is called *min-max m-connected k-coverage* and is described as follows:

Problem: *min-max m-connected k-coverage*
Instance: A SF, a set S of sensors, and a positive integer k.
Question: Select a minimum subset $S_{\min} \subset S$ of sensors such that each location in CF is k-covered, the network induced by all sensors in $S_{\min}$ is m-connected, and $\sum_{s_i \in S_{\min}} E_{\mathrm{rem}}(s_i)$ is maximized.

The problem of selecting a minimum subset of sensors to remain active for k-coverage of a sensor field is NP-hard [21], and so is *min-max m-connected k-coverage*. Hence, we propose efficient approximation algorithms to solve it.

4.2   Network Slicing-Based m-Connected k-Coverage

This section provides our solution to the sensor field slicing problem, where all sensors have the same sensing and communication disks whose radii are r and R, respectively. First, we provide a characterization of k-coverage of a SF. To this end, we need to compute the maximum size of a convex area A that is guaranteed to be k-covered when exactly k sensors are deployed in it. Lemma 1 gives an upper bound on the width of such a k-covered area.

Lemma 1. *Let r be the radius of the sensing disk of sensors and $k \geq 3$. A convex area A is guaranteed to be k-covered when k homogeneous sensors are deployed in it, if the width of A does not exceed r.*

Proof. Each point $p \in A$ is k-covered if $|\xi_i - p| \leq r$, for all $1 \leq i \leq k$. In particular, this should be true for the locations of sensors. Thus, for any pair of sensors s_i and s_j covering A the maximum distance between s_i and s_j is r so that any location in A is covered by k sensors. Otherwise, there must be a pair of sensors s_i and s_j such that $|\xi_i - \xi_j| > r$, meaning that the locations of the two sensors are not being covered by both sensors at the same time. This contradicts the hypothesis that all $p \in A$, including the locations of sensors, are k-covered by all sensors s_l, for all $1 \leq l \leq k$, and in particular s_i and s_j. Thus, the width of region A cannot exceed r.

Lemma 2 (instance of Helly's Theorem [4]) will help us compute the minimum sensor spatial density required to guarantee k-coverage of a SF. More specifically, this lemma together with a nice geometric structure, called *Reuleaux triangle* [23], will be used to characterize k-covered WSN, i.e., how a WSN can guarantee k-coverage of a SF.

Lemma 2. *The intersection of k sensing disks is not empty if and only if the intersection of any three of those k sensing disks is not empty, where $k \geq 3$.*

Theorem 1, which exploits the results of Lemma 1 and Lemma 2, computes the minimum sensor spatial density necessary for complete k-coverage of a SF.

Theorem 1. *Let $k \geq 3$. The minimum sensor spatial density required to guarantee k-coverage of a SF is computed as $\lambda(r, k) = \frac{2k}{(\pi - \sqrt{3}) r^2}$, where r is the radius of the sensing disks of sensors.*

Proof. First, we compute the maximum area that is guaranteed to be k-covered provided that k sensors are deployed in it. Let A be the intersection area of the

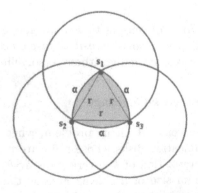

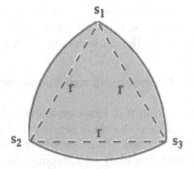

Fig. 1. Intersection of three disks   **Fig. 2.** Reuleaux triangle

sensing disks of k sensors. From Lemma 1, it is clear that the width of A should be upper-bounded by r so that any location in A is k-covered by these k sensors. Using the Venn diagram given in Figure 1, the maximum size of the intersection of the sensing disks of sensors s_1, s_2, and s_3, called *Reuleaux triangle* [23] and denoted by $RT(r)$, is obtained when s_1, s_2, and s_3, are symmetrically located from each other so that the distance between any pair of sensors is equal to r (Figure 2). We refer to this model as the *Reuleaux Triangle* model. As can be seen from Figure 1, a WSN is connected if each active sensor senses the location of at least another active sensor. Thus, the maximum size of A denoted by $A_{max}(r)$ is upper-bounded by the area of $RT(r)$, which is given by $A_{max}(r) = A_1 + 3A_2$, where $A_1 = \sqrt{3}\, r^2/4$ is the area of the central equilateral triangle of side r and $A_2 = (\pi/6 - \sqrt{3}/4)\, r^2$ is the area of each of the three curved regions α. Hence, to achieve k-coverage of a SF, k sensors should be deployed in an $RT(r)$ area. Thus, the *minimum sensor spatial density* that guarantees k-coverage of SF is equal to $\lambda(r, k) = k/A_{max}(r) = 2\, k/(\pi - \sqrt{3})\, r^2$.

Notice that $\lambda(r, k)$ depends only on r and k, and decreases as r increases, thus reflecting the expected behavior. Adlakha and Srivastava [1] also showed that the number of sensors required to cover an area of size A is in the order of O $(A/\hat{r}^2_2)$, where $\hat{r}_2$ is a good estimate of the radius r of the sensing disk of sensors. Specifically, r lies between $\hat{r}_1$ and $\hat{r}_2$, where $\hat{r}_1$ overestimates the number of sensors required to cover A, while $\hat{r}_2$ underestimates it.

Theorem 2, which follows from Theorem 1, states a necessary and sufficient condition for complete k-coverage of a SF.

Theorem 2. *Let $k \geq 3$. A SF is guaranteed to be k-covered if and only if any Reuleaux triangle region in the SF contains at least k active sensors.*

Theorem 3, which follows from the proof of Theorem 1, states that k-coverage implies connectivity only if $R \geq r$.

Theorem 3. *Let $k \geq 3$. A k-covered WSN is guaranteed to be connected if the radius R of the communication range of sensors is at least equal to the radius r of their sensing range, i.e., $R \geq r$.*

Theorem 4 computes the network connectivity of k-covered WSNs.

Theorem 4. *Assume a uniformly random distribution of sensor in a square sensor field and let r and R be the radii of the sensing and communication disks of sensors, respectively, $\alpha = R/r$ and $k \geq 3$. The connectivity m of a k-covered WSN is given by $m = \pi\, \alpha^2\, k/2\, (\pi - \sqrt{3})$.*

Proof. Consider a *boundary sensor* s_b (i.e., sensor located at one corner of a square field that has the least communication neighbor set). Although it has been proved that the optimum location of the sink in terms of energy-efficient data gathering is the center of the field [11], the sink could be located anywhere in the field. Thus, s_b can be either a sensor or the sink itself. Following the same approach used by Xing et al. [16], sensor s_b can be isolated by removing all of its communication neighbors. In other words, at least $\lambda(r, k) \times \pi R^2/4$ sensors should be removed. Thus, the network connectivity of k-covered WSNs is equal to $m = \pi \alpha^2 k/2 (\pi - \sqrt{3})$.

Given that $\alpha = R/r \geq 1$, it is easy to check that $m \geq 1.11k > k$. However, Xing et al. proved in [16] that the connectivity of k-covered WSNs is equal to k provided that $R \geq 2r$. Moreover, Xing et al. [16] assumed in their analysis that there are k coinciding sensors at some location. Our measure of network connectivity of k-covered WSNs, however, is based on the minimum sensor spatial density necessary for complete k-coverage of a SF. Thus, our network connectivity measure is more realistic and tighter. Furthermore, we only require that $R \geq r$ for a k-covered WSN to be m-connected, where $m \geq 1.11k$. It is worth noting that m-connectivity implies m disjoint paths between any pair of sensors although the proof of Theorem 4 considers the number of communication neighbors a sensor has. Indeed, under the assumption of uniform sensor distribution, each sensor has at least m communication neighbors, where $m \geq 1.11k$ since $R \geq r$.

Previous Work on k-Coverage Characterization. According to [16] ([20], respectively), a SF is k-covered if all *intersection points* (*crossing points*, respectively) between the boundaries of sensing disks of sensors and all the *intersection points* between the boundaries of sensing disks of sensors and the boundary of a SF are k-covered. This is a generalization of the result for 1-coverage [5]. Hence, if two sensing disks intersect, at least one more sensing disk needs to cover their intersection/crossing point. In case of 1-coverage, a location that coincides with an intersection/crossing point would be 3-covered instead of 1-covered. Thus, both approaches [16], [20] require more than enough sensors to k-cover a SF. In addition to characterizing k-coverage, our approach *quantifies* the minimum sensor density $\lambda(r, k)$ required to k-cover a SF.

Slicing Approach. Let SF be a square sensor field and $k \geq 3$. Based on the minimum sensor spatial density $\lambda(r, k)$, it is easy to check whether a given WSN can k-cover SF. For this purpose, we propose a *slicing* scheme of CF by dividing it into overlapping Reuleaux triangles of width r, called *slices*, such that two adjacent slices intersect in a region shaped as a *lens* (also known as the *fish bladder*) as shown in Figure 3. This implies that SF is sliced into regular triangles of side r. The result of this slicing operation is called *slicing grid*. Figure 4 shows a slicing grid of SF.

4.3 Impact of Network Slicing on Sensor Selection

Slicing a WSN can be *static* or *dynamic*. Next, we show the problems caused by a static slicing approach and propose a dynamic one as a remedy to the former.

Static Network Slicing. Our sensor selection scheme exploits the overlap between adjacent slices to select a minimum number of active sensors in each round for complete k-coverage of a SF. As can be seen from Figure 3, sensors

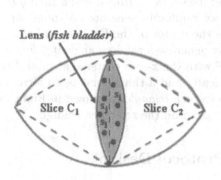 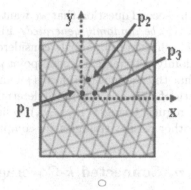

Fig. 3. Intersection of adjacent slices   **Fig. 4.** Random slicing grid of a field

located in the lens of two adjacent slices participate in the k-coverage of the area associated with the union of these two slices. Lemma 3 states this result.

Lemma 3. *Sensors located in a lens participate to k-cover its adjacent slices.*

Notice that each slice overlaps with at most three others. By Lemma 3, sensors located in the three lenses of a given slice should be selected first in each round. This process is repeated until all slices in a SF are k-covered. We assume that each slice has a unique *id*.

The sensor selection scheme described earlier generates only one subset of active sensors to k-cover a SF. If this scheme is executed in each round on the same slicing grid, such as the one given in Figure 4, sensors located in the lenses would suffer from a severe energy depletion problem. Thus, it would be more efficient if in each round a different subset of sensors is selected for k-coverage of a SF. Next, we describe a strategy based on dynamic network slicing in order to achieve this goal.

Dynamic Network Slicing. Our goal is to select different subsets of sensors S_i, $i \geq 1$ such that each subset S_i is selected to remain active in the ith round to k-cover a SF. Notice that in order to achieve a better load balancing among the sensors, we could add a restriction that the selected subsets are mutually disjoint. However, the disjointness constraint yields a small number of mutually disjoint subsets of sensors. Thus, we only require that those selected subsets of sensors be *partially disjoint*.

The first question that we want to address now is: *How would partially disjoint minimum subsets of sensors be selected to k-cover a SF?* To address this question, we consider the *dynamics of slicing grid* from one round to another. Since our scheme for selecting active sensors highly prioritizes the ones located in the lenses of all slices, it is important that those lenses be able to scan the entire SF, and hence include distinct subsets of sensors in different rounds. Thus, the slicing grid undergoes some dynamics to achieve balanced load among sensors during the operation of T-CRACC$_{mk}$ and D-CRACC$_{mk}$.

The second question that we want to address now is: *How would a slicing grid of a SF be randomly generated?* First, we randomly generate one point p_1 in a *SF*, which is temporarily considered as the center of the Euclidean plane. To randomly determine a second point p_2, we generate a random angle $0 \leq \theta \leq 2\pi$ so that the segment $\overline{p_1 p_2}$ forms an angle θ with the x-axis centered at p_1 and the length of $\overline{p_1 p_2}$ is r. Then, we deterministically find a third point p_3 to form the first regular triangle (p_1, p_2, p_3), called *reference triangle*, as shown in Figure 4. All other regular triangles are computed based on the reference triangle.

5 m-Connected k-Coverage Protocol Design

In this section, we describe our T-CRACC$_{mk}$ and D-CRACC$_{mk}$ protocols for m-connected k-coverage in WSNs based on their network clustering granularity. Then, we relax some widely used assumptions to enhance their practicality.

In general, the sink is connected to an infinite source of energy, such as a wall outlet, and thus has no energy constraint. In both T-CRACC$_{mk}$ and D-CRACC$_{mk}$, the sink is responsible for randomly generating a slicing grid of a *SF* and selecting a cluster-head for each cluster in each round. Each cluster-head is physically located within its cluster and is in charge of selecting some of its sensing neighbors to k-cover it. To this end, the sink should be aware of all sensors' locations. Moreover, we do not assume any strict ordering of the cluster-heads that determines the order in which cluster-heads select their active sensors. However, neighboring cluster-heads need to coordinate between themselves through message exchanges in order to select a minimum number of sensors to k-cover their clusters. The slicing grid generation and cluster-head selection could be assigned to each sensor in a *round-robin* fashion. However, this solution would be costly for sensors in terms of energy and space.

5.1   The T-CRACC$_{mk}$ Protocol

In T-CRACC$_{mk}$, a cluster is a *slice* ("T" for Reuleaux *triangle*) in a slicing grid and a cluster-head is called *slice-head*. Given that each slice has at most three adjacent slices (Figure 5), the T-CRACC$_{mk}$ protocol requires that each slice-head coordinates its activity with its adjacent slice-heads in order to select a minimum total number of sensors to k-cover a *SF*. Figure 5 shows slice-head sh_0 sharing three lenses with slice-heads sh_1, sh_2, and sh_3. For instance, sh_0 could k-cover its slice by selecting sensors located in its three lenses. Then, it communicates the numbers n_1, n_2, and n_3 of sensors selected from lenses *Lens 1*, *Lens 2*, and *Lens 3*, respectively, to its adjacent slice-heads sh_1, sh_2, and sh_3, respectively. Slice-head sh_1 would need to select $k - n_1$ more sensors from its lenses to k-cover its slice. It would definitely coordinate with its adjacent slice-heads to k-cover its slice and so does each slice-head. Theorem 5 states that T-CRACC$_{mk}$ is a minimum-energy protocol.

Theorem 5. *T-CRACC$_{mk}$ is a minimum energy-consuming protocol.*

Proof. Each slice-head ensures that each slice of a SF is k-covered by exactly k sensors. Thus, by Theorem 2, T-CRACC$_{mk}$ guarantees that a SF is k-covered with a minimum number of active sensors, and hence consumes a minimum amount of energy in each round.

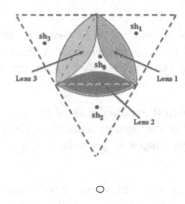
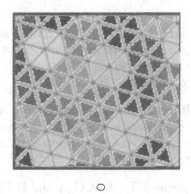

Fig. 5. Slice-heads for T-CRACC$_{mk}$ **Fig. 6.** Clustering for D-CRACC$_{mk}$

5.2   The D-CRACC$_{mk}$ Protocol

D-CRACC$_{mk}$ ("D" for *disk*) has higher network clustering granularity than T-CRACC$_{mk}$. Precisely, each cluster consists of six adjacent slices forming a *disk* (Figure 6). In each round, the sink selects for each cluster a sensor, called *disk-head*, which is located nearer the center of its disk to k-cover it. Similarly, each disk-head needs to coordinate with at most six adjacent disk-heads to k-cover its disk with a minimum number of sensors. Each disk-head manages at most six *interior lenses* (i.e., lenses between adjacent slices of the same disk) and at most six *boundary lenses* (i.e., lenses between adjacent slices of two adjacent disks). Hence, a disk-head should select sensors from its interior lenses with no coordination with other disk-heads but should coordinate with its adjacent disk-heads to select sensors from its boundary lenses. Theorem 6, which is similar to Theorem 5, states that D-CRACC$_{mk}$ is a minimum-energy protocol.

Theorem 6. *D-CRACC$_{mk}$ is a minimum energy-consuming protocol.*

5.3   Promoting T-CRACC$_{mk}$ and D-CRACC$_{mk}$

In this section, we relax the sensing and communication disk (*Assumption 2*) and homogeneous sensor (*Assumption 3*) models. Our goal is to promote the use of T-CRACC$_{mk}$ and D-CRACC$_{mk}$ in real-world scenarios.

Relaxing the Unit Sensing and Communication Disk Models. Zhou et al. [22] found that the communication range of radios is highly probabilistic and irregular. In this section, for tractability of the problem, we consider convex sensing and communication models, where sensors have the same sensing and communication ranges, which are convex but not necessarily circular.

The following results correspond to Lemma 1 and Theorem 1, respectively. Their proof is literally the same as that in Section 4.2 by using the notion of largest enclosed disk of the sensing ranges of sensors instead of their sensing disk.

Corollary 1. *Let $k \geq 3$. A convex area A is guaranteed to be k-covered when exactly k homogeneous sensors are deployed in it, if the width of A does not exceed r_{led}, where r_{led} is the radius of the largest enclosed disk of the sensing range of sensors.*

Corollary 2. *Let r_{led} be the radius of the largest enclosed disk of the sensing range of sensors and $k \geq 3$. The minimum sensor spatial density required to k-cover a SF by homogeneous convex sensing ranges is given by $\lambda(r_{\text{led}}, k) = 2\,k/(\pi-\sqrt{3})\,r_{\text{led}}^2$.*

To implement T-CRACC$_{mk}$ and D-CRACC$_{mk}$ with the above convex models, the sink should slice a SF into triangles of side r_{led}. Assumption 2 can thus be relaxed using the largest enclosed disk of the sensing ranges of sensors. It is worth noting that even if the sensing and communication ranges of sensors do not have the same convex shape, our results about coverage implying connectivity still hold as long as the communication range of sensors is larger than their sensing range, i.e., the sensing range is entirely included in the communication range. This assumption is realistic and conforming to previous work [20] reporting that the communication range of Berkeley motes is much higher than the sensing range of several typical sensors.

Relaxing the Homogeneous Sensor Model. Real-world applications may require heterogeneous sensors in terms of sensing and communication capabilities in order to enhance network reliability and extend its lifetime [18]. In this section, we consider heterogeneous sensors with different yet convex sensing and communication ranges.

The following results correspond to Lemmae 1 and 2, and Theorem 1, respectively. They can be proved using the concept of largest enclosed disk instead of sensing disk.

Corollary 3. *Let $k \geq 3$. A convex area A is guaranteed to be k-covered when exactly k heterogeneous sensors whose sensing ranges are convex but not necessarily circular are deployed in it, if the width of A does not exceed $r_{led}^{\min}$, where $r_{led}^{\min}$ is the smallest radius of the largest enclosed disks of the sensing ranges of sensors.*

Corollary 4. *Let $k \geq 3$. The intersection of k heterogeneous convex sensing ranges is not empty if and only if the intersection of any smallest three largest enclosed disks of these k heterogeneous convex sensing ranges is not empty.*

Corollary 5. *The minimum sensor spatial density required to k-cover a SF by heterogeneous sensors whose sensing ranges are convex but not circular is given by $\lambda(r_{led}^{min}, k) = 2\,k \big/ (\pi - \sqrt{3})\,r_{led}^{min^2}$, where r_{led}^{min} is the minimum radius of the largest enclosed disks of the sensing ranges of heterogeneous sensors and $k \geq 3$.*

In this case, the sink slices a SF into regular triangles of side r_{led}^{min} and applies the same processing as in Section 4.2. Therefore, the assumption of homogeneous sensors can also be relaxed with slight updates to T-CRACC$_{mk}$ and D-CRACC$_{mk}$. Notice that while these corollaries hold, they may greatly overestimate the sensor spatial density required for guaranteeing full k-coverage of a sensor field. For instance, even if a single sensor with a very small sensing range is deployed, the entire network would be required to have a large sensor spatial density. In this case, it is important that the CRACC$_{mk}$ protocols adapt the sensor spatial density to the sensing ranges of sensors in the area. Due to space limitations, we will address this issue in our future work.

6 Performance Evaluation

In this section, we present the simulation results of T-CRACC$_{mk}$ and C-CRACC$_{mk}$ using a high-level simulator written in the C programming language. We consider a square field of side length 1000 m. We use the energy model given in [19], where the sensor energy consumption in transmission, reception, idle, and sleep modes are 60 mW, 12 mW, 12 mW, and 0.03 mW, respectively. Following [20], *one unit of energy* is defined as the energy necessary for a sensor to stay idle for 1 second. We assume that the initial energy of each sensor is 60 Joules enabling a sensor to operate about 5000 seconds in reception/idle modes [19]. All simulations are repeated 20 times and the results are averaged.

Figure 7 plots $\lambda(r, k)$ versus k, where $r = 30$ m. Figure 8 plots $\lambda(r, k)$ versus the r, where $k = 3$. We observe a perfect match between simulation and analytical results in both experiments. As expected, $\lambda(r, k)$ decreases with r for a fixed k, and increases with k for a fixed r. As can be observed from Figures 7 and 8,

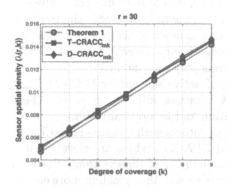

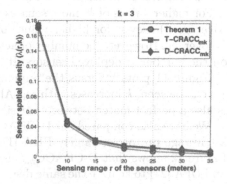

Fig. 7. $\lambda(r, k)$ vs. k **Fig. 8.** $\lambda(r, k)$ vs. r

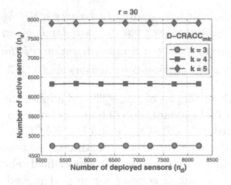

Fig. 9. n_a vs. n_d while varying k

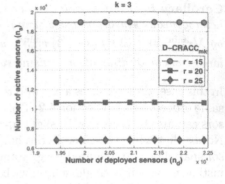

Fig. 10. n_a vs. n_d while varying r

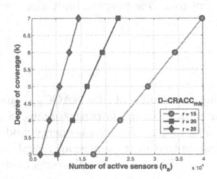

Fig. 11. k vs. n_a

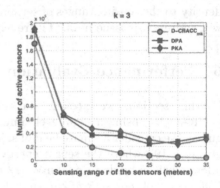

Fig. 12. Performance comparison

both T-CRACC$_{mk}$ and D-CRACC$_{mk}$ require the same number of active sensors. From now on, we focus only on the performance of D-CRACC$_{mk}$ protocol.

Figures 9 and 10 show the number of active sensors versus the total number of deployed sensors in the field for the D-CRACC$_{mk}$ protocol. In Figure 9, we consider different values of k, while in Figure 10, we consider different values of r. For higher values of k, more sensors need to be active to achieve the required coverage. However, for higher values of r, less number of sensors is needed for k-coverage. However, the number of active sensors for a given k does not depend on the number of deployed sensors. It depends only on k and r.

Figure 11 plots k versus the number n_a of active sensors for D-CRACC$_{mk}$. As can be seen, k increases with n_a. Also, k increases with r for fixed n_a. There is also a perfect match between our simulation and theoretical results.

We have also compared our D-CRACC$_{mk}$ protocol with two other distributed k-coverage protocols, namely PKA [17] and DPA [21], which are close to ours. Figure 12 shows that D-CRACC$_{mk}$ uses less number of sensors than PKA [17] and DPA [21] to achieve the same degree k of coverage, thus yielding more energy savings.

7 Conclusion

We have addressed the problem of energy-efficient m-connected k-coverage configuration in WSNs. We have characterized k-coverage in WSNs based on the intersection of sensing disks of k sensors. We have also computed the minimum sensor spatial density required to k-cover a SF. We have proved that k-coverage of a SF implies m-connectivity with $m \geq 1.11k$ when the radius R of the communication disks of sensors is at least equal to the radius r of their sensing disks, i.e., $R \geq r$. Since it is based on the minimum sensor density necessary to achieve full k-coverage of a sensor field, our bound on connectivity of k-covered WSNs is tighter than the one provided by Xing et al. [16] and adopted by all subsequent approaches for coverage and connectivity in WSNs. We have proposed two minimum energy-consuming protocols, called T-CRACC$_{mk}$ and D-CRACC$_{mk}$, for complete k-coverage of a SF while all active sensors remain m-connected. Finally, we have extended our analysis by relaxing several assumptions to promote the use of our CRACC$_{mk}$ protocols in real scenarios. Simulation results have showed perfect match with our theoretical ones and that our CRACC$_{mk}$ protocols outperform other existing k-coverage protocols.

Our future work is four-fold. First, we plan to conduct more simulations to compare our protocols with existing ones with respect to energy savings. Second, we also plan to extend T-CRACC$_{mk}$ and D-CRACC$_{mk}$ to three-dimensional (3D) WSNs. For instance, underwater WSNs [2] require design in 3D rather than 2D space. Third, we focus on joint m-connected k-coverage and routing in WSNs. Indeed, most of the routing protocols for WSNs assume that *all* sensors are always *on* during data forwarding. This assumption, however, is not valid in real-world scenarios, where sensors are turned *on* or *off* to save energy. Fourth, we intend to study m-connected k-coverage in WSNs using stochastic models of sensing and communication ranges, and considering shadowing.

Acknowledgments. The authors would like to thank the anonymous reviewers for their careful reading and helpful comments, which have helped improve this paper greatly. This work is partially supported by grants from the NSF under award numbers IIS-0326505 and CNS-0721951, and a grant from Texas ARP under award number 14-748779.

References

1. Adlakha, S., Srivastava, M.: Critical Density Threshold for Coverage in Wireless Sensor Networks. In: Proc. IEEE WCNC, pp. 1615–1620 (2003)
2. Akyildiz, I.F., Pompili, D., Melodia, T.: Underwater Acoustic Sensor Networks: research Challenges. Ad Hoc Networks 3, 257–279 (2005)
3. Bai, X., Kumar, S., Xuan, D., Yun, Z., Lai, T.H.: Deploying Wireless Sensors to Achieve Both Coverage and Connectivity. In: Proc. ACM MobiHoc, pp. 131–142 (2006)
4. Bollobás, B.: The Art of Mathematics: Coffee Time in Memphis. Cambridge University Press, Cambridge (2006)

5. Hall, P.: Introduction to the Theory of Coverage Processes. John Wiley, Chichester (1988)
6. Huang, C., Tseng, Y., Wu, H.: Distributed Protocols for Ensuring Both Coverage and Connectivity of a Wireless Sensor Network. ACM TOSN 3(1), 1–24 (2007)
7. Ji, X., Zha, H.: Sensor Positioning in Wireless Ad-hoc Sensor Networks Using Multidimensional Scaling. In: Proc. IEEE Infocom, pp. 2652–2661 (2004)
8. Kumar, S., Lai, T., Balogh, J.: On k-Coverage in a Mostly Sleeping Sensor Network. In: Proc. ACM MobiCom, pp. 144–158 (2004)
9. Lazos, L., Poovendran, R.: Stochastic Coverage in Heterogeneous Sensor Networks. ACM TOSN 2(3), 325–358 (2006)
10. Li, X., Wan, P., Frieder, O.: Coverage in Wireless Ad-Hoc Sensor Networks. IEEE TC 52, 753–763 (2003)
11. Luo, J., Hubaux, J.-P.: Joint Mobility and Routing for Lifetime Elongation in Wireless Sensor Networks. In: Proc. IEEE Infocom, pp. 1735–1746 (2005)
12. Megerian, S., Koushanfar, F., Potkonjak, M., Srivastava, M.: Worst and Best-Case Coverage in Sensor Networks. IEEE TMC 4(1), 84–92 (2005)
13. Shakkottai, S., Srikant, R., Shroff, N.: Unreliable Sensor Grids: Coverage, Connectivity and Diameter. Ad Hoc Networks 3(6), 702–716 (2005)
14. Shih, E., Cho, S.-H., Ickes, N., Min, R., Sinha, A., Wang, A., Chandrakasan, A.: Physical Layer Driven Protocol and Algorithm Design for Energy-efficient Wireless Sensor Networks. In: Proc. ACM MobiCom, pp. 272–287 (2001)
15. Tian, D., Georganas, N.: Connectivity Maintenance and Coverage Preservation in Wireless Sensor Networks. Ad Hoc Networks 3, 744–761 (2005)
16. Xing, G., Wang, X., Zhang, Y., Lu, C., Pless, R., Gill, C.: Integrated Coverage and Connectivity Configuration for Energy Conservation in Sensor Networks. ACM TOSN 1(1), 36–72 (2005)
17. Yang, S., Dai, F., Cardei, M., Wu, J.: On Connected Multiple Point Coverage in Wireless Sensor Networks. International Journal of Wireless Information Networks 13(4), 289–301 (2006)
18. Yarvis, M., Kushalnagar, N., Singh, H., Rangarajan, A., Liu, Y., Singh, S.: Exploiting Heterogeneity in Sensor Networks. In: Proc. IEEE Infocom, pp. 878–890 (2005)
19. Ye, F., Zhong, G., Cheng, J., Lu, S., Zhang, L.: PEAS: A Robust Energy Conserving Protocol for Long-Lived Sensor Networks. In: Proc. ICDCS, pp. 1–10 (2003)
20. Zhang, H., Hou, J.: Maintaining Sensing Coverage and Connectivity in Large Sensor Networks. Ad Hoc & Sensor Wireless Networks 1(1–2), 89–124 (2005)
21. Zhou, Z., Das, S., Gupta, H.: Connected k-Coverage Problem in Sensor Networks. In: Proc. ICCCN, pp. 373–378 (2004)
22. Zhou, G., He, T., Krishnamurthy, S., Stankovic, J.: Impact of Radio Irregularity on Wireless Sensor Networks. In: Proc. MobiSys, pp. 125–138 (2004)
23. http://mathworld.wolfram.com/ReuleauxTriangle.html

Activity Recognition from On-Body Sensors: Accuracy-Power Trade-Off by Dynamic Sensor Selection

Piero Zappi[1], Clemens Lombriser[2], Thomas Stiefmeier[2], Elisabetta Farella[1], Daniel Roggen[2], Luca Benini[1], and Gerhard Tröster[2]

[1] Department of Electronic Informatic and System,
University of Bologna, Italy
{pzappi,efarella,lbenini}@deis.unibo.it
www.micrel.deis.unibo.it
[2] Wearable Computing Lab., ETH Zürich, Switzerland
{lombriser,stiefmeier,droggen,troster}@ife.ee.ethz.ch
www.wearable.ethz.ch

Abstract. Activity recognition from an on-body sensor network enables context-aware applications in wearable computing. A guaranteed classification accuracy is desirable while optimizing power consumption to ensure the system's wearability. In this paper, we investigate the benefits of dynamic sensor selection in order to use efficiently available energy while achieving a desired activity recognition accuracy. For this purpose we introduce and characterize an activity recognition method with an underlying run-time sensor selection scheme. The system relies on a meta-classifier that fuses the information of classifiers operating on individual sensors. Sensors are selected according to their contribution to classification accuracy as assessed during system training. We test this system by recognizing manipulative activities of assembly-line workers in a car production environment. Results show that the system's lifetime can be significantly extended while keeping high recognition accuracies. We discuss how this approach can be implemented in a dynamic sensor network by using the context-recognition framework *Titan* that we are developing for dynamic and heterogeneous sensor networks.

1 Introduction

Wearable computing aims at supporting people by delivering context-aware services [1]. Gestures and activities are an important aspect of the user's context. Ideally they are detected from unobtrusive wearable sensors. Gesture recognition has applications in human computer interfaces [2], or in the support of impaired people [3]. Developments in microelectronics and wireless communication enable the design of small and low-power wireless sensors nodes [4]. Although these nodes have limited memory and computational power, and may have robustness or accuracy limitations [5,6], unobtrusive context sensing can be achieved by integrating them in garments [7,8] or accessories [9].

R. Verdone (Ed.): EWSN 2008, LNCS 4913, pp. 17–33, 2008.
© Springer-Verlag Berlin Heidelberg 2008

In an activity recognition system, high classification accuracy is usually desired. This implies the use of a large number of sensors distributed over the body, depending on the activities to detect. At the same time a wearable system must be unobtrusive and operate during long periods of time. This implies minimizing sensor size, and especially energy consumption since battery technology tends to be a limiting factor in miniaturization [10].

Energy use may be reduced by improved wireless protocols [11,12], careful hardware selection [13], or duty cycling to keep the hardware in a low-power state most of the time [14]. Energy harvesting techniques may also complement battery power [15], although the unpredictability of energy supply typical of harvesting makes it difficult to manage duty cycling schedules [16].

Activity recognition requires fixed sensor sampling rate and continuous sensor node operation, since user gestures can occur at any time and maximum classification accuracy is desired. Therefore adaptive sampling rate and unpredictable duty cycling can not be used to minimize energy use. Current approaches typically rely on a small, fixed number of sensors with characteristics known and constant over time [17]. Once one sensor runs out of energy the system is not able to achieve its objective and maintenance is needed.

Here we investigate how to extend network life in an activity recognition system, while maintaining a desired accuracy, by capitalizing on an redundant number of small (possibly unreilable) sensors placed randomly over the user arms. We introduce an activity recognition system with a metaclassifier-based sensor fusion method that exploits the redundancy intrinsic in the sensor network. We modulate the number of sensors that contribute to activity recognition at runtime. Most sensor nodes are kept in low power state. They are activated when their contribution is needed to keep the desired classification accuracy, such as when active nodes fail or turn off due to lack of energy. This approach copes with dynamically changing networks without the need for retraining and allows activity recognition even in the presence of unexpected faults, thus reducing the frequency of user maintenance. The algorithm can be easily parallelized to best use the computational power of a sensor network. We show how this approach fits the *Titan* framework that we are developing for the execution of distributed context recognition algorithms in dynamic and heterogeneous wireless sensor networks.

The paper is organized as follows. In sec. 2 we describe the activity recognition algorithm with dynamic sensor selection. In sec. 3 we analyze the performance of the system in terms of classification accuracy and system life time. In sec. 4 we describe the *Titan* framework and how the activity recognition algorithms fit in it. We discuss results in sec. 5 and conclude in sec. 6.

2   Activity Recognition with Dynamic Sensor Selection

We introduce a method to recognize activities (gestures) from on-body sensors. This method relies on classifier fusion to combine multiple sensor data and comprises a dynamic sensor selection scheme. It exploits the intrinsic redundancy in a network of small and inexpensive acceleration sensors distributed on the body to achieve a desired recognition accuracy while minimizing the number of used sensors. Gesture classification is performed on individual nodes using Hidden Markov Models (HMM) [18]. A Naive Bayes classifier fuses these individual classification results to improve classification accuracy and robustness. This method is tested by recognizing the activities of assembly-line workers in a car production environment. Activity recognition enables the delivery of context-aware support to workers [19,17].

2.1   Metaclassifier for Activity Recognition

The activity recognition algorithm is based on a metaclassifier fusing the contributions from several sensor nodes [20]. The sensor nodes comprise a three-axis accelerometer to capture user motion (Analog Device ADXL330). Each axis of the accelerometer is considered as an independent sensor. Fig. 1 illustrates the activity recognition principle.

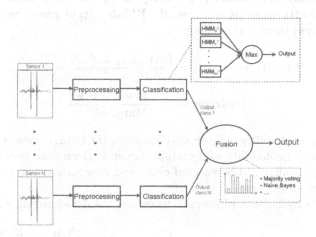

Fig. 1. Activity recognition architecture. Features extracted from the sensor data are classified by competing Hidden Markov Models (HMM), each one trained to model one activity class. The most likely model yields the class label. The labels are fused to obtain an overall classification result. Two fusing scheme have been compared: naive Bayesian and majority voting.

First on isolated instances, features are extracted from the raw acceleration data. The features are the sign of the acceleration magnitude (positive, negative or null). This is obtained by comparing the acceleration value with corresponding thresholds (-400mg and +400mg)[1]. Each sample is thus converted in one out of three possible symbols.

The features are then classified using discrete HMMs which model the gesture dynamics in the feature space. HMMs, together with Dynamic Time Warping

---

[1] Use of alternative features will be investigate in future works.

(DTW) [21] and neural networks [22], are a common approach to handle temporal dynamics of gestures. Our choice is motivated by previous work which showed HMMs to be a good approach [17,23]. We use ergodic HMMs with 4 states. For each accelerometer axis we train one HMM per class using the Baum-Welch algorithm starting with 15 random initial models and selecting the one that shows best classification accuracy on the training set. During activity recognition, the HMMs compete on each input sequence. The HMM best modelling the input sequence indicates the gesture class label. Training and evaluation of sequences is done using the Kevin Murphy's HMM Toolbox.

Finally, in order to end up with a single classification result we fuse the class label output from each accelerometer using a naive Bayes technique. The naive Bayes classifier is a simple probabilistic classifier based on the Bayes' theorem and the (strong) hypothesis that the input features are independent. The classifier combines the Bayes probabilistic model with a decision rule. A typical decision rule is to classify an instance as belonging to the class that maximizes the *a posteriori* probability [24].

Given the conditional model $P(C|A_0, A_1, ..., A_n)$, where C denotes the class and A_i n input attributes (in our case, the HMMs output from the sensors), we can use the Bayes theorem to define:

$$P(C|A_1, A_2, ..., A_n) = \frac{P(A_1, A_2, ..., A_n|C)\, P(C)}{P(A_1, A_2, ..., A_n)}$$

$$\text{Posterior} = \frac{\text{Likelihood} \times \text{Prior}}{\text{Marginal}} \qquad (1)$$

Posterior is the probability of a certain class given the input sequence. *Likelihood* is the conditional probability of a certain sequence given a certain class, *Prior* is the prior probability of the selected class, and *Marginal* is the probability of having the input sequence.

Applying the hypothesis of independence and the decision rule we obtain:

$$C_{out}(a_1, a_2, ..., a_n) = argmax_c \frac{P(C = c) \prod_{i=1}^{n} P(A_i = a_i|C = c)}{P(A_1 = a_1, A_2 = a_2, ..., A_n = a_n)} \qquad (2)$$

As the denominator in equation 2 is identical for every class we only need to compute the numerator for each class and find argmax. Also, since all the classes in our experiments have the same probability, we do not need to compute $P(C = c)$. The *Likelihood* is thus the only parameter that has to be calculated. This step is achieved during training by building the confusion matrix[2] for each HMM and defining $P(A_i = a_i|C = c) = \frac{t_c}{t}$, where t_c is the number of training instances for which the class $C = c$ and the attribute $A_i = a_i$ and t is the number

---

[2] A confusion matrix is a visualization tool typically used in supervised learning. Each column of the matrix represents the classifier output (predicted class), while each row represents the actual class of the instances. One benefit of a confusion matrix is that it clearly shows whether the system is confusing two classes (i.e. commonly mislabeling one as another).

of training instances for class c. However, depending on the training data, for some classes c we may not have a sample for which $A_i = a_i$. In this situation, $\prod_{i=1}^{n} P(A_i = a_i | C = c)$ of that class is always zero, despite the value of the other input attribute. For this reason we used the *M-estimate* of the *Likelihood* presented in Eq. 3, where p is an *a priori* probability of a certain value for an attribute, while m is the number of virtual sample per class added to the training set. In our experiment $p = \frac{1}{10}$ and $m = 1$.

$$P(A_i = a_i | C = c) = \frac{t_c + m\,p}{t + m} \qquad (3)$$

As we deal with dynamic networks where the number of active nodes varies during time, the *Posterior* probability is calculated including only the contribution of the active nodes in the network.

Feature extraction and classification can be computed in parallel on all the sensor nodes, thus allowing the exploitation of intrinsic parallelism within the sensor network, while sensor fusion is performed on a single node.

2.2   Evaluation of Activity Recognition Performance

In order to assess our approach, we consider the recognition of the activities of assembly-line workers in a car production environment. We consider the recognition of 10 activity classes (Table 1) performed in one of the quality assurance checkpoint of the production plant. These classes are a subset of 46 activities performed in this checkpoints [25].

Table 1. List of activity classes to recognize from body-worn sensors

Class	Description
0	write on notepad
1	open hood
2	close hood
3	check gaps on the front door
4	open left front door
5	close left front door
6	close both left door
7	check trunk gaps
8	open and close trunk
9	check steering wheel

We evaluate the performance of the approach in terms of correct classification ratio as a function of the number of nodes in the network. We perform a set of experiments using 19 nodes placed on the two arms of a tester (10 nodes on the right arm and due to a fault during the tests, 9 on the left arm) as illustrated in Fig. 2. Since we do not want to rely on particular positioninig and orientation of the nodes, the sensors were placed to cover the two arms without any particular

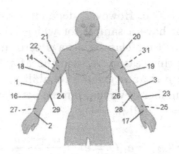

Fig. 2. Placements of the nodes on the right and left arm (dashed lines indicate nodes placed behind the arm, numbers represent the unique ID of each node)

constraints, as it is difficult to achieve such a placement for sensors unobtrusively integrated into people's garments. The subject executed 19 times each gesture listed in Table 1. Data from such trials has been recorded on a PC for subsequent analysis. Cross validation techniques have been used to extend the validation test up to all 19 instances. To perform cross validation, the input instances from the sensors have been divided into 4 folds (3 made up of 5 instances for each class and 1 of 4 instances for each class). We built 4 distinct sets of HMMs and confusion matrices. During the evaluation, for the classification of an instance we use a model obtained from a training set that did not include that specific instance.

To evaluate the correct classification ratio as a function of the number of nodes, we applied our algorithm to clusters of nodes with increasing size (one to 19 nodes). Although we consider each accelerometer axis as an independent sensor, the clusters are created in a nodewise manner. In other words a node is

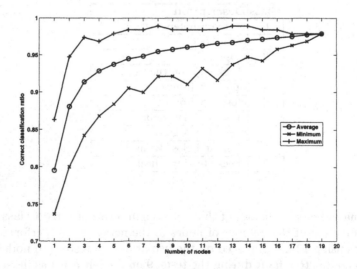

Fig. 3. Average, maximum and minimum correct classification ratio among random cluster as a function of cluster size

randomly selected and the contribution of its three axis is considered and fused. The reason is that when a node runs out of energy, the contributions of all its axes vanish. For each size we created 200 clusters from randomly selected sensor nodes. For each cluster size the average, maximum and minimum classification accuracy is recorded.

Figure 3 shows the correct classification ratio as a function of the cluster size. We achieve 98% correct classification rate using all 19 nodes and, on average, 80% using a single node. For smaller clusters the nodes composing the cluster influence the performance variance. For example, fusing the contributions from nodes 1, 3, and 24 results in 97% correct classification ratio, a value close to the accuracy that we can obtain using all the 19 nodes (Maximum curve in Fig. 3). On the other hand, fusing the outputs from nodes 20, 22 and 25 results in 84% accuracy (Minimum curve in Fig. 3) which is below what can be achieved using only one "good" node, e.g. node 16 (86%).

2.3 Dynamic Sensor Selection

We introduce a dynamic sensor selection scheme to select at run-time the sensors which are combined to perform gesture classification. This scheme seeks to achieve a desired classification accuracy while prolonging the system lifetime by minimizing the number of sensor used.

A minimum set of sensors to achieve the desired classification accuracy is first selected. Then the sensor set is updated at run-time when a sensor is removed from the network (e.g. due to failure or power loss). Since sensor nodes can fail while a gesture is performed, the algorithm ensures that the loss of a any single sensor still guarantees a performance above the desired minimum. In other words, a cluster of size D must satisfy the following condition: all subclusters of size $D - 1$ must still achieve the desired minimum correct classification ratio. When a node fails, we first test wether the remaining nodes fulfill this condition. If not, all the clusters of size $D + 1$ that can be built by adding one idle node to the given cluster are tested. The one that achieves the best performance is selected. If this new cluster fulfills the condition the system continues operation. If not, another idle node is added to the cluster and the process is repeated until a cluster that fulfills the condition is found or no idle nodes are left. In the latter case the system is not able to achieve the desired performance anymore.

The training instances are used to computed the expected performance of new clusters. This approach does not need system retraining, although it is valid only as long as the training set is a good representation of the user's gestures.

3   Characterization of Network Lifetime

Tests were done to assess the network lifetime (defined as the time until there are no more sensors available to achieve the desired classification accuracy) by simulating the evolution of the selected sensor set as nodes fail. For the sake of generality, we do not rely on a particular power consumption or fault model for network nodes, as it depends on the hardware and protocols chosen. In particular we are not interested in specifically identifying how long each sensor uses its radio or whether employs any kind of energy saving techniques. Instead we want to assess how our dynamic sensor selection algorithm extends network lifetime independently of these factors.

Since we assume that all nodes are identical and perform the same activity, we model node lifetime as a random variable following a Gaussian distribution with mean μ (arbitrary time units) and standard deviation as a percentage of the mean: $\alpha \times \mu$ $(\alpha < 1)^3$. Network lifetime is then calculated as a multiple of μ. The lifetime of all the nodes is fixed at the beginning of the simulation according to this model.

The dynamic sensor selection algorithm then generates a subset of nodes able to achieve a desired accuracy even if any node of the subset fails. Then at each time step, we decrease the life of all the active nodes by one time unit. When the lifetime of a node is over, we assume that it takes a controlling unit one time unit to generate the next cluster. When no cluster matching the desired performance requirement is found the lifetime of the system is reached.

With this lifetime model only μ influences the overall system lifetime. The standard deviation has no effect on the overall system lifetime since augmenting this parameter augments the probability to see both nodes with shorter and longer lifetime thus compensating each other (see Table 2). In our tests we selected $\alpha = 0.3$.

Table 2. Network life as a function of the standard deviation chosen. Network life is calculated as a multiple of the mean node life (μ).

Standard deviation (% of mean)	10	20	30	40	50	60
Average life (time)	4.010μ	4.154μ	3.986μ	4.049μ	4.134μ	4.136μ

We compare the system lifetime when the dynamic sensor selection scheme is used to the system lifetime when all the sensors are used simultaneously (with the same node life model). In Fig. 4 the results of one trial are illustrated when the minimum accuracy required is 90%. The plot shows the performance of the network in two situations: (i) all the 19 nodes are active at the same time (dashed line); (ii) only a subset is used (continuous line). Since the objective of the network is to keep performances above 90% it can be considered expired when, due to node faults, is not possible to find a subset of nodes able to achieve such accuracy. Using all the 19 nodes together, the starting performance is higher, but quickly drops as the average node life (μ) is reached. With the dynamic sensor selection scheme, as the nodes fail (drops in the continuous line) they are replaced by inactive nodes, thus keeping the minimum required performance. Even when nodes fail, the performance never drops below the fixed threshold.

---

[3] The consequences of using other distribution to model the node lifetime will be explored in the future.

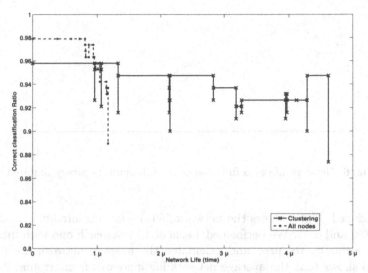

Fig. 4. Performance of the network versus time in the case of 90% minimum correct classification ratio. The network expires when its accuracy decreases under the fixed threshold (horizontal line at 0.9). Using all 19 sensors together results in a shorter life (dashed line), slightly above μ, while using dynamic sensor selection increases network life above 4μ. In the latter case, when a node fails, the performance never decreases below the fixed minimum.

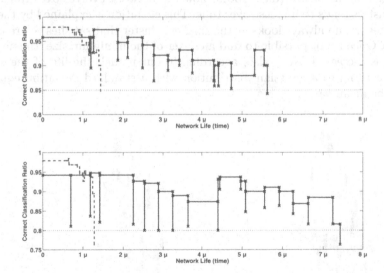

Fig. 5. Performance of the network versus time in the case that 85% (top) and 80% (below) minimum correct classification ratio

With a minimum classification accuracy of 90% the dynamic sensor selection scheme leads to a system lifetime about four times longer than when all the nodes are active. Network lifetime increases when the the minimum classification

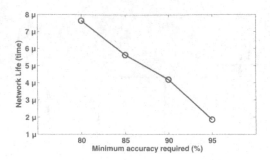

Fig. 6. Network life as a function of the minimum accuracy required

ratio is reduced. Fig. 5 shows the network lifetime for a minimum classification ratio of 80% and 85%. We performed 4 sets of 10 tests each one with increasing minimum accuracy required and calculated the average network life for each set. Fig. 6 shows that the average network life increases from around 2μ when minimum accuracy is 95% up to more than 7μ when minimum accuracy is 80%.

Without dynamic sensor selection all the sensors are used at the same time and the minimum classification accuracy does not play a role. As the nodes approach their average lifetime μ, they will fail within a short time window (related to the lifetime variance).

In Fig. 7 we illustrate (dark spots) how the network evolves over time. The size of clusters tends to increase over time. This evolution is explained by the fact that the algorithm always looks at the smallest cluster that satisfies the required accuracy. Once is not possible to find a cluster of the minimum size, the number of nodes is increased. Note also, according to our model, the life of the nodes varies according to a gaussian distribution with a standard deviation equal to 30% of the mean value.

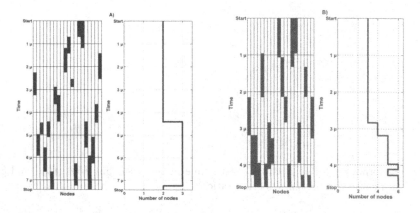

Fig. 7. Evolution of the network. On the left, in dark, are the active nodes at a certain time highlighted. On the right, the number of active nodes at a certain time is shown. A) 80% minimum accuracy. B) 90% minimum accuracy.

4   Implementation Using Tiny Task Networks (Titan)

The algorithm described above needs to be mapped on a wireless sensor network. The *Titan* framework that we are developing for context recognition in heterogeneous and dynamic wireless sensor networks can be used for this purpose [26]. We develop Titan as part of the ongoing e-SENSE project as a tool to enable and explore how context awareness can emerge in a dynamic sensor network. Titan simplifies the algorithm description, automates data exchange between selected sensor nodes, and adapts execution to dynamic network topologies. It thus qualifies for the implementation of the algorithm presented before.

Most context recognition algorithms can be described as a data flow from sensors, where data is collected, followed by feature extraction and a classification algorithm, which produces the context information. Within Titan, context recognition systems are represented as *Task Graphs*. It offers for each processing step (sampling, feature extraction, and classification) a set of predefined tasks. A task is usually a simple signal processing function, such as a filter, but may also be a more complex algorithm such as a classifier. A context recognition algorithm can be composed from those modular building blocks, which are provided by the nodes participating in the network.

A set of tasks are programmed into the sensor network nodes as a *Task Pool*. These tasks are instantiated when they are needed (i.e. they use RAM and CPU cycles only when they are used by a *Task Graph*). In a heterogeneous network, node processing power may vary, and nodes with higher processing power can provide more complex *Task Pools* than simpler nodes.

Figure 8 shows the Titan architecture and illustrates how a classification task graph is distributed on the sensor network; the *Task Graph Database* contains the classification algorithm description containing sensor tasks S_i, feature tasks F_i, a classification task C, and an actuator A_1 receiving the end result. Upon request to execute the algorithm, the *Network Manager* inspects the currently available nodes in the network, and decides on which node to instantiate what tasks,

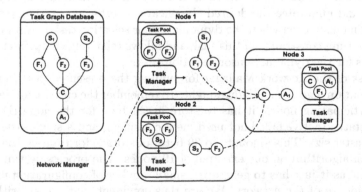

Fig. 8. Titan configures an application task graph by assigning parts of the graph to participating sensor nodes depending on their processing capabilities

such as to minimize processing load, overall power consumption, or maximise network lifetime. The Network Manager then sends a configuration message to the *Task Managers* on the sensor nodes, which instantiate the tasks on the local node. The Task Manager assigns a share of dynamic memory to the tasks for their state information and configures the connections between tasks, including transmitting data to other nodes.

During execution of the task graph, the Network Manager receives error messages from tasks or sensor nodes, and checks whether all participating sensor nodes are still alive. If changes to the current configuration are required, it adapts the distribution of the task graph on the network.

Titan provides several advantages. Ease of use, since a designer can describe his context recognition algorithm simply by interconnecting different tasks and selecting a few configuration parameters for those tasks. Portability, because it is based on TinyOS [27] which has been ported to a range of sensor network hardware and due to the abstraction of tasks, it is able to run on heterogeneous networks. Flexibility and speed, since it can reconfigure nodes in less than 1ms in order to quickly react to changes in dynamic sensor networks.

The meta classifier with dynamic sensor selection presented above can be incorporated into Titan by dividing it into a set of tasks that can be instantiated on different nodes. In particular, we define three new tasks: 1) a "gesture classification" task, which implements the HMM algorithm, 2) a "meta classification" task that performs Bayesian inference and decides the gesture class, 3) a "dynamic sensor selection" task that defines the set of sensors contributing to the meta classification task.

The initial cluster of nodes is created by the dynamic sensor selection task. The Network Manager instantiates on each of the nodes within this cluster the gesture classification task. The system runs as-is until a node fails (i.e. runs out of power). When the meta classification tasks senses that a node fails to send data it sends an error message to the Network Manager. The Network Manager instantiates the dynamic sensor selection task on a device with sufficient computational power (PDA, mobile phone), and then adapts the configuration of the nodes as needed. Since the cluster can tolerate the failure of any one of his nodes and guarantee the desired classification performance, the system can work continuously even when the dynamic sensor selection task is running. This relaxes the time constraint on this task and allows relatively complex clustering algorithms for the dynamic sensor selection task.

The task of the Network Manager for running the presented distributed gesture recognition algorithm is light-weight. To remember the current configuration of the participating nodes, it has to store just 1 byte for the node ID, 1 byte for their status (active,failed,not used,meta classifier), and a single byte for the current cluster size. This amounts to 39 bytes of storage for running the gesture recognition algorithm on our example of 19 nodes. The processing time is limited as well, as it just has to generate a small number of configuration messages at every update of the network. We are thus confident that the algorithm presented here is able to run on sensor network nodes, with the exception of the non-optimized dynamic sensor selection task which runs on a PDA or mobile phone.

5 Discussion

We have shown that by combining the fusion of classifier outputs operating on single sensors with a dynamic sensor selection scheme it is possible to extend the network lifetime while still achieving a minimum desired accuracy.

This technique may be easily used to adjust the number of sensors according to dynamically changing application constraints. Such change can be adopted as a consequence of changes in the user context (i.e. change in user location).

Active sensors may also be selected according to other criteria, such as the performance of a node as a function of the gesture. If we integrate information from the environment with the data of the sensor network, we may identify a subset of gestures that are most likely performed at a certain time. Thus active nodes may be selected among those which promise better classification performances only on that subset of gestures. However, since any change in configuration requires a set of messages to be sent among the nodes of the network, further investigation must validate this choice.

This metaclassifier is highly parallelizable and thus well suited for wireless sensor networks. Computation is shared among all active sensor nodes and none of the them is a single point of failure of the whole system. This is very important as we consider devices prone to fault or operating in environmental conditions that may severely alter the topology of the network.

Our activity recognition algorithm can find similar application in other fields of research. For example, sensor selection techniques try to extend network life by using a subset of nodes able to achieve the minimum desired performances. Such techniques are mainly used in environment monitoring [28] where dense networks cover the area of interest and sensors coverage area are overlapped.

Clustering is a fundamental research topic in sensor networks as it makes it possible to guarantee a basic level of system performance in presence of a large number of dynamically changing nodes [29]. Clustering algorithms vary depending on their application, such as guaranteeing certain latency, or balancing the activity among nodes and reducing power consumption. Energy aware clustering algorithms typically aim to reduce power consumption of the nodes either by reducing the messages sent over the wireless link by aggregating redundant data [30] or by keeping nodes in a low power state when there are other resources able to provide the same information [31].

Another research area closer to our work is feature selection. Feature selection includes a variety of techniques that aim to reduce the dimensionality of the input instances of a classifier. Some of its objectives are: reducing the measurement and storage requirements, reducing training and utilization times, defying the curse of dimensionality to improve prediction performance [32]. If we consider the HMM ouput as features, our approach may also be seen as a feature selection technique: since we dynamically select only a subset of the available ones.

Energy scavenging techniques can also take advantages from our approach. In fact now the nodes can rely on long periods when the application does not need their contribution. In such period they can collect energy and this relaxes the constraints on energy consumption due to the limited amount of energy that can be harvested from the environment. For example we showed an example of a network whose lifetime was extended by a factor 4 while still achieving 90% correct classification ratio. Since the average node life is one fourth of the total network life, each node may rely on three times its average life in order to harvest energy.

6   Conclusion

Wearable computing seeks to empower users by providing them context-aware support. Context is determined from miniature sensors integrated into garments or accessories. In a general setting the sensor network characteristics may change in unpredictable ways due to sensor degradation, interconnection failures, and jitter in the sensor placement. The use of a dense mesh of sensors distributed on the body may allow to overcome these challenges through sensor fusion techniques. Since such systems must remain unobtrusive, the reduction of node dimension and node interconnection is of high importance. Wireless sensor networks help achieving this unobtrusiveness since they do not require any wire connection. However, this implies that each sensor node must be selfpowered. In order to reduce obtrusiveness, the battery dimension must be kept at minimum, which results in low power availability.

Energy aware design aims to extend sensor nodes life by using low power devices and poweraware applications. Poweraware applications typically rely on duty cycling: they reduce the amount of time when the radio is active, and they increase the amount of time when the node can be placed in a low power state. In wearable computing, unpredictable duty cycles are proscribed. We described a different approach to extend network life while achieving desired accuracy. We capitalized on the availability of large number of nodes to implement a dynamic sensor selection scheme together with a metaclassifier that performs sensor fusion and activity recognition. This technique copes with dynamically changing number of sensor without need to retrain the system.

The method minimizes the number of nodes necessary to achieve a given classification ratio. Active nodes recognize locally gestures with hidden Markov models. The output of active nodes is fused by a naive Bayes metaclassifier. Inactive nodes are kept in a low power state. Once an active node fails the system activates one or more additional nodes to recover the initial performance. Compared to a system where all sensor nodes are continuously active, our approach can extend up to 4 times the network life while reaching 90% correct classification ratio, and up to 7 times while reaching 80% correct classification ratio. This method is highly parallelizable and well suited for wireless sensor networks.

We described how this method fits within the Titan framework that we develop to support context-aware applications in dynamic and heterogeneous sensor networks. Titan allows fast network configuration and is well suited for our technique as it allows to easily exploit network resources dynamically.

We now have demonstrated the advantage of a dynamic sensor selection scheme for accuracy-power trade-off in activity recognition. The implementation of this algorithm on wireless sensor nodes is still an open point. With qualitatively identical results, alternate classifiers and sensor selection methods that minimize computational power may be investigated. We also plan to extend the current method in order to be able to increase the inital number of nodes with on-line learning. Other future works can explore the use of an heterogeneous network that include different kind of sensors such as strain sensors or tilt sensors. Finally energy scavenging techniques benefit from our activity recognition algorithm: more time is available to harvest energy thanks to dynamic sensor selection. Evaluation of network performance with dynamically changing power availability needs to be carried out.

Acknowledgment

This work was supported by EU project WearIT@Work, contract number 004216, http://www.wearitatwork.com, and the 6th European Framework Programme Integrated Projects e-SENSE, contract number 027227, http://www.ist-e-SENSE.org.

References

1. Lukowicz, P., Junker, H., Staeger, M., von Bueren, T., Troester, G.: WearNET: A distributed multi-sensor system for context aware wearables. In: Borriello, G., Holmquist, L.E. (eds.) UbiComp 2002. LNCS, vol. 2498, pp. 361–370. Springer, Heidelberg (2002)
2. Kallio, S., Kela, J., Korpipää, P., Mäntyjärvi, J.: User independent gesture interaction for small handheld devices. International Journal of Pattern Recognition and Artificial Intelligence 20(4), 505–524 (2006)
3. Hernandez-Rebollar, J.L.: Gesture-driven american sign language phraselator. In: ICMI 2005. Proceedings of the 7th international conference on Multimodal interfaces, pp. 288–292. ACM Press, New York (2005)
4. Benini, L., Farella, E., Guiducci, C.: Wireless sensor networks: Enabling technology for ambient intelligence. Microelectron. J. 37(12), 1639–1649 (2006)
5. Watteyne, T., Augé-Blum, I., Ubéda, S.: Dual-mode real-time mac protocol for wireless sensor networks: a validation/simulation approach. In: Proceedings of the first international conference on Integrated internet ad hoc and sensor networks (2006)
6. Römer, K., Mattern, F.: The design space of wireless sensor networks. IEEE Wireless Communications 11(6), 54–61 (2004)
7. Van Laerhoven, K., Gellersen, H.W.: Spine versus porcupine: a study in distributed wearable activity recognition. In: McIlraith, S.A., Plexousakis, D., van Harmelen, F. (eds.) ISWC 2004. LNCS, vol. 3298, pp. 142–149. Springer, Heidelberg (2004)
8. Harms, H., Amft, O., Tröster, D.R.G.: Smash: A distributed sensing and processing garment for the classification of upper body postures. In: Third interational conference on body area networks (submitted, 2008)

9. Roggen, D., Bharatula, N.B., Stäger, M., Lukowicz, P., Tröster, G.: From sensors to miniature networked sensorbuttons. In: INSS 2006. Proc. of the 3rd Int. Conf. on Networked Sensing Systems, pp. 119–122 (2006)

10. Paradiso, J.A., Starner, T.: Energy scavenging for mobile and wireless electronics. IEEE Pervasive Computing 4(1), 18–27 (2005)

11. van Dam, T., Langendoen, K.: An adaptive energy-efficient mac protocol for wireless sensor networks. In: SenSys 2003: Proceedings of the 1st international conference on Embedded networked sensor systems, pp. 171–180. ACM Press, New York (2003)

12. Zigbee Alliance: Zigbee specification (2006), http://www.zigbee.org

13. Hill, J., Culler, D.: Mica: A Wireless Platform for Deeply Embedded Networks. IEEE Micro 22(6), 12–24 (2002)

14. Dai, L., Basu, P.: Energy and delivery capacity of wireless sensor networks with random duty-cycles. In: IEEE International Conference on Communications, pp. 3503–3510 (to appear)

15. Moser, C., Thiele, L., Benini, L., Brunelli, D.: Real-time scheduling with regenerative energy. In: ECRTS 2006. Proceedings of the 18th Euromicro Conference on Real-Time Systems, pp. 261–270. IEEE Computer Society Press, Washington (2006)

16. Vigorito, C.M., Ganesan, D., Barto, A.G.: Adaptive control of duty cycling in energy-harvesting wireless sensor networks. In: SECON 2007. 4th Annual IEEE Communications Society Conference on Sensor, Mesh and Ad Hoc Communications and Networks, June 18–21, 2007, pp. 21–30 (2007)

17. Stiefmeier, T., Ogris, G., Junker, H., Lukowicz, P., Tröster, G.: Combining motion sensors and ultrasonic hands tracking for continuous activity recognition in a maintenance scenario. In: 10th IEEE International Symposium on Wearable Computers (2006)

18. Rabiner, L.R.: A tutorial on hidden Markov models and selected applications in speech recognition. Proceedings of the IEEE 77(2), 257–285 (1989)

19. Maurtua, I., Kirisci, P.T., Stiefmeier, T., Sbodio, M.L., Witt, H.: A wearable computing prototype for supporting training activities in automative production. In: IFAWC. 4th International Forum on Applied Wearable Computing (2007)

20. Zappi, P., Stiefmeier, T., Farella, E., Roggen, D., Benini, L., Tröster, G.: Activity recognition from on-body sensors by classifier fusion: Sensor scalability and robustness. In: 3rd Int. Conf. on Intelligent Sensors, Sensor Networks, and Information Processing (2007)

21. Ming Hsiao, K., West, G., Vedatesh, S.M.K.: Online context recognition in multisensor system using dynamic time warping. In: Proc. of the 2005 International Conference on Intelligent Sensors, Sensor Networks and Information Processing, pp. 283–288 (2005)

22. Mitra, S., Acharya, T.: Gesture recognition: A survey. IEEE Transactions on Systems, Man and Cybernetics - Part C 37(3), 311–324 (2007)

23. Ganti, R.K., Jayachandran, P., Abdelzaher, T.F., Stankovic, J.A.: Satire: a software architecture for smart attire. In: MobiSys, pp. 110–123 (2006)

24. Rish, I., Hellerstein, J., Thathachar, J.: An analysis of data characteristics that affect naive bayes performance. In: ICML-01 (2001)

25. Stiefmeier, T., Roggen, D., Tröster, G.: Fusion of string-matched templates for continuous activity recognition. In: 11th IEEE International Symposium on Wearable Computers, pp. 41–44 (October 2007)

26. Lombriser, C., Stäger, M., Roggen, D., Tröster, G.: Titan: A tiny task network for dynamically reconfigurable heterogeneous sensor networks. In: KiVS. Fachtagung Kommunikation in Verteilten Systemen, pp. 127–138 (2007)

27. Hill, J., Szewczyk, R., Woo, A., Hollar, S., Culler, D., Pister, K.: System architecture directions for network sensors. In: Architectural Support for Programming Languages and Operating Systems (November 2000)

28. Chen, H., Wu, H., Tzeng, N.F.: Grid-based approach for working node selection in wireless sensor networks. In: IEEE International Conference on Communications, June 20–24, 2004, vol. 6, pp. 3673–3678 (2004)

29. Yu, J.Y., Chong, P.H.J.: A survey of clustering schemes for mobile ad hoc networks. IEEE Communications Surveys 7(1), 32–48 (2005)

30. Pham, T., Kim, E.J., Moh, M.: On data aggregation quality and energy efficiency of wireless sensor network protocols - extended summary. In: Proceedings of the First International Conference on Broadband Networks, pp. 730–732 (2004)

31. Guo, Y., McNair, J.: An adaptive sleep protocol for environment monitoring using wireless sensor networks. In: Communications and Computer Networks, pp. 1–6 (2005)

32. Guyon, I., Elisseeff, A.: An introduction to variable and feature selection. J. Mach. Learn. Res. 3, 1157–1182 (2003)

Predictive Modeling-Based Data Collection in Wireless Sensor Networks*

Lidan Wang and Amol Deshpande

Computer Science Department, University of Maryland,
A.V. Williams Building, College Park, MD 20742, USA
{lidan,amol}@cs.umd.edu

Abstract. We address the problem of designing practical, energy-efficient protocols for data collection in wireless sensor networks using predictive modeling. Prior work has suggested several approaches to capture and exploit the rich spatio-temporal correlations prevalent in WSNs during data collection. Although shown to be effective in reducing the data collection cost, those approaches use simplistic corelation models and further, ignore many idiosyncrasies of WSNs, in particular the broadcast nature of communication. Our proposed approach is based on approximating the joint probability distribution over the sensors using *undirected graphical models*, ideally suited to exploit both the spatial correlations and the broadcast nature of communication. We present algorithms for optimally using such a model for data collection under different communication models, and for identifying an appropriate model to use for a given sensor network. Experiments over synthetic and real-world datasets show that our approach significantly reduces the data collection cost.

1 Introduction

Wireless sensor networks (WSNs), comprising of tiny, radio-enabled sensing devices open up new opportunities to observe and interact with the physical world, and have been applied in domains ranging from patient health monitoring through the use of biomedical sensors to military applications such as battlefield surveillance [1]. In this paper, we address the problem of designing energy-efficient protocols for collecting all data observed by the sensor nodes in a wireless sensor network at an Internet-connected base station at a specified frequency [2,25,22,4]. The key issue in designing such data collection protocols is modeling and exploiting the strong spatio-temporal correlations present in most sensor networks (see Figure 1). In most sensor network deployments, especially in environmental monitoring applications, the data generated by the sensor nodes is highly correlated both in time (future values are correlated with current values) and in space (two co-located sensors are strongly correlated). Naive data collection protocols tend to be significantly suboptimal in the presence of such correlations. These correlations can usually be captured quite easily by constructing predictive models using either prior domain knowledge or historical data traces. However, because of the distributed nature of data generation in sensor networks, and the resource-constrained

* This work was supported by NSF Grants CNS-0509220 and IIS-0546136.

nature of sensor nodes, traditional data compression techniques cannot be easily adapted to exploit such correlations.

The distributed nature of data generation has been well-studied in the literature under the name of *Distributed Source Coding* [26,30,31,27]. In their seminal work, Slepian and Wolf [26] prove that it is theoretically possible to encode the correlated information generated by distributed data sources (in our case, the sensor nodes) at the rate of their joint entropy *even if the data sources do not communicate with each other*. However this result is non-constructive, and constructive techniques are known only for a few specific distributions [23]. More importantly, these techniques require precise and perfect knowledge of the correlations. This may not be acceptable in practical sensor networks where deviations from the modeled correlations must be captured accurately (we use DSC to provide a lower bound on the data collection cost; see Section 2.2). Pattem et al. [22] and Chu et al. [4], among others, propose practical data collection protocols that exploit the spatio-temporal correlations while guaranteeing correctness; however, these protocols may exploit only a subset of the correlations, and further require the sensor nodes to communicate with each other (increasing the overall cost).

Sensor networks, especially wireless sensor networks, exhibit other significant peculiarities that make the data collection problem challenging. First, sensor nodes are typically computationally constrained and have limited memories. Hence, it may not be feasible to run sophisticated data compression algorithms on them. Second, the communication in wireless sensor networks is typically done in a broadcast manner – when a node transmits a message, all nodes within the radio range can receive the message. As we will see later, this enables many optimizations that would not be possible in a one-to-one communication model.

In this paper, we present an approach to exploit all the spatial correlations in the data by approximating the joint probability distributions using a subclass of undirected graphical models called *decomposable models*. We develop algorithms for performing data collection using such a model, and for choosing an appropriate decomposable model for a given sensor network. Our data collection protocols are also naturally able to exploit the broadcast nature of communication among wireless sensors. Finally, we present an extensive experimental study over several synthetic and real-world datasets, and demonstrate that the expressiveness of our data collection model leads to a significant reduction in the total transmission cost.

2 Background

We begin with presenting preliminary background on data compression in sensor networks, and discuss the prior approaches. We then present an overview of the class of decomposable models.

2.1 Notation and Preliminaries

We are given a sensor network with n nodes that continuously monitors a set of distributed attributes $\mathcal{X} = \{X_1, \cdots, X_n\}$, and generates a discrete data value vector

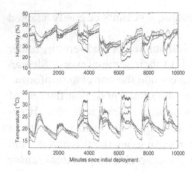

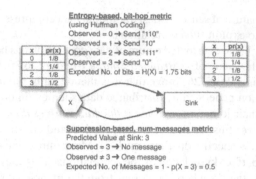

Fig. 1. A plot of several traces from the Intel Lab Dataset [18] shows the strong spatiotemporal correlations in the data

Fig. 2. Two extremes in the spectrum of communication model and data encoding options

$\mathbf{x}^t = \{x_1^t, \cdots, x_n^t\}$ at every time instance t^1. Each attribute, X_i, may be an environmental property being sensed by the node (e.g., *temperature*), or it may be the result of an operation on the sensed values (e.g., in an anomaly-detection application, the sensor node may continuously evaluate a filter such as "*temperature* > 100" on the observed values). If the sensed attributes are continuous, we assume that an error threshold ϵ is provided and the readings are binned into intervals of size 2ϵ to discretize them. In this paper, we focus on optimal exploitation of spatial correlations at any given time t and drop the superscript in the rest of the paper; however we note that our ideas can be easily generalized to handle temporal correlations as well.

Predictive modeling-based approaches to data compression begin by building a predictive model over the sensor network attributes that is used to obtain a joint probability distribution (pdf) over the attributes. We denote this pdf by $p(X_1, ..., X_n)$.

We denote the communication graph of the sensor network by $\mathcal{G}_C = (\mathcal{X}, E)$, where E consists of the pairs of vertices that are within communication radius of each other. We denote by $d(X, Y)$ the minimum distance between X and Y in terms of number of hops. For simplicity, we assume all communication links to be perfect and identical[2], and consider two alternatives for computing communication costs:

(1) *bit-hop metric:* The total cost of sending a message containing n bits from X to Y is given by $n * d(X, Y)$. In practice, this can be approximated reasonably well by batching multiple messages together (at the cost of increasing latency).
(2) *num-messages metric:* The total cost of sending a message (that can contain at most 32 bytes) from X to Y is given simply by $d(X, Y)$. In other words, we only count the number of messages that are transmitted.

In many practical sensor network deployments, the cost of *receiving* a message at the sensor node can be quite high (sometimes as high as the *transmission* cost). For

---

[1] The time instances at which data is acquired depends on the application-specified frequency of data collection.

[2] Both these assumptions can be relaxed by assigning appropriate weights to the communication links and adjusting the cost metric formulas accordingly.

simplicity, in our analysis and algorithm descriptions, we assume that the cost of receiving a message at a sensor node is zero; we however present several experiments where we account for receiving cost as well.

The choice of cost metric is closely tied with how the data is encoded during data collection. We consider two extremes in the spectrum of possibilities:

Joint Entropy-Based Data Collection (bit-hop metric): Assuming that it is possible to compress the data optimally according to the joint pdf (e.g. using Huffman coding), the number of bits that need to be transmitted from a sensor node X (also called *source*) to the base station (called *sink*) is given by the *information entropy* of the distribution:

$$H_p(X) = \Sigma_x - p(x) \log(p(x))$$

where $p(X)$ denotes the probability distribution (pdf) over the attribute X.

If an approximation, $q(X)$, is used instead to compress, the number of bits transmitted is given by $H(p) + D(p\|q)$, where $D(p\|q)$, called *relative entropy*, is given by: $D(p\|q) = \Sigma - p(x) \log(p(x)/q(x))$.

Suppression-Based Data Collection (num-messages metric): Full-scale data compression may not be feasible in a sensor network; hence prior work in this area has typically considered a suppression-based approach [21,25,4], where the base station uses the pdf to predict a value for the attribute X. The sensor node, which has access to the same distribution, also predicts the same value and only sends a message if the predicted value is different from the actual observed value. We denote the expected number of messages by $M_p()$, and note that:

$$M_p(X) = 1 - \max_x p(x)$$

Note that we assume here that only a single message is needed to update the base station with the correct values.

Figure 2 illustrates these two approaches for an example distribution. Our algorithms are invariant to the approach used for compression. However, we assume the ability to compute an analogous function to $H_p()$ or $M_p()$ for any distribution p. We use the former metric when analyzing the problem and for experiments on synthetic datasets, but use the latter, more practical, metric for our experiments on real datasets.

2.2 Predictive Modeling-Based Data Compression in Sensor Networks

Given a joint pdf over the sensor network attributes, the key problem in using it for data compression is the distributed nature of data generation. The natural way to use the joint pdf, $p(X_1, \ldots, X_n)$, would be to gather the sensed values at a central sensor node, and compress the data there. The data gathering cost, however, would typically dwarf any advantages gained by doing joint compression.

The prior research in this area has suggested several approaches that utilize a subset of correlations instead. One approach, called *Independent (IND)*, is to ignore the spatial correlations and to compress the data from each sensor node independently of the others (Figure 3 (i)). In other words, an approximate distribution $q_1(X_1, ..., X_n) = p(X_1)p(X_2)...p(X_n)$ is used for compression (where $p(X_i)$ denotes the marginal probability distribution of X_i, computed by summing over the remaining variables in $\mathcal{X}$).

The second approach, that we call *Clustering (CLSTR)* [22,4], is to group the sensor nodes into clusters, and to compress the data from the nodes in each cluster jointly. Figure 3 (ii) shows an example of this using three clusters $\{X_1\}, \{X_2, X_5\}, \{X_3, X_4\}$, which corresponds to using the distribution $q_2(X_1, ..., X_5) = p(X_1)p(X_2, X_5)p(X_3, X_4)$. In this approach, the intra-cluster spatial correlations are exploited during compression; however, the correlations across clusters are not utilized.

Several other approaches based on *routing driven compression* [22,24,6] have also been suggested. However, these approaches typically require joint compression and decompression of large numbers of data sources inside the network, and hence are not suited for resource-constrained sensor networks. We leave a detailed comparison of these approaches with our proposed approach to future work.

Distributed source coding (DSC), although not feasible in this setting for the reasons discussed earlier, can be used to obtain a lower bound on total communication cost as follows [7,6,27]. Let the sensor nodes be numbered in the increasing order of their distances from the base station (i.e., for all i, $d(X_i, sink) < d(X_{i+1}, sink)$). Then, the optimal scheme for using DSC is as follows: X_1 is compressed according to $p(X_1)$, and transmitted directly to the sink (incurring a total cost of $d(X_1, sink) \times H(X_1)$). X_2 is compressed according to $p(X_2|X_1)$ (since the sink already has the value of X_1, it is able to decode according this distribution). Note that, according to the distributed source coding theorem [26], sensor node X_2 does not need to know the actual value of X_1. Similarly, X_i is compressed according to $p(X_i|X_1 \ldots X_{i-1})$ and so on. The total communication cost incurred by this scheme is given by:

$$DSC(p) = \Sigma_{i=1}^n d(X_i, sink) \times H_p(X_i|X_1, \ldots, X_{i-1})$$

Figure 3 (iii) shows this for our running example (note that X_5 is closer to sink than X_3 or X_4).

As we can see in Figure 3, if the spatial correlation is high, both IND and CLSTR would incur much higher communication costs than DSC. As an example, if $H(X_i) = h, \forall i$, and if $H(X_i|X_j) \approx 0, \forall i, j$ (ie., if the spatial correlations are almost perfect), the total communication costs of IND, CLSTR(as shown in the figure), and DSC would be $8h, 6h$, and h respectively.

2.3 Discussion: Factors Affecting Data Compression Quality

The difference between the data compression ratios achieved by DSC and other techniques can be attributed to two factors.

Approximation Loss: If a data collection scheme only uses a subset of the correlations, then even if the scheme was optimal (ie., was able to compress as well as DSC), more bits would have to be communicated than minimally needed. For the example setup in Figure 3, since IND assumes independence between the sensor nodes, the node X_2 must transmit $H(X_2)$ bits to the sink compared to $H(X_2|X_1)$ that DSC transmits; in fact, the difference between IND and DSC ($8h - h = 7h$), can be attributed entirely to Approximation Loss. Although CLSTR is able to exploit some of the spatial correlations, it does not exploit inter-cluster correlations. Since the clusters are typically small (for reasons discussed below), the Approximation Loss can be quite high for CLSTR as

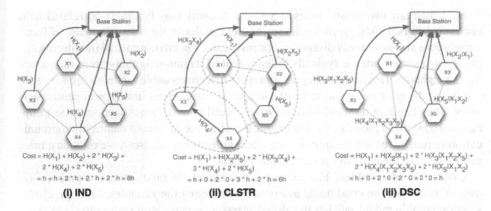

Fig. 3. Illustration of three prior approaches to data commmpression for a 5-node network (CLSTR uses 3 clusters $\{X_1\}, \{X_2, X_5\}, \{X_3, X_4\}$). If spatial correlations are perfect, total communication costs (using the *bit-hop* metric) for IND and CLSTR can be very high compared to the theoretical optimal DSC.

well. Of the $5h$ difference between CLSTR and DSC in Figure 3, $3h$ can be attributed to Approximation Loss.

Formally, let p denote the joint pdf that captures all spatial correlations in the network, and let q denote an approximation to p that captures a subset of those correlations. Let $DSC(p)$ denote the cost incurred by DSC when compressing according to the pdf p. Then the Approximation Loss for a data collection scheme that only exploits the correlations in q is given by: $DSC(q) - DSC(p)$.

Intra-source Communication: If two or more nodes are compressed jointly to exploit the spatial correlation, then the data from these nodes must be gathered at a single location. For the example shown in Figure 3, CLSTR communicates X_4 to X_3 to compress them jointly. We call this Intra-source Communication cost (the remaining $2h$ difference between CLSTR and DSC in Figure 3 can be attributed to intra-source communication).

By increasing the expressive power of the model used and thus capturing larger subsets of spatial correlations (for example, by increasing the cluster sizes), we can reduce the Approximation Loss, but the increase in the Intra-source Communication cost will typically outweigh the benefits (e.g. in Ken [4], the optimal cluster sizes were found to be < 4).

2.4 Decomposable Models and Junction Trees

In this paper, we propose using a subclass of *undirected probabilistic graphical models* [10], called *decomposable models* [8], to capture the spatial correlations and to perform data compression in a sensor network. Decomposable models capture and exploit the *conditional independences* in the data to compactly represent joint pdfs over a large number of variables. Two random variables X_1 and X_2 are conditionally independent of each other given X_3 iff:

$$p(X_1, X_2 | X_3) = p(X_1 | X_3)p(X_2 | X_3)$$

Even though any two sensor nodes in a sensor network may be highly correlated with each other in isolation, given the values of other nodes in the network, many of these correlations almost entirely disappear. For instance, in an environmental monitoring application, a sensor node is typically independent of its non-neighbors given the values of its neighbors. Hence, by using an appropriate decomposable model to approximate the joint pdf, we can exploit most of the spatial correlations in a typical sensor network while keeping the Intra-source Communication cost low. As we will see in the next section, these models can also naturally utilize the broadcast nature of communication to further reduce the Intra-source Communication cost. Next, we provide a brief introduction to the class of decomposable models.

Given a set of variables, $\mathcal{X}$, a decomposable model, denoted $\mathcal{M}$, uses a graph, $\mathcal{G}_\mathcal{M}$, over $\mathcal{X}$ to encode the conditional independences among the variables. More precisely, a decomposable model satisfies the global Markov property with respect to $\mathcal{G}_\mathcal{M}$ [28]:

> *If two node sets A and B are separated by a third node set C, i.e., if removing the nodes in C and all the edges attached to the nodes in C results in the node sets A and B getting disconnected, then A and B are conditionally independent given C.*

Further, the graph $\mathcal{G}_M$ must be *decomposable* (also called *chordal* or *triangulated*): every cycle of length greater than 3 must posses a *chord* – an edge joining two non-consecutive vertices of the cycle. Figure 4 shows two examples of decomposable graphs over 5 nodes. In the first graph, removing X_1 will separate the remaining vertices from each other; thus, we can say that X_2, X_3, X_4, X_5 are all conditionally independent of each other given X_1. In the second graph, if the edge (X_1, X_5) were missing, then it would not be chordal (since the 4-cycle $(X_1, X_2, X_5, X_4, X_1)$ would have no chord).

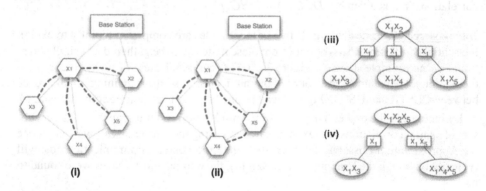

Fig. 4. (i, ii) Two example decomposable graphs superimposed on the communication network. Solid lines are network edges; dashed lines are model edges. (iii, iv) Junction trees for the two models rooted at cliques $X_1 X_2$ and $X_1 X_2 X_5$, respectively.

A compact and particularly useful representation of decomposable graphs is provided by *junction trees* (also known as *clique trees*) [3,16]. Briefly, given a decomposable graph $\mathcal{G}_\mathcal{M}$, a rooted junction tree $J_C(\mathcal{G}_\mathcal{M})$ is a tree whose vertex set consists of the *maximal cliques* of $\mathcal{G}_\mathcal{M}$, and whose root is the clique C. The edges in a junction tree are required to satisfy the following *clique-intersection property*:

For every pair C_i and C_j of cliques in $\mathcal{G}_M$, the set $C_i \cap C_j$ is contained in every clique on the path connecting C_i and C_j in $J(\mathcal{G}_M)$.

We denote by C the set of all maximal cliques of $\mathcal{G}_M$. Without loss of generality, we will assume that C_1 denotes the root of the junction tree. For a clique C, let $parent(C)$ denote the parent of the C, and let $S_C = C \cap parent(C)$ be the *separator* between the node and its parent (it is easy to see that S_C separates the vertex sets $parent(C) \setminus S_C$ and $C \setminus S_C$.). We denote by $\mathcal{S}$ the set of all separators. Although junction trees are not unique, all junction trees of a decomposable graph have the same set of separators.

Figure 4 shows one junction tree each for the two example decomposable graphs.

Approximating a Joint PDF Using a Decomposable Model: A decomposable graph, $\mathcal{G}_M$, can be used to approximate a joint probability distribution, $p(X_1, \ldots, X_n)$, as follows. For a set of variables, $C \subset \mathcal{X}$, let $p(C)$ denote the the marginal probability distribution over the variables in C (computed by summing over the remaining variables in $\mathcal{X}$). Let $q_{\mathcal{G}_M}(X_1, \ldots, X_n)$ be the probability distribution computed using the decomposable graph as follows:

$$q_{\mathcal{G}_M}(X_1, \ldots, X_n) = \frac{\Pi_{C \in \mathcal{C}}p(C)}{\Pi_{S \in \mathcal{S}}p(S)} = \Pi_{C \in \mathcal{C}}p((C - S_C)|S_C) \qquad \text{(Equation(1))}$$

For example, for the junction tree shown in Figure 4 (iii), we get that:

$$q_1(X_1, \ldots, X_5) = p(X_1X_2)p(X_3|X_1)p(X_4|X_1)p(X_5|X_1) \qquad \text{(Equation(2))}$$

We note that existence of such a closed form expression is perhaps the biggest advantage of using a decomposable graph over an arbitrary graph. Further, for any clique $C \in \mathcal{C}$, it is easy to see that q satisfies the following property: $q_{\mathcal{G}_M}(C) = p(C)$. In other words, $q_{\mathcal{G}_M}$ and p agree on the marginal distributions over the maximal cliques of $\mathcal{G}_M$.

If the approximation quality was the sole concern, we would like to use a decomposable model that minimizes the relative entropy between $q_{\mathcal{G}_M}$ and p, given by: $D(p||q_{\mathcal{G}_M}) = (\Sigma_{C \in \mathcal{C}}H(C) - \Sigma_{S \in \mathcal{S}}H(S)) - H(\mathcal{X})$. This is also the commonly used metric in probabilistic modeling [8], and further will result in low Approximation Loss. However, as we will see in next section, when using such a model for data compression, we also need to be cognizant of the communication topology.

3   Using Decomposable Models for Data Collection in WSNs

A decomposable model typically captures a subset of the correlations present in the sensor network. In this section, we first consider the problem of designing data collection protocols for optimally exploiting those correlations for a given decomposable model. We then address the problem of choosing a decomposable model for a given sensor network.

3.1   Data Collection Using a Decomposable Model

Example. We begin with the example decomposable model shown in Figure 4 (i) and the corresponding junction tree (Figure 4 (iii)). For this model, Equation (2) provides us with the way to fully exploit the captured correlations as follows:

- For each of the cliques in the model, $\{X_1, X_2\}$, $\{X_1, X_3\}$, $\{X_1, X_4\}$, $\{X_1, X_5\}$, gather the values of the attributes in the clique at some sensor node (this can be different for each clique).
- Use the marginal probability distribution $p(X_1 X_2)$ to jointly compress X_1 and X_2 (the clique at the root), and send them to the sink.
- Let the observed value of X_1 be x_1. Use the distribution $p(X_3|X_1 = x_1)$ to compress and transmit the observed value of X_3. Since $X_1 = x_1$ is already known to the sink, it can decompress using the appropriate distribution.
- Similarly, use the distributions $p(X_4|X_1 = x_1)$ and $p(X_5|X_1 = x_1)$ to transmit the values of X_4 and X_5 respectively.

The total number of bits received by the sink can be shown to be exactly:

$$H(p) + D(p\|q_1) = H(X_1 X_2) + H(X_3|X_1) + H(X_4|X_1) + H(X_5|X_1)$$

However, to be able to compute the total communication cost incurred during this protocol, we need to "place" the cliques at the sensor nodes (ie., decide which sensor nodes to collect the data for each clique at). Figure 5 shows an example placement that optimally exploits the broadcast nature of the communication. In this case, we place the clique $(X_a X_1)$ at the sensor node X_a for $a \in \{2...5\}$. With one broadcast from node X_1 (at a cost of $H(X_1)$), the value of $X_1 = x_1$ will be known to each of the remaining nodes (including the sink).

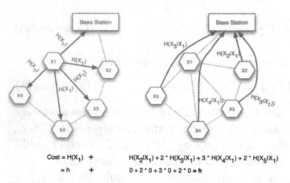

Fig. 5. Data compression using the example decomposable model from Figure 4 (i)

The total communication cost in the second step after this broadcast is given by:

$$H(X_2|X_1) + 2H(X_3|X_1) + 2H(X_4|X_1) + 2H(X_5|X_1)$$

For the case of perfect correlations considered in Figure 3, the total cost for this model can be seen to be h as well (same as DSC). However, the cost would be higher if the receiving costs were non-zero (whereas the cost for DSC would remain h).

Given an arbitrary decomposable model $\mathcal{M}$ and a rooted junction tree for it, the data collection is done as follows:

- Place the cliques of $\mathcal{M}$ on to the sensor network nodes (Section 3.2).
- For each node X_i, let D_{X_i} denote the sensor nodes which have been assigned a clique that contains X_i.
- Find a *broadcast tree* to communicate X_i to the nodes in D_{X_i} (we use a *breadth-first search* algorithm for this in our implementation).
- At the sensor node that has been assigned a clique C, compress the values of the sensor nodes in $(C - S_C)$ according to the distribution $p((C - S_C)|S_C)$.

3.2 Clique Placement Algorithms

We first present an optimal algorithm for the case when the decomposable model graph $(\mathcal{G}_M)$ is a subgraph of the communication graph $(\mathcal{G}_C)$. We then consider the more general case, and show that it is NP-Hard. We then present an efficient heuristic that we use in our experimental study.

CASE: $\mathcal{G}_M$ is a subgraph of $\mathcal{G}_C$. In most sensor networks, geographically co-located sensors tend to exhibit stronger spatial correlations than sensors that are far away from each other. As a result, in many cases, the decomposable model graph may only contain the edges between neighboring sensor nodes. We present an optimal algorithm to solve this case below.

Consider a clique C_i in $\mathcal{M}$. Since we must gather together all sensor nodes in C_i at one location, we can either (1) transmit some $|C_i| - 1$ of these nodes to the remaining node, or (2) transmit all of them to another node not in C_i (combined $|C_i| + 1$ alternatives). However, all the nodes in C_i are within communication radius of each other (since the decomposable model graph is a subgraph of the communication graph). Hence, each of the sensor nodes whose value needs to transmitted only needs to broadcast its value once. In other words, multi-hop transmissions are not needed to get the values in C_i together at one location. Thus, we only need to make binary decisions for each node (whether to broadcast, or not)[3]. Given these decisions, the placement of cliques follows (assuming sufficient nodes broadcast their values).

Our dynamic programming-based algorithm uses the following observation: once the broadcast decisions for the nodes in a separator S_i are made, the decisions for the nodes in the subtree below S_i can be made independently of the decisions for the remaining nodes in the graph. Algorithm 1 shows the pseudo-code for the main recursive procedure. Briefly, the algorithm starts at the root of the junction tree C_1 $(ComputeOptimalCost(C_1, \phi))$, and tries each of the $|C_1| + 1$ alternatives, recursing down the junction tree for each of the alternatives. It is easy to see that the algorithm runs in time $O(n^3)$.

If the receiving costs are non-zero, then the number of different possible decisions for a separator S_i is $O(|S_i|2^{|S_i|})$ (since we not only have to decide which of the nodes in S_i will broadcast, but we also must decide which of the nodes in S_i will receive those values). Overall the complexity of the algorithm increases to $O(n^3 2^s)$, where s denotes the maximum separator size. Although it is exponential in the worst case, in practice, we expect the value of s to be quite small (< 3), and hence this algorithm is quite feasible even in that case.

CASE: $\mathcal{G}_M$ is not a subgraph of $\mathcal{G}_C$

Theorem 3.1. *The general case of the clique placement problem is NP-Hard.*

Proof Sketch: We reduce a variant of the *minimum connected dominating set* problem to the clique placement problem. Given a graph $G = (V, E)$ and a set of nodes $S \subset V$, we construct a clique placement problem as follows. The communication graph over

---

[3] Note that we assume here that only the transmission costs are counted, and that the cost of receiving a message is zero.

Algorithm 1. Procedure ComputeOptimalCost(C_i, bc)

Input: C_i: A clique in $\mathcal{M}$; $bc[X_j] = true$ if $X_j \in S_{C_i}$ is broadcast

Let $key = (C_i, bc)$;

if key exists in cache **return** $cached\ cost$;

Let $D_1, \ldots, D_k$ denote the children of C_i;

if *there exists* $X \in S_{C_i}$ *such that* $bc[X] = false$ **then**

    /* All nodes in $C_i - S_i$ must be broadcast */

    $c = \Sigma_{Y \in C_i - S_i} H(Y) + H(C_i | S_i) \times d(X, sink)$;

    for $j = 1, \ldots, k$ **do**

        Construct a bit-vector bc_j of size $|S_{D_j}|$ and set all entries to $true$;

        if $X \in D_j$ **then** set $bc_j[X] = false$;

        $c = c + ComputeOptimalCost(D_j, bc_j)$;

    end

    Insert $\langle key, cost \rangle$ into cache;

    return c;

else

    /* We must try all possible placements for C_i. */

    for $X \in C_i - S_{C_i}$ **do**

        Let c_X denote the total cost assuming all nodes in C_i except X are broadcast;

        Compute c_X as above;

    end

    Compute c_{all} = the cost assuming all nodes in C_i are broadcast (C_i may be placed at a node $\notin C_i$);

    Insert $\langle key, \min(\min_X(c_X), c_{all}) \rangle$ into cache;

    return c_{min}

end

---

the sensor network is set to be G. For a node $X \notin S$, we set $H(X) = 0$. For $X \in S$, we set $H(X) = c$ for some constant c, and for each pair $(X, Y), X \in S, Y \in S$, we set $H(X|Y) = 0$. In other words, all nodes in S are perfectly correlated with each other. Further, we choose a node $A \in S$, and use a decomposable model with cliques $(A, X), X \neq A, X \in S$, and further choose an arbitrary junction tree for this model. It is easy to see that, for any junction tree, the optimal solution involves broadcasting A to all the other nodes in S. The problem of constructing the broadcast tree is identical to the problem of computing the *Steiner connected dominating set* for S, a problem that is known to be NP-Hard [11]. $\qquad\square$

We next present an efficient greedy heuristic that we use for solving the clique placement problem (Algorithm 2). Intuitively, Algorithm 2 starts off by placing all cliques as close to the sink as possible. Then, starting with the node closest to the sink, it makes local, cost-based decisions about whether to broadcast the value of each node away from the sink, into the sensor network (in effect, moving the cliques away from the sink).

Example. In our running example (Figure 4 (i) and (iii)), the four cliques $\{X_1, X_2\}$, $\{X_1, X_3\}, \{X_1, X_4\}, \{X_1, X_5\}$ would initially be placed at node X_1. The algorithm then checks if it would be beneficial to broadcast X_1 instead, which would result in placement of cliques as shown in Figure 5. After making the decision for X_1 (which is not changed afterwards), the algorithm then checks to see if X_2 should be set to broadcast and so on.

Algorithm 2. Heuristic Clique Placement Algorithm

Input: A decomposable model $\mathcal{M}$; a rooted junction tree of $\mathcal{M}$
Output: An assignment of cliques to the nodes in $\mathcal{G}_C$
Let bc denote current broadcast decisions ($bc[X] = true \implies X$ is broadcast);
Initialize $bc[X] = unknown$ for all nodes;
for $C \in \mathcal{M}$ **do**
    if $\exists X \in C$ such that $bc[X] \neq true$ **then**
        Let $X_r \in C$ be the node closest to the sink such that $bc[X_r] \neq true$;
    else
        Let $X_r \in C$ be the node farthest away from sink;
    Place C at X_r;
end
Let c denote the cost of the above clique placement;
Let X_i be the ith closest node to the sink;
for $i = 1, \ldots, n$ **do**
    Set $bc[X_i] = true$ and re-assign each clique currently placed at X_i as above;
    Let c_i be the new total cost;
    if $c_i < c$ **then** set $c = c_i$; **else** set $bc[X_i] = false$;
end

3.3 Choosing a Decomposable Model

The problem of finding an optimal decomposable model for a given data sample to minimize an error metric such as *Chi-squared error*, is known to be intractable [10], and heuristic algorithms are typically used for this purpose [8]. Although our metric (which accounts for the communication topology) is quite different from the Chi-squared error metric, we adapt a similar heuristic search procedure in our system. More specifically, we use a *forward stepwise selection* [8] algorithm to find an appropriate decomposable model. The algorithm starts with an *empty* decomposable model, i.e., a model with no edges. It then incrementally adds eligible edges in the order of their benefits until there is no improvement in the total expected communication cost. (An edge is said to be eligible if the model remains decomposable after adding it.) Algorithm 2 is used as a subroutine for evaluating the total expected communication cost of the model after adding a candidate edge in the incremental step.

To make the search problem tractable, we observe that disconnected components of the decomposable model do not influence the placement or junction tree decisions of each other. Hence, when a new edge is added, only the costs of the connected components that are affected by the addition need to be re-evaluated using Algorithm 2; a connected component is affected if the new candidate edge is incident on a vertex (or two vertices) in the component. We also memoize (cache) the total costs of all connected components encountered during search, as computed by Algorithm 2. Employing these two optimizations results in significantly reduced total execution time for the selection process. Due to space constraints, we omit a more detailed description of the algorithm.

4 Experiments

We conducted a comprehensive experimental study over several synthetic and real-world sensor network datasets. In this section, we present the results of that study.

Data Sets: Our first synthetic dataset (SYNTH-1, a 30-node network) is generated using a multivariate Gaussian distribution; each variable follows the standard normal distribution (with variance 1), and the covariance between attributes X_i and X_j is set to be a function of the distance between them, $c^{d(X_i, X_j)}$ (where c $(0 \leq c \leq 1)$ denotes the correlation strength). The sensor nodes are placed randomly in a 20x20 square and have an average hop count of 8.5 to the sink (placed at $(0, 0)$).

For the second and third synthetic data sets (SYNTH-2 and SYNTH-3, two 72-node networks), we use an analytical expression for computing the entropy for a precipitation data model (presented and used by Pattem et al. [22] in their study). The network topologies are generated by placing the nodes randomly within a 66x66 square and a 3x24 rectangle respectively, with average hop counts of 6.5 and 13.5 to the sink.

The first real-world data set, *Lab* [18], contains traces from 49 sensors deployed in the Intel Research Lab at Berkeley. The data contains roughly 23 days of recordings on light, humidity, temperature and voltage. We use the temperature readings between 9pm to 3am for our experiments. The data from first 15 days is used for training (for constructing the model and the pdfs), and the data from next 8 days is used for testing. Our second real-world data set, *Precipitation*, contains precipitation data in the states of Washington and Oregon collected during 1949-1994 [29]. Fifty stations are randomly selected from the deployment. We discretize the observed values into three categories: *light rain, medium rain,* and *heavy rain*. The initial two thirds of the data is selected as the training set, and the remaining data is used for testing.

Comparison Systems:
We compare the following data collection methods.

- NAIVE: No compression is done while collecting the data.
- IND (Section 2.2): Each node compresses its data independently of the others.
- CLSTR (Section 2.2): The clusters are chosen using the greedy algorithm presented in Chu et al. [4].
- KEN [4]: This is similar to above, except that no compression is performed while collecting the data for each cluster at the cluster-head (this will always perform worse than CLSTR).
- DECOMP: An appropriate decomposable model is chosen using the algorithms presented in Section 3, and is used for data collection.
- DSC: Where applicable, the theoretical lower bound is plotted (Section 2.2).

Methodology: We investigate the performance under different data and network characteristics including correlation, error threshold ϵ (for SYNTH-1 and Lab), network topology, and the sensor receiving costs. Unless otherwise mentioned, we set $\epsilon = 0.5$. To avoid model over-fitting, we limit the clique/cluster size $S \leq 3$ for DECOMP, KEN, and CLSTR. For the synthetic datasets, we restrict the models learned by DECOMP to be subgraphs of the communication network since the spatial correlations are strongest for neighboring nodes. We remove this restriction for the real-world data sets. For the

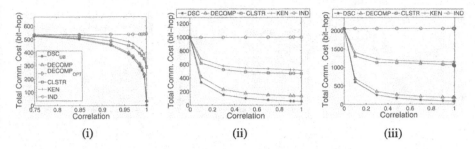

Fig. 6. Total data collection costs for (i) SYNTH-1, (ii) SYNTH-2, and (iii) SYNTH-3

synthetic datasets, we use the joint-entropy based data collection – for SYNTH-1, we estimate the entropy using the training dataset, whereas for SYNTH-2 and SYNTH-3, we use the analytical expressions presented in Pattem et al. [22]. For real-world datasets, we use suppression-based data collection.

Results: Synthetic Datasets. Figure 6 compares the effectiveness of the different schemes at reducing the total transmission cost on the three synthetic datasets for varying correlation characteristics. We also plot an estimate of the cost of DSC; for SYNTH-1, we can only compute an upper bound since accurate estimation of entropy over large sets of variables is not feasible. For SYNTH-1, we plot two graphs for DECOMP, one where we use the optimal clique placement algorithm and the other using the heuristic algorithm (Section 3.2). There is however almost no difference in the total transmission cost, and the two graphs overlap entirely. We use the heuristic algorithm in the rest of the section as it is much more efficient than the optimal algorithm.

Several facts become clear from these figures. At low correlations, the techniques perform fairly similarly; the intra-source communication cost outweighs the benefits of joint compression, and hence all techniques degenerate to IND. As the correlation strength increases, the total costs of the techniques that exploit the correlations decrease rapidly, with DECOMP performing much better than CLSTR or KEN. In fact, the total cost for DECOMP is very close to that of DSC; not only is the Approximation Loss of DECOMP very low, but, because it exploits broadcast communication, the Intra-source communication cost of DECOMP is also very low. We again note that, if the receiving costs are factored in, the performance of DECOMP is noticeably worse than DSC, although it is still much superior to CLSTR or KEN (see below).

Another interesting aspect is how network topologies affect the qualitative behaviors of the schemes. Comparing Figure 6(iii) with Figure 6(ii), we see that it is more expensive to transmit data in the deep network (Figure 6(iii)) since the average hop count is larger. Forming spatial cliques for doing in-network compressions becomes more attractive in such a network; if correlations are ignored, the Approximation Loss in such networks can be very high.

Figure 7(i) presents the effects of varying the user-defined error threshold ϵ (for the SYNTH-1 dataset, with correlation $c = 0.9$). As expected, the total cost decreases when ϵ is increased for all techniques. We note that the performance of DECOMP remains close to the upper bound on DSC for a wide range of error thresholds.

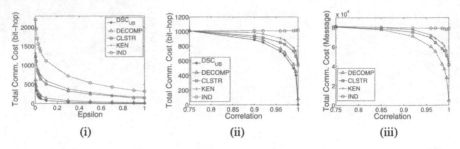

Fig. 7. (i) Effects of ϵ on the total cost for SYNTH-1, (ii) Impact of receiving cost for SYNTH-1, (iii) Total message-based transmission cost for SYNTH-1

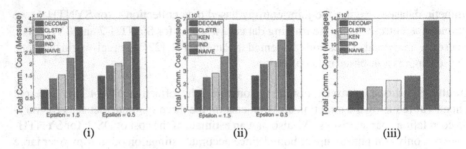

Fig. 8. The total communication costs for: (i) Lab dataset (over $\approx$ 1300 runs), (ii) Lab dataset including receiving costs, (iii) Precipitation dataset (over 5600 runs)

We next present the results from an experiment where the receiving cost was set to be the same as the transmission cost (as is common in many deployments). Figure 7(ii) shows the total communication cost with the receiving cost included for SYNTH-1. Similarly to Figure 6(i), both DECOMP and the clustering based methods stay at their upper bound, IND, till $c = 0.75$[4]. As we can see, the relative performance of DE-COMP, IND and CLSTR remains essentially unchanged; however, the relative cost of DECOMP increases slightly compared to DSC. This is because DECOMP exploits broadcast communication, which gets penalized when receiving costs are non-zero.

Finally, Figure 7(iii) presents the total cost in terms of the message-based metric for 500 test tuples in SYNTH-1. Messages, instead of bits, are used to quantify the communication costs. We note that the graph shows similar trends as the entropy-based metric (Figure 6(i)), with DECOMP resulting in much fewer total messages transmitted than the alternatives.

Results: Real-World Datasets. Figure 8(i) present the results for Lab's test traces when receiving costs are not considered. The results are for $\epsilon = 0.5$ and $\epsilon = 1.5$. DECOMP achieves the best performance in both cases. A small value of ϵ (i.e. $\epsilon = 0.5$) results in higher entropy and the total cost of all techniques increases. The increase in ϵ

---

[4] Although $c = 0.75$ might seem large, we note that the 30-node network resides in a 20×20 square, resulting in large pairwise node distances.

results in sharp drops in communication costs: DECOMP achieves a 41% drop in total cost, CLSTR has a 29% drop, and KEN has a 25% drop. More subtle, a small value of ϵ introduces higher variances in the quantized data, and hence the correlations across sensors are weaker. As a result, the relative performance of all modeling-based techniques, relative to IND, is slightly worse for small values of ϵ.

Introducing receiving costs (Figure 8(ii)) results in a higher total communication cost for all schemes. DECOMP continues to outperform the other methods, and the amount of performance differences for all modeling-based methods with respect to NAIVE stays relatively unchanged.

Finally, Figure 8(iii) plots the results of exact data collection for the precipitation data (i.e. $\epsilon = 0$). The spatial correlations in this data are not high, but as Figure 8(iii) shows, the modeling-based approaches significantly outperform Naive, and DECOMP achieves the lowest total communication cost among all four modeling-based approaches.

5 Related Work

Wireless sensor networks have been a very active area of research in recent years (see [1] for a survey). Due to space constraints, we only discuss some of the most closely related work on data collection in sensor networks here. Directed diffusion [15], Cougar [32], TAG [19], TinyDB [20], LEACH [14] are few of the general purpose data collection mechanisms that have been proposed in the literature. The focus of that work has been on designing protocols and/or declarative interfaces to collect data, and not on optimizing continuous data collection. Aside from the work by Pattem et al. [22] and Chu et al. [4], the BBQ system [9] also uses a predictive modeling-based approach to collect data from a sensor network. However, the BBQ system only provides probabilistic, approximates answers to queries, without any guarantees on the correctness. Scaglione and Servetto [24] also consider the interdependence of routing and data compression, but the problem they focus on (getting all data to all nodes) is different from the problem we address. Cristescu et al. [6] consider the problem of finding a near-optimal tree-based communication structure to minimize the total transmission cost; their approach is similar to routing driven compression (RDC) [24,22] and may require repeated compression and decompression over large numbers of data sources at the sensor nodes, which may make it unsuitable for resource-constrained sensor networks. In a seminal work, Gupta and Kumar [13] proved that the transport capacity of a random wireless network scales only as $O(\sqrt{n})$, where n is the number of sensor nodes. Although this seriously limits the scalability of sensor networks in some domains, in the kinds of applications we are looking at, the *bandwidth* or the *rate* is rarely the limiting factor; to be able to last a long time, the sensor nodes are typically almost always in sleep mode.

Several approaches not based on predictive modeling have also been proposed for data collection in sensor networks or distributed environments. Kotidis [17] and Gupta et al. [12] consider approaches based on using a representative set of sensor nodes to approximate the data distribution over the entire network. Constraint chaining [25] is a suppression-based exact data collection approach that monitors a minimal set of node and edge constraints to ensure correct recovery of the values at the base station.

More recently, Cormode et al. [5] have proposed a similar approach of using replicated predictive models to solve the problem of maintaining accurate quantile summaries over distributed data sources.

6 Conclusions

In this paper, we presented an approach that uses a subclass of undirected graphical models called *decomposable* models for continuous sensor data collection with accuracy guarantees. Compared to previous predictive modeling-based approaches, our approach is more effective at exploiting the spatial correlations in the data, and thus reducing the total communication cost incurred during the process. Our proposed approach also naturally exploits the broadcast nature of communication in sensor networks. An extensive experimental study using both synthetic and real-world data sets demonstrates the effectiveness of our approach.

There are several directions of future work that we are planning to pursue. We are developing more efficient algorithms that can scale to very large sensor networks, and that can efficiently exploit both spatial and temporal correlations. So far we have assumed that the sensor nodes do not fail; extending our protocols to function correctly in presence of such faults remains a challenge. Finally, although our approach performs very well compared to the lower bound provided by DSC, understanding the fundamental reasons behind the gap between the two and how we can bridge that gap remains an open question.

References

1. Akyildiz, I.F., Su, W., Sankarasubramaniam, Y., Cayirci, E.: Wireless sensor networks: a survey. Computer Networks 38 (2002)
2. Arici, T., Gedik, B., Altunbasak, Y., Liu, L.: PINCO: A pipelined in-network compression scheme for data collection in wireless sensor networks. In: IEEE Intl. Conf. on Computer Communications and Networks (2003)
3. Blair, J.R.S., Peyton, B.: An Introduction to Chordal Graphs and Clique Trees. In: Graph Theory and Sparse Matrix Computation, pp. 1–29. Springer, New York (1993)
4. Chu, D., Deshpande, A., Hellerstein, J., Hong, W.: Approximate data collection in sensor networks using probabilistic models. In: Proceedings of the International Conference on Data Engineering (ICDE) (2006)
5. Cormode, G., Garofalakis, M., Muthukrishnan, S., Rastogi, R.: Holistic aggregates in a networked world: Distributed tracking of approximate quantiles. In: SIGMOD (2005)
6. Cristescu, R., Beferull-Lozano, B., Vetterli, M., Wattenhofer, R.: Network correlated data gathering with explicit communication: Np-completeness and algorithms. IEEE/ACM Transactions on Networking 14(1), 41–54 (2006)
7. Cristescu, R., Beferull-Lozano, B., Vetterli, M.: Networked slepian-wolf: Theory and algorithms. In: Karl, H., Wolisz, A., Willig, A. (eds.) Wireless Sensor Networks. LNCS, vol. 2920, pp. 44–59. Springer, Heidelberg (2004)
8. Deshpande, A., Garofalakis, M., Jordan, M.: Efficient stepwise selection in decomposable models. In: UAI (2001)
9. Deshpande, A., Guestrin, C., Madden, S., Hellerstein, J., Hong, W.: Model-driven data acquisition in sensor networks. In: VLDB (2004)

10. Edwards, D.: Introduction to Graphical Modeling. Springer, New York (1995)
11. Guha, S., Khuller, S.: Approximation algorithms for connected dominating sets. Algorithmica 20(4), 374–387 (1998)
12. Gupta, H., Navda, V., Das, S., Chowdhary, V.: Efficient gathering of correlated data in sensor networks. In: MobiHoc (2005)
13. Gupta, P., Kumar, P.R.: The capacity of wireless networks. IEEE Transactions on Information Theory 46, 388–404 (2000)
14. Heinzelman, W.R., Chandrakasan, A., Balakrishnan, H.: Energy-efficient communication protocol for wireless microsensor networks. In: HICSS 2000. Proceedings of the 33rd Hawaii International Conference on System Sciences, vol. 8, p. 8020 (2000)
15. Intanagonwiwat, C., Govindan, R., Estrin, D.: Directed diffusion: A scalable and robust communication paradigm for sensor networks. In: ACM MobiCOM (2000)
16. Jensen, F.V., Jensen, F.: Optimal Junction Trees. In: Proceedings of the Tenth Annual Conference on Uncertainty in Artificial Intelligence, Seattle, Washington (July 1994)
17. Kotidis, Y.: Snapshot queries: Towards data-centric sensor networks. In: ICDE (2005)
18. Madden, S.: Intel lab data (2003),
    http://db.csail.mit.edu/labdata/labdata.html
19. Madden, S., Franklin, M.J., Hellerstein, J.M., Hong, W.: TAG: A tiny aggregation service for ad-hoc sensor networks. In: OSDI (2002)
20. Madden, S., Hong, W., Hellerstein, J., Franklin, M.: TinyDB web page,
    http://telegraph.cs.berkeley.edu/tinydb
21. Olston, C., Loo, B., Widom, J.: Adaptive precision setting for cached approximate values. In: SIGMOD (2001)
22. Pattem, S., Krishnamachari, B., Govindan, R.: The impact of spatial correlation on routing with compression in wireless sensor networks. In: IPSN (2004)
23. Pradhan, S., Ramchandran, K.: Distributed source coding using syndromes (DISCUS): Design and construction. IEEE Trans. Information Theory (2003)
24. Scaglione, A., Servetto, S.: On the interdependence of routing and data compression in multi-hop sensor networks. In: Mobicom (2002)
25. Silberstein, A., Braynard, R., Yang, J.: Constraint-chaining: On energy-efficient continuous monitoring in sensor networks. In: SIGMOD (2006)
26. Slepian, D., Wolf, J.: Noiseless coding of correlated information sources. IEEE Transactions on Information Theory 19(4) (1973)
27. Su, X.: A combinatorial algorithmic approach to energy efficient information collection in wireless sensor networks. ACM Trans. Sen. Netw. 3(1), 6 (2007)
28. Whittaker, J.: Graphical Models in Applied Multivariate Statistics. In: Wiley Series in Probability and Mathematical Statistics, John Wiley, Chichester (1990)
29. Widmann, M., Bretherton, C.: 50 km resolution daily precipitation for the pacific northwest (2003), http://www.jisao.washington.edu/data_sets/widmann
30. Wyner, A.D., Ziv, J.: The rate-distortion function for source coding with side information at the decoder. IEEE Transactions on Information Theory (1976)
31. Xiong, Z., Liveris, A.D., Cheng, S.: Distributed source coding for sensor networks. IEEE Signal Processing Magazine 21, 80–94 (2004)
32. Yao, Y., Gehrke, J.: Query processing in sensor networks. In: CIDR (2003)

Distributed Inference for Network Localization Using Radio Interferometric Ranging

Dennis Lucarelli[1], Anshu Saksena[1], Ryan Farrell[1,2], and I-Jeng Wang[1]

[1] Applied Physics Laboratory, Johns Hopkins University, Laurel, MD
[2] Computer Science Department, University of Maryland, College Park, MD

Abstract. A localization algorithm using radio interferometric measurements is presented. A probabilistic model is constructed that accounts for general noise models and lends itself to distributed computation. A message passing algorithm is derived that exploits the geometry of radio interferometric measurements and can support sparse network topologies and noisy measurements. Simulations on real and simulated data show promising performance for 2D and 3D deployments.

1 Introduction

Self-localization is a fundamental, yet not completely solved, problem in the design and deployment of sensor networks. It is *fundamental* because sensor networks are envisioned to provide visibility and monitoring with inexpensive devices in GPS denied areas. Despite many localization algorithms and improvements in device hardware, one can argue that the problem is not completely solved since no single method has been widely adopted for such a fundamental problem. Most notably, there is a need for a localization system capable of handling the multipath effects encountered indoors and in dense urban areas. The main impediment to the creation of such a system is an effective means of obtaining range measurements in a multipath environment and the development of localization algorithms that can account for these effects.

Various technologies such as ultrasound/RF TDOA ranging [1], acoustic TOA (e.g. [2]), and received radio signal strength (e.g. [3]), have been proposed and demonstrated for acquiring pairwise distance estimates. Broadly speaking and despite the ingenuity of these approaches, these methods are plagued by short range, poor precision, or the requirement of an ancillary system devoted just to ranging. Given these limitations, researchers have proposed methods for network localization that do not rely on ranging at all. These so-called *range free* methods, see for example [4,5,6], use either a camera system or in the case of [5] a steerable laser to localize the nodes. Again, these solutions require additional hardware and calibration to solve the problem.

A recent breakthrough has changed the localization landscape considerably. Researchers at Vanderbilt University have proposed and demonstrated a surprisingly simple, yet powerful, method for ranging using only the radio that produces centimeter ranging accuracy at ranges up to 160 meters [7,8]. This technique,

R. Verdone (Ed.): EWSN 2008, LNCS 4913, pp. 52–73, 2008.

known as radio interferometric ranging, exploits electromagnetic interference to obtain an observable that is a function of the locations of four nodes sensors (known here as a *quad*) involved in the measurement. As such, it does not directly produce pairwise distance measurements, but rather a linear combination of four of the possible six pairwise distances. This fact renders localization algorithms that rely on pairwise distances unable to capitalize on this new technique. Perhaps the most remarkable feature of this technique is that it can be implemented with coarse time synchronization on inexpensive radios found on widely available sensor network devices.

In this paper, we propose a distributed algorithm for network localization using radio interferometric ranging. We derive and exploit the geometry underlying the ranging technique that enables the algorithm. In the next section we show how the location of a node is constrained conditional on the location of the three other nodes involved in the ranging measurement. We show that, in the two dimensional case, knowing the location of three nodes constrains the fourth to a branch of a hyperbola. By taking two independent measurements on those four nodes, one can obtain another distinct hyperbola thus further constraining the nodes location to lie on the intersection of these conics. Given that the knowledge of three nodes and two independent interferometric range measurements (RIMs) reduces the uncertainty of the fourth node to just one or two intersection points, it seems plausible that a multilateration procedure can be derived akin to trilateration in systems with pairwise measurements. Indeed, assuming a 2D deployment with four anchor nodes[1] and a sensor within RIM's range of the four anchors, the unknown node can participate in up to three separate independent quads [8]. Further assuming that for each quad two independent measurements are obtained, a set of intersections points can be computed for the unknown sensor and this set of points could then potentially be used to determine the location of the unknown node.

In contrast, we adopt a probabilistic approach. Given the nonlinear relationships defined by the ranging procedure, their resulting uncertainty and our ultimate goal of developing a robust means of network localization in multi-path environments, a nonparametric probabilistic approach is preferred. We embed the underlying geometry in a flexible probabilistic model that lends itself to distributed computation. With the appropriate definition of the model, the distributed inference algorithm, known as *belief propagation*, in a sense, "comes for free." In this regard, our approach is very much in the spirit of Ihler et al. [9], but adapted to the subtleties of dealing with radio interferometric ranging.

2 Conditional Geometry of Radio Interferometric Measurements

The functional form of the radio interferometric range measurement presents a unique challenge in designing a distributed localization algorithm. On a set of

---

[1] Three anchors will not suffice, since, in the general case, the uncertainty of the unlocalized node can only be reduced to two distinct intersection points.

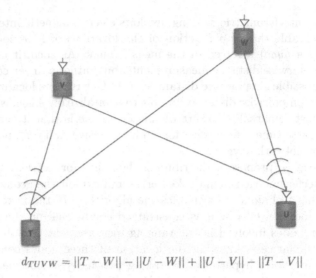

$$d_{TUVW} = \|T - W\| - \|U - W\| + \|U - V\| - \|T - V\|$$

Fig. 1. Radio interferometric measurement

four sensors labeled T, U, V, and W, after post processing the RIM is given by [7,8]

$$d_{TUVW} := \|T - W\| - \|U - W\| + \|U - V\| - \|T - V\| + \eta \tag{1}$$

where η represents an additive noise term. However, if three of the four nodes involved in the measurement are known, say for example, $\{T, V, W\}$, the measurement reduces to a quadratic equation in the coordinates of the unknown node,

$$d_{TUVW} = - \|U - W\| + \|U - V\| + k' + \eta \tag{2}$$

where k' is the constant given by $\|T - W\| - \|T - V\|$. As is evident, in two dimensions the locus of points satisfying this equation is a conic section. Specifically, by setting $d_{TUVW} = k^*$ and neglecting the noise term for a moment, the equation

$$k = k^* - k' = - \|U - W\| + \|U - V\| \tag{3}$$

describes the location of node U conditional on the measurement and the locations of the nodes $\{T, V, W\}$.

Equation 3 defines one branch of a hyperbola with foci at the points $\{V, W\}$. There are two independent RIMs on four nodes [8] corresponding to two distinct hyperbolae, thus the uncertainty of the unknown sensor location can be further reduced by taking an additional measurement. For example, the measurement $d_{TVUW} := \|T - W\| - \|V - W\| + \|U - V\| - \|T - U\|$ defines a second hyperbola with the unknown node location at the intersection points of the hyperbolae defined by the measurements $\{d_{TUVW}, d_{TVUW}\}$. Figure 2 depicts the

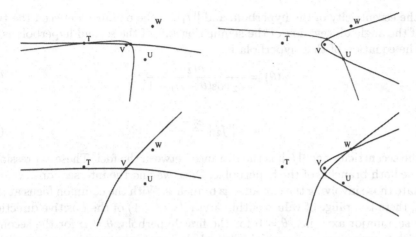

Fig. 2. Intersection points of hyperbolae defined by two independent RIMs

scenario with the unknown sensor cycling through all four possibilities with the two measurements fixed. From the figure we can get a feel for the sensitivity of the intersections to the input data. For example, the figure in the upper left quadrant (where T is the unknown node location) we see that not only two intersection points exist but also the hyperbolae almost coincide on the arc where T lies. Clearly this geometry is very susceptible to noise in the input data and hints to the difficulty in crafting a localization algorithm for ad-hoc networks with interferometric ranging. A favorable geometry is depicted in the lower left quadrant, where the hyperbolae intersect in a unique isolated point V.

Computing the intersection points of two conics, in general, requires solving a quartic equation that does not admit a convenient closed form solution. However, if the hyperbolae share a common focus, as is the case for the measurement set $\{d_{TUVW}, d_{TVUW}\}$, this system reduces to a quadratic equation and the intersection points can be computed exactly and efficiently. For example, the location of sensor V is a common focus of the hyperbolae defined by d_{TUVW} and d_{TVUW}, if sensor U is the unknown node.

Since a literature survey did not uncover the procedure for computing intersection points of conics sharing a focus, a derivation is presented here. If a translation and rotation are applied to bring the common focus to the origin and the other focus of one of the hyperbolae to the x-axis, then the equation in polar coordinates of the hyperbola with both foci on the x-axis is

$$r_1(\theta) = \frac{m_1}{e_1 \cos(\theta) - 1}, \tag{4}$$

where

$$m_1 = \|f_1\| \frac{e_1^2 - 1}{2e_1}, \tag{5}$$

e_1 is the eccentricity of the hyperbola and $\|f_1\|$ is the distance between the two foci. If the angle of elevation of the semimajor axis of the second hyperbola is ϕ, then the equation of that hyperbola is

$$r_2(\theta) = \frac{m_2}{e_2 \cos(\theta - \phi) - 1}, \tag{6}$$

where

$$m_2 = \|f_2\| \frac{e_2^2 - 1}{2e_2}, \tag{7}$$

e_2 is the eccentricity and $\|f_2\|$ is the distance between the foci. These expressions describe both branches of the hyperbolae. Once we find the intersections, we will eliminate those involving the extraneous branches. With the common focus at the origin, there is a range of values within $\arctan(\sqrt{e^2 - 1})$ of the positive direction of the semimajor axis (i.e., $\theta = 0$ for the first hyperbola, $\theta = \phi$ for the second) for which there are two points of the hyperbola – one corresponding to a positive value of r_i and lying on one branch of the hyperbola, and one corresponding to a negative value of r_i for θ halfway around the circle on the other branch. In order to find all intersections of the hyperbolae, we need to set $r_1(\theta) = r_2(\theta)$ to find intersections of portions of each hyperbola with the same sign of r_i and $-r_1(\theta + \pi) = r_2(\theta)$ to find intersections of the negative part of one hyperbola with the positive part of the other.

These equalities each yield a quadratic expression in $\cos(\theta)$ whose standard form coefficients are:

$$a_1 = \left(\frac{e_1}{m_1} - \frac{e_2}{m_2}\right)^2 + 2\frac{e_1 e_2}{m_1 m_2}(1 - \cos(\phi)) \tag{8}$$

$$b_1 = 2\left(\frac{e_1}{m_1} - \frac{e_2}{m_2}\cos(\phi)\right)\left(\frac{1}{m_2} - \frac{1}{m_1}\right) \tag{9}$$

$$c_1 = \left(\frac{1}{m_2} - \frac{1}{m_1}\right)^2 - \left(\frac{e_2}{m_2}\right)^2 (1 - \cos^2(\phi)) \tag{10}$$

for the first equality and

$$a_2 = \left(\frac{e_1}{m_1} - \frac{e_2}{m_2}\right)^2 + 2\frac{e_1 e_2}{m_1 m_2}(1 - \cos(\phi)) \tag{11}$$

$$b_2 = 2\left(\frac{e_1}{m_1} - \frac{e_2}{m_2}\cos(\phi)\right)\left(\frac{1}{m_1} + \frac{1}{m_2}\right) \tag{12}$$

$$c_2 = \left(\frac{1}{m_1} + \frac{1}{m_2}\right)^2 - \left(\frac{e_2}{m_2}\right)^2 (1 - \cos^2(\phi)) \tag{13}$$

for the second. If the discriminant $d_i = b_i^2 - 4a_i c_i$ is negative, zero, or positive, that equality has no solutions, one solution, or two solutions, respectively. Therefore, the total number of intersections of the hyperbolae can be anywhere between zero and four. If there are solutions, they are given by:

$$\cos(\theta_i) = \frac{-b_i \pm \sqrt{d_i}}{2a_i} \tag{14}$$

for $i = 1$ or 2 indicating which hyperbolic intersection equality we are evaluating. In order to solve for θ_i, we must calculate $\sin(\theta_i)$ as well to ensure we determine the correct quadrant.

$$\sin(\theta_1) = \frac{\cos(\theta_1)(e_1 m_2 - e_2 m_1 \cos(\phi)) - m_2 + m_1}{e_2 m_1 \sin(\phi)} \qquad (15)$$

$$\sin(\theta_2) = \frac{\cos(\theta_2)(e_1 m_2 - e_2 m_1 \cos(\phi)) + m_1 + m_2}{e_2 m_1 \sin(\phi)} \qquad (16)$$

The solutions for θ_i then can be calculated by taking the arctangent of the quotient of the sine and cosine, maintaining the correct quadrant. We eliminate those values that are outside the range of values for the branch of each hyperbola that correspond to the measurement constraint. After doing so we will have zero, one, or two values of θ_i remaining. Although for the most part we will have a nonzero number of intersections remaining since the nodes are embedded in the space and the measurements are derived from their positions, noise in the measurements can occasionally cause a situation where no intersections are possible. This indicates that the positions of at least one of the three foci is inconsistent with the measurements. When intersections remain, plugging their values back into Eq. (6) and rotating and translating back to the original coordinate system gives us the possible locations of the unknown sensor node.

The radio interferometric technique is not restricted to two dimensions. Moreover, the geometry associated with the measurements generalizes as well. In the 3D case, the conditional uncertainty of a node given the location of the three others is a hyperboloid. Two RIMs reduce the uncertainty to the intersection curve of the hyperboloids. Again if two hyperboloids share a common focus, solving a simple quadratic equation leads to an analytic parameterization of the intersection curve [10]. It turns out that this intersection curve is a hyperbola or an ellipse. Examples of the geometry of 3D RIMs is depicted in Figure 3 where a total of four measurements are taken, two generating a hyperbolic intersection and

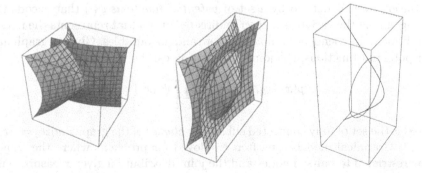

Fig. 3. Intersection curves of hyperboloids defined by RIMs in 3D

the other two generating an elliptical intersection. The location of the unknown sensor lies on the intersection of these two curves as depicted in the figure.

3   Problem Formulation

In the preceding section, the geometric intuition behind the proposed algorithm was outlined. These considerations, even in the 2D case, do not suffice to design a robust, scalable localization algorithm. Our approach embeds the multilateration primitive into a probabilistic model that allows for *soft assignments* of the sensor locations that are iteratively refined over time.

In addition to the nonlinearity introduced by the form of the interferometric measurement, noise and errors from a variety of sources affect the measurement value [7]. These sources of error, such as multipath effects, carrier frequency inaccuracy, time synchronization error and signal processing errors, are modeled by a noise distribution in our algorithm. These errors manifest in the post processing of the interferometric measurements as a possible error that is a multiple of the wavelength of the carrier frequency. This distribution can therefore be modeled as a small Gaussian mixture with components centered at integer multiples of the wavelength of the carrier frequency. It has been shown that iterative filtering techniques can be applied to the radio interferometric ranging procedure to produce high precision range estimates in a mild multipath environment that effectively remove the non-Gaussian nature of the errors [8]. Though it has not been explicitly demonstrated, an RSSI technique such as radio interferometry will likely suffer performance degradation in a high multi-path environment such as indoors or in a dense urban area. Our approach attempts to explicitly handle the effects of ranging error by associating a random variable to each sensor location and defining the joint distribution of the sensor locations that incorporates the intrinsic geometry of the radio interferometry technique.

The formalism used to capture the uncertainty and the measurement model is a probabilistic graphical model. Let $\mathcal{X} = \{x_1, x_2 \ldots x_n\}$ be a collection of random variables. A graphical model is a factored representation of the joint distribution over $\mathcal{X}$ defined by a set of *potential functions* $\psi(\cdot)$ that encode the coupling among the variables and an undirected graph that represents the notion of conditional independence among sets of random variables. Given a graph and set of potential functions, the joint distribution can be written as

$$p(x_1, x_2, \ldots, x_n) \propto \prod_{c \in \mathcal{C}} \psi_c(x_c) \tag{17}$$

where $\mathcal{C}$ is the set of fully connected subsets or *cliques* of the graph and $x_c = \{x_u : x_u \in c\}$. Graphical models are often employed for problems where the cliques can be restricted to pairs of nodes and the joint distribution given measurements is given by

$$p(x_1, x_2, \ldots, x_n | \mathcal{D}) \propto \prod_{(u,v) \in \mathcal{E}} \psi_{uv}(x_u, x_v, d_{uv}) \prod_u \psi_u(x_u, d_u) \tag{18}$$

where $\mathcal{E}$ is the set of edges in the graph and $\mathcal{D}$ denotes the entire set of measurements , $d_{uv}, d_u \in \mathcal{D}$ and $\psi(x_u, d_u)$ is a local potential function that is used to capture any *a priori* knowledge for a node or to model a local measurement.

The graphical representation of the joint distribution has inspired many inference algorithms that exploit this graphical structure to achieve greater efficiency. An iterative message passing algorithm known as *belief propagation* is one of the best known of these methods for computing marginal distributions due to its simplicity and excellent empirical results on high dimensional problems. For problems involving spatial data in ad-hoc sensor networks, one can exploit the analogy of a *communications* graph, where an edge signifies a communication channel between sensors, and identify these two graphical representations to develop a probabilistic model for fusing measurement data that includes a simple message passing algorithm for performing inference on that model.

For continuous systems with pairwise couplings, the belief propagation update equations are given by an expression for computing a message from node u to node v, denoted $m_{uv}(x_v)$, and an expression for computing the belief at a node, β_v, which is an estimate of the marginal distribution of the random variable x_v. At iteration n, the message update is given by

$$m_{uv}^n(x_v) \propto \int \psi(x_u, x_v)\, \psi(x_u) \prod_{(w,u) \in \mathcal{E} \backslash (v,u)} m_{wu}^{n-1}(x_u)\, dx_u \tag{19}$$

Note that the message sent from node x_v in the previous iteration is excluded from the message product for consistency of the marginalization procedure.

Roughly speaking, Eq. (19) represents node u's *belief* about the marginal of node v given its measurements and the messages from its neighbors in the graph from the previous iteration. Fusion of these messages to approximate its marginal is achieved by simply taking the product of received messages and the local potential function,

$$\beta^n(x_v) \propto \psi(x_v) \prod_{(w,v) \in \mathcal{E}} m_{wv}^n(x_v) \tag{20}$$

In the context of sensor networks, the attraction of belief propagation in a graphical model is evident since it is a simple way to perform *global* inference using *local* communications and *distributed* computation. However, the correctness of belief propagation is not guaranteed unless one restricts the graphical structure to a tree. Fortunately, the so called *loopy* version of belief propagation, where one carries out the message and fusion updates of Eqs. (19) and (20) without regard to the existence of loops in the graph, has shown excellent empirical performance in a variety of settings. There has been some progress in understanding the convergence of loopy belief propagation. The most useful characterization for this discussion is that if the loopy algorithm converges, it will converge to fixed points of the so called *Bethe free energy* [11]. Alternatively, one may always aggregate random variables into a *junction tree* and conduct message passing on that tree to perform inference exactly; however, the complexity of the algorithm is exponential in a graphical property of the junction tree known as the *tree width*.

As may be intuitively obvious, a graphical model formulation of the network localization problem with interferometric ranging will not have pairwise couplings since the variables are coupled by the measurement that involves four nodes to obtain one observable. The joint distribution factors according to this coupling and is given by

$$p(x_1, \ldots x_n | \mathcal{D}) \propto \prod_t \psi(x_t) \prod_{(tuvw) \in \mathcal{Q}} \psi(x_t, x_u, x_v, x_w, d_{TUVW}) \tag{21}$$

where $\mathcal{Q}$ is the set of quads in the graph.

There are a number of ways to define *higher order* belief propagation. One method, as mentioned above, is to aggregate variables into a junction tree. This technique has been extended for distributed inference problems in sensor networks with lossy communications in [12]. In this work, we follow a derivation obtained by minimizing the Bethe free energy in a manner analogous to the case with pairwise potential functions [13].

Let $\mathcal{T}_w$ be the set of index triples that share an interferometric range measurement with node x_w. Formally, if $(tuv) \in \mathcal{T}_w$, we can express the message from the set $\{x_t, x_u, x_v\}$ to node x_w, denoted $m_{tuvw}^n(x_w)$, as

$$m_{tuvw}^n(x_w) \propto \int \psi(x_t)\psi(x_u)\psi(x_v)\psi(x_t, x_u, x_v, x_w) \prod_{(qrs) \in \mathcal{T}_v \setminus (tuw)} m_{qrsv}^{n-1}(x_v)$$

$$\prod_{(qrs) \in \mathcal{T}_u \setminus (tvw)} m_{qrsu}^{n-1}(x_u) \prod_{(qrs) \in \mathcal{T}_t \setminus (uvw)} m_{qrst}^{n-1}(x_t) \, dx_t dx_u dx_v \tag{22}$$

Analogous to the pairwise case, the estimate of the marginal is simply the product of the incoming messages with the local potential function

$$\beta^n(x_w) \propto \psi(x_w) \prod_{(tuv) \in \mathcal{T}_w} m_{tuvw}^n(x_w) \tag{23}$$

While being functionally simple, the expression defining the messages suffers from two serious drawbacks. First, the integral is clearly intractable for densely connected networks of resource constrained devices such as sensor networks. We defer the discussion of this important consideration until the next section where a suitable approximation technique is presented. The second drawback of such an expression, which is clearly exacerbated in the case of four node couplings, is the complexity and coordination required among the sensors to implement the message passing. While being decentralized, a direct implementation of an algorithm utilizing (22) would be a poor *distributed* algorithm due to the complexity of the message passing. For example, as depicted in Figure 4, to pass a message from the triple $(ijk) \in \mathcal{T}_l$ to x_l, the sending triple would have to elect a leader node to recieve the individual nodes' contributions and perform the product and integral in (22). Following the approach suggested in [14,9,15], we can simplify

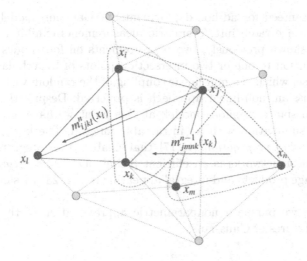

Fig. 4. Higher-order belief propagation message passing

the message passing to broadcast communications at the cost of local memory. To see this, note that the beliefs (23) contain much of the information required to form the message (22), except for the four variable potential function and the correction required for consistency. Thus, given the measurements, each node can reconstruct the incoming messages from the collection of beliefs broadcast by nodes who share measurements with it by forming,

$$m_{tuvw}^n(x_w) \propto \int \psi(x_t, x_u, x_v, x_w) \frac{\beta^{n-1}(x_t)\beta^{n-1}(x_u)\beta^{n-1}(x_v)}{m_{uvwt}^{n-1}(x_t)m_{tvwu}^{n-1}(x_u)m_{tuwv}^{n-1}(x_v)} \, dx_t dx_u dx_v \, .$$

(24)

In this formulation, a node updating its belief reconstructs the incoming messages by using neighboring nodes' beliefs and forming (24). These messages are then used in the node's belief update. It then calculates messages it would send to each of its neighbors using (22) and stores them locally to use in (24) in the next iteration while broadcasting its newly calculated belief instead of sending $\{m_{uvwt}(x_t), m_{tvwu}(x_u), m_{tuwv}(x_v)\}$.

4 Nonparametric Belief Propagation

In the previous section, formal expressions were presented for performing distributed inference over continuously valued random variables. A continuous model is favored over a discrete model, arising from a discretization of the sensor field, for a variety of reasons. First, the resolution of the localization solution is dictated by the size of the grid and thus the state space of the random variable grows quadratically with the precision of the solution. This would force an intractable summation in the discrete analogue of the BP equation (22). A discrete model also implies *a priori* knowledge of the size of the field which cannot be guaranteed for ad-hoc deployments. A Gaussian model is inappropriate as well, since radio interferometric measurements exhibit non-Gaussian errors and, as shown previously, two measurements on four nodes restrict the localization solution to one or two intersection points of hyperbolae in the two dimensional case, which is a non-linear coupling of the random variables. Therefore a non-Gaussian, non-linear approach is preferred. Despite the advantages of the non-Gaussian continuous model, at this point we have only exchanged an intractable summation with an intractable integral. The key innovation of *nonparameric belief propagation* [16,17] that enables the integration of these methods to sensor networks is an efficient technique to *stochastically approximate* the message products and integral appearing in (22, 23) by sampling based methods.

To this end, we pursue a nonparametric approximation of the beliefs and messages as mixtures of Gaussians,

$$m_{tuvw}(x_w) = \sum_i^N \alpha_w^i \mathcal{N}(x_w, \mu_w^i, \Lambda) \tag{25}$$

where $\mathcal{N}(x, \mu, \Lambda)$ is a Gaussian random variable centered at the sample μ and covariance Λ, α_w^i is the weight of the ith Gaussian component of the mixture, and N is the number samples. Since the product of Gaussian mixtures is a Gaussian mixture and further assuming that the potential function can be modeled as a Gaussian mixture, the products appearing in (22, 23) are well defined and again Gaussian mixtures, albeit with $\mathcal{O}(N^q)$ components for products of q messages. If N is large enough to represent the distribution and for $q > 2$ messages, exact sampling of (22, 23) would be intractable. Several techniques for approximate sampling from Gaussian mixtures were presented in [18]. In our simulations we used an approach from [18] known as *mixture importance sampling*, though other methods performed similarly. Covariances are determined by the so-called *rule of thumb*, which is simply an estimated weighted variance of the samples.

5   Description of the Algorithm

Given the machinery of nonparametric belief propagation and analytic expressions for the intersection sets resulting from the underlying geometry, the distributed algorithm is relatively straightforward to define. To do so, we must define the probabilistic model specified by the graph and its single and four node potential functions. The graph describing the coupling of the random variables is given by the ad-hoc deployment of the sensor nodes and the radio interferometric measurements collected in the field. Thus for each measurement, we define a clique on the four participating nodes. In this work, we also assume that this graph is contained in the communications graph so that there is a communications link between all nodes sharing a measurement. In practice this may not be the case as it has been demonstrated that interferometric measurements can be obtained with relatively weak signals that are not of sufficient fidelity

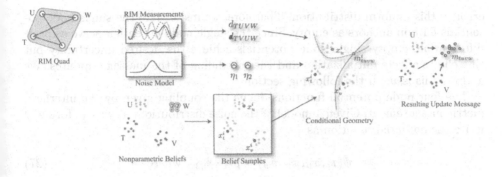

Fig. 5. Belief update

to support communications [8]. In this case, the probabilistic graphical model and the communications graph would not coincide. In our simulations we did not explicitly model the communication channel and therefore do not make this distinction here.

Figure 5 graphically depicts the belief update process for a single sample from a single quad. To update node W, the nodes $\{T, U, V, W\}$ perform the interferometric procedure to obtain the measurement set $\{d_{TUVW}, d_{TVUW}\}$. These measurements are perturbed by a sample from the noise distribution and with a sample from the belief of nodes T, U, and V the intersection set is formed to obtain one sample estimate of W's location. The sampling procedure is repeated for all samples. As described above, the mechanics of belief propagation generalize this process for fusing the contributions from multiple quads to further refine the belief estimate and mitigate the impact of noise and multi-modality.

In the localization algorithm, the single node potentials, $\psi(x_u)$, serve as a way of incorporating a node's prior location information into the probabilistic model. As in most network localization algorithms, we ground the problem by employing *anchor nodes* which know their precise location. This information is given by some other procedure outside of the algorithm; for example, these nodes are localized using GPS. Thus for a $d-$dimensional anchor node the potential is given by

$$\psi(x_{anchor}) = \mathcal{N}\left([x_1^{gt}, \ldots, x_d^{gt}], \Lambda_{anchor}\right) \qquad (26)$$

where x_i^{gt} denotes *ground truth* and Λ_{anchor} is a diagonal covariance matrix encoding the uncertainty in the anchor's position. In our simulations we assume that the anchors have perfect knowledge of their location, thereby effectively assigning a delta function to the position covariance, though this assumption can be easily relaxed. Also, in our implementation, anchor nodes do not update their beliefs. Whereas the anchors have perfect location information, the non-anchor nodes have total ignorance. This can be modeled by specifying the single node potential as a uniform random variable over the entire sensor field. In addition to implying some *a priori* information about the size of the field, in our experiments we found that estimates were adversely affected by sampling error of this uniform distribution. Therefore, we instantiate the single node potentials for non anchors as empty. Since the single node potentials serve as prior information, empty single node potentials achieve the desired uncertainty but this choice affects initialization and the scheduling of the message updates. We address this issue in the following section.

The four node potential functions define the coupling given by the interferometric measurement. Given a model of the noise distribution, p_η we can formally write the potential function as

$$\psi(x_t, x_u, x_v, x_w) = p_{\eta 1} \cdot p_{\eta 2} \quad \text{where} \tag{27}$$

$$p_{\eta 1} = p_\eta \left(d_{TUVW} - \left(\|x_t - x_w\| - \|x_v - x_w\| + \|x_u - x_v\| - \|x_t - x_v\| \right) \right) \tag{28}$$

$$p_{\eta 2} = p_\eta \left(d_{TVUW} - \left(\|x_t - x_w\| - \|x_u - x_w\| + \|x_u - x_v\| - \|x_t - x_u\| \right) \right) \tag{29}$$

Thus given an instantiation of the random variables and the potential functions defined as above, the joint distribution (21) expresses its likelihood. In our algorithm, these formal expressions are instantiated by the analytic expressions obtained by solving for the intersection set of the hyperbolae as described in the following.

The algorithm is initialized by performing the radio interferometric ranging procedure. Currently the coordination and estimation is executed at a base station [7,8,19]. Frequency and phase estimation is performed at the node level and from that information an estimate of the measurement d_{TUVW} can be computed. In this paper, we assume a situation where the range estimates can be obtained in the network and so that with the following algorithm, the entire localization procedure is distributed and performed in the network. In this scenario, local messages are sent so that all nodes involved in a measurement receive the range estimate. Also, as described previously, we only consider quads where two independent interferometric measurements have been taken. For simplicity, we assume that these are of the form d_{TUVW} and d_{TVUW}.

The expression defining the four node potential function is now made more concrete. The messages appearing in (24) are reconstructed at a node according to the following. Upon receiving a collection of weighted samples

$$\{\beta^n(x_t),\ \beta^n(x_u),\ \beta^n(x_v)\} = \left\{ (x_t^i, \alpha_t^i),\ (x_u^i, \alpha_u^i),\ (x_v^i, \alpha_v^i) \right\}_{i=1}^{N} \tag{30}$$

representing a current set of beliefs for which measurements exist, node x_w propagates these samples through the potential function to construct the message m_{tuvw}. The basic idea is to use the measurements and the three sample points to form the intersection set. To this end, the updating node x_w uses the ordering of the measurement to determine the common focus of the two hyperbolae (hyperboloids). For example, for the measurements d_{TUVW} and d_{TVUW} the common focus is x_t since we have

$$d_{TUVW} = \|x_t^i - x_w^i\| - \|x_u^i - x_w^i\| + \|x_u^i - x_v^i\| - \|x_t^i - x_v^i\| \tag{31}$$

$$= \|x_t^i - x_w^i\| - \|x_u^i - x_w^i\| + k_{TUVW} \tag{32}$$

and

$$d_{TVUW} = ||x_t^i - x_w^i|| - ||x_v^i - x_w^i|| + ||x_u^i - x_v^i|| - ||x_t^i - x_u^i|| \quad (33)$$

$$= ||x_t^i - x_w^i|| - ||x_v^i - x_w^i|| + k_{TVUW} \quad (34)$$

since using the i-th sample from current beliefs sets $\{x_t^i, x_u^i, x_v^i\}$, the last two terms in each expression evaluate to constants. Note that the ordering of the measurement matters. In the interferometric ranging procedure this ordering is determined by which nodes are transmitters and which are receivers and therefore easily obtained and stored in memory. The sample set is translated and rotated so that the common focus is at the origin and another focus lies on the x axis. Now for each measurement a sample is drawn from the noise model $\eta_j \sim p_\eta$ and the constants defining the hyperbolae (hyperboloids) are perturbed by this sample. Thus we have the quadratic equations defining our constraints on the location of the updating node as

$$d_{TUVW} - k_{TUVW} + \eta_1 = ||x_t^i - x_w^i|| - ||x_u^i - x_w^i|| \quad (35)$$

and

$$d_{TVUW} - k_{TVUW} + \eta_2 = ||x_t^i - x_w^i|| - ||x_v^i - x_w^i|| . \quad (36)$$

From the left hand sides of these equations and the samples defining the foci, the intersection set of the hyperbolae (hyperboloids) can be computed. In the 2D case, it is possible that the intersection set is a single point, however in general the intersection set itself must be sampled to produce the message sample m_{tuvw}^i. Note that this point must now be transformed back to the original coordinates system of the input data. Recall that the notation m_{tuvw} denotes the message "sent" from $\{x_t, x_u, x_v\}$ to x_w.

Finally the samples from the intersection set are weighted to complete a faithful approximation to (24).

$$\alpha_{tuvw}^i = \frac{\alpha_t^i \alpha_u^i \alpha_v^i \mathcal{R}(m_{tuvw}^i)}{m_{uvwt}(x_t) m_{vwtu}(x_u) m_{wtuv}(x_v)} . \quad (37)$$

In the expression defining the weight for the message sample m_{tuvw}^i we have introduced the function $\mathcal{R}(\cdot)$. This function serves to weight samples based on the notion of *range*. Because the intersection sets are sensitive to noise in the defining data, it can be the case that some samples are placed far outside the sensor field. This function limits the impact of these outliers by taking the max distance of the new sample from the incoming beliefs samples and evaluates an exponentially decreasing function on that distance. In the 3D case, the notion of maximum range also defines intervals to sample the unbounded hyperbola intersection curves so that only a segment of that hyperbola is ever used in the message update. This procedure is performed for all samples to construct a sample based estimate of the message $m_{tuvw} \approx \{m_{tuvw}^i, \alpha_{tuvw}^i\}_{i=1}^N$. When all messages have been similarly constructed, samples are drawn from the message product (23) to form the estimate of the marginal $\beta(x_w)$ as described in the previous section. Finally, now that node x_w has an updated belief, it broadcasts its belief to neighbors and the messages appearing in the denominator of the weighting expression (37) are computed and stored in memory for use in the next iteration of belief updating. This completes one iteration of belief propagation for a single node.

6   Broadcast Scheduling

After the interferometric ranges have been computed, the message passing algorithm is initiated by localized nodes broadcasting their beliefs to neighbors (neighbors with respect to the graph defining the probabilistic model). Since non-anchor nodes are initialized with an empty prior distribution, they are silent until updating their beliefs. Clearly, since anchors are the only nodes initialized with their location, they initiate the message passing. Since in general, a singe quad measurement does not suffice to localize an unknown node, it is likely that the first nodes receiving messages from the anchors will not be uniquely localized. In any case, these nodes broadcast their (perhaps multi-modal) belief. In this way, the belief updating grows out from the anchor nodes as shown in Figure 6. In the figure, the anchor nodes are depicted by diamonds and labeled as $1, 2$, and 3. The complete graph on four nodes denotes the first quad and therefore the first belief update. Subsequent nodes in range can use utilize the computed beliefs or the locations of the anchors to update their own belief. This process continues until covering the entire graph and repeats with the next iteration, however now that all nodes have a nonempty belief there will likely be more quads available to refine their belief estimates. Note that we also assume that at least 3 anchors are involved in at least one quad measurement, otherwise the process would not initiate. This assumption will be relaxed in future implementations by giving all nodes some prior distribution, however it is not currently implemented and it is expected that many iterations of belief propagation will be required to localize the node sufficiently. Even with 3 anchors sharing a measurement with a non-anchor node, it is reasonable to ask under what conditions the algorithm will grow out to cover the entire network. For a partial answer we quote a result derived for localization with trilateration with pairwise range estimates. In [20], necessary and sufficient conditions were derived for network localizability using trilateration. Using a *random geometric graphs* model of the ad-hoc configuration of sensor nodes and the existence of

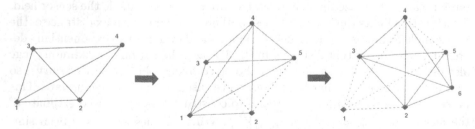

Fig. 6. Graph growing out from the anchors

pairwise range measurements between nodes, asymptotic results were obtained for determining the existence of a so-called *trilaterative ordering* of the vertices in a graph. A trilaterative ordering in dimension d for a graph is an ordering of the vertices $1, \ldots, d+1, \ldots n$ such that $1 \ldots d+1$ are fully connected and from every vertex $j > d+1$, there are least $d+1$ edges to vertices in the ordering. By appealing to graph rigidity theory, the authors show that the existence of trilaterative ordering is a necessary and sufficient condition for unique localizability of the network. Moreover, they establish an asymptotic result that for a network of n nodes with measurement range r, if $\lim_{n \to \infty} \frac{nr^2}{\log n} > 8$, then there exists a trilaterive ordering with high probability. In our case, this is a *necessary* condition for the broadcast schedule to cover the entire graph in the first iteration of belief propagation. Given the underlying geometry of the ranging procedure and the uncertainty in the measurements, additional iterations of message passing are needed for sufficient localization. However, this result which is satisfied by dense (measurement) graphs yields a theoretical assurance that our algorithm will terminate with all nodes being involved.

7 Simulation Results

To assess the performance of the algorithm we performed simulations with real and simulated data. We implemented the algorithm as described in the previous sections in MATLAB. This centralized version of the algorithm retains all the components necessary for a distributed implementation, but the simplicity of a centralized algorithm allowed for the focus to be on the algorithm and not on technical (albeit important) issues regarding wireless communications and limited computational power. We used the KDE Toolbox [21], a MATLAB toolbox with optimized data structures and sampling procedures, for the Gaussian mixture product sampling.

For a point of comparison, the real data used in our experiments was the "football field" data provided by Vanderbilt University [19]. This data set contains over 7000 RIM's for a network of 16 nodes placed in an approximate grid.

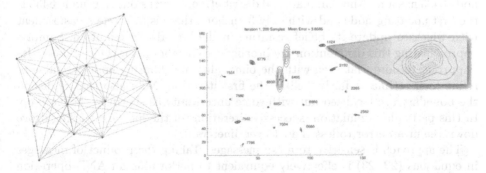

Fig. 7. Nearest neighbor quads graph from the football field data set and first iteration marginals

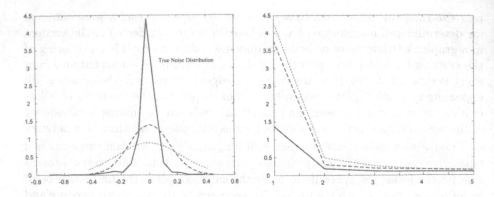

Fig. 8. Noise distributions used in simulations and average localization results

This data set benefits from the filtering technique proposed in [8] to refine the range estimates resulting in an error distribution that is nearly Gaussian with variance approximately .007, depicted by the solid (blue) curve in Figure 8. Excellent localization results with this data set were obtained in [8] using a centralized genetic algorithm executed at a base station. The genetic algorithm of [8] does not exploit the geometric structure of the problem, but rather does something akin to exhaustive search to find a minimum of the associated optimization problem. To obtain the centimeter localization accuracy reported in [8], this 7000 element data set was used.

From this data set we generated a random *nearest neighbor* graph simulating measurements in our simulation. This graph represents just 53 quads or equivalently 106 interferometric measurements. Three central nodes, labeled {6680, 6838, 6957} were chosen as anchors. Figure 7 shows the quad graph constructed from the football field data set and the marginals from the first iteration of belief propagation. As in all our simulations, the final localization results is taken as the maximum of the marginal distribution. Note that in the results plot, node 6435 has a multimodal marginal distribution. It turns out that node 6435 is the first updating node and with only 3 anchors, there is only one measurement with which to update its belief resulting in the bimodal distribution. Samples approximating this distribution are broadcast to neighbors for their updates. Its important to note that even with the bimodality, neighboring nodes are able to refine their estimates fairly well in the first iteration. Note also that nodes on the boundary are localized but with some uncertainty as shown in the close-up. In this particular simulation, successive iterations of the message passing drove down the mean error to less than 15 centimeters.

The approach is sensitive to noisy messages. Taking the product of messages in equations (22, 23) is effectively equivalent to performing an AND operation on the messages and looking mostly at the intersection region of all messages. A single noisy message has a heavy hand in altering this region. The result is a smaller region of support from the message product that leads to samples that are closely clustered, possibly lending misplaced confidence in their locations. Additionally, these locations can be removed from the true location of the node, leading to a situation where a node is confidently localized to the wrong location. Setting the bandwidths to capture the spread of the incoming messages may help to aleviate this situation.

From a Bayesian point of view, our algorithm relies on two sources of prior knowledge: the noise distribution and the maximum measurement range. Since these quantities can be estimated but never known with certainty before deployment, it is interesting to investigate the impact of our certainty of these quantities on the localization results. To test this, we performed 5 iterations of the belief propagation over 10 trials to get average localization results for various noise distributions. The results of this experiment are shown in Figure 8. The true noise distribution calculated from ground truth information from the entire data set is depicted by the solid (blue) curve in the left panel of Figure 8. The solid (blue) curve in the right panel shows the mean error per iteration in meters when the true noise distribution is used in the algorithm. Recall that we use our knowledge of the noise distribution by perturbing the measurements before solving for the intersection set (Eqs. (35) and (36)). Similarly, if we assume *a priori* that the noise distribution is given by the dashed (red and green) curves in the right panel , the corresponding localization estimates suffer somewhat. Not surprisingly, perfect knowledge of the noise distribution sharpens the localization results. However, in these experiments, even though our noise distribution assumptions are qualitatively different from the true distribution, the results are not affected too severely. A similar analysis with respect to our prior knowledge regarding the maximum range showed similar robustness.

In an effort to understand the impact of the grid layout of the football field data set, we created simulated data sets with ad-hoc deployments by placing nodes according to a uniform distribution over the field. A grid layout supports favorable geometries of the quads and limits the adverse situations depicted in Figure 2. These experiments exposed the dependence on the message schedule – if

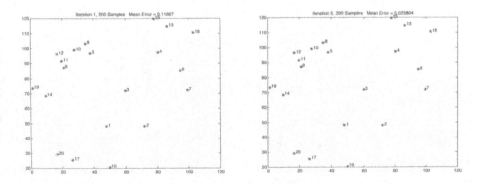

Fig. 9. Localization results ad-hoc deployment

in the first iteration of belief propagation most nodes update with only one quad measurement, it can cause instability in the updates of nodes not involved in measurements with anchors. Thus, merely satisfying the necessary condition stated in Section 6, may result in poor estimates. This is especially true with noisy measurements and "unfavorable" geometries as depicted in the first quadrant of Figure 2. However, we found empirically that if in the first iteration of belief propagation most nodes had at least 2 quad measurements, results were comparable to the football field data set simulations. As an example, Figure 9 depicts a scenario where most nodes updated with almost 3 quads in the first iteration with an mean of 7.4 quads for subsequent iterations.

As a final simulation, we investigated the performance of the algorithm on a three dimensional network. Initial results show success as a proof of concept, however more work is needed for the algorithm to be a viable method for three dimensional localization. However, given that there is no physical limitation to precise interferometric ranging in 3D and the scarcity of non-planar localization techniques, we find these initial simulations promising. As a test set we created a 3D lattice of 27 nodes and designated nodes 1 through 5 as anchors. Ideally, four non-planar anchors should suffice, however in our initial simulations with 4 anchors a fraction of the nodes could not localize with less than 2 units of error. This test set contained only 66 quads (for a total of 112 measurements). Results from 2 iterations of belief propagation are shown in figure 10. We also experimented with irregular configurations as well, with similar performance, however it was difficult to avoid nearly co-planar quads that adversely affected some nodes localization. Figure 11 is an output from the simulation showing 3 messages contributing to the belief update of node 12. Though perhaps difficult to see, there are 3 hyperbola segments contributing the belief pictured in the left panel of the figure. Two of these are messages constructed from triples consisting entirely of anchors, hence the thin curve representing the message. One message is constructed from messages from non-anchor nodes that have updated previously in the iteration of belief propagation. This message is clearly corrupted by noise and the location uncertainty of the sending nodes.

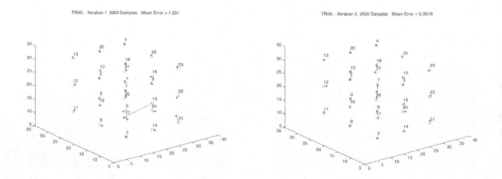

Fig. 10. Localization results for 4 iterations of belief propagation

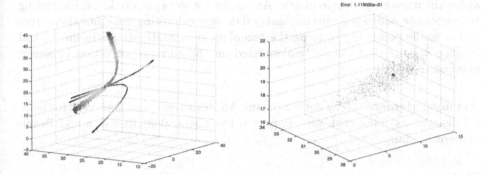

Fig. 11. Three messages and the marginal estimate from the product sampling

A significant drawback in the 3D case is the number of samples required for sufficient approximation of the messages. In our simulations we used 2000 samples. Associated with this high number of samples would be a significant communication cost that would likely limit the algorithm's effectiveness in a sensor network deployment. It would be interesting, though not considered here, to apply a message compression technique as in [22] to limit the number of samples transmitted.

8   Conclusion

The localization problem in sensor networks generally involves two separate tasks: ranging and the localization algorithm itself. Ranging is a fundamentally physical problem limited by power constraints, process noise and device characteristics. Radio interferometry is a significant advance that does not produce pairwise ranges, but rather a distance measurement that is a function of the locations of four nodes. This technique can produce very precise measurements at relatively long ranges. In this paper, we have contributed to the other half of the localization problem. Namely, we have proposed an algorithm that exploits the radio interferometry technique and we have shown centimeter localization accuracy on real and simulated data sets. We have defined a flexible probabilistic model that can account for non-Gaussian noise models and lends itself to distributed computation. Aside from the advantages of a distributed implementation, we have shown that the performance of our method compares favorably with the current centralized algorithm while using far fewer interferometry measurements. We have proposed nonparametric belief propagation as the machinery that enables an efficient solution. Nonparametric belief propagation is an approximation based on Monte Carlo sampling whose trade-off between efficiency and accuracy is dependent on the number of samples being used. As technological improvements continue to make faster computation cheaper and smaller, distributed sensor systems will increasingly be able to perform the necessary calculations associated with nonparametric belief propagation to satisfy approximation error requirements. As for future work, it would be interesting to investigate additional interferometry data sets exhibiting non-Gaussian errors to assess the possibility of using the technique in a multipath environment and explore designs that can be implemented on the current generation of sensor network devices.

Acknowledgments. The authors thank Andreas Terzis and Dan Wilt for helpful discussions. This work was supported by Independent Research and Development funding.

References

1. Priyantha, N., Chakraborty, A., Balakrishnan, H.: The cricket location-support system. In: Proceedings of the 6th ACM MOBICOM Conference (2000)
2. Girod, L., Estrin, D.: Robust range estimation using acoustic and multimodal sensing. In: IEEE International Conference on Intelligent Robots and Systems (2001)
3. Bahl, P., Padmanabhan, V.N.: RADAR: An in-building RF-based user location and tracking system. In: Proceedings of INFOCOM 2000, pp. 775–784 (March 2000)
4. Barton-Sweeney, A., Lymberopoulos, D., Savvides, A.: Sensor Localization and Camera Calibration in Distributed Camera Sensor Networks. In: Proceedings of IEEE BaseNets (October 2006)
5. Stoleru, R., He, T., Stankovic, J.A., Luebke, D.: A high-accuracy, low-cost localization system for wireless sensor networks. In: SenSys 2005. Proceedings of the 3rd International Conference on Embedded Networked Sensor Systems, pp. 13–26. ACM Press, New York (2005)
6. Farrell, R., Garcia, R., Lucarelli, D., Terzis, A., Wang, I.-J.: Localization in multimodal sensor networks. In: Third International Conference on Intelligent Sensors, Sensor Networks, and Information Processing, December 2007 (to appear)
7. Maróti, M., Völgyesi, P., Dóra, S., Kusý, B., Nádas, A., Lédeczi, Á., Balogh, G., Molnár, K.: Radio interferometric geolocation. In: SenSys 2005. Proceedings of the 3rd International Conference on Embedded Networked Sensor Systems, pp. 1–12. ACM Press, New York (2005)
8. Kusý, B., Maróti, Á.L.M., Meertens, L.: Node density independent localization. In: IPSN 2006. Proceedings of the Fifth International Conference on Information Processing in Sensor Networks, pp. 441–448. ACM Press, New York (2006)
9. Ihler, A.T., Moses, R.L., Fischer III, J.W., Willsky, A.S.: Nonparametric belief propagation for self-localization of sensor networks. IEEE Journal on Selected Areas in Communications 23(4), 809–819 (2005)
10. Fang, B.: Simple solutions for hyperbolic and related position fixes. IEEE Transactions on Aerospace and Electronic Systems 26(5), 748–753 (1990)
11. Yedidia, J.S., Freeman, W.T., Weiss, Y.: Understanding Belief Propagation and its Generalizations. In: International Joint Conference on Artificial Intelligence (August 2001)
12. Paskin, M.A., Guestrin, C., McFadden, J.: A robust architecture for distributed inference in sensor networks. In: IPSN. Proceedings of the Fourth International Conference on Information Processing in Sensor Networks, pp. 55–62 (2005)
13. Zhang, D.-Q., Chang, S.-F.: Learning to Detect Scene Text Using Higher-order MRF with Belief Propagation. In: IEEE Workshop on Learning in Computer Vision and Pattern Recognition (June 2004)

14. Koller, D., Lerner, U., Angelov, D.: A general algorithm for approximate inference and its application to hybrid bayes nets. In: Proceedings of the Conference on Uncertainty in Artifical Intelligence (1999)
15. Bickson, D., Dolev, D., Weiss, Y.: Modified belief propagation algorithm for energy saving in wireless sensor networks. Technical Report TR-2005-85, The Hebrew University (2005)
16. Sudderth, E., Ihler, A., Freeman, W., Willsky, A.: Nonparametric belief propagation. In: CVPR (2003)
17. Isard, M.: Pampas: Real-valued graphical models for computer vision. In: Proceedings of CVPR (2003)
18. Ihler, A.T., Sudderth, E.B., Freeman, W.T., Willsky, A.S.: Efficient multiscale sampling from products of Gaussian mixtures. In: Thrun, S., Saul, L., Schölkopf, B. (eds.) Neural Information Processing Systems 16, MIT Press, Cambridge (2004)
19. Kusy, B., Balogh, Gy., Ledeczi, A., Sallai, J., Maroti, M.: http://tinyos. cvs.sourceforge.net/tinyos/tinyos-1.x/contrib/vu/tools/java/isis/nest/ localization/rips/
20. Eren, T., Aspnes, J., Whiteley, W., Yang, Y.R.: A theory of network localization. IEEE Transactions on Mobile Computing 5(12), 1663–1678 (2006)
21. Ilher, A.: Kde toolbox, http://ttic.uchicago.edu/~ihler/code/kde.php
22. Ihler, A.T., Fisher III, J.W., Willsky, A.S.: Communication-constrained inference. Technical Report 2601, MIT, Laboratory for Information and Decision Systems (2004)

Speed, Reliability and Energy Efficiency of HashSlot Communication in WSN Based Localization Systems

Marcel Baunach

University of Würzburg, Department of Computer Engineering,
Am Hubland, 97074 Würzburg, Germany
baunach@informatik.uni-wuerzburg.de

Abstract. Precise localization of mobile objects is a common problem in WSN research for which various approaches exist. However, apart from technical aspects and the location estimation itself, speed, reliability and energy efficiency are central but barely addressed aspects within such systems.

We will point out, that the applied wireless communication affects these aspects significantly before comparing some well-known and commonly used radio protocols to the self-organizing HashSlot approach which was optimized for efficiency in wireless information aggregation. Besides some theoretical considerations, this paper presents practical results from a real-world testbed based on the ultrasound localization system SNoW Bat.

1 Introduction

Efficient wireless data aggregation is a frequent problem in WSN research. In this paper we compare the HashSlot communication protocol introduced by Baunach et al. in [1] to some other approaches for data transmission and centralization between several sources and a common destination under real-world conditions. HashSlot allows extremely fast, reliable, selective and energy saving wireless information aggregation without prior active coordination of the senders, acknowledgments or clear channel assessments.

For our examinations we selected the field of WSN based localization systems, as we found out, that wireless communication within such systems is a central factor concerning energy consumption of the nodes, reliability of the estimated position, speed and localization frequency respectively. In fact, most systems like Active Bat [2], AHLoS [3], Cricket [4] [5], Dolphin [6] and SNoW Bat [7] focus on hardware and algorithms for position estimation or even tracking of mobile objects but hardly discuss wireless communication regarding the effects just mentioned.

Yet, a frequent scenario in such systems is to quickly transmit measured spatial information from sensor nodes within the environment or infrastructure to the node that estimates the position of the mobile object to be localized. For our theoretical considerations we refer to the SNoW Bat localization system as we used a real-world installation of this system comprising 37 nodes as testbed for our experimental comparisons.

This paper is organized as follows. First, we will give a short overview over the SNoW Bat localization system and present some considerations about useful features for an appropriate wireless communication protocol. Then we'll review some

R. Verdone (Ed.): EWSN 2008, LNCS 4913, pp. 74–89, 2008.
© Springer-Verlag Berlin Heidelberg 2008

approaches for wireless information transmission in localization systems and explain the basic concepts of the HashSlot protocol. Finally, we'll describe the criterions and the testbed we used for comparison before opposing the results. A conclusion and an outlook to further work will close this paper.

2   The SNoW Bat Localization System

The SNoW Bat system is optimized for fast and precise 2D/3D localization and tracking of mobile objects. As it follows a WSN approach, it relies on an infrastructure of static sensor nodes (called anchors) within the environment to monitor and at least one mobile sensor node (called client) mounted on each object under surveillance. SNoW Bat scales very well with the number of anchors and clients and supports simultaneous tracking of mobile objects. Furthermore each mobile client may initiate its localization autonomously just when required.

Basically, several ultrasonic (US) distance measurements between the mobile client and some anchors together with a progressive position estimation algorithm are employed for each localization and achieve a precision of up to 4 mm for each dimension. These distances between the client and the anchors in its US range are always measured simultaneously. Figure 1 shows a single localization process and designates SNoW Bat as a decentralized system of four stages: (P1) combined initiation and node synchronization via radio broadcast (Chirp Allocation Vector, CAV), (P2) distance computation via TDoA (Time Difference of Arrival) measurement between radio (CAV) and ultrasound signal (chirp), (P3) return of measured distances via one-hop radio transmission (Distance Vector, DV) from the anchors directly back to the client and (P4) location estimation by the mobile node itself.

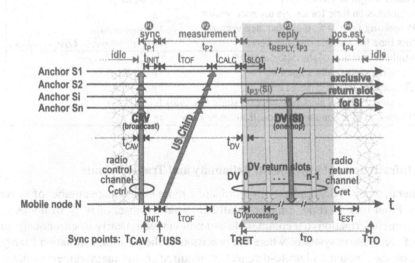

Fig. 1. The SNoW Bat localization process

3 Scalability and Communication Protocol

Before we take a closer look to various communication protocols for data centralization, we will motivate, why this aspect is that important for localization systems.

There are several ways to centralize the distance information from the anchors at a common node to estimate the mobile object's position. In case of SNOW BAT, each mobile node always derives its own position and thus collects the required distance vectors itself.

We will now analyze how much information must be transferred at least and how much time is required for this process. Table 1 summarizes the used abbreviations and symbols and helps to keep an overview.

Table 1. Abbreviations and formula symbols

Total number of sensor nodes in the network	m
Number of sending nodes	n
Desired number of spatial information (DVs)	g
Received number of spatial information (DVs)	$r \leq n$
Probability for a sufficient number of received DVs	$P(r \geq g)$
Time in radio TX / RX mode	t_{TX}, t_{RX}
Time for single CCA	t_{CCA}
The US coverage zone	Z
Ultrasound beam angle	φ
Distance of mobile node from anchor plane	h, h_{min}, h_{max}
Radius of US coverage zone Z	r, r_{min}, r_{max}
Grid constant	L
Radio TX speed	s_{radio}
Packet length of a DV / CAV	L_{DV}, L_{CAV}
Transimssion time for a sigle distance vector	t_{DV}
Processing time of a single distance vector	$t_{DVprocessing}$
Slot time for a single distance vector	$t_{SLOT} = t_{DV} + t_{DVprocessing}$
Minimal duration of the reply stage P3	$\Phi(g) = g \cdot t_{SLOT}$
Duration of the reply stage P3	$t_{P3} \geq \Phi(g)$
Timeout for the reply stage P3	$t_{TO} \geq \Phi(g)$
Duration of the localization process (static / mobile)	t_{locS}, t_{locM}
Proportion of P3 on the total localization process	$p(g)$

3.1 Infrastructure Deployment, Reliability and Traffic Volume

In general, many WSN applications consist of a more or less huge number of m sensor nodes. From time to time, a rather small but variable subset of $n \leq m$ nodes wants to transmit information to a common destination via radio nearly isochronously. In the case of localization systems, where the precision of the position estimation highly depends on the amount and up-to-dateness of acquired spatial measurements (distances, angles, etc.), it is important to guarantee the availability of a certain minimum of information. Yet, too much information is equally unwanted as this won't improve the estimation significantly but the resulting traffic volume will jam the radio channel and wastes time and energy for transmission and processing.

For most distance dependent position estimation algorithms in a dim-dimensional space, at least $g \geq dim + 1$ distances respectively anchors are required. Overestimating this system to a certain degree commonly yields increased precision and fault tolerance with each additionally measured distance and is also supported by SNoW BAT. Yet in most cases, $n \gg g$ nodes will start to transmit information. Thus, it would be most suitable to collect information progressively just until a sufficient precision or a certain timeout is reached. This however requires a progressive position estimation algorithm with the ability to iteratively improve the estimation with each new information. Moreover, limiting the amount of measurements and information in advance would allow a trade-off between the current requirements (localization speed/frequency, precision) and available resources (time, energy) individually for each localization. Obviously, both methods would lead to a significant speedup and energy saving which is of particular importance in WSNs.

Within an US localization system like SNoW BAT, exactly the $n \leq m$ anchors that obtained a distance information (i.e. the ones that received a CAV and the subsequent US chirp) will try to return a DV back to the mobile node. Obviously, n depends on the coverage zone Z of the US transmitter and the density of the static anchors within the environment. In turn, the density of the anchors depends on the movement space of the mobile clients. This effect can be seen clearly in figures 2a,c. Figure 2c shows a SNoW BAT helicopter landing platform with the anchors deployed on the ground. They are settled more densely towards the central landing point as a function of the helicopter's minimal height according to its entry lane.

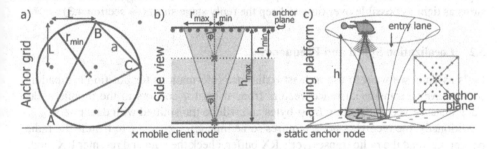

Fig. 2. Environmental observations for ensuring a sufficient number of DV transmissions

In [1], Baunach et al. suggest a special 2D grid alignment of the anchor nodes to guarantee that at least four anchors are always within a mobile node's US coverage zone Z independent from its position within the monitored environment ($\rightarrow$ fig. 2a). This grid – the so called *anchor plane* – can either be installed on the ceiling or on the floor of the environment depending on the application scenario. Their approach bases on calculating an upper bound L_{max} for the grid constant L depending on the ultrasound transmitter's beam angle φ and the minimal distance h_{min} of the mobile node from the anchor plane, as these values define the minimal radius r_{min} of the US coverage zone Z ($\rightarrow$ fig. 2b):

$$L \leq \frac{1.2 \cdot h_{min} \cdot \tan(\varphi)}{\sqrt{2}} = \frac{1.2 \cdot r_{min}}{\sqrt{2}} = L_{max}$$

By using L_{max} as grid constant, a sufficient number of distance measurements is ensured in whatever distance $h \geq h_{min}$ from the anchor plane the mobile client is located. Of course, the US coverage zone expands with increasing distance h ($h_{min} \leq h \leq h_{max}$) of the mobile node from the anchor plane and then contains more and more anchors ($\rightarrow$ fig. 2b).

This arouses the problem, how to select an adequate subset of the anchors within the US coverage zone Z for distance measurement. Allowing the mobile client to select anchors explicitly via radio prior to the localization is impossible as it does not yet know its current position and which anchors might be considered at all.

The naive method is to simply receive the distance informations greedily from all anchors in Z and discard some of them during position estimation. However, this does not only mean heavy radio traffic causing increased packet loss probability and energy consumption but also blocks the anchors from serving other mobile clients. Another possibility is to allow the anchors to arrange themselves via some distributed algorithm and to choose adequate anchors for distance information transmission. Yet, this requires communication among the anchors for each localization and even amplifies the disadvantages just described.

The HashSlot method allows implicit selection of anchors depending on the current estimated distance h of the mobile client from the anchor plane or a user definable quality of service level. It needs no communication between the anchors and uses a sophisticated technique based on a simple metrics for concentrating the radio transmissions as tight as possible over time to keep the reply stage short ($\rightarrow$ section 4.3).

3.2 Localization Speed and Frequency

Let's assume, we want to use at least g distance informations for position estimation, so we have to transmit distance vectors from at least g anchors to the mobile node. Each distance vector contains L_{DV} bytes and will be transmitted with data rate s_{radio}. Additionally, the receiving node requires some time $t_{DVprocessing}$ to handle the radio packet, i.e. read the radio transceiver's RX buffer, check the data and re-enter RX mode ($\rightarrow$ fig. 1). During this time $t_{DVprocessing}$, the radio transceiver can't receive further packets. Thus, the transmission of a single DV requires at least the time t_{SLOT}:

$$t_{SLOT} = t_{DV} + t_{DVprocessing} = \frac{L_{DV}}{s_{radio}} + t_{DVprocessing}$$

Finally, the reply stage P3 for the g desired DVs requires at least the time

$$t_{P3} \geq \Phi(g) = g \cdot t_{SLOT}$$

for transmission if all packets are received in direct succession (which is rather unlikely for most communication protocols). This arouses three questions:

1. Can the theoretical optimum $\Phi(g)$ for P3 really be achieved?
2. If not, which timeout $t_{TO} \geq \Phi(g)$ should be chosen to limit the duration of the reply stage P3?
3. How many DVs must really be transmitted to guarantee the successful arrival of at least g DVs at the mobile client when considering a certain packet loss rate of some radio protocols?

Just to get an idea: In case of SNoW BAT the information returned within a DV takes $L_{DV} = 64$ B. The radio transceiver operates at $s_{radio} = 250$ kbit/s and the DV processing time on the receiving SNoW^5 sensor node is $t_{DVprocessing} = 2$ ms. Thus, $t_{SLOT} = 4$ ms and $\Phi(g) = g \cdot 4$ ms for g desired DVs.

We will now show, that the time a node spends in the reply stage P3 contributes significantly to the maximal localization frequency and differs between static and mobile nodes. As the engagement of each static node S ends with its DV transmission, its reply stage $P3'$ is no longer than P3 of the mobile node. A mobile node involved in localization is occupied for t_{locM}, a static node for t_{locS} ($\rightarrow$ fig. 1):

$$t_{locM} = t_{SYNC} + t_{MEASUREMENT} + t_{P3} + t_{EST} \quad (t_{EST} \geq 0, t_{P3} \geq \Phi(g))$$
$$t_{locS} = t_{SYNC} + t_{MEASUREMENT} + t_{P3'} \quad\quad\quad\quad\quad (t_{P3'} \leq t_{P3})$$

The resulting maximal localization frequencies f_M, f_S are

$$f_M = \frac{1}{t_{locM}} \leq \frac{1}{t_{locS}} = f_S.$$

It is obvious, that k mobile nodes that share a static one may each still achieve a localization frequency f_M if $f_S \geq k \cdot f_M$ or if a certain number of other static nodes is available to guarantee a sufficient number of distance measurements for location estimation of each client. Yet, deploying a rather large amount of sensor nodes means high costs, maintenance effort, energy consumption and may cause much more impact on the environment than necessary. Thus, there are two further questions:

4. How many nodes are really required to ensure an area wide service coverage?
5. How can t_{locM} and t_{locS} be kept short?

Question 4 was already addressed in [1] and briefly reviewed in section 3.1. We will now address question 5 by analyzing the four stages P1 to P4 of the localization process ($\rightarrow$ fig. 1) regarding their complexity, minimal duration and proportion of the total time.

P1. $t_{P1} = t_{SYNC} = t_{CAV} + t_{INIT}$ and mainly depends on the transmission time of the chirp allocation vector and the activation time of the ultrasound hardware.
P2. $t_{P2} = t_{MEASUREMENT} = t_{TOF,max} + t_{CALC}$ mainly depends on the physical properties of ultrasound, i.e. its maximal time of flight, which, in turn, depends on the maximal distance h_{max} of the clients from the anchors and the surrounding temperature. t_{CALC} is the time required by the anchors to calculate the distance corresponding to the delay between CAV and chirp reception.
P3. $t_{P3} = t_{REPLY}$ is subject of this paper as it is the duration of the most critical stage. It occupies each static node until it has transmitted its distance information, requires energy for wireless communication and causes traffic on the radio

channel. Furthermore, a certain percentage of successfully delivered distance informations must be guaranteed to allow precise location estimation.

P4. $t_{P4} = t_{EST}$ also offers great optimization potential and depends on the amount of information to be processed and the type of used algorithm. Yet, as position estimation is done by the clients only, it does not affect the anchors at all and thus does not block them for another localization process. Furthermore, it is hardly energy critical, as plain CPU operation without any further communication is sufficient.

It is obvious, that the stages P1 and P2 are independent from g but are quite fixed in time due to physical constraints of electronics, radio and sound. In case of SNoW BAT, which uses a preemptive multitasking operating system and a fast position estimation algorithm, omitting P4 in our calculations is acceptable as this stage can entirely be executed in parallel to the stages P1 to P3 of the next localization process. Stage P3 is addressed now. Again, we'll take SNoW BAT as reference and evaluate some timings according to figure 1:

$$t_{P1} = t_{CAV} + t_{INIT} = \frac{L_{CAV}}{s_{radio}} + t_{INIT} = \frac{512bit}{250kbps} + 3ms = 5ms$$

$$t_{P2} = t_{TOF,max} + t_{CALC} = \frac{h_{max}}{v_{sound}} + t_{CALC} = \frac{8m}{343\frac{m}{s}} + 1ms \approx 24.3ms$$

$$t_{P3} \geq g \cdot t_{SLOT} = g \cdot 4ms$$

The proportion $p(g)$ of the reply stage on the total time without position estimation is bounded by the number of desired packets g and the given timeout t_{TO} as follows:

$$\frac{g \cdot t_{SLOT}}{t_{P1} + t_{P2} + g \cdot t_{SLOT}} \leq p(g) \leq \frac{t_{TO}}{t_{P1} + t_{P2} + t_{TO}}$$

As we will see in section 5.2, it is impossible for most radio protocols to achieve the optimal return time due to e.g. radio collisions. Thus, allowing some extra time for DV transmission by specifying a timeout is useful but even worsens the results. In the following we'll use $t_{TO} = 2 \cdot \Phi(g) = 2 \cdot g \cdot t_{SLOT}$. The blue graphs ($\blacksquare$ / $\square$) in figure 3 show strikingly, that returning just 4 DVs back to the anchor for 3D position estimation already consumes between 35% and 52% of the whole localization time for the maximal distance $h_{max} = 8$ m of the clients from the anchors. If $h_{max} = 2$ m as in the red graphs ($\blacktriangle$ / $\triangle$), this worsens $p(g)$ to be between 57% and 73% as t_{P2} is reduced due to a shorter maximal time of flight t_{TOF} of the US chirp. If some fault tolerance is desired and we want to receive e.g. three additional DVs, the transmission will already take up between 49% and 66% ($h_{max} = 8$ m) or between 70% and 83% ($h_{max} = 2$ m) of the total time. Finally, the green graphs ($\bullet$/$\circ$) show the highest achievable localization frequency $f_{M,max}$ for the clients.

As we have seen in this section, the reply stage in WSN based localization systems like SNoW BAT has significant influence on the maximum localization frequency of anchors and clients. Especially for fine grained node tracking in movement control systems f_M is of particular relevance. Furthermore, the concurrent support for several

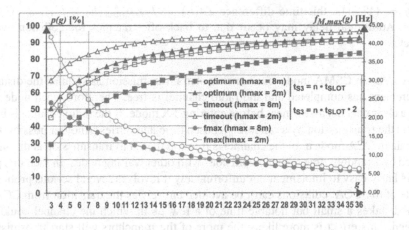

Fig. 3. Percentage of the reply stage duration from the complete localization time without position estimation in relation to the number of returned DVs

mobile nodes highly depends on f_S. Thus we will now review and compare the Hash-Slot and some other well-known communication protocols regarding speed, reliability and energy efficiency.

4 Radio Protocols for Data Aggregation

We will now discuss HashSlot and five other MAC protocols for data aggregation during the reply stage P3. Three of them use fixed time slots for transmission, three depend on the time when the US chirp was detected. As described, n anchors try to send whereas the client desires g DVs.

For each method we'll give a lower and an upper bound for the time t_{RX} the client and each of the n sending anchors will stay in radio RX mode. As this time depends on the timeout for the reply stage P3, we'll also present t_{TO} we used for comparison within our testbed ($\rightarrow$ section 5.2). The time each node stays in radio TX mode is fixed as each distance vector will be sent exactly once and neither acknowledgments nor retransmissions are used. Thus, during P3, $t_{TX} = t_{DV}$ for anchors and $t_{TX} = 0s$ for clients. The minimal time required for performing a clear channel assessment (CCA) is t_{CCA}. Recall, that the reply stage in SNoW BAT always uses a dedicated radio channel for each mobile node. Thus, no interference with any other radio communication is to be expected.

4.1 Non-slotted Methods

As non-slotted protocols don't need to synchronize to any clock, transmission might start in general as soon as the information is available. In case of SNoW BAT this is between $t_{TOF,min}(h) = \frac{h}{v_{sound}}$ and $t_{TOF,max}(h) = \frac{h}{\cos\varphi \cdot v_{sound}}$ after chirp emission. With the specifications from the SNoW BAT system ($h_{max} = 6.9$ m, $\varphi = 30°$) and

$v_{sound} = 343$ m/s, this time difference $\Delta t(h) = t_{TOF,max}(h) - t_{TOF,min}(h) \leq$ 3.2 ms. Additional delay may occur due to back-off strategies for collision avoidance, etc.

CSMA/CA: In CSMA mode, each anchor starts transmission as soon as the distance measurement has completed and the radio channel is free. Therefore, each node performs a clear channel assessment before entering TX mode. If the radio channel is busy, it defers the transmission by a randomly chosen time and retries. Another possibility is to remain in CCA mode until the channel is free and then start transmission additionally delayed by a random time to avoid collisions with other waiting nodes. In fact, this protocol is fairly easy to implement but unfortunately it involves several serious problems. Despite of the CCA, collisions can't be avoided entirely as the transition from CCA to TX mode takes a small but notable time of a few µs in which the channel could get occupied. This effect is more likely the more of the n anchors will start transmission roughly at the same point in time. Using acknowledgments to safeguard the transmission would not only slow down the whole process but also result in even more traffic, collisions and energy consumption. Another point to consider is, that packets might arrive in quick succession at the client, especially before the last one was completely processed and RX mode was re-entered. This also causes packet loss and eliminates the usage of progressive position estimation algorithms as described in section 3.1.

Timeout: $t_{TO} = g \cdot t_{SLOT}$
Anchor: $t_{RX,min} = t_{CCA}$ $\quad$ $t_{RX,max} = \Delta t(h) + t_{TO}$
Client: $\quad t_{RX,min} = g \cdot t_{DV}$ $\quad t_{RX,max} = \Delta t(h) + t_{TO}$

Brute Force: In brute force mode, each anchor starts transmission as soon as the distance measurement has completed without performing any CCA. As the US chirp reaches the anchors slightly delayed in time, it might be possible that this $\Delta t(h)$ allows a successful transmission of the distance information. In fact, this keeps T_{TO} short, but when taking a closer look at this approach, it turns out as unreliable. Since we have seen, that $\Delta t(h) \leq 3.2$ ms is almost equal to $t_{SLOT} = 4$ ms ($\rightarrow$ section 3.2) this would inevitably cause radio collisions and no information would finally arrive at the client.

Timeout: $t_{TO} = t_{DV}$
Anchor: $t_{RX,min} = t_{RX,max} = 0$
Client: $\quad t_{RX,min} = t_{RX,max} = \Delta t(h) + t_{TO}$

Random Start + CSMA: For this approach, the mobile node sends the number of desired DVs g along with the CAV to the anchors. Each anchor selects a random transmission delay $d_{DV} \in [0; (\gamma \cdot g - 1) \cdot t_{SLOT}]$. The sender will perform a CCA at t_{DV} after chirp reception and start transmission as soon as the channel is free. $\gamma \in \mathbb{N}\backslash\{0\}$ can be used to reduce the chance of collisions but also stretches the reply stage P3.

Timeout: $t_{TO} = \gamma \cdot g \cdot t_{SLOT}$
Anchor: $t_{RX,min} = t_{CCA}$ $\quad t_{RX,max} = \Delta t(h) + t_{TO}$
Client: $\quad t_{RX,min} = g \cdot t_{DV}$ $\quad t_{RX,max} = \Delta t(h) + t_{TO}$

The approaches so far used no uniform transmission slots and can not guarantee the successful transmission of the g desired DVs. Thus, the mobile node must stay in RX mode during the whole reply stage, i.e. until the desired amount of information was received or the timeout was reached.

4.2 Slotted Methods

In contrast to non-slotted protocols, the slotted ones need to synchronize to defined slot boundaries and thus require a precise time management and at least one synchronization point. In SNoW BAT, the sync point T_{CAV} is already given by the CAV radio packet which is also used for distance measurement via TDoA ($\rightarrow$ fig. 1). The first return slot starts at time $T_{RET} = T_{CAV} + t_{INIT} + t_{TOF,max} + t_{CALC}$ which is in fact a fixed time after CAV reception.

An important advantage of slotted methods is the possibility to allow progressive position estimation by selecting a sufficient slot length. Additionally, the slotted approaches allow the receiver to enter radio RX mode only for a short time at the beginning of each slot to save energy. Remains the question, how many slots must be reserved for a reliable DV transmission and how many of these slots will really be used.

Random Slot: Again, the mobile node sends the number of desired DVs g along with the CAV to the anchors. Each anchor S selects a random slot $b_S \in [0; \gamma \cdot g - 1]$ for DV transmission and sends the DV at time $t_{DV} = t_{RET} + b_S \cdot t_{SLOT}$. Like in random start, $\gamma \in \mathbb{N} \backslash \{0\}$ is used to provide more slots for reducing the chance of collisions.

Timeout: $t_{TO} = \gamma \cdot g \cdot t_{SLOT}$
Anchor: $t_{RX,min} = 0$ $t_{RX,max} = 0$
Client: $t_{RX,min} = g \cdot t_{DV}$ $t_{RX,max} = \gamma \cdot g \cdot t_{DV}$

NodeID: As node IDs in WSNs are expected to be unique, each anchor selects a unique and thus collision free return slot for the DV by using its NodeID as slot number. This way, the DV return time computes as $t_{DV} = t_{RET} + nodeID \cdot t_{SLOT}$. Though this method is definitely collision free, it might take up to $nodeID_{max}$ slots and should be avoided despite of its reliability.

Timeout: $t_{TO} = nodeID_{max} \cdot t_{SLOT}$
Anchor: $t_{RX,min} = 0$ $t_{RX,max} = 0$
Client: $t_{RX,min} = g \cdot t_{DV}$ $t_{RX,max} = nodeID_{max} \cdot t_{DV}$

4.3 The HashSlot Protocol

It is quite common in sensor networks, that information emerges (locally) at various sensor nodes almost simultaneously (e.g. in seismic surveillance, weather observation, etc.) and must be sent to a common processing unit as quick as possible. Obviously, this leads to several transmission problems like radio collisions and real-time aspects. We have employed and analyzed HashSlot for DV transmission from anchors to a client in the reply stage P3 of the SNOW BAT system as the distance information emerges almost at the same time (i.e. when the chirp is detected by the anchors) and must arrive at the client very quickly to allow precise localization in real-time.

The HashSlot radio communication protocol was designed for extremely reliable, fast, deterministic, energy efficient and selective data aggregation in WSNs and allows collision-free one-hop transmission from multiple sources to a common destination within a constant and predictable time. As it uses time slots, it is particularly suitable for progressive processing of the transmitted information at the receiver.

HashSlot is a self-organizing approach and thus allows to limit the amount of desired information with respect to the requirements of the receiver dynamically at runtime. Therefore each receiver may send its individual demands to the data sources when required and allows all involved nodes to calculate the exact total transmission time of all requested radio packets as well as the corresponding energy requirement in advance. Note, that this QoS request might also be used for synchronizing the senders to the transmission slots. However, at no time HashSlot needs active coordination between the senders as each node calculates its individual transmission slot autonomously. Yet, it demands each sender to adhere to the slot boundaries.

The basic idea is to use some sender S specific information $a_S \in A$ as input for a hash function $\mathcal{H} : A \mapsto B \subset \mathbb{N}_0$. As the resulting hash value $b_S \in B$ is used as slot number for S it is desirable to receive tightly packed values starting from 0. Depending on the application, $\mathcal{H}$ must be constructed to always produce pairwise different hash values $b_S, b_{S'} \in B$ for any two nodes S, S' which need to transmit concurrently, i.e. at the same time and radio frequency.

In case of our localization system we selected a special grid alignment for our anchors to guarantee at least four distance measurements for each position estimation ($\rightarrow$ section 3.1). Thus we also know the (unique) geometric position of each anchor S and the corresponding cell coordinate $(C_{Sx}|C_{Sy})$ within the grid.

In [1] it was proved, that if the grid constant L of the anchor grid and the maximal radius r_{max} of the US coverage zone Z over the grid is known, the minimal square around Z contains exactly $n_{max} = \Gamma^2 = \left(\left\lfloor \frac{2 \cdot r_{max}}{L} \right\rfloor + 1 \right)^2$ senders. Thus, at most n_{max} slots must be reserved for transmission and each sender S can calculate its individual transmission slot $b_S \in B$ depending on its cell coordinate $(C_{Sx}|C_{Sy})$ and Γ:

$$b_S = \mathcal{H}(C_{Sx}, C_{Sy}) = (C_{Sy} \bmod \Gamma) \cdot \Gamma + (C_{Sx} \bmod \Gamma)$$

Some further characteristics of HashSlot were also proved:

1. Two or more senders with the same slot number can never interfere with each other as they would never reside within the same US coverage area.
2. For n_{max} reserved slots, the slot numbers are always in range $[0; n_{max} - 1]$. Thus, a tighter packing is never possible and the time required for the n_{max} transmissions is $t_{n,max} = n_{max} \cdot t_{SLOT}$.

However it is not always useful to reserve n_{max} slots. When moving orthogonal to the anchor grid, the US coverage zone becomes smaller with decreasing distance from the anchor plane and thus contains less potential senders. Therefore, the grid module Γ is temporarily adjusted to Γ_{ad} ($1 \leq \Gamma_{ad} \leq \Gamma$) and limits the number of senders to $n_{ad} = \Gamma_{ad}^2 \leq n_{max}$ with $g \leq n_{ad}$. With increasing distance from the anchor plane there might be much more senders within the US coverage zone than required for successful position estimation. Therefore, a QoS level q ($1 \leq q \leq \Gamma$) can be specified to limit the number of senders to $n_q = q^2 \leq n_{max}$ with $g \leq n_q$.

By using an estimation for the distance from the anchor plane based on the last localization, the HashSlot protocol allows automatic calculation of a useful QoS level q and Γ_{ad} value to limit the number of senders to any value $g \leq n_{max}$. If g is no square number, $n = \left\lceil \sqrt{g} \right\rceil^2 \leq n_{max}$ slots are reserved.

This way, precision and speed of the localization can be adjusted. Furthermore, anchors can detect very early if they are not demanded for localization and omit the distance measurement entirely to save energy and to be available for other mobile nodes. Hence, HashSlot scales with g and is entirely independent from n.

Timeout: $t_{TO} = \left\lceil \sqrt{g} \right\rceil^2 \cdot t_{SLOT}$

Anchor: $t_{RX,min} = t_{RX,max} = 0$

Client: $t_{RX,min} = t_{RX,max} = \left\lceil \sqrt{g} \right\rceil^2 \cdot t_{DV}$

In this section we discussed several radio protocols regarding their efficiency for DV aggregation and showed, that HashSlot scales with g whereas all other protocols scale with g and n or even with $nodeID_{max}$. Table 2 summarizes these protocols.

Table 2. Comparison of various radio protocols for data aggregation in stage P3

	HashSlot	NodeID	Random Slot	Random Start+CSMA	Brute Force	CSMA/CA
slotted	yes	yes	yes	no	no	no
deterministic	yes	yes	no	no	no	no
colission free	yes	yes	no	no	no	no
CS necessary	no	no	no	yes	no	yes
anchor needs radio RX	no	no	no	yes	no	yes
client need radio TX	no	no	no	no	no	no
supports progressive position estimation	yes	yes	yes	no	no	no
requires	anchor position	unique NodeID	randomizer	randomizer, CCA	-	CCA
scalability depends on	g	$nodeID_{max}$	g, n	g, n	g, n	g, n
#replying nodes	$\left\lceil \sqrt{g} \right\rceil^2$	n	n	n	n	n

5 Real World Implementation

5.1 The Sensor Node Platform

The SNOW BAT hardware is based on the SNOW[5] wireless sensor node [8] which employs a TI MSP430 MCU [9]. The radio transceiver TI CC1100 [10] is configured to operate at 915 MHz, allows data rates up to 500 kbit/s and automatic clear channel assessment. The operating system SMARTOS [11] offers preemptive multitasking and real-time operation. The time management and automatic timestamping of external events with a resolution of 1 µs and a precision of 0.6 µs contributes significantly to the node synchronization and calculation/preservation of the distance vector transmission slots. Fig. 4 shows a SNOW[5] sensor node with stacked ultrasound extension.

P_{RX}	53.06 mW
P_{TX}	152.39 mW

Fig. 4. SNOW[5] sensor board with stacked ultrasound extension and receiver capsule

Fig. 5. Power consumption for SNOW[5] radio RX/TX (excluding the node itself)

5.2 Testbed and Results

For comparison of the communication protocols from section 4 regarding speed, reliability and power consumption under real world conditions, we set up a SNOW BAT testbed comprising $n \in \{4, 9, 16, 25, 36\}$ anchors and one client. For each combination of protocol and anchor count we executed 400 localization processes (without acknowledgments or retransmissions) and accomplished the following measurements at the client:

a) **Average packet loss rate** $\Lambda(n)$ for n sending nodes
b) **Average sufficiency rate** $\Sigma(g) = P(r \geq g)$ for $g = n$
c) **Average reply stage duration** t_{P3} for $g = n$
d) **Average RX mode duration** t_{RX} for the client and $g = n$

$\Lambda(n)$ is the average percentage of n packets from all n anchors, that did not arrive at the client. $\Sigma(g)$ is the percentage of localizations for which we received at least the desired number of g DVs. t_{P3} was determined with a resolution of 1 µs by using the SMARTOS timing functionality. The same holds for t_{RX} which is the total time the radio RX mode was active per localization. Figure 6a-d visualizes the results.

We focused on the client, since the energy supply for the anchors within the infrastructure is most commonly less critical compared to the e.g. battery powered mobile nodes. Additionally we were particularly interested in the maximum temporal resolution we could achieve for tracking the mobile node.

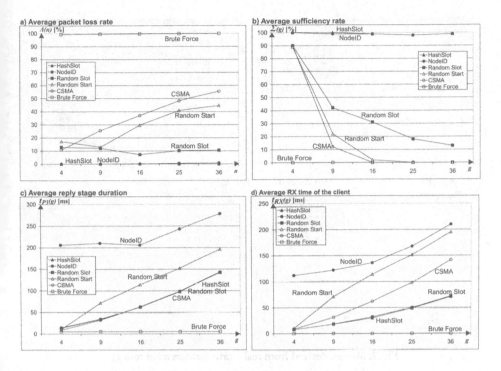

Fig. 6. Measurement results from the real world testbed

First, it becomes obvious, that the Brute Force method indeed performs as bad as expected, since the short reserved time for P3 leads to many collisions and an average packet loss rate of nearly 100%. In contrast, the NodeID and HashSlot approaches achieved the expected packet loss rate of about 0%, since they use collision free slots. Yet the first is extremely slow and comsumes a lot of energy due to many reserved slots ($nodeID_{max}$ was 69 in our testbed) whereas HashSlot dynamically adjusts the length of P3 to the number of desired DVs g. Apart, it reaches a much better sufficiency rate than Random Slot or CSMA which are sometimes subject to radio collisions but rank close to HashSlot when regarding t_{P3} and t_{RX}.

These measurements together with the power consumption values from the SNoW[5] specifications ($\rightarrow$ fig. 5) allowed us to calculate some more interesting values which are visible in figure 7e-h. This time, we also considered the energy required for transmitting the initial CAV in stage P1 but explicitly omitted the energy required by the MCU or the ultrasonic hardware:

e) Achievable localization frequency: $f_{loc} = \dfrac{1}{t_{P1} + t_{P2} + t_{P3}} \cdot \Sigma(g)$

f) Radio energy consumption per localization attempt: $W_{loc} = t_{RX} \cdot P_{RX} + t_{TX} \cdot P_{TX}$

g) Radio energy consumption per received DV: $W_{DV} = \dfrac{W_{loc}}{n \cdot (1 - \Lambda(n))}$

h) Radio energy wasting per localization: $W_{loc,waste} = W_{loc} \cdot (1 - \Sigma(g))$

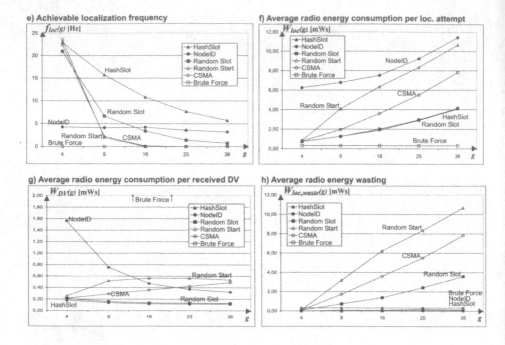

Fig. 7. Metrics derived from real world measurement results

f_{loc} is the achievable number of localizations per second for which at least the desired amount g of information would be available. W_{loc} is the required radio energy for each localization attempt regardless of success or failure due to an insufficient number of DVs. W_{DV} shows, how much radio energy is necessary in average to gain a single DV. Finally, $W_{loc,waste}$ is the wasted energy when assuming that the reception of less than the desired g DVs are insufficient for the intended operation. In this case, all effort is lost and the whole process must start over again.

Now it becomes visible, that HashSlot was the most reliable transmission protocol under test and consequently allowed the highest frequency of successful localizations. Though it requires nearly the same amount of energy per localization than Random Slot it significantly wastes less energy by virtue of canceled localizations due to an insufficient number of received DVs. In our opinion, the most remarkable result is, that HashSlot is independent from the total number of anchors n and the number of desired DVs g when regarding the average packet loss rate, sufficiency rate, energy consumption per DV and energy wasting. Just the localization time and consequently the frequency and total energy requirement is not constant but depends on the g. Finally, we can state, that the theoretically expected characteristics of HashSlot were indeed verifiable within our real world testbed.

6   Conclusion and Outlook

In this paper we addressed the impact of wireless communication on speed, reliability and energy consumption in WSN based localization systems by using SNoW BAT as an example. We pointed out, that information aggregation consumes a significant part of the total localization time and also widely influences localization frequency and system scalability regarding the number of mobile nodes. Real world experiments with various communication protocols showed, that an adequate adaption to the current requirements (speed, precision) of the mobile client node yields the best results. As the position of anchor nodes within localization systems is most commonly known anyway, it is no problem to compute collision-free transmission slots by using the HashSlot approach.

Further research in the general field of information aggregation aims on finding appropriate hash functions for collision free radio communication within arbitrary applications. In the specific field of WSN based localization, we are currently extending our testbed to comprise 70 anchors and various mobile nodes for real world results in multi-node localization and tracking.

References

1. Baunach, M., Kolla, R., Mühlberger, C.: A Method for Self-Organizing Communication in WSN Based Localization Systems: HashSlot. SenseApp, Dublin (Ireland) (accepted, October 2007)
2. Ward, A., Jones, A., Hopper, A.: A New Location Technique for the Active Office. IEEE Personal Comm. 4(5), 42–47 (1997)
3. Savvides, A., Han, C.-C., Strivastava, M.B.: Dynamic fine-grained localization in Ad-Hoc networks of sensors. In: MobiCom 2001. Proceedings of the 7th annual international conference on Mobile computing and networking, pp. 166–179. ACM Press, New York (2001)
4. Priyantha, B.N.: The Cricket Indoor Location System. PhD Thesis, Massachusetts Institute of Technology (2005)
5. Priyantha, N.B., Miu, A.K.L., Balakrishnan, H., Teller, S.: The Cricket Compass for Context-Aware Mobile Applications. In: MobiCom 2001. Proceedings of the 7th annual international conference on Mobile computing and networking, pp. 1–14. ACM Press, New York (2001)
6. Fukuju, Y., Minami, M., Hirasawa, K., Yokoyama, S., Mizumachi, M., Morikawa, H., Aoyama, T.: DOLPHIN: A Practical Approach for Implementing a Fully Distributed Indoor Ultrasonic Positioning System. In: Davies, N., Mynatt, E.D., Siio, I. (eds.) UbiComp 2004. LNCS, vol. 3205, pp. 347–365. Springer, Heidelberg (2004)
7. Baunach, M., Kolla, R., Mühlberger, C.: SNoW Bat: A high precise WSN based location system. Technical Report 424, Institut für Informatik, Universität Würzburg (May 2007)
8. Baunach, M., Kolla, R., Mühlberger, C.: SNoW^5: a modular platform for sophisticated real-time wireless sensor networking. Technical Report 399, Institut für Informatik, Universität Würzburg (January 2007)
9. Texas Instruments Inc., Dallas (USA): MSP430x1xx Family User's Guide, 2006.
10. Texas Instruments Inc., Dallas (USA): CC1100 Single Chip Low Cost Low Power RF Transceiver, 2006
11. Baunach, M., Kolla, R., Mühlberger, C.: Introduction to a Small Modular Adept Real-Time Operating System. In: Distributed Systems Group (ed.): 6. Fachgespräch Sensornetzwerke Aachen, July 16–17, 2007, pp. 1–4. RWTH Aachen University (2007)

Spatiotemporal Anomaly Detection
in Gas Monitoring Sensor Networks

X. Rosalind Wang[1,*], Joseph T. Lizier[1,2], Oliver Obst[1],
Mikhail Prokopenko[1], and Peter Wang[1]

[1] CSIRO ICT Centre, Locked Bag 17, North Ryde, NSW 1670, Australia
Rosalind.Wang@csiro.au
[2] School of Information Technologies, The University of Sydney, NSW 2006, Australia

Abstract. In this paper[1], we use Bayesian Networks as a means for unsupervised learning and anomaly (event) detection in gas monitoring sensor networks for underground coal mines. We show that the Bayesian Network model can learn cyclical baselines for gas concentrations, thus reducing false alarms usually caused by flatline thresholds. Further, we show that the system can learn dependencies between changes of concentration in different gases and at multiple locations. We define and identify new types of events that can occur in a sensor network. In particular, we analyse joint events in a group of sensors based on learning the Bayesian model of the system, contrasting these events with merely aggregating single events. We demonstrate that anomalous events in individual gas data might be explained if considered jointly with the changes in other gases. Vice versa, a network-wide spatiotemporal anomaly may be detected even if individual sensor readings were within their thresholds. The presented Bayesian approach to spatiotemporal anomaly detection is applicable to a wide range of sensor networks.

1 Introduction

Since the 1980s, electronic gas monitoring sensor networks have been introduced in the underground coal mining industry. However, no current system can provide site specific anomaly detection. This means monitoring systems often give false alarms, which can be costly to the mining operation. The periodic variation in the gas concentration also increases the number of false alarms in these flat line threshold based systems. Further, current systems ignore the spatial relations between data gathered at different sensor network nodes. These spatial relationships between data could identify anomalies missed by individual sensors. Conversely, the spatial relationships could explain away the anomalies identified by the individual gas sensors, thus avoiding false alarms.

Currently, the existing system integrates and interprets incoming data in accordance with a pre-determined set of rules, produces a risk profile, and autonomously initiates a response to a breach of these rules. A problem with this approach is that no clear-cut definitions of abnormal situations with respect to the concentration of different gases exist, so that it is difficult to produce a good set of rules.

---

* Corresponding author.
[1] The authors list after the lead author is in alphabetical order.

R. Verdone (Ed.): EWSN 2008, LNCS 4913, pp. 90–105, 2008.

The underground coal mining industry has been struggling with the issues of site-based moving threshold levels for critical gases since the introduction of electronic gas monitoring systems in the 1980s. No satisfactory, scientifically validated methodology is in existence that can provide a mine with its own specific moving threshold levels. Best guess estimates, universal rules-of-thumb and experience-based trigger points are the industry norm [1]. In this paper, we used Bayesian Networks as a means for unsupervised learning of temporal and spatiotemporal patterns in underground coal mining gas data, and applied the approach to spatiotemporal anomaly detection.

Section 2 presents the problem of anomaly detection in general sensor networks. In Sec. 3, we define the problem specifically for underground coal mining sensor networks. Section 4 describes the approach we took to learn and analyse the data. The results of identified anomalies are shown in Sec. 5. Finally, Sec. 6 presents the conclusions and future work.

2 Background

In order to be successful, sensor networks must detect, evaluate and diagnose patterns in diverse situations, forecast likely future scenarios, make decisions, initiate actions based on these decisions, and adapt to change. Adaptive anomaly detection in spatiotemporal sensor network data is, thus, one of the main challenges in this field. Conventional control theory and SCADA (Supervision Control And Data Acquisition) systems are employed for anomaly detection in these sensor networks, however, they are inadequate to deal with scenarios which require flexible acquisition and distribution of information.

For our particular application, each node in the sensor network monitors several different kinds of gases in order to ensure safety and productivity in a coal mine. We consider an existing system which takes measurements and interprets incoming data. The single nodes in the sensor networks cover wide areas. Since they are used for the prevention of hazards, rather than for recovery after a hazard, the position of each node is fixed and known. Our scenario also allows for the use of non-wireless communication between single nodes, whereas for applications in hazard recovery, cable-based communication could possibly be disrupted by collapsed roofs or explosions.

The application of sensor networks in coal mines seems to be natural, because several different kinds of data have to be collected for safety reasons. For example, in [2], a sensor network is used to detect leakages of gas, dust or water, and to monitor the density of oxygen in different areas. For this particular application, data from different nodes is used to create a qualitative overview, describing for example the extent of water leakages or areas with a high density of oxygen. For our application, monitoring gases at each node separately from each other is not sufficient to detect anomalies: densities of single gases at one location might appear normal, but the simultaneous measurement of densities of other gases at other locations could in fact indicate a potentially dangerous situation. Other properties of the scenario make the detection of abnormal situations more difficult: as mentioned above, there is no good definition of an abnormal situation, and one of the reasons for this is the rarity of abnormal events in the available data. Moreover, not only does the spatial distribution of gases have to be considered, but so too does the development of gas distributions over time.

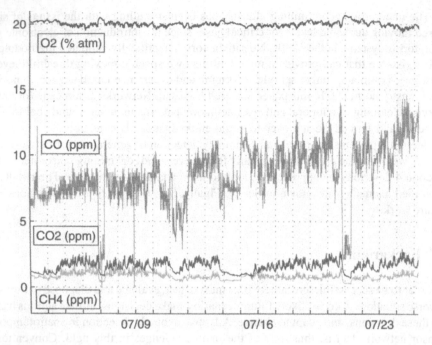

Fig. 1. Gas concentration data from a sensor node in an Australian coal mine. Data gathered for oxygen is in units of percentage of air, the other gases are in of parts per million. The horizontal axis indicates the time (mm/dd) the data was taken.

For the research presented in this paper, we are using data gathered from deployed sensor networks in existing Australian coal mines for testing the algorithms. Each sensor node measures gas concentration, e.g. at 30 second intervals, of a number of gases, e.g. methane (CH_4), carbon dioxide (CO_2), carbon monoxide (CO) and oxygen (O_2). Figure 1 shows the data from a sensor node in the first mine for three weeks in July 2006.

Intuitively, anomalies in our data are irregular patterns in multiple time series, e.g. a combination of $CH_4 - CO_2 - CO - O_2$. In general, the problem is to detect an abnormal event distributed over different sensors, although it is not clear what exactly "abnormal" means a priori. In our particular coal mine sensor network, all data is passed on to a central node, so that currently the problem of a distributed computation of abnormal situations is not pressing. Nevertheless, we pursue a method that has the potential to be distributively computed if required.

Methods to identify previously unseen, i.e. abnormal situations in data have previously been investigated [3,4]. The method in [3] uses self-organising maps (SOM) to describe normal system behavior, and to detect abnormal behavior. In order to use SOM, the authors present a new measurement to find out if a dataset and a map are matching based on a k-nearest neighbor approach.

The method introduced in [4] detects abnormal events in signals using Support Vector Machines (SVM). The method can be used online, i.e. without using a fixed training set: the last n observed input vectors are used for training. In the first of the proposed algorithms, a special kind of distance measure is used to compare the distance of a new vector to a region created by the last n input vectors. A distance greater than a given threshold is considered as abnormal. The second algorithm is similar, but delays the output by a small number of measurements N. Then, the *set* of N new vectors is tested for abnormality in a similar way to the first algorithm, leading to a more robust approach.

Both approaches expect all the data to be present in a single node, i.e. they could be used in the centralised fashion that coal mine sensor network deals with the data currently. We have, however, chosen to use a method based on Bayesian networks, because it would support inference in both distributed and centralised settings (see also [5]). In addition, our approach directly computes a likelihood measure for new data, thus allowing unsupervised learning for anomaly detection.

3 Problem Definition

One of the major road blocks we face in anomaly detection inside underground coal mines is complete lack of ground truth. This is because every mine is unique, so what is considered to be an anomaly in one mine may not be an anomaly in another. Mining experts do not have general purpose rules for anomaly detection that are applicable to every site. Therefore, our purpose is to devise an adaptive system that learns from the data specific to a mine, and identifies anomalies that are specific to the mine.

3.1 Temporal Anomalies in a Single Gas

Many current automatic detection systems use a flat baseline or threshold for anomaly detection. However, gas concentration in mines have a moving baseline depending on factors such as atmospheric pressure. That is, the mine "breathes" through the day, and the concentration of the various gases increases and decreases periodically. A flat baseline system does not capture this characteristic of the data, thus giving many false alarms and false negatives.

We consider an anomalous event or simply **event** in the time series data as a data point that results in a low likelihood given a model we have constructed of the time series. That is, the resulting likelihood value of the data point is an outlier from the general distribution of likelihood values of the other data. We will define likelihood, outliers and consequently the term 'event' formally after presenting the approach to the problem in Sec. 4.

This problem can be easily seen in the CO data in Fig. 1. For example, the data from July 16th to July 20th show a cyclical pattern in the concentration. A flat baseline system might assume the peak around July 18th is an anomaly, while we can see it's just a part of the moving cycle. Figure 4 also illustrates cyclical patterns.

3.2 Joint Temporal Anomalies in Multiple Gases

When several single events occur at the same time, they indicate a higher importance event. The current literatures identifies these as composite events and group events. A **composite** event, as defined by Kumar *et al.* [6] is a combination of two or more single events. Jiao *et al.* [7] used the term "group level event" in similar fashion to the composite event, that is the aggregation of multiple local events. Informally, a **group** event occurs when in a group of sensors, each sensor identifies an event.

While the aggregation of single events might be adequate for the situations described in the papers above, we need to define other types of events for our data. In Fig. 1 for example, we can see around July 7th, the concentrations of CO, CO_2 both dropped, however, at the same time the concentration of O_2 increased. These single events, as a combination, is considered safe by mining experts. Conversely, while no events may be identified by isolated analysis of single gases, as a combination, they may be considered an event. We define three new terms in event detection for sensor networks: joint, explained and implicit events. Below we describe each event informally, they will be defined mathematically in Sec. 4.4.

A **joint** event is a combination of data from sensors that results in a low likelihood given the model for the combination of single sensors. Consequently, we define explained and implicit events where there is a difference of opinion in joint event and single events.

An **explained** event is where there are detected anomalies in single gases, but the combination of time series do not result in a joint event. The CO-CO_2-O_2 event situation described above would be classified as an explained event. The opposite to an explained event is an **implicit** event. This is when isolated analysis of single gases do not cause any alarms, however, as a joint event, these measurements are significant enough to trigger an alarm.

3.3 Network-Wide Spatiotemporal Anomalies

The events described above relate to gases at a single spatial location, however, they also apply to data of different sensor nodes in the network. In situations involving different sensor nodes in the network, a composite event would involve two or more single events at different nodes, and a group event is one where every sensor node in the group identified an event [7,6].

A network-wide "explained" event is when a truck passes through the mine. The exhaustion gases may trigger alarms in individual gases as concentration will increase suddenly. However, this event should not be considered a network-wide anomaly in the data, as other nodes jointly explain it away. An example of an "implicit event" in the network is an increase of methane at one location of the mine, accompanied by an increase in oxygen at another location. Thus no joint event is identified at each sensor node, but a network-wide joint event could be identified for the combination of the sensor nodes.

4 Approach to the Problem

Our approach to the problem of anomaly detection is to use Bayesian Networks (BNs). The networks are constructed via a learning process from some training data. When new observations are made, we can use inference on the network to find a likelihood value of the network given the new observations. An anomaly is identified if the likelihood value is low.

4.1 Bayesian Networks

A Bayesian Network is a graphical model that takes a statistical approach to learning. Statistical learning uses probability distributions to model variables that represent the gathered data, thus taking into account the stochastic nature of real data. Graphical models expose the underlying relationship between probabilistic variables in a simple and clear form.

Specifically, Bayesian Networks are a form of acyclic directed graph (ADG) [8] in that if one variable of the network is dependent on another, then the reverse cannot be true. This relationship between two variables is represented in BNs by the direction of an arrow connecting the two. The variables of a BN are called *nodes* of a BN. The node with an arrow pointing to it is dependent on the node with the same arrow pointing away from it. The nodes connected by an arrow have a parent/child relationship, where the *child* node is dependent on its *parent* node. (See Fig. 2 for one of the network structures used in this paper.)

In a Bayesian network, each random variable is independent of its non-descendants in the graph given the state of its parents. This independence can be exploited to reduce the number of parameters needed to characterise the network. Thus it is possible to efficiently compute posterior probabilities given some evidence or observations. One set of probability parameters are encoded for each variable, in the form of the local conditional distribution given the variable's parent. Using the independence statements encoded in the network, the joint probability distribution is uniquely determined by these local conditional distributions [9,10]. We present the general form of this joint probability distribution in the following paragraphs.

We use capital letters such as X, Y for names of random variables, and lower cases x, y for values taken by these variables. A set of variables such as $\{X_1, X_2, X_3\}$ are written as $\mathbf{X}$, likewise, a set of values such as $\{x_1, x_2, x_3\}$ are written as $\mathbf{x}$. Thus, $\mathbf{x}$ are values taken by $\mathbf{X}$.

Let $P(\mathbf{U})$ be a joint probability distribution over $\mathbf{U} = \{X_1, \ldots, X_k\}$, where X_i is a random variable expressed by a node of the network. A Bayesian Network for $\mathbf{U}$ is a pair $B = \langle G, \Theta \rangle$. The first component, G, represents the graph structure of the network. G is an ADG whose nodes correspond to the random variables $X_1, \ldots, X_k$, and whose edges represent direct dependencies between the variables. The second component, Θ, represents the set of conditional probabilities that quantify the nodes of the network. It contains a set of parameters $\theta_{X_i|\Pi_{X_i}} = P_B(X_i|\Pi_{X_i})$ for each node X_i, where Π_{X_i} denotes the set of parents of X_i in G. A Bayesian Network B defines a unique joint probability distribution over $\mathbf{U}$ given by

$$P_B(\mathbf{U}) = \prod_{i=1}^{k} P_B(X_i|\Pi_{X_i}) = \prod_{i=1}^{k} \theta_{X_i|\Pi_{X_i}}. \tag{1}$$

In a Bayesian Network the learning process is to estimate the parameter set Θ as well as to find the structure of the network, G. The objective in the learning is to find a $B = \langle G, \Theta \rangle$ that "best describes" the probability distribution over the training data [11]. In this paper, however, we will not be learning the structure of the networks.

4.2 Network Structures for the Problem

Let a single variable time series be $\mathbf{X} = \{x_1, x_2, \ldots, x_N\}$, where N is the total number of data points in the series. We can embed this data in a d-dimensional phase space as follows [12]:

$$\mathbf{y}_t = \left(x_t, x_{t-\tau}, \ldots, x_{t-(d-1)\tau}\right),\tag{2}$$

where τ is the time delay, d is the embedding dimension, and $t = d, d+1, \ldots, N$. Henceforth, we set $\tau = 1$, thus Eqn. 2 becomes:

$$\mathbf{y}_t = \left(x_t, x_{t-1}, \ldots, x_{t-d+1}\right),\tag{3}$$

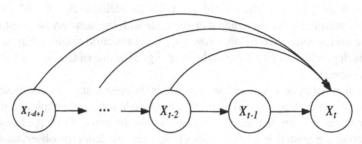

Fig. 2. Bayesian Network model used for learning and inference data in embedded phase space

Figure 2 shows the model used to learn this data. The network is constructed from the underlying dependencies in a time series, that is the data at time t is dependent on the data at time $t - 1, \ldots, t - d + 1$.[2] The joint distribution of the model is:

$$P(\mathbf{U}) = P(X_t|X_{t-1}, \ldots, X_{t-d+1})P(X_{t-d+1}) \prod_{k=1}^{d-2} P(X_{t-k}|X_{t-(k+1)})\tag{4}$$

where $\mathbf{U} = \{X_{t-1}, \ldots, X_{t-d+1}\}$. All the nodes are modelled as one dimensional Gaussians. For example, a BN model of Fig. 2 with $d = 3$ has the dependencies as $X_{t-2} \rightarrow X_{t-1} \rightarrow X_t$ as well as $X_{t-2} \rightarrow X_t$. The joint distribution of the model will be $P(\mathbf{U}) = P(X_t|X_{t-1}, X_{t-2})P(X_{t-1}|X_{t-2})P(X_{t-2})$, where each $P(\cdot)$ is a Gaussian or a conditional Gaussian distribution.

Figure 3 shows a model that may be used to learn and inference the combination of three sensors in the system. In this case, the network is composed of three 'subnets', that is the sets of nodes $\{A_t, A_{t-1}, \ldots, A_{t-m}\}$, etc. Each subnet has the same network configuration as that of the network in Fig. 2. The value for m, that is, the length of the subnet, is not necessarily the value of d, which is the number of nodes for the network in Fig. 2. Since $\{B_{t-1}, \ldots, B_{t-m}\}$ is independent of A_i, and $\{C_{t-1}, \ldots, C_{t-m}\}$ is independent of A_t or B_t, we can write the joint distribution of the model as:

$$P(\mathbf{U}) \propto P(\mathbf{A})P(\mathbf{B})P(\mathbf{C})P(B_t|A_t)P(C_t|A_t)P(C_t|B_t),\tag{5}$$

where $P(\mathbf{A})$ is the joint distribution of $\{A_t, A_{t-1}, \ldots, A_{t-m}\}$, and similarly for $P(\mathbf{B})$ and $P(\mathbf{C})$.

---

[2] The network in Fig. 2 is simply a $d - 1$-th order Markov model presented in the Bayesian Network representation.

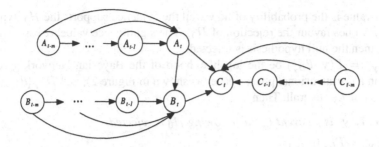

Fig. 3. Bayesian Network model used for learning the combined data from three sensors

Figure 3 describes a network for anomaly detection in the combination of gases at one spatial location, however, it can be easily adapted for detection across different spatial locations. For example, with the same network, A_t could be gas 1 from location 1, while B_t and C_t are gases 2 and 3 from location 2.

4.3 Learning and Inference

Since the structure of the network is known, only the parameter set Θ needs to be learnt. The Maximum Likelihood [13,14] algorithm is thus used to estimate Θ. In the ML estimator, the likelihood function, $p(\mathbf{x}|\theta)$, is treated as a function of θ for fixed $\mathbf{x}$, where x_j^t is the j-th data sample for the node X_t in the Bayesian Network. This *likelihood function* can be used to evaluate the choices of θ. The ML estimator chooses the value of θ that maximises the probability of the data $\mathbf{x}$:

$$\hat{\theta}_{ML} = \arg\max_\theta p(\mathbf{x}|\theta). \tag{6}$$

This learnt network can then be used to do inference on new data. That is, given the observed values of some of the nodes in the network, compute the probability distribution of the other nodes. Inference allows us to perform three types of analyses on the data:

1. *Prediction*, where the probability distribution of the child node can be computed given the values of the parents. In our case, the prediction of values in X_t in Figure 2 given the values of $\{X_{t-1}, \ldots, X_{t-d+1}\}$.
2. *Diagnosis*, where we can find the probability distribution of the parent node given the value of the child. In Figure 3 for example, given the values of B_t and C_t, we can find the values of A_t.
3. *Anomaly detection* using the likelihood values, which is actually a byproduct of inference operation. The likelihood value measures how well the observations fit the Bayesian Network model. Anomalies would result in a low likelihood value, while data that fit the model well will result in high likelihood values.

4.4 Anomaly Definitions

We will now define anomalies and the various events described in Sec. 3 formally. For all definitions below, the null hypothesis, H_0 is the hypothesis that the evidence is true, and the p-value is the probability of how well the evidence supports the H_0 hypothesis (smaller p-values favour the rejection of H_0). The significance value, α is set such that if $p < \alpha$, then the null hypothesis is rejected.

Let $L_{\mathbf{y}_t} = L(\mathbf{y}_t | \theta_{B_{\mathbf{y}}})$ be the log likelihood of the Bayesian Network given data point $\mathbf{y}_t$ in a d-dimensional phase space (as shown in Figure 2), and $P_{L_{\mathbf{Y}}}(\theta_{L_{\mathbf{Y}}})$ be the distribution of $L_{\mathbf{y}_t}$ overall. Then

Definition 1. $\mathbf{y}_t$ *is an* **event** *iff the following H_0 is rejected:*

$$H_0 : L_{\mathbf{y}_t} \sim P_{L_{\mathbf{Y}}}(\theta_{L_{\mathbf{Y}}})$$

For the spatiotemporal events, let $\mathbf{u}_t = \{\mathbf{y}_t^1, \mathbf{y}_t^2, \ldots, \mathbf{y}_t^n\}$ be the set of n data points in the d-dimensional phase space at time t. For example, with three gases A, B, and C, $\mathbf{u}_t = \{\mathbf{a}_t, \mathbf{b}_t, \mathbf{c}_t\}$, where $\mathbf{a}_t = \{a_t, a_{t-1}, \ldots, a_{t-(d-1)}\}$, etc.

Definition 2. $\mathbf{u}_t$ *is a* **composite event** *when two or more of $\{\mathbf{y}_t^1, \mathbf{y}_t^2, \ldots, \mathbf{y}_t^n\}$ is an event.*

Definition 3. $\mathbf{u}_t$ *is a* **group event** *iff $\mathbf{y}_t^i$ is an event, $\forall \mathbf{y}_t^i \in \mathbf{u}_t$.*

In Definitions 1–3, we use log likelihood of the BN for data from a single sensor. Now we utilise the log likelihood of the BN for combined sensors. Let $L_{\mathbf{u}_t} = L(\mathbf{u}_t | \theta_{B_{\mathbf{u}}})$ be the log likelihood of the Bayesian Network for $\mathbf{u}_t$ (e.g. as shown in Figure 3), and $P_{L_{\mathbf{U}}}(\theta_{L_{\mathbf{U}}})$ be the distribution of $L_{\mathbf{U}_t}$.

Definition 4. $\mathbf{u}_t$ *is a* **joint event** *iff the following H_0 is rejected:*

$$H_0 : L_{\mathbf{u}_t} \sim P_{L_{\mathbf{U}}}(\theta_{L_{\mathbf{U}}})$$

Definition 5. $\mathbf{u}_t$ *is an* **explained event** *iff $\mathbf{u}_t$ is not a joint event but any one of $\{\mathbf{y}_t^1, \mathbf{y}_t^2, \ldots, \mathbf{y}_t^n\}$ is an event.*

Definition 6. $\mathbf{u}_t$ *is an* **implicit event** *iff $\mathbf{u}_t$ is a joint event but none of $\{\mathbf{y}_t^1, \mathbf{y}_t^2, \ldots, \mathbf{y}_t^n\}$ is an event.*

The possibility of explained and implicit events is due to the fact that in general, $L_{\mathbf{u}_t}$ and $\sum_{i=1}^n L_{\mathbf{y}_t^i}$ may differ significantly.

5 Results and Discussion

To learn the Bayesian Network using the phase space representation of Eqn. 2 we used $d = 20$ and $\tau = 1$. The process of finding d is described in detail in Appendix A. Fraser and Swinney suggested to use the mutual information method to find τ [15]. However, we found through experiments, that $\tau = 1$ gives much better inference results. We trained the networks using the first half of the data as presented in Fig. 1, and run inference on the second half of the data. Table 1 shows the normalised root mean square error (NRMSE) of the inference. NRMSE gives a useful scale-independent measure of error between data sets of different ranges.

Figure 4 illustrates a cyclical baseline for a 7 day period of CH_4 sensor data from a second mine in Australia, contrasting actual and predicted data. A cyclical baseline can

Table 1. Prediction errors (NRMSE) for the data using the Bayesian Network in Fig. 2

Methane	Carbon dioxide	Carbon monoxide	Oxygen
0.0404	0.0210	0.0468	0.0302

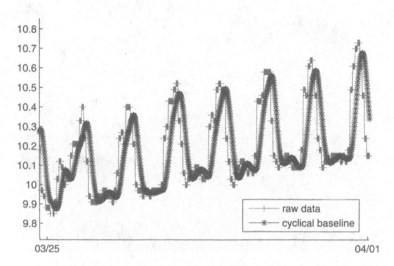

Fig. 4. Cyclical prediction of CH_4 for a 7 day period. Data are from a second mine in Australia.

be used to set moving thresholds around it, so that the fluctuating sensor data are within the thresholds. This in general will reduce false alarms.

Figure 5 shows the results of likelihood computation for the four gases in the data. For each sub-figure, we plot the actual data (bottom plot, left scale) with the logarithm of the likelihood (top plot, right scale). The Kolmogorov-Smirnov (KS) hypothesis test [16] was used to determine the anomalies from the likelihood values. The KS test is used because it can compare the test sample against any distribution, and it can be seen from Fig. 5 the log likelihoods do not fit a normal distribution, which is assumed by t-test or z-test. We applied the KS test using the extreme value distribution, which is a distribution skewed to the left as fitting for the likelihood results. The parameters of the distribution are set to be the mean and standard deviation of the likelihood values in each set of results.

It should be pointed out that in reality, there are no anomalies of real concern in this data set. That is because in an actual mining operation, events that are significant enough to raise an alarm and evacuate the mine are very rare. In most cases, any significant change in data would result in an immediate investigation of the situation and so the potential anomaly event would be avoided in the real data. To demonstrate the algorithm, we ran the KS test using $\alpha = 0.012$, that is the null hypothesis H_0 is rejected if $p < 0.012$. Normally, $\alpha = 0.01$ would be the first choice for anomaly detection through hypothesis tests [5,17], however with our data set, at $\alpha = 0.01$ no events were identified. The value we've chosen, $\alpha = 0.012$ allow us to demonstrate the flexibility of the method. The resulting events detected by the KS test are plotted as red dots in Fig. 5 above the likelihood values.

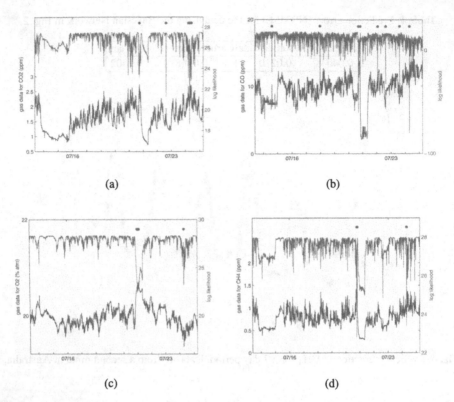

(a)   (b)

(c)   (d)

Fig. 5. Results of anomaly detection for single gases: (a) CO_2, (b) CO, (c) O_2, and (d) CH_4. For each plot, the bottom curve shows the data collected from the gas sensor, the top curve shows the log likelihood found given the data, and the dots at the top show the anomalies as determined by the algorithm.

Figure 5(a) shows there are three distinctive candidate anomaly events in the CO_2 data for this time period. Note the second anomaly identified by the system around July 23rd. This corresponds to a sudden jump in gas concentration during an interval where the gas concentration is decreasing. This highlights the advantage of using a system that has learnt from past events. This type of anomaly cannot be detected with a flat baseline benchmark, as at this particular time the gas concentration is lower than the two nearby peaks. Another interesting feature is that the large drop in gas concentration around July 21st was not identified as an anomaly, while a threshold system may do otherwise. Figure 1 showed that a similar event happened two weeks earlier around July 7th. However, the peak in gas concentration just before this dip was identified as an anomaly as this was an unusual event in the history of the data set.

Results of anomaly detections in CO, O_2 and CH_4 in Fig. 5(b)–(d) show similar anomalous and normal events as those of CO_2 results. Of particular interest is the last anomaly identified in the CO data, since at the scale presented, it is difficult to see why this particular region was identified as an anomaly with such a low log likelihood. However, upon closer inspection, we found that this is caused by a difference of 1.7 ppm between two consecutive data points. That is, in 30 seconds, the CO concentration

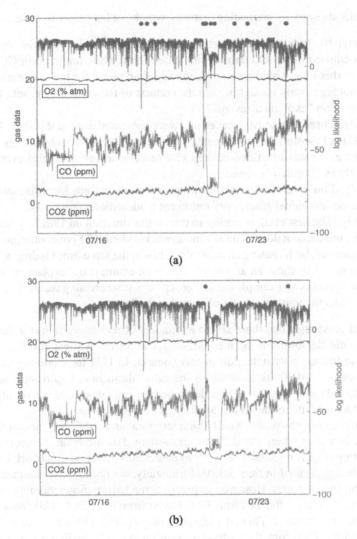

(a)

(b)

Fig. 6. Results of anomaly detection for the joint event of the gases, by using KS test setting (a) $\alpha = 0.012$; (b) $\alpha \approx 0.011$. The top curves show the log likelihood and the dots above show the anomalies determined by the algorithm.

jumped by 1.7 ppm, while the average difference is 0.035 ppm. This is roughly a 5000% increase in growth rate of CO, which is clearly anomalous.

For investigating joint events, we use the network structure shown in Fig. 3 with **A** as the data from CO_2, **B** as data from CO and **C** as the data from O_2. Figure 6(a) shows the inference results for the joint event of CO_2-CO-O_2 using this network. We used a history of 5 data points, that is, $m = 5$ in Fig. 3. We have conducted experiments with different m values from $m = 2$ to $m = d = 20$, finding that the inference results do not vary much. The anomalies were again identified by employing the KS test using extreme value distribution with $\alpha = 0.012$.

The results show many interesting features, which we list below in order of dates:

1. 14th July: No joint event was detected on this date, while Fig. 5(b) showed one event identified in the CO data on this date. Thus, while the jump in CO concentration at this time would be enough to trigger an alarm for the single gas system, it was not significant enough within the context of the combined gases. This is an example of an "explained" event.
2. 18th July: Three distinctive joint events were identified around this date. However, Fig. 5 (a)-(c) showed that no anomalies were detected in the CO_2 and O_2 data, and only one event was identified in the CO data. The second and third events would exemplify as "implicit" events.
3. 21st July: Four events closely following one another were identified around this date. In the individual gases, only one event is identified in each gas.
4. 22nd July: The first event is similar to that of the situation on 18th July, where only CO data were anomalous. The second event is where CO concentration dropped, CO_2 increased, both causing an anomaly (while at the same time O_2 dropped slightly but not enough to cause an anomaly). This is an example of "explained" event.
5. 24th July: This is an example of the "group" event where all gases had an anomaly detected and the joint event was observed as well.

We noted previously that there are no anomalies of real concern in this data set. To demonstrate the flexibility of the method, we set α for the KS test at 0.012, which is a large value for anomaly detection in this context. In [17] for example, the authors needed to set $\alpha = 0.00001$ to decrease the false alarm rate. Figure 6(b) shows the anomalies found using $\alpha \approx 0.011$ in order to demonstrate this value can be adjusted by operators at a mine site to identify anomalies specific to a mine.

The results shown above are that of "joint temporal anomaly" detection as discussed in Sec. 3.2, in which where the different gas sensor data are from the same location. It is more important for a sensor network to detect anomalies on a network level, such as the problem described in Sec. 3.3. Unfortunately, we do not have data taken at the neighbouring sensor nodes. However, in practice, the two spatiotemporal problems are almost identical. That is, the data from CO_2 can be from location 1, while data from CO and O_2 are from location 2. Then, the learning, inference and likelihood calculation are exactly the same. Therefore, the method we presented can be easily ported to groups of sensor nodes at different locations.

6 Conclusion and Future Work

In this paper, we used a combination of dimensionality analysis and a Bayesian Network to learn models for gas data from underground coal mine's sensor networks. We identified and defined new types of events for a sensor network. We showed that the anomalies in the data can be identified through inference of the Bayesian Network. Further, we showed that our model is able to identify events in a combination of sensor data that cannot be identified through simple aggregation. For example, it was demonstrated that anomalous events in individual gas data might be explained if considered jointly with the changes in other gases. Vice versa, a network-wide spatiotemporal anomaly may be detected even if individual sensor readings were within their thresholds. The application of this approach leads to a reduction in the number of false alarms without compromising the safety of monitored mines.

Let us briefly outline possible spatiotemporal extensions of the approach. First of all, a Bayesian Network corresponding to a physical location (for example, shown in Fig. 3 with three subnets A, B, C) can be extended with extra subnets for each new sensor at the same physical location, e.g. D and E. In this case, dependencies between existing and new subnets can be revealed by methods such as transfer entropy.

Transfer entropy [18] identifies a possible relationship between time series, say A and D, denoted $T_{A \rightarrow D}$, by estimating the amount of information that a source A_t provides about the next state of a destination D_{t+1} that was not contained in the k past states of the destination $D_{t-k}, \ldots, D_t$. In other words, transfer entropy provides a measure of the predictive influence of one element over another — hence, it may help in finding dependencies between sensor data. The active information storage, a measure of the amount of information in the past of a process that is used in determining its next state [19] may be used in addition to transfer entropy.

Secondly, a Bayesian Network can include subnets corresponding to different physical locations, for example, $A^{(1)}$ and $B^{(1)}$ for location 1, and $B^{(2)}$ and $C^{(2)}$ for location 2, where A, B, C are different gases. In such a case, there may be a temporal dependency between A and B relevant to location 1, a temporal dependency between B and C relevant to location 2, and a spatial dependency between $B^{(1)}$ and $B^{(2)}$. Our approach easily handles situations like this, provided that spatial and temporal dependencies are identified by methods such as transfer entropy. The challenge, however, is in preventing long chains of dependencies spanning the whole sensor network. To address this challenge, an information threshold $\bar{T}$ can be used to distinguish between different transfer entropies. For example, transfer entropy $T_{B^{(1)} \rightarrow B^{(2)}} \geq \bar{T}$ would indicate a need to include spatial dependency between $B^{(1)}$ and $B^{(2)}$, while $T_{C^{(2)} \rightarrow C^{(3)}} < \bar{T}$ would indicate that there is no need to include a dependency between $C^{(2)}$ and $C^{(3)}$ — thus, breaking a potential chain.

Constructing Bayesian Networks that correspond to dominant information flows in a sensor network is a subject of future research.

Acknowledgement

We would like to thank Greg Rowan and Russell Packham for their generous help with understanding gas behaviour in underground coal mines. We would also like to thank Olivier Fillon and Kerstin Haustein for their help with the data. We would also like to thank the reviewers for their comments that helped to make this a better paper.

References

1. Wang, P., Wang, X.R., Guo, Y., Gerasimov, V., Prokopenko, M., Fillon, O., Haustein, K., Rowan, G.: Anomaly detection in coal-mining sensor data, report 2: Feasibility study and demonstration. Technical Report 07/084, CSIRO, ICT Centre (2007)

2. Xue, W., Luo, Q., Chen, L., Liu, Y.: Contour map matching for event detection in sensor networks. In: Proceedings of the 2006 ACM SIGMOD international conference on Management of data, Chicago, IL, USA, pp. 145–156 (2006)
3. Ypma, A., Duin, R.P.W.: Novelty detection using self-organizing maps. In: Progress in Connectionist-Based Information Systems, vol. 2, pp. 1322–1325. Springer, London (1997)
4. Davy, M., Desobry, F., Gretton, A., Doncarli, C.: An online support vector machine for abnormal events detection. Signal Processing 86(8), 2009–2025 (2006)
5. Mamei, M., Nagpal, R.: Macro programming through Bayesian Networks: Distributed inference and anomaly detection. In: PerCom 2007. Fifth Annual IEEE International Conference on Pervasive Computing and Communications, Los Alamitos, CA, USA, pp. 87–96 (2007)
6. Kumar, A.V.U.P., Reddy, A.M.V., Janakiram, D.: Distributed collaboration for event detection in wireless sensor networks. In: Proceedings of the 3rd international workshop on Middleware for pervasive and ad-hoc computing, pp. 1–8 (2005)
7. Jiao, B., Son, S.H., Stankovic, J.A.: GEM: Generic event service middleware for wireless sensor networks. In: Second International Workshop on Networked Sensing Systems (2005)
8. Friedman, N., Koller, D.: Being Bayesian about network structure: A Bayesian approach to structure discovery in Bayesian Networks. Machine Learning 50, 95–126 (2003)
9. Friedman, N., Geiger, D., Goldszmidt, M.: Bayesian network classifiers. Machine Learning 29, 131–163 (1997)
10. Jensen, F.V.: Bayesian Networks and Decision Graphs. Springer, New York (2001)
11. Pearl, J.: Probabilistic reasoning in intelligent systems: networks of plausible inference. Morgan Kaufmann, San Francisco (1988)
12. Packard, N.H., Crutchfield, J.P., Farmer, J.D., Shaw, R.S.: Geometry from a time series. Phys. Rev. Lett. 45(9), 712–716 (1980)
13. MacKay, D.J.: Information Theory, Learning and Inference. Cambridge University Press, Cambridge (2003)
14. Myung, I.J.: Tutorial on maximum likelihood estimation. Journal of Mathematical Psychology 47, 90–100 (2003)
15. Fraser, A.M., Swinney, H.L.: Independent coordinates for strange attractors from mutual information. Phys. Rev. A 33(2), 1134–1140 (1986)
16. Massey, F.J.: The Kolmogorov-Smirnov test for goodness of fit. Journal of the American Statistical Association 46(253), 68–78 (1951)
17. Menzies, T., Allen, D., Orrego, A.: Bayesian anomaly detection. In: ICML 2006. Workshop on Machine learning Algorithms for Surveillance and Event Detection, PA, USA (June 2006)
18. Schreiber, T.: Measuring information transfer. Phys. Rev. Lett. 85(2), 461–464 (2000)
19. Lizier, J.T., Prokopenko, M., Zomaya, A.Y.: Detecting non-trivial computation in complex dynamics. In: Almeida e Costa, F., et al. (eds.) ECAL 2007. LNCS (LNAI), vol. 4648, pp. 895–904. Springer, Heidelberg (2007)
20. Grassberger, P., Procaccia, I.: Estimation of the Kolmogorov entropy from a chaotic signal. Phys. Rev. A 28(4), 2591–2593 (1983)
21. Takens, F.: Detecting strange attractors in turbulence. Lecture Notes in Mathematics, vol. 898, pp. 366–381. Springer, Heidelberg (1981)
22. Takens, F.: Invariants related to dimension and entropy. In: Atas do 13 Colóquio Brasiliero do Matemática, Rio de Janeiro (1983)
23. Theiler, J.: Spurious dimension from correlation algorithms applied to limited time-series data. Phys. Rev. A 34(3), 2427–2432 (1986)
24. Dhamala, M., Lai, Y., Kostelich, E.: Analyses of transient chaotic time series. Phys. Rev. E 64(5), 56207–56216 (2001)
25. Kugiumtzis, D., Lillekjendlie, B., Christophersen, N.: Chaotic time series part I: Estimation of some invariant properties in state space. Modeling, Identification and Control 15, 205–224 (1994)

A Dimensionality Analysis

Grassberger and Procaccia [20] showed that the correlation integral of a time series, $C_d(r)$ can be estimated as:

$$C_d(N, r) = \frac{1}{(N-1)N} \sum_{j=1}^{N} \sum_{\substack{i=1 \\ i \neq j}}^{N} \Phi(r - \|\mathbf{y}_i - \mathbf{y}_j\|). \tag{7}$$

Here Φ is the Heaviside function (equal to 0 for negative arguments and 1 otherwise). The vectors $\mathbf{y}_i$ and $\mathbf{y}_j$ contain elements of the observed time series $\{x_t\}$ with the dynamical information in one-dimensional data converted or reconstructed to spatial information in the d-dimensional embedding space $\mathbf{y}$ [21] as presented in Equation 2. The norm $\|\mathbf{y}_i - \mathbf{y}_j\|$ is the distance between the vectors in the d-dimensional space, e.g., the maximum norm [22]:

$$\|\mathbf{y}_i - \mathbf{y}_j\| = \max_{\tau=0}^{d-1}(x_{i+\tau} - x_{j+\tau}) \tag{8}$$

Put simply, $C_d(r)$ computes the fraction of pairs of vectors in the d-dimensional embedding space that are separated by a distance less than or equal to r. In order to eliminate auto-correlation effects, the vectors in Equation 7 should be chosen to satisfy $|i - j| > L$, for some positive L, and at the very least $i \neq j$ [23].

The correlation dimension ν is found by:

$$\nu = \lim_{r \to 0} \lim_{N \to 0} \frac{\ln C_d(N, r)}{\ln r} \tag{9}$$

That is, within certain ranges of r and d, the correlation integral $C_d(r)$ may be proportional to some power of r, $C_d(r) \sim r^\nu$ [20]. If the dynamical process is unfolded by choosing a sufficiently large $d > d_\nu$, a typical slope of the plot $\ln C_d(r)$ versus $\ln r$ becomes independent of d. Thus the common numerical practice of finding the embedding dimension d of the data set is to compute the slope from a linear region of the $C_d(N, r)$ plot. For $d \leq \lfloor \nu \rfloor$, where $\lfloor \nu \rfloor$ denotes the largest integer less than or equal to ν, the slope is equal to d. For $d > \lfloor \nu \rfloor$, the slop saturates at a constant value which is usually taken to be the estimated value of ν [24].

The data is from telemetric sensors, the time difference between two data point is 30 seconds, thus between 3rd July 0100 and 25th July 0556, we have 68194 data samples. To find the embedding dimensions, we divide the data into 1 day periods, this gives us 2880 data points per period. Kugiumtzis et al.[25] showed that this is a reasonable number for calculating embedding dimensions. We found the embedding dimension to be $d = 20$.

Discovery of Frequent Distributed Event Patterns in Sensor Networks*

Kay Römer

Institute for Pervasive Computing, ETH Zurich, Switzerland
roemer@inf.ethz.ch

Abstract. Today it is possible to deploy sensor networks in the real world and collect large amounts of raw sensory data. However, it remains a major challenge to *make sense of sensor data*, i.e., to extract high-level knowledge from the raw data. In this paper we present a novel in-network knowledge discovery technique, where high-level information is inferred from raw sensor data directly on the sensor nodes. In particular, our approach supports the discovery of frequent distributed event patterns, which characterize the spatial and temporal correlations between events observed by sensor nodes in a confined network neighborhood. One of the key challenges in realizing such a system are the constrained resources of sensor nodes. To this end, our solution offers a declarative query language that allows to trade off detail and scope of the sought patterns for resource consumption. We implement our proposal on real hardware and evaluate the trade-off between scope of the query and resource consumption.

1 Introduction

Systems research in sensor networks has reached a point where we can build and deploy medium-sized sensor networks and collect large amounts of raw or preprocessed sensor data during months of unattended operation. However, it remains a major challenge to make sense of the collected data, i.e., to extract the relevant knowledge from the raw data. Most existing techniques for knowledge discovery from sensor data are centralized and require the extraction of raw sensor data from the network. However, this can be very costly due to the large data volume and does not scale to large networks.

In a previous position paper [20] we sketched an in-network knowledge extraction technique that supports the discovery of frequent distributed event patterns. In this paper, we turn this idea into a complete system, implement it on sensor nodes and study important performance metrics. The key advantage of our in-network approach is that the extracted knowledge is directly available to the sensor nodes and can be used to control the behavior of the sensor nodes (e.g., to prioritize processing of event patterns that occur infrequently). Also, the extracted knowledge is often much more compact than raw sensor data and can therefore be more efficiently extracted from the sensor network than raw sensor data.

Our approach is based on events, that is, each sensor node locally analyzes the output of its sensors to find relevant real world occurrences. In many applications it is

---

* The work presented in this p aper was partially supported by the Swiss National Science Foundation under grant number 5005-67322 (NCCR-MICS).

R. Verdone (Ed.): EWSN 2008, LNCS 4913, pp. 106–124, 2008.

important to put such events into a spatial and temporal context, i.e., to consider the correlation of an event observed by a sensor node with events observed by surrounding sensor nodes in the recent past. In an equipment monitoring application (e.g., [1]), for example, one is interested in understanding if abnormal vibration signatures are correlated with nearby abnormal temperature readings. In a bird monitoring application (e.g., [21]), one is interested in understanding if certain events in the neighborhood of a nesting burrow (e.g., noise, motion) are correlated with birds leaving their nests.

Our approach supports this type of application by providing a framework to analyze the correlation of a certain type of event on a sensor node with *context events* observed by nodes in a confined neighborhood of this node in the recent past. For example, we might find that in 30% of the cases where a bird left its nest, motion has been detected by at least one sensor located within 10 meters of the nest no more than 3 minutes in the past. We call such a correlation of events a *distributed event pattern*. Our technique discovers such distributed event patterns that occur with a frequency not less than a user-specified minimum. Besides a minimum frequency, a user has to specify local events of interest and certain temporal and spatial constraints using a declarative query language.

The discovered set of frequent event patterns can be considered as a compact characterization of the "common behavior" observed by a set of sensor nodes over long periods of time. Likewise, an event pattern that is not frequent can be considered as an exceptional occurrence. Frequent event patterns can be used in two primary ways: Firstly, by a user to learn about the common behavior, or to be notified of exceptional behavior or of significant changes to the common behavior. Secondly, as the event patterns are computed on the sensor nodes, the latter can use this information to control or adapt their behavior, for example, to allocate more resources for the processing and communication of rare event patterns than for more common ones.

In this paper we focus on how frequent event patterns can be efficiently computed on resource-constrained sensor nodes. Although sensor nodes are becoming more powerful over time, constrained node resources are the primary challenge in designing and implementing our in-network knowledge extraction technique. Our approach to deal with this challenge lies in the query language, which allows the user to define the detail (e.g., granularity of temporal and spatial relationships between local events) and scope (e.g., minimum pattern frequency, involved local events, maximal temporal or spatial distance between local events) of sought patterns: the more detailed or the larger the scope of sought patterns, the more expensive is pattern discovery. Thus, we offer the user a turning knob to trade off detail and scope for resource consumption.

Note that the above *discovery of frequent events patterns* is different from *detection of event patterns*. For the latter, the user needs to specify in advance and exactly which event patterns the system should detect. With our approach, the system itself identifies event patterns that occur frequently given certain constraints on the sought event patterns. As such, our approach can be considered as a relaxation of detection of event patterns.

We begin with an overview of the system in Sect. 2 and introduce patterns and queries in Sect. 3, before presenting the core algorithms in Sect. 4. Important implementation aspects are discussed in Sect. 5. We evaluate our proposal in Sect. 6.

2 System Overview

The overall architecture of the proposed system is as follows. A user can pose a query to the system using a declarative language. Such a query defines the local events of interest and additional constraints on the sought frequent distributed event patterns, see Sect. 3 for details. A query is compiled into executable code (containing both the query parameters and the pattern discovery algorithm) at the gateway of the sensor network and the resulting executable is distributed to each node in the sensor network using a code distribution protocol.

Using the query parameters, the pattern discovery algorithm executing at a sensor node continuously collects event notifications from nodes in a confined network neighborhood and computes the set of frequent distributed events patterns as detailed in Sect. 4. This set can now be used in a number of different ways as discussed in Sect. 1.

Depending on the application scenario, the pattern discovery algorithm may be executing at some sensor nodes (e.g., only on nest nodes in the bird monitoring example in Sect. 1) or on every node of the sensor network.

3 Patterns and Queries

We will illustrate the notion of distributed event patterns using the bird monitoring example given in Sect. 1. Here, sensor nodes are deployed in and around the nest and can detect two types of events: motion (of creatures) and a bird leaving its nest. We are interested in understanding how *leave* events are correlated with *motion* events in the vicinity of the nest. Here, our system might find a frequent distributed event pattern such as

```
(motion, <10m, <3min, >=1) : leave [30%]
```

This pattern has to be read as follows: In 30% of the cases where a bird left its nest, motion has been detected by at least 1 sensor located within 10 meters of the nest sensor no more than 2 minutes in the past.

In general, a pattern consists of a *local event* (right of the pattern's column) and a term that summarizes occurrences of *context events* (left of the pattern's column) in a spatial and temporal neighborhood of the above event. The frequency or *support* of a pattern equals the number of occurrences of the local event for which the left-hand term of the pattern also applies, divided by the number of occurrences of the local event (regardless if the left-hand side of the pattern applies or not). A frequent pattern is a pattern whose support is greater than or equal to a given *minimum support*.

In order to discover such patterns, a user has to specify a query. The query defines events and context events of interest and a number of constraints on the sought patterns. These constraints are needed to cut down the otherwise huge search space for possible patterns to allow an implementation of the pattern discovery algorithm on resource-constrained sensor nodes. Fig. 1 shows a possible query for our bird monitoring example.

In our system, time is divided into epochs of fixed length. Nodes are synchronized such that epochs begin and end at approximately the same real-time instants at all nodes across the network. Since typical epoch durations are in the order of seconds or tens of seconds, required synchronization is rather loose and easily achieved with existing synchronization protocols. In our example query, epoch length is 60 seconds as specified in line 2. Epochs are identified by monotonically increasing integer numbers starting with zero.

In each epoch, a sensor node can generate at most one instance of each possible event type. In our sample query, two event types motion and leave are defined in lines 4 to 6, respectively. A *motion* event (i.e., ground is vibrating) is generated in an epoch if the maximum output value of the accelerometer sensor in that epoch is greater than a threshold (i.e., max:accel[0] > threshold is true, where the "0" in square brackets refers to the current epoch). A leave event is generated in the current epoch if the passive infrared

```
1   // epoch length
2   epoch = 60 // [seconds]
3   // event definitions
4   event motion { max:accel[0] > threshold }
5   event leave { max:pir[0] == 0 &&
6                         max:pir[1] == 1}
7   // events and context events
8   levents {leave}
9   cevents {motion}
10  // temporal and spatial scope
11  neighborhood = 1 // [hop]
12  history  = 6 //epochs
13  // minimum support and error bound
14  minsupport = 30 // [%]
15  error  = 5 // [%]
16  // distance  partitions  [meters]
17  distance { near =(0,10], far =(10,20) }
18  // time interval  partitions  [epochs]
19  time { now=0, recent =[1,3], old=[4,6] }
20  // frequency  partitions  [number]
21  frequency { none=0, some=[1,infty] }
```

Fig. 1. An example query

sensor (PIR) detected presence of a bird in the previous epoch (i.e., max:pir[1] == 1 is true, where the "1" in square brackets refers to the previous epoch), but not in the current epoch (i.e., max:pir[0] == 0 is true). We assume that PIR is a binary sensor that outputs either zero or one. The set of all events given in a query will be denoted by E.

The builtin event definition language only supports simple predicates over aggregated sensor values in the current and past epochs. In every epoch, sensor values are aggregated in predefined ways (e.g., minimum, maximum, average). For more complex and realistic events, the query language supports external events whose detection is implemented outside of our system (e.g., using more elaborate sensor signal processing techniques).

Lines 8 and 9 in our sample query define leave as a local event and motion as a context event, respectively. Note that an arbitrary numbers of local events and context events can be specified and event types may be declared as both local events and context events. The set of all context and local events defined in a query will be denoted by E_c and E_l, respectively.

Lines 11 and 12 define the spatial and temporal scope that should be considered for the correlation analysis. The spatial scope, denoted by $SSCOPE$, is given as a maximum hop count, such that only correlations between events generated by nodes at most $SSCOPE$ hops apart are considered. The temporal scope, denoted by $TSCOPE$ is given as a number of epochs, such that only correlations between events that occurred within a time window of $TSCOPE$ epochs are considered. In the example, if the node in the nest executing the pattern discovery algorithm observes a local event during a given epoch, only context events generated no more than 6 epochs in the past by nodes no more than one hop away (including the nest node itself) will be considered for the correlation analysis.

Recall that our system will only discover patterns that occurred with a given minimum support, which is given in line 14 of the sample query. Further, we allow a certain error (given in line 15 of the sample query), such that a pattern may be reported as being frequent by our system if its true support is greater than or equal to minimum support minus error bound. We will denote minimum support and error bound as MS and MS_e, respectively.

Finally, the query contains a quantization of Euclidean distances between nodes, time intervals (between event occurrences, where time is measured in epochs), and frequency of event occurrences into a set of discrete partitions. Each partition is an interval that is either open (parenthesis) or closed (bracket). Note that the set of distance (time, frequency) partitions does not need to cover the whole domain of distances (time, frequency). By this, a user can constrain the search space for patterns to certain distances and time intervals between events as well as to certain frequencies of events. We assume the existence of an implicit, possibly non-continuous or empty partition $\perp$ that covers the part of the domain that is not covered by partitions that have been explicitly defined. The sets of all distance, time, and frequency intervals defined in a query will be denoted by DP, TP, and FP, respectively. We assume the existence of mapping functions map_d, map_t, and map_f, which map a given distance, time interval, and frequency to elements of $DP \cup \{\perp\}, TP \cup \{\perp\}$, and $FP \cup \{\perp\}$, respectively.

We can now specify the general form of a pattern in terms of the query parameters as follows:

$$\bigwedge_{i=1..N} (e_i^c, dp_i, tp_i, fp_i) \quad : \quad \bigwedge_{j=1..M} e_j^l \quad [s] \tag{1}$$

Here, $e_i^c \in E_c$ is a context event, $dp_i \in DP$ is a distance partition, $tp_i \in TP$ is a time partition, and $fp_i \in FP$ is a frequency partition. $e_j^l \in E_l$ is a local event and s is the support of the pattern. Note that the above pattern is equivalent to M patterns with only one local event and identical terms on the left-hand sides, but with possibly different support values. The pattern is frequent if $s \geq MS$. One example pattern would be:

```
(motion, near, recent, some) AND
(motion, near, now, some) : leave [30%]
```

Note that while the above discussion is based on the notion of events (defined as a state change), patterns can also be used to reason about correlations between different *states* as well as between states and events. In our bird monitoring example, we could define an event *present* as follows: event present { max:pir[0] == 1 }. This event would fire in every epoch as long as a bird is in the nest, thus implementing the *state* "a bird is in the nest".

4   Discovery of Frequent Patterns

The pattern discovery algorithm executing at a sensor node consists of several components which will be discussed in this section. Firstly, a sensor node collects event occurrences from a confined network neighborhood and transforms this information into a pattern for each epoch (Sect. 4.1). These patterns are represented as sets of small integers, so-called itemsets (Sect. 4.2). From the resulting stream of itemsets, frequent itemsets are discovered (Sects. 4.3 and 4.4).

4.1 Data Collection and Pattern Generation

The pattern discovery algorithm is executing at one or more sensor nodes (as specified by the user using mechanisms outside of the scope of this paper) to discover frequent event patterns. We will denote such sensor nodes as *discovery nodes*. Sensor nodes that are within the spatial scope $SSCOPE$ of a discovery node are called *client nodes*. Note that a single sensor node may both act as a discovery node and as a client node to one or more other discovery nodes. Also note that the set of client nodes may change over time due to fluctuation of wireless links and due to nodes dying or being added. Throughout this section we consider a single discovery node.

The pattern discovery algorithm executing on the discovery node proceeds as follows. After each epoch t, the algorithm checks if any local events occurred locally during t. If so, a pattern is constructed for epoch t. Otherwise, nothing needs to be done.

To construct the pattern, a request message is sent to all client nodes containing the identity and location of the discovery node and epoch t. Client nodes reply a message containing the event occurrences during $TSCOPE$. Essentially, a reply message from node i contains values $freq_i(e, dp, dt)$ for each context event e, distance partition dp, and time partition dt that have been defined in the query. This value equals 1 iff event e occurred on node i in the distance partition dp during time partition dt with respect to the requesting discovery node and is zero otherwise. The discovery node computes the sums $freq(e, dp, dt) = \sum_i freq_i(e, dp, dt)$ over all client nodes to obtain the following pattern for epoch t:

$$\bigwedge_{\forall e \in E_c, dp \in DP, tp \in TP} (e, dp, tp, map_f(freq(e, dp, tp))) \; : \; \bigwedge E_l(t) \qquad (2)$$

where $E_l(t)$ refers to the set of local events that occurred at the discovery node during epoch t.

If $SSCOPE = 1$ (i.e., a spatial scope of one hop), then the request is implemented by a broadcast message from the discovery node to all child nodes and the replies are implemented by unicast messages from the child nodes to the discovery node. If $SSCOPE > 1$, then networking abstractions such as Abstract Regions [23] may be used which support the above communication pattern also for multi-hop neighborhoods. Also, in-network aggregation [18] may be used to compute the sums $freq(e, dp, tp)$ in the network rather than at the discovery node.

4.2 Pattern Representation

Patterns are represented by so-called *itemsets*, i.e., a set of items. Conversion of patterns to itemsets and vice versa is accomplished as follows. Each term on the left-hand side of a pattern is mapped to an item by concatenating the event identifier, distance partition identifier, time partition identifier, and frequency partition identifier. Each local event is mapped to an item consisting of the respective event identifier. The reserve mapping is analogous. In the remainder of the paper, we will use the terms pattern and itemset synonymously. For example, the pattern (motion, near, recent, some) AND (motion, near, now, some) : leave maps to the itemset {motion.near.recent.some, motion.near.now.some, leave}. It is easy to see that the maximum size of an itemset is

$$|E_c| \times |DP| \times |TP| \times |FP| + |E_l| \tag{3}$$

Hence, itemsets can be implemented as sets of small integers by mapping each possible item to an integer between 1 and the above maximum size. In our system, itemsets are implemented as bitvectors.

4.3   Frequent Patterns

The procedure described in Sect. 4.1 produces a stream of patterns (one for each epoch where a local event occurs), each of which is represented as an itemset as described in Sect. 4.2. We now need to find itemsets which are frequent with respect to this stream S of itemsets.

We will constrain our search to frequent itemsets is which contain only one local event $e \in E_l$. The support of such an itemset is defined as the number of itemsets in S of which is is a subset, divided by the number of itemsets in S which contain e as a local event. An itemset is frequent if its support is greater than or equal to the minimum support MS given in the query. Note that frequent itemsets are not necessarily elements of S, but they are subsets of one or more elements of S. Also note that every subset of a frequent itemset is also frequent and its support is greater than or equal to the support of the superset.

Several algorithms have been proposed to discover frequent itemsets from a stream of itemsets (e.g., [7,10,15]). The difficulty of this problem lies in the fact that only one pass over S is possible as S grows without bounds over time and hence cannot be stored completely on resource-constrained devices. Much better algorithms exist if multiple passes over S are possible. Typical single-pass algorithms therefore use a so-called *synopsis data structure*, which is essentially a compressed version of the data stream. Frequent itemsets can then be computed from the synopsis data structure which can be randomly accessed. However, synopsis data structures used by the above algorithms are still too large to fit into the constrained memory of a sensor node. Also, as we are ultimately interested in frequent itemsets (and not in the synopsis), memory is needed for both the synopsis data structure *and* frequent itemsets.

We therefore developed an algorithm that directly generates frequent itemsets without using a separate synopsis data structure. The algorithm basically splits S into small blocks B of fixed size which fit into main memory. An efficient multi-pass algorithm is used to discover frequent itemsets FIB_i in each block B_i. Each itemset $is \in FIB_i$ is associated with a counter $is.c$ that holds the number of itemsets in B_i of which is is a subset. That is, the support of is in B equals $is.c \times 100\%/|B|$. The frequent itemsets in all blocks are then merged in an incremental fashion to obtain the frequent itemsets

FIS of S. Initially, FIS is empty. To merge FIB_i into FIS, we merge each frequent itemset $is \in FIB_i$ into FIS by either inserting is into FIS if $is \notin FIS$, or by adding $is.c$ to the counter value of the existing itemset in FIS. The support of an itemset $is \in FIS$ then equals $is.c \times 100\%/|S|$.

For the ease of exposition we assume that the query contains only a single local event, i.e., $|E_l| = 1$. If more than one local event has been defined, the data stream will be split into $|E_l|$ data streams each of which contains only patterns with a single type of local event. These streams will then be processed separately as described above, but the resulting frequent itemsets will all be merged into a single instance of FIS.

Although simple, it is not clear that the above approach obtains the correct result, as an itemset that is frequent in S may not be frequent in some blocks B_i, such that the support of an itemset in S is not computed correctly. To fix this problem, we will use a smaller support value $\overline{MS} < MS$ when discovering frequent itemsets in a block. We will select $\overline{MS}$ such that we meet the error bound MS_e given in the query. That is, the support $\bar{s}$ we compute for an itemset with respect to S will be not less than the true support s of that itemset minus MS_e. Due to this, all itemsets in FIS with $\bar{s} \geq MS - MS_e$ will be considered frequent. This set of itemsets includes all true frequent itemsets (i.e., for which $s \geq MS$) plus additional ones that are actually not frequent with bounded error $s - \bar{s} \leq MS_e$.

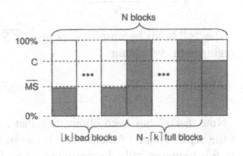

Fig. 2. Stream of itemsets that maximizes $s - \bar{s}$. Grey bars indicate the support s in a block on a scale from 0 to 100%.

How do we compute $\overline{MS}$ given MS and MS_e? For this, let us assume we have chosen some value $\overline{MS} < MS$. Let us consider an itemset is which is frequent in the stream S with support s. Our algorithm will output a value $\bar{s} \leq s$ for the frequency of is. We are interested in computing an upper bound for the error $s - \bar{s}$. For this, let us assume for now that S is split into N equal-sized blocks. We will see later that the actual length of the stream is irrelevant. Let us further consider a worst-case stream S that maximizes $s - \bar{s}$, i.e., which minimizes $\bar{s}$. Note that our algorithm only makes an error if the support of is in a block is smaller than $\overline{MS}$. In this case, is will not be considered a frequent itemset in this block and its support in this block will not be considered when computing $\bar{s}$. That is, to maximize the error, there should be as many blocks as possible where the support of is is just below $\overline{MS}$. To maximize the number of such "bad" blocks, is must have a support of 100% in the remaining blocks ("full" blocks), such that the global support of is for the whole stream is s. It follows that the (fractional) number k of bad blocks in the worst-case stream must satisfy the constraint $k \times \overline{MS} + (N - k) \times 100\% = N \times s$, which can be solved for k to obtain

$$k = N\frac{100\% - s}{100\% - \overline{MS}} \qquad (4)$$

It follows that the worst-case configuration includes $\lfloor k \rfloor$ bad blocks, $N - \lceil k \rceil$ full blocks, and optionally one block with support $C = (k - \lfloor k \rfloor) \times \overline{MS} + (\lceil k \rceil - k) \times 100\%$ with $\overline{MS} < C < 100\%$ unless k is an integer. If k is an integer then that block doesn't exist and $C = 0$. The worst-case configuration of S is illustrated in Fig. 2. Note that the order of the blocks in the stream is irrelevant.

We can now express the error $s - \overline{s}$ as follows:

$$s - \overline{s} = s - \frac{(N - \lceil k \rceil) \times 100\% + C}{N} = s - \frac{(N - k) \times 100\% + (k - \lfloor k \rfloor) \times \overline{MS}}{N}$$
$$\leq s - \frac{(N - k) \times 100\%}{N} \tag{5}$$

The "$\leq$" holds because $(k - \lfloor k \rfloor) \times \overline{MS} \geq 0$. Inserting Eq. 4 into Eq. 5 and rearranging terms we obtain

$$s - \overline{s} \leq s - (s - \overline{MS}) \frac{100\%}{100\% - MS} \tag{6}$$

Note that N has been eliminated, that is, the derived error bound is independent of the actual length of the stream. It can be easily verified that the right-hand side of Eq. 6 is monotonically decreasing in s for all $MS > 0$. That is, we obtain the largest error $s - \overline{s}$ for the smallest possible value of s, which is MS. s cannot be smaller than MS, since itemset is would then not be frequent in contradiction to our assumption. Replacing s by MS and rearranging terms we obtain

$$s - \overline{s} \leq MS - \frac{MS - \overline{MS}}{100\% - \overline{MS}} 100\% \tag{7}$$

To ensure that $s - \overline{s} \leq MS_e$, we require that the right hand side of Eq. 7 equals MS_e. Solving for $\overline{MS}$ we obtain

$$\overline{MS} = \frac{MS_e \times 100\%}{100\% + MS_e - MS} \tag{8}$$

Using Eq. 8, we can compute the minimum support $\overline{MS}$ to be used for discovering frequent itemsets in a block, such that the resulting error $s - \overline{s}$ is never greater than MS_e.

4.4 Closed Patterns

Since there may be a large number of frequent itemsets, we will consider so-called *closed itemsets* instead [22,24]. A closed itemset is a frequent itemset which has only proper supersets with smaller support than itself. In can the shown that the set of closed itemsets of S contains the same information as the set of frequent itemsets of S. In practice, the number of closed itemsets can be orders of magnitude smaller than the number of frequent itemsets. In our algorithm, FIB and FIS will be sets of closed itemsets.

The algorithm for discovering closed itemsets of S proceeds as follows. It collects itemsets (generated as described in Sect. 4.1) into a block B until a complete block of size BN has been filled. Then, the block is compressed by removing duplicate itemsets $B[i] = B[j]$ (equality does not consider the counter values $B[\_].c$): we set $B[i].c \leftarrow B[i].c + B[j].c$ and remove $B[j]$.

We can now implement a function $isfreq(is)$ as depicted in Fig. 3 that computes the support of an itemset is for B and checks whether or not that itemset is frequent in B by iterating over the compressed block and computing the number of itemsets in B of which is is a subset (lines 7 and 8). The function terminates early (lines 9 and 10) if the number of unprocessed itemsets in B is too small to make is frequent.

To find closed itemsets in block B that contain local event e_l, function $block()$ is used as depicted in Fig. 4 (left). After execution, FIB will hold all closed itemsets. With the help of $traverse()$ (also given in Fig. 4), $block()$ basically enumerates all possible itemsets which contain local event e_l, computes their support and stores closed itemsets in FIB. However, two properties of closed itemsets are exploited to prune the huge search space significantly. Firstly, if itemset is is not frequent, no superset of is is frequent. Secondly, if adding an item i to itemset is does not change the support of is, then is cannot be a closed itemset. Exploiting these properties for pruning is a standard

```
1   bool isfreq (itemset &is) {
2       int rest ← BN;
3       int minc ← BN × MS/100%
4       is.c ← 0;
5       foreach bis ∈ B {
6           rest ← rest − bis.c;
7           if (is ⊂ bis)
8               is.c ← is.c + bis.c;
9           else if (is.c + rest < minc)
10              return false ;
11      }
12      return true ;
13  }
```

Fig. 3. Algorithm to compute the support of itemset is in the current block

technique [5]. Additional techniques exist, but these require significant amounts of memory [24] or do not have a large impact on runtime according to our experience.

In more detail, $block()$ creates the itemsets is which contain only local event e_l in line 27, computes the support of this itemset in line 28, and invokes $traverse(is, tail)$ in line 29, which recursively enumerates supersets of is by incrementally moving items from $tail$ to is. Initially, $tail$ contains all possible items except items that represent local events (line 25). The first loop in $traverse()$ implements pruning by moving all items from $tail$ to is that do not change the support of s (lines 5 - 8), exploiting the second of the properties mentioned above. Also, if adding an item from $tail$ to is makes is infrequent, then that item is removed from $tail$ (line 10). The second loop (line 12) implements the recursion step for all items remaining in $tail$. Finally, is is added to FIB if the latter doesn't contain an itemset which is a superset of is and has same support (lines 19-21). If such a superset exists in FIB, then is cannot be a closed itemset. Note that $traverse()$ implements a depth-first search of the itemset space, that is, before is is considered for insertion into FIB, all supersets of is are considered first.

Next, function $merge()$ as depicted in Fig. 4 (right) is used to merge the closed itemsets in FIB for the current block into FIS. The latter set of itemsets holds closed itemsets of the stream S seen so far.

Basically, merging is implemented by considering each possible intersection of itemsets from FIS and FIB (is in line 35). If $is \notin FIS$, then the support of is with respect

```
1   void traverse (itemset is, tail) {        32   void merge () {
2     foreach item i ∈ tail {                 33     foreach itemset fis ∈ FIS {
3       itemset nis ← is ∪ {i};               34       foreach itemset fib ∈ FIB {
4       if (isfreq (nis)) {                   35         itemset is = fis ∩ fib;
5         if (nis.c = is.c) {                 36         if (is ∩ E_l ≠ ∅) {
6           is ← nis;                         37           if (is ∉ FIS) {
7           tail ← tail \ {i};                38             is.c ← fis.c;
8         }                                   39             is.c2 ← 0;
9       } else                                40             FIS ← FIS ∪ {is};
10        tail ← tail \ {i};                  41           }
11    }                                       42           if (FIS[is].c < fis.c)
12    foreach item i ∈ tail {                 43             FIS[is].c ← fis.c;
13      itemset nis ← is ∪ {i};               44           if (FIS[is].c2 < fib.c)
14      tail ← tail \ {i};                    45             FIS[is].c2 ← fib.c;
15                                            46   } } }
16      if (isfreq (nis))                     47
17        traverse (nis, tail);               48   foreach fib ∈ FIB {
18    }                                       49     if (fib ∉ FIS) {
19    if (∄fib ∈ FIB : is ⊂ fib               50       fib.c2 ← fib.c;
20                 ∧is.c = fib.c)             51       fib.c ← 0;
21      FIB ← FIB ∪ {is};                     52       FIS ← FIS ∪ {fib};
22  }                                         53     } else
23                                            54       FIS[fib].c2 ← fib.c;
24  void block (event e_l) {                  55   }
25    // ◇ = complete itemset                 56
26    itemset tail ← ◇ \ E_l;                 57   foreach fis ∈ FIS {
27    FIB ← ∅;                                58     FIS[fis].c ← FIS[fis].c
28    itemset is ← {e_l};                     59                  + FIS[fis].c2;
29    isfreq (is);                            60     FIS[fis].c2 ← 0;
30    traverse (is, tail);                    61   }
31  }                                         62 }
```

Fig. 4. Algorithm to discover closed itemsets

to FIS equals the support of the superset $sis \supset is$ with maximum support among all supersets $sis \in FIS$. The analog applies for the support of is with respect to FIB. The support of each intersection is is incrementally computed in lines 37-45 and stored in the fields $is.c$ (support with respect to FIS) and $is.c2$ (support with respect to FIB). An separate loop in lines 48-55 is used to add all itemsets $fib \in FIB$ to FIS. To compute the support values $fib.c$ and $fib.c2$, we can assume that either $fib \in FIS$, or fib has support 0 in FIS. If fib has nonzero support in FIS and is not contained in FIS, then a superset of fib must be contained in FIS. However, in this case fib has already been added previously as an intersection, because the intersection of fib with a superset of itself equals fib.

Finally, the new support values of all itemsets in FIS are computed in lines 57-61 by adding the support in FIS (counter c) and the support in FIB (counter c2). All itemsets $is \in FIS$ that satisfy $is.c \geq (MS - MS_e) \times |S|/100\%$ afterwards are output as closed itemsets of the stream S seen so far.

4.5 Maximal Patterns

In some cases it is sufficient to know whether or not an itemset is frequent, that is, the exact support does not matter. In these cases, we can compute the set of *maximal itemsets* [11,14] given the set of closed itemsets computed as described in the previous section. A frequent itemset is is maximal if there are no supersets of is which are frequent. Note that an itemset is frequent if and only if it is a subset of a maximal itemset. Hence, knowing the set of maximal itemsets a user knows all frequent itemsets and he could send inquiries to the sensor network to learn the frequencies of specific frequent itemsets.

The number of maximal itemsets is often orders of magnitude smaller than the number of closed itemsets. Maximal itemsets are typically an extremely compact and human-readable summary of the "common behavior" observed by a sensor network, see Sect. 6 for an example.

5 Implementation Aspects

We have developed two implementations of the proposed system. The first implementation is based on the BTnode [25] sensor node platform and supports a spatial scope of one hop. We chose the BTnode platform mainly because it provides 256 kB of RAM. Otherwise, the BTnode is similar to a MICA2: the microcontroller is an Atmel AT Mega 128L and the radio is a ChipCon CC1000.

The second implementation uses pre-recorded logs of sensor values instead of real sensors. The log contains sensor data also from neighbor nodes, such that communication between nodes is not required. This implementation runs both on BTnodes and on PCs and is mainly used for evaluation. Apart from these differences, the two implementations are identical. We will refer to these implementations as *DistributedImpl* and *SimulatorImpl*. Below we discuss some important implementation aspects that are shared by both programs.

5.1 Data Structures

The performance of our system significantly depends on an efficient implementation of itemsets and sets of itemsets (i.e., FIB and FIS), as operations on these data structures are frequently performed in the inner loops of algorithms for discovering and merging closed itemsets.

Itemsets are represented as bitvectors, which are implemented as an array of bytes. The size of the array is a compile-time parameter, such that the compiler can apply loop-unrolling to optimize itemset operations. Most operations on itemsets (such as union, intersection, subset tests) operate on bytes (i.e., 8 items at a time) rather than on individual bits and are thus efficient. Note that itemsets in S are densely populated. Eq. 2 implies that a fraction of about $1/|FP|$ of the bits are non-zero. That is, bitvectors are also a space-efficient representation.

Sets of itemsets (i.e., FIB and FIS) only need to support insertion, lookup, deletion of all elements, but *not* deletion of individual elements. Since FIS dominates the memory footprint of our system, it is also important that per-element memory overhead of these data structures is minimized. For example, many typical data structures (linked lists, trees) require one or more pointers per element. Since a typical itemset is rather small in the context of our work (typically < 10 bytes), this would represent a significant overhead. We therefore decided for hash tables that are implemented with a fixed-size array, which requires no per-element memory overhead. The hash function for FIS is based on the bitvector contents of the itemset, while the hash function for FIB is based on the support value of the itemset to support search for supersets (line 19 in Fig. 4).

5.2 Query Compilation

The query compiler reads a query as given in Fig. 1 and generates C code. The output consists of functions to generate events from sensor output according to the definitions given in the query (i.e., lines 4 to 6 in Fig. 1), mapping functions $map_d()$, $map_t()$, $map_f()$ that map distances, time intervals and event frequencies to partitions, as well several constant definitions (e.g., for minimum support, temporal and spatial scopes, epoch length). Among the latter is also the size of the bitvectors of itemsets, which is computed using Eq. 3.

6 Evaluation

We study code size, runtime, memory footprint, and the output of the pattern discovery algorithm for a typical query using sensor data logs [26]. In particular, we investigate the trade-off between the scope of the query (i.e., minimum support and number of local events) and resource consumption (i.e., runtime and memory footprint).

6.1 Code Size

We report the size of the code and data segments of *DistributedImpl* in Bytes. The program consists of two main parts. The first part includes algorithms and data structures for discovering frequent itemsets. The second part contains code for reading out sensors and generating events, the protocol for data collection from a one-hop neighborhood, as well as time synchronization. The latter simply uses the request messages of the data collection protocol which are broadcast by the discovery node to synchronize all nodes in the one-hop neighborhood to the time of the discovery node. Code has been compiled by avr-gcc 3.4.5 using optimization flags -O3 -funroll-loops.

Function	Code	Data
pattern discovery	10628	260
data collection, sensors, time sync	5498	707
total	16126	967

6.2 Runtime and Memory Footprint

To evaluate runtime and memory footprint of the pattern discovery algorithm, we use *SimulatorImpl* executing on a BTnode, using sensor data collected during one month from 54 sensor nodes in the Intel Research Lab Berkeley [26]. This dataset was collected with an epoch duration of about 30 seconds (resulting in a total of about 65000 epochs) and contains, among others, temperature and light readings. Using this dataset, we investigate how two key query parameters, namely minimum support and the number of local and context events, affect the resource consumption of our system in terms of runtime and memory footprint.

Fig. 5 shows the relevant query parameters. We consider two types of events: *warm* and *light* events. Each sensor node with a temperature reading > 23 degrees Celsius in an epoch emits a *warm* event in this epoch. Every sensor node with a light reading > 300 Lux emits a *light* event. Note that with these event definitions we are actually investigating correlations between *states* "it is light" and "it is warm" as discussed in Sect. 3. Both events are declared as both context and local events, which means that we are interested in how light on a node correlates with light and temperature in its neighborhood and how temperature on a node correlated with light and temperature in its neighborhood.

For our experiment, we selected the node with ID 1 as the discovery node executing the pattern discovery algorithm. We obtained very similar results when selecting other nodes as the discovery node. With the above settings, mote 1 generates a *warm* event in about 23% of all epochs and a *light* event in about 14% of all epochs.

```
1  epoch = 30
2  event warm { temp[0] > 23 }
3  event light { light [0] > 300 }
4  cevents {warm, light}
5  levents {warm, light}
6  history = 10
7  distance { near =(0,5), far =[5,10] }
8  time { now=0, recent =[1,4], old=[5,10] }
9  frequency { none=0, some=[1,infty] }
```

Fig. 5. Query used for evaluation

To evaluate runtime and memory footprint of the pattern discovery algorithm, we compiled a preprocessed version of the sensor data for the first 30254 epochs into the text segment of the *SimulatorImpl* executable that is running on a BTnode (more data didn't fit into the program flash). We then repeatedly ran the pattern discovery algorithm on this data set with different values for MS and MS_e, measuring execution time, the number of itemsets in FIS, the number of closed itemsets among the itemsets in FIS, as well as the number of maximal itemsets among the itemsets in FIS. We also studied how the size of FIS grows over time as more and more blocks are processed. Fig. 6 shows the results. The runtime is given as the ratio between execution time of the algorithm and total time of data collection (i.e., 30254 epochs × 30 seconds). In all cases, the resulting CPU duty cycle is very small (subfigure (a)). The number of itemsets in FIS strongly depends both on minimum support MS and on error bound MS_e (subfigure (b)). Interestingly, the number of closed itemsets in FIS is also strongly dependent on MS, but less so on MS_e (subfigure (c)). This indicates that reducing MS_e results in the generation of additional itemsets that are frequent in some blocks, but not frequent for the whole data stream. Also note that the number of closed itemsets does also depend on structure of frequent itemsets, such that increasing the error bound MS_e may actually result in more closed itemsets as it is the case in subfigure (c). Also note that only about half of the itemsets in FIS are actually frequent. Again, this indicates that there are many itemsets which are frequent in individual blocks, but not for the whole data stream. The number of maximal itemsets is at most 10 in all experiments (diagram not shown). That is, a very small number of maximal itemsets is sufficient to characterize the "common behavior" observed by the sensor network.

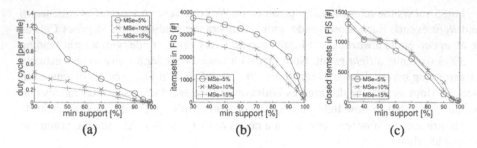

Fig. 6. Results for pattern discovery: (a) runtime (b) size of FIS (c) closed itemsets in FIS

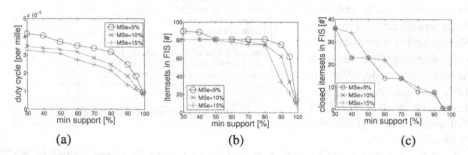

Fig. 7. Results for pattern discovery with simplified query: (a) runtime (b) size of FIS (c) closed itemsets in FIS

The size of an itemset for the experiment query is 8 bytes (4 bytes for the bit vector, 2 bytes each for the counters c and $c2$). With this, the total RAM required for itemsets in FIS was at most 30 kB in the course of our experiments.

Fig. 7 shows the same diagrams for a simplified query, which considers only *light* as a context event and *warm* as a local event, but is otherwise identical to the query in Fig. 5. We observe a qualitatively similar behavior as in Fig. 6, but at much lower absolute values. This illustrates the capability of our system to trade off scope for resource consumption by constraining the search to fewer local events.

To understand the reason for the above quantitative differences, let us estimate how the number of discovered itemsets (i.e., patterns) increases when adding additional context or local events to a query. For this, let us define $Q(E_c, E_l)$ as the number of patterns discovered for a query with context events E_c and local events E_l. Since our algorithm only considers patterns with a single local event, adding a new local event results in an additive increase of patterns:

$$Q(\{e_1\}, \{e_2, e_3\}) = Q(\{e_1\}, \{e_2\}) + Q(\{e_1\}, \{e_3\}) \tag{9}$$

However, when adding an additional context event, we obtain a multiplicative increase in patterns in the worst case:

$$Q(\{e_1, e_2\}, \{e_3\}) \leq Q(\{e_1\}, \{e_3\}) \times Q(\{e_2\}, \{e_3\}) \tag{10}$$

The reason for this is that potentially every frequent pattern that contains only e_1 as a context event could be combined with every frequent pattern that contains only e_2 as a context event to obtain a frequent pattern which contains both e_1 and e_2 as context events. However, in practice this number is often significantly smaller as event patterns with e_2 and events patterns with e_1 have to occur during the same epochs in the data stream – otherwise the combined event pattern may not be frequent.

6.3   Communication Overhead

During the experiment duration of 30254 epochs, only in 8000 epochs a local event occurred on the discovery node (i.e., mote 1). Recall that only when a local event occurs, then the discovery node requests event occurrences during the last $TSCOPE$ epochs (i.e., 10 epochs for our experiment) from client nodes. In our experiment, event occurrences for 12418 epochs have been requested by the discovery node. As each event is represented by a single bit, every client node would have to transmit 24836 bits (since there are two context events defined in the query) or about 3 kB. Assuming that every sensor reading requires one byte, the raw sensor data generated by each node during the experiment would be about 60 kB. Also note that with our approach communication among nodes is constrained to small neighborhoods, whereas traditional data gathering applications require to transmit raw sensor readings through the whole network to the sink.

6.4   Discovered Maximal Patterns

We would expect a strong correlation of the occurrence of *light* and *warm* events on the discovery node with *light* and *warm* events on client nodes. The discovered patterns confirm this expectation. For $MS = 90\%$, for example, we obtain two maximal itemsets that map to the following patterns:

```
(W,now,far,some) AND (W,recent,*,some) AND
(W,old,*,some) : L [96%]

(W,*,far,some) AND (L,now,far,some) AND
(L,{old,recent},*,some) : L [92%]
```

Here, "W" and "L" refer to *warm* and *light* events as defined above. The notations "{... , ...}" and "*" mean that the enclosing term is valid for the set of given partition identifiers or for all possible partition identifiers, respectively.

Packet loss is an issue in most multi-hop data collection sensor networks [9]. In particular, the dataset used for the experiments also had missing entries. In the context of our work, packet loss may affect the correctness of discovered frequent patterns. In particular, three cases can be distinguished. Firstly, a wrong frequency may be reported for a frequent pattern. Secondly, an infrequent pattern may be reported as being frequent. Thirdly, a frequent pattern may not be reported as being frequent. The latter two problems apply predominantly to patterns with a frequency close to MS, where "close to" is a function of the amount of packet loss. Hence, the likelihood of missing frequent patterns due to packet loss can be decreased by reducing MS to a lower value. A quantitative study of this aspect is the subject of future work.

7 Related Work

While data stream mining techniques have been used for other purposes in sensor networks, we are not aware of similar in-network approaches to discover frequent distributed event patterns. There are systems that support *detection* of given distributed event patterns (e.g., [2,16]), but this is a fundamentally different problem as mentioned in Sect. 1.

The authors of [17] apply itemset mining to find sensors that show the same value concurrently for significant portions of time, which can be considered as a very specific instance of distributed event patterns. However, their approach is centralized. Resource requirements of their solution are too high to allow an implementation on sensor nodes.

In a more general context, data stream mining techniques have also been applied to outlier detection [4] or to in-network reduction of sensor data streams [3] such that certain properties of the original data stream are preserved. However, these are fundamentally different problems. Also, while the authors claim that their algorithms can be implemented on resource-constrained sensor nodes, they resort to simulations.

Another approach that is loosely related to our work is *distributed regression* [12], where sensor nodes cooperate locally to fit a global function to their measurements. Implicitly, such a global function represents the correlation between sensor data of different nodes. However, this work is based on continuous sensor time series and makes the fundamental assumption that sensor data is strongly correlated both spatially and temporally. In contrast, our approach is based on discrete events and we make no assumptions about the correlation of sensor data – instead, we want to find out whether and how events on different sensor nodes are correlated.

There is a large amount of work regarding discovery of frequent itemsets from a data stream. Many approaches are based on sliding windows (e.g., [6,8]), where frequent itemsets are discovered from a small, moving fraction of the data stream. However, we are interested in discovering patterns from the whole data stream. Several proposals exist for this problem (e.g., [7,10,15,13,19]). However, these approaches use synopsis data structure in addition to the sought frequent itemsets, resulting in a memory footprint that led us to develop an approach that fits the specific constraints of sensor nodes. For discovery of closed itemsets from a small block of itemsets, we borrowed techniques from existing multi-pass algorithms, most notably [5].

8 Conclusions

We presented a novel in-network knowledge discovery technique that supports the discovery of frequent distributed event patterns in sensor networks, where event patterns characterize the spatial and temporal correlations between events observed by sensor nodes in a confined network neighborhood. To deal with the constrained resources of sensor nodes, our system offers a declarative query language to specify the level of detail and the scope of sought patterns, thus offering a turning knob to trade off detail and scope for resource consumption. We implemented our proposal on the BTnode platform and and showed that the resources of this platform are sufficient to handle typical problem instances. We also showed that by reducing the scope of the query we could decrease resource consumption.

References

1. Adler, R., Buonadonna, P., Chhabra, J., Flanigan, M., Krishnamurthy, L., Kushalnagar, N., Nachman, L., Yarvis, M.: Design and Deployment of Industrial Sensor Networks: Experiences from the North Sea and a Semiconductor Plant. In: Sensys 2005, San Diego, USA (November 2005)
2. Ahn, S., Kim, D.: Proactive Context-Aware Sensor Networks. In: Römer, K., Karl, H., Mattern, F. (eds.) EWSN 2006. LNCS, vol. 3868, Springer, Heidelberg (2006)
3. Akcan, H., Brönnimann, H.: Deterministic Data Reduction in Sensor Networks. In: MASS 2006, Vancouver, Canada (October 2006)
4. Branch, J., Szymanski, B., Gianella, C., Wolff, R., Kargupta, H.: In-Network Outlier Detection in Wireless Sensor Networks. In: ICDCS 2006, Lisboa, Portugal (July 2006)
5. Burdick, D., Calimlim, M., Gehrke, J.: MAFIA: A Maximal Frequent Itemset Algorithm for Transactional Databases. In: ICDE 2001, Heidelberg, Germany (April 2001)
6. Chang, J.H., Lee, W.S.: Finding Recent Frequent Itemsets Adaptively over Online Data Streams. In: SIGKDD 2003, Washington, USA (August 2003)
7. Cheung, W., Zaiane, O.R.: Incremental Mining of Frequent Patterns Without Candidate Generation or Support Constraints. In: IDEAS 2003, Hong Kong, China (July 2003)
8. Chi, Y., Wang, H., Yu, P.S., Muntz, R.M.: Moment: Mainatining Closed Frequent Itemsets over a Stream Sliding Window. In: Perner, P. (ed.) ICDM 2004. LNCS (LNAI), vol. 3275, Springer, Heidelberg (2004)
9. Choi, J., Lee, J., Wachs, M., Levis, P.: Opening the sensornet black box. Technical Report SING-06-03, Stanford Information Networks Group (2006)
10. Giannella, C., Han, J., Pei, J., Yan, X., Yu, P.S.: Mining Frequent Patterns in Data Streams at Multiple Time Granularities. In: NSF Workshop on Next Generation Data Mining 2002, Baltimore, USA (November 2002)
11. Gouda, K., Zaki, M.J.: Efficiently Mining Maximal Frequent Itemsets. In: ICDM 2001, San Jose, USA (November 2001)
12. Guestrin, C., Bodik, P., Thibaux, R., Paskin, M., Madden, S.: Distributed Regression: an Efficient Framework for Modeling Sensor Network Data. In: IPSN 2004, Berkeley, USA (April 2004)
13. Jin, R., Agrawal, G.: An Algorithm for In-Core Frequent Itemset Mining on Streaming Data. In: ICDM 2005, New Orleans, USA (November 2005)
14. Bayardo, Jr., R.J.: Efficiently Mining Long Patterns from Databases. In: SIGMOD 1998, Seattle, USA (June 1998)
15. Li, H.-F., Lee, S.-Y., Shan, M.-K.: An Efficient Algorithm for Mining Frequent Itemsets over the entire History of Data Streams. In: First Intl. Workshop on Knowledge Discovery in Data Streams 2004, Pisa, Italy (September 2004)
16. Li, S., Son, S.H., Stankovic, J.A.: Event Detection Services Using Data Service Middleware in Distributed Sensor Networks. In: Zhao, F., Guibas, L.J. (eds.) IPSN 2003. LNCS, vol. 2634, Springer, Heidelberg (2003)
17. Loo, K.K., Tong, I., Kao, B.: Online Algorithms for Mining Inter-Stream Associations from Large Sensor Networks. In: Ho, T.-B., Cheung, D., Liu, H. (eds.) PAKDD 2005. LNCS (LNAI), vol. 3518, Springer, Heidelberg (2005)
18. Madden, S.R., Franklin, M.J., Hellerstein, J.M., Hong, W.: TAG: a Tiny Aggregation Service for Ad-Hoc Sensor Networks. In: OSDI 2002, Boston, USA (December 2002)
19. Manku, G.S., Motwani, R.: Approximate Frequency Counts over Data Streams. In: Bressan, S., Chaudhri, A.B., Lee, M.L., Yu, J.X., Lacroix, Z. (eds.) CAiSE 2002 and VLDB 2002. LNCS, vol. 2590, Springer, Heidelberg (2003)

20. Römer, K.: Distributed Mining of Spatio-Temporal Event Patterns in Sensor Networks. In: Workshop on Middleware for Sensor Networks, San Francisco, USA (June 2006)
21. Szewczyk, R., Polastre, J., Mainwaring, A., Culler, D.: Lessons from a Sensor Network Expedition. In: Karl, H., Wolisz, A., Willig, A. (eds.) Wireless Sensor Networks. LNCS, vol. 2920, Springer, Heidelberg (2004)
22. Wang, J., Han, J., Pei, J.: Searching for the Best Strategies for Mining Frequent Closed Itemsets. In: SIGKDD 2003, Washington, USA (August 2003)
23. Welsh, M., Mainland, G.: Programming Sensor Networks Using Abstract Regions. In: NSDI 2004, Boston, USA (March 2004)
24. Zaki, M.J., Hsiao, C.: CHARM: An Efficient Algorithm for Closed Itemset Mining. In: SDM 2002, Arlington, USA (April 2002)
25. BTnodes, www.btnode.ethz.ch
26. Intel Lab Sensor Data, http://berkeley.intel-research.net/labdata/

Tracking Dynamic Boundary Fronts
Using Range Sensors

Subhasri Duttagupta, Krithi Ramamritham,
Purushottam Kulkarni[1], and Kannan M. Moudgalya[2]

[1] Dept. of Computer Science and Engineering
Indian Institute of Technology, Bombay
{subhasri,krithi,puru}@cse.iitb.ac.in
[2] Dept. of Chemical Engineering
kannan@che.iitb.ac.in

Abstract. We examine the problem of tracking dynamic boundaries occurring in natural phenomena using range sensors. Two main challenges of the boundary tracking problem are energy-efficient boundary estimations from noisy observations and continuous tracking of the boundary. We propose a novel approach which uses a regression-based *spatial estimation* technique to determine discrete points on the boundary and estimates a confidence band around the entire boundary. In addition, a Kalman Filter-based *temporal estimation* technique is used to selectively refresh the estimated boundary to meet the accuracy requirements. Our algorithm for dynamic boundary tracking (DBTR) combines *temporal* estimation with an aperiodically updated *spatial* estimation and provides a low overhead solution to track boundaries without requiring *prior* knowledge about the dynamics of the boundary. Experimental results demonstrate the effectiveness of our algorithm and estimated confidence bands achieve *loss of coverage* of less than $2 - 5\%$ for a variety of boundaries with different spatial characteristics.

1   Introduction

Large scale sensor networks are being deployed for real-time monitoring applications, such as detecting leakage of hazardous material, tracking forest fires and environmental phenomena. Consider a poisonous gas or plume monitoring application [1], tracking a spreading plume requires continuous updates regarding extent of the plume, its direction and its distance from habitats. The plume can be considered to be delineated by a boundary such that tracking the movement of the plume involves estimating a dynamically changing boundary. Strategically deployed range sensors can coordinate to track boundaries associated with such natural phenomena.

The solution space for boundary estimation using a sensor network can be examined along four orthogonal dimensions: (i) the *characteristic* of sensors - static [2], [3] or mobile [4]; (ii) *sensing capabilities* - in-situ sensing or range/remote sensing; (iii) the *accuracy* of estimation; and (iv) the *nature* of the boundary - static or

R. Verdone (Ed.): EWSN 2008, LNCS 4913, pp. 125–140, 2008.
© Springer-Verlag Berlin Heidelberg 2008

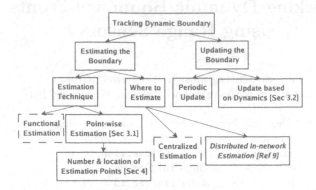

Fig. 1. Issues related to tracking dynamic boundaries. (Solid boxes indicate problems addressed in this paper).

dynamic. In this paper, we address the problem of estimating dynamic boundaries using static sensors with range/remote sensing capabilities. Previous techniques to estimate boundaries have employed *in-situ* [2] static or mobile sensors. In applications like tracking a plume, or predicting trajectory of weather parameters [5], in-situ sensing is not feasible due to difficulty in remote access or requirement of a large-scale deployment of sensors. In such situations, techniques based on range or remote sensing using radar or laser pulses are better suited. The basic difference between in-situ and range sensing is that, in the former approach a sensor measures the value of the field at its current location whereas in the latter approach a sensor finds approximate distance to a remote location where the field value equals some specific threshold. Radars used in [5] scan an angular area by swiping upto 360 degrees and gather reflectivity and wind velocity information. Lidars (LIght Detection and Ranging) are being used for detecting forest fires [6], [7] in the last few years. Lidars detect fire by analysing the energy back-scattered from smoke particles resulting from fire and measure the distance between lidar sensor and a point on the target(smoke) using simple principle of light. While today lidars are not capable of wireless communication, we envision in near future low power, inexpensive sensors with radar/lidar distance sensing and wireless/optical communication capability will be available. In the rest of the paper, we assume such sensors are used to detect boundaries occurring in natural phenomena.

Figure 1 is a pictorial representation of the issues involved in tracking a dynamic boundary. The two main issues are estimating the boundary and updating the estimates as the boundary moves. There are two broad techniques to estimate boundaries, *(i) Functional estimation and (ii) Point-wise estimation*. Unlike a functional estimation technique, a point-wise estimation technique assumes that boundaries consist of discrete points and individual points are estimated without reference to any specific functional form. The effectiveness of this technique depends on the number and locations of boundary estimation points. Our proposed point-wise technique exploits spatial variations to determine locations of estimation points and minimizes the number of estimation points.

Error in range estimation due to inherent inaccuracy of sensors introduces error in estimating points on the boundary. The challenge is to estimate an accurate boundary in the presence of noisy observations. In this paper, we use a *kernel smoothing* technique that exploits spatial correlation between proximate sensors so as to reduce the effect of range sensing errors. Further, a centralized technique for estimating boundaries suffers from high communication overheads. We explore a decentralized solution that utilizes local computation capability and performs *in-network* aggregation at sensors within the network to significantly reduce the communication overhead for boundary estimation.

In order to track a dynamic boundary, the boundary estimates need to be updated periodically. The ability to use the temporal characteristics of the boundary to update its estimate only when required is another challenge we address in this paper. The instances when a boundary estimate is updated depend on the dynamics of the boundary. But, unless there is clairvoyance, optimal choice of periodicity at each point is not possible in real-time tracking scenarios. Our approach uses a Kalman Filter based mechanism to *predict the movement* of the boundary and updates estimates only when error in the current estimate exceeds a pre-defined threshold.

We address the problem of accurate dynamic boundary estimation with observations from range sensors incurring low communication overhead. By way of *contributions*,

– We propose DBTR, a novel technique that intelligently combines both spatial and temporal estimation techniques for accurate dynamic boundary estimation. Our spatial estimation scheme is designed such that it lends itself to in-network aggregation.
– We demonstrate the effectiveness of DBTR for tracking a dynamic boundary without *prior* knowledge about the dynamics of the boundary. The performance of DBTR in terms of communication overheads and accuracy is comparable with the best *optimal* periodic update scheme.
– We experimentally show that the estimated confidence band around a boundary has *loss of coverage* (defined in Section 2) less than $2-5\%$ for a spectrum of boundaries with different spatial characteristics.

2   System Model and Problem Formulation

We assume n sensor nodes distributed randomly over a two dimensional field measuring a phenomenon (e.g., viscosity or reflectivity). Further, each sensor has directional range sensing capability to estimate the closest point whose field value matches the definition of a boundary. An observation (x_i, y_i) of the ith sensor represents the location of a boundary point. We assume that sensors can align their sensing antennas at any angle to locate a point on the boundary. Further, all sensors are located on one side of the boundary tracking the *front* of a phenomenon. Figure 2(a) shows a typical scenario of sensors detecting various points on the boundary. A sensor at location (x_s, y_s) positions its beam at an

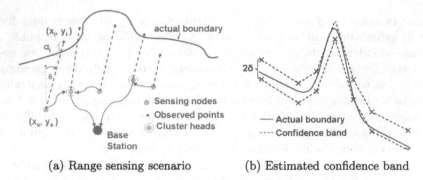

(a) Range sensing scenario   (b) Estimated confidence band

Fig. 2. Tracking dynamic boundary using range sensing observations

angle θ [1] w.r.t. the y axis and detects a point (x_i, y_i) on the boundary with error α_i along the sensing direction.

Given n observations $\{(x_i, y_i)\}_{i=1}^{n}$ with errors, we address the problem of estimating a confidence band of a specific width δ (the distance between the estimated boundary and limit of the band) as shown in Figure 2(b). The confidence band should cover the dynamic boundary at all times and with high probability. We measure the accuracy of coverage in terms of *loss of coverage* (*LOC*), the probability of the band not covering the actual boundary. If $(x_i, d(x_i))$ is a point on the actual boundary, *LOC* over a set of n sensors is defined as:

$$LOC(\delta) = \frac{1}{n} \sum_{i=1}^{n} I(|\hat{d}(x_i) - d(x_i)| > \delta) \qquad (1)$$

where $I(a)$ is an indicator function, i.e., $I(a) = 1$ if a is true, $I(a) = 0$ otherwise and $d(x_i)$ is the actual distance from estimation point x_i and $\hat{d}(x)$ is its estimate. Minimizing *LOC* helps maximize accuracy of coverage.

Our model assumes that sensor nodes are equipped with wireless radios. Further, these nodes use clustering for aggregation and multi-hop routing techniques for communication with a base station. Finally, since sensors are energy-limited, we aim to minimize the communication overhead at nodes to increase lifetime of sensor networks.

3   DBTR: Dynamic Boundary Tracking Algorithm

A dynamic boundary has mainly two types of variations: spatial and temporal. Effective tracking of dynamic boundaries requires handling both of these variations. In this section, we describe DBTR, a point-wise algorithm for dynamic boundary tracking which combines a *spatial estimation* technique and a *temporal estimation* technique to effectively track a dynamic boundary.

---

[1] In this paper, we assume the antennas are aligned to the y axis i.e., $\theta = 0$. Please refer to [8] for a discussion on using non-zero sensing angles.

The first step of DBTR is to estimate the boundary at a location x_{pj} using a spatial estimation technique. It uses spatial correlations among observations at a given time by sensors within a small *neighborhood* of x_{pj}. Cluster heads perform aggregation operations on sensor observations to estimate a number of boundary points. Partial information of the boundary from cluster heads is then sent to the base station where the final estimates are computed. A confidence band is estimated from multiple boundary points around the entire boundary using an interpolation scheme.

The second component of DBTR is a temporal estimation technique which ensures that the estimates are updated whenever due to changes in the boundary the confidence band does not cover the boundary with a desired accuracy. DBTR uses a Kalman Filter based technique to predict future boundary locations based on its model of the boundary dynamics. Once the boundary has moved by more than a certain threshold, DBTR invokes the spatial estimation technique to get an accurate estimate of the boundary. As a result, boundary estimates are updated based on only the local dynamics of the boundary and partial estimates track changes in sections of the boundary. Both of these lead to reduction in communication overhead for accurate boundary estimation.

3.1 Regression-Based Spatial Estimation Technique

This section briefly sketches the non-parametric regression method used by the spatial estimation technique as discussed in [9].

For each sensor observation (x_i, y_i), the independent variable x_i and the dependent variable y_i can be modeled as a non-parametric regression relation. For n observations at the n sensors, the regression relation is stated as,

$$y_i = d(x_i) + \alpha_i, \quad i = 1, \ldots, n \tag{2}$$

where d is the regression relation between x_i and y_i, and α_i the observation error. If the error distribution has mean zero, then the expected value of the distance to the boundary at x_i is $d(x_i)$. We assume the error distribution to be normal $N(0, \sigma^2)$, where σ^2 is the observation error variance. Note that in reality, observations from range sensors may not satisfy this assumption but in experiments with real sensors [9], we verify that the mathematical technique is applicable even when the assumption does not hold.

For a point on the boundary estimated at location x_{pj}, $d(x_{pj})$ is the actual distance of boundary from x_{pj} and $\hat{d}(x_{pj})$ is the estimated distance. Assuming a smooth boundary, it is possible to use a local average of the observations near x_{pj} to construct an estimate for $d(x_{pj})$. The *kernel smoothing* [10] technique that uses observations in the neighborhood of x_{pj} is applied to estimate $\hat{d}(x_{pj})$. Thus $\hat{d}(x_{pj})$ is,

$$\hat{d}(x_{pj}) = \frac{1}{n} \sum_{i=1}^{n} W_i(x_{pj}) y_i \tag{3}$$

where $\{W_i(x_{pj})\}_{i=1}^{n}$ denotes a sequence of weights defined using a *kernel* function. The weight for x_{pj} is non-zero in the neighborhood from $(x_{pj} - h)$ to

$(x_{pj} + h)$, referred to as the *h-neighborhood* of x_{pj}. Using the observations in the *h-neighborhood* of x_{pj}, the variance of the y-component of the observations is also estimated. This variance $\hat{\sigma}^2(x_{pj})$ captures the spatial variations of the boundary and is an estimate of the actual observation error variance σ^2.

$$\hat{\sigma}^2(x_{pj}) = \left(\frac{1}{n} \sum_{i=1}^{n} W_i(x_{pj}) y_i^2 \right) - \hat{d}^2(x_{pj}) \tag{4}$$

A crucial step in estimating the boundary is choosing the parameter h that controls how much of the neighborhood around x_{pj} has to be considered. An iterative *plug-in* approach (refer [11] for details) is used to estimate the optimal value of h that minimizes the error in estimation. Evaluation of optimal h involves estimation of the boundary for all x values of the sensors. This is the reason we recommend a centralized approach for evaluating the optimal h initially.

Since both expressions, Equation (3) and Equation (4), are summations, they are amenable to distributed evaluation. All observations contributing to the estimation of $\hat{d}(x_{pj})$ and $\hat{\sigma}^2(x_{pj})$ may not be available at a single cluster head. Each cluster head computes partial expressions for $\hat{d}(x_{pj})$ and $\hat{\sigma}^2(x_{pj})$, referred to as *partial aggregates*. Whenever possible, partial aggregates from multiple cluster heads for a specific x_{pj} are combined at intermediate nodes and forwarded to the base station. The base station collects all partial aggregates and estimates $\hat{d}(x_{pj})$ and $\hat{\sigma}^2(x_{pj})$ for all estimation points x_{pj}. Using the above technique, k distinct points x_{pj}, $j = 1, \ldots, k$ along a boundary are estimated. These k points on the boundary are used as input to an interpolation scheme that estimates the confidence band at δ distance around the entire boundary. DBTR uses smoothing spline [10] interpolation to estimate the boundary.

3.2   Model-Based Temporal Estimation Technique

The temporal estimation technique uses a model for the dynamics built using a time sequence of observations of the distances to the boundary. Typically the model is dependent on the exact application scenario. But the distinction in our approach is that here the sensors are not performing *in situ* measurements. Specifically, we are interested in modeling the *velocity* of the boundary which may be affected by factors such as the prevailing weather conditions, surrounding topography etc. If the combined effect of these factors can be modeled as a Gaussian error, and the actual physical process has a linear dynamics, then traditional tracking models like Kalman Filter can be used. A sensor maintains a state representation of distances to the boundary that is updated at each time step. Assuming that the boundary at a discrete point changes in a linear fashion with time, we use Kalman Filters to predict future boundary locations.

Process state $s(x_{pj}, t_i)$ consists of the actual distance $d(x_{pj}, t_i)$ to the boundary at x_{pj} and the velocity of the boundary along the y axis at time instant t_i.

$$s(x_{pj}, t_i) = \begin{bmatrix} d(x_{pj}, t_i) \\ \dot{d}(x_{pj}, t_i) \end{bmatrix}$$

$\dot{d}(x_{pj}, t_i)$ denotes the change in $d(x_{pj}, t_i)$ with respect to time. Irrespective of the actual movement of the boundary, we are interested in knowing only the change in $d(x_{pj}, t_i)$, i.e., the y component of the velocity of the boundary at x_{pj}. The principle of remote or range sensing helps in reducing the *dimensionality* of the problem because a range sensor can always find the distance to a moving boundary irrespective of its own location. For simplicity, here we assume that the boundary moves with a *constant mean velocity* having a mean zero random acceleration. Then the state space equation becomes:

$$s(x_{pj}, t_i) = F \times s(x_{pj}, t_{i-1}) + G \times \alpha_p(x_{pj}, t_{i-1}) \tag{5}$$

where $\alpha_p(x_{pj}, t_{i-1})$ is a Gaussian error with distribution $N[0, \sigma_p^2]$. The matrix F relates the state at time t_i to the state at time t_{i-1}. The term $G \times \alpha_p(x_{pj}, t_{i-1})$ represents the noise component in the process model and matrices F and G can be obtained using simple laws of motion:

$$F = \begin{bmatrix} 1 & t_s \\ 0 & 1 \end{bmatrix} \text{ and } G = \begin{bmatrix} \frac{t_s^2}{2} \\ t_s \end{bmatrix}$$

where t_s is the duration between time instant t_i and t_{i-1}. In this case, it can be same as the sampling period of sensors. Assuming that the model accurately represents the dynamics of the boundary, σ_p^2 can be taken as a small quantity as compared to the observation error variance σ^2. If $\alpha(x_{pj}, t_i)$ is the error in sensor observations as given in Equation (2), the observation $y(t_i)$ at x_{pj} is linearly related to the state using the observation matrix as:

$$y(t_i) = H \times s(x_{pj}, t_i) + \alpha(x_{pj}, t_i) \tag{6}$$

where $H = [1 \ 0]$ is the observation matrix. This relationship is helpful to derive the distance $d(x_{pj}, t_i)$ information from the current state. The observation error covariance for the Kalman Filter at estimation point x_{pj} is obtained from observation error variance $\sigma^2(x_{pj})$ estimated in Equation (4).

While the boundary can be estimated at any k points using the spatial estimation technique irrespective of whether sensors are located at those points, the temporal estimation has to be associated with a specific sensor and its observations. Assuming that the boundary has similar temporal variation within the *h-neighborhood* of a location, any sensor having observations within h distance from x_{pj} can perform the temporal estimation for x_{pj}. Moreover, by applying distinct Kalman Filter-based estimates for each of the k points, it is possible to track a boundary that has different sections moving at different velocities.

3.3 DBTR – Combining Spatial and Temporal Estimations

The proposed algorithm combines both spatial estimation as well as Kalman Filter-based temporal estimation and is illustrated in Figure 3 for a specific estimation point x_{pj} (x_{pj} is omitted from all terms for clarity). In this block diagram, two stages of Kalman Filter, state *prediction* and state *update*, are

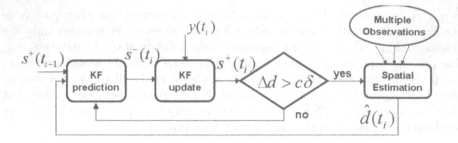

Fig. 3. Details of combining the Spatial and Temporal Estimation Techniques

shown separately. The prediction stage is used to predict the $s^-(t_i)$ from the state $s^+(t_{i-1})$ at previous time instant t_{i-1}. The output from the prediction stage and the new sensor observation are used to obtain the updated output $s^+(t_i)$. Both the prediction and update stages are needed for maintaining the current distance information. From the state information, the distance to the boundary as predicted by the Kalman Filter is obtained using $H \times s^+(t_i)$. This is compared with $\hat{d}(t_{Last})$, the last updated estimate obtained using the regression technique. Then, the difference Δd is estimated as:

$$\Delta d = H \times s^+(t_i) - \hat{d}(t_{Last}) \tag{7}$$

If the difference is more than $c \times \delta$ (where c is a constant and δ is the user specified width of the confidence band), it implies the boundary at x_{pj} has moved a distance larger than $c \times \delta$. Then the boundary is updated with the latest observations from all sensors in the *h-neighborhood* of x_{pj}. The estimate from the spatial technique is taken as the latest best estimate of the distance to the boundary at x_{pj} and is used by future temporal estimations for more accurate prediction. In Figure 3, $\hat{d}(t_i)$, the output from spatial estimation is used to update the distance information in state $s^+(t_i)$. The intelligent combination of spatial and temporal estimation techniques not only minimizes wasted boundary updates but also avoids updates to sections of the boundary that have not moved significantly.

4   Minimizing Number of Estimation Points

Our technique uses an interpolation scheme over a finite set of boundary points to estimate a confidence band around the boundary. The interpolation error of the confidence band reduces as the number of estimation points is increased. However, this will lead to an increased communication overhead. Our goal is two fold: (i) to estimate boundary at a minimal number of points, and (ii) to ensure that the *interpolated band* as mentioned in Section 2 covers the actual boundary with high confidence. We use k to denote the number of estimation points.

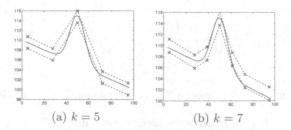

(a) $k = 5$ (b) $k = 7$

Fig. 4. Confidence band with different number of estimation points

Since the variance $\hat{\sigma}^2(x)$ captures the local spatial changes within the *h-neighborhood*, a higher value of the variance indicates a larger spatial variation of the boundary. We hypothesize that the sections of the boundary with higher variance contribute primarily to a higher *LOC*. Thus adding more estimation points in the high variance sections of the boundary is likely to reduce the *LOC*.

Our algorithm initially estimates the boundary at a small number of equidistant points. We can set $k = \lceil X_{range}/2h \rceil$ such that the boundary is estimated at every $2h$ interval, where X_{range} is the range of x values over which the boundary is being observed. Next, the sections of the boundary are sorted according to decreasing order of spatial variation and estimation points are incrementally added in that order. As more boundary points are estimated, the interpolation error reduces and *LOC*, the probability of the band not covering the boundary, is lower. This iterative process *converges* when additional boundary points do not lead to a further reduction in *LOC*. In absence of knowledge of the actual *LOC*, the heuristic uses another metric, *prediction error*, to decide the termination criterion for additional estimation points.

The prediction error at a specific location is the absolute difference between the observation and the estimated boundary at that location. When estimated over a set of n sensors, the probability of the prediction error being greater than δ can be used as a representative of *LOC*. This probability is evaluated as follows:

$$prediction\ error(\delta) = \frac{1}{n} \sum_{i=1}^{n} I(|\hat{d}(x_i) - y_i| > \delta) \tag{8}$$

Figure 4 illustrates the main aspect of our algorithm. It shows that with 5 points some sections of the boundary is outside the confidence band but with two additional points in sections of high variance, portions of the boundary outside the band reduces. We experimentally find that the trend of *prediction error* is similar to the *LOC* of boundaries (see Section 5.4 for details).

5   Experimental Evaluation of DBTR

In this section, we evaluate the performance of DBTR and its sensitivity to various parameters. The goals of our experimental evaluation are as follows: (i) to verify the effectiveness of DBTR as a combination of both spatial and

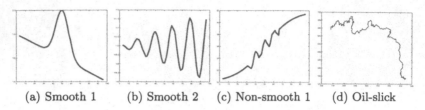

(a) Smooth 1   (b) Smooth 2   (c) Non-smooth 1   (d) Oil-slick

Fig. 5. Boundaries used to evaluate DBTR

temporal estimation techniques, (ii) to test its sensitivity to parameters such as specified width of band, number of estimation points and dynamics of the boundary, and (iii) to verify the effect of the adaptive update policy of DBTR on communication overheads.

5.1   Experimental Setup

Extensive simulation-based experiments are used to evaluate DBTR. DBTR algorithm is implemented in a MATLAB-based simulator. In addition, the spatial estimation technique is verified in a TOSSIM [12] based simulator and the results from these two simulators are similar. Sensors are randomly deployed in a two-dimensional field with dimension 100 units × 50 units. The communication range of sensors is 10–12 units. The maximum number of hops from the base station to sensors in a multi-hop network varies between 7–12 for different networks. We assume each sensor message contains a single observation and a single partial aggregate (explained in Section 3.1). Transmission of messages is assumed to be error-free. The error in sensor observations is assumed to be a Gaussian distribution $N(0, \sigma^2)$, where σ^2 is the error variance.

The performance of DBTR is evaluated with several boundaries generated using mathematical functions and real data traces from sensors. The boundaries in Figure 5 having different spatial variations are used as a representative set to evaluate DBTR. For example, the boundaries in Figure 5(a) and 5(b) are smooth while that in 5(c) is non-smooth. In addition, we also use a boundary (Figure 5(d)) obtained based on a real oil-slick[2]. The boundary Smooth 1 is used as the default boundary in all experiments unless specified otherwise. Dynamic boundaries are generated using a constant mean velocity model. Assuming a continuous boundary consists of several discrete points, at every time instant, each of the boundary points is displaced by a finite distance based on the model. We consider two scenarios: (i) all points on the boundary move with the same velocity and (ii) different points move with different velocities.

5.2   Evaluation Metrics

DBTR is evaluated using two metrics: (i) *communication overhead* and (ii) *accuracy of estimated boundary*. The overall communication overhead is the cumulative number of transmissions required for the spatial estimation technique

---

[2] Data for Lake Maracaibo http://modis.marine.usf.edu/index.html

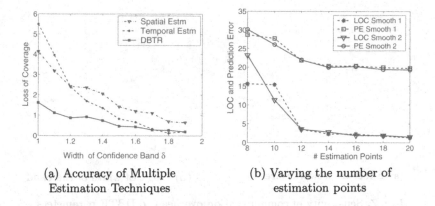

(a) Accuracy of Multiple
Estimation Techniques

(b) Varying the number of
estimation points

Fig. 6. Effect of the width of band and the number of estimation points on LOC

and the temporal estimation technique. This reflects the energy expenditure of
our solution. Accuracy of the estimated boundary is measured in terms of LOC
that is defined in Section 2. LOC reported is the mean value over at least 100
sets of observations.

5.3   Comparison of Boundary Estimation Techniques

In this section, we compare the performance of DBTR with both temporal and
spatial estimation techniques. In the temporal *only* and spatial *only* scenarios,
the confidence intervals around the boundary are updated at time instants when
the boundary is expected to move by greater than $0.5 \times \delta$, as predicted by the
temporal estimation. Figure 6(a) plots the LOC with varying δ, the width of
the confidence band (LOC for this experiment is the mean over 20 estimated
boundary points). Total duration of the experiment is 100 seconds. The velocity
of boundary is 1 unit/sec and sampling interval for the sensors is 0.5 sec. We
observe that for $\delta = 1 - 1.2$, DBTR performs better than both Temporal and
Spatial techniques by a factor $2.8 - 2.5$. For $\delta < 1.2$, DBTR as well as spatial estimation provide better performance as compared to temporal estimation. This
is because the error in sensor observations is reduced due to aggregation from
multiple sensors. For $\delta > 1.2$, the temporal technique provides better performance than the spatial technique. This is due to the fact that the accuracy of
the temporal estimation improves if the boundary changes by $0.5 \times \delta$ less frequently. However, we observe that DBTR performs best for *all values* of δ. This
is attributed to the feedback from the spatial estimation to the temporal estimation, due to which DBTR predicts the future boundary changes most accurately.
This experiment demonstrates the effectiveness of combining the temporal and
spatial estimation techniques in DBTR.

5.4   Impact of Estimation Points on Prediction Error and LOC

This experiment verifies correctness of the heuristic-based algorithm used to select
k, the number of estimation points. The goal is to ensure that the prediction error

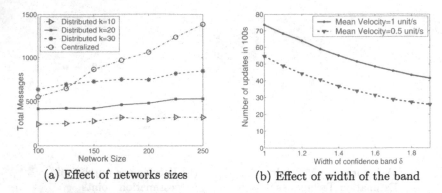

(a) Effect of networks sizes   (b) Effect of width of the band

Fig. 7. Sensitivity of communication overhead to DBTR parameters

can accurately capture the trend in LOC. Figure 6(b) plots the prediction error function and the LOC for boundaries Smooth 1 and Smooth 2. We observe that with increase in k, the prediction error function (see Section 4) and LOC both reduce and finally stabilize for $k > 14$. Initially LOC decreases much more sharply (85%) as compared to prediction error (29%), but for $k > 14$, both the prediction error and LOC reduces by a small amount ($0.5 - 0.2$). The value of k for which prediction error stabilizes can be used as a good choice for the number of estimation points. Since prediction error stabilizes earlier, a few more boundary points can be further added in order to achieve the minimized LOC. This experiment shows that the prediction error function represents LOC with high fidelity.

5.5 Communication Overhead of DBTR

The communication overhead of DBTR has two components: the number of messages required by the spatial estimation technique and the number of updates as indicated by the temporal estimation technique.

Overhead due to Spatial Estimation Technique. The result of this experiment is included from [9] to show the communication overhead of the spatial estimation component of DBTR. This overhead is compared with a solution where all the observations are sent to a central server for the estimation of the confidence band. Figure 7(a) plots the total number of messages for different sizes of the network. For 20 estimation points, the communication overhead for DBTR is lower than that of the centralized solution by a factor $3.3 - 2.6$. The communication overhead for the spatial estimation depends on the *h-neighborhood* and with increase in network size, the value of h reduces. Thus, the distributed solution of DBTR is easily scalable to larger networks. However, the communication overhead of DBTR increases in proportion with the number of estimation points which justifies reducing the number of estimation points to minimize communication overheads.

Overhead Due to Boundary Dynamics. In this experiment, we observe how the communication overhead of DBTR varies with different velocities of the boundary. The communication overhead depends on how frequently the estimation is updated. The number of updates depend mainly on two factors: (i) the width of the estimated band and (ii) velocity of the boundary along the y axis. Figure 7(b) depicts the number of updates required for two different velocities in an interval of 100 seconds as δ is varied. All the boundary points are assumed to be changing at the same velocity. The boundary is updated only when it is expected to have changed by more than $0.5 \times \delta$. We observe that the number of updates reduce by a factor of half as δ doubles, allowing for the boundary to be updated less frequently. As expected, a faster moving boundary requires more updates and as velocity changes from 0.5 to 1 unit/s, the number of updates increase by a factor more than 1.35. The experiment is also conducted with *different* portions of the boundary changing at different velocities and it shows that DBTR is able to capture boundary dynamics for adaptive updates.

5.6 Effect of Update Policies on Accuracy

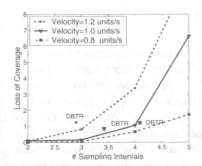

Fig. 8. Comparison of update schemes

The goal of this experiment is to compare the adaptive estimation technique of DBTR with a technique that periodically estimates the boundary. In such a scheme, the estimation based on regression is performed periodically rather than being based on the continuously predicted changes in the boundary (DBTR). The experiment is conducted for three scenarios– boundaries changing at velocities of 0.8, 1.0, 1.2 units/s. Figure 8(b) plots LOC versus periodicity of boundary updates for schemes with different periods. The period of updates is stated in terms of the number of sensor sampling intervals. We observe that for a certain velocity, there is an optimal period that should be used to obtain a LOC of 1% or less. For example, when velocity= 1.0 unit/s, LOC is 1.06% for a period of 4 sampling intervals. For each of the boundaries, the performance of DBTR is also shown. The period of DBTR is obtained by dividing the total duration with the number of times DBTR updates the boundary. The LOC is different in all three scenarios. For velocity of 1.0 unit/s, on an average DBTR updates the boundary at every 3.42 sampling intervals and achieves LOC of 0.86%. We note that DBTR may require lower communication overhead as it uses aperiodic updates without sacrificing accuracy obtained in a periodic scheme. Thus, the performance of DBTR is comparable with a periodic update scheme while not requiring *prior* knowledge about the dynamics of the boundary.

5.7 Summary of Results

Experimental evaluation of DBTR reveals the following important results: (i) DBTR consistently estimates boundaries more accurately than the Spatial-only and the Temporal-only estimation techniques. (ii) The distributed in-network estimation strategy significantly reduces the communication overhead as compared to the centralized solution by a factor about 2.6 to 3.3. (iii) The accuracy and communication overhead of DBTR are similar to the optimal periodic update scheme. (iv) The heuristic for simultaneously minimizing LOC and the number estimation points achieves a LOC of less than 2% for smooth boundaries.

Additional results from a more comprehensive experimental evaluation reported in [8] are: (i) A good choice of threshold for amount of change in the boundary (in Figure 3) is $0.5 \times \delta$. It implies that for low LOC, the boundary should be updated before the temporal estimation technique indicates that the boundary is changed by $0.5 \times \delta$. (ii) While non-smooth boundaries require higher number of estimation points, the efficacy of DBTR is demonstrated for smooth as well as non-smooth boundaries. (iii) Initial evaluation suggests that DBTR is applicable for non-zero sensing angles provided sensors detect an adequate set of points on the boundary.

6 Related Work

DBTR uses the *spatial-temporal* correlations among sensor readings to estimate the boundary efficiently. An alternative to non-parametric regression based technique is to use parametric regression as in [13] where sensor network data is modeled in terms of basis functions. The non-parametric approach reduces the effect of observation errors by aggregation. In the parametric case, the observations are taken to be the actual values of the sensed quantity and the coefficients of basis functions are computed to obtain an estimation with minimized mean square error (MSE). The system BBQ [14] exploits correlation among sensor attributes and a probabilistic model to answer queries. While our approach works for a boundary of arbitrary shape, the multivariate gaussian distribution used by BBQ may not be applicable.

An alternative to the model-based approach using Kalman Filter is simple state space models [15]. If the individual boundary points follow non-linear dynamics or have non-Gaussian errors more advanced techniques like particle filter [16] can be used. Switching Kalman Filters can be used to monitor boundaries with non-stationary dynamics (e.g., a storm) as discussed in [17].

There is a large amount of work dealing with contour extraction [18] using sensor networks. While a boundary detection technique is useful in detecting the presence of a phenomenon (either plume or fire), a contour extraction technique can provide more detailed information about the phenomenon. DBTR is most similar to the boundary estimation technique proposed by Nowak et al. [2]. The main difference is that DBTR tracks a dynamic boundary without incurring significant communication overhead, but there is no easy way for extending their technique to track dynamics apart from periodically recomputing the boundary. While DBTR provides a non-parametric estimation of the boundary, their technique provides a staircase-like approximation of the boundary. DBTR's adaptive selection of estimation points is also similar to the adaptive sampling method [19] which consists of two phases- a preview phase of collecting observations followed by a refinement phase in regions containing the boundary. DBTR attempts to minimize the locations for estimation points whereas their approach achieves a minimax bound on MSE.

DBTR makes use of sensors with range/remote capabilities for detecting a moving boundary. Another application using remote sensing is CASA [5], where a network of radars is used for meteorological monitoring to detect tornadoes.

7 Conclusion

We have developed a technique for dynamic boundary estimation in sensor networks where observations from range sensors are aggregated and a confidence band around the true boundary is obtained from estimates at a few selected locations. In addition, the temporal correlation among observations at certain points is utilized to develop a Kalman Filter based technique for estimating the changes in the boundary. This strategy updates the estimates before the boundary is expected to move out of the confidence band. Thus, our solution provides confidence band with high accuracy around the actual boundary at all times with low communication overheads that a suitable periodic scheme cannot achieve without prior knowledge about the dynamics of the boundary.

As part of future work, we propose to study the parametric regression technique for estimating boundaries in sensor networks. We propose to explore the impact of non-zero sensing angles on the accuracy of estimation. We also plan to extend our strategy to include in-situ measurements for detecting a boundary. Another way to extend our work is to consider more complex models for the dynamics of the boundary.

Acknowledgment. We would like to thank Parmesh Ramanathan of University of Wisconsin, Madison for his valuable suggestions.

References

[1] Akyildiz, I.F., Su, W., Sankarasubramaniam, Y., Cayirci, E.: Wireless sensor networks: a survey. Elsevier Journal of Computer Networks 38, 393–422 (2002)
[2] Nowak, R., Mitra, U.: Boundary Estimation in Sensor Networks: Theory and Methods. In: Zhao, F., Guibas, L.J. (eds.) IPSN 2003. LNCS, vol. 2634, Springer, Heidelberg (2003)
[3] Ding, M., Chen, D., Xing, K., Cheng, X.: Localized Fault-Tolerant Event Boundary Detection in Sensor Networks. IEEE INFOCOM 2, 902–913 (2005)
[4] Hsieh, C.H., Jin, Z., et al.: Experimental validation of an algorithm for cooperative boundary tracking. In: Proc. of American Control Conference (2005)
[5] Zink, M., Westbook, D., Abdallah, S., Horling, B.: Meteorological command and control: An end-to-end architecture for a hazardous weather detection sensor network. In: EESR. Workshop on End-to-End, Sense-and-Respond Systems, Applications, and Services (2005)

[6] Utkin, A.B., Lavrov, A.V., Costa, L., Simoes, F., Vilar, R.: Detection of Small Forest Fires by Lidar. Applied Physics B 74, 77–83 (2002)

[7] Lavrov, A., Vilar, R.: Application of lidar at 1.54 μm for forest fire detection. In: Remote sensing for earth science, ocean, and sea ice applications, vol. 3868, pp. 473–477 (1999)

[8] Duttagupta, S., Ramamritham, K., Kulkarni, P.: Tracking dynamic boundaries using sensor networks. In: IIT Bombay, CSE department Technical Report TR-CSE-2007-7 (2007)

[9] Duttagupta, S., Ramamritham, K., Ramanathan, P.: Distributed Boundary Estimation using Sensor Networks. In: The 3rd IEEE Conf. on Mobile Ad-hoc and Sensor Systems (2006)

[10] Härdle, W.: Applied Nonparametric Regression. Cambridge University Press, Cambridge (1990)

[11] Gasser, T., Kneip, A., Kohler, W.: A Flexible and Fast Method for Automatic Smoothing. Journal of the American Statistical Association 86(415), 643–652 (1991)

[12] Levis, P., Lee, N., Woo, A., Welsh, M., Culler, D.: TOSSIM: Accurate and scalable simulation of entire tinyos applications. In: Sensys. Proc. of 1st ACM Conf. on Embedded Networked Sensor Systems (November 2003)

[13] Guestrin, C., Bodik, P., Thibaux, R., Paskin, M., Madden, S.: Distributed Regression: an Efficient Framework for Modeling Sensor Network Data. In: IPSN (2004)

[14] Deshpande, A., Guestrin, C., Madden, S., Hellerstein, J.M., Hong, W.: Model-based Approximate Querying in Sensor Networks. VLDB Journal (2005)

[15] Liu, J., Chu, M., Liu, J.: Distributed State Representation for Tracking problems in Sensor Networks. In: IPSN (2004)

[16] Coates, M.: Distributed Particle Filtes for Sensor Networks. In: IPSN (2004)

[17] Manfredi, V., Mahadevan, S., Kurose, J.: Switching Kalman Filters for Prediction and Tracking in an Adaptive Meteorological Sensing Network. In: SECON. IEEE Conference on Sensor and Ad Hoc Communications and Networks (2005)

[18] Liao, P., Chang, M., Kuo, C.J.: Contour Line Extraction with Wireless Sensor Networks. In: IEEE Conference on Communications (2005)

[19] Singh, A., Nowak, R., Ramanathan, P.: Active Learning for Adaptive Mobile Sensing Networks. In: IPSN (2006)

Network-Coding-Based Cooperative Transmission in Wireless Sensor Networks: Diversity-Multiplexing Tradeoff and Coverage Area Extension*

Dereje H. Woldegebreal and Holger Karl

University of Paderborn, Paderborn, Germany
Tel.: +49-5251-605376; Fax: +49-5251-605377
{dereje.hmr,holger.karl}@upb.de

Abstract. In Wireless Sensor Networks large number of nodes and limited energy available per node calls for designing efficient transmission protocols. Cooperative transmission is one of the protocols which helps wireless nodes to achieve spatial diversity, which translates into reduction in transmission power or increase in coverage area. Cooperative protocol can be realized with or without (called conventional afterward) network coding; and the network-coding-based (respectively the conventional) protocol can be operated in either static or adaptive manner. For an efficient operation of cooperative protocols, good quality inter-source channels are required, which in turn depend on relative location of nodes within a network. In this work, a three-node cooperative network consisting of source, relay, and destination nodes is considered. At high signal-to-noise ratio values, we first approximate the outage probability result when the network-coding-based adaptive protocol is implemented. Then, based on the approximate probability result, a diversity-multiplexing tradeoff is studied; the result shows that this protocol performs similar to an amplify-and-forward protocol. Next, for the various protocols, the coverage area and relative location of the relay that minimizes the outage are studied; for that the exact outage probability results are used. Over wider geographic area, network-coding-based static and adaptive protocols perform better than their conventional counterparts, and this happens when the relaying node is positioned closer to the destination than the source. The conventional protocols perform better when the relay is positioned closer to the source. In Wireless Sensor Networks, assuming that relay nodes which are closer to both the source and destination exist, these results help as a guide in selecting with which node to cooperate (relay selection) when one cooperative scheme is implemented.

1 Introduction

Wireless Sensor Networks (WSNs) consist of large number of spatially distributed and low-power nodes, which are envisioned for a wide range of applications [1]. In WSN, wireless channel impairments added with limited available

---

* This work is supported by the German Academic Exchange Service DAAD.

R. Verdone (Ed.): EWSN 2008, LNCS 4913, pp. 141–155, 2008.

energy demands designing efficient transmission schemes and protocols [25]. Co-operation among nodes can be exploited in WSN so as to save transmission en-ergy, increasing network life, or extend nodes' coverage area. Various cooperative transmission protocols have been proposed and studied in the literature, mainly taking outage probability, channel capacity, diversity-multiplexing tradeoff, and coverage area as performance measures [7, 8, 10, 19].

In a three-nodes cooperative transmission, two nodes which we call as source and relay and both with messages of their own, assist by relaying each other's message cyclically while transmitting to a common destination.[1] In cooperative protocol the total transmission consists of two phases: in a first phase both the source and relay nodes broadcast their messages (using orthogonal channels) and simultaneously receive each other's transmission. In a second phase, both nodes forward the messages received in the first phase.

Amplify-and-forward and decode-and-forward are two of the widely used re-laying strategies. In the amplify-and-forward, the relay receives a noisy version of the source's message, amplifies and re-transmits it to the destination [10]. In the decode-and-forward scheme, the relay decodes the source's message, re-encodes and relays it to the destination; the relayed message could be in the form of incremental redundancy (transmitting additional information), repetition cod-ing (repeating the same message), or network coding (mixing the source's and relay's messages using a modulo-2 summation). Based on their level of adaptive-ness to decoding error, the decode-and-forward protocols are further categorized either as static or adaptive [19]. In the static protocol, the relay always forwards the source's message without checking errors; in the adaptive protocol, the re-lay decides whether to forward or not, depending on its success of decoding the source's message. If decoding fails, then the relay has the options to switch to the amplify-and-forward, transmit its own message, or even to remain silent [7]. In this work, we consider protocols based on network coding and repetition coding (called conventional protocol hereafter); both protocols are further subdivided into static and adaptive, therefore there are four protocols under consideration.

Diversity-multiplexing tradeoff is one performance measure used to study multiple-input, multiple-output (MIMO) and cooperative systems. It illustrates the relationship between reliability of data transmission in terms of *diversity gain*, and spectral efficiency in terms of *multiplexing gain* [10, 24]. In this work, the diversity-multiplexing tradeoff of the adaptive network-coding-based proto-col is derived; this is done by approximating the exact outage probability result in [18] at high signal-to-noise ratio (SNR) values. From the result, this network-coding-based and the amplify-and-forward protocols perform the same [10].

Cooperation between the source and relay nodes requires the presence of good quality source-relay (or inter-user) channels, which in tern depend on relative location of the nodes [19]. The conventional and network-coding-based protocols perform differently when the source and relay nodes are closer to each other

---

[1] In this definition of cooperative transmission, the terms 'source' and 'relay' are loosely used as the two nodes alternate each other in the relaying role. Our sub-sequent discussions are based on transmission of the source's message only.

than the destination, and vice versa. Hence, relative location of nodes and coverage area extension are other performance measures, which are also used in this work to compare the protocols under consideration. Similar comparisons have been made in previous literature. The decode-and-forward and a compress-and-forward protocols were compared in [15]. The results show that the former scheme works better when the relay is closer to the source, and the later is preferred when the relay is closer to the destination. Similarly, in [16] protocols were compared with additive white Gaussian noise (AWGN) channel and various channel state information assumptions. In [12], coded cooperation and point-to-point transmission were compared using *user cooperation gain*, which is the ratio of frame error rates of the two schemes. Range of channel conditions for which the coded cooperation performs better than the point-to-point transmission were found. Similar approaches were used in [5] for a Gaussian relay channel, and in [23] for a cooperative scheme with HARQ.

In this work, we study the coverage area and location of the relay where outage is minimized; the exact outage probability results in [19] are used. In relation to these coverage and relay deployment issues, we address the following questions. For the given network topology (i.e. location of the source, relay, and destination nodes), which cooperative protocol to use? In which geographic region is the network-coding-based protocol performs better than the conventional one? Within the network-coding-based (respectively the conventional) protocol, how do the static and adaptive protocols perform? The following approach is used: the channel coefficient is split into pathloss and fading coefficients. Then in all channels, the fading coefficient is assumed to have unity mean power, but the pathloss varies as it depends on nodes location. The source-destination separation and the transmit power at both the source and relay nodes are fixed. The relay's location is varied, such that the source-relay and relay-destination links quality vary because of the pathloss. When the relay is deployed closer to the source a *transmitter cluster* is formed, and when deployed closer to the destination a *receiver cluster* is formed. Let us define the following two terms.

Definition 1. Coverage area: *is defined as the region or area in which the relay can be placed, such that for a given resources allocation (i.e transmission power, bandwidth, and end-to-end spectral efficiency) the outage probability (or ratio of outage probabilities) is less than or equal to some threshold value.*

Definition 2. Intra-cooperation gain: *is the ratio of outage probabilities of two protocols; a gain of unity demarcates the region into two, where one protocol performs better than the other.*

The contributions of this work are summarized as follow. By approximating the outage probability result of the network-coding-based protocol at high SNR values, we study the diversity-multiplexing tradeoff. The study is then extend into the coverage area and relay deployment issues. Also, by comparing the network coding protocol and point-to-point transmission, we show that an energy saving can be achieved by using the network coding; this shows that sensor networks can benefit from the network coding.

This is how the remainder of the paper is organized. Section 2 briefly describes the system and channel models used in this work; the outage analysis at high SNR values of the adaptive protocol with network coding is given in Sect. 3. In Sect. 4 results are presented, and conclusions are drawn in Sect. 5.

2   System Description

2.1   System Model

Consider the network model shown in Fig. 1, where 's','r', and 'd' are the source, relay, and destination nodes, respectively. The source's and relay's messages are expressed as X_s and X_r, respectively. The network coding is implemented by the modulo-2 summation of X_s and X_r as in $X_s \oplus X_r$. The motivation behind the network coding is X_s can be recovered from either the source's direct transmission in the first phase or by further combining the relay's and network-coded message, i.e. $X_r \oplus (X_s \oplus X_r) = X_s$, provided both are correctly received.

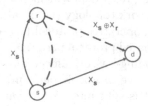

Fig. 1. Network-coding-based cooperative transmission scheme, where X_s, X_r, and $X_s \oplus X_r$ are the source's, relay's, and network-coded messages, respectively. In the conventional cooperation scheme, the transmission by the relay should have been X_s. Solid (dashed) lines show the transmission by the source (relay).

The information rate and energy per symbol in the cooperative and point-to-point transmission are related as follows. If R (bits/s/Hz) is the rate in the point-to-point transmission, then the rate in each phase of the conventional protocols is $2R$. This is also true in the network-coding-based protocols, provided the network coding is done before the channel coding [19]. The total energy can also be shared in the two phases. Let E_s be the radiated energy per symbol in the point-to-point transmission. In the cooperative protocols, if β is the fraction of the total energy allocated in the first phase, then $2\beta E_s$ and $2(1 - \beta)E_s$ are the energy per symbol in phases one and two, respectively. These rate and energy per symbol relationships of the point-to-point transmission and cooperative protocols are used in the next section to compute outage probability.

2.2   Channel Model and Outage Probability

The channels used in the system are assumed to be spatially independent, flat-fading, with additive white Gaussian noise (AWGN) and modeled as

$$y_{i,j} = h_{i,j}x_{i,j} + n_{i,j} \tag{1}$$

where $x_{i,j}$ and $y_{i,j}$ are the inputs and outputs of the channels, respectively. The sources $i \in \{s,r\}$; destinations $j \in \{s,r,d\}$ with $i \neq j$; $h_{i,j} = p_{i,j}q_{i,j}$ is the channel coefficient containing the fading term $p_{i,j}$, which is random, and the distance dependent pathloss coefficient $q_{i,j}$; $n_{i,j}$ is the AWGN component which is distributed as $N(0, N_0)$. The pathloss is modeled as $q_{i,j}^2 = \left(\frac{d_o}{d_{i,j}}\right)^\alpha$, where $2 < \alpha < 5$ is the pathloss exponent, $d_{i,j}$ is the distance between nodes i and j, and d_o is the reference distance. In this work, $|h_{i,j}|$ is assumed to be **block fading** and Rayleigh distributed such that $|h_{i,j}|^2$ is exponentially distributed. For a unity mean power $p_{i,j}$, the average power of $h_{i,j}$ is dictated by the average power of $q_{i,j}$, which in turn depends on node's location in the network.

Consider the point-to-point transmission of messages from the source to the destination. When the instantaneous SNR of the channel given as $\gamma_{s,d} = |h_{s,d}|^2 \frac{P_t}{N_o}$ is less than some threshold value, where $\frac{P_t}{N_o}$ is the transmit SNR, then the destination wrongly decodes messages and an outage is said to occur. For $|h_{s,d}|^2$ exponentially distributed, the outage probability $P_{out,s}$ is given as [8]

$$P_{out,s} = P\left(\gamma_{s,d} < 2^R - 1\right) = 1 - \exp\left(-\frac{2^R - 1}{\Gamma_{s,d}}\right) \qquad (2)$$

where $\Gamma_{s,d}$ is the average SNR of the channel. In cooperative scheme, R will be replaced by $2R$ and $\Gamma_{s,d}$ will be replaced by either $2\beta\Gamma_{s,d}$ or $2(1-\beta)\Gamma_{s,d}$ depending on the transmission phase.

2.3   Diversity and Multiplexing Gains

In the point-to-point transmission with the source's rate R (bits/second/Hz), the multiplexing gain m is defined as [24]

$$m := \lim_{SNR \to \infty} \frac{R(SNR)}{\log_2(SNR)} \qquad (3)$$

and the diversity gain d as

$$d := -\lim_{SNR \to \infty} \frac{\log_2 P_{out,s}(SNR)}{\log_2(SNR)}. \qquad (4)$$

The diversity-multiplexing tradeoff illuminates the relationship between the reliability of data transmissions in terms of the diversity gain and the spectral efficiency in terms of the multiplexing gain. This relationship can be characterized by mapping d as a function of m. As will be explained in Section 3, at large values of $\Gamma_{s,d}$ if we approximate (2) by $P_{out,s} \approx \frac{2^R}{\Gamma_{s,d}}$, then we get

$$d := -\lim_{SNR \to \infty} \frac{\log_2 P_{out,s}(SNR)}{\log_2(SNR)} \approx 1 - m. \qquad (5)$$

3   Performance Analysis of Network-Coding-Based Protocol

In this section, the network-coding-based adaptive protocol's outage probability result is approximated at high SNR values. In this protocol, the adaptiveness is implemented by letting the source and relay remain silent if they fail to decode each other's transmission. The diversity-multiplexing tradeoff, based on the approximate outage probability result, is computed next. For the analysis, the same four-cases classification as in [18] is used.

Table 1. The four cases and the corresponding transmissions

Case	s → r	r→s	s → d		r → d	
			Phase 1	Phase 2	Phase 1	Phase 2
1	works	works	X_s	$X_s \oplus X_r$	X_r	$X_s \oplus X_r$
2	fails	fails	X_s		X_r	
3	works	fails	X_s		X_r	$X_s \oplus X_r$
4	fails	works	X_s	$X_s \oplus X_r$	X_r	

As shown in (2), the outage probability is the function of the rate and average SNR. In the cooperative transmission, there are four spatially-separated channels (two uplink and two inter-source channels), which makes the outage computation involved. So, let us assume symmetrical inter-user (i.e. $\Gamma_{s,r} = \Gamma_{r,s}$) and identical uplink channels (i.e. $\Gamma_{s,d} = \Gamma_{r,d}$).[2] Hence, in the following we use only $\Gamma_{s,r}$ and $\Gamma_{s,d}$. The transmitted messages in the two phases and in the four cases are summarized in Table 1.

Case 1: Both the source and relay succeed in correctly decoding each other's message. For this to happen, the source-relay channel instantaneous SNR given as $\gamma_{s,r}$, should be greater than a threshold value. This success probability is obtained by subtracting the outage probability from unity; the outage probability is computed from (2) by replacing $\Gamma_{s,d}$ and R by $2\beta\Gamma_{s,r}$ and $2R$, respectively. At high $\Gamma_{s,r}$ values this success probability is given as

$$P\left\{2\beta\gamma_{s,r} > 2^{2R} - 1\right\} = P\left\{\beta\gamma_{s,r} > g(R)\right\}$$

$$= \exp\left(-\frac{g(R)}{\beta\Gamma_{s,r}}\right) \approx 1 - \frac{g(R)}{\beta\Gamma_{s,r}} \tag{6}$$

where $g(R) = \frac{1}{2}\left(2^{2R} - 1\right)$ is the threshold value; the equation next to the inequality in (6) results by using the approximation $\exp^{-x} \approx 1 - x$ for small x. As mentioned in Sect. 2.1, at the destination X_s can be recovered from either the source's first-phase transmission or by combining X_r and $X_s \oplus X_r$. The outage probabilities of the messages X_s and X_r are equal and given as

$$P\left\{\beta\gamma_{s,d} < g(R)\right\} \approx \frac{g(R)}{\beta\Gamma_{s,d}}. \tag{7}$$

---

[2] Note that the instantaneous SNRs of the channels are not necessarily the same.

Referring Table 1, at the destination the message $X_s \oplus X_r$ is received twice from the source and relay; if Maximum-Ratio combining is used to combine these two messages, the outage probability of $X_s \oplus X_r$ is given by the second equation in [18, equation (30)] as

$$P\left\{(1-\beta)(\gamma_{s,d}+\gamma_{r,d}) < g(R)\right\} = 1 - \left(1 + \frac{1}{\Gamma_{s,d}}\frac{g(R)}{(1-\beta)}\right)\exp\left(-\frac{1}{\Gamma_{s,d}}\frac{g(R)}{(1-\beta)}\right)$$

$$\approx \left(\frac{g(R)}{(1-\beta)\Gamma_{s,d}}\right)^2. \tag{8}$$

The source's message outage occurs, for the given inter-source channels condition, when X_s and at least one of X_r and $X_s \oplus X_r$ are in outage. Using logical operations, the outage event is expressed as $\overline{X_s} \wedge [\overline{X_r} \vee \overline{X_s \oplus X_r}]$, where the bar (indicates the outage), $\wedge$, and $\vee$ are logical 'NOT', 'AND', and 'OR' operations, respectively. The probability that this event occurs is then

$$P(\overline{X_s})[P(\overline{X_r}) + P(\overline{X_s \oplus X_r})(1 - P(\overline{X_r}))]. \tag{9}$$

The probabilities $P(\overline{X_s})$ and $P(\overline{X_r})$ are given by (7) and $P(\overline{X_s \oplus X_r})$ by (8). The overall outage probability under case one, denoted as $P_{out,s1}$, is the product of outage probability (9) and the probability that the source and relay decode each other correctly (or the probability that case one occurs) given by (6).

$$P_{out,s1} \approx \left(1 - \frac{g(R)}{\beta\Gamma_{s,r}}\right)^2 \frac{g(R)}{\beta\Gamma_{s,d}}\left[\frac{g(R)}{\beta\Gamma_{s,d}} + \left(\frac{g(R)}{(1-\beta)\Gamma_{s,d}}\right)^2\left(1 - \frac{g(R)}{\beta\Gamma_{s,d}}\right)\right]$$

$$= \left(1 - \frac{g(R)}{\beta\Gamma_{s,r}}\right)^2 \left(\frac{g(R)}{\beta\Gamma_{s,d}}\right)^2\left[1 + \frac{\beta}{(1-\beta)^2}\frac{g(R)}{\Gamma_{s,d}}\left(1 - \frac{g(R)}{\beta\Gamma_{s,d}}\right)\right]. \tag{10}$$

The terms $\left[1 - \frac{g(R)}{\beta\Gamma_{s,r}}\right]$ and $\left[1 - \frac{g(R)}{\beta\Gamma_{s,d}}\right]$ approach 1 for high $\Gamma_{s,r}$ and $\Gamma_{s,d}$ values, and (10) reduces to

$$P_{out,s1} \approx \left(\frac{g(R)}{\beta\Gamma_{s,d}}\right)^2\left[1 + \frac{\beta}{(1-\beta)^2}\frac{g(R)}{\Gamma_{s,d}}\right] \approx \left(\frac{g(R)}{\beta\Gamma_{s,d}}\right)^2. \tag{11}$$

When the source-relay channels are reliable, the outage-probability decay is proportional to the square of $\Gamma_{s,d}$; hence a diversity order of two is achievable with network-coding-based cooperative scheme.

Case 2: Neither the source nor the relay decodes each other's message correctly. If nodes remain silent during decoding failure, then the outage probability is determined from the first-phase transmission only. The outage probability $P_{out,s2}$ is obtained from (6) and (7) as

$$P_{out,s2} \approx \left(\frac{g(R)}{\beta\Gamma_{s,r}}\right)^2 \frac{g(R)}{\beta\Gamma_{s,d}}. \tag{12}$$

Case 3: The relay correctly decodes the source's message, but the source cannot decode the relay's message correctly. In this case, $X_s \oplus X_r$ is received from the relay only, and the outage probability is then

$$
\begin{aligned}
P_{out,s3} &\approx \left(1 - \frac{g(R)}{\beta\Gamma_{s,r}}\right) \frac{g(R)}{\beta\Gamma_{s,r}} \frac{g(R)}{\beta\Gamma_{s,d}} \left[\frac{g(R)}{\beta\Gamma_{s,d}} + \frac{g(R)}{(1-\beta)\Gamma_{s,d}}\left(1 - \frac{g(R)}{\beta\Gamma_{s,d}}\right)\right] \\
&= \left(1 - \frac{g(R)}{\beta\Gamma_{s,r}}\right) \frac{g(R)}{\beta\Gamma_{s,r}} \left(\frac{g(R)}{\beta\Gamma_{s,d}}\right)^2 \left[1 + \frac{\beta}{(1-\beta)}\left(1 - \frac{g(R)}{\beta\Gamma_{s,d}}\right)\right] \\
&\approx \frac{g(R)}{\beta\Gamma_{s,r}}\left(\frac{g(R)}{\beta\Gamma_{s,d}}\right)^2 \frac{1}{(1-\beta)}.
\end{aligned}
\tag{13}
$$

Case 4: The source correctly decodes the relay's message, but the relay cannot decode the source's message correctly. From outage probability point of view, this is the same as **Case 3** above as $\Gamma_{s,d} = \Gamma_{r,d}$ assumed. (Refer Table 1.)

The total outage probability is the sum of the outage probabilities under **Cases 1–4** and given as

$$
P_{out,s} \approx \left(\frac{g(R)}{\beta\Gamma_{s,d}}\right)^2 + \left(\frac{g(R)}{\beta\Gamma_{s,r}}\right)^2 \frac{g(R)}{\beta\Gamma_{s,d}} + \frac{g(R)}{\beta\Gamma_{s,r}}\left(\frac{g(R)}{\beta\Gamma_{s,d}}\right)^2 \frac{2}{(1-\beta)}.
\tag{14}
$$

If we further assume that $\Gamma_{s,r} = \Gamma_{s,d}$, then (14) becomes

$$
P_{out,s} = \left(\frac{g(R)}{\beta\Gamma_{s,d}}\right)^2 \left[1 + \frac{g(R)}{\beta\Gamma_{s,d}} + \frac{g(R)}{\beta\Gamma_{s,d}}\frac{2}{(1-\beta)}\right] \approx \left(\frac{g(R)}{\beta\Gamma_{s,d}}\right)^2.
\tag{15}
$$

So, we can see from (15) that the outage probability decays proportional to the square of the source-destination SNR, hence the diversity order of two can be

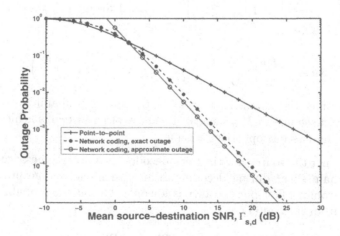

Fig. 2. Outage probability curves of the point-to-point transmission and the network-coding-based cooperative protocol (both approximate and exact)

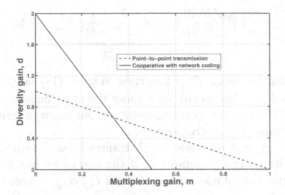

Fig. 3. Diversity-multiplexing tradeoff plots of the network-coding-based cooperative protocol (solid line) and point-to-point transmission scheme (dashed line)

achieved. Plotted in Fig. 2 are the exact and the approximate outage results based on (15).

Substituting (15) into (4) and using (3), we can extend the analysis into the diversity-multiplexing tradeoff such that

$$d := -\lim_{\Gamma_{s,d} \to \infty} \frac{\log_2 P_{out,s}(\Gamma_{s,d})}{\log_2(\Gamma_{s,d})} = -\lim_{\Gamma_{s,d} \to \infty} 2 \left[\frac{\log_2(g(R)) - \log_2(\beta) - \log_2(\Gamma_{s,d})}{\log_2(\Gamma_{s,d})} \right]$$
$$\approx 2(1 - 2m) \tag{16}$$

were m and d are the multiplexing and diversity gains defined in (3) and (4), respectively. To get (16), $g(R) = \frac{1}{2}(2^{2R} - 1)$ is substituted and the high SNR approximation used. For the point-to-point transmission, it was shown in (5) that $d \approx 1 - m$. Figure 3 shows the tradeoff curves.

One way to compare the energy saving by using the network coding instead of point-to-point transmission is to calculate the required received SNRs in the two schemes such that, for the same rate R, the resulting outage probabilities are the equal. Let $\Gamma_{s,d}^n$ and $\Gamma_{s,d}^p$ be the source-destination SNRs when the network coding and point-to-point transmissions are used, respectively. Similarly we have the outage probabilities $P_{out,s}^n$ and $P_{out,s}^p$. The point-to-point outage probability is calculated from (2) as $P_{out,s}^p = \frac{2g(R/2)}{\Gamma_{s,d}^p}$, and $P_{out,s}^n$ is given by (15). If we take the ratio of these outage probabilities, we get

$$\frac{P_{out,s}^p}{P_{out,s}^n} = 2\beta^2 \frac{g(R/2)}{g^2(R)} \frac{(\Gamma_{s,d}^n)^2}{\Gamma_{s,d}^p}. \tag{17}$$

If we require the two outage probabilities to be equal, and additionally assume the energy allocation term $\beta = 0.5$, then (17) results[3]

---

[3] $\beta = 0.5$ means the total energy is equally split in the two phases, and hence identical energy per symbol as in the conventional cooperative systems.

$$\frac{\Gamma_{s,d}^p}{\Gamma_{s,d}^n} = 2\beta^2 \frac{g(R/2)}{g^2(R)} \Gamma_{s,d}^n = \underbrace{\frac{2^R - 1}{(2^{2R} - 1)^2}}_{<1} \Gamma_{s,d}^n > 1. \tag{18}$$

This indicates that for large $\Gamma_{s,d}^n$, the right side of (18) is greater than one and hence $\Gamma_{s,d}^p > \Gamma_{s,d}^n$. This means, to achieve the same outage probability, the average SNR required in the point-to-point transmission is large than in the network-coding-based cooperative system.

This energy saving can be traded with transmission distance. For the same transmit energy in the two schemes (i.e. if the energy budget is fixed), the received SNR is a function of nodes separation as $\Gamma_{i,j} \propto \frac{1}{d_{i,j}^\alpha}$, where α and $d_{i,j}$ are pathloss coefficient and distance between nodes i and j, respectively. If we keep the same energy budget and equal outage probabilities in the two schemes, then we can communicate over longer distance by using one scheme than the other. This relationship is obtained by substituting the pathloss into (18), and we get

$$\left(\frac{d_{s,d}^n}{d_{s,d}^p}\right)^\alpha > 1 \tag{19}$$

where $d_{s,d}^n$ and $d_{s,d}^p$ are the distances covered using the network coding and point-to-point transmission, respectively. This shows that $d_{s,d}^n > d_{s,d}^p$, hence we can transmit further by using the network-coding-based cooperative system than the point-to-point transmission. Identical comparison can also be done from the rate point of view. The above discussions illustrate the tradeoff between energy saving, reliability of data transmission (in outage probability), coverage extension (transmission distance), and transmission rate (through R). In the next section, based on the exact outage probability formulas in [19], we study the coverage area and relay node deployment when various protocols are implemented.

4   Results and Discussion

In this section, the results based on the discussion done in the previous section are presented. Results are based on rate $R = 1/2$ bit/s/Hz, energy allocations $\beta = 1/2$, pathloss coefficient $\alpha = 4$, and symmetrical source-relay channels, i.e. $\Gamma_{s,r} = \Gamma_{r,s}$.

Figure 2 shows the outage probability curves based on the exact and approximate formulas. Here, all the uplink and source-relay channels have identical average SNR values, i.e. $\Gamma_{s,r} = \Gamma_{s,d} = \Gamma_{r,d}$. One can see that at higher $\Gamma_{s,d}$ values, the approximation captures the exact result, and the approximation error is in the order of 1 dB. Moreover, at these SNR values, the curves for the network-coding-based protocol decay faster than the point-to-point transmission curves; hence diversity order of two is achieved using the former scheme. Figure 3 shows the diversity-multiplexing curves of the point-to-point and cooperative scheme with network coding.

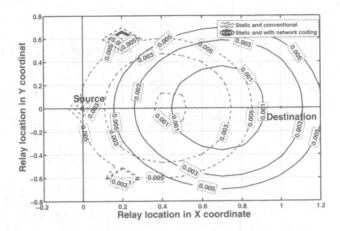

Fig. 4. Outage probability contours of static protocols: conventional (dashed lines) and with network coding (solid lines). The source and the destination are placed at the coordinates $(0,0)$ and $(0,1)$, respectively.

The outage probability and intra-cooperation gain contours of the conventional and network-coding-based static and adaptive protocols are discussed next. The transmit SNR at the source and relay is set to 20 dB; the fading coefficient is assumed to unity mean power, but the pathloss is varied by changing the relay's position (the uplink channels become asymmetric). The contours show the locations of the relay in which the outage probability (respectively the intra-cooperation gain) is the same. As defined in Sect. 1, the area enclosed by a contour forms the coverage area. Taking the source-destination distance as a reference, i.e. $d_{s,d} = 1$, the other channels' pathloss coefficients become $q_{i,j}^2 = \left(\frac{1}{d_{i,j}}\right)^\alpha$, where $i, j \in \{s,r,d\}$. Questions that will be addressed next are: for a fixed outage probability (or intra-cooperation gain) value, what is the improvement in coverage area when the network-coding-based protocol is used instead of the conventional one? What is the relative location of the relay that minimizes the outage probability? In which geographic region is network-coding-based protocol perform better than the conventional protocol, the adaptive protocol is better than the static protocol?

Figure 4 depicts the outage probability contours of the conventional (dashed lines) and network-coding-based (solid lines) static protocols. For a given outage probability value, e.g. 0.001, the area span by the protocol with network coding is larger than the conventional protocol. As long as the relay is confined to these areas, we are guaranteed that the outage probability does not exceed 0.001. The probability contours of the network-coding-based and conventional static protocol are approximately concentric to the coordinates $(0, 0.7)$ and $(0, 0.45)$, respectively. The coordinates $(0, 0.7)$ and $(0, 0.45)$ can also be seen as the outage contours where the outage probability approaches 0. Hence, the network-coding-based static protocol is more appropriate when a node closer to the destination

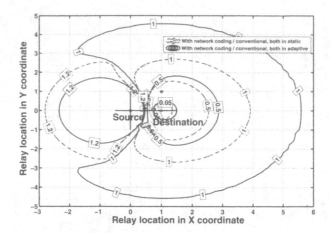

Fig. 5. Intra-cooperation gain contours, where the gain is computed by dividing the outage probability results of the network-coding-based static protocol by the conventional static protocol (dashed lines) and network-coding-based adaptive protocol by the conventional adaptive protocol (solid lines)

is selected as the relay; and at such locations the quality of the source-relay channels is poor and the uplink channels are more asymmetrical. In the conventional protocol, a node closer to the source (or in the center) should be selected as the relay.

Shown in Fig. 5 is the intra-cooperation gain contours of the static protocols (solid lines) and adaptive protocols (dashed lines). The gain is computed by dividing the outage probability of the network-coding-based and conventional protocols, when both are either in static or adaptive manner. These contours help to answer the question, given the location of the relay, is it better to use the conventional or network-coding-based protocol. When the gain is greater than 1 (outside the unity-gain contour), the conventional protocol performs better; when it is less than 1 (inside the unity-gain contour), the protocol with network coding performs better. From the figure, we note that the region in which the gain is greater than 1 (or the conventional protocols perform better) is located closer to the source, and the region in which the gain is less than 1 is located closer to the destination. Moreover, the gain is less than one for sufficiently large geographic area.

Finally shown in Fig. 6 is the intra-cooperative gain contours, where the comparison is performed within the conventional and network-coding-based protocols, i.e. by dividing the outage probability of the conventional (respectively with network coding) adaptive protocol by the the conventional (respectively with network coding) static protocol. These contours help to illustrate the advantage, within either the conventional or network-coding-based protocol, when we switch from static to adaptive. We see that as we go from the bigger to the smaller contours, the intra-cooperation gain approaches unity. This means that over such large area, adaptive protocols are more suited than the static protocols.

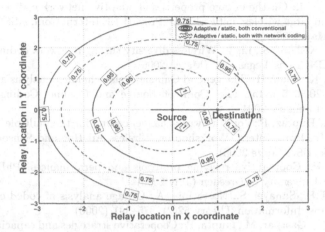

Fig. 6. Intra-cooperative gain contours, where the gain is computed by dividing the outage probability of the conventional adaptive protocol by the conventional static protocol (solid lines) and the network-coding-based adaptive protocol by the network-coding-based static protocol (dashed lines)

We conclude that, in general adaptive protocols outperform their static counterparts over wider geographic area.

5 Conclusion and Remarks

Throughout this paper, we have presented the approximate outage probability analysis of the network-coding-based cooperative protocol, and discussions were made from the diversity-multiplexing, coverage area, and relay location perspectives. The results show that the network-coding-based protocol can achieve the same diversity-multiplexing gain as the amplify-and-forward protocol. Coverage area extension can be obtained using network coding, and the protocols with network coding are more suited when the relay is located closer to the destination than the source. Comparing static vs. adaptive, adaptive protocols outperform their static counterparts both in conventional and network-coding-based realizations. Based on the presented results, sensor networks will definitely benefit from cooperation and network coding by saving transmission energy and/or extending the coverage area. To exploit the dense number of potential cooperative nodes in sensor networks, extending the current work into multi-source and multi-relay cases would be an area to explore in the near future.

References

[1] Karl, H., Willig, A.: Protocols and Architectures for Wireless Sensor Networks. Wiley, Chichester (2005)
[2] Ahlswede, R., Cai, N., Li, S.-Y.R., Yeung, R.W.: Network information flow. IEEE Trans. Information Theory 46, 1204–1216 (2000)

[3] Bao, X., Li, J.: On the outage properties of adaptive network coded cooperation (ANCC) in large wireless networks. In: Proc. IEEE Intern. Conf. ASSP, Toulouse, France (May 2006)

[4] Chen, Y., Kishore, S., Li, J.: Wireless diversity through network coding. In: Proc. IEEE WCNC, Las Vegas, NV (March 2006)

[5] Dawy, Z., Kamoun, H.: The general Gaussian relay channel: analysis and insights. In: SCC 2004. 5th Int. ITG Conf. on Source and Channel Coding, Erlangen, Germany (January 2004)

[6] Hausl, C., Dupraz, P.: Joint network-channel coding for the multiple-access relay channel. In: Proc. Intern. Workshop on Wireless Ad Hoc and Sensor Networks, New York, USA (June 2006)

[7] Herhold, P.: Cooperative relaying protocols and performances. PhD Thesis at Technical University of Dresden (July 2005)

[8] Hunter, T.E., Sanayei, S., Nosratinia, A.: Outage analysis of coded cooperation. IEEE Trans. Information Theory 52(2), 375–391 (2006)

[9] Kramer, G., Gastpar, M., Gupta, P.: Cooperative strategies and capacity theorems for relay networks. IEEE Trans. Inform. Theory 51(9) (September 2005)

[10] Laneman, J.L., Tse, D.N.C., Wornell, G.W.: Cooperative diversity in wireless networks: efficient protocols and outage behavior. IEEE Trans. Information Theory 50(12) (December 2004)

[11] Lin, Z., Erkip, E.: Relay search algorithms for coded cooperative systems. In: Proc. GLOBECOM Communication Theory Symposium, St. Louis (December 2005)

[12] Lin, Z., Erkip, E., Stefanov, A.: Cooperative regions for coded cooperative systems. In: Proc. GLOBECOM Communication Theory Symposium, Dallas (December 2004)

[13] Lin, Z., Erkip, E., Stefanov, A.: Cooperative regions and partner choice in coded cooperative systems. IEEE Transactions on Communications 54(7), 1323–1334 (2006)

[14] Yu, M., Li, J.T., Sadjadpour, H.: Amplify-forward and decode-forward: The impact of location and capacity contour. In: MILCOM. Military Communications Conference, vol. 3, pp. 1609–1615. IEEE, Los Alamitos (2005)

[15] Stankovic, V., Host-Madsen, A., Xiong, Z.: Cooperative diversity for wireless ad hoc networks: capacity bounds and code designs. IEEE Signal Processing Magazine 22, 37–49 (2006)

[16] Ng, C.T.K., Goldsmith, A.: Capacity Gain from Transmitter and Receiver Cooperation. In: ISIT. Proc. IEEE International Symposium on Information Theory, Adelaide, Australia, pp. 397–401 (September 2005)

[17] Shuguang, C., Goldsmith, A.: Energy-efficiency of MIMO and cooperative MIMO techniques in sensor networks. IEEE Journal on Selected Areas in Communications 22(6), 1089–1098 (2004)

[18] Woldegebreal, D., Karl, H.: Network-Coding-based Adaptive Decode and Forward Cooperative Transmission in Wireless Networks: Outage Analysis. In: Proc. 13th European Wireless Conf. (April 2007)

[19] Woldegebreal, D., Valentin, S., Karl, H.: Outage Probability Analysis of Cooperative Transmission Protocols without and with Network Coding: Inter-User Channels based Comparison. In: Proc. of the 10th ACM/IEEE International Symposium on Modeling, Analysis and Simulation of Wireless and Mobile Systems (MSWiM), Oct. 2007 (to appear)

[20] Wu, Y., Chou, P.A., Kung, S.-Y.: Information exchange in wireless networks with network coding and physical-layer broadcast. In: 39th Annual Conference on Information Sciences and Systems (March 2005)

[21] Yu, M., Li, J.: Is Amplify-and-Forward Practically Better than Decode-and-Forward or Vice Versa? In: ICASSP. Proceeding of IEEE International Conference on Accoustic, Speech, and Signal Processing, Philidelphia, PA (March 2005)

[22] Zhao, B., Valenti, M.C.: Some new adaptive protocols for the wireless relay channel. In: Proc. Allerton Conf. Communication, Control, and Comp., Monticello, IL (October 2003)

[23] Zimmermann, E., Herhold, P., Fettweis, G.: The impact of cooperation on diversity-exploiting protocols. In: Proc. of 59th IEEE Vehicular Technology Conference (VTC Spring 2004), Milan, Italy (2004)

[24] Zheng, L., Tse, D.N.C.: Diversity and multiplexing: a fundamental tradeoff in multiple-antenna channels. IEEE Trans. Information Theory 49(5), 1073–1096 (2003)

[25] Coso, A., Spagnolini, U., Ibars, C.: Cooperative distributed MIMO channels in Wireless Sensor Networks. IEEE Journ. Selected Areas in Communication 25(2) (February 2007)

Resilient Coding Algorithms for
Sensor Network Data Persistence

Daniele Munaretto[1], Jörg Widmer[1], Michele Rossi[2], and Michele Zorzi[2]

[1] DoCoMo Euro-Labs, Landsberger Strasse 312 – 80687 Munich, Germany
[2] DEI, University of Padova, via Gradenigo 6/B – 35131 Padova, Italy

Abstract. Storing and disseminating coded information instead of the original data can bring significant performance improvements to sensor network protocols. Such methods reduce the risk of having some data replicated at many nodes, whereas other data is very scarce. This is of particular importance for data persistence in sensor networks. While coding is generally beneficial, coding over all available packets can be detrimental to performance, since coded information might not be decodable after a network failure. In this paper we investigate the suitability of different codeword degree distributions with respect to the dynamics of the underlying wireless network and design a corresponding data management algorithm. We further propose a simple buffer management scheme for continuous data gathering. The performance of the protocols is demonstrated by means of simulation, as well as experiments with an implementation on MICAz motes.

1 Introduction

Data collection is the primary task of a wireless sensor network. To this end, the sensed data has to be transported to the sink node(s) or should be stored within the network in case no sink node is currently available. Due to the power and memory constraints of the sensor nodes, this has to be done as efficiently as possible. Network coding [1] was shown to provide significant benefits in such networks. Several papers have analyzed the benefits of random network coding [2] for information dissemination and data persistence [3] (the amount of information that can be decoded at any give time). These methods reduce the risk of having some data replicated at many nodes, whereas other data is very scarce (in analogy to the coupon collector's problem [4]). The robustness that can be achieved through the diversity of available information by coding at intermediate nodes can be crucial in sensor networks, where node failures may be common.

While coding is generally beneficial, coding over all available packets might leave coded information undecodable after a network failure, thus reducing data persistence. Algorithms such as Growth Codes (GC) [5], a variant of LT codes [6], address this issue by using low complexity coding algorithms together with a code degree distribution that maximizes data persistence. These concepts are generalized in [7], considering coding over multiple snapshots of data and more general random mixed coding schemes. Growth Codes are designed for networks where the information available at neighboring nodes is uncorrelated, i.e., very sparse networks with a topology that changes significantly from one transmission to the next.

R. Verdone (Ed.): EWSN 2008, LNCS 4913, pp. 156–170, 2008.

In this paper we investigate the suitability of different codeword degree distributions with respect to the dynamics of the underlying wireless network. In particular, we also investigate more static settings than those analyzed in previous research and discuss their implications on the optimum degree distribution. We then design a corresponding data dissemination algorithm that works well over a wide range of different network scenarios. To allow autonomous operation over an extended period of time in the face of a small amount of available RAM, nodes usually use their on-board flash memory. Since writing to (and to a lesser degree also reading from) the flash is very energy consuming, the coding algorithm has to make sure that the data required for encoding and decoding is available in RAM, and only data that is unlikely to be used again in the near future is written to the flash. We propose a simple buffer management scheme that allows for continuous data gathering, without using an excessive amount of writes to the flash memory.

The protocol is implemented on the MICAz mote platform. We perform a range of experiments to demonstrate its performance and compare it to previously proposed solutions. We further use simulation to investigate the scalability of the proposed approach in larger networks.

The paper is structured as follows. In Section 2 we review related work. Section 3 gives a brief overview of network coding. In Section 4 we present our novel algorithm based on network coding, analyzing suitable degree distributions for coding. Section 5 provides detailed simulation and experimental results on real sensor nodes for the different coding algorithms and degree distributions. In Section 6 we present a buffer management scheme to handle multiple temporal generations of data and Section 7 concludes the paper.

2 Related Work

The usefulness of network coding for data storage was investigated in [3], where the authors showed that a simple distribution scheme using network coding and only based on local information can perform almost as well as the case where there is complete coordination among nodes. Similar considerations also apply to sensor networks.

Growth Codes [5] were specifically designed to enhance data persistence, i.e., to maximize the amount of information that can be decoded at any time instant. Sensor nodes send out codewords that can be coded over multiple original information units. Nodes exchange codewords with their neighbors and combine received codewords with the existing local information, such that the stored information is coded over more and more information units over time.

The number of original information units a stored codeword is coded over is referred to as codeword degree. The authors in [5] propose to gradually increase the codeword degree with the amount of received information, hence the name "Growth Codes". This codeword degree distribution optimizes sensor network data persistence in the presence of node failures, as it allows to decode the joint information of any subset of nodes with high probability. Intuitively, a high degree increases the probability that transmissions are innovative in that they bring new information to neighbors, while a low degree increases the probability that the information can be decoded immediately upon reception, thus decreasing the likelihood that nodes will be left with undecodable information in case parts of the sensor network fail. As mentioned in the introduction, Growth Codes work well in case the information available at neighboring nodes is uncorrelated. As shown in [8], performance degrades in less dynamic situations, which are more likely to be found in sensor networks scenarios.

An extension of the Growth Codes work is described in [7], where the problem of collecting multi-snapshots spatial data in a resource constrained sensor network is addressed. Starting from [5], which provides an example of single snapshot data collection, the authors of [7] combine coding and scheduling to maximize the system's utility. They implement two algorithms, with and without mixing the snapshots, where only in the latter case a schedule is needed to improve the total utility gain. The scheduling problem is modeled through the Multi-Armed Bandit theory and solved optimally using Gittins Indices. They also demonstrate that there exists an optimal degree for the snapshots-mixed coding, which achieves maximum utility gain and data persistence.

We observe that without coding, data collection becomes equivalent to a coupon collector problem [9] which takes $O(N \log N)$ coupons (symbols) for recovering the N original symbols. Existing coding techniques help avoiding the related heavy tail collector effect. However, channel codes such as LT Codes [6] and Reed-Solomon Codes [10] start decoding only after accumulating a large number of received packets, which is not suitable for resource constrained sensor nodes (due to, e.g., limited memory) and for data persistence. Persistence and reliability of cached data can be improved through Fountain Codes, as shown in [11]. The authors use Belief Propagation (BP) for a low decoding complexity. Random walks are used to disseminate coded data in a scalable way. The paper is related to our work, addressing the problem of data persistence when sinks are not available, but it uses the Robust Soliton degree distribution, which limits the range of applicable scenarios. Close to this work, [12] proposes a decentralized implementation of fountain codes. Erasure codes lead to reduced communication, storage and computational cost over random linear coding. One main drawback is to consider only one data packet stored in each node, and then multiplied in loco with incoming new symbols, which wastes the capability of the sensor nodes and increases rapidly codeword degrees without taking into account the network topology. Another drawback is the data dissemination process via pre-routing, in particular geographic routing, which requires each node to know its own location. Pre-routing is the process by which each node, before the data collection can take place, routes its data packet to d randomly selected nodes, which will be XORing what they receive. In [13], the authors extend this approach by showing that if these conditions are slightly relaxed, a constant pre-routing degree suffices.

The main difference of our work with respect to previous research is that we specifically analyze codeword degree distributions providing a high degree of resilience to node/network failures for a much wider range of scenarios (than, e.g., in [5]). In addition, we present a thorough discussion on the degree distributions that work well, designing a full data dissemination algorithm, which we complete with a buffer management scheme. Finally, we provide a performance analysis through experiments with a real-world implementation of the algorithm on sensor motes.

3 Network Coding

With network coding, nodes transmit packets coded over multiple original packets, instead of uncoded data. Coded packets can contain information from many different data sources. For coding, sets of s consecutive bits of a packet are treated as a symbol over the Galois field $GF(q)$, with $q = 2^s$, and an L bits long packet consists of L/s symbols. Note that coded packets have the same length as uncoded data packets. Due to its simplicity, usually *linear* network coding is used, where packets are linear combinations of the original packets.

For random linear network coding, a packet Y coded over the original packets $X^1, ..., X^n$ is generated by multiplying each with a random coding coefficient g_i to obtain $Y = \sum_{i=1}^{n} g_i X^i$. This is done individually for each symbol in the data packet. It is not necessary to first decode received data in order to create new coded packets, but the same operations can be applied recursively to already coded data.

Decoding requires knowledge of the coding coefficients. For simplicity, assume that a packet contains both the coefficients $g = (g_1, ..., g_n)$ and the encoded data [14]. Assume a node has received $(g^1, Y^1), ..., (g^m, Y^m)$. Decoding requires solving the system of equations $\{Y^j = \sum_{i=1}^{n} g_i^j X^i\}$ to retrieve the original X^i. In case $m \geq n$ and n of the equations are linearly independent, all data can be recovered.

The special case $GF(2)$ with a field size of 2 is very appealing for sensor networks since it only requires addition over a finite field (which corresponds to a simple xor) and no multiplication. Also the coding coefficients are only a single bit which reduces overhead and decoding complexity. Different algorithms are suitable for decoding. Network coding schemes often use Gaussian elimination to invert the matrix of coding coefficients, but also methods with lower computational complexity (e.g., message passing [6]) can be effectively used in some cases.

To cope with the limited node memory, it is necessary to limit n, the number of packets that can be coded over at the same time. Packets are grouped into generations [14], and only packets from the same generation can be combined in the encoding process.

4 Coding Degree Distributions for Static and Mobile Networks

4.1 Description of the Algorithm

In this section we present a novel network coding (NC) algorithm, called *adaptive network coding* (ANC). In contrast to previous schemes ANC uses specific degree distributions (specified in detail later) in order to adapt its behavior to the type of mobility in the network. Each node has a buffer of limited and known size, which should be however larger than the size of the current generation (i.e., of the number of packets that are to be processed together and eventually distributed to all nodes). This buffer may contain encoded as well as original information packets, which may be combined to produce additional encoded packets through random linear coding. Whenever a transmission opportunity occurs, NC schemes usually (see, e.g., [15]) code over all packets in the buffer. We however advocate that coding over *all* available linearly independent packets (maximum degree encoding) at all times is not always optimal in terms of performance. This was observed in [5], where the authors showed that depending on the number of decoded or *recovered* packets r at a specific node there exists an optimal number of packets to combine to get close to optimal performance in terms of number of decodable packets at each instant in time. The optimum degree distribution however depends on the dynamics of the underlying network and in [8] the authors show the deficiencies of Growth Codes in scenarios other than the very specific one they were designed for.

In this section, we design suitable network coding algorithms based on our findings on the impact of network dynamics such as node mobility and channel conditions. We use the following definitions. The *packet degree* is the number of original information packets which are combined together to form a packet. The degree distribution gives the degree that a packet to be sent should have to give maximum performance under certain network conditions: if r is the number of packets recovered at a given node, the degree distribution returns $\mathcal{D}(r)$, i.e., the degree of the next output packet.[1]

We further say that a transmission opportunity for a node occurs when this node is selected for transmitting a new encoded packet. The actual transmission schedule is not specified in detail here and could be, e.g., either TDMA based or event based. In the former case, a distributed or centralized TDMA schedule is assumed, whereas in the latter a new encoded packet is usually sent as the node receives innovative information from its neighbors (see [15]). An example of a fully distributed approach for the selection of transmission schedules can be found in [16], where the authors propose Proactive Network Coding (ProNC). According to this strategy, every node infers transmission times as well as the data rate to use, based on incoming innovative information and on messages it receives from its neighbors. This scheme has been proven to perform very close to a mechanism exploiting partially centralized and optimal transmission schedules.

ANC works as follows. When a transmission opportunity occurs, the node randomly combines a number of packets in its buffer, so that the resulting packet has a degree that is as high as possible while being less than or equal to $\mathcal{D}(r)$. If this degree can not be obtained, the algorithm combines all packets in the buffer, obtaining a degree strictly lower than $\mathcal{D}(r)$. It is easy to determine the degree of a packet from the number of non-zero entries in the corresponding coding vector. At the first transmission, the buffer is empty and the node generates and transmits a packet containing only the node's own information. Upon receiving a new packet, a node first checks whether this packet increases the rank of the decoding matrix (which is formed by the packets in the node's buffer). If this is the case, this packet is stored in the first empty position of the buffer. Otherwise, the packet is discarded as it is useless for data recovery purposes. In the decoding process, early decoding of some information packets may occur before all packets have been recovered, thereby increasing r, the number of packets recovered by a given node so far. This often happens in practice due to the manner in which information propagates and is *gradually* coded over more and more other information (i.e., there is a codeword degree distribution inherently given by the information dissemination process).

---

[1] The name degree *distribution* is used to recall the stochastic nature of the encoding process by which $\mathcal{D}(r)$ packets are randomly and uniformly picked among those in the node's buffer. There is, however, an abuse of notation here. In fact, differently from [6] the number of packets to encode $\mathcal{D}(r)$ is deterministic once we know r.

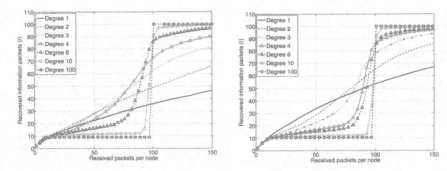

Fig. 1. Average number of packets recovered per node vs. number of packets received for a network of size $N = 100$, static (left) and moderate mobility (right) scenario

The use of a topology-dependent degree distribution is the main difference between the present algorithm and previous schemes. This modification has a significant impact and the improvements in terms of dissemination time and total number of decoded packets sent are substantial, as can be seen from the experiments later on. In the next section we discuss the properties that a good degree distribution should have as a function of the network dynamics.

4.2 Discussion on Degree Distributions

We use the network coding scheme presented in the previous section for our analysis of the degree distribution's impact on the performance of the dissemination algorithms. For the analysis, we first consider a static grid topology (referred to as STATIC in the experimental results of Section 5). Subsequently, we study the effects of node mobility in a moderate random mobility scenario and a so called *random encounter* mobility scenario (RE in Section 5). In the former, nodes move according to a random way point mobility model with speeds uniformly distributed in the interval [2, 4] m/s, whereas in the latter they move in a completely uncorrelated fashion such that the neighbors of a given node at any time instant are independent of the neighbors of the same node at any other instant. This latter case corresponds to the scenario analytically investigated in [5]. It is somewhat unrealistic in practice, except for extremely sparse and highly mobile networks with very sporadic data exchange.

We start our investigation with the static network case. We consider $N = 100$ nodes in a grid, where every node has exactly 8 neighbors. For the degree distribution we keep the encoding degree $\mathcal{D}(r)$ at a fixed value, independent of r, during the entire dissemination process. Hence, we run simulations by varying the encoding degree from 1 to N in steps of one unit.[2] The simulation results for this case are shown in Fig. 1, on the left side, where we only plot results for a few selected degrees for the sake of clarity. In particular, this figure shows the average number of packets recovered per node, r, as a function of the number of packets received. This plot, as well as the plots that remain to discuss in this section, were obtained through a large number of simulations, so as to get sufficiently tight confidence intervals (within $\pm 3\%$ of the plotted values). These

---

[2] A customized C++ simulator was written to this end.

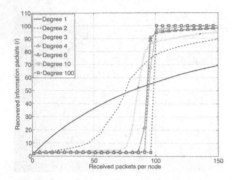

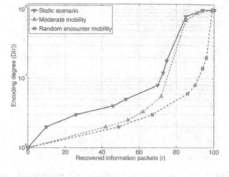

Fig. 2. Average number of packets recovered per node vs. number of packets received for a network of size $N = 100$, random encounter mobility scenario

Fig. 3. Comparison among the optimal degree distributions in the three mobility scenarios: $\mathcal{D}(r)$ vs recovered packets, r

intervals, for the sake of readability, are not shown inside the figures. Fig. 1 clearly emphasizes that the actual degree in use does matter. Very large degrees (e.g., $N = 100$) tend to have good performance, in that they allow full recovery very early on. However, they typically present a step behavior, i.e., very little can be decoded up to a certain point, and then the recovery rate suddenly jumps to 100%. By contrast, smaller degrees give a smoother recovery curve. Due to the static nature of the network and the fixed node density, there is little difference for very high degrees (around 50 and above). The early recovery of useful information through a lower degree coding is preferable in some cases. In particular, in case of a network failure or partition before full recovery, nodes with such heavily coded information cannot make any use of what they retrieved so far.

In the right side plot of Fig. 1, we show similar results for the moderate mobility scenario (again with an average node density of 8 neighbors per node). From the figures we can see that mobility helps to disseminate information more quickly, in the same way as a higher degree distribution does. For example, the curve for degree 6 in the static scenario coincides with the curve for degree 4 in the mobile one. In particular, the performance of low coding degrees is improved through mobility. Finally, in Fig. 2 we report the same results for the random encounter case. Here, the trend is even more pronounced, and very low degrees of 1, 2, and 3 perform extremely well, compared to their performance in the static case.

In all of these graphs, the curves intersect at specific points. Using these crossing points it is therefore possible to define an "optimal" degree distribution by moving along the x-axis of each graph and selecting the curve (i.e., the degree) which maximizes the number of packets recovered, r. Such a distribution is plotted in Fig. 3 for all of the three scenarios considered here.

Note that the "optimal" distributions we obtain in this way only approximate the true optimal curves. Our distributions were obtained offline through the analysis of the sim-ulation results we obtained for fixed degrees and, in turn, we neglected the dynamics in-volved in varying the codeword degree during the dissemination process. Nevertheless, we observe that the distribution for the random encounter scenario very closely matches the true optimal distribution in this case, see [5,7]. This provides evidence about the validity of our approach. An exact analysis for the static and moderate mobility cases is still missing in the literature and is one of the objectives of our future research.

Notably, these optimal distributions increase $\mathcal{D}(r)$ slowly for small r. However, their degree $\mathcal{D}(r)$ increases sharply as r approaches N. This makes sense as when the number of recovered packets becomes sufficiently large, it is convenient to code over packets with large degree (large $\mathcal{D}(r)$) in order to maximize the probability that the few missing packets are included with high probability in the new encoded packets. Moreover, in the random encounter case, this sudden increase of the encoding degree $\mathcal{D}(r)$ occurs for higher values of r. This is mainly due to the fact that mobility contributes to the redistribution of data in the network. Such a redistribution is however absent in the static case and should be compensated for by the dissemination protocol through a more aggressive encoding (i.e., a larger $\mathcal{D}(r)$). Moreover, we verified that the seemingly small difference, for small values of r, between the distributions in the static and in the moderate mobility scenarios is however very important in terms of performance. For the moderate mobility case which, in terms of mobility, lies between the static and the random encounter scenario, we observe a further interesting fact. In particular, its distribution is very close to that of the random encounter case up to a certain value of r ($r \approx 70$ in Fig. 3), while it approaches the optimum distribution of the static case for larger r. The mobility in this scenario provides a sufficient mixing of the information in the initial delivery phase, whereas this is insufficient to ensure a prompt complete recovery when there is only a small number of packets left to recover.

Finally, given the importance of picking the right distribution as a function of the type of mobility, we may think of a distributed algorithm to monitor the dynamics in the set of neighbors in order to select, and possibly change, the degree distribution in use. This scheme is also part of our future research.

5   Experimental Results

In this section we discuss and present our experimental results on real sensor nodes. Our tests are run on MICAz XBow motes with a CC2420 radio chip (working at 2.4 GHz) [17] and an MPR2400CA processor based on the Atmel ATmega128L. The transmission range of these sensor nodes for indoor transmission is about 25 meters. As we obtained our experimental results in a laboratory or 36 square meters, we had to scale down the transmission power so as to get a proper multi-hop environment. Because of the limited number of sensors available, TOSSIM simulations were run to analyze our protocol in networks with a larger number of nodes, e.g., $N = 100$ (see below for a short description of the TOSSIM simulator). Hence, we measure the average number of recovered information packets as a function of the number of packets received per node for grid (with four neighbors per node), line and random topologies. For each scenario we obtain the performance of our algorithm, ANC. For comparison, we also plot results for the scheme proposed in [5], referred to here as *growth codes based dissemination GC* and the pure network coding based scheme in [15], referred to here as *network coding*. ANC is then evaluated considering the optimal distributions discussed above for the random encounter (ANC-RE) and the static scenario (ANC-STATIC). Note again that *network coding* encodes data through the linear combination of all packets (of a given generation) in the node's buffer. *Growth codes based dissemination* uses the RE distribution, i.e., the optimal distribution in the random encounter scenario. However, in this scheme only one packet, which must contain the node's own information packet, can be used to increase the encoding degree at any given time (if allowed by the RE distribution). Hence, even though the distribution in use is the same as in ANC-RE, the time instants in which the encoding degree is increased differ. Hence, the distribution for Growth Codes almost always returns lower degree packets than what the optimal encoding policy would do, even for the random encounter scenario. This, as we show shortly, leads to substantial differences in terms of performance. These schemes, as well as the different distributions we consider for ANC, are selected to isolate the impact of the adopted degree distribution and of the coding strategy in use, respectively.

In our experiments, interference due to the channel access mechanism, temporal and spatial modifications of the transmitting/receiving radio range, energy consumption due to transmissions and memory usage are all accounted for. Also, for each setting of the involved parameters we repeated a number of experiments so as to get sufficiently tight confidence intervals about our performance measures. In particular, the confidence intervals for the subsequent plots are all within $\pm 10\%$ of the values we show in the graphs. Once again, these intervals are not shown in the graphs for improved readability. In this section, we show results for the case where each sensor generates a single information packet. Hence, we focus on the network-wide dissemination of a single generation of data. Algorithms for more complex scenarios, where nodes generate multiple information packets, are given later in Section 6, where we discuss schemes for *generation and buffer management*.

Before proceeding with the description of the obtained results, we give a short introduction to the TOSSIM TinyOS simulator, which we used to validate our experimental findings and to obtain results for large networks. TOSSIM is the simulator that is distributed with TinyOS. It is used to run TinyOS software thereby emulating the behavior of actual sensor nodes, their timers, the wireless channel, etc. It can be used to test the code to be eventually run on actual sensors, as well as to simulate the behavior of a given protocol in large networks. Packets are transmitted according to a standard CSMA channel access scheme, channel errors can be emulated through any (user defined) channel model and the correctness of received packets is assessed through a CRC check. Errors on acknowledgments, missed start symbols, noise, etc., are also accounted for [18].

5.1 Small Scale Experiments

In this section we consider a small network of 9 sensor nodes, showing results for grid, line and random topologies. The transmission power is set to the same value for all sensor nodes. In the experiments each node broadcasts either uncoded or coded packets to its neighbors, where coding is executed by means of one of the above algorithms. To access the channel, we use a standard CSMA scheme. At the end of each experiment, all sensors communicate the collected statistics transmitting a *trace file* to the sink node. Trace files contain information about received/transmitted packets as well as their degrees.

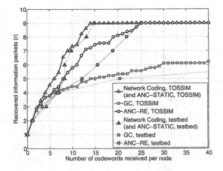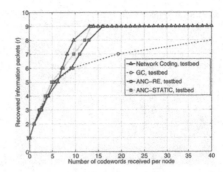

Fig. 4. Average number of packets recovered, r, for 9 sensor nodes placed on line (left) and grid topologies (right). Results are obtained for GC [5], *network coding* [15] and the proposed ANC encoding schemes.

9 Sensor Nodes, Line and Grid Topologies: Positioning the nodes so as to exactly obtain line or grid topologies is difficult in practice, due to the dynamics of the wireless channel. MICAz motes are in fact quite sensitive to antenna positioning and interference. Transmitting and receiving radio ranges change significantly in space and time, see [19]. Given these facts, the actual connectivity graph we get in our experiments does not perfectly match the corresponding graph we would obtain in a simulation with a deterministic channel model. To smooth out part of these variations, we average the results over a sufficient number of experiments.

In Fig. 4 we show the results for line (left plot) and grid (right plot) topologies. For the grid case we considered four neighbors per node. Notably, GC gives unsatisfactory performance in both cases. In particular, the fact that the degree can only be increased adding the node's own information packet to the received packets is insufficient for a proper mixing of the information in static networks. This problem was not observed in [5] as in this paper the authors only focused on extremely dynamic topologies, where the growth codes encoding strategy performs well. *Network coding* performs well and very close to ANC-STATIC. For this reason, only one curve is plotted for both mechanisms. ANC-RE does not perform equally well due to the conservative degree distribution, but it clearly outperforms Growth Codes with the same distribution. Performance in the simulations is slightly higher than in real networks for all algorithms, due to the "more well-behaved" channel mode, but overall TOSSIM simulation data points are reasonably close to the outcomes of our experiments (as seen in the left plot of Fig. 4). A similar agreement between TOSSIM and experiments was found for the results in Fig. 4, plot on the right (and thus they were omitted for the sake of readability). When comparing the two curves, one can see that the less connected the topology is, the more important the high node degree becomes (as done by pure network coding [15]). In the line scenario, pure network coding outperforms all other algorithms. The increase in the number of neighbors in the grid topology helps information dissemination and allows ANC to perform as well as network coding. Growth Codes have worse performance here.

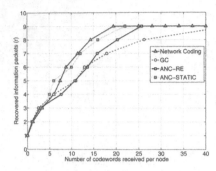 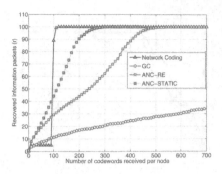

Fig. 5. Average number of packets recovered for *network coding*, ANC and GC. Experimental results for $N = 9$ nodes, random topology.

Fig. 6. Average number of packets recovered for *network coding*, ANC and GC. TOSSIM simulations with $N = 100$ nodes on a grid.

9 Sensor Nodes, Static Random Topology: Next, we present our experimental results for a simple random topology. This topology is somewhere in between the grid and and the line network and is set up so as to obtain a connected graph. The results for this scenario are given in Fig. 5. A comparison with TOSSIM is not shown due to the difficulties in reproducing the exact random scenario in the simulator. Once again, ANC (ANC-STATIC) performs very close to *network coding*. We can also observe the gap between ANC-STATIC and ANC-RE: the performance of the latter suffers as its degree distribution is not optimal in a static scenario. Finally, GC still gives the worst performance among the considered schemes.

At this point, one might observe that there is little reason for using ANC, as standard *network coding* (i.e., encoding over all available packets) performs very well. However, note that this comes from the fact that nodes gradually accumulate information, and even with full network coding will send out lower degree packets in the beginning, due to the unavailability of further information. This is not the case for larger networks, as we show below.

5.2 Large Scale Experiments

In this section we show results for a network with $N = 100$ nodes. Simulation points are obtained with TOSSIM, the TinyOS simulator. In this simulator, the training sequence (start symbols) of every packet is transmitted at 10 Kbps, whereas the payload is transmitted at the higher rate of 40 Kbps. Hence, sending a packet of, say, 128 bytes will take about 25.6 ms. Assuming that nodes take turns to transmit, an ideal TDMA would require 2.56 s to schedule the transmission of all nodes. Since we use a random access protocol, we let nodes pick a random transmission time within an interval of $[0, 10]$ s for each transmission slot. In detail, when a node receives an information packet, it stores such packet in its buffer. Hence, before sending a new packet, it waits for the next transmission slot. Transmissions are finally triggered by picking a random transmission time within each time slot. This results in a reasonably low collision rate. We used these settings in all our TOSSIM simulations. The results for 100 nodes are shown in Fig. 6 where we report the performance of ANC, *network coding* and GC. It shall be observed that in this case *network coding* presents the same step-like behavior we discussed previously. This is however detrimental to the performance in terms of *data persistence* as discussed in [5]. In fact, assume that some nodes (or even the whole network) stop working after the dissemination of, e.g., 80 packets so that the network becomes fragmented. In this case, *network coding* would give a recovery rate close to zero. ANC-STATIC, instead, would provide a delivery rate of about 33% (i.e., one third of the packets to be delivered). The same applies if the network generates data faster than it can be transported to the sink nodes. In this case, coding over all packets will prevent the sink node from decoding since it cannot gather enough data for each generation. Also in settings where requests for aggregate information occur at random times and at random nodes in the sensor network, always being able to decode most of the received data is beneficial. Otherwise, the request could only be served after all data has been decoded. Thus, in practical settings a smooth recovery is advisable. Moreover, encoding over *some* packets, as we do in ANC, leads to sparse decoding matrices. These can be inverted with a lower complexity through, e.g., heuristic algorithms, thus leading to lower energy consumption. In addition, with sparse matrices early decoding occurs with higher probability (which is the actual reason for the smooth recovery of ANC).

As a further remark, we note that there is a substantial difference between ANC-STATIC and ANC-RE for a static network with $N = 100$ nodes. This is a further indication of the importance of the selected degree distribution, especially for large networks. Finally, we observe that GC still gives unacceptable performance. Once again, the selected encoding strategy matters and its importance becomes apparent with increasing network size.

6 Handling Multiple Generations Via Buffer Management

In this section we consider a more general scenario, where nodes generate a large number of observations, at different time instants. We use the concept of *generations* as introduced in Section 3. How packets are subdivided into generations can be decided for example based on spatial or temporal criteria. With the term *spatial generation* we refer to the data generated within the same cluster of nodes, i.e., within a well characterized geographical region (over a certain period of time). With *temporal generation* we refer to the data generated within the same time interval by all the nodes in the network: for the sake of simplicity we consider that the first readings of all sensor nodes belong to the first generation, the second readings to the second generation and so on. Here, we present a simple buffer management scheme based on temporal generations. This buffer management scheme is included in the real-world implementation used in the previous section.

MICAz nodes have very limited RAM capabilities. Sensor nodes may only be able to hold a single generation in their memory at a time. This is especially true when the number of nodes in the network, N, is large. Moreover, energy consumption is an important consideration in wireless sensor networks and we thus need to devise energy efficient solutions to handle multiple generations with the given memory constraints. In case multiple generations can be stored in the RAM, the following discussion still holds with minimal modifications.

Let N be the number of nodes in the network, which we consider to be connected. Our ANC protocol is used to select the degree distribution for encoding. Moreover, assume that our nodes are processing the first generation of data. As per our ANC algorithm, as nodes receive new codewords (i.e., new packets), these are stored in the main buffer in RAM (one codeword, one row in the buffer). When a transmission opportunity occurs, the rows in the buffer are randomly combined as dictated by the degree distribution in use, following the procedure we described in the previous sections.

For the sake of explanation, consider now the instant in which a given node recovers the first generation. Note that any further packet this node may receive for this generation will be discarded since the packet can not be innovative. Also, the packets currently stored in the buffer (i.e., the recovered generation) can be safely copied to the flash memory as the decoding process is complete for this generation at this specific node. However, these packets are not deleted right away from the buffer, but are rather kept there to further assist the node's neighbors that have not yet recovered the generation.

Upon the complete decoding of the old data, the node can start processing a new generation (i.e., encoding new readings) but the neighbors of this node that are still using the old generation might need additional packets to be able to decode. In order to help these nodes, we propose a novel algorithm referred to here as *cooperative distribution management*. According to this scheme, the node successively overwrites the old data in the RAM, with data from the new generation, from the top row of the buffer to the bottom one. When information belonging to the new generation is received, the node in question stores it in the first row of its buffer. The old packet that previously occupied this position in the buffer is not deleted, but it is rather combined with the packet in the last position of the buffer, as shown in Fig. 7, figure on the left. Upon the reception of subsequent packets belonging to the new generation, the node sequentially stores them in the second, third, etc. position of the buffer, by combining the old packets in these positions with the old packets that are still in the buffer. This combination is done in such a way that the degrees of the old packets that are retained in the buffer resemble, as close as possible, the power of two sequence $1, 2, 4, 8, \ldots$, see Fig. 7, figure in the middle. This specific sequence allows a sufficient variety of degrees among the retained old packets to be able to send out packets of different degrees if necessary. As long as neighbors require packets from the old generation, the node may alternately send out packets from the new and the old generation.

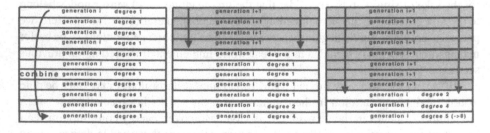

Fig. 7. Example of buffer management. Generation i is fully recovered, the new generation $i + 1$ is being processed. Packets belonging to generation i are still retained, through their linear combination, upon the reception of packets pertaining to the new generation.

We now consider the nodes which may receive packets belonging to the new generation without, however, having switched to it yet. These nodes may just store these packets in an extra buffer of small size for later use (in case such additional storage space is available). This allows a prompt switch to the new generation, as soon as the recovery of the old generation is complete.

We observe that the above mechanism extensively uses the RAM memory, whereas the flash memory is written only upon the complete recovery of a given generation of data. Limiting the access to the flash is an important consideration as it is characterized by rather long writing times as well as substantial energy consumption (compared to writing to the RAM).

We intend to investigate further buffer management schemes in future work. In particular, we believe that a more flexible scheme that is able to handle multiple generations simultaneously, while adhering to the same memory constraints, may improve the performance. Writing coded data to the flash is undesirable since it needs to be rewritten once it has be decoded. However, it is not necessary to only write full generations to the flash in a single pass. As partial data is recovered, it can be written to the flash in case it is not needed very often for the decoding of further packets for a given generation. Note that reading from the flash is substantially less expensive than writing to it. We also intend to explore spatial generations, coded over the packets of a specific region.

7 Conclusions

In this paper we proposed a novel network coding-based algorithm with adaptive degree distribution, with the aim of achieving a high degree of data persistence in static and mobile networks. We believe this is an important first step towards a practical self-adaptive coding algorithm for sensor networks. We provide insights into the relationship between degree distributions and network mobility. We also characterized the performance of different encoding schemes and related degree distributions through simulations and experiments on real nodes.

A more thorough analysis on how to adapt the degree distribution to the specific dynamics of the network (and how to "measure" these dynamics) is still necessary and kept under study. Moreover, buffer management is another important avenue for future research, which we briefly introduced here and which needs to be addressed further to successfully distribute multiple snapshots of data in large networks.

References

1. Ahlswede, R., Cai, N., Li, S.-Y., Yeung, R.: Network information flow. IEEE Trans. on Information Theory 46(4), 1204–1216 (2000)
2. Ho, T., Medard, M., Shi, J., Effros, M., Karger, D.R.: On Randomized Network Coding. In: 41st Annual Allerton Conference on Communication Control and Computing, Monticello, IL, US (October 2003)
3. Acedanski, S., Deb, S., Medard, M., Koetter, R.: How good is random linear coding based distributed networked storage? In: NetCod, Riva Del Garda, Italy (April 2005)

4. Deb, S., Medard, M.: Algebraic gossip: A network coding approach to optimal multiple rumor mongering. In: 42nd Annual Allerton Conference on Communication Control and Computing, Monticello, IL (October 2004)
5. Kamra, A., Misra, V., Feldman, J., Rubenstein, D.: Growth Codes: Maximizing Sensor Network Data Persistence. In: ACM SIGCOMM, Pisa, Italy (September 2006)
6. Luby, M.: LT Codes. In: 43rd Ann. Symp. on Foundations of Computer Science, Vancouver, Canada (November 2002)
7. Liu, J., Liu, Z., Towsley, D., Xia, C.H.: Maximizing the data utility of a data archiving and querying system through joint coding and scheduling. In: IPSN 2007, Cambridge, MA, US (April 2007)
8. Munaretto, D., Widmer, J., Rossi, M., Zorzi, M.: Network coding strategies for data persistence in static and mobile sensor networks. In: WNC3, Limassol, Cyprus (April 2007)
9. Motwani, R., Raghavan, P.: Randomized Algorithms. Cambridge University Press, New York, NY, US (1995)
10. Lin, S., Costello, D.: Error Control Coding: Fundamentals and Applications. Prentice-Hall, Englewood Cliffs (1982)
11. Lin, Y., Liang, B., Li, B.: Data persistence in large-scale sensor networks with decentralized fountain codes. In: INFOCOM 2007, Anchorage, AK, US (May 2007)
12. Dimakis, A.G., Prabhakaran, V., Ramchandran, K.: Decentralized Erasure Codes for Distributed Networked Storage. IEEE/ACM Trans. on Networking 52(6), 2809–2816 (2006)
13. Dimakis, A.G., Prabhakaran, V., Ramchandran, K.: Distributed Fountain Codes for Networked Storage. In: IEEE ICASSP, Toulouse, France (May 2006)
14. Chou, P.A., Wu, T., Jain, K.: Practical network coding. In: 41st Annual Allerton Conference on Communication Control and Computing, Monticello, IL, US (October 2003)
15. Widmer, J., Fragouli, C., LeBoudec, J.-Y.: Low-complexity energy-efficient broadcasting in wireless ad-hoc networks using network coding. In: NetCod (April 2005)
16. Fasolo, E., Widmer, J., Rossi, M., Zorzi, M.: A Proactive Network Coding Strategy for Pervasive Wireless Networking. In: IEEE GLOBECOM, Washington, DC, US (November 2007)
17. CC2420 data sheet. [Online]. Available: http://www.ti.com/
18. Levis, P., Lee, N.: TOSSIM: A Simulator for TinyOS Networks (June 26, 2003)
19. Tinyos community forum. [Online]. Available: www.tinyos.net

Radio Characterization of 802.15.4 and Its Impact on the Design of Mobile Sensor Networks

Emiliano Miluzzo, Xiao Zheng, Kristóf Fodor, and Andrew T. Campbell

Computer Science Department
Dartmouth College
Hanover, NH 03755, USA
{miluzzo,zhengx,fodor,campbell}@cs.dartmouth.edu

Abstract. Future mobile sensing systems are being designed using 802.15.4 low-power short-range radios for a diverse set of devices from embedded mobile motes to sensor-enabled cellphones in support, for example, of people-centric sensing applications. However, there is little known about the use of 802.15.4 in mobile sensor settings nor its impact on the performance of future communication architectures. We present a set of initial results from a simple yet systematic set of benchmark experiments that offer a number of important insights into the radio characteristics of mobile 802.15.4 person-to-person communication. Our results show that the *body factor* - that is to say, the human body and where sensors are located on the body (e.g., on the chest, foot, in the pocket) - has a significant effect on the performance of the communications system. While this phenomenon has been discussed in the context of other radios (e.g., cellular, WiFi, UWB) its impact on 802.15.4 based mobile sensor networks is not understood. Other findings that also serve to limit the communication performance include the effective contact times between mobile nodes, and, what we term the *zero bandwidth crossing*, which is a product of mobility and the body factor. This paper presents a set of initial findings and insights on this topic, and importantly, we consider the impact of these findings on the design of future communication architectures for mobile sensing.

1 Introduction

Wireless sensor networks have gained remarkable interest among researchers and application developers in the past ten years. Several studies have been conducted in order to best understand and characterize the radio environment of cheap low-power wireless sensor nodes and their impact on communication protocols such as the media access, routing, and transport. Early sensing platforms [1] presented a number of challenging radio issues. In [2] [3] the authors studied the performance of low-power radio transceivers found in sensor networks where nodes were static, closely situated, and presented obstacle-free communications in the same neighborhood. These studies demonstrated the existence of grey areas and strong asymmetric links among other findings which have had considerable impact on the design of robust MAC and routing protocols for static sensor networks. While these findings have had an important impact for the design of static sensor networks there has been no equivalent study in the case

R. Verdone (Ed.): EWSN 2008, LNCS 4913, pp. 171–188, 2008.

of mobile sensor networks, particularly, for a class of emerging people-centric, mobile sensor networks [4] [5] [6] [7] [8] that are built on low-power short-range radio such as 802.15.4 [9]. Many of these applications use mobile-to-mobile and mobile-to-static communications using a variety of devices including sensor-enabled cellphones and embedded sensors.

In this paper, we study the impact of 802.15.4 radio characteristics on the communication performance of mobile sensor networks. We aim to answer two questions in this study: what are the dominant factors that impact the overall communication performance of mobile-to-mobile, and mobile-to-static people-centric sensor networks? And, what is the impact on the design of future communication architectures based on these findings? We take a systematic approach and analyze inter-node communications when people are mobile (e.g., at walking speed of 1.5-2 meters/sec) in different radio environments such as indoors (i.e., walking along the hallway in an office building), in an unimpeded outdoor space (i.e., a soccer field), and walking in an outdoor urban environment (i.e., along a sidewalk). We consider a number of positions on the body that a sensor could be placed including around the neck and in the pocket. We characterize the performance of the radio link based on a number of known metrics including throughput between devices, received signal quality and signal strength for mobile-to-mobile and mobile-to-static communications under the different radio environments discussed above. For all experiments we use Tmote Invent nodes, based on the Telos platform [21], and their 802.15.4 radio as representative of a class of 802.15.4 devices that could be used in cellphones [11] and embedded sensor devices. Note, in our project we integrated the Tmote Mini [10] into the Nokia N800 and have recently acquired Intel/Motorola PSI [24] 802.15.4 linux phones. We plan to further extend our study to these devices as part of future work. To the best of our knowledge this is the first paper to present a set of detailed benchmark experiments to characterize 802.15.4 in a mobile people-centric setting and its impact on communications.

Our results show that the *body factor* - that is to say, the human body and where sensors are located on the body (e.g., on the chest, foot, in the pocket) - has a significant effect on performance of the communications system particularly in outdoor experiments where it effectively halves the transmission range of a device. While the body factor has been discussed in the context of other radios its impact on 802.15.4 based mobile sensor networks is not understood. Other findings that also serve to limit the communication performance include the effective contact time between mobile nodes, and, what we term the *zero bandwidth crossing*, which is a product of mobility and the body factor. In summary, the contribution of this paper is as follows:

- We present the first detailed set of empirical 802.15.4 benchmark experiments for mobile sensor networks where the nodes are carried by people;
- We present experimental results showing that the body factor, mobile-to-mobile contact times, and zero bandwidth crossing are dominant in mobile, people-centric sensor networks; and
- We discuss a set of architectural considerations to be taken into account when designing protocols, applications, and radio models for mobile sensor networks, when the nodes are carried by people.

The data traces collected during our study are publicly available at [36].

The paper is structured as follows. In Section 2 we present the related work followed by a detailed description of our experiments and results in Section 3. We present a short discussion on the impact of our findings on the design of future communication architecture for mobile sensor networks in Section 4 and finish with some concluding remarks and future work in Section 5.

2 Related Work

A number of studies have discussed interference caused by the human body and differing environments on radio communications. In [14] the authors model the influence of the human body for cellular radio as a function of the terminal-person distance. However, the model only holds for the cellular devices discussed and the cellular frequencies used. In other studies, models of human body shadowing for indoor radio environments that apply to humans crossing the line of sight (LoS) links between a transmitter and receiver for transmissions in the 10 GHz [15], 900 MHz, and 60 GHz [16] have been developed. The specifics of the devices, cellular radio, operating frequencies and models differ from what we study in this paper.

A number of papers discuss issues more closely related to our work. In [17] the authors show the effect of people crossing a link between a transmitter and a receiver operating at 2.4 GHz. However, they use a customized RF transmitter that generates signals with a power of 20 dB, which is very different from the low power devices (i.e., 2.4 GHz based Tmote Invents [21]) that we consider in this study. The authors found that a person's body causes signal attenuation at the receiver. The shadowing effect caused by a person's body has also been discussed in [18] for the 802.11 radio. Even in this case the experiments consist of having a person crossing the transmitter-receiver link. It is shown that the body creates severe attenuation and that the transmitter-receiver orientation matters. Our work differs from both [17] and [18] in that we present results for a different class of devices, low power, short-range radio 802.15.4 nodes, in a broader set of environments (outdoor open space, outdoor urban environment, indoor) adopting realistic mobility patterns to characterize the radio behaviour as a function of the transmitter-receiver distance, and considering different position of the nodes on the body. In [28] the degradation of the radio signal when passing through the human body is described.

A large body of work discusses the impact of the surroundings and interference on the same radio bands as 802.11, 802.15.4, and Bluetooth technologies proposing in some cases radio models for these environments. In these studies only the impact of obstacles such as buildings, trees, foliage, walls, etc., in outdoor and indoor environments is presented. The authors of [25] analyze an indoor home deployment of six 802.11a and 802.11b nodes. The study highlights the predominance of asymmetric links, the effect of obstacles being more severe than distance between nodes, the impact of the node orientation, and the interference caused by microwaves radio sources. The result of an investigation to characterize Bluetooth propagation in an indoor environment is presented in [27] showing the impact of the receiver's speed on the bit error rate.

The work in [19] [20] [21] [26] discuss the indoors and outdoors evaluation of 802.15.4 radio for static sensing platforms through a characterization of the Radio Signal

Strength Indicator (RSSI) and Link Quality Indicator (LQI) for different transmitter-receiver distances. RSSI and LQI are both parameters retrievable from the 802.15.4 hardware upon the reception of a radio packet [21] [20]. In [26] [25], the authors state that the antenna orientation greatly impacts the RSSI and the incidence of the asymmetric links. In [26] [30] the authors show that multipath fading is another important cause of indoor performance degradation. Impact of 802.11 on the Zigbee radio is analyzed in [29]. In [2] [3] the authors present a detailed study of communication limitations for static sensor networks including findings associated with grey areas and link asymmetry. In [23] the authors also discuss the radio irregularities in wireless sensor networks and show that the battery level of a node impacts the signal strength at the receiver.

Within the context of pocket-switched networks [12] [22] work has been done to analyze Bluetooth traces in order to understand people's mobility patterns, the distributions of the rendezvous times between mobile nodes, and the inter-contact time (i.e., the time interval between two consecutive rendezvous). Our work provides similar results associated with contact times but for 802.15.4, and includes a broader study of the mobile-to-mobile and mobile-to-static nodes rendezvous showing detailed RSSI, LQI, and throughput maps as a function of nodes distance for different experimental scenarios, as discussed in Section 3. We also record the contact time and effective contact time measurements during the mobile-to-mobile and mobile-to-static interactions, and consider the body factor and the position of sensors on the body.

3   Experiments: Methodology and Results

In this section, we discuss the methodology we follow for experimentation and the results derived from the measurements. For all experiments we use two Tmote Invents operating in the 2.4 GHz band, one acting as a transmitter and the other as a receiver. A different two are chosen for each experiment from a large pool of Invents to avoid biases specific to a particular Invent's hardware. The transmitter is programmed to send packets at the maximum transmission power (0 dBm) and transmission rate. We investigate the same metrics, (viz. RSSI, LQI, and throughput) as previous work targeting studies to characterize the radio environment in wireless sensor networks [2] [3] [19] [21] [26] [20]. We also measure the effective contact time, i.e., the time window during which nodes are in radio contact with each other and have enough available bandwidth between them to support data transfer (this is somewhat application specific and it will be defined in Section 3.2). Here we extend the results discussed in [12] [22] where contact time is simply defined as the time interval in which nodes are in radio contact, saying nothing about communication potential between nodes. The contact time is an important parameter to consider in mobile sensor networks because it is the time interval when nodes can exchange data. The contact time is obviously a function of the speed the nodes are moving at, i.e., it decreases as the speed increases and viceversa. Throughout our evaluation, however, we notice that when nodes move at walking speed (i.e., relatively low speeds of 1.5-2 meters/sec) the 802.15.4 radio and link performance in terms of signal quality and throughput is similar to static nodes communicating. This is because of the relatively low speed people move at. So, in our evaluation speed is not considered as a factor that impacts the RSSI, LQI, and throughput.

We carry out our experiments according to three benchmarks: *i)* outdoor experiments in a soccer field away from obstacles and radio interference in the 802.15.4 radio band, *ii)* outdoor experiments along a sidewalk which is an example of urban environment, and, *iii)* indoors experiments in a 55 meter hallway in an office building. In all the cases people were moving at walking speed. We repeat the experiments positioning the transmitter and receiver nodes at different places on the body, (i.e., on the chest front hanging on from a necklace, inside a pocket). This choice is motivated by the fact that we are also interested in quantifying the impact of the position on the body where the nodes are more likely to be carried. A third position, i.e., where the node is clipped onto a belt on the side of the body, is evaluated. Given the similarity of the results with the node carried in the pocket (due to the side position on the body in both cases), we omit results of the belt experiment due to space limitations. We run each experiment five times and calculate the 95% confidence interval (represented by the error bars in the plots presented in this paper). In what follows, we describe the experimental setup for each of the scenarios discussed above.

Outdoor open space benchmark. We perform this benchmark experiment in a soccer field out of town in a rural setting away from obstacles and radio activity to minimize any external source of interference and perturbation on the measurements. We implement a TinyOS [13] application to make the transmitter send 18 byte long packets (note, this size is selected for experimental reasons) as fast as possible and the receiver retrieve and store the RSSI and LQI from each packet received from the sender. We also record the throughput of the sender measured at the receiver. We draw concentric circles with different radii on the ground, the center being the position of the sender node during the measurements. The radii are: {5, 10, 20, 30, 40, 50, 60} meters. Along the circumference of each circle we place equally spaced markers that identify the distance walked along the circles. The experiment consists of a stationary person standing in the center of the circles wearing a necklace mote (transmitter) and facing a fixed direction while the other person walks along each circle wearing a necklace mote (receiver). Each time the person carrying the receiver passes a marker the user button on the receiver mote is clicked and a counter, which represents an abstraction of the distance walked along the circle, is incremented. Every RSSI and LQI sample is stamped with the latest marker value which means that the RSSI, LQI, and throughput values are stored in bin structures identified by the number of markers minus one. The RSSI, LQI, and throughput values for a position denoted by *i* in the circle are an average of the RSSI, LQI, and throughput values between position *i* and *i+1* (assuming the receiver moves according to the *i* to *i+1* direction). This way we are able to produce 360 degree RSSI, LQI, and throughput maps around the transmitter. To have a set of comparison points we also perform LoS measurements between the transmitter and the receiver where the transmitter is placed in the center of the circles in such a way so there are no obstacles in the proximity, and the transmitter and receiver are lifted 1.5 meters above the ground. The receiver is slowly moved along the concentric circles keeping the LoS condition with the transmitter. This way we obtain 360 degree LoS maps around the transmitter for throughput, LQI, and RSSI measured at the receiver.

Outdoor urban environment benchmark. The second benchmark experiment aims to show the radio behaviour during a mobile-to-mobile communication rendezvous in the common case of people carrying short-range radio nodes and passing each other in a typical urban environment: a sidewalk. In this case, we record RSSI, LQI, and throughput values measured at the receiver as a function of the transmitter and receiver distance. The experiments consists of having two people respectively carrying a transmitting and a receiving mote walking toward each other from a long distance and eventually passing each other. The sidewalk runs along a street which is about 15 meters away from buildings on both sides making this environment distinct from the open soccer field experiments. Since the measurements are reported as a function of the distance between the sender and the receiver we mark a 160 meter portion of the sidewalk. Each marker is 2 meters apart and every measurement starts with the two people located at a distance of 160 meters (in order to start the experiment by having them out of radio contact). Every time each person encounters a marker, the user button of the mote is clicked and a counter, which again represents an abstraction of the distance walked, is incremented. Every RSSI and LQI sample is stamped with the latest marker value which means that the RSSI and LQI values fall into bins identified by the number of markers minus one. The RSSI, LQI, and throughput values at the receiver at position i with the transmitter at position j are calculated as the average of the RSSI, LQI, and throughput values collected by the receiver between position i and $i+1$ (assuming the receiver moves according to the i to $i+1$ direction). By knowing the starting location of the nodes it is possible to determine the relative sender-receiver distance and an RSSI, LQI, and throughput map for each distance.

Indoor long hallway benchmark. We carry out this benchmark experiment in a building hallway of an office building. The hallway represents one of the common indoor scenarios where people approach each other from a long distance, get in radio contact and pass each other. Because we are interested in evaluating scenarios when nodes rendezvous, the hallway allows us to repeatably control and record this situation. Even in this case we take RSSI, LQI, and throughput measurements at the receiver as a function of the transmitter-receiver distance. To investigate the mobile-to-mobile interaction in this environment the experiment setup is the same manner as the sidewalk setup, with the 55 meter hallway marked by equally spaced markers and starting the experiments with the people at the far edges of the hallway. Furthermore, we perform some experiments having a static transmitter hanging from the ceiling while the receiver is mobile and carried by a person. The aim of these experiments is to analyze the mobile-to-static interaction in the case where a short-range mobile node performs rendezvous with a static gateway placed in an indoor environment for either data upload or tasking purposes [4] [8]. Before we start each experiment we measure the noise floor in the 2.4 GHz band. In order to do this we modify the TinyOS source code (CC2420ControlM.nc and CC2420RadioC.nc files).We observe the noise floor values oscillating between -98.79 dBm and -100.28 dBm.

3.1 Body Factor and Zero Bandwidth Crossing

In Figure 1, the results of the measurements for the soccer field LoS experiment and nodes carried by people experiment are shown. In both cases the transmitter is located at (x,y) = (70 meters, 70 meters). Given the limited size of the soccer field we do not

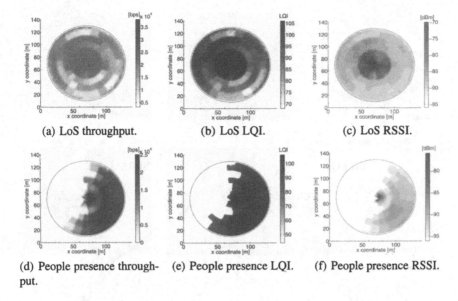

(a) LoS throughput.   (b) LoS LQI.   (c) LoS RSSI.

(d) People presence through-   (e) People presence LQI.   (f) People presence RSSI.
put.

Fig. 1. 360 degree LQI, RSSI, and throughput maps for the soccer field benchmark in the LoS and people presence cases

show the maximum outdoor transmission coverage, which is almost 70 meters for a Telos platform with a transmission power of 0 dBm [21]. Instead, we are interested in the RSSI, LQI, and throughput map around the transmitter given the impact of the body factor. For this reason a maximum radius of 60 meters around the transmitter fulfills our needs. Thus, the plots in Figure 1 do not show the boundary of the radio cell of the transmitter, but just a portion of it, namely within a 60 meter radius. Figures 1(a), 1(b), and 1(c) confirm the non-uniform nature of radio signal LoS propagation and symmetric regions around the transmitter present very different radio patters, as also discussed in [3] [23]. It is of more interest when we compare these data to the case when the transmitter and the receiver are worn by people as a mote necklace. The person wearing the transmitter is standing at (x,y) = (70, 70) facing the right hand side of the circle (e.g., watching the point of coordinates (x,y) = (130,70)). The person wearing the receiver node moves along each circle in a counter-clock wise fashion. The dotted boundary circle delimits the area where the measurements are taken. The results are shown in Figures 1(d), 1(e), and 1(f). From the plots the impact of the body factor on the radio signal is evident. The white color in almost the entire left hand side of each map of Figures 1(d), 1(e), and 1(f) indicates no data reception in that area. This is due to the fact that the transmitting node's signal is blocked by the person wearing the node so that when the receiver is carried to the back of the transmitter (i.e., from the upper left side to the lower left side of the circle) no radio signal is actually received. This phenomenon occurs independent of the distance between the transmitter and the receiver. The interesting result is that the body factor, that is mainly caused by the fact that radio frequencies in the 2.4 GHz band are strongly attenuated by water which is the main constituent of the human body, significantly limits the radio performance when

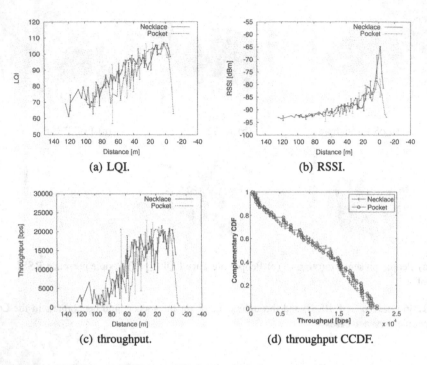

(a) LQI.

(b) RSSI.

(c) throughput.

(d) throughput CCDF.

Fig. 2. Sidewalk urban environment: LQI, RSSI, throughput, and throughput Complementary CDF measured at the receiver as a function of the transmitter-receiver distance

the nodes are carried by people. In fact, the radio contact opportunity is significantly reduced given the radio coverage asymmetry shown in Figures 1(d), 1(e), and 1(f). We define the *zero bandwidth crossing* point as the relative position(s) between a transmitter and a receiver beyond which the throughput drops to zero because of the body factor. In Figure 1(d) the zero bandwidth crossing points for the receiver moving counter-clock wise are encountered on average along the radius of coordinates $(x_1,y_1)=(70,70)$ and $(x_2,y_2)=(80,130)$.

The implications of the zero bandwidth crossing point are more evident when analyzing the case of nodes performing a rendezvous along a straight path. This is the case where people are walking along a sidewalk according to the experimental setup described earlier. The LQI, RSSI, and throughput measurements as a function of the transmitter-receiver distance are shown in Figure 2. The coordinate x=0 on the x-axis in Figures 2(a), 2(b), and 2(c) denotes the point where the two people cross along the sidewalk.

If we first analyze the mote necklace case we can see from Figures 2(a), 2(b), and 2(c) that the RSSI, LQI, and throughput increase as the transmitter and receiver move to the crossing point at x=0. Right after the crossing point the receiver stops receiving data (note the absence of data for the mote necklace case on the right of x=0). The x=0 coordinate represents the zero bandwidth crossing point for the sidewalk experiment. This result confirms the trend shown in the soccer field (Figure 1) where no signal is

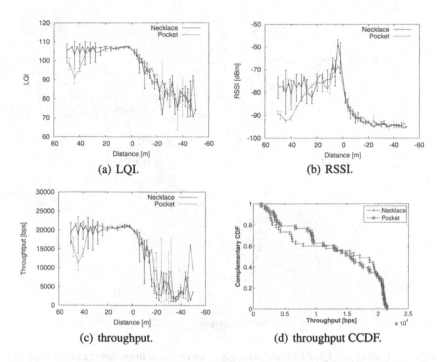

(a) LQI.   (b) RSSI.

(c) throughput.   (d) throughput CCDF.

Fig. 3. Indoor (hallway): LQI, RSSI, throughput, and throughput Complementary CDF measured at the receiver as a function of the transmitter-receiver distance

received by the receiver node when the body of the person carrying the transmitter is between the transmitter and the receiver.

When the nodes are carried in the pant/trouser pocket (akin to a sensor-enabled cellphone) the results are different. Being in a pocket, which implies a node position slightly to the side of the person's body, the performance degradation particularly at large transmitter-receiver distances is larger. In Figures 2(a), 2(b), and 2(c) it is shown that when the nodes are in the pocket the LQI and throughput increase slower than the necklace case when the distance decreases reducing the time window in which nodes experience high throughput. The complementary CDF of the throughput is also shown in Figure 2(d). Having the node more towards the side of the body translates into a positive effect as well, i.e., the nodes have the opportunity to remain in radio contact beyond the crossing point at x=0. This occurs because the position of the nodes, which now experience some degree of LoS contact being on the side of the body, allows some radio signal to be received even when the nodes pass each other extending the zero bandwidth crossing point by 10 meters beyond x=0 (this can be seen in Figures 2(a), 2(b), and 2(c) for the pocket related curves).

The zero bandwidth crossing point is pushed even further in indoor scenarios. This is shown in Figures 3(a), 3(b), and 3(c) where the x-coordinate x=0 represents the point where the people carrying the nodes cross in the hallway. Note the asymmetry in Figures 3(a), 3(b), and 3(c) for LQI, RSSI, and throughput signatures respectively as the mobile nodes pass each other at x=0. This is again due to the bodies of the two

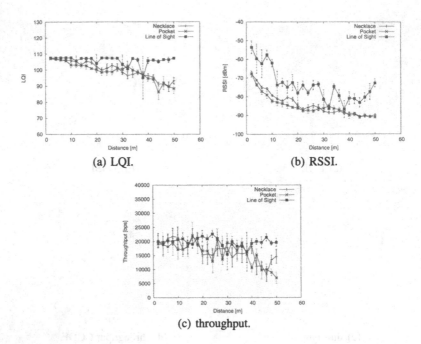

(a) LQI.   (b) RSSI.

(c) throughput.

Fig. 4. Indoor (hallway): LQI, RSSI, and throughput measured at the receiver as a function of the transmitter-receiver distance. The transmitter is static and positioned at one edge of the hallway.

people between the transmitter and the receiver. The interesting aspect is that the zero bandwidth crossing point is extended for more that 50 meters (up to the end of the hallway) beyond the physical crossing point. Even when the people's bodies attenuate the LoS component of the signal propagation, we believe that radio signal reflections off walls and other obstacles provide a non-LoS propagation path to the receiver. For this scenario, again the necklace case produces LQI, RSSI, and throughput patterns slightly better than the pocket case when the people approach each other from a long distance.

Modeling the Body Factor. In order to quantify the impact of the body of the person carrying the node we perform the following experiment: we position the transmitter node at one edge of the hallway, hanging from the ceiling and in LoS contact with the rest of the hallway. The receiver node is carried starting under the transmitter to the other end of the hallway as a mote necklace at first and then as a pocket mote. As a term of comparison, we also carry out LoS measurements along the whole hallway having the receiver lifted 50 cm above the ground. The LQI, RSSI, and throughput measurements for the LoS and body factor experiments are reported in Figures 4(a), 4(b), and 4(c) respectively.

We can see that the LQI degrades almost linearly with the distance for both the mote necklace and pocket mote cases. The throughput, which in general mirrors the LQI pattern [21], also degrades with the transmitter-receiver distance and in the necklace case it almost follows a linear decay. The RSSI for both the necklace and pocket cases

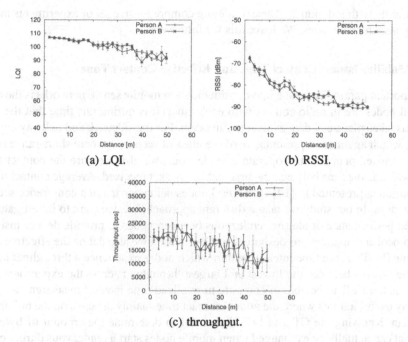

(a) LQI.

(b) RSSI.

(c) throughput.

Fig. 5. Indoor (hallway): LQI, RSSI, and throughput measured at the receiver when the receiver is carried by two different people as a function of the transmitter-receiver distance. The transmitter is static and positioned at one edge of the hallway.

remains on average 15 dBm below the nominal value measured in the LoS case and presents an exponential decay [21]. Given these findings we believe that it is possible to model the impact of the body factor over distance. The results suggest that probably linear interpolation for LQI and throughput and exponential interpolation with a known offset for the RSSI might be used in order to design models that consider the impact of the body factor for indoor scenarios. At the moment this is out of the scope of this work but we are planning to continue our research to consolidate our findings and present radio models that take such insights into account.

Body factor for different people. We conduct experiments to quantify the body factor caused by different people with different body sizes. We design an experiment where the transmitter is positioned at one edge of the hallway, hanging from the ceiling in LoS contact with the rest of the hallway. The receiver node is carried, starting under the transmitter node, to the other end of the hallway by two people with different body sizes. Person A's weight and height are 55 kg and 1.65 meters respectively, whereas Person B's weight and height are 78 kg and 1.79 meters, respectively. We measured LQI, RSSI, and throughput on the receiver node carried as a mote necklace and the results are reported in Figures 5(a), 5(b), and 5(c). From the plots no substantial difference exists between Person A and Person B in terms of LQI, RSSI, and throughput patterns. As for this result, we conjecture that for a broad class of people's figure, at least falling in the same category as the people we have experimented with, the body factor does not vary significantly with individuals. Clearly, a more comprehensive set of experiments might highlight such differences. We leave this for future work.

3.2 Mobility Issues: Contact Time and Effective Contact Time

An important parameter to take into consideration in mobile sensor networks is the time interval nodes are in radio contact with each other. It is during this time that the rendezvous takes place and data exchange can occur. For the sidewalk and hallway experiments, which again are representative of the class of scenarios where short-range radio devices carried people could operate a rendezvous, we also measure the contact time (CT) which is the time between the first and last packet received. Average contact times distribution is presented in [12] for several nodes being carried in a conference setting for few days. In our study we take a different approach, i.e., we want to investigate the detailed performance of atomic rendezvous between nodes to provide deeper insights for protocol and applications designers. For this reason we also define the effective contact time (ECT) as the time interval within which nodes experience a throughput larger than the median between the lowest and largest throughput across the experiment. We introduce the ECT to be able to compute normalized time interval measurements particularly useful indoors where the nodes' contact time mainly depends on the building's floorplan. Knowing the CT and ECT is helpful to determine the amount of bytes of data that can actually be exchanged when mobile nodes start a rendezvous during common walking patterns, like in a sidewalk or hallway. The average CT and ECT values measured in the sidewalk along with their confidence intervals are reported in Table 1.

Table 1. Contact Time and Effective Contact Time measured on the sidewalk

Scenario	CT (sec)	ECT (sec)	CT Conf. Interv. (sec)	ECT Conf. Interv. (sec)
Necklace	59.42	33.64	10.65	8.08
Pocket	31.14	17.21	10.29	2.73

What is interesting about this result is that the amount of time during which two mobile nodes performing a rendezvous can exchange data is limited to few tens of seconds consequently limiting the overall amount of data that can be exchanged. This has to be taken into consideration when designing applications that require peering interaction and data exchange between mobile nodes with short-range radios, as can be found in delay tolerant networks [12] for example. The short contact time also impacts the performance of the mobile-to-static node rendezvous that occurs when mobile nodes interact with static gateways to upload data or receive tasks [8] [4]. The average CT and ECT values along with their confidence intervals for the mobile-to-mobile rendezvous in the hallway are reported in Table 2.

Although the CT becomes less important in an indoor scenario because it depends on the topology of the environment which impacts the maximum physical distance the nodes can be placed at, the ECT is still meaningful. In fact, no matter how big the indoor space is, when two mobile nodes approach each other we would always observe

Table 2. Contact Time and Effective Contact Time measured in the straight part of the hallway

Scenario	CT (sec)	ECT (sec)	CT Conf. Interv. (sec)	ECT Conf. Interv. (sec)
Necklace	39.14	27.21	2.63	2.09
Pocket	37.24	27.64	1.46	1.67

the following performance: the throughput, first increasing and then decreasing. By applying the median throughput thresholding technique as part of the ECT definition, the ECT provides a normalized measure of the time interval when the throughput is above a certain threshold (in our case the median value between the highest and lowest throughput during the measurement). In Table 2 it is shown that even for the indoor case the ECT is in the order of less than 30 seconds. Clearly, different definitions of ECT could be determined. We plan to study this issue as part of future work.

Impact of obstacles on the contact time. So far results are related to the case when the nodes are moving along a straight path from one end to the other end of the hallway. We conduct an experiment to analyze the effect of obstructions, in particular the L-shape corners at each end of the hallway when a person turns them. The transmitter node is positioned in the middle of the hallway hanging from the ceiling and the receiver is carried as a mote necklace and pocket mote. The results are shown in Figures 6(a), 6(b), and 6(c) for LQI, RSSI, and throughput, respectively. The corners are turned at coordinates x=20 meters and x=70 meters.

Table 3. Contact Time and Effective Contact Time measured in the hallway turning corners

Scenario	CT (sec)	ECT (sec)	CT Conf. Interv. (sec)	ECT Conf. Interv. (sec)
Necklace	43.66	36.59	0.82	1.86
Pocket	42.55	35.40	0.73	1.87

It is shown that the receiver stops receiving the transmitter's packets almost immediately as the corners are turned. If we look at Table 3 the CT and ECT are below 45 seconds and 37 seconds, respectively. Given the short amount of time nodes are in contact with each other, data exchange or task download could be challenging. Even in this case the CT depends on the length of the hallway whereas the ECT assumes a more general validity.

As shown in Figure 6(b), the RSSI measured at the receiver approaching the transmitter increases (from 15 to 42 meters), whereas it decreases when the receiver moves away from the transmitter (from 42 to 72 meters). Although the RSSI signature might not present a monotonic pattern (note the necklace case RSSI at 25 meters) when either approaching or moving away from a node, it might still be used as an input to ranging algorithms to coarsely determine the distance between two nodes or at least their relative position variation. In fact, it may be possible to filter the local maximum at 25 meters in Figure 6(b) by applying an exponentially weighted moving average over the

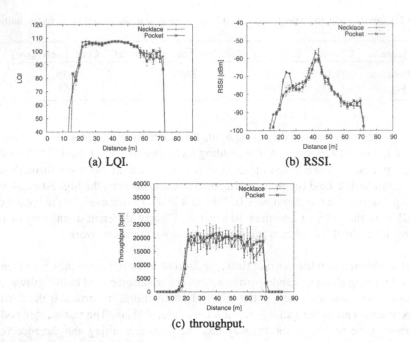

(a) LQI.

(b) RSSI.

(c) throughput.

Fig. 6. Indoor (hallway): LQI, RSSI, and throughput measured at the receiver as a function of the transmitter-receiver distance turning around corners. The transmitter is static, hanging from the ceiling in the middle of the hallway.

RSSI samples. Then, by looking at the increasing RSSI gradient the receiver could infer that it is approaching the transmitter. At the same time, as the receiver moves away from the transmitter at its back, the decreasing RSSI gradient could make the receiver infer that it is leaving the radio coverage of the transmitter. From our experiments the RSSI and LQI signatures have similar patterns if the receiver is static (in the middle of the hallway) and the transmitter mobile (i.e., the RSSI measured at the static receiver increases as the transmitter approaches the receiver while it decreases as the transmitter moves away from the receiver). For this reason we do not show the results for the latter scenario but we can draw the same conclusion as the static transmitter and mobile receiver case.

4 Architectural Considerations

All the experiments discussed so far lead us to assert that characterizing short-range low power radio performance in mobile sensor networking scenarios is complicated. This is particularly true when considering arbitrary static and mobile node positions across the experimental field because of the dependence on the surrounding environment, the background noise in the same radio band, neighboring obstacles, etc. However, we take a systematic approach to experimentally investigate and quantify the effect of a person's body and mobility on short-range radio transmissions by designing a number of simple benchmark tests.

We believe that the findings of this work could be considered as an important step towards understanding the complex radio behaviour of mobile 802.15.4 devices carried by people. In particular, the results discussed in Section 3 could drive application and protocol design for mobile people-centric sensor networks [4] and delay tolerant networks [12]. In what follows, we discuss some of the implications of our results on the communication protocol stack for short-range radio mobile node architectures.

Application layer. The data exchanged between nodes is limited by the short mobile-to-mobile and mobile-to-static rendezvous times, i.e., the CT and ECT metrics discussed in Section 3. The former includes scenarios such as a peering application or the result of delay-tolerant data exchange [12]. The latter includes the case when mobile nodes engage in a rendezvous with static nodes for uploading data to the Internet or receiving tasks [8] [4].

In our experiments, at most 96 kBytes and 73 kBytes can be exchanged in the sidewalk and hallway scenarios, respectively, given the average throughput achieved during the nodes interaction and the measured contact time at normal walking speed. For this reason, an application should minimize the number of data bytes to be exchanged. This could be achieved by implementing fusion and filtering algorithms directly on the nodes to minimize the amount of data produced (and/or locally stored) by the on-board sensors.

Transport layer. Any communication protocol should minimize the signaling overhead to maximize the data transmission opportunities during the rendezvous time. A transport protocol must act quickly and a NACK-ing or cumulative acknowledgment solution would be preferred over a per-packet ACK-ing scheme. The transport protocol should be opportunistic in the sense that it should be able to rely, for example in the mobile-to-static case, on multiple static nodes to accomplish the job. The mobile-to-static interaction in fact is most likely associated with data upload or task download sessions [8] [4], where the static node acts as a gateway between the static and mobile infrastructure.

If the mobile node goes out of the radio range of a static node, then the data upload or tasking session must be able to recover/complete when the next static node in the neighborhood is encountered. For example, this could be done by having a static node involved in a mobile uploading or tasking session propagate the state of the ongoing session to its neighboring nodes (e.g., to the static nodes in the same building or on the same street). As the mobile node enters the radio cell of one of the notified static nodes the uploading/tasking session would eventually complete.

Network layer. Any routing protocol must be reactive enough to the strong asymmetry on the radio signature caused by the body factor (Section 3). In particular, given this asymmetry, maintaining multi-hop paths between nodes is challenging. This is because when a link is established between two mobile nodes approaching each other, this link could suddenly disappear as the nodes pass each other (as we have seen in Section 3) causing a sudden disruption of the path. There is a need then for proactive routing protocols that, by monitoring the radio channel conditions (for example the RSSI gradient as the nodes approach each other) and maintaining alternative paths if possible, can quickly recover from any sudden links loss due to the body factor.

MAC layer. The body factor could make the hidden terminal problem more severe in mobile people-centric sensor networks than in the static LoS grid topology. Imagine node A approaching node B (having the two nodes facing each other), and imagine node A passing node B and eventually stopping behind B. Assume that B is static and it is willing to start communicating with a node C approaching node B from the front. As we have seen in Section 3, given this configuration node A will not be able to overhear B's transmission to C. Assuming a CSMA access scheme, A hears a clear channel and assumes it can start transmitting packets to a node D in the neighborhood. This means that even if nodes A and B are physically close to each other, by not being able to sense the respective radio activity their radio transmissions will possibly interfere with each other. We plan to experimentally investigate the impact of the body factor on the MAC layer design in future work.

Physical layer. Our findings can be leveraged to develop more accurate radio models for the short-range, low power 802.15.4 radio networks when the nodes are carried by people. These models could have applications in: *i)* improving network simulators widely used in the research community (e.g., NS-2 [31], Omnet++ [32], and Tossim [33]) to include radio models that take into account the body factor and the zero bandwidth crossing point; *ii)* in the domain of opportunistic communications; there have been studies to characterize mobility and radio contact patterns between people [34] [35] where nodes are assumed to be in radio contact if they are in the same venue at the same time [34]; delay tolerant routing protocols using routing functions based on nodes distance have been proposed [35]. However, we show that given the body factor nodes that are almost co-located and near each other are not guaranteed to have radio contact. Our work could be used to enhance the radio models for opportunistic communication networks.

5   Conclusion

In this paper, we have studied the impact of the human body on 802.15.4 radio communication under a variety of experimental conditions (mounting positions, indoor/outdoor environments, body size, etc.). We show how the body factor, and particularly the zero bandwidth crossing point phenomenon, combined with mobility, makes people-centric sensor networking based on low-power 802.15.4 radios challenging. Our work underscores the importance of taking the body factor into consideration when designing applications, networking protocols, and radio models in the people-centric sensing domain [4]. Our experimental data are publicly available in the CRAWDAD repository [36].

As part of future work we plan to investigate the body factor in the context of more sophisticated scenarios, for example, in multihop, multi-node environment with simultaneous transmissions. Additionally, we hope to demonstrate the extent of the body factor in other short- to mid-range radio networks (e.g., Bluetooth and 802.11abg).

Acknowledgments

This work is supported in part by Intel Corp., NSF NCS-0631289, ARO W911NF-04-1-0311, and the Institute for Security Technology Studies (ISTS) at Dartmouth College. Kristóf Fodor is supported as a Fulbright Scholar. ISTS support is provided by the U.S. Department of Commerce under Grant Award Number 60NANB6D6130. The views and conclusions contained in this document are those of the authors and should not be interpreted as necessarily representing the official policies, either expressed or implied, of the U.S. Department of Commerce, NIST, NSF, ARO, and Intel.

References

1. Hill, J., Culler, D.: Mica: A wireless platform for deeply embedded networks. IEEE Micro 22(6), 12–24 (2002)
2. Zhao, J., Govindan, R.: Understanding Packet Delivery Performance in Dense Wireless Sensor Networks. In: Proc. of SenSys 2003, Los Angeles, CA, USA (November 5–7, 2003)
3. Woo, A., Tong, T., Culler, D.: Taming the Underlying Challenges of Reliable Multihop Routing in Sensor Networks. In: Proc. of SenSys 2003, Los Angeles, CA, USA (November 5–7, 2003)
4. Campbell, A.T., Eisenman, S.B., Lane, N.D., Miluzzo, E., Peterson, R.A.: People-Centric Urban Sensing. In: Proc. of WICON 2006, Boston, USA (August 2006)
5. Eisenman, S.B., Miluzzo, E., Lane, N.D., Peterson, R.A., Ahn, G.S., Campbell, A.T.: The BikeNet Mobile Sensing System for Cyclist Experience Mapping. In: Proc. of SenSys 2007, Sydney, Australia (November 6–9, 2007)
6. Miluzzo, E., Lane, N.D., Eisenman, S.B., Campbell, A.T.: CenceMe – Injecting Sensing Presence into Social Networking Applications. In: Proc. of EuroSSC 2007, Lake District, UK (2007)
7. Abdelzhaer, T., et al.: Mobiscope for Human Spaces. In: IEEE Pervasive (April/June 2007)
8. Wood, A., et al.: ALARM-NET: Wireless Sensor Networks for Assisted-Living and Residential Monitoring. TR CS-2006-11, Dep. of Computer Science, University of Virginia (2006)
9. IEEE 802.15.4,
   http://standards.ieee.org/getieee802/download/802.15.4-2006.pdf
10. Sentilla Corp., http://www.sentilla.com
11. Telecom Italia Zigbee SIM,
    http://www.zigbee.org/imwp/download.asp?ContentID=10403
12. Hui, P., Chaintreau, A., Scott, J., Gass, R., Crowcroft, J., Diot, C.: Pocket Switched Networks and Human Mobility in Conference Environments. In: Proc. of SIGCOMM 2005 Workshop, Philadelphia, PA, USA (August 22–26, 2005)
13. TinyOS, http://tinyos.net
14. Lin, F.-L., Chuang, H.-R.: Performance Evaluation of a Portable Radio close to the Operators Body in Urban Mobile Environments. IEEE Trans. Vehicular Technology (March 2000)
15. Ghaddar, M., Talbi, L., Denidni, T.A.: Human body modelling for prediction of effect of people on indoor propagation channel. Electronics Letters (December 2004)
16. Obayashi, S., Zander, J.: A body-shadowing model for indoor radio communication environments. IEEE Transactions on Antennas and Propagation 46, 920–927 (1998)
17. Kara, A., Bertoni, H.L.: Blockage/Shadowing and Polarization Measurements at 2.45GHz for Interference Evaluation between Bluetooth and IEEE 802.11 WLAN. In: Proc. of IEEE Antennas and Propagation Society International Symposium (July 2001)

18. Gaertner, G., ONuallain, E., Kulpreet, A.B., Cahill, S.V.: 802.11 Link Quality and Its Prediction – An Experimental Study. In: Niemegeers, I.G.M.M., de Groot, S.H. (eds.) PWC 2004. LNCS, vol. 3260, Springer, Heidelberg (2004)
19. Srinivasan, K., Dutta, P., Tavakoli, A., Levis, P.: Understanding the Causes of Packet Delivery Success and Failure in Dense Wireless Sensor Networks. Technical Report SING-06-00
20. Srinivasan, K., Levis, P.: RSSI is Under Appreciated. In: Proc. of EmNets 2006 (May 2006)
21. Polastre, J., Szewczyk, R., Culler, D.: Telos: Enabling Ultra-Low Power Wireless Research. In: Proc. of IPSN/SPOTS 2005 (April 25–27, 2005)
22. Leguay, J., et al.: Opportunistic Content Distribution in an Urban Setting. In: CHANTS 2006. ACM SIGCOMM 2006 – Workshop on Challenged Networks, Pisa, Italy (September 2006)
23. Zhou, G., He, T., Krishnamurthy, S., Stankovic, J.A.: Models and Solutions for Radio Irregularity in Wireless Sensor Networks. ACM Transactions on Sensor Networks (2006)
24. Pering, T., Zhang, P., Chaudhri, R., Anokwa, Y., Want, R.: The PSI Board: Realizing a Phone-Centric Body Sensor Network. In: Proc. of BSN 2007 (March 2007)
25. Yarvis, M., Papagiannaki, K., Conner, W.S.: Characterization of 802.11 Wireless Networks in the Home. In: Proc. of Winmee 2005, Riva del Garda, Italy (April 2005)
26. Lymberopoulos, D., Lindsey, Q., Savvides, A.: An empirical characterization of radio signal strength variability in 3-d ieee 802.15.4 networks using monopole antennas. In: Römer, K., Karl, H., Mattern, F. (eds.) EWSN 2006. LNCS, vol. 3868, pp. 326–341. Springer, Heidelberg (2006)
27. Madhavapeddy, A., Tse, A.: A Study of Bluetooth Propagation Using Accurate Indoor Location Mapping. In: Beigl, M., Intille, S.S., Rekimoto, J., Tokuda, H. (eds.) UbiComp 2005. LNCS, vol. 3660, pp. 105–122. Springer, Heidelberg (2005)
28. Ruiz, J.A., Xu, J., Shimamoto, S.: Propagation Characteristics of Intra-body Communications for Body Area Networks. In: Proc. of CCNC 2006, Las Vegas, USA (January 2006)
29. Petrova, M., Riihijarvi, J., Mahonen, P., Labella, S.: Performance Study of IEEE 802.15.4 Using Measurements and Simulations. In: Proc. of WCNC 2006, Las Vegas, USA (2006)
30. Werb, J., Newman, M., Berry, V., Lamb, S., Sexton, D., Lapinski, M.: Improved Quality of Service in IEEE 802.15.4 Mesh Networks. In: Proc. of the International Workshop on Wireless and Industrial Automation, San Francisco, California, USA (March 2005)
31. Network Simulator – 2, http://www.isi.edu/nsnam/ns
32. Omnet++, http://www.omnetpp.org/
33. Tossim, http://www.cs.berkeley.edu/~pal/research/tossim.html
34. Srinivasan, V., Motani, M., Ooi, W.T.: Analysis and Implications of Students Contact Patterns Derived from Campus Schedules. In: Proc. of MobiCom 2006 (September 23–29, 2006)
35. Leguay, J., Friedman, T., Conan, V.: Evaluating Mobility Pattern Space Routing for DTNs. In: IEEE Infocom 2006, Barcelona, Spain (April 2006)
36. Crawdad, http://crawdad.cs.dartmouth.edu/dartmouth/zigbee_radio

Analysis of Audio Streaming Capability
of Zigbee Networks

Davide Brunelli[1], Massimo Maggiorotti[2], Luca Benini[1], and Fabio Luigi Bellifemine[2]

[1] Dept. of Electronics, Computer Science and Systems, University of Bologna, Italy
{davide.brunelli,luca.benini}@unibo.it
[2] Telecom Italia Lab, Italy
{massimo.maggiorotti,fabioluigi.bellifemine}@telecomitalia.it

Abstract. Although formerly conceived for industrial sensing and control over Wireless Sensor Networks, LR-WPANs are registering an increasing interest in experimenting multimedia applications, with particular emphasis on evaluating the streaming capability of Zigbee networks. Due to their limited throughput they are not expected to provide high QoS, nevertheless there are several application scenarios such as distributed surveillance, emergency and rescue where audio and video streaming over low cost Zigbee networks is highly desirable. In this paper we first investigate the feasibility of Zigbee-like networks for low-rate voice streaming applications. We analyze important streaming metrics such as throughput, packet loss and jitter in multi-hop topologies. We propose some improvements in the stack implementation and show the performance in order to determine the streaming capacity limits of LR-WPAN networks.

1 Introduction and Contribution

The past few years have seen an explosion of research studies on Wireless Sensor Networks (WSN) and in particular on low-rate wireless personal area network (LR-WPAN) conforming to the IEEE 802.15.4 standard. WSNs have been confirmed as an important embedded computing platform and in the next future it is expected that LR-WPANs will be used in a wide variety of embedded applications, including home automation, industrial sensing and control and environmental monitoring. In this paper we focus on Zigbee [1], which is one of the most promising standards for LR-WPAN. It relies on IEEE 802.15.4 and it is specifically designed to address the need of low cost, low power solutions and flexible network routing and management. Although most of the past and the current applications for WSN focus on simple sensing and reporting activities , there is a growing demand to make WSNs really ubiquitous and in particular there is the need to support multimedia streaming for audio, voice and low-rate video. A wireless sensor network is a collection of low-cost sensor nodes that can be deployed very quickly in the environment and can communicate with each other via radio interface. To allow large networks some nodes act usually as routers for multi-hop connections without relying on any pre-existing infrastructure. For all these features together with low-power consumption, WSNs are very attractive for many applications such as conferences, intra-building communications as well as surveillance and emergency scenarios (e.g. law enforcement, rescue activities ...) and voice streaming communication is an attractive feature for many of these network scenarios.

R. Verdone (Ed.): EWSN 2008, LNCS 4913, pp. 189–204, 2008.
© Springer-Verlag Berlin Heidelberg 2008

Since so far much attention has been paid to low duty-cycle applications, to the best of our knowledge, streaming capabilities have not been yet extensively studied for multi-hop LR-WPAN. Moreover, if we consider that multimedia streaming is very different from data communication, assuring effective audio communication over LR-WPAN is an important new challenge in the sensor network arena. In particular our case study is an emergency scenario where a rescue team must go inside hostile and unknown environments (e.g. collapsed or blazing buildings, caves, long tunnels ...) and where classic long distance wireless communications might be hampered by the nature of the environment. The idea is therefore to disseminate small wireless sensor nodes while the rescuers advance and explore the environment in order to build dynamically a network for on-site data transmission and voice streaming between the place of the disaster and the base station. Of course the network will not be stable and long-term operating, but low-power characteristics of LR-WPAN are essential to guarantee the maximum life-time during the rescue activity, and the low cost of the Zigbee devices makes the loss or the destruction of some nodes affordable.

There are several limits for achieving an effective streaming capability over Zigbee-like networks. Wireless streaming is generally an expensive operation for the limited energy budget of the nodes and it is often infeasible replacing batteries of the devices. The energy reservoir problem seems will be solved by recent studies on hardware/software power harvesting techniques which attempt to realize perpetual powered systems [2,3]. Another well-known restriction in wireless networks is the high probability of transmission errors due mainly to multi-path fading or electromagnetic interference and its intrinsic location-dependency, which make wireless communication links to have fluctuating quality levels and time-varying characteristics. Finally time constraints are also very important, because audio/video streaming applications are delay-sensitive. Usually a late arriving packet is not useful to the end node, and it is better to drop such data rather than sending it several times.

The overall goal of this paper is to describe the audio streaming capability of a Zigbee-like network over the IEEE 802.15.4 framework. In particular we examine several metrics of multi-hop communication such as throughput, jitter, latency and packet loss, using different paths and routers to deliver the information. All the measurements are performed through the analysis of a real setup using Zigbee-enabled devices deployed in the environment.

The remainder of the paper is organized as follows. Related works are reviewed in the next section whereas an overview of the Zigbee protocol is presented in Section 3. We will also argue about the decision to adopt a free protocol stack for our work. Section 4 describes the experimental hardware we use, followed by Section 5 which illustrates the results during the analysis of the Zigbee network for streaming activity. The discussion on improvements and tuning of the protocol stack is reported in Section 6, finally Section 7 concludes the paper.

2   Related Work

Streaming over sensor networks makes power management, bandwidth, memory and energy supply very challenging especially in a multi-hop domain rather than in a direct link. Several studies have been already presented about performance analysis over IEEE 802.15.4 MAC framework. In [4] the author investigates the performance and feasibility of IEEE 802.15.4 for low bit-rate audio/video streaming applications. In particular he focuses on packet loss and latency in order to find a suitable operating rate value and he proposes a method for an adaptive streaming, based on a link quality indicator. The main weak point of the article is that the author presents only simulation results using a network simulator and does not perform real measurements with sensor nodes deployed in the environment. Formerly, [5,6,7] have presented overviews of the IEEE 802.15.4 standard showing simulations, experiments or combination of both.

Theoretical research about the real-time streaming capability in a generic multi-hop WSN is presented in [8]. The author defines the capacity of the network in order to estimate the amount of data sensor nodes can deliver real-time before packet deadlines.

Practical implementations of multimedia context transmission over WSNs are also available, but usually the information to deliver is just a still image and streaming issues are not tackled. An implementation of a sensor node that can deliver multimedia information is proposed in [9]. In [10,11] the authors present image transmission over WSN, but they mainly focuses on the point-to-point transmission and power management in order to minimize the overall compression-and-transmission energy consumption.

Finally a system for voice streaming over WSN is fully implemented in [12]. The authors do not exploit a Zigbee network but investigate a TDMA-based network scheduling to meet audio timing requirements. They provide 2-way voice communication with a 24 ms per-hop deterministic latency across 8 hops. The developed hardware has a dual-radio architecture for data communication and hardware-based global time synchronization.

None of the above references focuses on the streaming capabilities of a real Zigbee network, analyzing the performance of the stack protocol under different parameters or proposing changes and improvements to outperform the current characteristics. In this paper we fill this gap using a free Zigbee-like stack protocol.

3 Stack Overview

Zigbee and IEEE 802.15.4 wireless technology are specifically designed to provide cost-effective and flexible wireless networks, which supports low power consumption, interoperability, reliability for control and sensors acquisition with moderate data rates. The scalable capability is supported in particular by the IEEE 802.15.4 standard, which defines physical (PHY) specifications to operate into three ISM frequency bands (868 MHz, 915 MHz, 2.4 GHz) and can accommodate up to 27 channels with a maximum raw data rate of 250 Kbps for the 16 channels allocated in 2.4 GHz band. Clearly this might be a limiting factor if transferring larger amounts of data is required. Devices currently available on the market work with a transmission range between 10 and 70 m.

Medium access control (MAC) specifications are also provided by IEEE 802.15.4 standard. The network can operate in two configurations: beacon enabled and beaconless mode. Beacon mode defines synchronization and reliability of the transmission mechanism, whereas beaconless networks adopt a simple lightweight protocol based on CSMA-CA. Although using no beacons is generally preferred, this mode registers more power consuming communications because of the more collisions which make the node to wait for the retransmission of the frame.

Zigbee protocol relays on the underlying IEEE 802.15.4. It manages routing protocol in the network layer (NWK), security and name binding in the Application Support Sub-layer (APS), and defines the Application Framework (AF) for user applications. In our work we focus on streaming applications which are built over (AF) and are forwarded using multi-hop path by the network layer. Zigbee specifies three types of nodes, for different activities: the Zigbee End Device (ZED) which provides information to deliver, the Router (ZR) and the Coordinator (ZC) which is unique in a network. The coordinator has to synchronize the network, maintaining the routing table, has to accept new nodes in the network and has to manage the disconnections. Usually it is also employed as data sink.

In streaming communications the maximum packet size should be transmitted, because with the increase of the data unit size the overhead of the headers is reduced. Unfortunately IEEE 802.15.4/Zigbee protocols do not define large payload in their specification. For instance, the maximum payload data unit defined by PHY layer is limited to 127 bytes. Since the MAC header requires a maximum of 23 bytes, and up to 17 additional bytes are reserved for NWK, APS, and AF layers, the actual user data unit size at application level is limited to 89-93 bytes (depending if long or short addressing is adopted during communication). In this situation an efficient fragmentation mechanism becomes essential for a streaming application, but again Zigbee does not specifies data fragmentation and reassembling protocols, and the implementation of fragmentation and flow control mechanisms at application layer is up to the end-user development.

We tried several commercial solutions ranging from Freescale [13] to Telegesis [14]. So far we have found out that a real integration and interoperability among these systems is not yet completely fulfilled, since some devices do not provide all the features of Zigbee 1.0. Since our work is not focused on interoperability and Zigbee profiles compliance, we decided to adopt for our tests a Zigbee-like protocol stack in order to evaluate the performances of the streaming capability. In particular it is provided source free allowing the developers to look deep into the code. This is an interesting feature because one goal of this work is to investigate and flush inefficiencies, optimize performances and point out hardware and software lacks. The stack is developed by MS State University [15], and although it is not certified as compliant by the Zigbee Alliance, it does use the NWK, APS, AF frame formats from the Zigbee standard implementing static trees and routing as specified in the standard, so it actually performs all the main features that are fundamental for streaming analysis of the Zigbee protocol [1,16].

4   Experimental Setup

As hardware platform, we exploit a solution provided by Texas Instrument [17], using the system on chip (SoC) CC2430. The system operates at 2.4 GHz band and offers a raw bit rate of 250 Kbps. The device integrates all operational functions such as radio transceiver, data processing unit, memory and user-application features on one single silicon die and this contributes greatly to performance, power consumption and cost. High performance and reliability at lower power consumption is achieved due to the close interaction of dedicated on-chip functions minimizing overhead. In particular MAC timing operations are handled more effectively by dedicated circuitries, and the system integrates a significant set of the IEEE 802.15.4 requirements (e.g. CSMA-CA, preamble generation, synchronization, CRC-16) to off-load the micro-controller.

As we already remarked, audio streaming is very different from data and control communication due to the inherent delay constraints. If data arrives too late, information is no more useful for playing audio and this leads to the consideration that it is better to drop it at the sender or somewhere in the path. Too late packets could happen for various reasons, for example, the necessity of the sensor node to react to external events in a timely manner. To evaluate the audio streaming performances over a Zigbee network, we off-load the SoC device from audio conversion and compression processing using external dedicated devices. Audio information is sampled at 8 KHz and data is coded using 8bit A-law conversion, moreover we can dynamically perform additional compression using an external ADPCM processor and select dynamically the desired audio rate ranging from 16 Kbps to 64 Kbps. Of course this first step of data processing results in an increase of power consumption due to additional devices but it helps to separate and identify the cost of the Zigbee stack in power consumption, computation effort and its reactivity, without any interference of other on-board activities. On the other hand the power consumption of the CODEC is comparable to the consumption that the SoC CC2430 registers when it performs additional A/D conversions and processing. For audio processing, we use the PCM codec TLV320AIC1107 from TI which consumes no more than 20 mW when it performs coding/decoding procedures, while the DS2165Q ADPCM processor chip from Maxim is exploited for ADPCM compression at the desired data rate and may require up to 60 mW. To guarantee a complete decoupling between signal processing and streaming procedures, we adopt double buffers architecture between CODEC modules and the micro-controller as depicted in Fig. 1. To verify the quality of the voice transmitted over Zigbee we implemented a simple full-duplex push-to-talk (PTT) application between nodes in the network. The FSM used in our system is illustrated in Fig. 2.

Depending on the RF environment and on the required output power consumption, Zigbee compliant wireless devices are expected to transmit in a range of 10-70 m. The evaluations presented in this paper are selected between several measurements

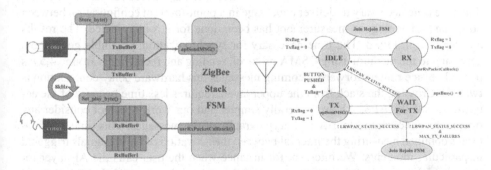

Fig. 1. Buffer architecture for audio streaming   **Fig. 2.** FSM of the PTT application

performed using distances ranging from 5 m to 35 m between nodes in the network and exploiting different payload sizes at AF level (varying between 8 and 93 bytes). We used a beaconless network and direct transfer mode to send messages. In order to minimize the influence of other ISM transmissions over 2,4GHz, the WPAN is formed using the channel 15 because it is pretty unaffected by IEEE 802.11 networks in Europe (as well as channels 16, 21 and 22).

The voice stream is delivered at constant bit-rate (CBR) and its value can be selected at the startup. For the experiments presented in this paper we vary the bit rate ranging from 24 Kbps to 128 Kbps. In every measurement session at least 10000 packets were sent over the network for each experimental test conditions and the results were averaged over a minimum of 20 trials. It is worth to specify that measurements are taken indoor with no particular attention to serious obstacles for signal propagation in order to approximate a real scenario of streaming infrastructure for emergency rescue in hostile environments.

5   Performance Evaluation

In this section, the experimental results are reported. We begin with a baseline analysis of the timing performance of the used devices, then we discuss throughput measurements, followed by some considerations on the deployment of the network in the environment and the problem of the shared channel. Finally further measurements aim to investigate the latency, the inter-packet delay, the jitter, the packet loss and the power consumption of a streaming LR-WPAN.

5.1   Time Analysis

In addition to simulation results, another useful way to estimate the best-case streaming performance over Zigbee is to analyze the time the platform needs to deliver the messages and to receive acknowledgments from the destination node. In this way we can separate the contribution of the latency between software implementation and hardware components of the protocol stack. As remarked, the module CC2430 executes several MAC and PHY operations directly on dedicated built-in hardware to guarantee the maximum efficiency in terms of power consumption and execution time. We investigate the time necessary to deliver a message in a point-to-point configuration between nodes and an analogous measurement has been done for a router device. The results are depicted in Fig. 3. The time necessary for synchronization, preamble generation, accessing to the medium using CSMA protocol, sending and receiving is around 4,5 ms per link. Since routers forward incoming messages this hardware delay contribution is twofold. Crossing the stack from the upper layers requires less time because of the activities of NWK, APS, AF are generally simpler and our work does not consider any operations concerning security and cryptography of the messages. This time information is obtained measuring the interval between the activation of GPIO signals triggered in particular moments. We intercept for instance when the user calls the AF layer for message delivery, when the software part of the stack writes to the FIFO TXFIFO of the SoC letting the hardware to complete the delivery of the packet, and when the signal

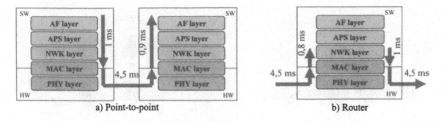

a) Point-to-point   b) Router

Fig. 3. Time to cross the HW and SW part of the protocol stack

IM_TXDONE of the MCU informs that the transmission has successful completed with acknowledgment.

Using a point-to-point configuration and exploiting the maximum data unit size of 93 bytes, the delivery of the message to destination takes 6,4 ms in the best case. We can use this information to find out a practical estimation of the best case data rate in a ZigBee network. Assuming that:

- We perform a single hop transmission;
- There is no overhead in the node activity;
- There are no lost packets.

we can compute that the highest data rate is expected to be

$$data\ rate = \frac{maximum\ payload}{time\ to\ deliver\ the\ message}$$

that is 116,25 Kbps. It means that the effective utilization of the channel for user information is limited to the 46,5% of the theoretical raw data rate (250 Kbps) claimed by the standard.

Under the same assumptions we could also compute the best forward rate of a Zigbee router in a network. In this case, if we consider a network with precompiled routing tables, the expected forward rate is

$$data\ rate = \frac{maximum\ payload}{time\ to\ cross\ the\ router}$$

that is 68,9 Kbps.

5.2 Throughput

In this work the throughput is defined as the amount of the data units (PDU) correctly arrived to the destination, divided by the length of the interval of the experiments (i.e. between the first and the last delivery $T_{end} - T_{start}$):

$$Throughput = \frac{\sum_i Length(PPDU_i)}{T_{end} - T_{start}} \tag{1}$$

The setup used for this experiments is a multi-hop string topology varying the number of the routers in the path as illustrated in Fig. 4.

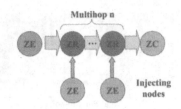

Fig. 4. Topology used for multihop tests   **Fig. 5.** Topology used for cross traffic tests

The throughput in a multi-hop path decreases quickly, as shown in Fig. 6. We performed measurements varying both the size of the user data unit (8, 20, 32, 46, 64, 93 bytes) and the number of hops using up to eight routers. In particular the plot shows that increasing the number of hops the throughput degrades faster for large sized payloads. This higher degradation is due to higher probability of collisions for large packets during CSMA, if there are several nodes of the WPAN in the same transmission area. No optimizations were implemented in the protocol stack during these experiments.

Considering that our scenario is intended the share the network infrastructure for other kind of data transmission (e.g. status of the rescuers, temperature in the blazing building ...), we performed experiments also with cross traffic. In particular, as illustrated in Fig. 5, other nodes, called injecting nodes, are joined to the same network and exchange data with the coordinator (ZC). We use different values of cross traffic, ranging the rate from 93 bps to the highest rate achievable by the node, using the maximum available payload and we change the position of the injecting nodes across the network. Figure 7 shows the degradation of the throughput when two hops divide the streaming sender from the receiver and only one injecting node was connected to the router. In the x-axis the different rates of the cross traffic packets are reported and considering that in the absence of cross traffic the measured throughput is 61,4 Kbps, the plot shows that only moderate injecting rate keep the degradation of the stream throughput reasonable low. Considerable reductions of over 40% are registered starting from 930 bps traffic rate.

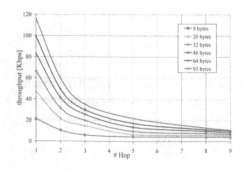

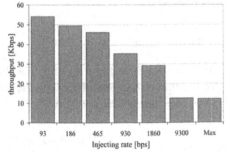

Fig. 6. Effective throughput varying the number of the hops

Fig. 7. Throughput in function of the cross traffic level

5.3   The Shared Channel Problem

The absence of a dynamic policy for channel switching between nodes belonging to the same PAN is one of the main shortcomings of the current Zigbee specifications. Once the coordinator has selected the channel for the personal area network, all the nodes will join the PAN will work and share the same channel. Of course nodes may join to different networks in the same time using different channels, but at the moment there are no specifications concerning frequency hopping within the same network. In other words, because the channel is fixed once the PAN is formed, if nodes are deployed too close to each other they have to share the same space and channel causing an uncoordinated access to it. To achieve high network utilization it is necessary maximize the number of nodes which can transmit concurrently and therefore exploiting spatial reuse becomes essential. As example we consider the deployments illustrated in Fig. 8. In a) a situation which does not take in account spatial reuse and can perform only one transmission is compared with the deployment b) where several nodes can communicate each other in the same time without interference, due to smart radio range coverage.

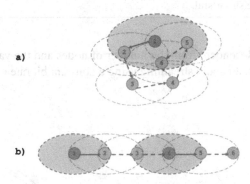

Fig. 8. Deployments: a) shared space and channel; b) network which exploits the spatial reuse

We propose algorithm 1 to enable this kind of smart coverage in a Zigbee network. The algorithm is solely designed for the initialization phase, when the PAN is already formed by the coordinator and sensor nodes are joining to the network. The main idea is to keep the transmission range of a sensor node as short as possible, avoiding the contention of the channel with other nodes of the PAN which are not directly linked to it. Obviously such a configuration may suffer of instable connections. but this problem can be solved with a dynamic tuning of the output power level using the Link Quality Indicator (LQI) of the connection as feedback information from the receiver. One of these method is presented in [4].

Using the proposed algorithm to build the network and maximizing the number of concurrent transmission, we repeat the measurements of throughput. The comparison between the two deployments is shown in Fig. 9. It confirms that adopting an intelligent distribution of the network may increase the throughput up to 30,5 Kbps. Since this kind of deployment defines a set of nodes which can transmit concurrently, this pattern can be repeated in the space with low effects on the throughput. In the figure we can see that

Algorithm 1. Spatial reuse algorithm

Require: Maintain an ordered set of increasing programmable RF output power level
　　　　for the Zigbee node $\{Pout_i : 1 \leq i \leq NMAX\}$;
　Output: Transmit power level TPL;
　Data: Joined node $JOINED$;
　initialize the Zigbee node;
　$n \Leftarrow 1$;
　$TPL \Leftarrow Pout_n$;
　$JOINED \Leftarrow$ FALSE;
　$JOINED \Leftarrow$ join_to_network();
　while $(JOINED =$ FALSE) **do**
　　if $TPL = Pout_{NMAX}$ **then**
　　　return Join procedure failed;
　　end
　　$n \Leftarrow n + 1$;
　　$TPL \Leftarrow Pout_n$;
　　$JOINED \Leftarrow$ join_to_network();
　end
　return Join procedure successful;

---

it becomes almost independent from the number of nodes and the values we measured could perfectly sustain an audio streaming using a constant bit rate of 24 Kbps.

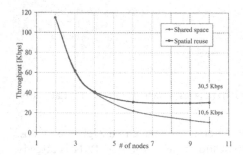

Fig. 9. Throughput of networks with different deployments

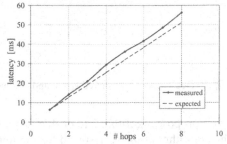

Fig. 10. Expected and measured latency varying the number of the hops

All the measurements presented in the following sections, are taken using this kind of setup which maximizes the number of concurrent transmissions.

5.4 Latency

The latency is also known as delay and it is usually defined as the amount of time required by a packet to travel from source to destination. Together, latency and throughput define the speed and capacity of a network. Real time and full-duplex streaming communications must consider this metrics very carefully in a network deployment. For example in full-duplex communication roundtrip delay of 300 ms is noticed by the final user and the human ear starts to detect delays of 250 ms. If such thresholds are exceeded the communication becomes annoying. Figure 10 depicts the measurements performed in order to characterize the end-to-end latency in our Zigbee testbed. Under ideal conditions and considering the timing analysis described in Section 5.1, we expected a linear increase of the delay with the number of the hops to the destination. The measured latencies validate this trend, registering also an additional overhead due to the not ideal environment. Our experiments is limited to 9 nodes and we covered a distance between sender and receiver of about 160 m, but considering that a transmission range of a Zigbee compliant device can arrive up to 70 m, these experiments confirm that a LR-WPAN could sustain voice transmission in a range of some hundreds of meters and fulfill the most common WSN multimedia application scenarios.

5.5 Inter-packet Delay

If voice streams are sent at constant bit rate, it is expected that also the receiver registers in average the same rate for arriving packets. Of course packets may be routed through different paths in the networks, take different time, and some of them may be lost during the travel to the destination, but in general it is possible to define an expected deadline for packet arrivals. For this reason we measure the average of inter-arrival time of the packets in Fig. 11. In streaming communication also the order of packet arriving is important, and in Fig. 12 we show the average of the interval time between consecutive packets.

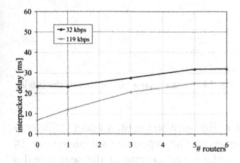
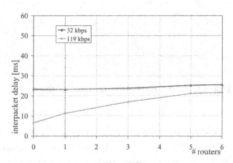

Fig. 11. Inter-packet delay varying the number of the hops

Fig. 12. Inter-packet delay between consecutive packets

The measurements were performed varying the number of the hops in the path and using different sending rate for voice transmission. Using an audio rate of 32 Kbps and exploiting the whole payload in the Zigbee messages, it is expected to receive a packet every 22,7 ms when no messages are lost. Higher values of delays are the consequence of packet loss, because missing messages at the receiver increase the inter-packet delay. To test the limits of the network, we perform the measurements also using a sender bit rate of 119 Kbps, that is the maximum rate we registered in a single hop connection (see Fig. 6). In this case the expected average inter-packet delay is only 6,2 ms, but the plot shows higher measured values in multi-hop configuration that is symptom of a high packet loss in the network.

5.6 Jitter

The jitter is a typical problem in connectionless networks and in particular in wireless infrastructure. It is closely connected to inter-packet delay since it is the measure of the variability over time of the latency across a network. Multimedia streaming has usually problems due to this effect, which affects the QoS. In a full-duplex voice service the jitter should be less than 100 ms. One of the solution to mitigate this effect is exploiting buffers between the network and the multimedia converters. A jitter buffer is basically a small queue where received messages are stored in order to give the information to the CODECs with a constant delay. Usually queue size may be dynamically modified and when it is tool small the packet loss increases. On the contrary a too large jitter buffer turns out in lower packet loss at the cost of a bigger delay experienced by final users. Figure 13 shows the maximum measured jitter varying the number of hops in the path and using different rates at the sender.

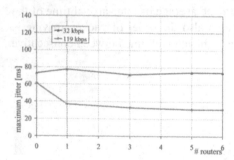
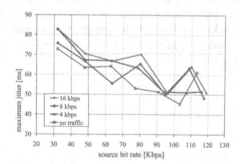

Fig. 13. Jitter varying the number of the hops   **Fig. 14.** Jitter varying the bit rate of the sender

Using the topology described in Fig. 5, we evaluated also the jitter under traffic condition with five routers between sender and receiver. The experiments depicted Fig. 14 show the maximum jitter measured with a variable source rate of the sender and a second node that injects data in the LR-WPAN with three different data rates. As expected, the jitter of the stream communication increases in average when cross traffic in the network grows. The evaluations are done over correctly consecutive arriving messages, therefore packet loss does not influence the measurement. All the experiments register a maximum jitter below the threshold of 100 ms for an acceptable QoS even in case of cross traffic configurations.

5.7 Packet Loss

Packet Loss can be due to several reasons, such as the congestion of the network, full buffers in some routers in the path and fails in the reception of packets (e.g. CRC fails, or channel interferences). Depending on the used audio compression level the loss of several consecutive packets may lead to a severe reduction of QoS. In fact if we use an audio rate of 64 Kbps, a single Zigbee packet contains 11 ms of audio stream, the information interval increases up to 46 ms adopting a more aggressive ADPCM compression of 16 Kbps. However voice is quite predictive and if the packet loss is isolated the voice can be heard in an optimal way. Moreover an emergency scenario accepts also low audio quality levels for the service, therefore even more lost packets are allowed if they do not occur in a burst way.

In this work we consider the packet loss as the number of the user messages that actually have never arrived to the destination at application level, divided by the total number of delivered packet:

$$Packet\ Loss = \frac{N_{sent\ packet} - N_{received\ packet}}{N_{sent\ packet}} \tag{2}$$

First of all in Fig. 15 we evaluated the dependence of the packet loss as a function of the distance using a direct link between two nodes. Measurements are taken in indoor environment with an uninterrupted burst of messages from the sender in order to emulate a critical scenario. For this reason the packet loss starts to grow quickly beyond 25 m.

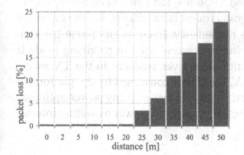
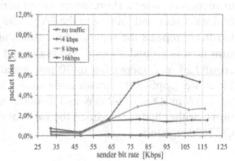

Fig. 15. Packet loss in function of the distance   **Fig. 16.** Packet loss under traffic condition

Using a fairer setup with small distances between nodes and the cross traffic scenario already adopted for jitter experiments, the plot in Fig. 16 shows how the traffic from other nodes affects the packet loss. We remark that in a voice over WSN application, even if the audio stream requires most of the resources in the path, other kind of data (such as environmental data) may be delivered. This auxiliary information is characterize by low data rate and this is the reason because of the effect of the traffic begin to influence the performance with sender rate over 64 Kbps.

In a multi-hop scenario the packet loss increases with the number of hops. As depicted in Fig. 17, the maximum source rate (119 Kbps) at the sender results in a dramatic packet loss even with only one router, meanwhile with a controlled bit rate of 32 Kbps the effect of losses is mitigated, but it is still important if high QoS is required. The reason of such a high rate of missing packets is investigated in Section 6.

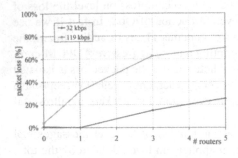
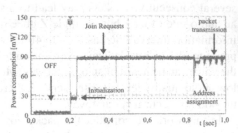

Fig. 17. Packet loss in multi-hop configuration

Fig. 18. Registered power consumption of the voice streaming node at the startup

5.8 Power Consumption

We analyzed the power consumption of the whole Zigbee transceivers, because the nature of the adopted SoC system does not allow to identify accurately the contribution of the micro-controller and the RF radio. If no low-power mode is adopted the Zigbee module operates always in receiving mode, after having joined a network. Figure 18 shows the power trace when the voice streaming module is switched on. It is possible to recognize, after a short initialization period of 36 ms, the voice node attempting to find a network and joining to the PAN. The join request lasts 200 ms, but the exploited hardware repeats the request three times as redundancy. Even in this phase the consumption is around 90 mW. We registered that the current used in receiving mode is around 28 mA, increasing to 30 mA when the transceiver switches to the TX mode. Since we supplied the sensor node with 3.3 V, the power consumed by the platform is 92,4 mW in RX, and 99 mW in TX. In our test we did not perform any power optimizations, neither had we modified the value of the RF transmitted power by setting internal CC2430 registers.

6   Refinements

In this section we investigate the adopted implementation for the Zigbee stack and we show how it is possible with small changes in the default parameters to improve the performance of the system. In particular we investigate the input and output buffer mechanism, varying the size of the queues in a Zigbee router device.

In Fig. 19 we analyze the causes of the packet loss in a multi-hop configuration. The main contribution to router losses is given by packet collisions at MAC level, whereas considering the messages actually received by a router, a small percentage is discarded by failure in the CRC verification. Finally a relevant amount of packets to forward are lost because the system buffers are not available to store them after a successful CRC.

The adopted stack implementation reserves memory space for 4 packets size both for the input and output queue by default. When these buffers are full, any further arriving packet is discarded. We tried to increase the buffer length and in particular we tested any combination using 4, 16, 32, 64, 128 packets as queue size. Results about the obtained

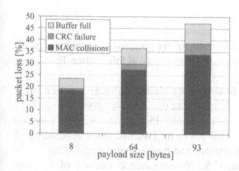

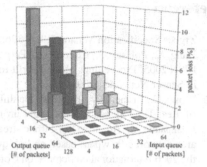

Fig. 19. Analysis of the causes of the packet loss

Fig. 20. How packet loss depends on the dimension of the input and output queues

performance are depicted in Fig. 20. In any measurements, we registered the number of arrived packets and correctly forwarded by the router, counting also the number of losses because of the full buffer. From the plot we deduce that the size of the input queue buffer does not really influence loss reduction (even the best size results to be 64) and it depends on the fact that the stack makes immediately a copy of the incoming message in the NWK space. Increasing the size of the NWK buffer, instead, helps to reduce the number of lost packets. With the adopted platform we found that a buffer size of 64 messages is enough to nullify the contribution of the stack to the packet loss.

7 Conclusion

This paper presented an accurate evaluation of streaming performance over LR-WPAN. All the experiments have been taken using a real Zigbee testbed with large LR-WPAN network deployed in indoor environment. We also discussed about methodology of network deployment in order to optimize the performance and we evaluated the optimal size for the input/output queues in a Zigbee router. Our investigation on metrics such as throughput, packet loss, jitter and power consumption demonstrates that it is possible to develop voice streaming applications over LR-WPANs network at the cost of an accurate deployment of the Zigbee network. Under these conditions the maximum throughput, which results almost unaffected by the number of hops, results to be around 30 Kbps and although it is not enough for high quality audio requirements, it suffices for the most common voice streaming applications. Main issues for an effective multimedia streaming over Zigbee are related not only to hardware improvements and smart deployments, but also to overcome drawbacks of the standard specifications such as an efficient low-level fragmentation mechanism and providing for larger data unit and for dynamic channel switching between nodes belonging to the same PAN.

Acknowledgements

The work presented in this paper was supported by a grant of Telecom Italia.

References

1. Zigbee Specification Version 1.0, p. 376, www.zigbee.org
2. Jiang, X., Polastre, J., Culler, D.E.: Perpetual environmentally powered sensor networks. In: IPSN 2005. Proceedings of the Fourth International Symposium on Information Processing in Sensor Networks (2005)
3. Moser, C., Brunelli, D., Thiele, L., Benini, L.: Real-time scheduling with regenerative energy. In: Real-Time Systems, 2006. 18th Euromicro Conference, pp. 261–270 (2006)
4. Deshpande, S.: Adaptive low-bitrate streaming over ieee 802.15.4 low rate wireless personal area networks (lr-wpan) based on link quality indication. In: IWCMC 2006. Proceeding of the 2006 international conference on Communications and mobile computing (2006)
5. Gang, L., Krishnamachari, B., Raghavendra, C.S.: Performance evaluation of the ieee 802.15.4 mac for low-rate low-power wireless networks. In: Performance, Computing, and Communications, 2004 IEEE International Conference, pp. 701–706 (2004)
6. Petrova, M., Riihijarvi, J., Mahonen, P., Labella, S.: Performance study of ieee 802.15.4 using measurements and simulations. In: IEEE WCNC 2006 (April 3–6 2006)
7. Lee, J.S.: An experiment on performance study of ieee 802.15.4 wireless networks. In: Emerging Technologies and Factory Automation, 2005. 10th IEEE Conference (2005)
8. Abdelzaher, T.F., Prabh, S., Kiran, R.: On real-time capacity limits of multihop wireless sensor networks. In: RTSS 2004. Proceedings of the 25th IEEE International Real-Time Systems Symposium, Washington, DC, USA, pp. 359–370. IEEE Computer Society Press, Los Alamitos (2004)
9. Huang, H.C., Huang, Y.M., Ding, J.W.: An implementation of battery-aware wireless sensor network using zigbee for multimedia service. In: Consumer Electronics, 2006. ICCE 2006. Digest of Technical Papers. International Conference, pp. 369–370 (January 7–11, 2006)
10. Yu, W., Sahinoglu, Z., Vetro, A.: Energy efficient jpeg 2000 image transmission over wireless sensor networks. In: GLOBECOM 2004. Global Telecommunications Conference (2004)
11. Pekhteryev, G., Sahinoglu, Z., Orlik, P., Bhatti, G.: Image transmission over ieee 802.15.4 and zigbee networks. In: ISCAS 2005. Circuits and Systems (2005)
12. Mangharam, R., Rowe, A., Rajkumar, R., Suzuki, R.: Voice over sensor networks. In: RTSS 2006. Proc. of the 27th IEEE International Real-Time Systems Symposium (2006)
13. Freescale Semiconductor, Inc., BeeKit Wireless Connectivity, http://www.freescale.com
14. Telegesis, Ltd., Telegesis ZigBee Technology, http://www.telegesis.com
15. Reese, R.B.: A Zigbee-subset/IEEE 802.15.4 Multi-platform Protocol Stack, http://www.ece.msstate.edu/~reese/msstatePAN/
16. IEEE Std. 802.15.4, Part 15.4: Wireless Medium Access Control (MAC) and Physical Layer (PHY) Specifications for Low-Rate Wireless Personal Area Networks (LR-WPANs).
17. Texas Instruments, Inc., TI ZigBee Solutions, http://www.ti.com

Efficient Resource Estimation During Mass Casualty Emergency Response Based on a Location Aware Disaster Aid Network

Ashok-Kumar Chandra-Sekaran[1], Gerd Flaig[1], Christophe Kunze[2], Wilhelm Stork[1], and Klaus D. Mueller-Glaser[1]

[1] Institute for Information Processing Technology, University of Karlsruhe (TH), Engesser Strasse-5, D-76128 Karlsruhe, Germany
Chandra@itiv.uka.de, gefla@pond.sub.org, stork@itiv.uka.de, kmg@itiv.uka.de
[2] FZI research center for information technologies, Haid-und-Neu-Strasse.10-14, 76131 Karlsruhe, Germany
kunze@fzi.de

Abstract. The mass casualty emergency response involves logistic impediments like overflowing victims, paper triaging, extended victim wait time and transport. We propose a new system based on a location aware wireless sensor network (WSN) to overcome these impediments and assists the emergency responders (ER) in providing efficient emergency response. We have developed a ZigBee-ready acceleration sensor node hardware which is energy efficient as shown by its current consumption results. ZigBee mesh network is setup and a RSSI-based localization solution is analyzed. The main functionality of this WSN is to collect real time data – patient/emergency doctor tracking, triage information, patient vital signs/activity and communicate it to the ER's Monitor Station device that runs the visualization software. We have implemented this software using the new 'Care Zone Count Algorithm' a dynamic mechanism based on localized events and data acquired from the WSN. This algorithm calculates and displays the patient count in each care zone, victim flow rate, transport capacity, thereby enabling the ER to efficiently estimate the resources required. The analysis of this algorithm verifies that the proposed system creates situation awareness to the ER.

Keywords: Emergency response system, care zone count algorithm, location aware WSN, ZigBee.

1 Introduction

During a mass casualty disaster, one of the most urgent problems that lead to chaos at the disaster site is the large number of patients [3]. Currently existing emergency response system mostly involves manual interpretation which is labor intensive, time consuming and error prone. A new emergency response system based on wireless sensor network (WSN) is proposed by us to solve these problems. The use of WSN emergency response system provides flexibility and usability.

R. Verdone (Ed.): EWSN 2008, LNCS 4913, pp. 205–220, 2008.

WSN's are perceived as dynamic, ad-hoc networks with thousands of sensor nodes communicating over radio channels, performing data sensing and collaborative processing [2]. Some of the important challenges of WSN are:

- Self-Sufficient operation: Typically, the sensor nodes are battery powered and left unattended at deployment site.
- Self Organization: The ability of the sensor nodes to spontaneously create an impromptu network, configure the network, dynamically adapt to device failure and degradation, manage movement of sensor nodes, and react to changes in task and network requirements [9].
- Scalability: A WSN should be able to adapt itself to the insertion of new nodes.

The new short range, low power, low rate wireless networking ZigBee standard open the door for many new applications [2].

The organization of the paper is as follows. Section 2 explains the disaster management strategy and problems that arise. Section 3 describes about the disaster aid network architecture and its functionalities. Section 4 elaborates the ZigBee ready sensor node and RSSI based localization solution analysis. Section 5 explains an algorithm for efficient resource estimation during emergency response and its results.

2 Disaster Management Scenario

The new emergency response system we propose is based on the disaster management strategy followed in Germany [11], but it can also be adapted to other disaster management strategies.

Mass Casualty events-"Massenanfall von Verletzten" (MANV) is the widely used process for handling disasters in Germany. The on-site organization chief (OOC) designates the disaster site into four care zones [12] as shown in Figure 1 and the chief emergency doctor plans for triaging the patients.

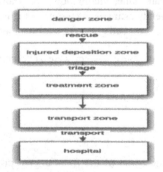

Fig. 1. Patient flow at the disaster site

Danger Zone (DZ): This is the zone where the actual disaster takes place. The search and rescue of the injured patients is carried on here.

Injured Deposition Zone (IDZ): The rescued patients are gathered and triaged. Triaging is a method to classify the patient according to the severity of their injury and prioritize them for evacuation. There are four different classes of triaging:

- Red: patients who require immediate attention
- Yellow: patients who require delayed attention
- Green: patients with light injuries
- Blue: patients with no hopes of survival
- Black represents patients who are dead and is not a triage class

Treatment Zone (TZ): The triaged patients are treated based on the short diagnosis in the triage and first aid.

Transport Zone (TRZ): The ambulances are present here to transport the patients from the disaster site to the hospital. The red triaged patients are moved to the Transport Zone first, followed by the yellow ones.

2.1 Field Study

A disaster simulation drill was conducted by state fire department Bruchsal, Germany and the MANV based emergency response for a train-bus collision was simulated. The drill comprised of around 60 patients, 35 emergency doctors including the paramedics, fire fighters and the Organization group.

The on-site organization chief (OOC) charted out a plan based on the resources available and the victim count. He manually drew a map (see Figure 2) and accounted the details of the number of medical responders, transport vehicles, care zones [10].

Fig. 2. OOC drawing manual map

The zones can be nearby or far away and may even overlap one over the other. The manual mapping done by the organization chief was time consuming, complex for updating real time changes and the resource estimation was hindered.

Medical responders conduct initial triage and then call their emergency medical chief (EMC) using their handheld radios, and verbally report the patient count. The officer manually tallies the patient counts on clipboards and verbally reports the patient count to transportation coordinators and requests for the necessary number of ambulances. After initial triage, patients wait at the scene until their ambulance arrives. With a resource limited response team, patients often wait for an extended period of time before transport. During this waiting period, patient conditions may deteriorate. Secondary injuries such as hypoxemia, hypotension, and cardiac tamponade can become life-threatening if not treated immediately. There is no continuous patient vital sign monitoring currently used [4]. The paper based triage is a bottle neck and makes the re-triaging difficult [3]. In addition, patients with minor injuries often depart the scene without notifying the response team, thus creating an organizational headache for EMC/OOC who is responsible for tracking the whereabouts of each patient.

3 Disaster Aid Network (DAN)

An emergency response system is proposed based on the DAN to solve the following main problems (see section 2.1) – no real time patient tracking and vital sign monitoring, triaging is a bottleneck, manual resource estimation is time consuming, extended patient wait time before transporting.

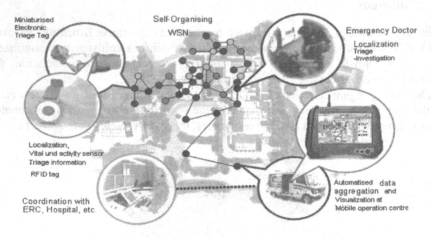

Fig. 3. DAN architecture

The DAN architecture (see Figure 3) consists of hundreds of nodes distributed in a disaster site and wirelessly interconnected through the new low-power ZigBee technology to form a mesh network. The DAN ZigBee network uses the 2.4 GHz band which operates worldwide, with a maximum data rate of 250 kbps [6].

ZigBee is chosen for DAN because it's a low power, low cost technology for sensor networks [6] [17]. ZigBee network can access up to 16 separate 5MHz channels in the 2.4GHz band, several of which do not overlap with US and European versions of IEEE 802.11 or Wi-Fi. It incorporates an IEEE 802.15.4 defined CSMA-CA protocol that reduces the probability of interfering with other users and automatic retransmission of data ensures robustness. Its self-forming feature enables the mesh network to be formed by itself thereby enabling the network to be easily scalable. Its Self-healing mesh network architecture permits data to be passed from one node to other node via multiple paths. Its security toolbox ensures reliable and secure networks. The MAC layer uses the Advanced Encryption Standard (AES) as its core cryptographic algorithm and describes a variety of security suites that use the AES algorithm. These suites can protect the confidentiality, integrity, and authenticity of MAC frames.

There are three logical device types in ZigBee namely- the Coordinators, Routers, and End Devices. The Coordinator initializes a network, manages network nodes, and stores network node information. The Router node is always active and participates in the network by routing messages between paired nodes. The routing is based on the simplified Ad-hoc on demand Distance Vector (AODV) method. The End Device is the low power consuming node as it is normally in sleep mode most of the time. It can take 15 ms (typical) to wake up from sleep mode [17].

DAN is a heterogeneous network [7] formed with the following type of nodes:

- 'Patient bracelet node' (End Device): Minimized electronic triage tag, localization support, ZigBee mote, vital and activity sensors, RFID tag, Localization
- 'Emergency Doctor's (ED) bracelet node' (End Device): Localization support and ZigBee mote
- 'Monitor station' (Coordinator): Collector node running a visualization software that displays the disaster site map with location, triage information and used by the EMC / OOC
- 'Router nodes': ZigBee motes with known location coordinates that can be deployed at the site (ex: attached to tents, ambulances)
- 'Emergency doctors PDA': For patient monitoring and data recording

Based on the instantaneous need during the emergency response the concerned nodes can form a Mobile Ad-hoc network (MANET) for accomplishing a specific task.

3.1 DAN Functionalities

The main functionalities of the Disaster Aid Network are efficient logistics at the disaster site (see section 5) and patient monitoring.

Patient Monitoring
The implementation of this functionality is not within the scope of this paper. The physical and physiological parameters are sensed, collected from the mesh network and displayed at the Monitor Station for continuous patient monitoring. If there is a change in patient status the EMC is informed at the monitor station and treats the corresponding patient swiftly. A passive RFID tag is integrated into the bracelet for patient identification.

In this paper we focus on the efficient logistics functionality. We have implemented a ZigBee mesh network for patient tracking. The care zone count algorithm for efficient resource estimation is also implemented and its performance is analyzed.

4   ZigBee Mesh Network

A ZigBee mesh network is implemented with acceleration sensor nodes acting as router or end device and a ZigBee dongle enabled laptop acting as coordinator.

4.1 ZigBee-Ready Acceleration Sensor Node

The Acceleration sensor node consists of a telemetry board connected to a sensor board via connector (see Fig 4).

The telemetry board is a generic platform since it can be connected to a sensor board comprising any sensor that supports SPI interface. The telemetry board is designed with a power supply, TI (Texas Instruments) CC2431 System on Chip (SOC), Arm Processor, chip antenna, High Frequency and low frequency oscillators. The CC2431 (see [15], [14]) consists of the location engine, 2.4 GHz IEEE 802.15.4 compliant RF transceiver, an enhanced 8051 MCU, 8 kB of RAM, 128 kB Flash memory. The ARM processor performs sensor data processing and transmits via UART to the 8051. The ZigBee stack from TI runs in 8051 microcontroller as object code on top of which we have developed the application layer.

The sensor board is designed with a three dimensional digital acceleration sensor LIS3LV from ST Microsystems. Data acquisition takes place at 160 Hz followed by a downsampling of 80 Hz. The packets transmitted consist of acceleration data collected over a period of 1 sec.

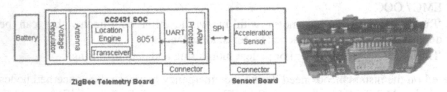

Fig. 4. ZigBee-ready Acceleration Sensor Node

The current consumption of this sensor node during activated and deactivated data communication states (see Table 1) are averaged over a period, by measuring the voltage across a 1 ohm shunt resistor using the LabView software.

Table 1. Current consumption of acceleration sensor node

ZigBee Sensor Node (supply voltage = 3.3 V)	Router	End Device
Data communication activated	50.8 mA	32.6mA
Data communication deactivated	-	22.4 mA

The ZigBee router is always active leading to higher current consumption. During inactive data communication, the data acquisition and transmission are stopped and the end device is in light sleep mode. In this mode the 8051 core and the oscillators are active while the RF transceiver is off. In DAN the nodes may need to have a battery lifetime of around 5 hours to one week. The current consumption values show that the sensor node can be used as the patient bracelets or doctor's node or routers and last atleast for few days.

4.2 Received Signal Strength Indicator (RSSI) Based Localization

The CC2431 Location Engine hardware from TI (Texas Instruments) implements a distributed computation algorithm that uses RSSI values from reference nodes whose coordinates are known to calculate the location of the blind nodes whose coordinates are to be determined. Performing location calculations at the node level reduces network traffic and communication delays otherwise present in centralized computation approach.

Functionality
The basis of this radio-based positioning solution is the relation between the distance from the transmitter and the received signal strength (see equation 1) considering the assumption that the propagation of the signal is approximately isotropic [16].

$$RSSI = -(10n \log_{10} d + A) . \qquad (1)$$

The parameters A and N determine the exactness of the blind node location. A is an empirical parameter determined by measuring the absolute RSSI value in dBm of an omni-directional signal at a distance of one meter from the transmitting unit. The Value of A ranges from 30 to 50 with resolution of 0.5.

The parameter N is defined as the path loss exponent and describes the rate at which the signal strength decreases with increasing distance from the transmitter. The value of N depend on the environment conditions and ranges from 1 to 8 [16].

In the open air and large absence of reflections the signal strength decreases almost squarely with the distance, while in closed areas deviations can occur due to increased absorption by obstacles or reflections. Thus the measured values clearly deviate from the ideal values particularly with individual measurements. For this reason, the positioning of blind node is done by averaging at least three and a maximum of eight references nodes.

Localization takes place in two steps, which are repeated in cycles. The cycle begins with the Burst-phase, in which the blind node broadcast a sequence of packages, requesting the reference nodes for their position and the averaged received signal strength of the packets sent to them. In the last phase the eight best received references will be sorted according to their signal strength and handed over to the localization hardware along with the parameters A and N values [16].

Analysis: Patient tracking using the RSSI based Localization
A primitive analysis of CC2431 hardware based location solution is undergone to find its suitability to the DAN. ZigBee ready acceleration sensor nodes are used as reference and blind nodes. The coordinator is a ZigBee hardware dongle enabled laptop running Location Graphical User interface (GUI) software to display the positions of nodes in the site map.

A 40 x 20 meters rectangular grid of six reference nodes each separated by 20 meters is formed at an indoor area (computer laboratory). Larger areas can be covered by forming rectangular grids with more number of nodes. The origin (0, 0) is in the upper left corner with x axis rightwards and y axis downwards. The value of A is measured as 49 and corresponds to an average of the RSSI values on the one meter radius circle from the ZigBee-ready acceleration sensor nodes. The value of N is selected as 3.875 from the vendor specification, based on the empirical measurement that best fits the environment. The blind node is moved within this grid to 10 different positions (centre of grid, corners) at an interval of 20 seconds and the corresponding position coordinates are measured via Location GUI.

The actual location and the measured location of the blind node are compared. The average deviation of the measured values from the actual values, for 10 different readings is calculated and shows an accuracy of 2 meters. The computation time for every blind node location with reliable location value is measured as 2 seconds.

Only the fundamental applicability of the localization solution is analyzed in this paper. The map of the disaster site can be obtained form external sources (example Google Earth) and the Global Positioning system (GPS) receivers equipped in the ambulances and emergency surgeon PDA's can configure the position of the reference nodes. ZigBee-ready acceleration sensor nodes are worn as bracelets by victims. In MANV, let's consider a scenario of 50 victim count/hour flowing into the treatment zone of area 40x50 meter [15]. In such a scenario, the accuracy (2 meters) and computation time (2 seconds) values obtained in this analysis indicate that the localization solution is suitable for victim tracking.

Since blind nodes can also serve as reference nodes for other blind nodes, measuring errors can reproduce within the system and affect the overall result. The converging time of the position estimations of the blind nodes can be a concern, if only a small number of nodes in one section are equipped with absolute reference coordinates and another section contains large nodes that are constantly mobile. These concerns will be examined under adverse RF conditions as part of future works.

5   Efficient Logistics at the Disaster Site

The visualization software implements the Care zone algorithm. It consists of a display and summary panel. The display panel shows a map of the disaster site with patient/ emergency doctor location and triage color, zones. The summary panel provides count of patients in each zone, transport vehicle count and overall count of patients/doctors.

5.1   Care Zone Algorithm

The care zone algorithm is a dynamically responding mechanism based on localized events [5]. The functionalities of this algorithm are – to estimate the overall count of patients/doctors in the disaster site, count of the un-triaged and different triage classes, to determine the operational areas and victim count of the disaster site zones. The algorithm is implemented in Python using NumPy (Numerical Python) for matrix processing and wxWidgets/wxPython for the graphical user interface.

The inputs to this algorithm are

- The location coordinates of patient/doctor bracelets, tent nodes and sign boards nodes.
- Events that commence during the emergency response: nodes coming online| storage of triage data| node entering transport| location update.
- Type of the node: doctor | ambulance | tent.

The outputs from the algorithm are:

- Overall count of patients
- Overall count of doctors
- IDZ count
- TTZ count
- Count of patient taken to the transport vehicle count
- Estimated geometric dimension, form and orientation of IDZ,TTZ,TZ

It is assumed that the victim's initial location is either in the DZ or IDZ, depending on where the network node is attached. The patient locations then follow one of the following sequences:

- Danger zone (DZ) $\rightarrow$ Injured Deposition Zone (IDZ) $\rightarrow$ Treatment Zone (TTZ) $\rightarrow$ Transport Zone (TRZ)
- DZ $\rightarrow$ TTZ $\rightarrow$ TRZ
- DZ $\rightarrow$ TRZ

Ideally, only the first flow occurs. However, in reality, it is possible that IDZ, TTZ and other elements of the disaster management process are not (yet) established and therefore the correlation method must be able to cope with diversions from the process. The following conditions hold high probability for the care zone algorithm:

- When triage data is initially stored, the node location should be inside the IDZ area
- Doctors who are near bracelets during triage time should be in the IDZ area and on triage duty
- When red and yellow triage classes are moved from IDZ to a different area with high doctor density, then this zone should be TTZ
- Only Red and yellow triage classes patients are transferred to transport vehicle
- Area with high density of ambulances should be TRZ

The algorithm has considered the following caveats

- The zone areas can be re-designated
- Doctor duties can change or be undefined
- Some inputs may not be available (ex: tent tags)
- Some events may enter the network in a delayed fashion (temporary dissociation from network and buffering)

The data structures used for the parameters in the algorithm are as follows:

- Location: (x, y)
- Event: Node Online I Storage of Triage Data I Node Enters Transport I Location update
- Type: (Doctor Tag I Patient Tag I Object Tag)
- Patient bracelet: Un-triaged I Red I Yellow I Green I Blue

5.2 Care Zone Algorithm-Method

The functional block diagram of care zone algorithm is as shown in figure 4.

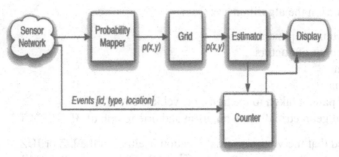

Fig. 5. Functional block diagram of care zone algorithm

Probability Mapper

The locations of nodes, events and type of nodes are given as input to the probability mapper. For every location coordinate received, depending on the events and type of node the probability mapper calculates the probability distribution of the node to belong to the zone (IDZ, TTZ, TRZ). Thereby an Event Probability vector $P_{ev}(x, y)$ is formed.

$$P_{ev}(x, y) = (p_{IDZ}(x, y), p_{TTZ}(x, y), p_{TRZ}(x, y)) . \qquad (2)$$

Where, (x, y): Location coordinates

$\quad p_{IDZ}(x, y)$: Probability that the location belongs to IDZ

$\quad p_{TTZ}(x, y)$: Probability that the location belongs to TTZ

$\quad p_{TRZ}(x, y)$: Probability that the location belongs to TRZ

For example let's say the algorithm gets the location of a node in IDZ, as input. The probability mapper identifies with the $P_{ev}(x, y)$ 'Storage of Triage Data' event that this node has high probability to belong to the IDZ and thus the $P_{ev}(x, y)$ will be as shown in figure 6.

$$P_{ev}(x, y) = (0.9, 0.1, 0.3) \qquad (3)$$

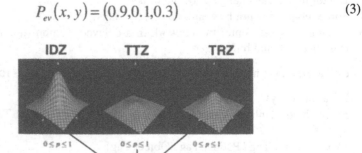

Fig. 6. Event Probability vector $P_{ev}(x, y)$ on a 'Storage of Triage Data' event

The probability values will be assigned to $p_{idz}(x, y), p_{ttz}(x, y), p_{trz}(x)$ in an empirical way based on experimentations.

Grid Block

The Grid block generates a three dimensional $\vec{p}(x, y, t)$ vector as output for every location coordinate given as input and stores this value in the grid. The value of $\vec{p}(x, y, t)$ in the grid is calculated by adding the output of probability mapper to the decayed previous grid value at that location (see equation 4). The values of the grid are instantaneously calculated and updated at each time step for all location coordinate inputs. The grid block functionality is mathematically shown below.

This is a representation of the grid:

$$\vec{p}(x, y, t) \mapsto \sum_{ev} \vec{p}_{ev}(x, y) \cdot decay(t - t_{ev}) \tag{4}$$

For efficient implementation, a decreasing exponential function is used.

$$decay(x) = a^x, \ 0 < a < 1 \tag{5}$$

By substituting the decay function in $\vec{p}(x, y, t)$ and expanding the summation, we get

$$\vec{p}(x, y, t) \mapsto \vec{p}_{ev_1}(x, y) \cdot a^{t - t_{ev_1}} + ... + \vec{p}_{ev_n}(x, y) \cdot a^{t - t_{ev_n}} \tag{6}$$

Extraction of a summands between 1 and n-1 yields

$$\vec{p}(x, y, t) \mapsto$$
$$a\left(\vec{p}_{ev_1}(x, y) \cdot a^{t - 1 - t_{ev_1}} + ... + \vec{p}_{ev_{n-1}}(x, y) \cdot a^{t - 1 - t_{ev_{n-1}}}\right) \tag{7}$$
$$+ \vec{p}_{ev_n}(x, y) \cdot a^{t - t_{ev_n}}$$

By substitution of $\vec{p}(x, y, t - 1)$ for events from 1 o n-1, we get

$$\vec{p}(x, y, t) \mapsto a \cdot \vec{p}(x, y, t - 1) + \vec{p}_{ev_n}(x, y) \cdot a^{t - t_{ev_n}} \tag{8}$$

When $t = t_{ev_n}$, this is further simplified to

$$\vec{p}(x, y, t) \mapsto a \cdot \vec{p}(x, y, t - 1) + \vec{p}_{ev_n}(x, y) \tag{9}$$

The above equation is a convenient and efficient form for implementation.

Estimator
This block maps the grid values to zone types. Generally, this is a function from three-dimensional probability vectors to zone types. A naive implementation just selects the zone with the highest probability in the vector.

Display
Zones are then displayed by assigning a color to each location of the output of the estimator. The resulting color of each output is calculated by multiplying the assigned color with the probability value of the estimated zone.

Counter
In each time step, the last known locations of all known patient nodes are mapped to a zone by using the estimator output and are subsequently counted per zone. Counting of the other node types is not done per zone and is trivial.

5.3 Simulation

In a real scenario the data (location, type and events) are generated by the disaster aid network but due to lack of large number of nodes at the time of this analysis, the data is provided through an event log (text file) to the algorithm (see Figure 7). The structure of the event log is as follows: Each line describes an event specifying its attributes separated by spaces. The first column contains the time of the event, followed by the originating node's identification, type and event parameters.

Fig. 7. Simulation model for care zone algorithm

Consider a disaster site of area 100 by 100 meters containing 50 nodes of types-patient, doctor, ambulance and transport. The time sequence starts at t=0 and stops at t = 500 seconds. One time step is equal to ten seconds. The display panel map origin (0, 0) is in the upper left corner with x axis rightwards and y axis downwards. The map grid size is 500 by 500 units of 0.2m. An event log with 116 events is generated for the above assumption with the following general flow:

1. At first, few injured patients are found. The first patient is directly taken to the first transport as an exception to the normal process.
2. Six more injured people are found. The EMC orders the patients to be triaged because there are not enough resources for individual treatment. IDZ, TTZ and TRZ are designated.
3. Injured people are moved to the IDZ. Two emergency doctors arrive and start triaging.
4. Two patients, triaged red and yellow respectively, are moved to the TTZ.

The output of the algorithm for the above generated event log is seen in the visualization software from t = 0 to 500 seconds. In order to describe the situation awareness that the visualization software can create for the OOC/EMC, the output of algorithm at time step t= 9, t= 31 and t = 40 are explained below.

Between t=0 and t=9 (90 seconds), patient nodes 1 to 4 have reported locations as well as an ambulance. The ambulance, coming in via the southwest access road, has parked in free space at (128,297). Patient 4 has been moved near to it (151,302). Figure 8 shows the output at t=9 (90 seconds).

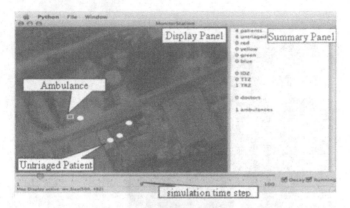

Fig. 8. Visualization software screenshot when t = 90s

At t=31 (310 seconds), two emergency doctors have arrived on the scene and triaged one patient as red and another as yellow. Also, a treatment zone sign with a radio tag has been placed which regularly sends location update events. Figure 9 shows how the input from these new events has superseded the former estimation for the transport zone. This display shows that more paramedics should be sent to the danger zone to shift patients to the IDZ for triaging. Thus the EMC can manage his paramedics efficiently.

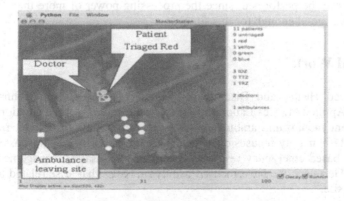

Fig. 9. Visualization software screenshot when t = 310s

By looking at the monitor station at simulation time t=400 seconds (see Figure 10), the EMC can quickly see that all currently available ambulances will soon be occupied because there are already two patients in red and yellow triage classes in the treatment zone and another triaged red patient in the Injured deposition zone. This means he will need at least one more ambulance, which he can immediately request from the ERC. He will probably also require at least one more emergency doctor in a timely manner, since there are still seven un-triaged patients and there are patients waiting for treatment in the treatment zone.

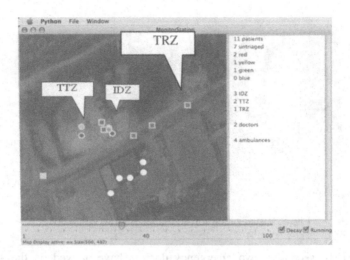

Fig. 10. Visualization software screenshot when t = 400s

Results
We generated events that provided a realistic set of data and gave as input to the algorithm which gave accurate counts that match the actual scenario. The simulation consumed 22.69 seconds of CPU time (19.02s user, 3.67s system) on a Mac Book Pro Core2Duo for *116 input events*. No optimization of the code after the initial working prototype had to be performed, since the processing power of more than five events per second was good enough for this simulator.

6   Related Work

The Advanced Health and Disaster Aid Network (AID-N) from Johns Hopkins University, Applied Physics Laboratory develops technology-based solutions for time critical patient monitoring, ambulance tracking, web portals for patient information flow etc. AID-N mainly focuses on critical patient monitoring [4] at disaster site. But in the DAN based emergency response system for the disaster management strategy followed in Germany, we have focused mainly on issues that arise related to logistics at a disaster site.

7 Conclusion

A new emergency response system based on the location aware DAN is proposed for assisting the mass casualty response providers in the disaster site. The ZigBee-ready acceleration sensor node current consumption results indicate that they can last longer lifetime as patient bracelet or doctor bracelet or routers in DAN. The primitive analysis of RSSI based localization solution shows its suitability to DAN even though intensive analysis is yet to be done. The result of the care zone algorithm analysis shows its effectiveness in providing situation awareness to the EMC/OOC enabling them to efficiently estimate and distribute resource. The patients can therefore be quickly evacuated from the disaster site. Thus the DAN based system is capable of solving the problems of the existing emergency response methods.

References

1. Ranjan, G., Kumar, A., Rammurthy, G., Srinivas, M.B.: A natural disaster management system based on location aware distributed sensor networks. MASS 2005, 0-7803-944-6/05/
2. Chandra-Sekaran, A., Mueller Glaser, K.D., Stork, W., Picioroaga, F., Brinkschulte, U.: Towards a self-organizing wireless hospital area network, World Congress in Medical Physics and Bio-Medical Engineering, Seoul, South Korea (2006)
3. Gao, T., White, D.: A next generation electronic triage to aid mass casualty emergency medical response. Applied Physics Laboratory, Johns Hopkins University
4. Gao, T., Greenspace, D., Welsh, M., Juang, R.R., Alm, A.: Vital sign monitoring and patient tracking over a wireless network. Applied Physics Laboratory, Johns Hopkins University
5. Tatomir, B., Rothkrantz, L.: Ant based mechanism for crisis response coordination. In: Dorigo, M., Gambardella, L.M., Birattari, M., Martinoli, A., Poli, R., Stützle, T. (eds.) ANTS 2006. LNCS, vol. 4150, Springer, Heidelberg (2006)
6. "ZigBee Specification 2006" ZigBee Alliance, Tech. Rep. Document 053474r13 (2006)
7. Hac, A.: Wireless Sensor Network Designs. University of Hawaii at Manoa, Honolula, USA
8. Zhao, F., Guibas, L.: Wireless sensor networks, an Information processing approach
9. Heylighen, F., Gershenson, C.: The Meaning of Self-organization in Computing. IEEE Inteligent Systems, Los Alamitos (2003)
10. Gesetz über den Rettungsdienst sowie die Notfallrettung und den Krankentransport durch Unternehmer (Rettungsgesetz NRW - RettG NRW) (Fn1) -Emergency response law in the German state NRW, vol. 24 (November 1992)
11. Strategische Neukonzeption der ergänzenden technischen Ausstattung des Katastrophen-schutzes im Zivilschutz - Bericht Entwurf März 2003 Bundesministerium des Innern Aktenz: O4 – 750100/1b RefL: MR Dr. Meyer-Teschendorf Projekt-Ref: P. Rechenbach - Disaster strategy concept report to the ministry of the interior
12. Organisationsrahmenplan für erste Maßnahmen am Unfallort, den Transport und die stationäre Versorgung Schwerbrandverletzter bei einem Massenanfall / [Hrsg.: Ministerium für Arbeit, Gesundheit u. Sozialordnung Baden-Württemberg]. - Stuttgart, 1982. - 24 S.; (dt.) - National alarm base plan to be used as a Framework for Organization planning of MANV

13. Texas Instruments CCC2431 - System-on-Chip for 2.4 GHz ZigBee/ IEEE 802.15.4 with Location Engine: Data sheet
14. Texas Instruments CCC2430 - System-on-Chip for 2.4 GHz ZigBee/ IEEE 802.15.4 with Location Engine: Data sheet
15. NRW, Behandlungsplatz-bereitschaft: Konzept BHP-B 50 NRW. Innenministerium des Landes Nordrhein-Westfalen - NRW state Treatment zone concept BHP-B 50 NRW (April 2006)
16. Texas Instruments CC2431 Location Engine: Application Note AN042
17. http://www.zigbee.org/

Efficient Clustering for Improving Network Performance in Wireless Sensor Networks

Tal Anker[1,2], Danny Bickson[1,*], Danny Dolev[1], and Bracha Hod[1]

[1] The Hebrew University of Jerusalem, Israel
{anker,daniel51,dolev,hodb}@cs.huji.ac.il
[2] Marvell Semiconductor, CA, USA
tala@marvell.com

Abstract. Clustering is an important mechanism in large multi-hop wireless sensor networks for obtaining scalability, reducing energy consumption and achieving better network performance. Most of the research in this area has focused on energy-efficient solutions, but has not thoroughly analyzed the network performance, e.g. in terms of data collection rate and time.

The main objective of this paper is to provide a useful fully-distributed inference algorithm for clustering, based on belief propagation. The algorithm selects cluster heads, based on a unique set of global and local parameters, which finally achieves, under the energy constraints, improved network performance. Evaluation of the algorithm implementation shows an increase in throughput in more than 40% compared to HEED scheme. This advantage is expressed in terms of network reliability, data collection quality and transmission cost.

Keywords: Wireless sensor networks, clustering, belief propagation.

1 Introduction

Organization of large multi-hop wireless networks into clusters is essential for achieving basic network performance. In wireless sensor networks (WSN), the clustering is primarily characterized by data aggregation by each cluster head, which significantly reduces the traffic cost. The hierarchial model requires two main methods: (1) periodic selection of cluster heads (CHs); and (2) assignment of each node to one or multiple clusters.

Optimal clusters' selection is equivalent to the minimum dominating set problem which is an NP-complete problem. The literature is extremely rich with many approximation algorithms based on several heuristics. The reader is referred to [1] and [2] for a review of previous work.

While most efforts thus far have focused on an energy-efficient clustering scheme, the attention to the performance of the multi-hop network was quite limited. An energy-efficiency algorithm may select a few CHs for energy-saving,

---

* Danny Bickson has been partially supported by EVERGROW, IP 1935 of the EU Sixth Framework.

R. Verdone (Ed.): EWSN 2008, LNCS 4913, pp. 221–236, 2008.
© Springer-Verlag Berlin Heidelberg 2008

but if these CHs do not have good connectivity or if they are not stable, the retransmission and the dropped packets may significantly degrade the network performance and the total energy wasted may end up to be higher. Therefore, taking reliable communication into account is essential for any clustering algorithm which aims to reduce the energy consumption in a network.

Moreover, the network lifetime should be measured not only by the time that the first or the last node dies, but also by the period of time that the network is available for providing services and operating appropriately. Since the network is usually dense and many nodes are redundant, the death of a few nodes does not affect the network. Thus, network lifetime is tightly coupled with the network performance.

The work presented in this paper uniquely addresses the clustering problem in multi-hop networks with a special focus on network performance, using the belief propagation (BP) algorithm. BP is an iterative algorithm for computing marginal probabilities on trees, by local message passing [3]. Mostly, it is used for efficiently solving inference problems. BP is a popular method for distributed inference because of its properties, such as fast convergence, accurate results, and good performance in asynchronous environment etc.

The main advantage of this method over existing algorithms for clustering is that BP considers not only local properties of a node, such as residual energy or degree, but also takes into account joint characteristics of a group of nodes, such as link quality and topology information. Utilization all available data, while maintaining small constant message and time overhead, leads to considerable increase in network performance and balanced power consumption among the nodes.

The contribution of the paper is two-fold. First, it introduces a new algorithm for efficient clustering that considers not only the power balancing among the nodes, but also the total transmission power aggregated in the multi-hop routing. The algorithm is fully decentralized and asynchronous, have fixed small convergence time and scales to large networks. Extensive simulation of the algorithm in environment of interferences, packet loss and node failures, which covers other synchronization issues, such as active node's duty cycle, demonstrates its robustness as well. In contrast to many algorithms in this area, our algorithm makes no a priori assumptions regarding the network size and distribution of nodes, link symmetry or topology.

Moreover, the paper presents a scalable and practical implementation of BP in WSN for inference goals. We propose a new broadcast variation that is tailored to fit Min-Sum algorithm, efficient implementation in hardware and effective network transmission. The message passing routine is highly energy-aware and provides distinctive combination of energy-efficient features. Our novel approach of using a broadcast communication paradigm and the use of only integer calculations, without any scheduling or message ordering, considerably decrease the general overhead relative to other BP frameworks that are used for WSN ([4], [5], and [6]).

The rest of the paper is organized as follows. Section 2 briefly presents relevant previous work. Section 3 describes the network model and formalizes the clustering problem. Efficient clustering, using belief propagation, is described in Section 4. Section 5 analyzes the algorithm using simulation. Section 6 concludes the paper with a discussion and directions for future work.

2   Related Work

Many research projects in the last few years have explored clustering in WSN from different perspectives. LEACH [7], is the first clustering algorithm that was proposed for reducing power consumption. In LEACH, the clustering task is rotated among the nodes, based on duration. Direct communication is used by each CH to forward the data to the base station (BS).

HEED [8] extends the basic scheme of LEACH by using residual energy and node degree or density as a metric for cluster selection to achieve power-balancing. It operates in multi-hop networks, using an adaptive transmission power in the inter-clustering communication.

Both schemes are fully-distributed, terminate in constant number of iterations and incur low message overhead. However, the cluster selection deals with only a subset of parameters, which can possibly impose constraints on the system. These methods are suitable for prolonging the network lifetime rather than for the entire needs of WSN.

VCA [9] is a voting-based clustering algorithm that enhances the criteria for cluster selection and combines load balancing consideration together with topology and energy information. VCA addresses inefficient cluster formation using a voting scheme, which enables the nodes to exchange information about their local network view. This method assumes a synchronization among the nodes. Similar to WCA [10], the time required for the nodes to gather information about all other nodes depends on the network size and is not constant.

In EEUC [11], the hot-spot problem in multi-hop networks is solved using clusters with unequal size. CHs that are closed to the BS tend to die faster, because they relay much more traffic than remote nodes. Setting smaller cluster sizes to the close CHs preserves their energy. Additional improvement for multi-hop networks is presented in [12], using a separation between the data gathering and aggregation task and the forwarding task.

All these algorithms try to prolong the network lifetime and to balance the load among the nodes, using some metrics for cluster selection and maintenance. Network performance of a multi-hop network is beyond the scope of these papers. A broader perspective is presented in [13], where three fundamental characteristics of multi-hop networks are clarified: power consumption distribution, the effect of the distribution on data collection rate, and data collection time. This work examines the network performance of direct communication, LEACH and HEED. It provides new metrics for measuring the quality of a clustering algorithm in multi-hop WSN. These metrics are used for evaluation of our algorithm as well.

3   System Modeling and Problem Formulation

We model the sensor network as a directed graph $G = (V, E)$, where V is a set of nodes, where each one is assigned a local unique identifier. E is a set of wireless links connecting two adjacent nodes. Nodes are defined as adjacent if and only if they are within each other's transmission range. The links may be asymmetric. A special node, v_0, is defined to be the base station (BS). The BS is distinguished from other nodes by its unlimited energy supply. The network is multi-hop, where nodes closer to the BS relay traffic of other remote nodes and probably consumes much more energy [11]. There are no assumptions about the distribution of the nodes, their homogeneity, location information etc.

The challenge of a clustering scheme is to efficiently form and maintain a connected disjointed groups of nodes in a local and distributed manner. Each group contains a single leader and several ordinary nodes.

The connectivity requirement may be achieved using one of two basic methodologies: either by an adaptive transmit power, where the CH increases its transmission power to reach the next CH or by the assignment of a set of nodes, covered by several CHs, to be gateway nodes. In this work, the second approach is used. This approach is more general because it does not assume any distribution of the nodes and it also takes into consideration interferences in the area.

An efficient scheme is used to select CHs that: (1) minimize the total transmission power aggregated over all nodes in the selected path; (2) balance the load among the nodes to prolong the network lifetime. These two requirements may contradict; e.g. a long path that consumes more energy than a short path may be selected in order to avoid battery depletion at some nodes. The network performance itself is obtained, in part, by the first requirement, where minimizing the total transmission cost results in a decrease of retransmissions as well as the data transmission time.

In order to achieve a scalable and feasible framework, the overhead of the scheme should have a constant message and time complexity per node, with low maintenance cost. Additionally, it should work well under constraints as topology changes, asynchronous environment, failures and duty cycle.

4   Efficient Clustering Using Belief Propagation

The idea of using BP for clustering was recently introduced in [14]. The affinity propagation method was set in that paper in a very general context and not in a practical manner for WSN. In this section we construct a novel BP framework for WSN and describe the algorithm for clustering.

4.1   Belief Propagation

In a probabilistic graphical model, an undirected graph $G = (V, E)$ is a set of nodes V and arcs E which represent dependencies among random variables. We denote by x_i the variable representing the set of possible states of a node i. $\psi_i(x_i)$

corresponds to a local (prior) distribution function of node i and $\psi_{ij}(x_i, x_j)$ refers to a joint function of two connected nodes i and j. These functions are also called potential functions.

In the BP method [15], [16], the inference is carried out in a local and distributed manner by each node, using a message passing technique. $m_{ij}(x_j)$ is a message from node i to node j about the state that node j should be. Node i calculates the massage using previous messages it receives from its adjacent neighbors $N(i)$. The message update rule performed by a node i in round t is:

$$m_{ij}(x_j)^t = \sum_{x_i} \psi_i(x_i)\psi_{ij}(x_i, x_j) \prod_{k \in N(i)\backslash j} m_{ki}(x_i)^{t-1}.$$

The update rule refereing to state x_j of node j is a sum over all the possible states x_i of node i. On each state, three elements are incorporated together: the local prior information $\psi_i(x_i)$, the joint function $\psi_{ij}(x_i, x_j)$ and the direct neighbors information $m_{ki}(x_i)^{t-1}$.

Upon termination, after round $\bar{t}$, the belief at a node i (the marginal of the variable) is the product of the local evidence together with all the incoming messages and a normalization constant α:

$$b_i(x_i) = \alpha\psi_i(x_i) \prod_{k \in N(i)} m_{ki}(x_i)^{\bar{t}}.$$

The BP algorithm for trees is an exact inference algorithm, which means that the belief converges to the correct marginal values in a finite number of iterations equals to the diameter of the tree.

Min-Sum Algorithm. For energy efficiency, a variation of the original BP algorithm, known also as the Min-Sum (MS) [17], is used. This algorithm uses only addition and subtraction operations, so it works well with integer values and saves the overhead of floating-point calculations. Additionally, the algorithm uses broadcast messages [18], in order to preserve communication resources.

The MS algorithm computes inference in the negative log domain, which can be equivalently viewed from the physics point of view as an energy, or cost minimization. Considering that, the goal of the MS algorithm is to minimize the overall cost over all the nodes in the network, based on the local cost functions and the constraints between the nodes. The algorithm is intuitive. Each node transmits to its neighbors a message with its local and joint costs. Each neighbor that receives the message updates its own belief accordingly and transmits the new belief, so gradually the information is propagated through the network until the nodes converge to a common belief. This convergence point minimizes the overall cost in the network. The algorithm, in its broadcast form has three basic steps:

1. *Message Passing*

   Each node i transmits its local evidence on the initial round, and its belief, based on incoming messages, on the successive rounds. Every broadcast message m_{i*} from node i includes a combined information for all its neighbors, replacing multiple unicast messages. The receivers extract the information intended for them.

$$m_{i*}(x_i)^0 = \psi_i(x_i),$$

$$m_{i*}(x_i)^t = \psi_i(x_i) + \sum_{k \in N(i)} m_{ki}(x_i)^{t-1}.$$

2. *Message Update Rule*

   Upon a reception of message $m_{j*}(x_j)^t$ from node $j \in N(i)$, node i updates its local belief by extracting the unicast information from the broadcast message of node j, using the following calculation:

$$m_{ji}(x_i)^t = \min_{x_j}\{\psi_{ij}(x_i, x_j) + m_{j*}(x_j)^t - m_{ij}(x_j)^{t-1}\}.$$

   The value of every message at round $t < 0$ is 0.

3. *Belief Calculation*

   At the end of round $\bar{t}$, where $\bar{t}$ can be chosen to be the network diameter or any other predefined limit, node i determines its final state x_i to be the one which minimizes the total cost.

$$b(x_i) = arg \min_{x_i}\{\psi_i(x_i) + \sum_{k \in N(i)} m_{ki}(x_i)^{\bar{t}}\}.$$

4.2   Cost Metrics

Basic metrics for energy-efficient and reliable communication are formulated in [19] for minimum energy path and maximum lifetime. Their analysis shows that an incorporation of the link error rates is required for reliable packet delivery, in both constant-power and variable-power scenarios. Using a similar method, two cost functions are defined. These cost functions consider residual energy, degree, topology and link quality, distance from BS (in terms of hops) and overall transmission cost, as the following.

A self cost of a potential CH is denoted by $C_i = \frac{E_i}{B_i}$, which is basically defined by the expected energy consumption in a period E_i and it's residual battery power B_i. The expected energy consumption is an estimation of the power used in the routing if that node becomes a CH. The estimation is based on the network topology: the degree of the node determines the expected reception and transmission; the distance from the BS in terms of hop count estimates the further transmission cost to the BS.

Transmission cost among two nodes or along a path is a function of the radio power level and the number of transmitted bits. Previous work [20], [21] has shown that the overall transmission cost cannot be estimated by the distance between the nodes, e.g. because of interferences, nor can be estimated by the received signal strength indicator (RSSI), due to in-correlation between low RSSI and reception rate. Link quality can evaluate the expected number of transmissions along the path. Each node estimates the quality of the links by observing packet success and loss events. Accordingly, the transmission cost between two neighbors $C_{ij} = \frac{E_{ij}}{B_i}$ is defined as a function of the energy consumption over the link E_{ij} and the remaining battery power of the transmitting node B_i.

4.3 Algorithm Description

Let x_i be a CH candidate of node i, i.e. $x_i = i$ or $x_i \in N(i)$ and x_i has a valid route to the BS and appropriate link quality.

We define $\psi_i(x_i)$ to be a local cost function of connecting node i to CH x_i.

$$\psi_i(x_i) = \begin{cases} C_i & for \ x_i = i \\ C_{ij} & for \ each \ x_i = j \in N_i. \end{cases}$$

$\psi_{ij}(x_i, x_j)$ represents the constraints between two neighbors i and j to eliminate improper assignment of CH association. The constraints are: (1) two neighbors cannot be both CHs; (2) a node can select another node to be its CH only if that node announces that it is a CH.

$$\psi_{ij}(x_i, x_j) = \begin{cases} \infty & one \ of \ the \ constraints \ is \ applied \\ 0 & otherwise. \end{cases}$$

Cluster selection is possible at each node after a period of initialization, when a route to the BS is constructed. The process is asynchronously triggered by two events: (1) when a regular node does not find a CH among its neighbors, e.g. because of topology changes; and (2) periodically, by a CH, to balance the power among the nodes in a local area. The second event also ensures that the number of CHs will not be too large, by preventing a CH from assuming that role if it is not re-selected.

The message passing algorithm is performed on a tree structure, which is a sufficient condition for convergence. The algorithm is executed in a restricted region of a 1-hop neighborhood, and as a result, it requires a constant number of messages. It stabilizes when the entire network is not affected by local changes anymore. The tree is a subtree of the general routing tree that is used in the network. In the first event, once a node triggers a clustering process because of no CH, it announces itself as a temporary CH and its 1-hop neighbors, which get its message and find it as an appropriate CH, selects it as a parent and performs the message passing on the resulting 1-hop tree. In the second event, the node is already a CH, so the message passing tree is already constructed, where all the children of that node participate in the message passing.

Each node i starts the process by broadcasting the message $m_{i*}(x_i)^0$. This message contains its cost for being a CH (infinite if it is not a valid CH) and the cost to connect other CH candidates among its neighbors. These costs are transmitted as 16-bit integer numbers together with 16-bits of identification.

The rest of the packet processing is performed according to the MS algorithm described above, where unordered messages are stored in a buffer until computation. The timer between the rounds is large enough to support asynchronous operation, but not too large, for not to adversely impact effective operation.

Topology changes during the message passing are taken into consideration as follows: (1) Cost of new neighbors is not added in the middle of the message passing operation; (2) Node who loses its parent during the message passing cannot converge with its new parent, so all its messages are ignored. The node should wait until the end of the process to find out a new CH; (3) Link breaks are marked by updating the joint cost to be infinite. A node determines which of its neighbors are in its routing subtree by inspection the messages of its parent and its descendants. A node discards cost information of nodes that are not in its subtree, because it does not have complete information about them. Messages with errors or those which are not synchronized with the messages of the node, are discarded as well.

One round before termination, a node calculates the belief about its final state - a CH or an ordinary node, and attaches the appropriate announcement to the message. After the last round a node operates according to its announcement; If it has previously announced itself as a CH it becomes a CH. Otherwise, it joins the cluster that minimizes the overall cost, according to the information it holds. In case of errors or convergence problem, it is possible that no node would declare itself as a CH. In such a scenario, nodes that do not have any alternative CH in their area start the clustering process again.

In contrast to the cost messages, which are propagated over the routing tree to avoid loops, the decision of a selected cluster is made by the information spread in the entire 1-hop neighborhoods, i.e. a node can select a CH that does not appear in its current subtree. Each node updates its clusters map according to all the broadcast messages it gets.

Once the clustering process is done, the routing tree is changed, where CHs operate as parents of the nodes who join them. Using the gateway approach to connect two clusters, a CH may choose a regular node to be its parent, if it does not have any CH that could operate as its parent. The hop metric is used to detect and avoid cycles, so after the process there is a new routing tree.

Convergence Time. BP has a fast convergence property, but when too many errors are involved, it is likely that the convergence will be more slow and into a wrong value. WSN are exposed to a large amount of communication and node failures, so the convergence to a correct state is not guaranteed. Therefore, in order to avoid impact of the physical and the MAC layers as well as other environment factors, we limit by design the number of rounds until termination to be a predefined small fixed value. On ideal environment, the convergence of the algorithm to a common belief, not including the CH announcement, is 2 rounds, equal to the diameter of the 1-hop vicinity graph. Actually, the predefined round number was set to 5. This value is robust against some synchronization and packet loss and it is sufficient in most of the cases to reach a convergence via three steps: detection of the nodes in the routing tree for correct cost calculations, computation of the belief based on cost functions and publication of the CH announcement. This number of rounds is very small in compared to other schemes and is not affected by the network size, therefore providing a scalable

Main

(1) If CH and timer expires or if ordinary node with no CH
    (1.1) Start clustering process with propagation limit of 1;
(2) Upon reception a first-round BP message from parent or from CH candidate
    and when the propagation limit is 1
    (2.1) Update your parent to be the sender node for the message passing;
    (2.2) Start clustering process with propagation limit of 0;

Clustering Process

(1) Compute local cost function and joint cost function of all the neighbors;
(2) Run the MS algorithm with the following rules:
    (2.1) Unordered messages will be stored in a buffer until computation;
    (2.2) Upon topology changes update the cost;
    (2.3) Messages with errors or synchronization problems are discarded;
(3) One round before termination attach the belief about final state to the message;
(4) Ending steps:
    (4.1) Set the power level according to the final state and update timers;
    (4.2) Select a parent: if ordinary node, select CH that minimizes the cost;
        if CH, select other CH if possible, otherwise choose an ordinary node
        as a gateway.

Fig. 1. Sketch of the Algorithm

solution in large networks. Moreover, the limitation on the number of messages means low delay and small message overhead.

5   Performance Evaluation

To evaluate the performance of clustering using BP, it has been compared with the clustering process of HEED [8], in a network model that uses gateway nodes to connect between the clusters, when two CHs cannot communicate directly.

In HEED, a node initially sets its probability to become the CH according to its residual energy. During each iteration, a node arbitrates among the CHs announcements it has received to select the lowest cost CH. If it has not received any announcements, it elects itself to become a CH with probability it has. If successful, it sends an announcement indicating its willingness to become CH. The node then doubles its probability, waits for a short iteration interval, and begins the next iteration. A node stops this process one iteration after its probability reaches the value of 1. Simulation results have shown that HEED is effective in prolonging the network lifetime and in supporting scalable data aggregation.

5.1 Simulation Model

TOSSIM, TinyOS simulator [22], was used for the analysis of the clustering algorithm. Link Estimation and Parent Selection (LEPS) [21] was used as the routing protocol in the multi-hop network. In this method, each node monitors all traffic received within the single hop range, including route updates from neighbors. Using shortest path heuristic, it manages the nearest available neighbors and decides the next hop. The Surge application was used for data aggregation, where every nodes periodically takes light sensor readings and sends them over the network to the BS. The simulator provides an environment which includes realistic properties of a network, like interferences and collisions, asymmetric links, changes in the link quality, nodes death and failure etc.

Evaluation of the communication cost, as well as the estimation of the remaining energy, were done based on the power information about Berkeley Mica2 mote [23] and using the credit point system, proposed by [24]. In this system, every node is assigned some number of points that reflect its residual energy. Each packet reception or transmission reduces points from the node, based on the packet size and the transmission power level.

Every plot was taken as an average of 27 different runs. In all the experiments, 250 nodes including a single BS were run. The simulated time was 20000 seconds, to observe the network in a stable state until it collapses when the major of the nodes die.

Every node starts with a random residual energy, ranges from 250 to 500 thousand points. The power level of a regular node was -20 dBm and the power level of a CH was -13 dBm. A timer of 540 seconds was set for periodic cluster selection triggered by each CH or by each node in BP and HEED, accordingly, and a timer of 11 seconds was used between the rounds of the message passing. Both the power levels and the timers are the default parameters used by HEED in TinyOS. We adapted the transmission rate and the aggregation rate to the network size, so the transmission rate by the application was increased to 6144 milliseconds. Every CHs that receives the packets aggregates them and transmit them every 3 minutes. The other parameters are taken to be the defaults defined in TOSSIM.

5.2 Network Performance

We first study the network performance of the two algorithms, in terms of data packets received by the BS. Each node constantly transmits data points to its CH which aggregates all the points into a single packet and forwards them toward the BS.

As one can see in Figure 2, clustering with BP achieves more than 40% higher throughput than HEED, where the data points received by the BS are significantly greater. This higher throughput is expressed by both data collection rate and time.

The trend of the data rate during the network lifetime is shown in Figure 3. In Figure 3(a), there is an increase in the data rate over time, both because the

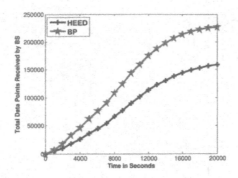

Fig. 2. Data collection time

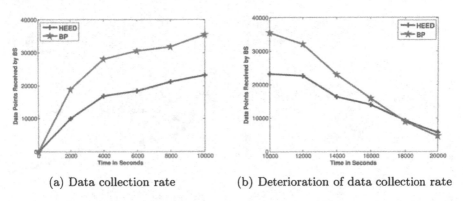

(a) Data collection rate   (b) Deterioration of data collection rate

Fig. 3. Data collection rate during the network lifetime

network becomes more stable and also because nodes start to die, so the network experiences less interferences. The number of live nodes in the system decreases to about 150 nodes at time 10000, but the network is still well connected and only the nodes' redundancy is removed. From this time, the nodes die quickly, so the connectivity of the network and its coverage rapidly decrease. Since the data rate of BP is larger than HEED, the deterioration is steeper.

The advantage of BP can be explained by several network parameters, which are all a result of the fact that BP selects CH better. The non-optimized routing of HEED can be shown by the average hop count of HEED, as presented in Figure 4 which is larger than BP. This means that the number of transmissions in the network may increase, so the number of interferences and the dropped packets increase as well.

Better deployment and network stability may be another reason for the advantage of BP over HEED. The estimated number of CHs in the system during each period of time is presented in Figure 5. Each period is about 540 seconds, with a single periodic clustering process. The figure shows the network state from the beginning with 250 nodes, until about 150 nodes are left, at which point (in periods 11-13) nodes start to die. At the beginning, BP has less CHs

Time (s)	HEED	BP
2000	5.11	3.04
4000	4.11	2.83
6000	3.61	2.73
8000	3.93	2.67
10000	3.88	2.55
12000	3.39	2.51
14000	3.81	2.44
16000	3.58	2.42
18000	3.46	2.38
20000	3.51	2.36

Fig. 4. Average hop count

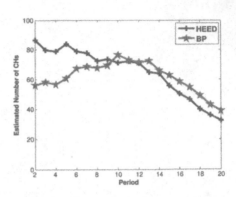

Fig. 5. Estimated number of CHs

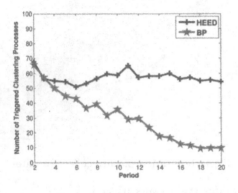

Fig. 6. Triggered clustering processes

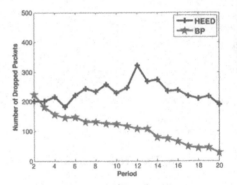

Fig. 7. Dropped packets

in the system which implies better aggregation, less transmission cost and interferences. Once nodes start to die, the number of CHs selected by BP in the system increases proportionally to the number of nodes that are alive and to the number of CHs which are selected by HEED. The intersection of BP and HEED in periods 11 and 12 is a result of the decrease in the number of CHs in HEED and the increased number of CHs, in proportion to the number of alive nodes, by BP. The increased number of CHs achieves better coverage and deployment and improves the network connectivity. The network with BP performs better even under conditions of topology changes, so as a result, less clustering processes are performed and less route failures exist, as it shown in Figure 6 and Figure 7.

The number of clustering processes that are triggered in HEED increases somewhat in period 11, which can be explained by the fact that nodes start to die, and consequently some of the nodes lose their CHs. Nonetheless, with the exception of that increase, during most of the duration, the number of clustering processes that are triggered is quite similar, even during the periods when there are much fewer nodes alive. This means that the network has proportionally more clustering processes and that it is not in a stable state. On the other hand, the

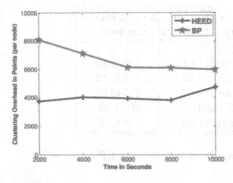
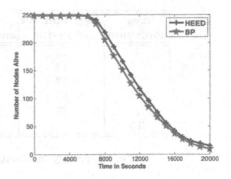

Fig. 8. Clustering process overhead   **Fig. 9.** Network lifetime

number of clustering processes that are triggered in the BP scheme decreases over time, which shows better stability even when nodes die. The number of packets that are dropped because of no route, correlates to number of clustering processes that are triggered because of no CHs, and presents the same trend.

It is important to note that no retransmission is done in the simulation. When retransmission is performed, HEED is expected to perform much worse than BP, since retransmission means more interferences and more energy consumption.

5.3 Clustering Overhead

Although BP and HEED have both a constant and consistent number of rounds in the clustering process, BP suffers from more overhead during the clustering process. This is because the messages of BP are larger than HEED. BP messages, at the extreme, might reach up to 74 Bytes (17 cost entries with identification of total 4 Bytes plus header of about 6 Bytes), while HEED message have size of 29 Bytes at most. In fact, BP messages are usually not that long, and do not reach that limit, but still the messages are longer than HEED, so the transmission cost is higher.

Figure 8 shows that at the start of the simulation, the overhead of BP is about double the HEED overhead. Later, when the network becomes more stable, BP performs less re-clustering than HEED. HEED performs more because nodes die, so this difference significantly decreases.

5.4 Energy Characteristics

Network Lifetime. BP achieves better network performance and reduces the transmission cost as well. However, the network lifetime, measured by the number of alive nodes of BP and HEED are quite similar, with a marginally (very small) advantage of HEED, as presented in Figure 9. This results from the fact that the total number of packets that are forwarded in the network is significantly greater in BP than HEED. This implies a higher total transmission cost. BP pays for transmission of a single packet much less than HEED pays, as a

Avg. hop count	Avg. number of nodes	Avg. initial energy (points)	Avg. lifetime (seconds)
1	13	374933.48	11673.37
1.5	14	394017.97	12727.69
2	57	388017.87	13047.62
2.5	81	388938.62	12546.50
3	76	335469.51	9587.23
3.5	8	292071.86	7800.46

Fig. 10. Energy information about the nodes in BP

result of the CHs' selection but over the network lifetime the overall transmission cost is similar.

When measuring the network lifetime as the time that the network is available for providing services, we can see in Figure 3(b) that BP succeeds in achieving better performance than HEED, until very close to the end. Only from time 18000, HEED has a slight advantage in the throughput, but this has no real meaning because there are about 20 nodes in the network and anyway the network does not operate appropriately. Therefore, from service availability point of view, BP has better overall network connectivity than HEED and thus better network lifetime.

Power and Load Balancing. In multi-hop communication, the nodes closest to the BS usually tend to be burdened with a heavy relay traffic load and to die first. This is the hot-spot problem and many clustering algorithms suffer from it. To verify that this problem does not occur in BP, we analyze the energy characteristics of the nodes based on their distance from the BS.

A node with some physical distance from the BS can have different hop distances over time. For example, a node with distance 1.5 from the BS, can sometimes be connected directly to the BS and sometimes connected via a CH. The different hop count is mostly a result of link quality, which is affected by many network parameters.

We explore on the general concepts that arise from Figure 10 and not from the specific values, since the nodes start with a random initial energy, which definitely affects the network lifetime, even when power balancing takes place.

As shown, both, nodes that are very close to the BS, with distance 1-1.5 and more remote nodes, with distance 2-2.5 (that start with comparable initial energy) have similar lifetime. This means that the BP method succeeds in achieving power-balancing in the core of the network and it does not suffer from the hot-spot problem.

It is interesting to see that more remote nodes (distance 3-3.5) not only start with significantly less residual energy, but their lifetime is shorter. The reason for the initial low energy is that nodes with low residual energy usually would not be selected as CH, and this means that their average distance is larger because they are constantly connected to a CH one hop farther. The explanation for the short lifetime of those nodes, in general, is that they are located at the edge of the network. Nodes at the edge, usually have less neighbors and less chance for having CHs around, so they experience more topology changes and usually perform further frequent clustering processes, which result in more overhead as well. This overhead have a considerable effect on the nodes' lifetime.

6 Conclusions and Future Work

This paper presents a novel distributed inference scheme, based on BP, for efficient clustering in multi-hop WSN. This inference scheme selects CHs that minimize the overall transmission cost and at the same time balance the power among the nodes, for a longer network lifetime. Utilization of all available information, is more optimal than current solutions, and leads to a significant improvement in the network performance.

Using simulations, we show that the BP algorithm succeeds in improving the data transmission time and rate, so at the same network lifetime as the HEED scheme, the overall throughput of BP is increased by more than 40%. Moreover, clustering using BP mitigates the hot-spot problem by providing power and load balancing among the nodes.

The BP framework that has been proposed is a feasible and realistic inference scheme, and can be effective for many other applications. The special attention to energy constrains and the fact that no assumptions were made regarding the network topology or size, differs this framework from other schemes for WSN that are based on BP, and makes it more practical and scalable to large networks with their dynamics.

Comparing the BP algorithm with an optimal clustering algorithm and applying methods in distributed inference to reduce the communication load, may be a useful area for future work.

References

1. Younis, O., Krunz, M., Ramasubramaian, S.: Node clustering in wireless sensor networks: Recent developments and deployment challanges. IEEE Network Magazine (2006)
2. Yu, J.Y., Chong, P.H.J.: A survey of clustering schemes for mobile ad hoc networks. IEEE Communications Surveys & Tutorials 7(1) (2005)
3. Pearl, J.: Probabilistic Reasoning in Intelligent Systems: Networks of Plausible Inference. Morgan Kaufmann, San Francisco (1988)
4. Crick, C., Pfeffer, A.: Loopy belief propagation as a basis for communication in sensor networks. In: UAI 2003. Proceedings of the 19th Annual Conference on Uncertainty in Artificial Intelligence (2003)
5. Ihler, A.T., Fisher III, J.W., Moses, R.L., Willsky, A.S.: Nonparametric belief propagation for self-calibration in sensor networks. IEEE Journal of Selected Areas in Communication (2005)
6. Schiff, J., Antonelli, D., Dimakis, A.G., Chu, D., Wainwright, M.J.: Robust message-passing for statistical inference in sensor networks. In: IPSN 2007. Proceedings of the 6th International Conference on Information Processing in Sensor Networks (2007)

7. Heinzelman, W.R., Chandrakasan, A.P., Balakrishnan, H.: An application-specific protocol architecture for wireless microsensor networks. IEEE Transactions on Wireless Communications 1(4) (2002)
8. Younis, O., Fahmy, S.: HEED: A hybrid, energy-efficient, distributed clustering approach for ad hoc sensor networks. IEEE Transactions on Mobile Computing 3(4) (2004)
9. Qin, M., Zimmermann, R.: VCA: An energy-efficient voting-based clustering algorithm for sensor networks. Journal of Universal Computer Science 13(1) (2007)
10. Chatterjee, M., Das, S.K., Turgut, D.: WCA: A weighted clustering algorithm for mobile ad hoc networks. Cluster Computing 5(2) (2002)
11. Li, C., Ye, M., Chen, G., Wu, J.: An energy-efficient unequal clustering mechanism for wireless sensor networks. In: MASS 2005. Proceedings of the 2nd IEEE International Conference on Mobile Ad-hoc and Sensor Systems (2005)
12. He, Y., Zhang, Y., Ji, Y., Shen, X.S.: A new energy efficient approach by separating data collection and data report in wireless sensor networks. In: IWCMC 2006. Proceedings of the International Wireless Communications and Mobile Computing Conference (2006)
13. Kiri, Y., Sugano, M., Murata, M.: On characteristics of multi-hop communication in large-scale clustered sensor networks. IEICE Transactions on Communications E90-B (2007)
14. Frey, B.J., Dueck, D.: Clustering by passing messages between data points. Science (2007)
15. Yedidia, J.S., Freeman, W.T., Weiss, Y.: Understanding belief propagation and its generalizations. Technical Report TR-2001-22, Mitsubishi Electric Research Laboratories (2002)
16. Jordan, M.I., Weiss, Y.: Probabilistic inference in graphical models. In: The Handbook of Brain Theory and Neural Networks, MIT Press, Cambridge (2002)
17. Wiberg, N.: Codes and Decoding on General Graphs. PhD thesis, Dept. of Electrical Engineering, Linköping, Sweden (1996)
18. Bickson, D., Dolev, D., Weiss, Y.: Modified belief propagation algorithm for energy saving in wireless and sensor networks. Technical report, The Hebrew University of Jerusalem (2005)
19. Banerjee, S., Misra, A.: Energy efficient reliable communication for multi-hop wireless networks. CM/Kluwer Journal of Wireless Networks (WINET) (2005)
20. Ault, A., Coyle, E., Zhong, X.: K-nearest-neighbor analysis of received signal strength distance estimation across environments. In: WiNMee 2005. Proceedings of the 1st Workshop on Wireless Network Measurements (2005)
21. Woo, A., Tong, T., Culler, D.: Taming the underlying challenges of reliable multihop routing in sensor networks. In: SenSys 2003. Proceedings of the 1st International Conference on Embedded Networked Sensor Systems (2003)
22. TinyOS, http://www.tinyos.net/
23. Shnayder, V., Hempstead, M., Chen, B., Allen, G.W., Welsh, M.: Simulating the power consumption of large-scale sensor network applications. In: SenSys 2004. Proceedings of the 2nd International Conference on Embedded Networked Sensor Systems (2004)
24. Younis, O., Fahmy, S.: An experimental study of routing and data aggregation in sensor networks. In: MASS 2005. Proceedings of the 2nd IEEE International Conference on Mobile Ad-hoc and Sensor Systems (2005)

Lifetime Maximization in Wireless Sensor Networks by Distributed Binary Search

André Schumacher, Pekka Orponen, Thorn Thaler, and Harri Haanpää

Lab. for Theoretical Computer Science, TKK – Helsinki University of Technology,
P.O. Box 5400, FI-02015 TKK, Finland
Andre.Schumacher@tkk.fi, Pekka.Orponen@tkk.fi,
Tthaler@tcs.hut.fi, Harri.Haanpaa@tkk.fi

Abstract. We consider the problem of determining the transmission power assignment that maximizes the lifetime of a data-gathering wireless sensor network with stationary nodes and static transmission power levels. We present a simple and efficient distributed algorithm for this task that works by establishing the minimum power level at which the network stays connected. The algorithm is based on a binary search over the range of feasible transmission power levels and does not require prior knowledge of network topology. We study the performance of the resulting BSPAN protocol by network simulations and compare the number of control messages required by BSPAN to two other recently proposed methods, the Distributed Min-Max Tree (DMMT) and Maximum Lifetime Spanner (MLS) algorithms. We find that BSPAN outperforms both DMMT and MLS significantly.

1 Introduction

Consider a group of sensors newly deployed in an environment. In many applications, it is desirable to have the network to self-configure, i.e. to have the nodes after wakeup contact their neighbors in order to decide where to forward the collected data, at what intervals, transmission power levels etc. One important goal of this self-configuration process is to determine data gathering and transmission protocols so that the operational time of the network, for given initial battery levels, is maximized [1, 2].

We address this lifetime maximization problem in the setting where it is the task for a network of stationary nodes to provide a roughly uniform, low-intensity stream of data to a designated sink node. Possible application scenarios include monitoring some environmental parameters (temperature, humidity, chemical concentrations) in a given region or, say, a forest-fire alarm network, where most of the data traffic consists of regular "status ok" messages.

More specifically, we consider the problem of determining transmission power levels for the nodes so that, under the assumption of uniform traffic load per node, all the nodes maintain connectivity to the sink for a maximum amount of time. In this paper we only consider the case of static power assignments, i.e. we assume that once the transmission power levels have been set, they stay the same

R. Verdone (Ed.): EWSN 2008, LNCS 4913, pp. 237–252, 2008.

throughout the operating life of the network. We also assume that transmission costs have a dominant effect on the lifetime on the nodes, which may operate a sleep-scheduling scheme [3].

Under these assumptions of stationary nodes, uniform traffic load and static power assignments, the goal of maximizing the lifetime of a network is in fact equivalent to finding the lowest possible transmission power levels for the nodes that suffice to make all of the network connected to the sink. This version of the problem was considered by Lloyd et al. [4] who presented a simple and efficient binary search based solution to it, assuming that the full internode transmission power threshold matrix of the network is centrally available.

Our Binary Search for Minmax Power Spanner (BSPAN) algorithm presented below is basically a distributed implementation of the "binary search over transmission power levels" idea of Lloyd et al. [4]. However, getting this natural approach to work in a fully distributed environment, starting in an initial state where the nodes upon wakeup know nothing about their neighbors, let alone the global topology of the network, is a somewhat nontrivial task. Nevertheless, we have implemented this approach down to the level of a protocol agent in the ns2 [5] simulator, and it shows quite competitive performance in comparison with other recently proposed approaches to the same task. In graph-theoretic terms the algorithm finds a spanning tree with maximum edge cost at most ϵ greater than the minimum maximum edge cost possible, where ϵ is a parameter of the algorithm. Thus we obtain a power assignment that, to arbitrary accuracy, maximizes the time for which we can keep the network connected.

The rest of the paper is organized as follows. The following section overviews some of the related work on lifetime maximization, and Section 3 gives a precise formulation of the version of the problem we consider. Section 4 describes our distributed method for finding a spanning tree of a given network with minimum maximum transmission cost. In Section 5 we evaluate our proposed BSPAN algorithm in terms of the number of required control messages, and compare it to the performance of the Distributed Min-Max Tree algorithm proposed in [6] and the Maximum Lifetime Spanner (MLS) algorithm proposed in [7]. For our experimental comparison we use the ns2 network simulator. Section 6 summarizes the paper.

2   Related Work

The problem of minimizing the maximum transmission power required to establish connectivity has been considered previously in the literature several times. One of the earliest papers on the topic is the work of Ramanathan and Rosales-Hain [8], which addresses the problem in the setting of maximizing the lifetime of a single-session broadcast. Ramanathan and Rosales-Hain propose a centralized algorithm for finding the minimum maximum (minmax) transmission power level that maintains network connectivity, as well as two simple distributed heuristics that aim at achieving the same. Their distributed heuristics, however, are suboptimal and do not necessarily guarantee connectivity in all cases.

Kang and Poovendran [9] discuss several problems related to dynamic lifetime maximization, such as the issue of non-uniform energy levels. They also emphasize the importance of considering the minmax energy metric rather than the more often addressed minimum total energy metric for the purpose of maximizing network lifetime. For a distributed implementation, Kang and Poovendran rely on distributed methods for constructing minimum spanning trees, such as the algorithm of Gallager, Humblet and Spira [10]. These techniques are, however, rather involved, and we complement this work by suggesting an efficient and much simpler method for computing the minmax edge cost required for connectivity. For a discussion of the two different objectives, minimizing total transmission power and minimizing maximum transmission power, see e.g. [4,9].

The problem of minimizing the *total*, as opposed to minmax, network transmission power required for connectivity has been studied extensively (cf. e.g. [4] and the references therein). Rodoplu and Meng [11] present a distributed algorithm for this problem that is based on the concept of *relay regions*: each node is aware of its own geographic location and the location of its neighbors. Based on a path-loss model, nodes can locally determine which neighbor they should forward the message to in order to minimize the total energy consumption. The algorithm proposed in [11] is optimal but requires extensive assumptions, such as the availability of location information and a specific path-loss model.

In a recent work, Guo, Yang, and Leung [6] proposed a distributed algorithm DMMT (Distributed Min-Max Tree) for the construction of multicast trees with minimum maximum transmission cost, following Prim's algorithm for constructing minimum spanning trees. Since their technique can easily be adapted also for the purpose of sensor network lifetime maximization, and seems to be the proposal in the literature closest to our BSPAN approach, we conducted an experimental comparison of the runtime behavior of the algorithms DMMT, the recently proposed Maximum Lifetime Spanner (MLS) algorithm [7] and our proposed BSPAN algorithm.

3   The Lifetime Maximization Problem

We consider a wireless sensor network composed of stationary nodes with distinct identifiers, operating in a data-gathering scenario. Each node is able to vary its transmission power, either using a possibly large set of discrete power levels, or by choosing the power from a continuous range of possible values. We further assume that each node has a finite energy budget that is consumed during the operation of the network and whose value is initially the same for all nodes. We consider a scenario where the energy consumed by wireless transmission dominates over energy consumed by computation or sensing. We further assume that traffic is generated uniformly over the nodes and that data aggregation techniques can possibly be applied, thereby yielding a close to uniform load within the network.

In order to maintain connectivity to a neighbor u, each node v has to spend some energy that depends on v's transmission power level. Each node has the same maximum transmission power p^{max} that must not be exceeded. We assume that the link costs are symmetric, so that if v can reach u at a certain power, then u can also reach v at the same power; this is the case for example if the costs represent signal attenuation resulting from a deterministic path-loss model that only depends on the pairwise distance of nodes. We consider the notion of lifetime that regards all nodes as equally important, so that the objective is to maximize the time span after which the first node runs out of energy [12].

The transmission structure of the network is modelled as a graph $G = (V, E)$ with an associated edge cost function $\delta : E \mapsto \mathbb{R}^+$. Here δ is scaled so that v can reach u as long as $\tau(v) \geq \delta(v, u) p^{max}$. A transmission power assignment $\tau : V \mapsto \mathbb{R}^+$ induces a graph $G(\tau) = (V, E(\tau))$ whose edges represent the radio links that are supported by the given assignment τ: an edge (v, u) is an element of $E(\tau)$ if and only if $\tau(v) \geq \delta(v, u) p^{max}$, i.e. if and only if node v transmits at a power that is sufficient for u to correctly receive messages from v. For simplicity, we assume that $G(\tau^{max})$ with $\tau^{max}(v) = p^{max}$ for all v is a connected graph.

We consider the problem of finding a static transmission power assignment $\tau : V \mapsto [0, p^{max}]$, such that the lifetime of the network is maximized while the network remains connected. Within the context of this problem, any power assignment τ that connects the network induces a spanning subgraph with some maximum edge cost $\alpha = \max_{(v,u) \in E(\tau)} \delta(v, u)$; we aim to find a power assignment that minimizes α. Although this condition generally does not uniquely determine τ, choosing $\tau(v) = \alpha p^{max}$ for all nodes v does not decrease the lifetime. The power assignment τ is considered to be fixed after it has been once determined during the initial network setup. Note that this problem is considerably different from the case of computing a dynamic assignment of power levels, which is a computationally more complex problem [13].

Definition 1. *Given a set of nodes V, and an edge cost function $\delta : V \times V \mapsto \mathbb{R}^+$, a graph $G = (V, E)$ is an α-spanner if G is connected and $\delta(v, u) \leq \alpha$ for each edge $(v, u) \in E$.*

In other words, an α-spanner is a connected spanning graph for the nodes in V where the no edge has cost greater than α. Note that since we normalize the edge costs for any network a 1-spanner exists exactly when the network can be connected by the nodes sending at full power.

Definition 2. *For given V and δ, an α-spanner is ϵ-optimal, if $\alpha' \geq \alpha - \epsilon$ for all α'-spanners.*

A 0-optimal α-spanner has a maximum edge cost α, but there are no spanners with only edges of cost less than α; thus, we also call such spanner a *minmax cost spanner*. Network lifetime can now be maximized by determining the minmax cost spanner (V, E) and choosing the power assignment $\tau(v) = p^{max} \max_{(v,u) \in E} \delta(v, u)$.

4 Binary Search for a Minmax Power Spanner

We propose a distributed algorithm for determining an ϵ-optimal α-spanner, given a graph with edge costs and the accuracy parameter ϵ. The algorithm determines transmission power levels that maximize the time until the first node runs out of energy.

The resulting protocol BSPAN consists of three stages. All stages are initiated by a designated reference node which also detects their termination (except for the final stage that only requires local termination), but otherwise the computations proceed without central coordination. The protocol thus admits an efficient implementation in a distributed setting such as a wireless sensor network.

In the first stage, nodes collect neighborhood information and estimate link costs by transmitting and receiving beacon messages. The reference node also obtains a count of the number of nodes in the network, assuming the transmission graph $G(\tau_{max})$ is connected. The second stage of the protocol performs a binary search over the range of possible transmission power levels. The final stage consists of a network broadcast in which the reference node notifies all other nodes of the global termination of the algorithm and the resulting minmax power level. The three stages of the BSPAN protocol are executed in the order indicated in Fig. 1. We now discuss the three stages of the protocol in more detail.

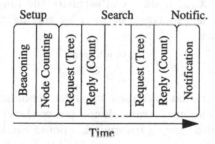

Fig. 1. Overview of the different stages of the BSPAN protocol

4.1 Setup Stage

The setup stage as described in Algorithm 1 first finds a spanning tree of the transmission graph by a process of beaconing at maximum transmission power p^{max}. Each node, once it has joined the spanning tree under construction, starts sending a sequence of beacon messages using random delays between consecutive messages. These beacons enable nodes to discover their neighbors, estimate the cost of their incident edges in the transmission graph and determine whether they are leaf nodes in the spanning tree. When the beaconing sequence has terminated, a reply message is transmitted along the attained spanning tree edges to the reference node, starting at the leaf nodes. This reply message contains a count of the number of child nodes of each node, so that the reference node eventually obtains a count of the total number of nodes in the network. More specifically, in a beacon message beacon(v, f) the parameter v denotes the identity of the beaconing node and f is its parent in the spanning tree being constructed; in a reply message reply(v, count) the parameter v is again the identity of the sender, and count represents the number of nodes in the subtree rooted at v.

The setup stage is initiated as if the reference node had received a beacon message. Upon receiving a beacon message from a node u for the first time, each node v sends the message beacon(v, u) and schedules a number of retransmissions using random delays. After transmitting the beacon for the first time, v starts listening for messages from neighboring nodes and records their presence in a neighbor list together with a flag indicating whether the neighbor is a child node in the spanning tree. Note that the neighbor u is a child of v, if u includes the information that it previously received the beacon from v in the message. For each received beacon, v also estimates a lower bound on the transmission power that is required to reach the neighboring node.

More specifically, we consider a message that a node v receives from node u, received with power p^{recv}, arrived successfully if $p^{\text{recv}} \geq p^{\text{thresh}}$, where p^{thresh} is the threshold power required for a successful transmission (disregarding interference). In our simulations, the power p^{recv} is computed by the propagation model under consideration. Assuming that the received power depends linearly on the sending power, $p^{\text{recv}} = X_{u,v} p^{\text{send}}$, and the receiver knows the sending power used, the receiver v can estimate the attenuation coefficient $X_{u,v} = p^{\text{recv}}/p^{\text{send}}$. Assuming that $X_{v,u} = X_{u,v}$, node v can estimate the minimum transmission power p^{min} it needs to use to transmit to u by solving $p^{\text{thresh}} = X_{v,u} p^{\text{min}}$. Combining these, we have

$$p^{\text{min}} = \frac{p^{\text{thresh}} \, p^{\text{send}}}{p^{\text{recv}}},$$

where p^{send} is the power that was used by u for sending. If the assumption does not hold or if the measured transmission power shows random variations, then beacon messages with varying transmission power can be used for the same purpose, similar to the techniques proposed in [14]. Recall that the link costs $\delta(v, u)$ are normalized so that the minimum power required for v to send to u is $p^{\text{min}} = \delta(v, u) p^{\text{max}}$; due to the normalization the link costs lie in the interval $[0, 1]$, and v can estimate the link cost as $\delta(v, u) = p^{\text{min}}/p^{\text{max}}$, or if the maximum power was used for sending, $p^{\text{send}} = p^{\text{max}}$ and $\delta(v, u) = p^{\text{thresh}}/p^{\text{recv}}$.

When v has sent a certain number of beacon messages, it decides that the setup phase has locally terminated. In the case that v discovers itself to be a leaf node of the constructed spanning tree, it sends a reply message to its father reporting a node count of one. If v is not a leaf node it waits until it receives replies from all its children before it sends a reply to its father that contains its child counts incremented by one, indicating the termination within the subtree rooted at v. When the reference node has received replies from all its child nodes the setup stage has terminated.

For measuring the strength of arriving radio signals, one can utilize for example Received Signal Strength Indication (RSSI) for a system with IEEE 802.11 network interfaces or, alternatively, methods similar to the ones proposed in [14].

Algorithm 1. Setup stage

node v with variables beacon_count, beacon_delay, expecting_reply_from, father,
neighbor_list, node_count, rand, timer;

at start
    node_count $\leftarrow$ 0; expecting_reply_from $\leftarrow \emptyset$;
    enter state IDLE;

in state IDLE   // wait for incoming beacon messages
    if beacon(u, f') is received with power p^{recv} **then**
        father $\leftarrow u$; $\delta \leftarrow p^{\mathrm{thresh}}/p^{\mathrm{recv}}$;   // estimate link cost
        neighbor_list $\leftarrow$ neighbor_list $\cup$ (u, δ);
        broadcast beacon(v, father) at power p^{max};
        timer $\leftarrow$ new beacon event after rand(0,beacon_delay);
        enter state BEACON;
    end

in state BEACON   // send beacon_repetitions many beacons with random delay
    if beacon(u, f') is received with power p^{recv} **then**
        $\delta \leftarrow p^{\mathrm{thresh}}/p^{\mathrm{recv}}$;   // estimate link cost
        neighbor_list $\leftarrow$ neighbor_list $\cup$ (u, δ);
        if $f' = v$ **then** expecting_reply_from $\leftarrow$ expecting_reply_from $\cup$ $\{u\}$;
    end
    if reply(u, count) is received with power p^{recv} **then**
        expecting_reply_from $\leftarrow$ expecting_reply_from $\setminus$ $\{u\}$;
        if expecting_reply_from $= \emptyset$ and beacon_count $=$ beacon_repetitions **then**
            unicast reply$(v, \text{node\_count} + \text{count} + 1)$ at power p^{max} to father;
            enter state SETUP_FINISHED;   // starts the next stage
        else
            node_count $\leftarrow$ node_count $+$ count;
        end
    end
    if timer triggers new beacon event **then**
        broadcast beacon(v, father) at power p^{max};
        if beacon_count $<$ beacon_repetitions **then**
            beacon_count $\leftarrow$ beacon_count $+ 1$;
            timer $\leftarrow$ new beacon event after rand(0,beacon_delay);
        else if expecting_reply_from $= \emptyset$ **then**
            unicast reply$(v, \text{node\_count} + 1)$ at power p^{max} to father;
            enter state SETUP_FINISHED;   // starts the next stage
        end
    end

To obtain the correct neighborhood information for all the nodes, in most cases
the number of retransmissions for the beacon messages can be fairly small. In the
absence of interference and resulting collisions, it would be even sufficient that
each node beacons exactly once. Thus, the message complexity of the beaconing
stage is $O(N)$, where N is the number of nodes in the network.

4.2   Search Stage

After the global termination of the setup stage, each node has information of all other nodes in its maximum transmission range and the costs of the incident edges. The reference node also knows the total number of nodes within the network. In the second stage Algorithm 2 performs a binary search over the range of possible transmission power levels, coordinated at the reference node. At each iteration of the algorithm, the reference node initiates the computation of a rooted tree spanning the nodes that can be reached from the reference node using paths with maximum edge cost at most α. The reference node then checks whether this tree spans all nodes in the network. After the search has terminated, the reference node informs all other nodes about the termination and the minimum edge cost necessary to connect all nodes. This cost can then be used to locally determine the transmission power level required at each node.

Each iteration of the binary search algorithm consists of two steps: The first step is initiated by the reference node and consists of a flooding of request messages over edges with cost at most α. The second step consists of a convergecast of reply messages back to the reference node in order to count the nodes in the tree computed in the first step. This count is then compared by the reference node to the total number of nodes in the network.

The request messages are of the form (v, α, f) where v is the identity of the sending node, α is the maximum allowable link cost in this iteration, and f is the parent of node v. In the first step, each node v, upon receiving a request from a neighbor u, broadcasts a request message at most(!) once by broadcasting it to all neighboring nodes. We assume that all messages are sent at maximum power, although that assumption is not critical to the algorithm: choosing a power corresponding to α would be possible as well. Node v decides that sending the message is required under the following conditions. Firstly, v must not have broadcast a request earlier in this iteration. If so, and the cost of the link (u, v) is less or equal to α, the current edge cost under consideration, u becomes the *father* of v. Note that the edge costs are assumed to be symmetric. Secondly, there must still be adjacent nodes w different from u such that the link (v, w) has cost less than or equal to α.

After sending the request (v, α, u), v waits for a request from any w that meets the condition above. In the case that v receives a request (w, α, v') from w, it will mark w as *child* if $v' = v$, and as *processed* otherwise. A neighbor marked *child* corresponds to w being v's child in the tree of the current iteration, and the label *processed* corresponds at this step to w being in the tree already with a different father node v'.

In the case that v has no child nodes, either because there are no adjacent nodes with low enough edge costs or if they all have different father nodes, it can determine that it is a leaf node in the current tree. Subsequently, it originates a reply message that contains its id and a node count of one, which it sends to its father node u. If v has at least one child w, v waits for replies from all its child nodes before sending a reply. After receiving a reply from w, node v marks w as *processed*.

Algorithm 2. Search stage

---

node v with variables α, $\alpha_{max} = 1$, ϵ, expecting_msg_from, father, lower, is_reference_node, $N(v)$, node_count, status, upper ;

at start
    if is_reference_node **then**
        $\alpha \leftarrow \alpha_{max}/2$; lower $\leftarrow 0$; upper $\leftarrow \alpha_{max}$;
    for $u \in N(v)$ **do** status$[u] \leftarrow$ processed;
    enter state RESET;

in state RESET
    father $\leftarrow$ none; node_count $\leftarrow 0$;
    if is_reference_node **then**
        if $\epsilon <$ upper $-$ lower **then enter state** SEND_REQUEST;
        else enter state SEARCH_FINISHED;
    else enter state IDLE;

in state IDLE   // wait for incoming requests
    if request(u, α', f') with $\alpha' \le \delta(u, v)$ is received **then**
        $\alpha \leftarrow \alpha'$; father $\leftarrow u$;
        enter state SEND_REQUEST;
    end

in state SEND_REQUEST   // broadcast a request to neighboring nodes
    expecting_msg_from $\leftarrow \{w \in N(v) \setminus \{\text{father}\} \mid \delta(v, w) \le \alpha\}$;
    for $w \in$ expecting_msg_from **do** status$[w] \leftarrow$ wait;
    if expecting_msg_from $\ne \emptyset$ **then**
        broadcast request$(v, \alpha, \text{father})$;
    enter state PROCESSING;

in state PROCESSING   // process requests, wait for replies
    if request(u, α', f') is received **then**
        if $f' = v$ **then**   // u has acknowledged v as its father
            status$[u] \leftarrow$ child;
        else   // u has father f' different from v
            status$[u] \leftarrow$ processed;
    end
    if reply(u, nodes) is received **then**
        status$[u] \leftarrow$ processed; node_count $\leftarrow$ node_count $+$ nodes;
    if status$[w] =$ processed for all $w \in N(v) \setminus \{\text{father}\}$ **then**   // end of iteration
        if is_reference_node **then**
            if total_nodes $=$ node_count **then** upper $\leftarrow \alpha$;
            else lower $\leftarrow \alpha$;
            $\alpha \leftarrow$ (upper $+$ lower)$/2$;
        else
            unicast reply$(v, \text{node\_count} + 1)$ to father;   // report node count
        enter state RESET;
    end

When v receives the last outstanding reply (all neighbors except its father are marked *processed* in v's neighbor table), v updates the last reply to contain the sum of all node counts received from its child nodes incremented by one and

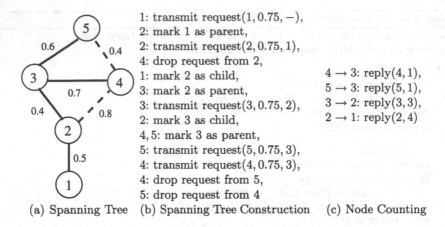

(a) Spanning Tree   (b) Spanning Tree Construction   (c) Node Counting

Fig. 2. Simple example of a single iteration of the search stage as described in Algorithm 2, initiated by reference node with id 1. (a) shows the spanning tree that results from the parent record at each node at the end of the iteration; edges that are not contained in the tree are shown dashed. (b) shows the request messages and the resulting actions of the nodes during the construction of the tree. (c) shows the replies that are sent along the attained spanning tree edges and the node counting operation. Note that requests reach all neighboring nodes (broadcast), while replies are sent from a child to its parent (unicast).

then forwards the reply to its father. Thus, the reference node can determine the number of nodes in the network reachable by edges with cost at most the current candidate edge cost α. By comparing this count with the count obtained during the setup stage, the reference node is able to determine whether α is an upper or lower bound of the minmax transmission cost and update α correspondingly. See Algorithm 2 for details and Fig. 2 for a toy example of a single iteration of the search stage.

In each iteration each node that has been reached by a request, except the reference node and nodes that have no adjacent neighbors that they could reach with cost at most α, sends exactly two messages, one request and one reply. The reference node sends a request but no reply. Therefore, the total number of messages sent in a single iteration is at most $2(N - 1) + 1$, where N is the number of nodes in the network. The binary search over intervals of size ϵ of the range $[0, 1]$ requires $\lceil \log(1/\epsilon) \rceil$ iterations, where the logarithm is taken in base 2. Thus, the search stage has message complexity $O(N \log(1/\epsilon))$.

Note that in a realistic setting the different costs resulting from the available transmission power levels are not necessarily equidistant. Instead, the possible power levels would be represented by an ordered set PL of real numbers. In this case, instead of using the range $[0, 1]$ to represent the edge costs, one would perform a search on the set of available power levels using their rank, rather than their cost value. The number of iterations required by the algorithm would then be $\lceil \log(|PL|) \rceil$, where $|PL|$ is the number of distinct power levels.

4.3   Notification Stage

The notification stage consists of a simple network-wide broadcast by which the reference node informs all other nodes about the termination of the algorithm and the final edge cost value α (the upper bound in Algorithm 2). Notification messages are sent at power α and nodes keep track from which node they first receive a notification message. In this way, similar to the previous stages, the notification stage constructs a spanning tree of the transmission graph that is an ϵ-optimal α-spanner. From the adjacency list and by listening to notification messages all nodes can infer locally their power level assignment.

The number of messages that are required for the notification stage is at most N. However, the search stage clearly dominates the message complexity of the protocol. We therefore conclude that the complete BSPAN protocol has message complexity $O(N \log(1/\epsilon))$.

5   Experimental Evaluation

We experimentally evaluated the algorithm described in the previous section using the **ns2** [5] network simulator and compared it to two previously proposed algorithms, Distributed Min-Max Tree (DMMT) [6] and Maximum Lifetime Spanner (MLS) [7]. To measure the performance of the algorithms, we considered both the number of control messages and the time it takes for the algorithms to finish. The network topologies were generated by scattering nodes randomly in a square, whose dimensions were chosen such that the expected node density was constant for all number of nodes. We used the TwoRayGround model as the propagation model, for it perfectly meets the conditions as outlined in Section 4.1. Instances for which the placement does not yield a connected network were discarded from the simulations. We also disregard simulation runs that result in an incorrect node count due to beacon collisions during the setup stage of BSPAN, as this event possibly invalidates results obtained during the later stages. During the experiments this event occurred in at most 0.5% of runs for any network size. Refer to Table 1 for the list of simulation parameters.

Table 1. Simulation parameters; the input graphs were generated by random placement of nodes within the area, while disconnected graphs and graphs for which the beaconing did not yield the correct node count were discarded

ns2 version	2.31	Node density	1 node per 130 m×130 m
Transmission range	250 m	Number of nodes	50-500
Number of nodes	50-500	Propagation model	TwoRayGround
Max jitter (BSPAN)	0.5 s	BSPAN iterations	7
Message timeout	2.1 s	ϵ	2^{-7}
Beacon delay (max)	1.5 s	Beacon repetitions	3

5.1   Distributed Min-Max Tree Algorithm

The DMMT algorithm proposed in [6] determines for a given set M of nodes (the *multicast group*) a spanning tree with minmax edge cost. Choosing $M = V$, DMMT can be readily applied to solve the lifetime maximization problem as formulated in Section 2. In this paper, we focus on the version of the algorithm that was proposed for omnidirectional antennas.

The DMMT algorithm borrows ideas from the well-known Prim's algorithm for constructing minimum spanning trees. Prim's algorithm grows a subtree of the original graph starting from an initial node, such that in each step the minimum cost edge is added that connects one node belonging to the tree and another node not yet in the tree. After all nodes have been added, the algorithm terminates and the resulting tree forms a minimum spanning tree.

The DMMT algorithm finds a minimum power spanner by adding an additional step to each iteration, the so-called *growth phase*: After the attempt of finding the minimum outgoing-edge-cost has terminated, this cost is propagated to all tree nodes in a *join request* message. Each tree node u then forwards this message to each neighbor v that u believes is not yet in the tree if the cost of the edge (u, v) is less or equal to the minimum outgoing edge-cost. This operation corresponds to growing the tree along edges with cost less or equal to the current threshold cost. After a non-tree node has been added via an edge adjacent to the tree node, the tree node becomes the *parent node* of the newly added node which becomes a *child node* of its parent.

However, the DMMT algorithm does not necessarily always find an outgoing edge in the *search phase* of the algorithm, as is the case for an iteration of Prim's algorithm. This is due to the fact that nodes only learn about their neighbors being in the tree when these forward request messages to them and can result in costly non-progress iterations of the algorithm.

The formulation in [6] employs timers at each node in order to let the nodes distributively estimate the termination of the growth phase. In our evaluation we considered a more synchronized method initiated by the reference node to notify the nodes to switch from the growth to the search phase. This modification was considered necessary, in order to make DMMT more resilient against network failures, such as packet drops at the MAC level. Additional control messages were not taken into account for the comparisons described below.

5.2   Maximum Lifetime Spanner Algorithm

The Maximum Lifetime Spanner (MLS) algorithm proposed in [7] uses a breadth-first search approach to construct paths with minmax edge cost, which are combined to form a minmax power spanner of the transmission graph. Starting from the reference node, messages containing the lowest edge cost known so far are propagated in the network. Upon receiving a request for the first time from a neighbor v containing the maximum edge cost α on the path the request has taken from the reference node to v, each node u keeps track of its father and forwards the message to its neighbors. When u forwards the message received from v, u updates α to be the maximum of α and the cost of the edge (v, u).

If a node learns about a better route during the execution of the algorithm, it informs the old father by sending a NAK message (negative acknowledgement) to its father. Then the node changes the father to the node it learns the better route from. As soon as it has received replies form each of its neighbors, the node sends an ACK message (positive acknowledgement) to its father.

These ACK and NAK messages serve two purposes. Firstly, they allow each node to be aware about both, its father and its children, and secondly, they guarantee the termination of the algorithm. As soon as the reference node has received acknowledgements, either positive or negative, from all its neighbors, the algorithm terminates. At termination each node u knows about which of its neighbors it is responsible for. Thus, it can decide which power level it has to choose to assure connectivity.

5.3 Network Simulations

We implemented the aforementioned algorithms, BSPAN, DMMT and MLS, as protocol agents in ns2. All three protocols are initiated by the designated reference node. DMMT and MLS require topology information in the form of neighbor lists and edge costs that are loaded into the nodes prior to the execution of the algorithms. For BSPAN, the reference node starts the protocol by initiating the setup stage to obtain the weighted neighbor lists and a count of the nodes in the network. The total message counts of BSPAN, DMMT and MLS are depicted in Fig. 3(a). Both DMMT and MLS require prior topology information in the form of neighbor lists. However, as opposed to BSPAN the number of messages required for obtaining this information are not included in the total message counts of DMMT and MLS. Despite this handicap, BSPAN outperforms MLS by a factor of 3 for 50 nodes and 5 for 200 nodes. DMMT even requires between 8 and more than 40 times more messages than BSPAN and therefore does not scale well with the size of the network. One should note that BSPAN also benefits from the broadcast advantage of wireless networks.

Recall that BSPAN is guaranteed to find an ϵ-optimal spanner. For a fixed ϵ the number of messages required by BSPAN is linear in the number of nodes, whereas for a fixed number of nodes the message count for BSPAN is linear in $\log 1/\epsilon$. Figure 3(b) illustrates the effect of different values for ϵ. As opposed to DMMT and MLS, BSPAN scales well with the number of nodes. For our further observations we fixed ϵ at 2^{-7} which corresponds to a difference of less than one percent compared to the optimal value.

When evaluating running time, one has to consider the effect of timers on the performance of the different protocols. Assuming a collision free network, BSPAN would only require a timer in the setup stage of the protocol. However, as this assumption is not necessarily realistic, one has to introduce a retransmission timer into the search stage of the protocol in order to avoid the following erroneous state: When a request that was sent by a node v is not received correctly at node u due to a collision at node u, or the later request sent by u is not received due to a collision at v, the node v will end up in a deadlock. This

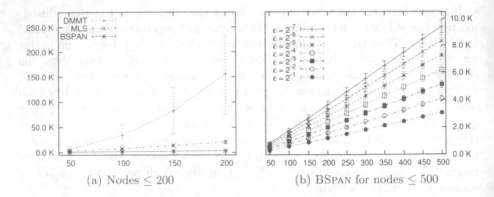

(a) Nodes ≤ 200   (b) BSPAN for nodes ≤ 500

Fig. 3. Number of messages required by BSPAN, DMMT and MLS for networks of increasing size. Errorbars represent standard deviations over 1000 repetitions. The number of messages for BSPAN includes the messages in the setup and search stages; the notification stage was excluded from the results, as it is not part of the DMMT and MLS algorithms, although required for global termination of the algorithms. The choice for ϵ in (a) is 2^{-7}. Note the different scale in (a) and (b).

is due to the fact that v waits for u to broadcast a request, possibly indicating v to be its parent, or unicast a reply message if u is in fact a leaf node.

To avoid the situation above, a retransmission timer ensures that v sends a copy of the last request by unicast every 2.1 s until the node receives any message from the particular neighbor, whose reply is outstanding. Unicast communication is sufficient as possibly not all neighbors of v are required to react. A node u that receives a retransmitted request from node v will either unicast its last transmitted request back to v in order to signal v that v is not u's parent in the

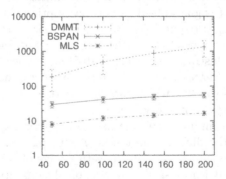

Fig. 4. Total simulated running time (in seconds). Errorbars represent standard deviations over 1000 repetitions; note that the total running times are plotted on a logarithmic scale. The duration of the notification stage of BSPAN was excluded from the results, as it is not part of the DMMT and MLS algorithms, although required for global termination of the algorithms.

current iteration, or process it as usual, if it has not processed any request in the iteration previously.

The second timer involved is used in the setup stage to allow a leaf node to wait some time before it starts to reply, in order to discover neighbors. This timer triggers after Δ = (Number of Beacons) × (Maximum Jitter) = 1.5 s after the node has broadcasted the request for the last time, since, unless all beacon messages were dropped, a potential neighbor sends its last broadcast message after Δs at the latest. In a collision free network this timer could be set to Δ = 2 × (Maximum Propagation Delay), for in the ideal case no jitter would be needed, and the only delay is due to radio propagation.

The DMMT protocol makes extensive use of timers, whose values naturally have a strong impact on the running time. Figure 4 shows that BSPAN is slightly slower than MLS, which - one could argue - is partly due to the absence of timers in MLS and that BSPAN significantly outperforms DMMT.

6 Conclusions

We have presented an efficient distributed algorithm for the problem of lifetime maximization in a wireless sensor network with stationary nodes and static transmission power assignments. Unlike many previously proposed algorithms for related problems, our algorithm does not rely on prior knowledge of the network, such as network size or neighbor lists. The algorithm is based on a binary search for the minimum maximum edge cost that is required to connect the network, where connectivity is determined in each iteration of the algorithm by counting the nodes reachable from the reference node.

The algorithm has been formulated as a network protocol BSPAN and implemented using the ns2 network simulator. In our experiments comparing the runtime behavior of BSPAN to the DMMT algorithm for constructing minmax trees and the previously proposed MLS protocol, BSPAN systematically outperforms both other algorithms in terms of number of control messages generated, and it also performs clearly better than DMMT in terms of execution times.

A natural extension of the present work would be to consider the task of lifetime maximization under dynamic transmission power assignments. This is, however, a computationally much more challenging problem than the static one considered here [13]. One possible (suboptimal) heuristic would be to build a dynamic schedule iteratively from solutions to appropriately scaled static problems, using the BSPAN protocol as an auxiliary routine.

References

1. Akyildiz, I.F., Su, W., Sankarasubramaniam, Y., Cayirci, E.: A survey on sensor networks. IEEE Communication Magazine 40(8), 102–114 (2002)
2. Cerpa, A., Estrin, D.: ASCENT: adaptive self-configuring sensor networks topologies. IEEE Transactions on Mobile Computing 3(3), 272–285 (2004)

3. Cao, Q., Abdelzaher, T., He, T., Stankovic, J.: Towards optimal sleep scheduling in sensor networks for rare-event detection. In: Proceedings of the 4th International Symposium on Information Processing in Sensor Networks, pp. 20–27. IEEE Press, Piscataway, NJ, USA (2005)
4. Lloyd, E.L., Liu, R., Marathe, M.V., Ramanathan, R., Ravi, S.: Algorithmic aspects of topology control problems for ad hoc networks. Mobile Networks and Applications 10(1-2), 19–34 (2005)
5. McCanne, S., Floyd, S., Fall, K., Varadhan, K.: The network simulator ns2 (1995) The VINT project (1995), http://www.isi.edu/nsnam/ns/
6. Guo, S., Yang, O.W.W., Leung, V.C.M.: Tree-based distributed multicast algorithms for directional communications and lifetime optimization in wireless ad hoc networks. EURASIP Journal on Wireless Communications and Networking. Article ID 98938, p. 10 (2007)
7. Haanpää, H., Schumacher, A., Thaler, T., Orponen, P.: Distributed computation of maximum lifetime spanning subgraphs in sensor networks. In: Zhang, H., Olariu, S., Cao, J., Johnson, D. (eds.) MSN 2007. LNCS, vol. 4864, Springer, Heidelberg (2007)
8. Ramanathan, R., Hain, R.: Topology control of multihop wireless networks using transmit power adjustment. In: INFOCOM. Proceedings of the Nineteenth Annual Joint Conference of the IEEE Computer and Communications Societies, pp. 404–413 (2000)
9. Kang, I., Poovendran, R.: Maximizing network lifetime of broadcasting over wireless stationary ad hoc networks. Mobile Networks and Applications 10(6), 879–896 (2005)
10. Gallager, R.G., Humblet, P.A., Spira, P.M.: A distributed algorithm for minimum-weight spanning trees. ACM Transactions on Programming Languages and Systems 5(1), 66–77 (1983)
11. Rodoplu, V., Meng, T.H.: Minimum energy mobile wireless networks. IEEE Journal on Selected Areas in Communications 17(8), 1333–1344 (1999)
12. Chang, J.H., Tassiulas, L.: Energy conserving routing in wireless ad-hoc networks. In: INFOCOM. Proceedings of the Nineteenth Annual Joint Conference of the IEEE Computer and Communications Societies, pp. 22–31 (2000)
13. Floréen, P., Kaski, P., Kohonen, J., Orponen, P.: Lifetime maximization for multicasting in energy-constrained wireless networks. IEEE Journal on Selected Areas in Communications 23(1), 117–126 (2005)
14. Kohvakka, M., Suhonen, J., Hannikainen, M., Hamalainen, T.D.: Transmission power based path loss metering for wireless sensor networks. In: 17th Annual IEEE International Symposium on Personal, Indoor and Mobile Radio Communications, pp. 1–5 (2006)

An Algorithm for Reconnecting Wireless Sensor Network Partitions

Gianluca Dini, Marco Pelagatti, and Ida Maria Savino

Dept. of Ingegneria della Informazione
University of Pisa
Via Diotisalvi 2, 56100 Pisa, Italy
{g.dini,m.pelagatti,i.savino}@iet.unipi.it

Abstract. In a Wireless Sensor Network, sensor nodes may fail for several reasons and the network may split into two or more disconnected partitions. This may deteriorate or even nullify the usefulness and effectiveness of the network. Therefore, repairing partitions is a priority. In this paper we present a method to repair network partitions by using mobile nodes. By reasoning upon the degree of connectivity with neighbours, a mobile node finds the proper position where to stop in order to re-establish connectivity. Factors influencing the method performance are singled out and criteria for their selection are discussed. Simulations show that the proposed method is effective and efficient notwithstanding packet loss.

1 Introduction

Networked Embedded Systems play an increasingly important role and affect many aspects of our lives. New applications are being developed in areas such as health-care, industrial automation, smart building and rescue operations. The European Integrated Project "Reconfigurable Ubiquitous Networked Embedded Systems" (RUNES) [1] brought together 21 industrial and academic partners with the aim of enabling the creation of large scale, distributed, heterogeneous networked embedded systems that inter-operate and adapt to their environments.

To illustrate the potential of the networked embedded systems, the project selected a disaster relief scenario, in which a fire occurs within a tunnel, much as happened in the Mont Blanc tunnel in 1999 [5]. The RUNES work in general and the disaster relief scenario in particular offer a number of interesting and challenging problems. In the rest of the paper we focus on the following.

A set of nodes with wireless communication capabilities are deployed inside the tunnel for monitoring purposes. As soon as an emergency situation occurs, for example an accident involving many cars, the nodes need to transmit data regarding the tunnel conditions to a base station responsible for tunnel control. In such a scenario, accurate and comprehensive information must be provided to the base station so that correct counter measures can be taken. It is of fundamental importance that the network would maintain connectivity, so that the

R. Verdone (Ed.): EWSN 2008, LNCS 4913, pp. 253–267, 2008.

flow of critical data to the base station is guaranteed. However, the network could be partitioned because of a malfunction of the nodes, caused by a fire, or because the presence of obstacles that deteriorate or even nullifies metrics of the Quality of Service. In such a critical situation, restoring network connectivity is a priority.

The problem of network partitioning in WSN is not entirely new even though so far has received limited attention [16]. Chong and Kumar raise the problem of partitions with a security focus [7]. So do Wood and Stankovic with respect to denial of service [17]. In [6], Cerpa and Estrin propose methods to self-configuring WSNs topologies. Although they mention the problem of network partitions as an important one, however, they leave such methods to future work. Finally, Shrivastava *et al.* propose a low overhead scheme to detect network partitioning, "cuts" in their parlance, but they do not propose any method to repair them [16].

With respect to Shrivastava *et al.*'s work, in this paper we focus on the complementary problem of restoring network connectivity. With reference to the tunnel scenario, we propose a method that uses autonomous mobile nodes. Once the base station determines the network partitioning, one or more mobile nodes are sent inside the tunnel. A mobile node is equipped with a radio transmitter-receiver so that it can communicate with the sensor nodes. Furthermore, it maintains connectivity with the base station through the wireless sensor network. By reasoning upon the degree of connectivity with neighbours, a mobile node navigates inside the tunnel until it reaches the optimal position to re-establish connectivity.

The paper is organized as follows. In Section 2 we state the system model. In Section 3 we define the problem. In Section 4 we present the algorithm the mobile nodes locally perform to restore the connectivity and we single out the main factors affecting the algorithm. In Section 5 we present a performance analysis based on simulations. Finally, in Section 6 we draw final conclusions.

2   System Model

According to the tunnel-disaster-scenario, the wireless sensor network is composed of a powerful base station and a set of low-end sensor nodes. Base station and sensor nodes have wireless capabilities and communicate through a wireless, multi-hop, ad-hoc network. We assume the resulting wireless network runs a routing algorithm that is able to cope with the failure of a "small" number of nodes by finding alternative routes [10,14,15]. However, in the case of a disaster, the number of failed nodes is "too large" and the network breaks into two or more disconnected partitions.

We assume the existence of a *Partition Detection System* (PDS), running on the base station and able to both detect the presence of network partitions and provide a rough estimation of their positions. More precisely, we assume the Shrivastava *et al.*'s partition detection system [16] that works as follows. The base station knows the position of a small subset of sensor nodes that are called the *sentinels*. Each sentinel communicates with the base station at regular

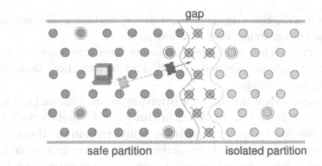

Fig. 1. The tunnel disaster-relief scenario. Double-circled nodes represent sentinels.

time intervals. Intuitively, the failure of the base station to communicate with a given sentinel is the proof that a partition containing that sentinel has formed (Figure 1). Furthermore, the sentinel position provides a rough estimation of the partition position.

Notice that even in structured environments such as a tunnel, the base station could not be able to define where exactly the failure occurs. Let us suppose that the base station knows the location of each node. So, the base station could broadcast a discovery message and then define the partition border on the basis of the not-responding nodes. Nevertheless, this solution is not suitable because too expensive in terms of time and communication overhead.

Our system includes mobile nodes (robots), that are used for repairing the network partitions. Upon detecting the presence of a partition and roughly estimating its position, the base station sends a mobile node to that position. The mobile node navigates inside the tunnel until it reaches the target position. Each mobile node is equipped with the same communication capabilities as sensor nodes so that it can communicate with sensor nodes in its neighbourhood and with the base station through the wireless sensor network. In this way, mobile nodes can reach positions that are far from the base station despite their limited radio range. We assume that the speed of a mobile node is such that its neighbourhood remains practically constant during a network round-trip time.

3   Problem Definition

Let us assume that the WSN splits in two partitions: a *safe partition*, containing the base station, and an *isolated partition*. The two partitions are separated by a *gap* of failed nodes (Figure 1). For brevity, we call *safe nodes* the nodes belonging to the safe partition and *isolated nodes* those belonging to the isolated one.

The PDS detects the network partitioning and knows that the inter-partition gap intersects the path leading to the not-responding sentinel, but the PDS is not able to exactly determine where the intersection actually occurs and how wide the inter-partition gap is. Hence, the mobile node has to determine itself the proper place where to stop according to the following conditions: 1) the mobile node is in contact with both the safe and the isolated partition; or, 2) the mobile node is in contact with the safe partition and any further movement makes the mobile node lose connectivity with that partition.

Condition 1 occurs when the safe and the isolated partition are so close to each other that a single mobile node is sufficient to reconnect them despite its limited communication range.

Condition 2 occurs when the inter-partition gap is too wide and a single mobile node is not sufficient to reconnect them. In this case the mobile node has to get as close as possible to the isolated partition while remaining always connected to the safe partition. This means the mobile node has to realise when it is about to lose connectivity with the safe partition and, consequently, stop before this event takes place.

4 Algorithm for Repairing Network Partitioning

As soon as the PDS has detected the network partitioning, the base station broadcasts a fresh number, called *epoch*, to identify the partitions. Safe nodes, that are connected with the base station, can receive the new epoch. In contrast, isolated nodes keep holding the old epoch. Notice that in real environments communication channels are not stable because of several factors including the distance between nodes, environment conditions, noise, and interference. So, a safe node could not be able to receive the new epoch.

As soon as the base station has distinguished the safe partition from the isolated one by broadcasting the epoch, it sends the mobile nodes towards the isolated partition. While navigating, each mobile node detects the partition boundary by monitoring its connectivity degree with the safe partition, i.e., the number of safe nodes it can communicate with. In fact, when the number of neighbours is below a certain threshold, it is likely that the mobile node is close to the partition boundary (Figure 2). However, a simple threshold-based approach may not be sufficient because of communication instability. In our model, we have a good communication link between a mobile node and a fixed node only if the probability for the former to receive a message is greater than a certain threshold

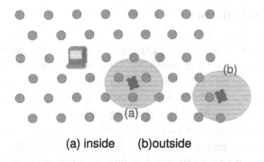

(a) inside   (b)outside

Fig. 2. Number of neighbour nodes vs. mobile node position

$\mathcal{P}_g$. So, the mobile node considers a fixed node as its neighbour if they have a good communication link.

During this phase, referred to as *Monitoring Phase*, the mobile node broadcasts an HELLO message. If a fixed node replies with a REPLY message containing the current epoch, the mobile node assumes that the fixed node certainly belongs to the safe partition. The mobile node counts how many REPLYs it receives from safe neighbours. As long as the mobile node is in the safe partition, the number of REPLYs it receives for each HELLO does not suffer strong variations. So, if the mobile node detects a decrease in the number of received REPLY messages, it could be about to lose connection with the safe partition.

It is worthwhile to notice that the mobile node may receive a REPLY message carrying an old epoch even from a safe node. In fact, a safe node could fail to receive the new epoch because of packet loss. So, if the mobile node has not detected any decrease in its neighbourhood during the Monitoring Phase, it can ignore the message containing the old epoch.

If the mobile node detects a decrease in its neighbourhood during the Monitoring Phase, it enters into the *Verification Phase*. In this phase, the mobile node verifies whether it is about to lose connection with the safe partition by broadcasting a burst of HELLO messages. If this is not the case, the mobile node returns into the Monitoring Phase. Otherwise, it verifies whether it has received a REPLY message containing the old epoch. If it is the case, the mobile node assumes that it has reached an isolated node so that the partitions have been bridged. Otherwise, the mobile node assumes that the gap is too wide and any further movement makes him lose the connectivity with the safe partition.

When the mobile node reaches the position to bridge the partitions or, at least, reduce the partition gap, it may stop and behave as an ordinary, fixed sensor node, so participating to routing and sensing, if it has sensing capabilities, and cooperating with other mobile nodes for network repairing. Alternatively, the mobile node may carry fixed sensor nodes and deploy one of them in the final position. These alternative choices influence the mobile node complexity from an electro-mechanical standpoint.

The mobile nodes could be equipped with an hardware device for the self-localization. In case of inter-partition gap too wide, the mobile node could broadcast its own position to the other mobile nodes so that they can use this information to adjust their final position. Nevertheless, each mobile node has to perform the algorithm to verify its connectivity degree with the safe partition.

Furthermore, repairing the network is not the only form of cooperation required to mobile nodes. Mobile nodes have also to cooperate to avoid crashing into one another or into obstacles. Of course, this influences the actual path of the mobile node to reach the final position. It should be noted that the actual path the node takes is independent of the problem addressed in this paper, namely finding the proper positions where to place nodes (mobile or not) to repair network partitions. For this reason we shall not consider these issues any further. Interested readers can refer to [2,4].

4.1   Algorithm for Finding the Proper Position

The Monitoring and the Verification Phase are implemented by the Monitor and Verify functions, respectively.

```
1: function Monitor(epoch)
2: begin
3:    ΔT_H = 0; replySet = ∅; round=random number;
4:    repeat/* round */
5:        wait(ΔT_H);
6:        broadcast(⟨HELLO, epoch, round⟩);
7:        setTimeOut(ΔT_R);
8:        repeat
9:            reply = receive();
10:           if (getRound(reply) == round) then
11:               replySet = replySet ∪ reply;
12:           end if
13:       until timeout strikes
14:       n_R = size(replySet);
15:       round++;
16:       ΔT_H = newInterval(n_R);
17:   until n_R > N_PS
18: end
```

Fig. 3. The Monitor function

A conceptual implementation of the Monitor function is in Figure 3. The Monitor function is organized as a sequence of rounds that starts every ΔT_H seconds. The sequence terminates when the mobile node is in the gap and about to lose connection with the safe partition. In every round, the Monitor function broadcasts an HELLO packet (line 6) and receives the corresponding REPLY packets for ΔT_R seconds from fixed nodes (lines 7-9,13). An HELLO packet has two fields: (i) an *epoch* field that specifies the epoch known to the mobile node; and (ii) a *round* field that specifies the round (of that epoch) in which the mobile node has transmitted the packet. A REPLY packet has three fields: (i) an *identifier* field that specify the fixed node identifier; (ii) an *epoch* field that specifies the epoch known by the fixed node; (iii) a *round* field that specifies the round of the HELLO packet to which the REPLY packet replies. We say that a REPLY packet is a *valid* reply for a given HELLO packet if the former carries the same round and the same epoch as the latter.

The Monitor function counts the number n_R of valid REPLY packets coming from safe nodes (line 14). If n_R is greater than a given threshold N_{PS}, Monitor assumes that the mobile node is still in the safe partition and calculates the new value for the interval ΔT_H on the basis of the n_R itself (line 16). Notice that such a computation does not take into account ΔT_R, that is usually negligible with respect to ΔT_H. On the contrary, if $n_R < N_{PS}$, the Monitor function assumes

that it is about to lose connectivity with the safe partition. So, the function ends
and the mobile node calls the Verify function to ascertain whether it is actually
in the gap between partitions.

```
1: function Verify(epoch) → [FalseAlarm, IsolatedNodeFound, InTheGap ]
2: begin
3:    replySet = ∅; round = random number; neighbours = 0
4:    while ((round < B)) do
5:        broadcast(⟨HELLO, epoch, round⟩)
6:        setTimeOut(ΔT_R);
7:        repeat
8:            reply = receive();
9:            if ((getEpoch(reply)==epoch) and (getRound (reply)==round)) then
10:               replySet = replySet ∪ reply;
11:           end if
12:           if (size(select(replySet,getId(reply)))==B_min) then
13:               neighbours++;
14:           end if
15:       until timeout strikes
16:       if (neighbours ≥ N_C) then
17:           return FalseAlarm;
18:       end if
19:       round++;
20:   end while
21:   for reply in replySet do
22:       if (getEpoch( reply ) ≠ epoch)  then
23:           return IsolatedNodeFound;
24:       end if
25:   end for
26:   return InTheGap;
27: end
```

Fig. 4. The Verify function

The conceptual implementation of the Verify function is in Figure 4. The function estimates the connectivity degree of the mobile node with the safe partition,
i.e. how many good links the mobile node has with safe nodes. The Verify function evaluates the neighbourhood by broadcasting a burst of B HELLO messages
(lines 4–20). If a fixed safe node replies with at least B_{min} valid messages, it
is considered a neighbour (lines 9–14). If the number of neighbours exceeds a
given threshold N_C, the mobile node has still enough neighbours. So, the function returns FalseAlarm (lines 16–17) and the mobile node returns to the Monitor
function.

If the number of neighbours is less than N_C, the function verifies whether it has
received a REPLY message from an isolated node. So, if it has received a REPLY
packet containing the old epoch, the function returns the value IsolatedNodeFound

(lines 21–25). Otherwise, the function assumes that the mobile node is about to disconnect from the safe partition and returns the InTheGap value (lines 26).

4.2   Algorithm Parameters

In order the algorithm performs as expected, the following parameters should be properly chosen: the *Connectivity threshold* N_C, the *Phase-Switch threshold* N_{PS}, the *Signalling interval* ΔT_H, the *Response interval* ΔT_R, and the *Burst parameters* B and B_{min}.

Let us define R_g the maximum distance covered by good links. We assume most of neighbouring nodes lie into a circle with radius R_g, whereas nodes placed outside suffer link instability. Given the radio communication range R, the parameter R_g could be defined as $R_g = \mathcal{P}_g \times R$, or calculated via experiments. Furthermore, let us define $\overline{N}_{neigh}$ the expected number of neighbours when the mobile node is in the safe partition. Given the initial node distribution δ_0, $\overline{N}_{neigh}$ can be defined as $\overline{N}_{neigh} = \lfloor \delta_0 \pi R_g^2 \rfloor$ or via experiments. Note that the nodes are subjected to failure and the network density could get not uniform. More in detail, in some areas the density could be less than the initial value δ_0.

The Connectivity Threshold N_C
The *Connectivity threshold* N_C is the minimum number of neighbours in the safe partition the mobile node has to be in contact with during the Verification Phase.

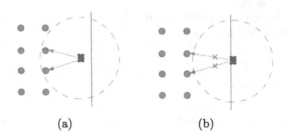

(a)   (b)

Fig. 5. A small N_C may result in disconnections

The Connectivity threshold N_C influences the algorithm performance because a too small value may cause disconnections from the safe partition. Let us consider the scenario depicted in Figure 5 where the mobile node is in contact with two neighbours. If $N_C = 1$ the mobile node keeps moving and loses the connectivity with the safe partition. Actually, the next time it checks for connections, it has already left the partition. For this reason, $N_C \geq 2$ is in general preferable. Nevertheless, a high N_C value could cause a premature stopping of the mobile node in the safe partition. So, N_C has to be below $\overline{N}_{neigh}/2$ that is the expected number of neighbours when the mobile node is crossing the border.

The Phase-Switch Threshold N_{PS}

The *Phase-Switch threshold* N_{PS} is the expected number of REPLYs the mobile node receives as it enters the gap between partitions. So, if the number of replies is lower than N_{PS}, the mobile node switches from the Monitoring Phase to the Verification phase. A high value of N_{PS} implies frequent switchings to the Verification Phase: many bursts are sent in order to verify the mobile node's connectivity, thus causing an excessive amount of messages. On the contrary, choosing a too low threshold reduces phase switchings and may cause disconnections from the safe partition if the Verification Phase is executed when the node has already crossed the border of the safe partition.

The mobile node uses this parameter to perform a first, rough detection of the partition boundary. When the mobile node crosses the border, half of the communication range lies outside the safe partition. Hence a reasonable value is $N_{PS} = \overline{N}_{neigh}/2$. Furthermore, during the Monitoring Phase, the mobile node could receive messages from poor link nodes. In order to avoid disconnections from the safe partition, the Phase-Switch threshold has to be greater than the Connectivity one. That is, $N_{PS} > N_C$.

The Signalling Interval ΔT_H

The *Signalling interval* ΔT_H is the time between two consecutive HELLO messages broadcast during the Monitoring Phase. It affects both the probability of disconnecting from the safe partition and the total number of messages exchanged during the repairing process. In order to stop in time, a mobile node needs to sample the number of its neighbours with a high frequency. Hence, a short ΔT_H is required. However, using a small interval implies an excessive amount of messages. For this reason, we opted for an adaptive calculation of ΔT_H in order to use shorter intervals only in the most critical region (i.e., when the mobile node is entering the gap between partitions).

As the mobile node gets near the safe partition boundary, the number of fixed nodes around it decreases because only a portion of its communication range lies within the safe partition. The signalling interval is calculated taking into account the worst case, when the partition border is perpendicular to the direction $\hat{v}$ of the mobile node (Figure 6).

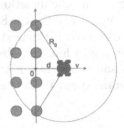

Fig. 6. Area containing neighbours

$$n_{cur}(d) = \begin{cases} \left\lfloor \frac{\overline{N}_{neigh}}{\pi} \left(\arccos \frac{d}{R_g} - \frac{d}{R_g} \sqrt{\frac{R_g^2 - d^2}{R_g^2}} \right) \right\rfloor & |d| \leq R_g \\ \overline{N}_{neigh} & d \leq -R_g \end{cases} \quad (1)$$

Let $n_{cur}(d)$ be the number of nodes within the R_g range when the mobile node is at a distance d from the safe partition border. A negative distance from the border means that the mobile node is still in the safe partition and has not crossed the border. With reference to Figure 6, $n_{cur}(d)$ is given by the Equation 1.

Since the number of neighbours assumes only discrete values in the range $[0, \overline{N}_{neigh}]$, the mobile node can construct a translation table containing the pairs $\langle n, \tilde{d}(n) \rangle$, where n is the number of neighbours and $\tilde{d}(n)$ is the maximum value so that $n_{cur}(\tilde{d}(n)) = n$. By using the translation table, the mobile node can estimate the maximum distance that can be covered without losing connectivity with the safe partition. More in detail, given the number of REPLYs n_R, the mobile node estimates its current distance from the border, $\tilde{d}(n_R)$. Note that the mobile node could receive more REPLY messages than $\overline{N}_{neigh}$ because the communication radius R is greater than R_g. In this case, the distance from the partition border is approximated with $\tilde{d}(\overline{N}_{neigh}) = -R_g$.

The next position is defined on the basis of how many nodes it has to be connected with. The mobile node has to be connected with almost N_C nodes, thus it has to stop at distance $\tilde{d}(N_C)$ from the border. Hence, the mobile node has to cover a distance $\tilde{D}$ so that $\tilde{D} \leq |\tilde{d}(n_R) - \tilde{d}(N_C)|$.

Table 1. Translation table ($\overline{N}_{neigh} = 7$)

n	2	3	4	5	6	7
$\frac{\tilde{d}(n)}{R_g}$	0.42	0.14	−0.11	−0.34	−0.56	−1

For example, with reference to Table 1, if the mobile node receives $n_R = 4$ replies and $N_C = 2$, the estimated distance that has to be covered is $\tilde{D} \leq |\tilde{d}(4) - \tilde{d}(2)| = |-0.11 - 0.42|R_g = 0.53R_g$.

Given the current position x_{cur} and the direction $\hat{v}$, the mobile node can calculate the next position $x_{nxt} = x_{cur} + \hat{v}\tilde{D}$. So, the Signalling interval ΔT_H is the time that the mobile node needs to reach the next position x_{nxt} starting from x_{cur}. It depends on the motion algorithm, i.e., obstacle advoidance algorithm, collision advoidance algorithm and so on. Let us suppose that the mobile node moves in a straight line at constant speed V. In this case, the Signalling interval is $\Delta T_H = \frac{\|x_{nxt} - x_{cur}\|}{V} = \frac{\tilde{D}}{V}$.

The Response Interval ΔT_R

The *Response time* ΔT_R is the time the mobile node waits for the REPLY messages. Since $\overline{N}_{neigh}$ is the expected number of replies when the node is in the safe partition, ΔT_R has to include at least $\overline{N}_{neigh}$ packet transmission intervals.

Furthermore, ΔT_R has to take into account the probability of collisions resulting from concurrent broadcasting. Usually, the MAC protocols use Random Backoff Scheme in order to reduce collisions. Each broadcast is delayed by a time period, called backoff time period. The protocols define how to select appropriately this backoff time. We define $\Delta T_{BO}(\overline{N}_{neigh})$ the expected backoff time period in presence of $\overline{N}_{neigh}$ nodes. So, the Response interval ΔT_R is defined as follows:

$$\Delta T_R = \overline{N}_{neigh}\Delta T_1 + \Delta T_{BO}(\overline{N}_{neigh})$$

where ΔT_1 is the time for transmitting a packet. Usually the Response interval ΔT_R is negligible with respect to the Signalling interval ΔT_H. In fact, the interval ΔT_R is a communication time, whereas ΔT_H is the time the mobile node needs to cover a given distance.

The Burst Parameters B and B_{min}
The parameter B is the number of HELLO messages the mobile node broadcasts during the Verification Phase. This burst of messages is used to find how many neighbours in the safe partition the mobile node is in contact with. The parameter B_{min} is the minimum number of REPLY messages the mobile node has to receive from a specific node in order to consider it as a neighbour.

As already specified, two nodes are neighbours if the probability of receiving a REPLY in response of a HELLO message is greater than or equal to a given $\mathcal{P}_g$. In order to evaluate this probability, a mobile node sends B HELLO messages and records how many REPLYs it receives from each fixed node. Let us suppose that r_j is the number of replies broadcast by the node j. This counter gives us a rough estimation of the reception probability: if the r_j/B ratio is greater than $\mathcal{P}_g$, we assume to have a good link.

The parameter B could be defined via experiments on the basis of $\overline{N}_{neigh}$. That is, B is the minimum burst size so that the expected number of replying nodes is $\overline{N}_{neigh}$. Furthermore, given B and $\mathcal{P}_g$, the parameter B_{min} is chosen so that $B_{min} \geq \mathcal{P}_g B$.

5 Simulation Results

We implemented our algorithm over TinyOS [13] using the *nes*C programming language [9] and carried out performance analysis through simulation using TOSSIM simulator [11,12]. The simulated environment is a wireless sensor network where nodes are uniformly distributed to form a grid. Grid spacing is 8 feet and the radio communication range is 12 feet. Furthermore, we suppose that every safe node holds the current epoch. The mobile node moves in a straight line with a constant speed $V=2$ feet/s.

We used TOSSIM's *empirical* radio model, which defines packet loss rates based on measurements made by Woo et al. on RFM radio [8]. For our experiments, we defined the reception probability for discriminating between good and poor links to $\mathcal{P}_g = 0.8$. Before testing the algorithm, we performed the preliminary calibration of parameters $\overline{N}_{neigh}$, R_g, and B. The mobile nodes broadcasts

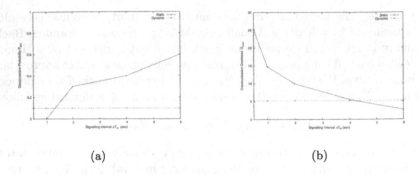

(a)   (b)

Fig. 7. $\mathcal{P}_{dsc}$ and O_{com} vs. static and dynamic ΔT_H (sec)

a burst of HELLO messages when it is within the safe partition. On the basis of the replying nodes and their position, the mobile node sets the parameters as follows: $\overline{N}_{neigh} = 10$, $R_g = 10$ feet, and $B=10$. Thus, given $\mathcal{P}_g =0.8$ we have $B_{min}=8$.

We evaluate the algorithm performance in terms of communication overhead O_{com} and disconnection probability $\mathcal{P}_{dsc}$. More in detail, the communication overhead O_{com} is the average number of HELLO messages that the mobile node broadcasts. The average is computed over ten repetitions of the experiment. For each repetition, the starting point of the mobile node is randomly selected. The disconnection probability $\mathcal{P}_{dsc}$ is defined as the ratio between the number of simulations resulted in a connection loss (no good links between the mobile node and the safe partition) and the total number of runs.

First, we examined the algorithm behaviour both whether the signalling interval ΔT_H is statically chosen and is adaptively calculated. In the case of a static predefined ΔT_H, the disconnection probability increases as the signalling interval exceeds a certain value. However, a short interval means a higher communication overhead. In fact, as shown in Figure 7, a static ΔT_H in the [0.5, 2] range limits the disconnection probability in the [0, 0.3] range. Nevertheless, in this case the communication overhead ranges from 9.9 to 25.2. On the other hand, the adaptive calculation of ΔT_H limits the disconnection probability to 0.1 and the communication overhead to 5.2. It is important to observe that an adaptive selection of ΔT_H is particularly effective when the safe partition is much larger than the communication range because the mobile node strongly reduces the amount of communication overhead it produces while traversing the safe partition.

Furthermore, we evaluated how the Phase-Switch threshold N_{PS} influences both the disconnection probability and the communication overhead. Figure 8(b) shows how small N_{PS} values reduce the communication overhead. In particular, they reduce the chance of false alarms, and thus unneeded bursts. Nevertheless, small N_{PS} values may cause an higher probability of disconnection from the safe partition (Figure 8(a)).

Our third experiment concerns how the connectivity threshold N_C affects the final position reached by the mobile node. We ran simulations with different

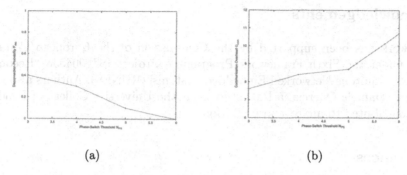

(a)   (b)

Fig. 8. $\mathcal{P}_{dsc}$ and O_{com} vs. N_{PS}

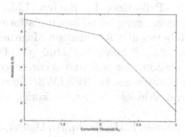

Fig. 9. Final distance d_f vs. N_C

values of N_C and measured the average distance d_f from the mobile node to the safe partition boundary. A negative value of d_f means that the mobile node is still in the safe partition and has not crossed the border. Results are shown in Figure 9. We notice that lower thresholds lead to higher distances (the node advances into the gap between partitions). On the other hand, higher thresholds make the mobile node stop early. For example, in case of $N_C = 3$, the mobile node does not cross the partition border ($d_f = -0.8\,ft$).

6   Conclusions

With reference to a WSN, we have presented a method for repairing network partitions based on mobile nodes. The paper has the following merits. First of all, it treats an important problem that, so far, has received limited attention. Furthermore, the paper suggests a method that is based on a few mobile nodes that move through the network reducing the communication overhead. The paper presents the main factors influencing the algorithm behaviour and performance and discusses their selection criteria. By simulation, the paper shows that the proposed method is effective in terms of disconnection probability and efficient in terms of communication overhead. Future steps consist in deploying an early prototype on the multi-agent platform we have been developing [3].

Acknowledgements

This work has been supported by the Commission of the European Communities under the Sixth Framework Programme Project IST-004536 "Reconfigurable Ubiquitous Networked Embedded Systems"(RUNES). Authors also wish to thank Daniele Quercia, a PhD student at the University College of London, who contributed to improve presentation.

References

1. Reconfigurable Ubiquitous Networked Embedded System (RUNES). European Integrated Project, FP6-IST-004536, http://www.ist-runes.org
2. Dini, G., La Porta, S., Pallottino, L., Savino, I.M., Bicchi, A., Danesi, A., Schiavi, R.: A safe and secure component-based platform for heterogeneous multi-robot systems. IEEE Robotics and Automation Magazine (to appear)
3. Pallottino, L., Savino, I.M., Schiavi, R., Dini, G., Danesi, A., Fagiolini, A., Bicchi, A.: A scalable platform for safe and secure decentralized traffic management of multi-agent mobile systems. In: REALWSN 2006. Proceedings of the ACM Workshop on Real-World Wireless Sensor Networks, Uppsala, Sweden (June 19 2006)
4. Alriksson, P., Nordh, J., Årzén, K.H., Bicchi, A., Danesi, A., Schiavi, R., Pallottino, L.: Component-based approach to the design of networked control systems. In: ECC 2007. Proceedings of European Control Conference, Kos, Greece (July 2–5, 2007)
5. Årzén, K.H., Bicchi, A., Dini, G., Hailes, S., Johansson, K.H., Lygeros, J., Tzes, A.: A component-based approach to the design of networked control systems. European Journal of Control 13, 261–279 (2007)
6. Cerpa, A., Estrin, D.: Ascent: Adaptive self-configuring sensor networks topologies. IEEE Transactions on Mobile Computing 3(3), 272–285 (2004)
7. Chong, C.-Y., Kumar, S.P.: Sensor networks: Evolution, opportunities and challenges. Proceedings of the IEEE 91, 1247–1256 (2003)
8. Ganesan, D., Krishnamachari, B., Woo, A., Culler, D., Estrin, D., Wicker, S.: An empirical study of epidemic algorithms in large scale multihop wireless networks (2002)
9. Gay, D., Levis, P., von Behren, R., Walsh, M., Brewer, E., Culler, D.: The nesC language: A holistic approach to network embeddedd systems. In: Proceedings of the ACM SIGPLAN 2003 Conference on Programming Language Design and Implementation, San Diego, California, USA, pp. 1–11 (June 9–11, 2003)
10. Johnson, D.B., Maltz, D.A.: Dynamic source routing in ad hoc wireless networks. In: Imielinski, Korth (eds.) Mobile Computing, vol. 353, Kluwer Academic Publishers, Dordrecht (1996)
11. Levis, P., Lee, N.: TOSSIM: A simulator for TinyOS networks (Novemeber 14 2003)
12. Levis, P., Lee, N., Welsh, M., Culler, D.E.: TOSSIM: accurate and scalable simulation of entire TinyOS applications. In: SenSys, pp. 126–137 (2003)
13. Levis, P., Madden, S., Gay, D., Polastre, J., Szewczyk, R., Woo, A., Brewer, E., Culler, D.: The emergence of networking abstractions and techniques in TinyOS. In: NSDI 2004. First Symposium on networked system design and implementation, San Francisco, California, USA, pp. 1–14 (2004)

14. Perkins, C., Bhagwat, P.: Highly dynamic destination-sequenced distance-vector routing (DSDV) for mobile computers. In: ACM SIGCOMM 1994 Conference on Communications Architectures, Protocols and Applications, pp. 234–244 (1994)
15. Perkins, C.E., Belding-Royer, E.M.: Ad-hoc on-demand distance vector routing. In: WMCSA, pp. 90–100. IEEE Computer Society, Los Alamitos (1999)
16. Shrivastava, N., Suri, S., Tóth, C.D.: Detecting cuts in sensor networks. In: IPSN, pp. 210–217. IEEE, Los Alamitos (2005)
17. Wood, A.D., Stankovic, J.A.: Denial of service in sensor networks. IEEE Computer (2002)

Typhoon: A Reliable Data Dissemination Protocol for Wireless Sensor Networks

Chieh-Jan Mike Liang, Răzvan Musăloiu-E., and Andreas Terzis

Computer Science Department
Johns Hopkins University
{cliang4,razvanm,terzis}@cs.jhu.edu

Abstract. We present Typhoon, a protocol designed to reliably deliver large objects to all the nodes of a wireless sensor network (WSN). Typhoon uses a combination of spatially-tuned timers, prompt retransmissions, and frequency diversity to reduce contention and promote spatial re-use. We evaluate the performance benefits these techniques provide through extensive simulations and experiments in an indoor testbed. Our results show that Typhoon is able to reduce dissemination time and energy consumption by up to three times compared to Deluge. These improvements are most prominent in sparse and lossy networks that represent real-life WSN deployments.

1 Introduction

One of the main end-user requirements for WSNs is the ability to reprogram the network after it has been deployed. In turn, the requirement to reprogram the network generates the need to reliably disseminate large objects (~50–100 KB) to every node in the network. This combination of large object sizes, 100% reliability, and network-wide distribution is not addressed by other WSN protocols and thus requires a custom protocol. This need has been identified by numerous researchers in the past (*e.g.*, [3,4,5,13,16] among others).

In this paper we present *Typhoon*, a reliable data dissemination protocol that represents a different set of choices in the design space. Our choices are motivated by the observation that *idle listening* is the major consumer of energy during dissemination. Thereby, all protocol decisions should be geared towards minimizing the time that nodes are not transmitting or receiving data packets (*i.e.* competing to request or waiting for the retransmission of a lost packet).

Unlike previous protocols, Typhoon sends data packets via unicast. This approach allows receivers to acknowledge the receipt of individual packets and thereby quickly recover lost packets. While data packets are sent via unicast, interested nodes can still receive them by *snooping* on the wireless medium. Through the combination of unicast transfers and snooping, Typhoon achieves the best of both worlds—prompt retransmissions and data delivery to all the nodes in a broadcast domain through a single transmission. Dissemination latency is also reduced by exploiting spatial reuse, through which nodes in different parts of the network can be transmitting at the same time. We enhance spatial

R. Verdone (Ed.): EWSN 2008, LNCS 4913, pp. 268–285, 2008.
© Springer-Verlag Berlin Heidelberg 2008

reuse through the combination of two techniques: setting timers in a way that encourages nodes further from the origin to propagate the object and the use of channel switching. Specifically, it has been shown that the minimum node distance necessary to avoid interference among concurrent transmissions is three hops [2]. On the other hand, if nodes switch frequency channels[1] during data transfer it is possible to reduce the distance to two hops in many cases. Typhoon leverages this observation to reduce object dissemination time.

We evaluate the performance of Typhoon through a combination of simulations and experiments on a testbed deployed in an office building. Performance is measured in terms of the time required and the energy expended to deliver an object to the whole network. We vary the size, diameter, and density of the network and test Typhoon using different object sizes and loss rates to understand the effects of these factors on the protocol's behavior. Moreover, we compare Typhoon's performance to that of Deluge—the de facto standard for data dissemination in TinyOS [3]. Our results show that Typhoon can be up to three times faster than Deluge in sparse and lossy networks.

This paper has five sections. We summarize related work in the section that follows and provide a detailed description of the Typhoon protocol in Section 3. We evaluate the protocol's performance and compare it with previous protocols proposed in the literature in Section 4. Finally, Section 5 outlines future research directions.

2 Related Work

The problem of designing protocols for reliably disseminating large data objects has received considerable attention in the past. One can divide existing protocols in two broad categories: randomized protocols in which nodes compete to acquire and subsequently transmit parts of the object, and protocols that avoid contention by scheduling node transmissions.

The genealogy of the first protocol family starts with PSFQ [18], a transport protocol for reliable delivery of objects from a sink to all the nodes in a wireless sensor network. PSFQ uses TTL-scoped broadcast to propagate messages from the sink and hop-by-hop retransmissions to recover from lost messages. Unlike PSFQ, Typhoon uses unicast messages to propagate objects, while leveraging overhearing to deliver packets to multiple receivers within the same broadcast domain. Moreover, PSFQ uses negative acknowledgments, whereas Typhoon uses postive acknowledgments and multiple frequency channels to increase spatial reuse. MOAP [16] transfers the complete object one hop at a time. After receiving the whole object a node can become a secondary source, delivering it to nodes further away from the origin. The design of MOAP is driven by the desire to trade latency for reliability and simplicity. Unlike MOAP, Typhoon uses pipelining in which nodes offer to further deliver *pages*) (*i.e.*, subsets of the object) as soon as they receive them. This approach dramatically reduces the network completion time, defined as the time by which all nodes receive the

---

[1] Current 802.15.4 radios can switch between 16 non-overlapping channels.

full image, thereby reducing energy consumption due to idle listening. MNP [5] reduces download time by using pipelining and reduces contention in dense networks through the use of a sender selection algorithm. Reliability is achieved through retransmissions, initiated by query messages sent by the packet source to nodes receiving the transmissions. Unlike MNP, Typhoon implements opportunistic overhearing for traffic of common interest. Moreover, Typhoon uses fast acknowledgments transmitted after each packet rather at the end of a page. Finally, Typhoon uses channel switching to reduce contention in the broadcast medium, amplifying the benefits of spatial reuse.

Deluge [3] is the de facto standard for data dissemination in TinyOS. It uses an epidemic protocol that eventually propagates the object to all the nodes in the network. Deluge relies on randomized *Trickle* timers [10] to reduce contention among transmission requests. Objects are transmitted as sequences of fixed-size pages via broadcast to leverage the broadcast nature of the wireless medium. NACKs trigger the retransmission of lost messages after a full page has been transmitted. NACKs also use Trickle timers to minimize the probability that multiple retransmission requests will collide. While beneficial in reducing the number of collisions, random timers can prolong the time required to propagate the image throughout the network. Typhoon also delivers data to multiple receivers whenever possible. On the other hand, receivers send acknowledgments after each data message instead of NACKs after each block transmission. This design choice enables nodes to start offering data to downstream destinations sooner, thereby minimizing completion time and thus energy costs. This is especially important in lossy networks in which the number of retransmissions is expected to be high. Moreover, Typhoon uses channel switching to reduce contention and to allow multiple concurrent transmissions over the same broadcast domain.

Protocols of the second family initially distribute the object to a subset of the network's nodes using a fixed schedule that avoids overlapping transmissions. The object is then broadcasted to the rest of the network. In order to minimize completion time, the initial set of nodes should be the minimum connected dominating set (MCDS) of the graph induced by the wireless network [13]. Calculating that set however is an NP-hard problem even for the unit graph connectivity model [1] and therefore approximation algorithms are necessary. Sprinkler uses a distributed approximation algorithm that computes a connected dominated set that is a multiplicative factor larger than the MCDS [13]. Infuse [4] follows a similar dissemination strategy and combines it with implicit acknowledgments for reliability. Furthermore, Infuse turns off the radios of nodes not participating actively in the dissemination thus reducing energy consumption due to idle listening. GARUDA [14] is a recent protocol that uses an efficient mechanism for constructing an approximate MCDS during the first packet transfer. Moreover, GARUDA nodes publish bitmaps indicating the packets they have received correctly. Downstream nodes use these bitmaps to send (re)transmission requests. Unlike protocols that rely on node coordination to prevent contention, Typhoon minimizes contention through the use of channel switching and implicit synchronization. This approach does not have the overhead of building the MCDS, is robust to node failures, and simplifies data dissemination to new nodes in the network.

3 Protocol Description

Typhoon is designed to reliably deliver large objects, such as code binaries, to all the nodes in a WSN. In this context, large objects are defined as objects that do not fit in the mote's main memory and can be as large as 50–100 KB. Typhoon divides an object to fixed-size pages (1 KB) which are further divided to fixed-size packets (28 bytes in our implementation) that can be atomically transmitted over the radio.

Even though protocols like Typhoon are unlikely to be invoked frequently, their inherent flooding nature and the need for 100% reliability, irrespective of loss conditions suggest that each invocation of the protocol could be resource intensive and thus its cost should be minimized. As has been argued before, idle listening is one of the largest energy consumers [19]. Therefore, the protocol should make every effort to "push" the object's pages through the network as fast as possible. In turn this means that the protocol should attempt to leverage spatial re-use, transmitting pages from multiple non-overlapping nodes and minimize contention that leads to node back-offs and thereby added latency.

We note that an alternative approach would be to use duty cycling, turning radios off when not in use. In this case network completion time is not as crucial, because energy consumption due to idle listening is minimized. However, we argue that duty cycling is not appropriate for reliable dissemination protocols. First, users want to reduce network downtime due to reprogramming. Second, duty cycling introduces complexity which should be minimized in protocols that serve a critical role to network operations.

3.1 Metadata Dissemination

We assume that the object to be disseminated is injected through an out-of-band mechanism to a single node from which it must propagate to the network. In this regard, the first necessary step is to notify the network about the existence of this new object. Typhoon uses separate mechanisms to disseminate data objects and metadata about these objects. By metadata, we mean information about the existence of a new object, codified into an object ID, size and version. Nodes decide whether they should attempt to download an advertised object by comparing the new object ID and version with those of previously retrieved objects. If a node decides to download the new object, the number of pages is determined by dividing the object's size by the page size.

The reason for using separate mechanisms stems from the difficulty of designing a single protocol that can efficiently serve both purposes. For example, since new nodes may join the network at any time, the metadata dissemination protocol must be always active. This means that, while it should quickly propagate

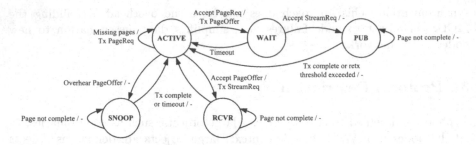

Fig. 1. State transition diagram for Typhoon. State transitions are marked using the condition/action notation in which a transition occurs when a condition is met and results in an action (or no action in case of '-').

updates to the whole network, it must minimize overhead during steady state. On the other hand, for reasons outlined above, the data dissemination protocol should disseminate the object as fast as possible and then terminate. Typhoon uses Trickle [10] to disseminate metadata.

For the remainder of the section we describe what happens once nodes become aware of the existence of a new object and attempt to retrieve it.

3.2 Data Request Handshake

Figure 1 represents Typhoon's state transition diagram. Nodes start in the ACTIVE state and return to this state while they have more pages to download. While in this state, a node will periodically broadcast `PageReq` requests that contain the object's ID and the number of the requested page. Nodes request pages sequentially. By doing so, nodes within the same broadcast domain are more likely to be in the same state, which increases the probability of overhearing traffic of common interest.

The broadcast period is uniformly chosen from $[t_a, t_b]$ to avoid collisions among multiple interested receivers[2]. Nodes that have copies of the requested page and receive a `PageReq` message, each respond with a unicast `PageOffer` message after waiting for a random time uniformly selected from $[t_c, t_d]$. The `PageOffer` message includes the object's ID as well as the number of the page offered. The random waiting period is used to prevent collisions among multiple potential offerers. They then transition to the WAIT state and wait for a `StreamReq` message. If no `StreamReq` arrives within T_s seconds the offerers return to the ACTIVE state[3]. Otherwise, upon receiving a unicast `StreamReq` message, one of the offerers will transition to the PUB state and start the data transfer. That offerer returns to the ACTIVE state after the page has been successfully downloaded or after a number (five) of unsuccessful data packet transfers. These failures are detected because the receiver acknowledges the receipt of individual data packets (see Section 3.3).

---

[2] We use, $[t_a, t_b] = [400, 500]$ msec.
[3] $T_s = 20$ msec in our implementation.

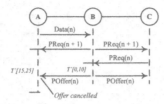

Fig. 2. Pipelining pages through the network

Conversely, a node that receives a `PageOffer` message matching its request, transitions to the RCVR state and signals the source of the `PageOffer` message to initiate the data download by transmitting a unicast `StreamReq` message. The receiver stays in that state while more packets from the requested page need to be retrieved and returns to the ACTIVE state either when the whole page has been successfully downloaded or when a timeout occurs. The second case protects the receiver against failures of the transmitting node.

Nodes that overhear a `PageOffer` message for a page they are missing, will transition to the SNOOP state in which they will attempt to receive the data packets from the offered page. While `PageOffer` messages are sent via unicast, interested nodes can still receive them. For example, the CC2420 radio provides the ability to disable *address filtering* enabling a node to receive all packets irrespective of their destination address. Similar to the RCVR state, the node leaves the SNOOP state when the page transfer has completed or when a timeout occurs. If a node does not successfully overhear all the packets from a page, it discards the page.

In addition to the base scheme described above, Typhoon optimizes its use of timers to enable the pipelining of pages through the network. We describe this optimization using the example presented in Figure 2. In this scenario, node A has finished transmitting page n to node B. In response, node B will transition to the ACTIVE state and transmit a `PageReq` for page $n + 1$. Node A receives this message and starts its timer to transmit the `PageOffer` message. However, node C also receives the request and deduces that node B already has page n (because pages are downloaded sequentially). C then sends its own `PageReq` for page n to B. From the perspective of pipelining, C's request has priority over B's original request, since it pushes pages further downstream. To encourage this behavior, Typhoon sets the timer at B to fire before A's timer[4]. Once B's timer expires, it transmits a `PageOffer` for page n. A overhears that offer and cancels its own `PageOffer`, implicitly deferring to B's data transmission.

3.3   Data Transfer

Typhoon achieves reliable transfer in the face of packet loss, through the use of retransmissions. However, unlike previous protocols that use negative

---

[4] In our implementation, $[t_c, t_d] = [15, 25]$ msec for a node that has just finished transmitted a page and $[0, 10]$ msec otherwise.

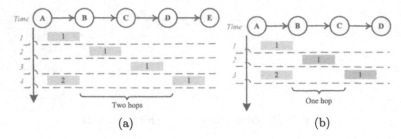

Fig. 3. (a) Propagation of consecutive pages on a linear topology when only one frequency channel is used. Notice that node A has to wait until time period 4 to transmit the second page in order to avoid colliding at B with node C's transmission of the first page. (b) When nodes can use different frequency channels to transmit data packets (indicated by different colors in the figure) the wait time is reduced by one time period.

acknowledgments after all packets in page have been transmitted, Typhoon acknowledges the receipt of individual data packets. If the sender does not receive an acknowledgment, it retransmits the last data packet thus implementing a stop-and-wait ARQ protocol.

A node can generate these acknowledgments in two different ways. First, modern radios offer the ability to automatically generate hardware acknowledgments [17]. The benefit of this approach is reduced latency because the ACK is generated as soon as the radio hardware correctly receives the packet. On the other hand, it is possible for an acknowledged packet to be dropped before it reaches the application. In this case, the hardware acknowledgment results in a false positive. Fortunately, TinyOS2 [8], on which Typhoon is developed, implements a mechanism called software ACK that can trigger this acknowledgment at the system level. It is thus possible to disable the hardware from automatically generating hardware ACKs and achieve equivalent functionality using software ACKs.

An additional benefit of disabling hardware ACKs is that it enables overhearing of unicast packets. This is because enabling hardware ACKs in the commonly-used CC2420 radio also enables destination address filtering, in which case the radio automatically discards all unicast frames not destined to the current node. With address filtering disabled, nodes in the SNOOP state can still receive data packets sent to the unicast address of the node that transmitted the **StreamReq** message, while the explicit receiver will generate ACKs for those data packets.

3.4   Channel Switching

As we already argued, data dissemination protocols should leverage spatial re-use to accelerate the propagation of pages through the network. Spatial re-use is achieved by having nodes retransmit pages as soon as they arrive. However, as Figure 3(a) demonstrates, in order to avoid collisions due to the hidden terminal problem a node must wait for two additional periods (a period is defined as the amount of time necessary to transmit a page) before it can transmit the next page. On the other hand, as Figure 3(b) shows, this bound can be further reduced if nodes have the ability to transmit at different frequency channels. Channel switching provides another benefit in addition to accelerating the pipelining process. Because nodes exchange PageReq and PageOffer messages on the default common channel, having data transfers on different frequencies eliminates the danger of ongoing data transfers colliding with these control messages.

Considering the advantages of channel switching, Typhoon incorporates it to the data request handshake described above. Rather than using an explicit agreement protocol in which nodes are assigned specific frequencies, Typhoon employs a randomized scheme to select transmission frequencies. Specifically, the publisher suggests a frequency channel in its PageOffer message by randomly selecting from one of the possible channels (e.g. 15 in the case of 802.15.4, since one channel is reserved for broadcast messages). If the receiver accepts the offer it replies with an acknowledgment (similar to the ACK used for data packets) and switches to the suggested frequency channel. After receiving the acknowledgment the publisher also tunes to the new channel and the data transfer starts. Note that the receiver transmits a StreamReq message after switching to the channel indicated in the PageOffer message. Although the channel is randomly chosen, it is still possible to have multiple publishers willing to serve the same receiver on the same channel. Therefore, the StreamReq message serves as an explicit indication of the receiver's decision. Although nodes randomly select data transfer channels, it is possible that more than one ongoing data transfers with overlapping radio coverage take place on the same channel. In this case, interference can cause higher packet loss and thus retransmissions and possibly failure to transmit the page due to the loss of multiple acknowledgments. In the second case, the sender and/or the receiver will timeout, return to the ACTIVE state, and retry downloading the original page.

While channel switching provides clear performance benefits, it also introduces new complications. For example, Typhoon uses Trickle for metadata dissemination, and both Typhoon and Trickle can be active at the same time. Since Trickle is not aware of the channel changes it will transmit over the channel selected by Typhoon. This means that if a node is transferring data on a channel other than the default one, the node's neighbors will not be able to receive any metadata sent via Trickle. Realizing this conflict, we implement two schemes to minimize its effects. First, upon receiving the initial notification via Trickle, nodes wait for a random period before they start Typhoon[5]. This delay allows Trickle to propagate the metadata downstream. Second, nodes switch to the default channel immediately after each page transfer, thus allowing the continued dissemination of metadata.

4   Evaluation

4.1   Evaluation Metrics and Methodology

We evaluate the performance of Typhoon using simulations and experiments performed on a testbed deployed in an office building. The results we report

---

[5] Set to [400, 500] msec in our implementation.

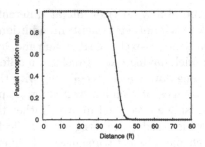

Fig. 4. Packet reception rate as a function of distance from a packet source. The path-loss exponent is 4.

are based on an implementation of Typhoon built on top of TinyOS 2 (T2) [8]. Moreover, we use the standard CSMA MAC protocol used in T2.

We use Deluge, the de facto standard for reliable bulk transfer in TinyOS, as the baseline for our comparisons. Since Deluge provides no guidelines for setting its parameters under different network conditions we use the default parameters provided with Deluge under all cases. All simulations were carried out in TOSSIM, a discrete event based simulator for TinyOS [9]. We leverage two of TOSSIM's features to improve the fidelity of our simulations. First, TOSSIM allows defining signal attenuation levels on a per link basis. We calculate these attenuations using the log distance path loss model [15]. In this model the path loss at distance d from the source, measured in dB, is, $PL(d) = PL(d_0) + 10n \log(d/d_0)$, where n is the path-loss exponent and $PL(d_0)$ is an experimentally measured path loss at reference distance d_0. Path loss exponent $n = 2$ corresponds to free space propagation, while $n = 3, 4$ model environments with reflections and refractions [15]. We use $n = 4$ for all our simulations. Figure 4 shows the packet reception rate at various distances from a source node. Second, we utilize TOSSIM's ability to emulate bursty noise due to interference.

We quantify the performance of Typhoon through two metrics: **(1) Completion time**, which captures the time necessary to disseminate an object. We measure both the time necessary for individual nodes as well as the network completion time, defined as the longest node completion time. **(2) Power consumption.** While completion time quantifies the level of disruption from executing the object dissemination protocol (assuming the network's operation is disrupted during the download), power consumption quantifies the impact of data dissemination on the network's lifetime.

Due to the lack of a direct mechanism for measuring power consumption in TOSSIM, we use the indirect approach of measuring the amount of time the nodes spend transmitting, in idle listening mode, as well as the number of packets it receives. Because the Tmote Sky data sheet [12] publishes only the current drawn in transmit mode (17.4 mA), and in idle listening mode (19.7 mA), we experimentally measured using a Tmote Sky mote [11] the average current drawn while receiving one packet to be 21.7 mA. Note that our energy estimates do not include the costs of reading and writing to flash. The reason is that they represent a fixed cost which is orthogonal to the operation of the data dissemination protocol and therefore it provides no insight into the impact of different protocol design decisions.

We run each experiment five times and use the two evaluation metrics to reason about the impact of different factors on the performance of Typhoon. Specifically, we investigate the impact that network density and size, object size, and loss rate have on data dissemination. Moreover, we evaluate the incremental benefits of overhearing and channel switching in Typhoon. Finally we present the behavior of Typhoon in practice through results from a small testbed.

4.2   Effect of Network Density and Size

Network density is a critical performance factor since it affects the level of contention when requesting and downloading pages. We first discuss the impact of network density on completion time. Figure 5(a) shows the effect of increasing the number of nodes per square foot by increasing the size of an $N \times N$ node grid, deployed on a fixed 180×180-foot field. Also shown in the same figure is the average node degree, defined as the set of nodes with $PRR > 0$, as network density increases. One can make two observations from this figure. First, the performance margin between Typhoon and Deluge increases in sparse networks. This is because Deluge uses timer values that reduce the number of messages sent and increase the probability of overhearing. However, in sparse networks, these timer values increase the idle listening time and thus completion time. Second, Typhoon is consistently faster throughout the density range despite its more aggressive timers. This indicates that channel switching is effective in relieving channel contention.

Both Typhoon and Deluge require nodes to keep their radios on for the duration of the data dissemination. Considering that the radio consumes considerable energy in idle listening state, completion time will influence energy consumption. Figure 5(b) verifies this intuition as it shows that energy consumption follows closely completion time. We found that for both protocols nodes spend less than 7% of their time transmitting further indicating that energy cost is dominated

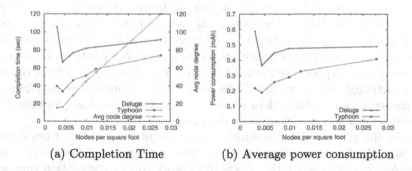

(a) Completion Time   (b) Average power consumption

Fig. 5. Average network completion time and average node power consumption for a 20 KB object, as a function of network density. Network nodes are placed on a grid over a 180×180-foot field.

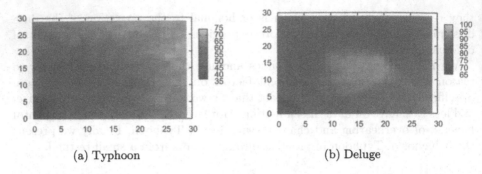

(a) Typhoon   (b) Deluge

Fig. 6. Node completion time for Typhoon and Deluge on a 180 × 180-foot field. The field had 30^2 nodes uniformly distributed with a density of 0.028 nodes per square foot. A 20 KB object was initially injected at the bottom left corner of the field.

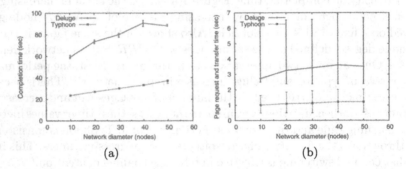

(a)   (b)

Fig. 7. (a). Network completion time of a 20 KB object, as a function of the diameter changes in $1 \times n$ linear topology. (b). Page acquisition time, including the page request phase and subsequent data transfer. The vertical lines represent the 5th and 95th quartiles.

by idle listening time. With this result in mind, we present only completion times for the remainder of the evaluation.

Figure 6 illustrates the propagation time for individual nodes in a dense grid. As reported in [3], Deluge propagates the data object faster around the edges than in the middle of the network. The main reason is that nodes in the middle of the network have more neighbors and thus higher probability of collisions. On the other hand, Typhoon generates a uniform wavefront pattern from corner to corner. Although nodes in the middle have more neighbors, the only messages broadcasted on the default channel are the first two handshake messages. The probability of collision is thus lower than Deluge.

Unlike the grid topology in which a node might receive data from different neighbors, the linear topology limits the propagation to only one direction. It is therefore easier to study the effects of network size on completion time using linear topologies.

A number of interesting observations can be made from Figure 7(a) that plots completion time as a function of network diameter in a linear topology. First, both Typhoon and Deluge benefit from pipelining, and the completion time does not increase at the same rate as the number of nodes. Second, Deluge exhibits faster increase compared to Typhoon. As the network diameter increases, the number of neighboring nodes for some nodes also increases, and thus the probability of contention increases. This has a larger influence on Deluge, because Typhoon sends packets on the common channel only during the page request phase. Figure 7(b), which shows the average time to request and download a single page as the network's diameter increases, verifies this conjecture. From the similarity between the two graphs, it is easy to see that page acquisition time dictates completion time. Furthermore, Typhoon has approximately constant page transfer time in all cases, which suggests that the shorter page request phase underlies the difference in completion time. Finally, Deluge exhibits larger variability in page acquisition time, due to the varying levels of contention that different nodes experience.

4.3   Effect of Object Size

Unlike metadata dissemination protocols for which network diameter dominates completion time, the size of the object transferred affects the completion time of bulk data dissemination protocols. Figure 8 shows the impact of object size on completion time in two cases: a sparse linear topology in which nodes can reach only their immediate neighbors, and a 20×20 grid topology with 10-feet node spacing. In both cases, the completion time grows linearly with the object size with Deluge yielding a steeper slope.

To understand the root cause for this behavior, we briefly present a model for data dissemination in sparse linear topologies. We assume ideal conditions in which pages are transferred in perfect synchrony with no collisions. In this case, the expected completion time for Typhoon is $\hat{T}_t = 2(n-1)P_t + d \cdot P_t$, where n is the number of object pages, d is the network diameter, and P_t is the time to request and receive a page (see Figure 3). Given the description of Typhoon from Section 4, we can estimate P_t and thus $\hat{T}_t$. A page transfer is preceded by

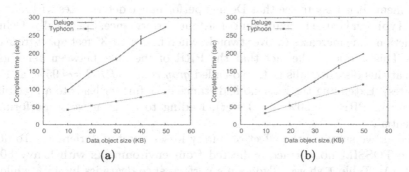

(a)   (b)

Fig. 8. Completion time as the object size varies in (a) 1×50 sparse linear topology where nodes can reach only their immediate neighbors, and (b) 20×20 grid topology with 10-feet node spacing

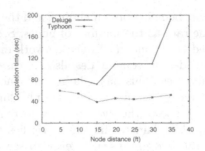

Fig. 9. Modeled and simulated completion time of Typhoon in 1 × 50 sparse linear topology

the data request handshake. According to TOSSIM, each handshake exchange of a 21-byte message followed by the ACK requires 1.68 msec to complete. Since the handshake consists of three messages and two back-off timers with maximum length of 25 msec each, it should take 55.04 msec. Moreover, according to TOSSIM, a page transfer requires approximately 428 msec and thus $P_t = 483.04$ msec. Figure 9 shows the modeled and simulated completion time for Typhoon with different object sizes. Since the modeled completion time is based on ideal conditions, it represents the lower bound on Typhoon's performance. At the same time, it explains that the lower completion time that Typhoon exhibits is due to the speedup that channel switching offers.

4.4   Impact of Packet Loss

Since reliability is a requirement for bulk data dissemination protocols completion time depends on how fast lost packets are recovered. We perform two experiments to estimate the effect of packet loss on completion time.

First, we increase the spacing between neighboring nodes in a 20 × 20 grid topology. This increase raises the path loss on the link and therefore decreases the packet reception rate (PRR). Figure 10 illustrates the completion time for this experiment. It is easy to see that Deluge performance deteriorates with distance while Typhoon is able to maintain consistent performance. Specifically, Deluge's completion time increases by over twofold when nodes are 35 feet apart from each other. This is due to the fact that the PRR of the links between neighboring nodes at this distance falls in the so-called *gray region* ($PRR =\sim 95\%$, as Fig. 4 indicates). Extending the inter-node distance even further leads to a precipitous decrease in PRR ($\sim 30\%$ at 40 feet), leading to an even worse performance differential.

Second, we simulate the effect of bursty losses due to interference. To do so, we use TOSSIM noise traces collected from environments with heavy 802.11 use [6]. As Table 1 shows, Typhoon's performance degrades by 48% while the completion time for Deluge increases threefold. Two main reasons underlie this trend. First, Typhoon requires all data packets to be individually acknowledged, and it bases the retransmission decision on this acknowledgment instead of a

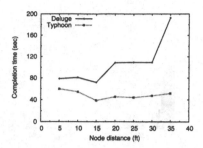

Fig. 10. Completion time as the inter-node distance varies in a 20×20-node grid topology

Table 1. Completion time under different loss environments for a 20×20-node grid topology with 10-feet node distance

	Quiet	Bursty loss
Typhoon	54.30	73.37
Deluge	80.79	241.43

timer. This allows lost packets to be recovered quickly. Second, compared to Deluge, Typhoon is more aggressive in sending packets, so the transfer moves at a faster pace.

4.5 Benefits of Overhearing and Channel Switching

In order to better understand the performance benefits that channel switching and overhearing offer, we selectively disable them in an experiment on a 5×5 grid topology.

Table 2 presents the results of this experiment. Disabling channel switching creates a larger performance deterioration compared to disabling overhearing. This degradation while large is expected because Typhoon assumes that data transfers take place on a channel that is free from interference caused by other data transfers and request handshakes. As a result, being aggressive hurts performance in this case. On the other hand, overhearing provides only modest improvement. The reason is that Typhoon performs opportunistic overhearing, in which nodes can snoop on a page transfer only when they overheard the preceding `PageOffer` message. In other words, if a node misses that message, it loses the opportunity to overhear since the transfer happens at another channel. Moreover, if a node in the SNOOP misses one or more packets from a page due to interference it discards the whole page. At the same time, when overhearing is combined with channel switching, it offers $\sim 30\%$ reduction in completion time.

Table 2. Completion time as channel-switching and overhearing are disabled in a 5×5-node grid topology with 20-feet node spacing for s 3 KB object

	Completion time (sec)
Channel-switching and overhearing	6.24
Channel-switching only	8.79
Overhearing only	945.80
None	1016.43

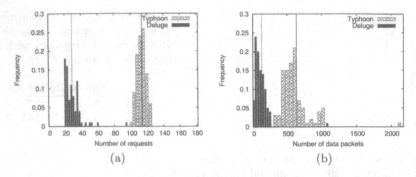

Fig. 11. Probability distribution of (a) Typhoon request messages and Deluge advertisements (b) Typhoon and Deluge data messages. The topology is a 10×10 node grid, with 10-feet node distance, and the object size is 20KB. The vertical lines show the average.

4.6 Protocol Overhead

The major design goal of Typhoon is to minimize completion time. It achieves this goal by being aggressive in requesting and transmitting object pages. Figure 11 illustrates the results of this aggressive behavior by comparing the per-node packet distributions for disseminating the same object using Typhoon and Deluge.

We focus on request and data transfer messages because they constitute the majority of traffic. Typhoon generates approximately three times more traffic than Deluge for both message types. The reason is that, unlike Deluge, Typhoon does not have a request suppression mechanism, so nodes broadcast requests more aggressively. Moreover, we found that 47% of the overhearing attempts failed (*i.e.* node had to discard the partially overheard pages). While one can suggest based on this result that nodes should sleep instead of performing opportunistic overhearing, sleep scheduling introduces complexity and overhead to the protocol. Furthermore, as Section 4.5 shows, overhearing when used in conjunction with channel switching, leads to $\sim 30\%$ reduction in completion time.

4.7 Testbed Evaluation

We complement the simulation results presented above, with experimental results from testing Typhoon and Deluge on a small testbed. While simulations are meant to explore the behavior of the protocols under various conditions, the testbed is used to compare their performance in a realistic environment. Given the two different goals, we do not compare results across simulations and the testbed. Rather, it is the relative performance of Typhoon and Deluge under the same testing scenarios that is of interest.

We test Typhoon on a testbed that consists of 22 motes deployed in an office building according to the topology shown in Figure 12. Due to the shape of the building, the testbed physically resembles a linear topology. Moreover, the center of the testbed around location 119 tends to have relatively bad connectivity to

Fig. 12. The testbed floor plan shows the locations of Tmote Connect boxes, which can have either one or two motes attached

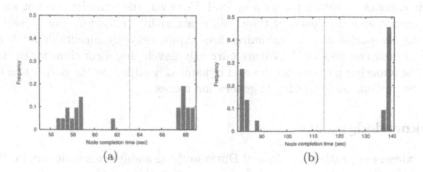

Fig. 13. PDF of node completion time on the testbed for (a) Typhoon and (b) Deluge. The green line shows the network average in each case.

the rest of the network. Dissemination starts by injecting a 20 KB object from location 118 on the right side of the testbed.

The average network completion time was 75.15 seconds using Typhoon and 145.57 seconds with Deluge. To understand how the object propagates through the network, Figure 13 shows the distribution of node completion times. For both protocols, the node completion time is divided into two groups, with one group taking longer to receive the entire object. Analysis of the experiment log shows that the group of slow nodes is located on the left side of the testbed. This is due to the the poor link connectivity in the center of the testbed. For example, in the case of Typhoon, most nodes on the left side of the testbed download pages from location 112. However, since the link connectivity between location 112 and nodes on the right side of the testbed was poor, location 112 becomes the bottleneck.

As explained above, Typhoon uses the Dissemination service to publish meta-data and T2 components for reading/writing to the Flash. The combined code foot-print of all three components is 14752 bytes of ROM and 413 bytes of RAM. At the same time, the incremental overhead of adding Typhoon to an application that uses Dissemination and the Flash is 3806 bytes of ROM and 112 bytes of RAM.

5 Looking Forward

We have shown how Typhoon leverages frequency diversity to reduce network contention and system-level ACKs to expedite recovery from lost data packets.

The combination of these two techniques provides significant performance benefits across a wide range of network sizes and conditions.

As we move forward, we plan to explore the benefits that dynamic packet size adjustment provides. Preliminary results from our testbed show that changing packet size can affect the packet reception rate by as much as 28%. The intuition is that the probability of bit errors and thereby corruption accumulates as the packet size increases. One should then transmit smaller packets in noisy environments to reduce the number of retransmissions and larger packets in 'quiet' environments to reduce packet overhead. However, the noise level is not known in advance and changes over time. While algorithms exist for dynamically adjusting the packet size to maximize throughput, they are unsuitable for WSNs due to their complexity [7]. We are currently developing algorithms for estimating the underlying bit error rates and dynamically adjusting the packet size that can be implemented on current generation motes.

Acknowledgments

We extend our gratitude to Prabal Dutta and the anonymous reviewers for their insightful comments and their help in improving this paper.

This research was supported in part by NSF grant CNS-0546648 and by the U.S. Department of Homeland Security (Grant Number N00014-D6-1-0991) through a grant awarded to the Center for Study of Preparedness and Critical Event Response (PACER) at the Johns Hopkins University. Any opinions, finding, conclusions or recommendations expressed in this publication are those of the author(s) and do not represent the policy or position of the Department of Homeland Security and the National Science Foundation.

References

1. Clark, B., Colbourn, C., Johnson, D.: Unit disk graphs. Discrete Mathematics 86, 165–177 (1990)
2. Couto, D.S.J.D., Aguayo, D., Bicket, J., Morris, R.: A High-Throughput Path Metric for Multi-Hop Wireless Routing. In: MobiCom 2003. Proceedings of the 9th ACM International Conference on Mobile Computing and Networking (September 2003)
3. Hui, J.W., Culler, D.: The dynamic behavior of a data dissemination protocol for network programming at scale. In: SenSys 2004. Proceedings of the Second ACM Conference on Embedded Networked Sensor Systems (November 2004)
4. Kulkarni, S.S., Arumugam, M.: Infuse: A TDMA Based Data Dissemination Protocol For Sensor Networks. Technical Report MSU-CSE-04-46, Michigan State University - Computer Science and Engineering (November 2004)
5. Kulkarni, S.S., Wang, L.: MNP: Multihop network reprogramming service for sensor networks. In: ICSCS. Proceedings of the 25th IEEE international Conference on Distributed Computing Systems (June 2005)
6. Lee, H., Cerpa, A., Levis, P.: Improving Wireless Simulation Through Noise Modeling. In: IPSN 2007. Proceedings of the Sixth International Conference on Information Processing in Wireless Sensor Networks (2007)

7. Lettieri, P., Srivastava, M.B.: Adaptive frame length control for improving wireless link throughput, range, and energy efficiency. In: Proceedings of IEEE INFOCOM 1998 (1998)
8. Levis, P., Gay, D., Handziski, V., Hauer, J.-H., Greenstein, B., Turon, M., Hui, J., Klues, K., Cory Sharp, R.S., Polastre, J., Buonadonna, P., Nachman, L., Tolle, G., Culler, D., Wolisz, A.: T2: A Second Generation OS For Embedded Sensor Networks. Technical Report TKN-05-007. Telecommunication Networks Group, Technische Universitat Berlin (2005)
9. Levis, P., Lee, N., Woo, A., Welsh, M., Culler, D.: TOSSIM: Accurate and scalable simulation of entire TinyOS Applications. In: Proceedings of Sensys 2003 (November 2003)
10. Levis, P., Patel, N., Culler, D., Shenker, S.: Trickle: A Self-regulating Algorithm for Code Propagation and Maintenance in Wireless Sensor Networks. In: Proceedings of NSDI 2004 (March 2004)
11. Moteiv Corporation. Tmote Sky. Available at http://www.moteiv.com/products/tmotesky.php
12. Moteiv Corporation. Tmote Sky Datasheet. http://www.moteiv.com/products/docs/tmote-sky-datasheet.pdf
13. Nail, V., Arora, A., Sinha, P.: Sprinkler: A Reliable and Energy Efficient Data Dissemination Service for Wireless Embedded Devices. In: RTSS 2005. Proceedings of the 26th International Real-Time Systems Symposium (2005)
14. Park, S.-J., Vedantham, R., Sivakumar, R., Akyildiz, I.F.: GARUDA: Achieving Effective Reliability for Downstream Communication in Wireless Sensor Networks. The IEEE Transactions on Mobile Computing (to appear, 2007)
15. Rappaport, T.S.: Wireless Communications: Principles & Practices. Prentice-Hall, Englewood Cliffs (1996)
16. Stathopoulos, T., Heidemann, J., Estrin, D.: A remote code update mechanism for wireless sensor networks. Technical Report CENS-TR-30, University of California, Los Angeles, Center for Embedded Networked Computing (November 2003)
17. Texas Instruments. 2.4 GHz IEEE 802.15.4/ZigBee-ready RF Transceiver (2006). Available at http://www.chipcon.com/files/CC2420_Data_Sheet_1_3.pdf
18. Wan, C., Campbell, A., Krishnahmurthy, L.: PSFQ: A Reliable Transport Mechanism for Wireless Sensor Networks. In: Proceedings of the ACM International Workshop on Wireless Sensor Networks and Applications (September 2002)
19. Ye, W., Heidemann, J., Estrin, D.: An Energy-Efficient MAC Protocol for Wireless Sensor Networks. In: Proceedings of IEEE INFOCOM 2002 (2002)

FiGaRo:
Fine-Grained Software Reconfiguration
for Wireless Sensor Networks

Luca Mottola[1], Gian Pietro Picco[2], and Adil Amjad Sheikh[2]

[1] Department of Electronics and Information,
Politecnico di Milano, Italy
mottola@elet.polimi.it
[2] Department of Information and Communication Technology,
University of Trento, Italy
{amjad,picco}@dit.unitn.it

Abstract. Wireless Sensor Networks (WSNs) are increasingly being proposed in scenarios whose requirements cannot be fully predicted, or where the system functionality must adapt to changing conditions. In these scenarios, the ability to reconfigure *portions* of the software running on WSN nodes becomes imperative. At the same time, recent WSN proposals often employ *heterogeneous* nodes (e.g., sensors and actuators), which require the deployment of different code on different devices, based on their characteristics. Unfortunately, existing work in the field largely focuses on simpler scenarios where the same, monolithic program is distributed to all the nodes in the WSN.

In this paper we present FIGARO, a programming model supported by an efficient run-time system and distributed protocols, collectively enabling an unprecedented fine-grained control over *what* is being reconfigured, and *where*. Using FIGARO, the programmer can deal explicitly with component dependencies and version constraints, as well as select precisely the subset of nodes targeted by reconfiguration, leaving the others unaltered. We show that our run-time support imposes a very limited processing and memory overhead, while the communication overhead lies within 9% of the theoretical optimum.

1 Introduction

The nodes of a wireless sensor network (WSN) are often deployed in large numbers and inaccessible places, making individual code uploading an impractical solution. This problem was early recognized in the WSN research field, leading to solutions exploiting the wireless link for on-the-fly, untethered software reconfiguration [1]. However, these solutions were designed to suit the needs of early WSN architectures, i.e., application-specific systems with homogeneous devices.

Problem and Motivation. Today, WSNs are proposed in contexts where their functionality changes over time and/or cannot be predicted a priori. For instance, in emergency response [2] systems the WSN must be reconfigured on-the-fly by mobile operators which demand customized behavior to carry out their activities. In similar scenarios, anticipating all expected needs, if at all possible, may lead to complex and unreliable code

R. Verdone (Ed.): EWSN 2008, LNCS 4913, pp. 286–304, 2008.

cluttered with rarely-used functionality. Therefore, software reconfiguration—even if representing a rare activity compared to the application operations—becomes a much-needed feature. For reconfiguration to be fully effective, however, programmers must retain fine-grained control over *what* is being reconfigured, by updating selected functionality to minimize energy consumption. However, most platforms allow updates only of the full application image. In the very few exceptions, programmers sorely miss proper constructs to deal with dependencies among different functionality, versions, and other fundamental aspects of reconfiguration [1].

Moreover, modern WSNs are typically heterogeneous, containing a mixture of sensing devices and/or actuators. In building monitoring, for instance, a wide range of sensor and actuators is deployed, e.g., to implement heating, ventilation, and air conditioning (HVAC) control [3]. As different nodes are likely to run different application code, software reconfiguration may be limited to a specified portion of the WSN. For instance, a structural engineer inspecting a building may want to load a new piece of functionality only on seismic sensors deployed in a specific location (e.g., the floor being inspected), to process the sensed data in a previously unanticipated manner [4]. In this case, fine-grained control over *where* the code is deployed, based on application attributes of the nodes, is largely missing from existing approaches, which instead are designed to distribute the *same* code to *all* the nodes, regardless of their function [1].

Contribution. In this paper we present FIGARO (FIne Grained softwAre RecOnfiguration), a novel approach enabling fine-grained control over *what* is reconfigured and *where*, to a degree unprecedented in WSNs. FIGARO tackles the two problems in an integrated way, spanning all the aspects from the programming model down to the node-level run-time support and the protocols for efficient code distribution. Its programming model, described in Section 2, has two core constituents:

- the *component model* defines constructs for structuring the code on the single nodes. Differently from other component models for WSNs (e.g., [5]), ours is designed with reconfiguration in mind, thus providing dedicated constructs to deal with component dependencies and versions, and to simplify the reconfiguration process.
- the *distribution model* defines constructs to restrict component dissemination only to a given subset of nodes—the reconfiguration target—based on programmer-specified characteristics of the nodes or their current software configuration.

Our implementation includes a lightweight node-level run-time system, discussed in Section 3, whose responsibility is to manage the local part of a reconfiguration process, along with an efficient protocol for code distribution, illustrated in Section 4. Both are evaluated in Section 5. As for the former, our results show that processing and memory overhead are almost negligible, while the energy overhead during reconfiguration is marginal. Similarly, our distributed protocol results in a communication overhead within 9% of the theoretical optimum, which is instead computed in a centralized manner and with global knowledge of the system topology.

In Section 6 we compare FIGARO against representative state-of-the-art systems. Finally, in Section 7 we conclude by illustrating directions for future work.

2   Programming Model

FIGARO is currently built on top of the Contiki [6] operating system, and therefore relies on the C programming language.

2.1   Specifying *What* Is Reconfigured

Components, Interfaces, and Dependencies. In FIGARO, a *component* represents a single unit of functionality and deployment. The services provided by a component are described by its *interface*. For instance, Figure 1 shows the declaration of an interface for data collection. This specifies the signature of two operations to broadcast interests and to report the data, respectively. Components must provide the code for all the operations in the interface declaration, as in the case of Figure 2. The **DECLARE_COMPONENT** macro is used to specify the name of the component (tree_routing), the interface it implements (data_collection_if), and the component version (2).

To accomplish its goal, a component normally interacts with others on the same node. Interaction occurs through function calls across components using **CALL**, as shown in the first operation of the component in Figure 2. However, it is not for granted that a component provides an (interface containing the) operation required by another, while the caller component may not be able to continue its execution without a callee component implementing the required interface. Therefore, the presence of a **CALL** statement determines a *dependency* between caller and callee.

In FIGARO, dependencies are explicitly declared by the programmer using the **DECLARE_DEPENDENCY** macro. The first parameter of this macro is a *receptacle*, the dual of an interface. An interface specifies a set of operations provided by a component to others, while a receptacle specifies the set of interfaces a component requires

```
DECLARE_INTERFACE(data_collection_if, {
  void (* broadcast_interest)(void* data,  u8_t len);
  void (* report)(uip_ipaddr_t dest, void* data,  u8_t len); })
```

Fig. 1. An example of component interface

```
DECLARE_COMPONENT(tree_routing, data_collection_if, 2)
DECLARE_DEPENDENCY(radio_receptacle, radio_if, 3, MANDATORY | STATIC)
void broadcast_interest(void* data,  u8_t len) {
  CALL(radio_receptacle, send(&broadcast_addr, &msg, 64));
  // ...
}
void report(uip_ipaddr_t dest, void* data,  u8_t len) {
  // ...
}
ON_RUNNING({ // ON_SUSPEND, ON_DESTROY are also available
  // ...
})
```

Fig. 2. A component implementing the interface of Figure 1

from others. In the case of Figure 2 the dependency being declared specifies the name of the receptacle (radio_receptacle), the interface required (radio_if), and the minimum component version allowed for a component (3). Moreover, the programmer can also specify a bit-masked constant describing the *nature* of the dependency. In the example, **MANDATORY** specifies that the component cannot run without relying on the needed interface. Otherwise, the dependency is considered optional, and the component is expected to work correctly also in absence of the specified interface. Instead, **STATIC** indicates that once a callee component is bound to the caller through the receptacle, the callee component cannot be changed. Otherwise, a reconfiguration can take place substituting the component with another providing the same interface.

Figure 3 shows an example of component configuration. The Sampling component is responsible for querying the sensor, and calling the report function in TreeRouting, which transmits the data to a sink. Note how TreeRouting satisfies only the **MANDATORY** dependency of Sampling,

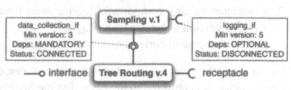

Fig. 3. An example of component configuration

while the **OPTIONAL** one is currently not satisfied. This information is reflected in the receptacle descriptor inside the run-time support, as described in Section 3.

Component Life Cycle. The life cycle of a component is illustrated in Figure 4. A component becomes **RUNNING** when all its dependencies on other components are satisfied, i.e., components implementing the required interfaces are available on the node. Note that dependencies are inherently recursive, i.e., a component may depend on some others, which in turn may depend on others, and so on. Therefore, the instantiation of a component may trigger the instantiation of an entire component *closure*, based on the declared dependencies. In practice, however, WSN applications are made of a small number of components with short dependency chains. The instantiation of a set of components bound by dependencies occurs atomically, i.e., control returns to the application only when the instantiation of *all* components is complete. When a component providing services to others undergoes a reconfiguration, the components exploiting those services move to the **SUSPENDED** state, and revert to the **RUNNING** state when the reconfiguration completes. Instead, the **DESTROYED** state is reached when the component has been replaced by another with the same interface.

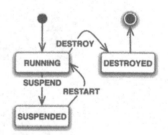

Fig. 4. The life cycle of a FI-GARO component

Programmers can intervene at each step of the life cycle by specifying code fragments to be executed when entering a given state, as shown in Figure 2. When starting a new component, for instance, the body of the **ON_RUNNING** macro is executed. Similar operations exist for each state. The ability to intercept run-time activities is particularly important in the case of **SUSPEND**, to give programmers the ability to release resources held by the suspended components, and avoid deadlocks and run-time faults.

Component Reconfiguration. In FIGARO, programmers do not need to manage the reconfiguration manually, e.g., using a dedicated API as in [7]. Instead, the underlying run-time automatically and transparently manages the reconfiguration process, based on dependencies and component versions. When components are instantiated at start-up, the run-time keeps track of their version, the interface they implement, and their dependencies. Upon receipt of a new component C, reconfiguration unfolds as follows. Provided C's **MANDATORY** dependencies can be satisfied:

1. C is instantiated if there is no running component with the same interface, or
2. C replaces another component C_{old} implementing the same interface as C if:
   (a) C's version is greater than C_{old}'s,
   (b) no component currently relying on C_{old} has a **STATIC** dependency on it.

If a component cannot be instantiated because of one or more unsatisfied **MANDATORY** dependencies, it is buffered in the hope that the necessary components will be received later on. If this does not happen, the component is discarded after a timeout.

As an example, Figure 5 shows a possible evolution of the configuration shown in Figure 3. When a Logging component is received, the node-level run-time determines that it can be used to satisfy the optional dependency of Sampling. However,

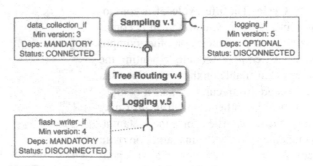

(a) Logging is received.

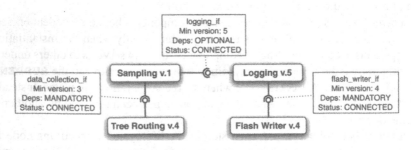

(b) FlashWriter is received.

Fig. 5. A sample evolution of the component configuration in Figure 3

Logging has a **MANDATORY** dependency of its own, which cannot be satisfied. Therefore, Logging is temporarily buffered and remains disconnected from the other components, yielding the configuration in Figure 5(a). In Figure 5(b), a FlashWriter component satisfying the dependency of Logging is received. The run-time determines, by recursively travelling the component graph, that all dependencies are now satisfied, and instantiates the new components in the correct order (i.e., FlashWriter before Logging), yielding the configuration shown in the figure.

Our automatic reconfiguration mechanism relieves the programmer from checking the conditions for the reconfiguration to take place, changing the component interconnections, and managing the coordination among the components involved. Although similar approaches (e.g., [8]) already proved their effectiveness in other contexts, to the best of our knowledge we are the first to enable this functionality in WSNs.

2.2 Specifying *Where* Reconfiguration Occurs

FIGARO empowers programmers with the ability to delimit the portion of the WSN where reconfiguration takes place. This is achieved with dedicated programming constructs that enable programmers to: *i)* declare the attributes characterizing a node; *ii)* specify the reconfiguration target—i.e., the subset of nodes for component deployment—by using boolean predicates over the nodes' attributes.

```
DECLARE_NODE({
    Function = SENSOR
    Type = TEMPERATURE
    Floor = 1
    Battery = getBatteryReading()
})
```

```
DECLARE_TARGET({
    Function == SENSOR && Battery >= 70 &&
    (Type == TEMPERATURE || Type == VIBRATION) &&
    RUNNING(TreeRouting) &&
    VERSION(TreeRouting) <= 11
})
```

Fig. 6. Declaring node attributes   **Fig. 7.** Declaring the reconfiguration target

Figure 6 shows an example where we use the **DECLARE_NODE** macro to specify that a node hosts a temperature sensor and is located on a given floor. Note how, in principle, attributes can be assigned any legal C expression, including C functions as in the case of the Battery field. The nodes targeted by the reconfiguration can be specified declaratively as an (arbitrary) boolean predicate over node attributes using the macro **DECLARE_TARGET**. In Figure 7, we specify as reconfiguration target the set of temperature or vibration sensors with at least 70% of battery left, and running a TreeRouting component with version less than 11. Notably, the latter requirement leverages off information automatically exported by our run-time layer, which describe the current component configuration on a node. Specifically, the parametric, built-in predicate **RUNNING** takes as input the name of a given component C, and yields true when evaluated on a node where C is currently in such state. Instead, the built-in function **VERSION** returns the version of the component given as parameter.

3   Node-Level Run-Time Support

FIGARO provides the constructs described in Section 2.1, concerned with node-level reconfiguration, by making extensive use of C macros, therefore moving at compilation time most of the added complexity while not requiring any dedicated pre-processing step. However, dynamic reconfiguration requires specialized run-time support, provided by library functions we developed, linked against the (unmodified) Contiki kernel.

Our run-time maps FIGARO components to Contiki services [6], and leverages off Contiki's dynamic linking facility [9] to install new code. Consequently, the implementation of the **CALL** macro uses Contiki look-up functions to find a pointer to the callee component, and perform the operation requested. Interfaces and receptacles are represented by descriptors (standard C structs) containing an array of function pointers. In the case of interfaces, these always point to the corresponding functions in the component currently implementing the interface. Instead, the pointers inside receptacles are assigned the function pointer values of the associated interface, when connected, or NULL otherwise. In addition, receptacle descriptors contain further fields to keep track of the nature of dependency, as well as the minimum version required by any component connected to it, as shown in Figure 5.

Based on the information gathered by our macros during the compilation phase, our run-time maintains on every node an internal representation of the exported attributes and current software configuration. This is represented as a graph where vertexes are components, and edges are labeled to reflect the nature of the dependency at hand, similarly to Figure 5. When a new component arrives, simple graph traversal algorithms are used to check the conditions for the installation of a new piece of functionality. If the new component can indeed be installed, the run-time fires the relevant state transitions on all involved components, installs the new component by reconfiguring the involved receptacles, and updates the graph accordingly.

Instead, the constructs concerned with the reconfiguration target, illustrated in Section 2.2, require a minimal amount of pre-processing. On the user base-station, reconfiguration is triggered using a dedicated executable, whose arguments are two files: one containing the component binary image and one with the reconfiguration target (e.g., as in Figure 7). A dedicated pre-processor we developed parses them together, generates a unique reconfiguration identifier, divides the binary image into smaller chunks fitting in single physical messages, and starts injecting them into the network. The details of the routing protocol determining their propagation are described next.

4   A Routing Protocol for Selective Code Distribution

Our dedicated distribution scheme revolves around two base mechanisms:

- While the application is running, we exploit its message traffic to build a *mesh* topology interconnecting all nodes with same attribute-value pairs, as in Figure 8, to identify all possible alternative paths connecting the relevant nodes.
- When a reconfiguration is requested, a subset of the mesh paths are exploited to build a tree rooted at the target node closest to the injection point, as in Figure 9. The tree is then used to propagate the component chunks to all target nodes.

In principle, the two mechanisms above could be designed independently. Nonetheless, our solution is explicitly conceived to take advantage of their mutual interplay. As our objective is to build shortest paths to the target nodes, we make all

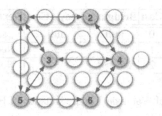

Fig. 8. A mesh connecting all target nodes

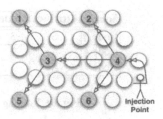

Fig. 9. A distribution tree exploiting the mesh

paths in the mesh itself *bi-directional*. This allows us to exploit the same shortest paths regardless of where the code is injected. Moreover, our solution is designed to create a *planar* mesh topology, i.e., one in which no two paths with different end-points cross at any intermediate node, as in Figure 8. Results in graph theory indeed demonstrated how planar graphs involve fewer routing loops [10]. As a result, the tree topology built atop the mesh easily identifies near-optimal paths, as we demonstrate in Section 5.

4.1 Building the Mesh Topology

Architecture and Data Structures. As the mesh is built during normal system operation, we must minimize the impact of the mesh-building protocol on the application behavior. We obtain this goal by designing a solution that does *not* generate explicit control messages. Rather, we leverage off the application traffic by piggybacking the current value of a node's attributes on every outgoing message[1]. This is achieved by interposing a thin software layer between the application and the underlying network layers whose interface is the same as the original network stack, making its use transparent to the application.

The information piggybacked is overheard by all nodes in range[2], and used to populate a simple routing routing table (e.g., as in Figure 10), that describes the paths of the mesh. Each entry in the table contains a node identifier and the associated attribute-value pair, the next hop to reach that node along with the corresponding cost in hops, and a timestamp to discriminate stale information. In addition, the Bridging and Bridge Cost fields are used to distinguish entries corresponding to bidirectional paths. The former possibly contains the identifier of another node with same attribute-value pair, representing the opposite end-point of the path itself, whereas the latter stores the total path length in hops. Each entry in the table is associated with a lease (not shown) that, if not refreshed, causes the entry removal.

Protocol Operation. Figure 11 describes an example of mesh construction. The initial situation, depicted in Figure 11(a), illustrates the physical network topology and the attributes defined in the node declarations, along with their corresponding values. Initially, all routing tables contain only entries relative to the local node. For instance, let us focus on the nodes having attribute A equal to 1 as target. When node 1 first

---

[1] In case a node is silent, we generate dummy messages at a pre-specified rate.

[2] A simple hook within the Contiki radio layers allows us to overhear also unicast messages.

Source	Attribute	Value	Cost	Bridging	Bridge Cost	Next Hop	Timestamp
Node 3	B	3	0	null	null	self	4
Node 4	A	1	1	Node 1	3	Node 4	25
Node 1	A	1	2	Node 4	3	Node 2	72

Fig. 10. Routing table at node 3 in the situation of Figure 11(c).

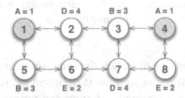

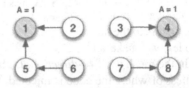

(a) Initial situation. Arrows describe the physical topology.

(b) Node 1, 4, 5 and 8 send application messages. Bold arrows describe the Next Hop field for A = 1.

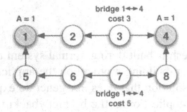

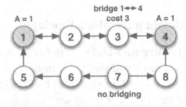

(c) Node 3 and node 7 recognize a chance to build a bidirectional path connecting node 1 and node 4.

(d) The path through node 3 is complete. The one through node 7 is pruned as unnecessary.

Fig. 11. Example of mesh construction (grey circles are target nodes)

sends an application message, we append a subset of node 1's routing table entries to it[3]. The nodes in range parse this information, increments all cost fields by one, and add these entries to their routing tables provided no other entry with same attribute-value pair but smaller or equal cost exists. By doing this at every node, node 1's specification spreads across multiple hops. For instance, node 5's piggybacked information also includes node 1's initial entry, as it was overheard from node 1's transmissions. Assuming node 4 and 8 eventually send some application message as well, the resulting situation is as depicted in Figure 11(b).

To recognize when a bidirectional path can be established, we look for received entries containing an attribute already stored in the local table, but from a different source and greater or equal cost. This is the case in Figure 11(c), where node 3 receives from node 2 an entry for attribute A with value 1 and cost 2. In this situation, a bidirectional path for the same attribute can be established, with node 1 and node 4 as end-points. To establish the bidirectional path in both directions, we insert the newly received entry in

---

[3] Entries are selected in round-robin, their number limited by a configuration parameter.

node 3's routing table with the Bridging field set to the identifier of the opposite end-point of the path (e.g., node 4 in case of node 3 in the last entry of Figure 10), and the Bridge Cost field set to the total cost of the path itself. Similarly, we update any entry already in the table that refers to the other end-point of the bidirectional path—as it is the case for the second entry in Figure 10—modifying the Bridging and Bridge Cost accordingly. Afterwards, entries with non-null Bridging fields are propagated only towards the node reported in the Bridging field itself. Thus, the second entry in Figure 10 is propagated only towards node 1, whereas the last entry spreads only towards node 4. This is as simple as appending an optional field to all outgoing messages stating what nodes propagate what entries.

As a side-effect of the above processing, more than a single bidirectional path connecting node 1 and node 4 could be established. For instance, a further path is eventually built through node 5, 6, 7 and 8, with a total cost of 5. This, however, poses unnecessary communication overhead. To alleviate this undesirable behavior, non-null Bridging entries are propagated only if the node is not aware of other (bidirectional) paths with smaller cost. In our example, node 7 eventually stops propagating its non-null Bridging entry after overhearing the last entry at node 3, which contains a smaller cost. This ultimately yields the situation in Figure 11(d). Although this scheme does not completely prune all redundant paths, it greatly diminishes their number. Pruning all the paths but the shortest one would indeed require propagating the minimum cost entry multiple hops away from the shortest path. How far to propagate is hard to determine without knowledge of the network topology. Also, the additional paths may be used as back-ups in case of sudden faults. We plan to investigate this in the near future.

Dynamic Attributes and Topology Changes. The protocol operation occurs whenever the application generates network traffic. Therefore, in the case of time-varying attributes, the accuracy provided by the mesh topology w.r.t. the current values of attributes is ultimately dictated by the amount of application traffic over time. Applications generating more traffic allow our protocol to build more accurate topologies, whereas it is difficult to do so if the amount of traffic flowing in the network is insufficient to keep up with the dynamics of the varying attribute. As for topology changes, e.g., due to failing nodes, invalid routes will eventually expire without being refreshed. As soon as the application generates further messages, our protocol identifies alternative routes according to the new topology. Still, the time taken to build the new routes is dependent on the amount of traffic generated by the application.

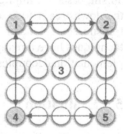

Fig. 12. Node 3 has equal cost to all target nodes

Enforcing Planarity. By construction, our scheme does not generate multiple paths with different end-points crossing at an intermediate node. Indeed, the only way this can be obtained is to have, in the same routing table, more than one non-null Bridging entry for the same attribute-value pair with different source. Consider Figure 12: node 3 may try to establish two crossing paths, e.g., connecting node 1 to node 5 and node 2 to node 4. This cannot occur in our protocol, as received entries with cost greater or equal to the local table for the same attribute-value pair are ignored, end every non-null Bridging entry can be used to establish a single bidirectional path. Therefore, node 3 in Figure 12 will never be able to generate crossing paths.

4.2 Distributing Code

When a reconfiguration takes place, code is distributed along a tree: redundant paths in the mesh are identified based on the position of the code injection point, using a *marker* message. This contains the reconfiguration identifier generated by our pre-processor, and an encoding of the predicate defining the required reconfiguration target. The former serves to support multiple concurrent reconfigurations. The latter is used by nodes to determine, based on their routing table, the next hop for the marker. Upon forwarding, target nodes add to the marker the cost accumulated along the last bidirectional path traversed. This way, the marker eventually reaches all the target nodes, making them aware of their distance from the injection point. This information is used at each target node to configure a dedicated distribution tree by selecting as parent the target node that, along the links of the mesh, is the closest to the injection point. The selection is communicated to the parent with a message containing the identifiers of the source target node and of the selected parent. Note how code dissemination can start before the entire tree is built. When receiving a code chunk, a node that has not yet determined its children simply defers forwarding and buffers the chunk. Buffering would happen in any case, since a component cannot be reconstructed until all chunks are received.

The code distribution phase demands reliable communication, e.g., because all code chunks must be correctly delivered. We employ a simple hop-by-hop reliability mechanism, based on implicit acks. Nodes on a tree path buffer every message, waiting for the downstream node to re-send it. When this occurs, the upstream node overhears the transmission, and concludes the message was received; otherwise, it is re-sent. Similar techniques have already been successfully employed in WSNs [11]. However, our implementation decouples this aspect, enabling the use of alternative reliability schemes.

5 Evaluation

To assess the effectiveness of our approach, in this section we separately evaluate the performance of the node-level run-time support, and of the code distribution protocol.

5.1 Evaluating the Node-Level Run-Time Support

Our objective here is to quantify the overhead imposed by FIGARO w.r.t. plain Contiki. We consider the following performance figures:

- The *memory occupation* caused by our component model, w.r.t. both program and data memory. We evaluated the former by looking at the size of binary images after compilation. As for the latter, we manually inspected the code managing components and their interconnections, looking for any data structure we defined.
- The additional *processing time* caused by the presence of components. This is affected both by the installation of a new component compared to the native Contiki

dynamic linker, and by function calls across components using **CALL** instead of a direct C call. As for the latter, we placed the call in a loop and repeated the operation a million times, since the single call is too quick to be measured precisely.

– The *energy consumption* during reconfiguration, which may increase as a result of the additional processing required to manage components and dependencies.

We measured processing time and energy consumption using real nodes as opposed to simulation environments, as similar fine-grained aspects are only partially modeled in existing simulators. Practically, we measured the processing overhead using a JTAG programmer attached to the node to measure the time elapsed between the execution of different instructions. Energy consumption was instead evaluated using an Agilent 54832B oscilloscope and a multimeter hooked to a node, which in our case was a TMote Sky [12]. We repeated the experiments concerning these metrics 5 times using 3 different nodes, and averaged the results. New components have been injected via a USB cable attached to the node, to avoid any bias due to the radio.

To gather the above metrics, we employed a Blinker component offering a single interface with two operations to start/stop the blinking of a led. We varied the number of receptacles within the component itself to evaluate our performance w.r.t. a varying number of dependencies. The processing within Blinker is the same as in [9], and is quite simple being described by only 17 lines of C code. This choice was intentional, as simpler components make the overhead more evident w.r.t. the above metrics.

Results. Figure 13 shows the memory overhead, which turns out to be quite reasonable, w.r.t. both program and data memory. As for the former, the binary code deployed in addition to the operating system accounts for less than 2 Kbytes in total. This cost, along with the overhead due to helper data structures, is paid once and for all, regardless of the number of components and the number of their interfaces/receptacles. Conversely,

Performance Measure	Memory	Footprint
Dependency Checks	Program	1.1 KB
Helper Functions	Program	802 bytes
Helper Data Structures	Data	230 bytes
Per-Component Data	Data	15 bytes
Per-Interface Data	Data	8 bytes
Per-Receptacle Data	Data	10 bytes

Fig. 13. Memory overhead

Function Type	Time Overhead %
Empty	157.5%
50 integer additions	20.1%
3 x 3 matrix inversion	5.4%
5 x 5 matrix inversion	0.98%
Fourier Transform (100 input values)	0.78%
Fourier Transform (1000 input values)	0.03%

Fig. 14. FiGaRo calls across components vs. native C function calls

Dependencies	Time (s)		Energy (mJ)	
	Absolute	Overhead	Absolute	Overhead
1	0.518 sec	+0.019	3.45	+0.07
2	0.520 sec	+0.021	3.45	+0.07
3	0.525 sec	+0.026	3.47	+0.09
4	0.528 sec	+0.029	3.49	+0.11
5	0.532 sec	+0.033	3.5	+0.12

Fig. 15. Time and energy to install the Blinker component

the bottom section of Figure 13 reports the memory consumption incurred every time a component, interface, or receptacle is loaded on a node. In this case as well, the overhead is fairly limited. Based on these results, we maintain that our approach can scale to a sizable number of components simultaneously running on the same node, presumably well beyond the current needs of common WSN applications. As for the amount of code to be deployed, we compared the size of the binary image of the plain-Contiki Blinker process used in [9] against ours, implemented as a FiGaRo component. The size increases from 1.01 Kbytes to 1.11 Kbytes, yielding an overhead of only 9.98%. We believe this value is good, given the little complexity of the processing at hand.

The overhead in performing calls across components against direct C function calls is reported in Figure 14. Interestingly, when the function called does not contain any real processing the overhead due to using **CALL** is high. In this case, performing the look-up of the Contiki service implementing the requested component dominates the processing time. In contrast, some even simple processing within the function called makes this metric drop abruptly. For instance, in the case of a Fourier transform (e.g., employed to perform in-network processing in WSN applications such as [4]) the overhead becomes less than 1%. Therefore, although our programming model does introduce an overhead, the performance penalty is expected to be negligible in real applications.

By the same token, the time for installing a new component, and hence the energy consumed during this process, increases only marginally w.r.t. the standard Contiki dynamic linker, as shown in Figure 15 for a varying number of dependencies in the component being installed. Note how these values are independent of the size of the component being deployed, as they represent the overhead imposed by our run-time layer in addition to the Contiki dynamic linker, which we left unmodified. Also, they scale well with the number of dependencies, showing only a very small increase. To place Figure 15 in context, consider that the energy *overhead* in the case with 5 dependencies is equal to only about 5% of the *total* energy required to transmit a 32-byte message.

5.2 Evaluating the Code Distribution

In this section we assess the effectiveness of our solution for code distribution by reporting about simulations performed using Cooja, the Contiki simulator.

node 3's routing table with the Bridging field set to the identifier of the opposite end-point of the path (e.g., node 4 in case of node 3 in the last entry of Figure 10), and the Bridge Cost field set to the total cost of the path itself. Similarly, we update any entry already in the table that refers to the other end-point of the bidirectional path—as it is the case for the second entry in Figure 10—modifying the Bridging and Bridge Cost accordingly. Afterwards, entries with non-null Bridging fields are propagated only towards the node reported in the Bridging field itself. Thus, the second entry in Figure 10 is propagated only towards node 1, whereas the last entry spreads only towards node 4. This is as simple as appending an optional field to all outgoing messages stating what nodes propagate what entries.

As a side-effect of the above processing, more than a single bidirectional path connecting node 1 and node 4 could be established. For instance, a further path is eventually built through node 5, 6, 7 and 8, with a total cost of 5. This, however, poses unnecessary communication overhead. To alleviate this undesirable behavior, non-null Bridging entries are propagated only if the node is not aware of other (bidirectional) paths with smaller cost. In our example, node 7 eventually stops propagating its non-null Bridging entry after overhearing the last entry at node 3, which contains a smaller cost. This ultimately yields the situation in Figure 11(d). Although this scheme does not completely prune all redundant paths, it greatly diminishes their number. Pruning all the paths but the shortest one would indeed require propagating the minimum cost entry multiple hops away from the shortest path. How far to propagate is hard to determine without knowledge of the network topology. Also, the additional paths may be used as back-ups in case of sudden faults. We plan to investigate this in the near future.

Dynamic Attributes and Topology Changes. The protocol operation occurs whenever the application generates network traffic. Therefore, in the case of time-varying attributes, the accuracy provided by the mesh topology w.r.t. the current values of attributes is ultimately dictated by the amount of application traffic over time. Applications generating more traffic allow our protocol to build more accurate topologies, whereas it is difficult to do so if the amount of traffic flowing in the network is insufficient to keep up with the dynamics of the varying attribute. As for topology changes, e.g., due to failing nodes, invalid routes will eventually expire without being refreshed. As soon as the application generates further messages, our protocol identifies alternative routes according to the new topology. Still, the time taken to build the new routes is dependent on the amount of traffic generated by the application.

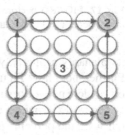

Fig. 12. Node 3 has equal cost to all target nodes

Enforcing Planarity. By construction, our scheme does not generate multiple paths with different end-points crossing at an intermediate node. Indeed, the only way this can be obtained is to have, in the same routing table, more than one non-null Bridging entry for the same attribute-value pair with different source. Consider Figure 12: node 3 may try to establish two crossing paths, e.g., connecting node 1 to node 5 and node 2 to node 4. This cannot occur in our protocol, as received entries with cost greater or

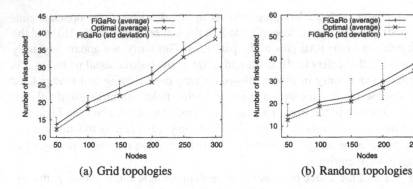

Fig. 16. FIGARO performance vs. topology and system size (target nodes are 10% of the total)

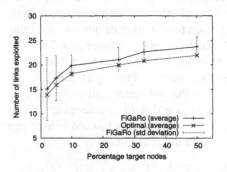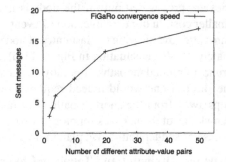

Fig. 17. FIGARO performance vs. number of target nodes (100 nodes arranged in a grid)

Fig. 18. FIGARO convergence speed (100 nodes arranged in a grid)

its planarity property, yields near-optimal routes in the distribution trees relying on it. Further, note how Figures 16(a) and 16(b) exhibit similar trends, although the results on random networks show higher variability due to the irregularity of the topology.

Figure 17 provides a different perspective by analyzing the behavior of our protocol w.r.t. the percentage of target nodes. As shown in the chart, our solution is barely affected by this parameter. The high variability observed with few target nodes is due to cases where nodes end up aligned w.r.t. the injection point, and the distribution tree degenerates in a chain. In these configurations, intermediate nodes are reached at essentially no cost. The probability of these configurations decreases as the number of target nodes grows. We limited our experiments to half of the nodes in the system as targets. Beyond this point, the scenario starts bearing similarities with traditional code distribution in homogeneous networks, where all nodes are target. In this case, existing solutions are better suited, e.g., [14].

Finally, we verified that the convergence speed of the mesh-building phase is not affected by the system scale. Indeed, the extent to which routing entries are propagated is not dictated by the overall number of nodes, rather by the amount of redundancy among attribute-value pairs. This claim is supported by Figure 18, showing the number of messages required to build the mesh against the number of (distinct) attribute-value pairs in the system. When the latter is small the mesh builds quickly, as the bidirectional paths connecting nodes with the same attribute-value pairs are likely to be short. Instead, when attribute-value pairs are highly heterogeneous the mesh takes more time, due to the dual argument. Overall, the values in the chart are good: only 17 messages need to be sent when 50 different attribute-value pairs are present, i.e., only 2 nodes in the 100-node network of Figure 18 have the same attribute-value pair—a rather unusual setting. In any case, the values in the chart should represent only a very little fraction of the overall system lifetime, typically measured over months or even years.

6 Related Work

Single-Node Reconfiguration. Several solutions enable the installation of new code on individual nodes. At the operating system level, besides Contiki also the SOS operating system [15] provides dynamic linking, while FlexCup [16] enables this functionality in TinyOS [17], where this was initially not possible. These solutions concentrate on efficient dynamic linking, and are therefore complementary to our approach. In principle, our component model can be re-applied in SOS and FlexCup with minimal modifications, as it is mostly based on standard C macros. We chose Contiki because, unlike FlexCup, it preserves the application state as it does not require a reboot after code loading and, in comparison to SOS, its service functionality eases the implementation of the FIGARO component model. Alternative approaches use interpreted languages and virtual machines (e.g., [18,19,20]), with some also allowing for extensible instruction sets, e.g, [21]. Nonetheless, the trade-offs between interpreting code and executing native binaries, as discussed in [18], suggest the use of the latter for long-running systems where reconfiguration is a rare event, as in the scenarios we target.

Most importantly, none of the above approaches provides support to the *programmer* for managing the interactions among the different functionality on a node during reconfiguration. Indeed, even though component models for WSN programming have already been proposed (e.g., [2, 5, 7]), they do not include any dedicated construct for managing mutable component configurations. Conversely, we made component dependencies and versions first-class citizens in the FIGARO programming model, and designed the reconfiguration mechanism by balancing automation and customizability.

Code Distribution. To the best of our knowledge, we are the first to provide efficient distribution of code to an arbitrary subset of nodes identified by programmer-provided information. Our distribution model is inspired by Logical Neighborhoods [22], a programming abstraction giving developers the ability to define system partitions based on application information. A message-passing API is then provided to interact with nodes in a given partition. Although [22] describes a generic communication layer for Logical Neighborhoods, tackling the issues germane to code distribution required a completely different routing support, as described in Section 4. In the field of code distribution, the approach closest to ours is the TinyCubus framework [23], where code can be distributed to all nodes with a given role, e.g., all cluster-heads. This is far less flexible than FIGARO's predicate logic over programmer-defined attributes, and does not encompass the ability to identify the target nodes based on their current software configuration, e.g., as provided by the RUNNING built-in-predicate. At the network level, TinyCubus assumes *a priori* knowledge of the system topology and of the location of nodes with a given role, as it requires to specify an upper bound on the number of hops separating nodes with the same role. In contrast, our solution is fully dynamic and decentralized.

Network-wide distribution of code has been widely investigated, tackling different facets of the problem. On one hand, solutions have been proposed to reduce the size of the code to be distributed by employing differential patching and smart linking mechanisms, e.g., [24, 25]. Still, similar concerns are orthogonal to the problem we tackle in this work, and the corresponding solutions may be integrated in our framework for even better performance, e.g., by injecting a patch instead of the whole binary when the new component is going to replace an older version. Instead, other approaches focused on routing. Trickle [14] uses a counter-based technique called "polite gossip", whose objective is to suppress redundant transmissions while guaranteeing eventual delivery. Deluge [26] uses a similar technique, with the addition of a negotiation phase to guarantee the proper sequencing of packets. This is also used in MNP [27] to address the hidden terminal problem before transmitting the actual code. Sprinkler [28] and Firecracker [29] instead leverage off node hierarchies, by first sending code to "core" nodes up in the hierarchy, which then forward the code to nodes in their vicinity. As the objective of all the above solutions is to distributed code to all nodes, they can avoid any background activity under normal operating conditions. For the same reason, however, these mechanisms are hardly applicable in our case. For instance, it would be fairly inefficient to add multi-hop negotiation in Deluge to address the case where the target nodes are multiple hops away.

7   Conclusion and Future Work

In this paper we presented FIGARO, a solution enabling software reconfiguration in WSNs at an unprecedented level of granularity, both w.r.t. the functionality to reconfigure on single nodes, and the subset of nodes targeted by the reconfiguration. We provide a component-based programming model with explicit support for component dependencies and versions, along with a dedicated component life cycle, and an intuitive yet expressive distribution model allowing programmers to identify what part of the network is affected by the reconfiguration. Our evaluation demonstrated how the overhead imposed on single nodes is negligible, while the communication overhead during reconfiguration lies within 9% from the theoretical optimum.

Our research agenda includes distributed mechanisms to provide more guarantees (e.g., atomicity) w.r.t. the reconfiguration process. For instance, the programmer may require that either all or none of the nodes in the reconfiguration target install the new component, to tolerate run-time faults where a node crashes and then reboots.

Acknowledgements. The authors wish to thank Fabio Fabbri for helping with the measures gathered on real nodes, Prof. Greg Frederickson for the insightful discussions on the shortest path problem on planar graphs, and Alessandro Ungari for his work on the implementation of the FIGARO run-time. The work described here was partially supported by the European Union under the IST-004536 RUNES project.

References

1. Wang, Q., Zhu, Y., Cheng, L.: Reprogramming wireless sensor networks: challenges and approaches. IEEE Network 20(3) (2006)
2. Costa, P., et al.: The RUNES middleware for networked embedded systems and its application in a disaster management scenario. In: PERCOM. Proc. of the 5th Int. Conf. on Pervasive Communications (2007)
3. Deshpande, A., Guestrin, C., Madden, S.: Resource-aware wireless sensor-actuator networks. IEEE Data Engineering 28(1) (2005)
4. Lynch, J.P., Loh, K.J.: A summary review of wireless sensors and sensor networks for structural health monitoring. Shock and Vibration Digest (March 2006)
5. Gay, D., Levis, P., von Behren, R., Welsh, M., Brewer, E., Culler, D.: The nesC language: A holistic approach to networked embedded systems. In: PLDI. Proc. of the ACM SIGPLAN Conf. on Programming Language Design and Implementation (2003)
6. Dunkels, A., Grönvall, B., Voigt, T.: Contiki - a lightweight and flexible operating system for tiny networked sensors. In: Proc. of 1st Wkshp. on Embedded Networked Sensors (2004)
7. Grace, P., Coulson, G., Blair, G., Porter, B., Hughes, D.: Dynamic reconfiguration in sensor middleware. In: MidSens. Proc. of Int. Wkshp. on Middleware for Sensor Network (2006)
8. Becker, C., Handte, M., Schiele, G., Rothermel, K.: PCOM - A component system for pervasive computing. In: PERCOM. Proc. of the 2nd Int. Conf. on Pervasive Computing and Communications (2004)
9. Dunkels, A., Finne, N., Eriksson, J., Voigt, T.: Run-time dynamic linking for reprogramming wireless sensor networks. In: SenSys. Proc. of 4th Int. Conf. on Embedded Networked Sensor Systems (2006)
10. Frederickson, G.: Fast algorithms for shortest paths in planar graphs, with applications. Siam J. Computing 16(6) (1987)
11. Stann, F., Hiedemann, J.: RMST: reliable data transport in sensor networks. In: Proc. of the 1st Int. Wkshp. on Sensor Network Protocols and Applications (2003)
12. MoteIV Technology, www.moteiv.com
13. Stoleru, R., Stankovic, J.: Probability grid: A location estimation scheme for wireless sensor networks. In: SECON. Proc. of the 1st Int. Conf. on Sensor and Ad-Hoc Communication and Networks (2004)
14. Levis, P., Patel, N., Culler, D., Shenker, S.: Trickle: a self-regulating algorithm for code propagation and maintenance in wireless sensor networks. In: NSDI. Proc. of the 1st Conf. on Networked Systems Design and Implementation (2004)
15. Han, C.C., Kumar, R., Shea, R., Kohler, E., Srivastava, M.: A dynamic operating system for sensor nodes. In: MobiSys. Proc. of the 3rd Int. Conf. on Mobile Systems, Applications, and Services (2005)
16. Marrón, P.J., Gauger, M., Lachenmann, A., Minder, D., Saukh, O., Rothermel, K.: FlexCup: A flexible and efficient code update mechanism for sensor networks. In: Römer, K., Karl, H., Mattern, F. (eds.) EWSN 2006. LNCS, vol. 3868, pp. 212–227. Springer, Heidelberg (2006)
17. Hill, J., et al.: System architecture directions for networked sensors. In: Proc. of the 9^{nt} Int. Conf. on Architectural Support for Programming Languages and Operating Systems (2000)
18. Levis, P., Culler, D.: Maté: a tiny virtual machine for sensor networks. In: ASPLOS-X: Proc. of the 10th Int. Conf. on Architectural Support for Programming Languages and Operating Systems (2002)
19. Müller, R., Alonso, G., Kossmann, D.: A virtual machine for sensor networks. In: Proc. of the EuroSys Conf. (2007)
20. Koshy, J., Pandey, R.: VM*: synthesizing scalable runtime environments for sensor networks. In: SenSys. Proc. of 3th Int. Conf. on Embedded Networked Sensor Systems (2005)

21. Levis, P., Gay, D., Culler, D.: Active sensor networks. In: NSDI. Proc. of the 2nd Conf. on Networked Systems Design & Implementation (2005)
22. Mottola, L., Picco, G.P.: Logical Neighborhoods: A programming abstraction for wireless sensor networks. In: DCOSS. Proc. of the the 2nd Int. Conf. on Distributed Computing on Sensor Systems (2006)
23. Marrón, P.J., Lachenmann, A., Minder, D., Hahner, J., Sauter, R., Rothermel, K.: Tinycubus: a flexible and adaptive framework sensor networks. In: Proc. of the 2nd European Workshop on Wireless Sensor Networks (EWSN) (2005)
24. Reijers, N., Langendoen, K.: Efficient code distribution in wireless sensor networks. In: WSNA. Proc. of the 2nd Int. Conf. on Wireless Sensor Networks and Applications (2003)
25. Koshy, J., Pandey, R.: Remote incremental linking for energy-efficient reprogramming of sensor networks. In: Proc. of 2nd European Workshop on Wireless Sensor Networks (EWSN) (2005)
26. Hui, J.W., Culler, D.: The dynamic behavior of a data dissemination protocol for network programming at scale. In: SenSys. Proc. of 2nd Int. Conf. on Embedded Networked Sensor Systems (2004)
27. Kulkarni, S., Wang, L.: MNP: Multihop network reprogramming service for sensor networks. In: ICDCS. Proc. of the 25th Int. Conf. on Distributed Computing Systems (2005)
28. Naik, V., Arora, A., Sinha, P., Zhang, H.: Sprinkler: A reliable and energy efficient data dissemination service for wireless embedded devices. In: RTSS. Proc. of the 26th International Real-Time Systems Symposium (2005)
29. Levis, P., Culler, D.: The Firecracker protocol. In: Proc. of the 11th ACM SIGOPS European Workshop (2004)

NanoECC: Testing the Limits of Elliptic Curve Cryptography in Sensor Networks

Piotr Szczechowiak[1], Leonardo B. Oliveira[2,*], Michael Scott[1], Martin Collier[1], and Ricardo Dahab[2]

[1] Dublin City University, Ireland
piotr@eeng.dcu.ie, mike@computing.dcu.ie, collierm@eeng.dcu.ie
[2] UNICAMP, Brazil
leob@ic.unicamp.br, rdahab@ic.unicamp.br

Abstract. By using Elliptic Curve Cryptography (ECC), it has been recently shown that Public-Key Cryptography (PKC) is indeed feasible on resource-constrained nodes. This feasibility, however, does not necessarily mean attractiveness, as the obtained results are still not satisfactory enough. In this paper, we present results on implementing ECC, as well as the related emerging field of Pairing-Based Cryptography (PBC), on two of the most popular sensor nodes. By doing that, we show that PKC is not only viable, but in fact attractive for WSNs. As far as we know pairing computations presented in this paper are the most efficient results on the MICA2 (8-bit/7.3828-MHz ATmega128L) and Tmote Sky (16-bit/8.192-MHz MSP-430) nodes.

Keywords: Wireless Sensor Networks, Elliptic Curve Cryptography, pairings, cryptographic primitives, implementation.

1 Introduction

Wireless sensor networks (WSNs) are ad hoc networks comprised mainly of small sensor nodes with limited resources and one or more base stations (BSs). Usually a BS is a much more powerful laptop-class node that connects the sensor nodes to the rest of the world [1,2]. WSN's are used for monitoring purposes, and provide information about the area being monitored to the rest of the system. Application areas range from battlefield reconnaissance and emergency rescue operations to surveillance and environmental protection.

Like any wireless ad hoc network, WSNs are vulnerable to many different attacks [3,4]. Besides the well-known vulnerabilities due to wireless communication and their distributed nature, WSNs face additional problems. Sensor nodes are usually small, cheap devices that are unlikely to be made tamper-resistant or tamper-proof and after deployment they are left unattended which makes them easily accessible to malicious parties. It is therefore crucial to add security

* Supported by CAPES (Brazilian Ministry of Education) grant 4630/06-8 and FAPESP grant 2005/00557-9.

to WSNs, especially in those applications where nodes are distributed in open environments.

Until recently it used to be thought that Public-Key Cryptography (PKC) was impractical in resource-constrained nodes and that security primitives must depend only on symmetric cryptosystems (e.g., RC5 [5] and SkipJack [6]). Although more efficient than PKC, symmetric cryptosystems suffer from some drawbacks (e.g., the *key distribution problem*[1]) which make them not well-suited for every WSN application.

This fact has motivated work on how to compute PKC efficiently in sensor nodes (e.g., [7,8,9,10]). The problem is challenging because those tiny devices have very limited battery life and we cannot afford to spend too much processor time on additional computations. By using Elliptic Curve Cryptography (ECC) [11,12] it has been shown (e.g., [8,9]) that PKC is indeed feasible in WSNs. This is because ECC demands considerably less resources than more conventional PKC (e.g. RSA/DSA), for a given security level. This feasibility, however, does not necessarily mean attractiveness, as the results presented so far are still too time consuming for some applications.

In this paper, we present updated results on implementing ECC, and PBC, over two of the most popular WSN platforms. By doing that, we show that these types of PKC are not only viable, but in fact attractive for resource-constrained sensor nodes. More specifically, we present results on computing point multiplication and pairings over MICA2 and Tmote Sky nodes. Our main contributions are

1. To show that ECC and PBC based PKC is not only viable, but in fact efficient for resource-constrained nodes;
2. To present the first known implementation of pairings over binary field for sensor networks.

Our code is based on Multiprecision Integer and Rational Arithmetic C/C++ Library (MIRACL) [13], which is a publicly available library written in C, and thus can be easily ported to other devices.

The remainder of this work is organized as follows. In Section 2, we discuss related work. In Section 3, we introduce some basic ECC and PBC concepts. Implementation issues and performance results are presented in Sections 4 and 5, respectively. Finally, we conclude in Section 6.

2   Related Work

WSNs are a subclass of MANETs, and much work (e.g., [14,15]) has been proposed for securing MANETs in general. These studies are not applicable to WSNs because they assume laptop or palmtop-level resources, which are orders of magnitude larger than those available in WSNs. Conventional public key

---

[1] The key distribution problem is the problem of how to set up secret keys between communicating nodes.

based methods are an example of a type of application which, while practical in a MANET, would be impracticable for a WSN.

Among the studies specifically targeted to resource-constrained WSNs, some (e.g,[4,3]) have focused on attacks and vulnerabilities. Wood and Stankovic [4] surveyed a number of denial of service attacks against WSNs, and discussed some possible countermeasures. Karlof and Wagner [3] focused on routing layer attacks, and showed how some of the existing WSN protocols are vulnerable to these attacks.

Many security proposals for WSNs (e.g., [5,16,17,18,19,20,21,22,23,24]) have focused on efficient key management of symmetric encryption schemes. Perrig et al. [5] proposed SPINS, a suite of efficient symmetric key based security building blocks. Eschenauer et al. [16] looked at random key predistribution schemes, which provoked a large number of follow-on studies [25]. In [17] Zhu et al. proposed LEAP, a rather efficient scheme based on local distribution of secret keys among neighboring nodes.

The studies specifically targeted to PKC have tried either to adjust conventional algorithms (e.g. RSA) to sensor nodes, or to employ more efficient techniques (e.g. ECC) in this resource-constrained environment. All the seminal papers of Watro et al. [7], Gura et al. [8], and Malan et al. [9] have used the ATmega128L microprocessor as the implementation platform. Watro et al. [7] proposed TinyPK. To perform key distribution, TinyPK assigns RSA efficient public operations to nodes and RSA expensive private operations to better equipped external parties. Gura et al. [8] reported results for ECC and RSA primitives on the ATmega128L and demonstrated convincingly that the former outperforms the latter. Their ECC implementation is based upon arithmetic in the prime finite field $GF(p)$. In order to speed up integer multiplication in this field they came up with the idea for the hybrid multiplication. In our work we exploit improvements to this method to make it even more efficient on both considered platforms. Malan et al. [9] have presented the first ECC implementation over binary fields $GF(2^m)$ for sensor nodes. They used polynomials basis and presented results for the ECDH key exchange protocol. More recently, Liu et al. developed TinyECC [26], an ECC library that provides elliptic curve arithmetic over prime fields and uses inline assembly code to speed up critical operations on the ATmega128 processor. Lately, they have also added support for the MSP430 and XScale platforms.

Some of the research in cryptographic implementation has focused specifically on the MSP430 processor. Guajardo et al. [27] have shown that scalar point multiplication over prime fields can be achieved efficiently without any stored/precomputed values. They used the MSP430x33x family of microprocessors which is not used in current WSN motes. Wang et al. [28] worked with the TelosB mote [29], which also features the MSP430 processor. They presented results for basic ECC operations over prime fields, such as point addition, point doubling and point multiplication.

In the literature we can find some papers (e.g [30,31,32,33,34,35,10]) that envision WSNs as a scenario in which to exploit Pairing-based Cryptography (PBC).

Of those related to pairing implementation on sensor nodes, McCusker *et al.* [33] have focused on a hardware solution that both implements primitives for computing the Tate pairing and meets the strict energy constraints of sensor nodes. Doyle *et al.* [32] presented simulation results on pairings on the ARM7TDMI [36] processor. This platform, however, is considerably more powerful than any of the devices that are used in WSN's at the moment. In [35] Oliveira *et al.* focused on the ATmega128L and described the possibility of implementing the Tate pairing on this platform. Nevertheless no actual implementation was presented. Finally, Oliveira *et al.* [10] recently presented TinyTate and showed that software implementation of PBC is indeed viable in resource-constrained nodes, even though its level of security was not adequate for all applications. TinyTate also targets the ATmega128L and uses TinyECC as the underlying library.

3   Concepts

ECC was independently introduced by Miller [11] and Koblitz [12]. As opposed to conventional PKC (e.g. RSA/DSA), there is no sub-exponential algorithm known to solve ECC's underlying hard problems and ECC can thus offer equivalent security using smaller parameters [37].

Cryptography using Pairings (PBC), on the other hand, is an emerging field related to ECC which has been attracting the interest of international cryptography community, since it enables the design of original cryptographic schemes and makes well-known cryptographic protocols more efficient. Pairings, such as the Weil pairing, were first used in the context of cryptanalysis [38], but their first use in cryptography is due to the works of Sakai [39] *et al.* and Joux [40].

In this section we briefly introduce some ECC and PBC concepts. For more information on this issues please refer to, for instance, López *et al.* [37] and Galbraith [41]. In what follows, let $E/\mathbb{F}_q$ be an elliptic curve over a finite field $\mathbb{F}_q$, and $E(\mathbb{F}_q)$ be the group of points on this curve, and $\#E(\mathbb{F}_q)$ be the group order.

Bilinear Pairing. Let ℓ be a positive integer. Let $\mathbb{G}_1$ and $\mathbb{G}_2$ be additively-written groups of order ℓ with identity $\mathcal{O}$, and let $\mathbb{G}_T$ be a multiplicatively-written group of order ℓ with identity 1.

A *bilinear pairing* is a computable, non-degenerate function

$$e : \mathbb{G}_1 \times \mathbb{G}_2 \to \mathbb{G}_T.$$

The most important property of pairings in cryptographic constructions is the bilinearity, namely:

$$\forall P \in \mathbb{G}_1, \forall Q \in \mathbb{G}_2 \text{ and } \forall a, b \in \mathbb{Z}^*, \text{ we have}$$

$$e([a]P, [b]Q) = e(P, [b]Q)^a = e([a]P, Q)^b = e(P, Q)^{ab}.$$

In practice, the groups $\mathbb{G}_1$ and $\mathbb{G}_2$ are implemented using a group of points on certain special elliptic curves and the group $\mathbb{G}_T$ is implemented using a multiplicative subgroup of an extension of the underlying finite field. For certain families of supersingular elliptic curves we have $\mathbb{G}_1 = \mathbb{G}_2$.

Discrete Logarithm Problem. Let $\mathbb{G} = \langle \alpha \rangle$ be multiplicatively-written group of order n with generator α and let β be an element of $\mathbb{G}$. The Discrete Logarithm Problem (DLP) is to compute an integer l such that $\beta = \alpha^l$.

Elliptic Curve Discrete Logarithm Problem. Elliptic Curve Discrete Logarithm Problem (ECDLP) is: given a point P of order n and $Q \in \langle P \rangle$, compute $l \in [0, n-1]$ such that $Q = lP$.

Elliptic Curve Diffie-Hellman Problem. Elliptic Curve Diffie-Hellman Problem (ECDHP) is: given a point P, $[a]P$, and $[b]P$ for some $a, b \in \mathbb{Z}^*$, compute $[ab]P$.

Embedding Degree. A subgroup $\mathbb{G}$ of $E(\mathbb{F}_q)$ is said to have an *embedding degree* k with respect to ℓ if k is the smallest integer such that $\ell \mid q^k - 1$.

Bilinear Diffie-Hellman Problem. Most of the pairing applications rely on the hardness of the following problem for their security [41]: given P, $[a]P$, $[b]P$, and $[c]P$ for some $a, b \in \mathbb{Z}^*$, compute

$$e(P, P)^{abc}.$$

This problem is known as the *Bilinear Diffie-Hellman Problem*. The hardness of the Bilinear Diffie-Hellman Problem depends on the hardness of the Diffie-Hellman problems both on $E(\mathbb{F}_q)$ and in $\mathbb{F}_{q^k}$. So, for most pairing applications the parameters q, ℓ, and k must satisfy the following security requirements:

1. ℓ must be large enough so that solving the ECDLP in an order-ℓ subgroup of $E(\mathbb{F}_q)$ is infeasible (e.g. using Pollard's rho algorithm);
2. k must be large enough so that solving the DLP in $\mathbb{F}_{q^k}$ is infeasible (e.g., using the index-calculus method).

The Tate Pairing. Let $E(\mathbb{F}_q)$ contain a subgroup of prime order ℓ coprime with q and with embedding degree k. (In most applications, ℓ is also a large prime divisor of $\#E(\mathbb{F}_q)$.) The *Tate pairing* is the bilinear pairing

$$\hat{e} : E(\mathbb{F}_{q^k})[\ell] \times E(\mathbb{F}_{q^k})/[\ell]E(\mathbb{F}_{q^k}) \rightarrow \mathbb{F}_{q^k}^* / (\mathbb{F}_{q^k}^*)^\ell.$$

4 Implementation

Our implementation of Elliptic Curve primitives targets two different platforms the 8-bit Atmel ATmega128L and the 16-bit Texas Instruments MSP430F1611, as these are most commonly used processors in Wireless Sensor Network nodes nowadays. Although both microcontrollers have RISC architectures, they differ in many ways. ATmega128L [42] has a very modern advanced RISC architecture where most of 133 instructions are executed in a single clock cycle. In contrast, the MSP430F1611 [43] has a more traditional architecture, offers 27 instructions in 7 addressing modes and uses mainly memory based operations. The former

CPU has 32 8-bit registers and three 16-bit pointer registers, the latter provides 16 16-bit registers from which only 12 are available for general purpose use. The Atmel product operates at 7.3828 MHz, and offers 4KB of RAM memory and 128 KB of program space, whereas MSP430 has 8.192 MHz frequency, 48 KB ROM and 10 KB RAM. The Texas Instruments microcontroller also embeds a 16×16 bit hardware multiplier and has an ultra-low power design, which makes it more efficient in terms of current consumption than the ATmega128L.

We chose two popular WSN motes to test the performance of our ECC based programs: The MICA2 [44] platform developed by Crossbow Technology and the Tmote Sky [45] developed by Moteiv corporation. MICA2 mote is build upon the ATmega128L processor, incorporates a 433 MHz radio and has 512 KB of FLASH memory to store measurement data. The Tmote Sky uses the MSP430F1611 microcontroller and Chipcon CC2420 wireless transceiver which operates in the 2.4 GHz ISM band and provides transmission speeds up to 250 Kbps. Using the TinyOS [46] operating system allowed us to run the same programs written in nesC [47] language on both WSN motes. Porting the code from one device to another was a lot easier with the use of TinyOS, which enables the use of features like timers, I/O interfaces, LED's, etc. in an unified way. This approach allowed us to hid most of the hardware dependencies for different platforms and simplified the programming.

Almost all of our code was written in the C/nesC language and can be easily ported to other 8, 16 or even 32-bit resource constrained platforms. This approach is a trade-off between size and re-usability of the code. In order to speed up the execution of particularly time-critical functions we have replaced standard C code with some assembly language specific for each platform. Even though we used inline assembly in our programs we made the whole process as portable as possible. Our assembler routines were generated automatically by special utility program from user defined macros. In this simple and convenient way appropriate assembler code can be quickly developed for new platforms and processors that are not yet supported.

4.1   Basic Primitives Implementation

NanoECC is based on MIRACL [13] (Multiprecision Integer and Rational Arithmetic C/C++ Library) which provides all the necessary Elliptic Curve primitives and functions to compute Pairings and to implement protocols like ECDH, ECDSA. MIRACL is a set of tools that supports standard symmetric-key and public-key cryptography. It handles big numbers arithmetic and offers full support for Elliptic Curve Cryptography over the prime field $GF(p)$, and the binary field $GF(2^m)$. MIRACL is also a good choice when implementing cryptographic services in an embedded environment. It has built in features that allows to run ECC even on very constrained environments and tiny architectures which do not support a heap. In this case all memory can be allocated exclusively from the stack. This allows maximum use and re-use of memory, and avoids fragmentation of precious RAM. We have optimized MIRACL library to achieve the best ECC performance on our WSN motes.

Different Elliptic Curve Cryptography implementations for sensor networks [27], [26], [28], [8] were mainly focused on the prime finite fields. The choice of the field was dictated by the fact that basic arithmetic operations can be effectively optimized if pseudo-Mersenne primes are used in $GF(p)$. $GF(2^m)$ fields were not favoured because binary polynomial arithmetic (multiplication in particular) is insufficiently supported by current CPU's. This paper compares results achieved using both types of finite fields and shows that in some cases in this constrained environments, ECC operations over binary polynomial field $GF(2^m)$ outperforms those in $GF(p)$. On top of that timings for binary field case would be significantly faster if a "binary polynomial multiplication" instruction was available on the considered architectures.

Modular arithmetic routines are fundamental operations in every Elliptic Curve system. The overall performance of ECC depends greatly on the speed of those primitives. In $GF(p)$ big integer multiplication and reduction modulo p of the result are the most time-critical operations and must be performed as quickly as possible. We have used a variant of the hybrid multiplication method proposed in [8] to achieve this goal. Our implementation minimizes the number of operations on memory and uses additional CPU registers for catching and storing the carry bits. The Hybrid method takes advantage of extra registers to avoid unnecessary load operations and becomes more efficient with the number of registers used. On ATmega128L we were able to implement hybrid multiplication with column size $d = 4$. Due to the small number of general purpose registers on MSP430F1611 we could only achieve $d = 2$, using all 12 available registers. For more details concerning the implementation of our improved hybrid method see the paper [48]. For modular reduction a fast algorithm was implemented that takes advantage of special form of $p = 2^{160} - 2^{112} + 2^{64} + 1$ (a Solinas prime) as the modulus, using a 160-bit Elliptic Curve. Multiplication and reduction along with squaring, modular addition and modular subtraction were all implemented in assembly language. All the results for those routines in instruction cycles, assuming 160-bit integer operands, are listed in Table 1. Taking into account the 7.3828 MHz clock on the ATmega128L and the 8.192 MHz clock on Tmote Sky, 160-bit numbers multiplication can be performed in 0.36 ms and 0.21 ms respectively.

The field $GF(2^m)$ is usually constructed using a polynomial basis representation. In this case binary polynomials multiplication and reduction modulo

Table 1. Timings in instruction cycles for basic modular arithmetic routines using 160-bit integers on ATmega128L and MSP430F1611

	ATmega	**MSP430**
hybrid multiplication	2654 (d=4)	1746 (d=2)
squaring	2193 (d=4)	1373 (d=2)
modular reduction	1228	990
modular addition	340-470	105-235
modular subtraction	340-470	105-235

an irreducible binary polynomial are the crucial operations. As described in [49] Karatsuba-Ofman multiplication algorithm were adopted for the polynomial case. This divide-and-conquer technique allowed us to reduce multiplication complexity by using word size polynomial multiplication and extra additions (which are very fast in $GF(2^m)$). Throughout our research we observed that assembler implementation of binary polynomials multiplication did not improve our timings as much as we had expected. This was due to the fact that binary polynomial word multiplication and variable length shifts instructions were not available on our target devices. In the end we decided to implement all binary field primitives and operations using the standard C language. In order to speed up reduction routines on both platforms we have developed fast field-specific code for the reduction modulo the irreducible polynomials $x^{163} + x^7 + x^6 + x^3 + 1$ (as recommended by NIST) and $x^{271} + x^{201} + 1$. For guidance on the optimal irreducible polynomials for $GF(2^m)$ arithmetic to use in given circumstances please refer to [50].

4.2   ECC Implementation

One difficulty in using ECC is that of finding a suitable Elliptic Curve. Curve parameters have to be carefully chosen to allow efficient computations and provide a reasonable level of security. NIST recommends using at least 160-bit keys in ECC systems to achieve security level equivalent to that offered by standard RSA based solutions with 1024-bit keys. In our example programs we decided to use NIST k163 Koblitz curve over $GF(2^{163})$ binary field and $y^2 = x^3 - 3x + 157$ curve with $p = 2^{160} - 2^{112} + 2^{64} + 1$ over $GF(p)$. The usage of Koblitz curve gives a significant speed up when performing a point multiplication, as no expensive point doublings are required. To satisfy security requirements mentioned in section 3 our pairing parameters were chosen as $k \cdot \ell > 1024$. In this inequality k stands for embedding degree and ℓ stands for number of bits in p (in the case of prime fields $GF(p)$) or m (in case of binary fields $GF(2^m)$). To satisfy these conditions we chose the supersingular curve $y^2 + y = x^3 + x^2$ with $k = 4$ and $x^{271} + x^{201} + 1$ as the reduction polynomial for the binary field. For the pairing program in the prime field we used a $y^2 = x^3 + Ax + B$ curve, $k = 4$ and 256-bit modulus p. Parameter A was set to -3 in order to reduce the number of operations for the point doubling routine.

ECC operations are based on arithmetic involving the points of the elliptic curve and as mentioned before it is essential to optimize basic arithmetic operations in underlying fields. Overall performance of the system is also highly dependably on efficient implementation of curve operations. Two of those fundamental operations are point addition and point doubling. Please see [49] for a geometrical explanation of those operations. The selection of points coordinate system has a big influence on the performance of the above mentioned operations. It has been shown that projective coordinate systems (x, y, z) are more efficient than affine (x, y) systems. Rules for point addition and point doubling in affine coordinates requires inversion in underlying field, which is usually much more expensive than multiplication. The same operations in projective coordinates uses greater number of cheaper multiplications and squarings in place of an inversion and thus makes it more suitable to our target platforms.

A common operation in ECC is the computation of sP, where s is an integer and P is a point on an elliptic curve. This operation is called point multiplication and can be decomposed into a sequence of point additions and point doublings. These operations dominate the overall execution time of elliptic curve cryptographic schemes, and so optimization is important. The ECDH and ECDSA protocols require multiplication by a scalar of a fixed base point on the selected curve, and this can be carried out more quickly using precomputation. Our example programs therefore implement a fixed point multiplication method using additional storage to accelerate the calculations. The Comb method for point multiplication described in [49] was used in this case. Precomputation was performed with window size $w = 4$ resulting in 16 elliptic curve points stored in ROM. With this approach point multiplication is a tradeoff between memory space and computation time.

Pairing based systems have become more and more popular in Public Key Cryptography schemes. At first it appeared that these operations are far too complex to be calculated in reasonable amount of time on tiny architectures like WSN nodes. However our implementation shows that pairings can by computed quickly and efficiently on small and constrained devices such as MICA2 or Tmote Sky. The Tate pairing denoted as $e(P, Q)$, on an elliptic curve $E(\mathbb{F}_{q^k})$, evaluates as an element of an extension field $\mathbb{F}_{q^k}$. This requires implementation of extension field arithmetic routines. We used $k = 4$, so special procedures for multiplication, squaring, exponentiation, inversion and calculation of square roots in quadratic extension fields ($\mathbb{F}_{p^4}$ and $\mathbb{F}_{2^{4m}}$) were developed. More detailed descriptions of those routines can be found in [51].

There has been a lot of work on efficient implementation of pairings on elliptic curves. This research shows that some of the best results can be achieved on supersingular curves over fields of low characteristic. For this reason we chose the improved Duursma-Lee algorithm to compute the Tate pairing over $GF(2^m)$ based on η_T pairing, which is one of the fastest known. Due to space limitations please refer to [52] for a detailed description and explanation of this method. The pairing operation in the prime field on MSP430 was implemented and optimized as described in [53] and is based on Miller's algorithm. We used a different approach on the ATmega128L, where more program space was available. Here we have implemented the Ate pairing on a non-supersinglar curve over $GF(p)$ as described in [54] with parameters $k = 4$, p a 256-bit prime, and a fixed point P. Knowing P's coordinates allowed us to use precomputation, which speeds up elliptic curve point multiplication. In the next section we will evaluate NanoECC and show results for computing pairings and point multiplications.

5   Results

Efficient implementation of ECC on such constrained devices as WSN nodes is not an easy task. Issues like the small amount of memory, limited CPU capabilities and scarce battery resources have to be taken into consideration. Program code needs to be highly optimized to meet all those demands. That is the reason why there is some confusion in the literature concerning timings of basic Elliptic Curve operations on those constrained platforms. The results presented in recent papers vary a lot. In our research we have tested the limits of ECC in sensor networks and our results give a clear answer to the question of how long Elliptic Curve Cryptography primitives take on standard WSN motes.

NanoECC is optimized for speed. Memory usage was our secondary concern as optimizing for code size lowers functionality and portability due to greater number of assembly routines. A large set of available library functions in NanoECC gives a lot of flexibility in writing ECC based programs. Most of the procedures were developed using standard C which favors speed and allows us to re-use the code on numerous other WSN platforms.

5.1 Point Multiplication

Our example programs were compiled under TinyOs operating system and run on the MICA2 and Tmote Sky motes, so all measurements were taken on actual devices. We decided to measure three most important parameters for sensor nodes: computation time, memory usage and energy consumption. Both devices had to be slightly modified to facilitate data acquisition. A precise one ohm resistor was soldered between the mote and its battery pack to measure the exact amount of current drained during program execution. Input/Output ports on MICA2 and Tmote Sky were used to pass trigger signals to the measuring device. We used National Instruments NI 5112 digitizer card to acquire measurement data from both nodes. In this way exact timings and precise power consumption information could be gathered without using the mote's timers and other features which increase computation overhead.

All experiments were carried out using LabVIEW software. Figure 1 shows an example graph of Tmote Sky voltage levels during Elliptic Curve Diffie Helman (ECDH) program execution. As we can see point multiplication takes a considerable percentage of the total duration of the program. Current drawn from the battery pack was calculated based on voltage levels. The average value of current consumption was taken from all the samples within the program execution period. Both motes were powered with two AA batteries, so a voltage equal approximately to 3 V was provided (assuming new batteries). Based on this information total energy consumption was calculated from the formula $E = U \cdot I \cdot T$, where T is code running time.

Results for point multiplication operation in binary and prime fields on MICA2 and Tmote Sky nodes are listed in Table 2. Precomputation was used in all cases to speed up the point multiplication routine. Point addition and point doubling operations were not considered independently because their computation time is insignificant comparing to point multiplication. As we can see point multiplication is faster on both platforms when using the prime field, but the difference is not as big as we might have expected. Results in $GF(2^m)$ are comparable to those in $GF(p)$, even though both CPU's don't support special

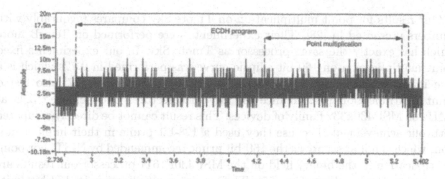

Fig. 1. Voltage levels on Tmote Sky during example ECDH program execution

Table 2. Performance evaluation of point multiplication on MICA2 and Tmote Sky

	MICA2		Tmote Sky	
	Binary field	Prime field	Binary field	Prime field
Computation time	2.16s	1.27s	1.04s	0.72s
Current draw	7.86mA	7.88mA	3.45mA	3.68mA
Energy consumption	50.93mJ	30.02mJ	10.76mJ	7.95mJ
ROM	32.4KB	46.1KB	32.1KB	31.3KB
RAM	1.7KB	1.8KB	2.8KB	2.9KB

instructions for binary field arithmetic. Achievements in binary field are even more competitive because no assembly language routines were used in this case. We used the hardware multiplier on Tmote Sky's CPU to improve timings for big numbers multiplication in the prime field. This fact has an influence on average current consumption, which is slightly higher when the multiplier unit is turned on. Operations in binary field of course do not require the hardware multiplier. On the MICA2 the average current drawn is almost the same using both fields. Total energy consumption in all experiments was lower for the prime field case, because of the faster execution time of point multiplication. Looking at the power consumption on both platforms, it is clear that Tmote Sky is far more efficient using even in some cases 5 times less energy for the same work carried out.

Program size figures given in Table 2 include only our ECC implementation without counting additional storage for TinyOs modules. The numbers for the RAM memory requirement were not taken directly from TinyOs output, because they did not include stack usage. Simulation environments such as AVR Studio and IAR Embedded Workbench for MSP430 allowed us to achieve precise information about RAM usage and stack size at any given time during our programs execution. Figures for RAM, presented in Table 2 show the maximum usage that we have encountered. Average RAM utilization was usually much lower than that.

Our results for point multiplication on Tmote Sky compares favourably with numbers presented in [28]. Their experiments were performed on TelosB mote which has exactly the same processor as Tmote Sky. In our experiments fixed point multiplication on 160-bit elliptic curve was performed in 0.72s which is a nice improvement comparing to 3.13s in [28]. Guajardo *et al.* [27] also tested point multiplication performance on tiny architectures and achieved 3.4s at 1MHz on MSP430x33x family of devices. This result cannot be directly compared with our achievements because they used a 128-bit prime in their implementation, which is not as secure as the 160-bit prime recommended by NIST. For point multiplication in the binary field on the MSP430F1611 processor our results are superior to those achieved in [55]. Their point multiplication in 163-bit finite field takes 32.5s which is quite a lot comparing to 1.04s in our implementation.

There were several attempts to implement ECC on MICA2 platform. Point multiplication in prime field was implemented by Gura *et al.* on ATmega128 [8]. They calculated point multiplication in 0.81s at 8MHz on secp160r1 curve. In our implementation same operation using a different curve takes 1.27s at 7.3828MHz on MICA2 mote. Malan *et al.* [9] implemented point multiplication in the binary field. However the result of 34.16s for this operation on a 163-bit curve is far from being optimal. In [56] the authors managed to perform fixed point multiplication in 6.74s on MICA2 but they used $GF(2^{113})$ arithmetic which should be much faster to calculate. Computation of the same routine in $GF(2^{163})$ in our implementation takes only 2.16s. To our knowledge, point multiplication results in binary field reported in this paper are the fastest known so far.

5.2 Pairing Evaluation

Table 3 shows all the results for pairing computation achieved on the MICA2 and Tmote Sky motes. Our timings show that pairing calculation can be performed in as fast as 5.25s on a resource constrained WSN node. As we can see pairing programs in binary field are much faster than in prime field on both our research platforms. The difference is quite significant, as much as 7s. Binary field pairings are also more efficient in terms of energy consumption and program size. Bigger code size for pairings in the prime field is due primarily to precomputation data. It is especially visible for MICA2 where constant precomputed values take 28K of a total 71.9K of program memory. We couldn't use that much of precomputation on Tmote Sky due to the 48KB memory limit. Otherwise the pairing program

Table 3. Results for pairing implementation on MICA2 and Tmote Sky

	MICA2		Tmote Sky	
	Binary field	Prime field	Binary field	Prime field
Computation time	10.96s	17.93s	5.25s	11.82s
Current draw	7.86mA	7.88mA	3.45mA	3.68mA
Energy consumption	258.44mA	423.87mJ	54.34mJ	130.49mA
ROM	53.5KB	71.9KB	30.3KB	47.0KB
RAM	2.8KB	2.5KB	3.7KB	3.0KB

on this platform would have been a bit faster. On the other hand RAM usage was a critical issue on ATmega128L. All variables and runtime objects had to be handled very carefully to fit 4KB of dynamic memory. All of our binary field pairing programs have a big advantage that they do not need any precomputation at all.

Although much research has been carried out in PBC, very little attention has focused on implementing those operations on resource constrained devices. Apparently pairings were considered as too heavyweight for WSN nodes. The first pairing implementation in WSN's was performed by Oliveira *et al.* [10]. In that work a $k = 2$ Tate pairing with a 256-bit prime was implemented over a supersingular curve $y^2 = x^3 + x$. The timing for this operation was estimated as 30.21s on 7.3828MHz MICAz mote (also ATmega128L CPU). Our implementation of the Tate pairing in the prime field on the MICA2 outperforms that result with 17.93s and offers a much higher level of security using bigger parameters. All of our results for pairing implementation show that those operations can be performed in a reasonable amount of time on small and constrained devices. As far as we know our pairing programs are at the moment the fastest implementations on popular WSN motes. Nevertheless we are pretty sure that further optimizations are possible in terms of memory usage as well as execution time.

6   Conclusion

Recent results in WSN research area show that PKC based on elliptic curves is indeed feasible in those constrained environments. However the performance of many ECC implementations is still a disappointment in terms of running time and resources usage. This fact prevents ECC based security protocols from being used in certain applications. Our achievements presented in this paper prove that ECC operations can be performed in a quick and efficient way on popular sensor network platforms. As our contribution, we present updated results on computing elliptic curve point multiplication and pairings. We also show that ECC over prime field is not always the best option as pairings over $GF(2^m)$ seem to be more efficient on this type of architecture. PBC offers a flexible cryptographic primitive that can be used in many new security protocols. Fast pairing computation enables Identity Based Encryption and thus opens new ways for achieving security in sensor networks. Future work will address this issue and will deal with some problems that need to be solved in order to develop a complete security protocol.

References

1. Estrin, D., Govindan, R., Heidemann, J.S., Kumar, S.: Next century challenges: Scalable coordination in sensor networks. In: MobiCom 1999. Mobile Computing and Networking, Seattle, WA USA, pp. 263–270 (1999)
2. Akyildiz, I.F., Su, W., Sankarasubramaniam, Y., Cayirci, E.: Wireless Sensor Networks: a survey. Computer Networks 38(4), 393–422 (2002)

3. Karlof, C., Wagner, D.: Secure routing in Wireless Sensor Networks: Attacks and countermeasures. Elsevier's AdHoc Networks Journal, Special Issue on Sensor Network Applications and Protocols 1(2-3), 293-315 (2003) (Also apeared in 1st IEEE International Workshop on Sensor Network Protocols and Applications)
4. Wood, A.D., Stankovic, J.A.: Denial of service in sensor networks. IEEE Computer 35(10), 54-62 (2002)
5. Perrig, A., Szewczyk, R., Wen, V., Culler, D., Tygar, J.D.: SPINS: Security protocols for sensor networks. Wireless Networks 8(5), 521-534 (2002) (Also appeared in MobiCom 2001)
6. Karlof, C., Sastry, N., Wagner, D.: Tinysec: A link layer security architecture for Wireless Sensor Networks. In: 2nd ACM SensSys., pp. 162-175 (2004)
7. Watro, R.J., Kong, D., fen Cuti, S., Gardiner, C., Lynn, C., Kruus, P.: Tinypk: securing sensor networks with public key technology. In: SASN 2004. 2nd ACM Workshop on Security of ad hoc and Sensor Networks, Washington, DC, pp. 59-64 (2004)
8. Gura, N., Patel, A., Wander, A., Eberle, H., Shantz, S.C.: Comparing Elliptic Curve Cryptography and RSA on 8-bit CPUs. In: Joye, M., Quisquater, J.-J. (eds.) CHES 2004. LNCS, vol. 3156, pp. 119-132. Springer, Heidelberg (2004)
9. Malan, D.J., Welsh, M., Smith, M.D.: A Public-Key Infrastructure for key distribution in TinyOS based on Elliptic Curve Cryptography. In: SECON 2004. 1st IEEE Intl' Conf. on Sensor and Ad Hoc Communications and Networks (2004)
10. Oliveira, L.B., Aranha, D., Morais, E., Daguano, F., López, J., Dahab, R.: TinyTate: Computing the TinyTate in resource-constrained nodes. In: 6th IEEE International Symposium on Network Computing and Applications, Cambridge,MA (2007)
11. Miller, V.: Uses of elliptic curves in cryptography, advances in cryptology. In: Williams, H.C. (ed.) CRYPTO 1985. LNCS, vol. 218, pp. 417-426. Springer, Heidelberg (1986)
12. Koblitz, N.: Elliptic curve cryptosystems. Mathematics of computation 48, 203-209 (1987)
13. Scott, M.: MIRACL—A Multiprecision Integer and Rational Arithmetic C/C++ Library. Shamus Software Ltd, Dublin, Ireland (2003), http://www.shamus.ie
14. Zhou, L., Haas, Z.J.: Securing Ad Hoc Networks. IEEE Network 13(6), 24-30 (1999)
15. Hubaux, J.P., Buttyán, L., Capkun, S.: The quest for security in mobile ad hoc networks. In: 2nd ACM international symposium on Mobile ad hoc networking & computing, pp. 146-155. ACM Press, New York (2001)
16. Eschenauer, L., Gligor, V.D.: A key management scheme for distributed sensor networks. In: CCS 2002. 9th ACM conf. on Computer and communications security, pp. 41-47 (2002)
17. Zhu, S., Setia, S., Jajodia, S.: LEAP: efficient security mechanisms for large-scale distributed sensor networks. In: CCS 2003. 10th ACM conference on Computer and communication security, pp. 62-72. ACM Press, New York (2003)
18. Pietro, R.D., Mancini, L.V., Mei, A.: Random key-assignment for secure Wireless Sensor Networks. In: SASN 2003. 1st ACM workshop on Security of ad hoc and sensor networks, pp. 62-71 (2003)
19. Kannan, R., Ray, L., Durresi, A.: Security-performance tradeoffs of inheritance based key predistribution for Wireless Sensor Networks. In: Castelluccia, C., Hartenstein, H., Paar, C., Westhoff, D. (eds.) ESAS 2004. LNCS, vol. 3313, Springer, Heidelberg (2005)

20. Çamtepe, S.A., Yener, B.: Combinatorial design of key distribution mechanisms for Wireless Sensor Networks. In: Samarati, P., Ryan, P.Y A, Gollmann, D., Molva, R. (eds.) ESORICS 2004. LNCS, vol. 3193, pp. 293–308. Springer, Heidelberg (2004)
21. Liu, D., Ning, P., Li, R.: Establishing pairwise keys in distributed sensor networks. ACM Transactions on Information and System Security (TISSEC) 8(1), 41–77 (2005)(Also appeared in ACM CCS 2003)
22. Du, W., Deng, J., Han, Y.S., Varshney, P.K., Katz, J., Khalili, A.: A pairwise key pre-distribution scheme for Wireless Sensor Networks. ACM Transactions on Information and System Security 8(2), 228–258 (2005) (Also appeared in ACM CCS 2003)
23. Oliveira, L.B., Wong, H.C., Dahab, R., Loureiro, A.A.F.: On the design of secure protocols for hierarchical sensor networks. International Journal of Networks and Security (IJSN) 2(3/4), 216–227 (2007) (Special Issue on Cryptography in Networks)
24. Oliveira, L.B., Ferreira, A., cca, M.A.V., Wong, H.C., Bern, M., Dahab, R., Loureiro, A.A.F.: Secleach-on the security of clustered sensor networks. Signal Process 87(12), 2882–2895 (2007)
25. Hwang, J., Kim, Y.: Revisiting random key pre-distribution schemes for Wireless Sensor networks. In: 2nd ACM workshop on Security of ad hoc and sensor networks, pp. 43–52. ACM Press, New York (2004)
26. Liu, A., Kampanakis, P., Ning, P.: Tinyecc: Elliptic Curve Cryptography for sensor networks (ver. 0.3) (2007), http://discovery.csc.ncsu.edu/software/TinyECC/
27. Guajardo, J., Bluemel, R., Krieger, U., Paar, C.: Efficient implementation of Elliptic Curve Cryptosystems on the TI MSP430x33x family of microcontrollers. In: Kim, K.-c. (ed.) PKC 2001. LNCS, vol. 1992, Springer, Heidelberg (2001)
28. Wang, H., Sheng, B., Li, Q.: Elliptic Curve Cryptography based access control in sensor networks. International Journal of Security and Networks (IJSN). Special Issue on Security Issues on Sensor Networks 1(3/4), 127–137 (2006)
29. Polastre, J., Szewczyk, R., Culler, D.: Telos: enabling ultra-low power wireless research. In: IPSN 2005. 4th international symposium on Information processing in sensor networks, p. 48. IEEE Press, Piscataway, NJ, USA (2005)
30. Zhang, Y., Liu, W., Lou, W., Fang, Y.: Securing sensor networks with location-based keys. In: WCNC 2005. IEEE Wireless Communications and Networking Conference (2005)
31. Oliveira, L.B., Dahab, R.: Pairing-based cryptography for sensor networks. In: 5th IEEE International Symposium on Network Computing and Applications, Cambridge, MA (fast abstract) (2006)
32. Doyle, B., Bell, S., Smeaton, A.F., McCusker, K., O'Connor, N.: Security considerations and key negotiation techniques for power constrained sensor networks. The Computer Journal 49(4), 443–453 (2006)
33. McCusker, K., O'Connor, N., Diamond, D.: Low-energy finite field arithmetic primitives for implementing security in Wireless Sensor Networks. In: 2006 Intl. Conf. on Communications, Circuits and systems. Computer, Optical and Broadband; Communications; Computational Intelligence, vol. III, pp. 1537–1541 (2006)
34. Bellare, M., Namprempre, C., Neven, G.: Unrestricted aggregate signatures. Cryptology ePrint Archive, Report 2006/285 (2006), http://eprint.iacr.org/
35. Oliveira, L.B., Dahab, R., Lopez, J., Daguano, F., Loureiro, A.A.F.: Identity-based encryption for sensor networks. In: PERCOMW 2007. 5th IEEE International Conference on Pervasive Computing and Communications Workshops, pp. 290–294 (2007)

36. Segars, S.: ARM7TDMI power consumption. IEEE Micro 17(4), 12–19 (1997)
37. López, J., Dahab, R.: An overview of Elliptic Curve Cryptography. Technical Report IC-00-10, Institute of Computing – UNICAMP (2000)
38. Menezes, A., Okamoto, T., Vanstone, S.: Reducing elliptic curve logarithms to logarithms in a finite field. IEEE Transactions on Information Theory 39(5), 1639–1646 (1993)
39. Sakai, R., Ohgishi, K., Kasahara, M.: Cryptosystems based on pairing. In: SCIS 2000. Symposium on Cryptography and Information Security, pp. 26–28 (2000)
40. Joux, A.: A one round protocol for tripartite diffie-hellman. J. Cryptology 17(4), 263–276 (2004) (Proceedings of ANTS-IV, 2000)
41. Galbraith, S.: Pairings. In: Blake, I., Seroussi, G., Smart, N. (eds.) Advances in Elliptic Curve Cryptography. London Mathematical Society Lecture Notes, pp. 183–213. Cambridge University Press, Cambridge (2005)
42. Atmel: ATmega128(L) datasheet (2006), http://www.atmel.com
43. TI: MSP 430F1611, Datasheet (2002), http://www.ti.com
44. Crossbow Technology, Inc. 41 Daggett Dr., San Jose, CA 95134: MPR/MIB Mote Hardware Users Manual – Document 7430-0021-05 (2003)
45. Moteiv: Tmote Sky datasheet (2006), http://www.moteiv.com
46. Levis, P., Madden, S., Polastre, J., Szewczyk, R., Whitehouse, K., Woo, A., Gay, D., Hill, J., Welsh, M., Brewer, E., Culler, D.: TinyOS: An operating system for Wireless Sensor Networks. In: Weber, W., Rabaey, J., Aarts, E. (eds.) Ambient Intelligence, Springer, New York (2004)
47. Gay, D., Levis, P., von Behren, J.R., Welsh, M., Brewer, E.A., Culler, D.E.: The nesC language: A holistic approach to networked embedded systems. In: ACM Conf. on Programming Language Design and Implementation, pp. 1–11 (2003)
48. Scott, M., Szczechowiak, P.: Optimizing multiprecision multiplication for Public Key Cryptography. Cryptology ePrint Archive, Report 2007/299 (2007)
49. Hankerson, D., Menezes, A., Vanstone, S.: Guide to Elliptic Curve Cryptography. Springer, Heidelberg (2004)
50. Scott, M.: Optimal irreducible polynomials for $GF(2^m)$ arithmetic. Cryptology ePrint Archive, Report 2007/192 (2007)
51. Scott, M.: Implementing cryptographic pairings (2006)
52. Barreto, P.S.L.M., Galbraith, S., hEigeartaigh, C.O., Scott, M.: Efficient pairing computation on supersingular abelian varieties. In: Designs Codes And Cryptography, Boston/Norwell (USA) (2006)
53. Scott, M.: Computing the Tate Pairing. In: Menezes, A.J. (ed.) CT-RSA 2005. LNCS, vol. 3376, pp. 293–304. Springer, Heidelberg (2005)
54. Hess, F., Smart, N., Vercauteren, F.: The Eta Pairing revisited. IEEE Transactions on Information Theory 52(10), 4595–4602 (2006)
55. Arazi, O., Qi, H.: Load-balanced key establishment methodologies in Wireless Sensor Networks. International Journal of Security and Networks (IJSN). Special Issue on Security Issues on Sensor Networks 1(3/4), 158–166 (2006)
56. Blaß, E.O., Zitterbart, M.: Towards Acceptable Public-Key Encryption in Sensor Networks. In: The 2nd Int'l Workshop on Ubiquitous Computing, ACM SIGMIS (2005)

Characterizing Mote Performance:
A Vector-Based Methodology

Martin Leopold, Marcus Chang, and Philippe Bonnet

Department of Computer Science,
University of Copenhagen,
Universitetsparken 1, 2100 Copenhagen, Denmark
{leopold,marcus,bonnet}@diku.dk

Abstract. Sensors networks instrument the physical space using motes that run network embedded programs thus acquiring, processing, storing and transmitting sensor data. The motes commercially available today are large, costly and trade performance for flexibility and ease of programming. New generations of motes are promising to deliver significant improvements in terms of power consumption and price — in particular motes based on System-on-a-chip. The question is how do we compare mote performance? How to find out which mote is best suited for a given application? In this paper, we propose a vector-based methodology for benchmarking mote performance. Our method is based on the hypothesis that mote performance can be expressed as the scalar product of two vectors, one representing the mote characteristics, and the other representing the application characteristics. We implemented our approach in TinyOS 2.0 and we present the details of our implementation as well as the result of experiments obtained on commercial motes from Sensinode. We give a quantitative comparison of these motes, and predict the performance of a data acquisition application.

1 Introduction

Sensor networks-based monitoring applications range from simple data gathering, to complex Internet-based information systems. Either way, the physical space is instrumented with sensors extended with storage, computation and communication capabilities, the so-called motes. Motes run the network embedded programs that mainly sleep, and occasionally acquire, communicate, store and process data. In order to increase reliability and reduce complexity, research prototypes [1,2] as well as commercial systems[1] now implement a tiered approach where motes run simple, standard data acquisition programs while complex services are implemented on gateways. These data acquisition programs are either a black box (Arch Rock), or the straightforward composition of building blocks such as sample, compress, store, route (Tenet). This approach increases reliability because the generic programs are carefully engineered, and reused across

---

[1] See http://www.archrock.com

R. Verdone (Ed.): EWSN 2008, LNCS 4913, pp. 321–336, 2008.

deployments. This approach reduces complexity because a system integrator does not need to write embedded programs to deploy a sensor network application.

Such programs need to be portable to accommodate different types of motes. First, a program might need to be ported to successive generations of motes. Indeed, hardware designers continuously strive to develop new motes that are cheaper, and more power efficient. Second, a program might need to be ported simultaneously to different types of motes, as system integrators need various form factors or performance characteristics.

Handzicki, Polastre et al. [5] address the issue of portability when they designed TinyOS 2.0 Hardware Abstraction Architecture. They defined a general design principle, that introduces three layers:

1. Mote Hardware: a collection of interconnected hardware components (typically MCU, flash, sensors, radio).
2. Mote Drivers: Hardware-specific software that exports a hardware independent abstraction (e.g., TinyOS 2.0 define such Hardware Independent Layer for the typical components of a mote).
3. Cross-Platform Programs: the generic data acquisition programs that organize sampling, storage and communication.

We rely on these three layers to reason about mote performance. Whether motes are deployed for a limited period of time in the context of a specific application (e.g., a scientific experiment), or in the context of a permanent infrastructure (e.g., within a building), power consumption is the key performance metric. Motes should support data acquisition programs functionalities within a limited power budget. We focus on the following questions:

1. What mote hardware to pick for a given program? The problem is to explore the design space and choose the most appropriate hardware for a given program without having to actually benchmark the program on all candidate platforms.
2. What is a mote hardware good for? The problem is to characterize the type of program that is well supported by a given mote hardware.
3. Is a driver implemented efficiently on a given hardware? The problem is to conduct a sanity check to control that a program performs as expected on a given hardware.

We are facing these questions in the context of the Hogthrob project, where we design a data acquisition infrastructure. First, because of form factor and cost, we are considering a System-on-a-Chip (SoC) as mote hardware. Specifically, we want to investigate whether Sensinode Nano, a mote based on Chipcon's CC2430 SoC, would be appropriate for our application. More generally, we want to find out what a CC2430 mote is good for, i.e., what type of applications it supports or does not support well. Also, we had to rewrite all drivers to TinyOS 2.0 on CC2430, and we should check that our implementation performs as well as TinyOS 2.0 core. Finally, we would like to use Sensinode Micro as a prototyping platform for our application as its toolchain is easier and cheaper to use (see Section 3.2 for details). We would like to run our application on the Micro, measure performance, and predict the performance we would get with the Nano.

In this paper, we propose a vector-based methodology to study mote performance. Our hypothesis is that energy consumption on a mote can be expressed as the scalar product of two performance vectors, one that characterize the mote (hardware and drivers), and one that characterize the cross-platform application. Using this methodology, we can compare motes or applications by comparing their performance vectors. We can also predict the performance of an application on a range of platforms using their performance vectors. This method will enable sensor network designers answer the questions posed above. Specifically, our contribution is the following:

1. We adapt the vector-based methodology, initially proposed by Seltzer et al. [4], to study mote performance in general and TinyOS-based motes in particular (Section 3).
2. We conduct experiments with two types of motes running TinyOS 2.0: Sensinode Micro and CC2430. We ported TinyOS to these platforms (see Section 4).
3. We present the results of our experiments (Section 5). First, we test the hypothesis underlying our approach. Second, we compare the performance of the Micro and CC2430 motes using their hardware vectors. Finally, we predict the performance of generic data acquisition programs from the Micro to the CC2430.

2   Related Work

Typically, analytical models, simulation or benchmarking are used to study the performance of a program [3]. In our opinion, simulation is best suited for reasoning about the performance and scalability of protocols and algorithms, not to reason about the performance of an application program on a given mote hardware. Indeed, simulators are best suited when they abstract the details of the hardware and driver layers. Standard benchmarks fall into two categories: application benchmarks (SPEC, TPC), or microbenchmarks (lmbench)[2]. There is no such standard benchmark for sensor networks. Micro benchmarks have been defined for embedded systems (EEMBC), but they focus at the automotive and consumer electronics markets – they do not tackle wireless networking or sensing issues.

The vector-based methodology proposed by Setlzer et al. [4] has been used to characterize the performance of web servers, OS utilities and Java Virtual Machines. Our paper is the first to propose this methodology in the context of sensor networks.

Performance estimation is of the essence for real-time embedded systems. The focus there is on timing analysis, not so much on energy consumption. We share a same goal of integrating performance estimation into system design [8].

---

[2] See http://www.tpc.org, http://www.spec.org, http://www.bitmover.com/lmbench, and http://www.eembc.org/ for details about these benchmarks.

In the context of sensor network, our work follows-up on the work of Jan Beutel that defined metrics for comparing motes[9]. Instead of using data sheets for comparing mote performance, we propose to conduct application-specific benchmarks.

Our work is a first step towards defining a cost model for applications running on motes. Such cost models are needed in architectures such as Tenet [1] or SwissQM [2] where a gateway decides how much processing motes are responsible for. Defining such a cost model is future work.

3   Vector-Based Methodology

The vector-based methodology[4], consists in expressing overall system performance as the scalar product of two vectors:

1. A system-characterization vector, which we call **mote vector** and denote $\underline{MV}$. Each component of this vector represents the performance of one primitive operation exported by the system, and is obtained by running an appropriate microbenchmark.
2. An application-characterization vector, which we call **application vector** and denote $\underline{AV}$. Each component of this vector represents the application's utilization of the corresponding system primitives, and is obtained by instrumenting the API to the system primitive operations.

Our hypothesis is that we can define those vectors such that mote performance can be expressed as their scalar product:

$$Energy = \underline{MV} \cdot \underline{AV}$$

Our challenge is to devise a methodology adapted to mote performance. The issues are (i) to define the mote vector components, and the microbenchmarks used to populate them, and (ii) to define a representative application workload, to collect a trace from the instrumented system API, and to convert an application trace into an application vector.

3.1   Mote Vector

We consider a system composed of the mote hardware together with the mote drivers. The primitive operations exported by such a system are:

- CPU duty cycling: the network embedded programs that mainly sleep and process events need to turn the CPU on and off[3].
- Peripheral units: controlled through the hardware-independent functions made available at the drivers interface.

---

[3] Note that we assume that the mote hardware relies on a single CPU to control all peripheral units. Peripheral units such as digital sensors might include their own micro-controller. Our assumption simply states that a mote program is run on a single CPU.

We choose this system because its interface is platform-independent. This has two positive consequences. First, we can use mote vectors to compare two different motes. Second, the application vector is platform-independent. We can thus use our vector-based methodology to predict the performance of an application across motes.

The mote vector components correspond to the CPU (when active or idle), and the peripheral units (as determined by the driver interfaces). Throughout the paper, we use an associative array notation to denote the mote (and application) vector components, e.g., $MV[active]$ corresponds to CPU execution, $MV[idle]$ corresponds to CPU sleep, $MV[PUi]$, correspond to peripheral units primitives where PUi is for example ADC sample, flash read, flash write, flash erase, radio transmit, radio receive.

We need to define a metric for the vector components. The two candidates are energy and time. We actually need both: (a) energy to compute the scalar product with the application vector and thus obtain mote performance, and (b) time to derive the platform-independent characteristics of an application (see Section 3.2). We thus need to define a microbenchmark for each mote vector component for which we measure time elapsed and energy spent. We distinguish between the energy mote vector, noted MV_e, and the time mote vector, noted MV_t.

The microbenchmarks must capture the performance of the system's primitive operations. The first problem is to represent CPU performance. The most formidable task for the CPU in a sensor network application is to sleep. This is why we distinguish sleep mode from executing mode in the mote vector. For the applications we consider, a single sleep mode is sufficient. Defining a microbenchmark to define the energy spent in sleep mode is trivial. However, we wish to use the time mote vector to compare the time spent in sleep mode by different motes. Intuitively, the time spent in sleep mode is a complement of the time spent processing. As an approximation, we thus consider that $MV_t[idle]$ is the complement of $MV_t[active]$ with respect to an arbitrary time period (fixed for all mote vectors), and that $MV_e[CPUsleep]$ corresponds to the energy spent in sleep mode during that time.

The second problem is to define an appropriate representation of CPU performance (in executing mode). Unlike peripheral units, for which drivers define a narrow-interface, the CPU has a rich instruction set. It is non-trivial to estimate the CPU resources used by a given application as it depends on the source code and on the way the compiler leverages the CPU instruction set. We choose a simple approach where we use a microbenchmark as a yardstick for the compute-intensive tasks of an application. We thus represent CPU performance using a single vector component. There is an obvious pitfall with this approach: we assume that the distribution of instructions used by the microbenchmark is representative of the instructions used by the application. This is unlikely to be the case. We use this simple approach, despite its limitation, as a baseline for our methodology because we do not expect CPU utilization to have a major impact on energy consumption. Our experiments constitute a first test of this assumption. Obviously much more tests are needed, and devising a more precise estimation of CPU utilization is future work.

The third problem related to the microbenchmarks is that driver interfaces often provide a wide range of parameters that affect their duration and energy consumption. Instead of attempting to model the complete range of parameters, we define microbenchmarks that fix a single set of parameters for each peripheral unit primitive. Each peripheral unit microbenchmark thus corresponds to calling a system primitive with a fixed set of parameters, e.g., a microbenchmark for radio transmit will send a packet of fixed length, and a microbenchmark for ADC sampling will sample once at a fixed resolution. We believe that this models the behavior of sensor network application that typically use a fixed radio packet length or a particular ADC resolution. This method can trivially be expanded by defining a vector component per parameters (e.g., replacing radio transmit with two components radio transmit at packet *length_1* and radio transmit at packet *length_2*).

For the sake of illustration, let us consider a simplistic mote with a subset of the TinyOS 2.0 drivers, that only exports two primitives: ADC sample and radio transmit (tx). The associated time mote vectors will be of the form:

$$MV_t = \begin{bmatrix} active \\ idle \\ adc \\ tx \end{bmatrix}$$

Where the mote vector components correspond to the time spent by the mote running the CPU microbenchmark, to the time spent in sleep mode (the complement of the time spent running the CPU benchmark with respect to an arbitrary time period that we set to 20 s), to the time spent running the ADC benchmark, and to the time spent running the transmit benchmark.

In order to express mote performance as the scalar product of the energy mote vector and the application vector, we need the components of the mote vectors to be independent. This is an issue here, because CPU is involved whenever peripheral units are activated. Our solution is to factor CPU usage in each peripheral unit component. As a consequence, the mote vector component corresponding to CPU performance (*active*) must be obtained without interference from the peripheral units. Another consequence is that we need to separate the CPU utilization associated to peripheral units from the pure computation, when deriving the platform-independent characteristics of an application. We thus register CPU time when benchmarking each peripheral unit primitive. We denote them as $CPU[PUi]$ for each peripheral unit primitive PUi.

We detail in the next Section, how we use those measurements when deriving the application vector from a trace.

3.2 Application Vector

Our goal is to characterize how an application utilizes the primitives provided by the underlying system. The first issue is to define a workload that is representative of the application. In the context of sensor networks, workload characterization is complicated (i) because motes interact with the physical world and (ii) because the network load on a mote depends on its placement with respect to the gateway, and (iii) because different motes play different roles in the sensor network (e.g., in a multihop network a mote located near the gateway deals with more network traffic than a mote located at the periphery of the network).

We consider that a sensor network application can be divided into representative epochs that are repeated throughout the application lifetime. For example, the application we consider in the Hogthrob project consists of one data acquisition epoch[4], where an accelerometer is sampled at 4 Hz, the samples are compressed, stored on flash when a page is full, and transmitted to the gateway when the flash is half-full. While sampling is deterministic, such an epoch is non-deterministic as compressing, storing or transmitting depends on the data being collected, and on the transmission conditions. Obviously, tracing an application throughout several similar epochs will allow us to use statistics to characterize these non-deterministic variations.

For each epoch, we trace how the application uses the CPU and the peripheral units. More precisely the trace records the total time spent by the mote in each possible mote state, defined by the combination of active mote vector components (*active* that represents the compute-intensive operations, *idle* that represents the CPU in sleep mode, and *PUi* that represents a peripheral unit interface call). We thus represent the trace as a vector, denoted $\underline{T}$. $\underline{T}$ is of dimension 2^m, where m is the dimension of the mote vector. Some of the mote states will not be populated because they are mutually exclusive (e.g., *active* and *idle*), or because the driver interfaces prevent a given combination of active peripheral units.

Let us get back to the simple example we introduced in the previous section. The trace vector for an epoch will be of the form:

$$\underline{T} = \begin{bmatrix} active \\ idle \\ adc \\ tx \\ adc \ \& \ tx \\ active \ \& \ adc \\ active \ \& \ tx \\ active \ \& \ adc \ \& \ tx \end{bmatrix}$$

Now the problem is to transform, for each epoch, the trace vector into a platform-independent application vector. The application vector, denoted $\underline{AV}$, has same dimension m as the mote vector, and each application vector compo-

---

[4] A sensor network deployed for collaborative event detection will typically consist of two epochs: one where motes are sampling a sensor and looking for a given pattern in the local signal, and one where motes are communicating once a potential event has been detected.

nent corresponds to the utilization of the system resource as modeled in the mote vector. The application vector components have no unit, they correspond to the ratio between the total time a system primitive is used in an epoch, by the time spent by this system primitive in the appropriate microbenchmark (as recorded in the time mote vector MV_t). Note that if the driver primitive is deterministic, then the ratio between the total time spent calling this primitive in an epoch and the microbenchmarking time is equal to the number of times this primitive has been called. However, drivers typically introduce non-determinism, because the scheduler is involved or because drivers embed control loops with side effects (e.g., radio transmission control that results in retransmissions).

We use a linear transformation to map the trace vector onto the application vector. This transformation can be described in three steps:

1. We use an **architecture matrix** to map the trace into a vector of dimension m, the **raw total time vector**, where each component correspond to the total utilization of the CPU and peripheral units. The architecture matrix encodes the definition of each state as the combination of active mote vector components. Note that this combination depends on the architecture of the mote. For example, a SPI bus might be shared by the radio and the flash. In this case, the time spent in a state corresponding to radio transmission and flash write is spent either transmitting packets or writing on the flash (there is no overlap between these operations). We assume fair resource arbitration and consider that both components get half the time recorded in the trace. In case of overlap between operations, both get the total time recorded in the trace.

   In our simplistic example, assuming that a SPI resource is shared between the radio and the ADC, the architecture matrix will be of the form:

$$
\mathbf{AM} = \begin{bmatrix} 1 & 0 & 0 & 0 & 0 & 1 & 1 & 1 \\ 0 & 1 & 0 & 0 & 0 & 0 & 0 & 0 \\ 0 & 0 & 1 & 0 & \frac{1}{2} & 1 & 0 & \frac{1}{2} \\ 0 & 0 & 0 & 1 & \frac{1}{2} & 0 & 1 & \frac{1}{2} \end{bmatrix}
$$

2. We use a **CPU matrix** to factor out of the *active* component the time spent by the CPU controlling the peripheral units. The CPU matrix, of dimension $m \times m$, is diagonal except for the column corresponding to the *active* component. This column is defined as 1 on the diagonal, 0 for the *idle* component, and $-CPU[k]/MV[k]$ for all other components. When multiplying the total time vector with the CPU matrix, we obtain a **total time** vector where the *active* component corresponds solely to the compute-intensive portion of the application.

   Using again our running example, we have a CPU matrix of the form:

$$
\mathbf{CPU} = \begin{bmatrix} 1 & 0 & 0 & 0 \\ 0 & 1 & 0 & 0 \\ -\frac{CPU[adc]}{MV_t[adc]} & 0 & 1 & 0 \\ -\frac{CPU[tx]}{MV_t[tx]} & 0 & 0 & 1 \end{bmatrix}
$$

3. We use the time mote vector to derive the application vector. The basic idea is to express the application utilization of the system primitive as the ratio between total time per component, and the time spent running a benchmark. We define the inverse mote vector, $\underline{MV^{-1}}$, as a vector of dimension m where each component is the inverse of the time mote vector component (this inverse is always defined as the time mote vector components are always non zero). We define the application vector as the Hadamard product of total time vector with the inverse mote vector.

With our running example, we obtain the equation:

$$\begin{bmatrix} totalactive/\underline{MV_t}[active] \\ totalidle/\underline{MV_t}[idle] \\ totaladc/\underline{MV_t}[adc] \\ totaltx/\underline{MV_t}[tx] \end{bmatrix} = \begin{bmatrix} totalactive \\ totalidle \\ totaladc \\ totaltx \end{bmatrix} \circ \begin{bmatrix} 1/\underline{MV_t}[active] \\ 1/\underline{MV_t}[idle] \\ 1/\underline{MV_t}[adc] \\ 1/\underline{MV_t}[tx] \end{bmatrix}$$

More generally, we derive the application vector from the trace vector using the following linear transformation:

$$\underline{AV} = (\mathbf{CPU} \times (\mathbf{AM} \times \underline{T})) \circ \underline{MV^{-1}}$$

And we obtain the mote performance as the scalar product of the application vector with the energy mote vector:

$$E = \underline{AV} \cdot \underline{MV_e}.$$

4   Implementation in TinyOS 2.0

We applied our vector-based methodology to two motes: Sensinode Micro, a Telos-like mote, and CC2430, which is the basis for a new generation of commercial motes[5]. We ported TinyOS 2.0 on both platforms.

4.1   CC2430 and Sensinode Micro

As a SoC Chipcon's CC2430[6] has a small form factor (7x7 mm) and promises to be mass-produced at a lower price than complex boards. Motes built around the CC2430 might constitute an important step towards reducing the price of sensor networks. The CC2430 is composed of the 8051 MCU with a wide range of common on-chip peripherals as well as an 802.15.4 radio very similar to the Texas Instruments CC2420. We run the system at 32 MHz. The CC2430 differs from the platforms on which TinyOS has been implemented so far in two important ways: the system architecture and the interconnect to the radio.

The Intel 8051 MCU architecture was designed in the early eighties and many oddities from the era remain. Not only is it an 8 bit, CISC style processor with a

---

[5] We experimented with a CC2430 development kit. Using commercial systems based on CC2430, such as Sensinode Nano, is future work.

[6] For details, see CC2430 data sheet: http://focus.ti.com/lit/ds/symlink/cc2430.pdf

Harvard architecture[7], but the main memory is further subdivided into separate address spaces that differ in size, are addressed differently and vary in access time. Simply put, the 8051 defines a fast memory area limited to 256 bytes, and a slow memory area of 8 KiB. In addition to variables, the fast access area contains the program stack. This limits the program stack to less than 256 bytes depending on the amount of variables in this area. Commonly, activation records of functions are placed on the stack, thus potentially limiting the call depth critically. To circumvent this problem, the compiler places stack frames in the slow data area, which imposes a high cost for storing and retrieving arguments that do not fit in registers when calling a function. The slow access RAM also penalizes dynamic memory allocation, and context switches and thus favor an event-based OS with static memory allocation such as TinyOS.

Because CC2430 is a SoC, there is no bus between the MCU and the radio. The MCU controls the radio via special function registers (instead of relying on a SPI bus as it is the case on Telos and Micro motes for example). The other peripheral units (ADC, UART, timers, flash, and pins) are accessed in the 8051 MCU as in other micro-controllers such as the MSP or Atmega.

The Sensinode Micro is built around the 16 bit, RISC style MSP430 MCU with combined code and memory spaces (Von Neuman). The platform can run up to 8 MHz, but we choose 1 MHz in our experiments. Apart from the built in common peripherals of the MSP, it features the Texas Instruments CC2420 radio which is connected though an SPI bus.

4.2 TinyOS 2.0 on CC2430 and Micro

TinyOS 2 has been designed to facilitate the portability of applications across platforms. First, it is built using the concept of components that use and provide interfaces. TinyOS is written in nesC, an extension of C that supports components and their composition. Second, TinyOS implements the Hardware Abstraction Architecture[5]. For each hardware resource, a driver is organized in three layers: the Hardware Presentation Layer (HPL) that directly exposes the functions of the hardware component as simple function calls, the Hardware Abstraction Layer (HAL) that abstracts the raw hardware interface into a higher-level but still platform dependent abstraction, and the Hardware Independent Layer (HIL) that exports a narrow, platform-independent interface. The TinyOS 2.0 core working group has defined HIL for the hardware resources of typical motes: radio, flash, timer, ADC, general IO pins, and UART.

Porting TinyOS 2.0 on CC2430 consisted in implementing these drivers[8]. For the timers, pins, UART and ADC we used the TinyOS HIL interfaces, however for the Radio and Flash diverge from the common interfaces.

Radio. We export the radio using a straightforward *SimpleMac* interface. This interface is well suited for the 802.15.4 packet-based radios of the CC2430. It allows to send and receive packets, and set various 802.15.4 parameters as

---

[7] Code and data are located in separate memory space.
[8] For details, see http://www.tinyos8051wg.net

well as duty cycling the radio. Note that we depart from the Active Message abstraction promoted by the TinyOS 2.0 core working group. Our SimpleMac implementation supports simple packet transmission, but does not provide routing, or retransmission. Implementing Active Messages is future work.

Flash. We export the flash using the *SimpleFlash* interface that allows to read and write an array of bytes, as well as delete a page from flash. Note that this interface is much simpler than the abstractions promoted by the TinyOS 2.0 core working group (volumes, logging, large and small objects). We adopted this simple interface because it fits the needs of our data acquisition application. Implementing the core abstractions as defined in TEP103 is future work.

Timer. The timers are exported using the generic TinyOS Timer interfaces *Alarm* and *Counter*. These two interfaces give applications access to hardware counters and allows the use of the TinyOS components to extend the timer width from 16 bit to 32 bit. Note that on the pre-release CC2430 chips we used for our experiments, timers do not work properly[9].

ADC. The Analog-to-Digital Converter is accessed through the core *Read* interface that allows to read a single value. In order to read multiple values, an application must issue multiple read calls or use DMA transfers.

Pins. The General IO pins are exported through the core *GeneralIO* interface, that allows to set or clear a pin, make it an input or an output.

UART. The UART is exported using the core *SerialByteComm* interface (that sends and receives single bytes from the UART) and *StdOut* interfaces (that provides a `printf`-like abstraction on top of SerialByteComm).

Note that we did not need to change the system components from TinyOS 2.0. However, supporting a sleep mode on the CC2430 requires implementing a low-frequency timer. On the pre-release CC2430 chips we used for our experiments, timers do not work properly. This is work in progress, as a consequence our experiments are conducted without low-power mode on the CC2430.

The main challenges we faced implementing TinyOS 2.0 drivers on CC2430 were to (i) understand the TEP documents that describe the core interfaces as we were the first to port TinyOS 2.0 on a platform that was not part of the core, and (ii) to define an appropriate tool chain. Indeed, the code produced by the nesC pre-compiler is specific to gcc, which does not support 8051. We had to (a) choose another C compiler (Keil), and (b) introduce a C-to-C transformation step to map the C file that nesC outputs into a C file that Keil accepts as input (e.g., Keil does not support inlining, the definition of interrupt handlers is different in Keil and gcc, Keil introduces compiler hints that are specific to the 8051 memory model). The details of our toolchain are beyond the scope of this paper, see [6] for details.

Because the Micro has many similarities with the Telos mote, on which TinyOS 2.0 was originally developed, porting porting TinyOS 2.0 was a simple exercise. However, the wiring of the radio does not feature all of the signals

---

[9] The timers miss events once in a while. This error is documented on a ChipCon errata, which is not publically available.

available on the Telos mote, meaning that the radio stack could not be reused. We implemented the simple MAC layer, *SimpleMac*, and simple flash layer *SimpleFlash* described above.

4.3   Mote Vectors and Benchmarks

The vector component are chosen by analyzing the components used by the applications. As a result, we choose the following components for their mote vectors: *active*, *idle*, *adc*, *radio_receive*, *radio_transmit*, *flash_read*, *flash_write*, and *flash_erase*. Doing so, we leave some of the peripheral unit primitives out of the mote vector (e.g., the primitives to set or get the channel on the 802.15.4 radio) and unused peripherals. The time spent executing primitives left out are factored as CPU execution time, while the unused peripherals are only considered to contribute the idle power consumption. We also leave timers, UART and general IO pins out of the mote vector. The time spent in the timers is factored in the CPU idle component. We leave general IO pins out because we do not use LEDs, or digital sensors. Similarly, we do not use the UART. Note that we do not consider a specific sensor connected to the ADC.

The benchmarks we defined for these mote vector components are:

- A compression algorithm to characterize CPU execution. This component contains a mix of integer arithmetic with many loads and stores and some function calls. Using this algorithm is a baseline approach.
- Simple function calls with a fixed parameter for each peripheral unit primitive[10]. Note that benchmarks, in particular for the radio and flash, contain some buffer manipulation. These are measured as $CPU[PUi]$ (see Section 2.1).

4.4   TinyOS API Instrumentation

We need to implement the CPU and peripheral units to collect the traces that are the basis for the application vectors. We implemented the following mechanisms:

- For the peripheral units, we introduce a platform-independent layer between the component that provides the driver interface and the component that uses it. As an example consider reading a value from the ADC using the TinyOS 2.0 *Read* interface. This interface starts an ADC conversion with a *Read* command and returns with a *readDone*, We insert a layer that records the time elapsed between the *Read* command is called and the *readDone* event is received. This is obviously an approximation of the time during which the ADC is actually turned on.
- For the CPU, we leverage the fact that TinyOS has a simple task scheduler that puts the CPU into sleep mode when the task queue is empty. The microprocessor is awoken via interrupts generated from internal or external peripherals. We record the time elapsed between the CPU enters sleep mode and the woke-up interrupt handler is executed as *idle* and the rest of the time as *active*.

---

[10] The source code is available through the TinyOS 2 contribution section.

In order to collect this trace, we encode each state as a combination of bits (our mote vector is of dimension 8) we thus use 8 bits to encode the states. Collecting this trace could be done internally on the mote being investigated, but this introduces a management overhead. Instead we output each bit of the state as an IO pin, using a second mote, which we call *LogRecorder*, that records the state transitions. This mechanism is very similar to the monitoring techniques devised for deployment-support networks[7].

4.5   Data Acquisition Applications

We use simple data acquisition applications as workload for our experiments. We build them from building blocks: sample, compress, store, and send. We create 4 applications that increase the parallel behavior of these tasks from isolation to parallel sample and transmission:

SampleCompressStore is a simple state machine, that runs each step in isolation. As each sample is retrieved, it is then compressed, and once 10 samples are retrieved they are stored to flash. This cycle is repeated 9 times.

DataAcquisition extends the state machine from SampleCompressStore to retrieve the data from flash and transmit it. Again, each step in isolation.

SampleStoreForward is similar to DataAcquisition, except without the compression step.

DataAcquisitionAdv performs the same tasks as DataAcquisition, but interleaves the sample and transmit processes. Store is done in isolation.

For our first experiments, we want a deterministic workload that exhibits reproducible results. One important source of variance in a sensor network applications is the environment. We choose a simple network topology and transmission scheme. Data is transmitted in 384 byte chunks (data and padding). The transmission does not expect acknowledgment that a packet is received, but only wait for the channel to be cleared (CCA) before sending. Sampling is at 10Hz and for compression we use the Lz77 algorithm.

5   Experimental Results

5.1   CC2430 and Micro

We ran the benchmarks described in the previous section on both the Micro and CC2430 motes. The time and energy mote vectors we obtain are shown in Figure 1 as spider charts. The results are somewhat surprising. CC2430 is much faster than the Micro when running the benchmarks and transmitting packets. Slow memory accesses is compensated by the high clock rate and direct access to the radio speeds up packet transmission. It means that the CC2430 can complete its tasks quickly, and thus be aggressively duty cycled. In terms of energy, we observe that:

1. CPU operations are two to three orders of magnitude more expensive on the CC2430 than on the Micro. This is due to the high clock rate (which

guarantees fast execution) and to the overhead introduced by the slow access RAM.

2. Flash operations are much more expensive on the Micro than on the CC2430. These results led us to check our driver implementation (which is a positive results in itself). We could not find any bug. We believe that the difference in performance can be explained by the difference in clock rate between both platforms (1 MHz for the Micro vs. 32 MHz for the CC2430) and with the fact that the CC2430 driver is hand coded in assembler and the Micro's is not.

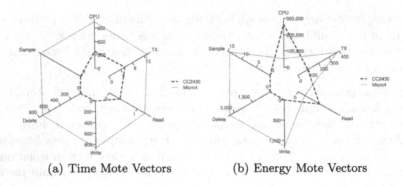

(a) Time Mote Vectors   (b) Energy Mote Vectors

Fig. 1. Time and energy mote vectors for CC2430 and Micro

5.2 Performance Prediction

We used our methodology to derive the application vectors for the four data acquisition applications described in the previous Section. The results are shown in Figure 2.

The profiles we get for the applications correspond to what we expect. Indeed, the application vector components for the ADC, flash and radio operations correspond roughly to the number of samples, flash and radio operations issued by the

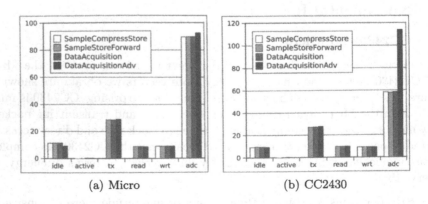

(a) Micro   (b) CC2430

Fig. 2. Application vectors for CC2430 and Micro

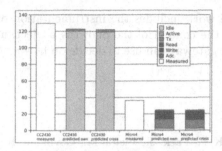

Fig. 3. Energy measurements and estimates

applications. The application vector is designed to be platform-independent. We thus expect that the application vectors derived from the CC2430 and Micro are similar. The good news is that they are at the exception of the ADC component. This is either a measurement error, a software bug in the driver, or a hardware bug. We focused on this issue and observed that the time it takes to obtain a sample on CC2430 varies depending on the application. Two different programs collecting the same data through the same ADC driver experience different sampling times. We observed as much as 50% difference between two programs. We believe that this is another hardware approximation on the CC2430.

Our initial hypothesis is that the energy spent by an application on a mote can be estimated using the scalar product of the application vector with the mote vector. We computed the energy estimate for the *DataAcquisitionAdv* application and we compared them to the measurements we conducted directly on the motes (using an oscilloscope). The results are shown in Figure 3.

The estimations are well into an order of magnitude from the actual energy consumption. This is rather positive. As expected, the contribution from the CPU in active mode is insignificant. The poor performance of the CC2430 is due to the fact that we did not implement sleep mode support on the CC2430. Much more work is needed to test our methodology. This experiment, however, shows that we can use our method to prototype a data acquisition application with the Micro and predict how much energy the CC2430 would have used in the same conditions.

6   Conclusion

We described a vector-based methodology to characterize the performance of an application running on a given mote. Our approach is based on the hypothesis that mote energy consumption can be expressed as the scalar product of two vectors: one that characterize the performance of the core mote primitives, and one that characterizes the way an application utilizes these primitives. Our experiments show that our methodology can be used for predicting the performance of data acquisition applications between Sensinode Micro and a mote based on the CC2430 SoC. Much more experimental work is needed to establish the limits of our approach. Future work includes the instrumentation of an application deployed in the field in the context of the Snowths project, and the development of a cost model that a gateway can use to decide on how much processing should be pushed to a mote.

References

1. Gwanali, O., Jang, K.Y., Paek, J., Vieira, M., Govindan, R., Greenstein, B., Joki, A., Estrin, D., Kohler, E.: The Tenet Architecture for Tiered Sensor Networks. In: Sensys 2006. Proc. ACM Intl. Conference on Embedded Networked Sensor Systems (2006)
2. Mueller, R., Alonso, G., Kossmann, D.: SwissQM: Next Generation Data Processing in Sensor Networks. In: Third Biennial Conference on Innovative Data Systems Research
3. Shnayder, V., Hempstead, M., Chen, B.-r., Welsh, M.: PowerTOSSIM: Efficient Power Simulation for TinyOS Applications. In: Sensys 2004. Proc. ACM Intl. Conference on Embedded Networked Sensor Systems (2004)
4. Seltzer, M., Krinsky, D., Smith, K., Zhang, X.: The Case for Application-Specific Benchmarking. In: Workshop on Hot Topics in Operating Systems (1999)
5. Handziski, V., Polastre, J., Hauer, J.-H., Sharp, C., Wolisz, A., Culler, D.: Flexible Hardware Abstraction for Wireless Sensor Networks. In: Proc. 2nd European Workshop on Wireless Sensor Networks (EWSN) (2005)
6. Leopold, M.: Creating a New Platform for TinyOS 2.x Technical Report 07/09, Depth. of Computer Science, University of Copenhagen (2007)
7. Beutel, J., Dyer, M., Yücel, M., Thiele, L.: Development and Test with the Deployment-Support Network. In: Langendoen, K., Voigt, T. (eds.) EWSN 2007. LNCS, vol. 4373, Springer, Heidelberg (2007)
8. Thiele, L., Wandeler, E.: Performance Analysis of Distributed Embedded Systems. In: The Embedded Systems Handbook. CRC Press, Boca Raton, USA (2004)
9. Beutel, J.: Metrics for Sensor Network Platforms. In: REALWSN 2006. Proc. ACM Workshop on Real-World Wireless Sensor Networks (2006)

Que: A Sensor Network Rapid Prototyping Tool with Application Experiences from a Data Center Deployment

David Chu[1], Feng Zhao[2], Jie Liu[2], and Michel Goraczko[2]

[1] CS Division, EECS Department, UC Berkeley, Berkeley, CA, USA
`davidchu@cs.berkeley.edu`
[2] Microsoft Research, Redmond, WA, USA
`{zhao,jie.liu,michelg}@microsoft.com`

Abstract. Several considerable impediments stand in the way of sensor network prototype applications that wish to realize sustained deployments. These are: scale, longevity, data of interest, and infrastructure integration. We present a tool, Que, which assists those sensor network deployments transitioning from prototypes to early production environments by addressing these issues. Que is able to simulate realistic deployments with faithful data, provide fast and iterative feedback on operations, and compose applications quickly in a platform-independent manner. We demonstrate Que's applicability via tests against our new data center environment-monitoring deployment, DataCenter.NET.

1 Introduction

Sensor networks are notoriously difficult to build, deploy and maintain. Early sensor network experiences are not without case studies of deployment that have failed to mature or taken considerably longer to arrive at fruition than originally anticipated.

For example, several geomorphologists, excited by the new science that sensor networks might bring to their field, targeted an initial test deployment in a modest desert cave to collect climatological data. They purchased a packaged sensor network product from a major sensor networking company. The package was billed as the most straightforward off-the-shelf solution offered, so their realistic expectations were that such a system would last several months given the energy provisions once deployed.

Unfortunately, the experiences were not encouraging. After spending several days in the field trying to determine why the product failed to deliver results, the geologists finally established connectivity and collected data for two hours before the product failed permanently. Disillusioned, these users have since reconsidered their sensor network efforts. While the brief two hours of data were beneficial, the costs were very significant [24].

What can we do to remedy this lack of sensor network usability? Let us pursue this question by first examining the development model surrounding sensor

R. Verdone (Ed.): EWSN 2008, LNCS 4913, pp. 337–353, 2008.

network deployments today. Sensor network deployment efforts typically follow a 4-step procedure:

1. *Goals and requirements specifications*
2. *Prototype deployment*
3. *Prototype to production transition*
4. *Production deployment*

Many scenarios are easy to prototype, but have difficulty achieving production standards. This indicates that there are significant factors in the production requirements that are unaccounted for in the prototype phase. To address these disparities effectively, it is often more important to know what is wrong *early, often and approximately* rather than late, infrequently and precisely.

We have built *Que*, a tool which provides a unified scripting and simulation/emulation framework for multi-tier sensor network systems. Que assists the transition from prototype to production by enabling fast iterations on whole-system assembly and system input/output testing.

Several important factors influence why this transition is not straight forward, and where a tool like Que aims to provide assistance:

Scale: In the prototype phase, it is important to get something working quickly. This often means over-instrumentation with dense arrays of sensors in a limited area rather than finely-tuned capacity planning. However, scale is driven upward in the production phase while the cost of ownership prohibits over-instrumentation. Thus, determining the minimum density of sensors is a necessary yet often unanswered question.

Longevity: In the prototype phase, the sensornet does not have to be long-lived nor particularly reliable. In production, lifetime and manageability requirements are dominant concerns. Frequently, longevity issues such as minimum sampling interval and duty-cycling are deferred until production deployment, an expensive phase in which to address a fundamental requirement of the sensor system. A short-lived sensing system is often simply not useful [7].

Data: In the prototype phase, raw data is useful especially for exploration. In production, distilled decision making information is most important. Thus, data processing operations which were not present in the prototype must be introduced in production. Furthermore, the operational dynamics are further complicated in the case of online or in-network data processing. Thus, it is important to test with realistic data input and control logic in the prototype phase.

Integration: Integration with the rest of infrastructure pyramid is not a priority during prototyping. However, realistic production systems often involve many elements in addition to the sensornet. Traditional sensornet development lacks such multi-tier systems integration testing.

The goal of Que is to help answer these question through a combination of two primary mechanisms. First, Que offers a scripting-based exploration environment for operator-based system assembly across multiple platform tiers. Quick scripting makes it easy for developers to retask their system for new data processing either on mote- or microserver-class devices. Second, Que provides a simulation and emulation environment for an entire multi-platform tiered system, so that retasking can be quickly tested on the entire system against realistic scenarios. The combination of these two mechanisms lends naturally to rich system and data exploration, which are important in the transition from prototype to production.

To validate our approach, we have applied Que to DataCenter.NET, an entirely new deployment at Microsoft Research with significant material impact. A significant problem in the modern computer data center is the lack of visibility into power-intensive cooling support systems. DataCenter.NET is a compelling application that assists data center operators with real-time high-granularity feedback into operational metrics such as facilities and server temperatures. As we worked toward a real production deployment with our operations colleagues, we realized that DataCenter.NET required addressing all of the key issues mentioned above: scale, longevity, data and integration; hence, providing a great testing environment for Que. Our main result here is that Que, positioned as a general rapid prototyping tool, does indeed provide fast insight into these system-wide issues, while leaving definitive and highly-refined answers for special-purpose tools.

The next section describes related work. Section 3 discusses the design principles that drive Que. Section 4 introduces the Que environment. Section 5 describes the system architecture. Section 6 and 7 discusses our deployment DataCenter.NET and our results in using Que to bring this system to production. Finally, section 8 presents discussion and conclusions.

2   Related Work

Observing the practical difficulty of deploying sensor networks, a number of projects provide "out-of-the-box" sensor network solutions [6,9]. Although these solutions are convenient for data collection tasks, they do not address the inherent customization necessary for many sensor network scenarios. Many proposed sensornet programming systems have aimed to facilitate customization with new programming models or APIs. Several have explicitly looked at the benefits toward rapid prototyping [5,4]. Also, customization may not mean programming each sensor node directly. They can be expressed in declarative ways, such as seen in TinyDB [23], Semantics Streams [26], and DSN [8]. Or, they can be specified via composition languages.

Composition languages, sometimes referred to as "programming by component wiring," is used in many embedded systems programming and designs [17, 14, 13, 10, 15, 22]. They are particularly useful at the system prototyping and testing stages, where the users have some ideas of how they system works, but need more hand tuning. EmStar [13] and Viptos [10] both provide two-tier simulation environments. However, Emstar does not provide ways to program at the sensor mote level. Sensors are primarily used as wireless interfaces for microservers. Viptos is a visual programming interface where microserver components are implemented in Java. Que is similar to Viptos in spirit, but by using a unified Python programming language at both sensor mote and microserver levels, users get access to the full capability of Python for experiment control, data archiving, and visualization purposes. The text based general purpose language gives users powerful and intuitive constructs like loops and conditions when building prototypes. Que also takes advantage of MSRSense to support web services and integration with web and enterprise applications.

Some of the preceding composition languages additionally provide model-based semantics in addition to operational semantics [8, 10, 23]. Model-based semantics often permit establishment of program guarantees beyond those available with purely operational semantics, which may help with ensuring that prototype and production systems both conform to user requirements. As a pure composition language, Que itself does not impose any models of computation. It relies on subsystems like TinyOS and MSRSense [22] to provide execution semantics.

Que's scripting environment is similar in spirit to those proposed in Marionette [25] and Tinker [11]. Whereas Marionette uses scripting for debugging and Tinker uses scripting for data exploration, Que employs this approach in whole system development, as well as data exploration. In fact, Que offers a convenient bridge to the server-side data manipulation operators offered by Tinker.

3   Design Goals

The Que functional interface is meant to be an extremely simple yet sufficiently flexible for operator composition and simulation execution.

Simplicity: Que does not provide yet another programming approach to sensor networks. Rather, Que directly provides the intermediate operator composition language while other languages (e.g., C) provide operator implementations. It has been argued that restricted coordination languages fit well for constructing systems when operator boundaries are well-defined [20]. Indeed, Que users benefit from the safety and simplicity of the language restrictions, yet retain the ability to create new operators in native systems languages. This programming paradigm is common in embedded systems [11, 14, 15, 22].

Leverage Existing Libraries: The lack of full node programmability means that Que relies on others to provide the bulk of operator implementations. By default, Que interfaces with three such operator libraries: MSRSense [22], TinyOS [15] and Tinker [11] and additionally offers a general adapter to integrate with other operator libraries.

Flexibility: Que exposes a Python-like shell for convenient interaction. We utilize it as a flexible platform from which to perform operator composition, sensor network to system integration, and data analysis.

There are some associated limitations with this model as well. Que is best suited for operator-based programming. This implies establishment of well-defined operator interfaces and libraries. Development of new device drivers for example must still be done in native environments.

```
 1 # Create tinyos operator graph
 2 op_man = toslib.create('tos/system/Main')
 3 op_osc = toslib.create('apps/Oscilloscope/OscilloscopeM')
 4 op_com = toslib.create('tos/system/UARTComm')
 5 link(op_man, 'StdControl', op_osc, 'StdControl')
 6 # ... (3 instantiations and 7 linkages elided)
 7 link(op_osc, 'DataMsg', op_com, 'SendMsg[AM_OSCOPEMSG]')
 8
 9 # Create microserver operator graph
10 op_tpr = mslib.create('ComplexTOSPacketReceiver')
11 op_tpr.setparam('messageType', 'ArrayOscopeMsg')
12 op_d2x = mslib.create('DataToXml')
13 link(op_tpr, 'output', op_d2x, 'input')
14
15 # Bind cross-platform ports
16 op_amp = toslib.createAMPort()
17 op_por = mslib.createTcpPort()
18 link(op_com, 'SendMsg', op_amp, '10')
19 link(op_amp, '10', op_por, '9002')
20 link(op_por, '6001', op_tpr, 'input')
21
22 # Execute emulator
23 emusrc1 = emulator.DataCenterEmulator(connstr)
24 net = openlocal(op_amp, op_por, emusrc=emusrc1)
25 results = run(net, time=60*10, appname='Oscilloscope', dosrcgen=True,
            docompile=True, dosimulate=True)
```

Listing 1.1. Instantiating and linking operators from operator libraries

4 Example User Session

Next we illustrate a user's interaction
with Que via an example session. This
comprehensive example session creates, executes and postprocesses the
operator graph shown in Figure 1 that
spans both mote and microserver
platforms, while simultaneously em-
phasizing the minimal mechanism

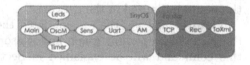

Fig. 1. Operator graph demonstrated in example session

presented to accomplish these objectives. The application corresponds to the
prototypical multi-sensor sampling application. Its function is to periodically
send all sensors' measurements over the serial port to the microserver for XML
canonicalization.

The user is able to instantiate operators from platform-specific libraries from
the interactive shell. Listing 1.1 begins by showing the instantiation and linking of
several operators from a particular library, the TinyOS platform library (lines 2–4
and lines 5–7 respectively). The two important functions above are the operator
library create call and the link call. The create call instantiates new operators from
the platform-specific operator library toslib. The link call binds the output port of
one operator to the input port of another operator. There is also a function unlink
provided to unlink an object. For example, the Main operator and the OscilloscopeM
operators are linked together through the StdControl interface (line 5). Parameterized interfaces, introduced in TinyOS, are also supported (e.g., line 7).

Que provides integrated support for both TinyOS and MSRSense. MSRSense is a .NET-based compenentized sensor network microserver. Lines 10–13 show the manipulation of MSRSense operators in Que which by intention is the same as manipulating the TinyOS operator library above. This uniform support for cross-platform operator composition is one point where Que facilitates system assembly.

Cross-platform operator composition such as MSRSense operator to TinyOS operator composition is also easy to accomplish. Lines 16–20 show the binding of ports between operators of different platforms. In particular, the special operators opamp and oppor for Active Message and TCP ports respectively, serve as conduits through which communication occurs between the two platforms. Que identifies and appropriately handles this case, as discussed in Section 5.

In addition to easing system assembly, Que also provides a simulator with great emphasis on ease of use (lines 23–25. The overall goal is to simulate the operator graph consisting of heterogeneous elements. We next explain these three important commands in detail.

First in line 23 of Listing 1.1, the user chooses an appropriate simulator for her concerns. The emulator.DataCenterEmulator in particular draws ADC values from traces collected in our new deployment which we describe subsequently in Section 6. Section 5 describes more about possible emulators.

Second in line 24, the openlocal initializes the network topology with a minimum of user intervention. Our ease of use criterion means that the user can either choose a predefined network or can query a preexisting network for its parameters[1]. In addition, openlocal accepts chains of operators and binds these to the nodes initialized in the network.

Third in line 25, the run simulates the given network, in conjunction with the particular operator graph and sensor inputs. The heavy lifting underlying this command will be explained in Section 5. The goal is to provide a very minimal interface through which the details of the simulation are abstracted, but the results are not. At the end of run, the results are brought from the particular platform-specific simulations into the Que environment. The results are naturally emitted by the endpoint(s) of the directed operator graph. For our running example, the results are at the MSRSense operator op_d2x.

The preceding three commands, and particularly the last one, present simple interfaces for simplicity of use. Yet these allow full flexibility for exercising a custom operator graph on a custom network topology with a custom simulation data source.

By default, simulation results are returned as a sequence of arrays, one for every message from the terminal operator in the graph. After some initial operator-specific data marshalling, the user is able to apply Que's script-based processing to achieve very fast turnaround time for getting initial results. For example, standard utility functions such as plotresults and plotcorrs generate scatter and topographical plots respectively. ewma computes a tunable exponential weighted moving average that is often useful in real-world data cleaning. In addition, the

---

[1] The latter option is not yet implemented.

wealth of native Python libraries is often a benefit for our scripting environment; corrcoef is a built-in Python function that computes correlation coefficients. Additionally, Que can interface to the Tinker and Matlab-like matplotlib Python tools in order to apply more standard data operations [11,16]. Section 7 demonstrates the utility of this rapid data processing.

5 System Architecture

Our architecture, shown in Figure 2, consists of several major components: operator libraries, network libraries, and the simulator. We next discuss the mechanics of each.

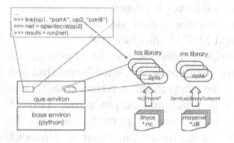

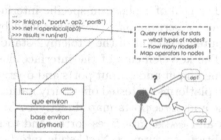

(a) Unified operator composition from interfaces of platform-specific operators.

(b) Creation of a network object based upon a static network configuration or querying of a live network. The operator graph is assigned to platform-specific network nodes.

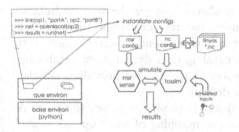

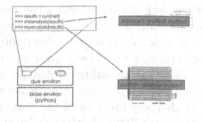

(c) The operator graph is run. This involves instantiating operators (possibly involving compilation) and invoking platform-specific simulation environments. Results are retrieved back into the Que environment.

(d) The results are fed into standard analysis and visualization tools. In addition, the user has very flexible options for scripting her own post-processing.

Fig. 2. The Que Architecture

5.1   Operator Libraries

Operator libraries permit the creation of operators for manipulation in Que. There is an operator library per platform which subclasses oplib. Often these libraries correspond directly to existing software libraries available on the corresponding platforms. For example, the TinyOS and MSRSense platforms both contain a fair number of operators in their distributions. In order to expose these platform-specific elements as operators in Que, we provide platform-specific *interface extractors* as illustrated in Figure 2(a). For TinyOS and MSRSense, this functionality is provided by the tools nc2moml and ServiceLibrary2Moml respectively. After instantiation from a platform-specific library, all operators behave consistently, resulting in a uniform user experience.

New platforms are straightforward to expose to Que. The only requirements are to subclass oplib for the platform's operator library and populate the library with a platform-specific interface extractor tool.

The goal of a platform-specific interface extractor is to generate *operator interface descriptor files* which are used by operator library subclasses. We have adopted a variant of the Ptolemy2 standard MOML interface [19].

The key elements of the interface descriptor interface are the exposition of named input and output ports and operator parameters. We have found that the two platforms we tested offer fairly natural mappings to this interface. MSRSense input and output ports map directly to MOML input and output ports; TinyOS uses and provides interfaces correspond to input and output ports respectively. In addition, to support NesC-style interface parameterization, input and output ports are permitted to be parameterized, such that a single port proxies for a number of instances of the port determined at compile time.[2]

5.2   Network Libraries

The network library provides the network abstraction for the user. Subclasses of netlib define a set of heterogeneous nodes and the interconnecting network. For example, a subclassed network object may correspond to a predefined static set of nodes, a set chosen from an asset catalog, or a dynamic set established from querying an online prototype network. Currently, we provide a subclass that supports a predefined static set as a default.

Another key function of the network object is to pin operators to nodes. As illustrated in Figure 2(b), this determines the mapping of what operators each node runs. Typically this assignment proceeds by associating platform-specific operators with the nodes on which they are capable of running. At present, every operator is targeted for only one platform so the mapping is straightforward. However, cross-platform operators are also possible (*e.g.*, with operator virtualization or platform-independent operator implementations). These then permit variable operator placement informed by metrics such as computational speed,

---

[2] Note that MOML parameters are distinct from parameterized ports. MOML parameters are more akin to NesC generics [12].

energy and sensitivity to network loss. Furthermore, they open the possibility of dynamic operator placement optimization.

5.3 Simulator

The heart of Que is the heterogeneous network simulator. The simulator is initiated with the run command. As shown in Figure 2(c), the simulator executes the following sequence of operations:

Operator configuration: The simulator first generates platform-specific configuration files from operator graph specifications given as input. For example, for TinyOS, the simulator generates NesC component wirings. For MSRSense, the simulator generates XML operator configuration files.

Binary compilation: The simulator then enacts platform-specific compilation for the configured system. This possibly involves multiple compilations for multiple platforms.

Native execution: The simulator next executes the compiled operator graphs in low-level native platform-specific simulators. The TOSSIM simulator is used for TinyOS binaries [21]. Since MSRSense microserver is already contained within the .NET virtual machine, it is natively executed. Also, the simulator draws data inputs from its user-specified data source for either preset, trace-driven, or emulated sensor readings. This provides for a customizable degree of fidelity. We highlight that similar emulator drivers can also be provided for the network.

Channel establishment: A myriad of communication channels are needed for interoperability in a mixed environment of heterogeneous platforms. For instance, appropriate connection bindings are needed between the MSRSense runtime and Serial Forwarder, a standard TinyOS communication channel, in order to achieve heterogeneous network simulation. As another example, data input from the user-specified data source also needs to be connected with the simulator. The Que simulator establishes all of these channels and extra plumbing on the user's behalf when the run command is invoked.

At the conclusion of this process, the operator graph is transformed into a set of results over the specified network and data source. These results are populated back into the Que environment as easy-to-manipulate arrays.

5.4 Analysis Tools

The standard analysis tools provide helpful first-level diagnostics that go toward answering the general prototype to production questions. These tools are: visualizing the resulting output for each node; calculating and visualizing the correlation map for the nodes of interest; and performing basic data cleaning of the resulting data. Examples of there application are shown in Figure 2(d). These are exposed as additional user scripts callable from Que. Likewise, we are able to readily adopt Tinker and Matlab-like matplotlib built-in tools [11, 16].

6   DataCenter.NET Deployment

6.1   The Problem

We focused the use of Que in a particular deployment, DataCenter.NET. The goal of DataCenter.NET is to reduce energy costs in the computer data center, a rapidly rising concern [1,3]. The typical data center is an intense environment consisting of thousands to tens of thousands of physical compute and storage servers, arranged in vertical racks. This density of servers creates two compounding problems. First, the servers require an intense amount of power to run. Hundreds of watts per square foot is not uncommon. Second, the density of machinery places an immense cooling requirement placed on the data center facilities; the Heating, Ventilation and Air Conditioning (HVAC) energy expenditure is a sizable fraction of the overall facilities energy expenditure. Therefore, both are significant sources of energy consumption, and hence present significant opportunities for energy reduction.

Unfortunately, data center managers have relatively scarce information on which to base facilities HVAC decisions. Traditional thermostats are generally deployed at a very coarse grain, with one thermostat canvassing several thousand servers. This means that HVAC settings are naturally adjusted to local phenomenon first, and only slowly adapt to global temperature changes. Since there is often a hard requirement to run all machines under certain machine-specific temperatures or else risk overheating and hardware failure, facilities managers are loathe to experiment aggressively with new thermostat settings. Unfortunately, zeroing in on the right temperature setting is exactly a key factor in saving data center energy consumption.

Further compounding the problem, data center operators often have little visibility into future request loads that are being executed by data center clients. In addition, each rack is configured to contain a mix of varied processing and storage elements, all of which exhibit different workloads. This leads to unpredictable fluctuations in the space of optimal HVAC settings over time.

6.2   Our Approach

To tackle this problem, we worked with data center managers to develop a wireless network for environment sensing. Wireless sensors are a suitable fit for this scenario for several reasons. First, the wireless sensors can be deployed incrementally and flexibly. This is important for gradual rollout and avoiding high upfront costs (e.g., of traditional thermostats or of upmarket environment sensing-enabled server racks). Second, wireless sensors can cover a very fine-grained spatial setting, and this density can be flexibly chosen and reconfigured.

With detailed temperature heat maps, data facilities managers are able to make more informed decisions affecting data center operations. First, managers gain visibility into better ways to design facilities, such as where to optimally place new racks and improve HVAC distribution systems. Second, managers and the server's users can control job scheduling better so as to not only take into account server load, but also heat displacement effects. With a flexible job allocation mechanism such as virtualization, we might even apply optimization algorithms to job placement.

Commissioned with these high level goals, we proceeded to build a modest prototype data center before embarking on a live pilot deployment. Our lab prototype, DataCenter.NET, contains 14 servers arranged in racks of 5, 5 and 4 servers each. They are located in a 10 ft by 15 ft contained testing environment. We fully instrumented each server with a wireless temperature sensor mote near the front intake fan, and a mote near the back exhaust fan. Similarly, we deployed 6 ambient temperature sensors along the ceiling in a grid arrangement. Along with a base station to transmit all the data, this formed a 35 mote deployment. Figure 3 shows the components of this setup.

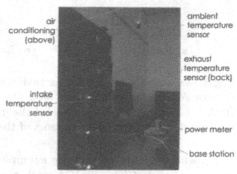

Fig. 3. The DataCenter.NET lab prototype server racks consist of 35 wireless sensors placed on the front and rear of 15 servers and on the ceiling. The servers compromise 3 racks, two of which are visible in the foreground and background here.

6.3   Using Que in DataCenter.NET

DataCenter.NET is a fitting scenario in which to test Que. In fact, DataCenter.NET highlights the importance of each of the areas of concern when transitioning from prototype to production which we previously outlined in Section 1:

Scale: Our initial prototype consists of 35 motes deployed on 3 racks. However, we are facing a massive scale-up to tens of thousand racks and a proportional increase in the number of wireless sensors.

Longevity: Energy requirements are not initially an issue. However, as we transition to production, battery replacement becomes an increasingly important concern. In particular, the number of radio messages sent, an energy intensive operation, becomes important to monitor.

Data: Our prototype is capable of delivering all of the data to the end users. However, facilities managers are only interested in faithful temperature trends as opposed to noisy and lossy raw readings.

Integration: Lastly, a wireless sensing system is but one part of many tools for facility managers. This must integrate cleanly with their other preexisting tools and infrastructure.

In the Section 7, we address how Que answers these questions we had about our deployment. Section 7 also shows how it was often necessary to modify existing mote and microserver operator graphs because some amount of customization was necessary. Hence, it was not feasible to use readily available off-the-shelf solutions [9, 2].

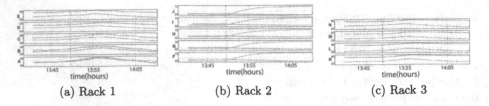

(a) Rack 1   (b) Rack 2   (c) Rack 3

Fig. 4. An entire rack, Rack 2, actuated simultaneously during the day. Notice the strange *decrease* in temperature after the initial temperature increase, especially at Rack 1. Later investigations revealed the involvement of the building thermostat AC, underscoring the nontrivial dynamics of the seemingly simple test deployment.

Presently, we illustrate some example temperature traces in Figure 4. Three subfigures 4(a), 4(b) and 4(c), each correspond to a rack of machines. For example, Subfigure 4(a) corresponds to five machines Server A, B, C, D and E whose physical arrangement corresponds to the vertical ordering of their plots. For each machine, the red plot indicates the exhaust temperature measurements and the blue plot indicates the intake temperature measurements across time.

In the experiment corresponding to Figure 4, all servers in Rack 2 are turned on at 1:50 PM. As expected, this causes a universal rise in room temperature which is seen at all racks. However, slightly after 1:55 PM, Racks 1 and 3 proceed to cool down(!). Further investigation revealed that as the temperature rose, the building thermostat sensed the change and actuated the building AC, causing a depression in temperature. This effect was more heavily felt at Rack 1 then at Rack 3 because the AC ventilation was much closer to Rack 1. This sort of complex interaction is common, yet difficult to identify without a rich coverage of sensors.

7   Evaluation

We first built an application that we ran on the nodes in the lab data center testbed. This application was previously described in Section 4 and shown in Figure 1. The application simply collects temperature readings periodically, and send these back to a base station where they are canonicalized into a standard XML format. We ran this application for approximately eighteen days.

Next we evaluated Que with respect to DataCenter.NET in the four important areas of concern for sensor networks that we have outlined: scale, longevity, data and integration. For evaluation purposes, we compare each area to the original base application of Figure 1; in an actual Que usage scenario, each iteration would improve upon the former. While rarely providing the final word on any single topic, we argue that Que delivers on its ability to retask and reevaluate systems quickly. We cover the results of each area of concern in-depth below, and illustrate how Que was applied.

7.1   Scale

Scaling up deployments introduces many new issues. Presently, we use Que to address just one particular issue in this process: what density of spatial coverage is necessary in a production deployment? This has previously been formulated as a theoretical optimization problem [18].

Our test environment, as described in Section 6, embeds motes in a wealth of locations in the environment: six on the ceiling, and two per server, for an average of ten motes per rack. While this finely captures transitions in temperature across space, the number of sensors may be saturating the environment for the utility of the information provided.

The task is then to determine which sensors to retain if one were to scale to many thousands of racks. We focus on a primitive to mutual information criteria used in [18],

```
1 net = openlocal(opgraph, ...)
2 results = run(net, ...)
3 z = myappconverter(results)
4 cc = corrcoef(z)
5 plotcorrs(cc)
```

Listing 1.2. Que script to compute correlations between monitoring nodes in the server room. Some optional parameters have been omitted.

the correlation coefficients between every pair of sensors. We are less concerned with network costs since a single-hop base station suffices for all communication in our scenario.

Listing 1.2 and Figure 5 show the steps we performed in Que to drill down on this question, and the results generated respectively. The correlations between pairs of nodes are illustrated in a 3D histogram where darker intensities correspond to stronger correlations. For example, in Figure 5(a), two clusters emerge: one which contains the majority (eight nodes) and another

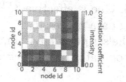 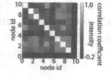

(a) Clustered sensors   (b) Weakly correlated sensors

Fig. 5. Histogram visualization of node correlations

that contains the minority (two nodes). The larger cluster corresponds to the front and back of one rack during a period of time when no server in the rack was active. The smaller cluster corresponds to two nodes associated with another rack which did have servers activated during the investigated period. Hence, we can start to suspect that if the server workload is highly localized to particular racks, then clusters emerge around nodes of the same rack. In Figure 5(b), we tested a different workload that varied across racks. Here, no clear clusters immediately emerge. While more thorough investigation is warranted to determine the optimal configuration for various server workloads, Que's ease of data analysis permitted us to quickly gain valuable ballpark intuition on the scaling issue.

7.2 Data

The data is the key benefit that draws clients to use sensor networks. One prerequisite of providing data of interest is extracting first level base data from noisy sensor measurements. In particular, data cleaning and calibration is often a mundane but necessary step.

There are two approaches to data cleaning in Que for the data collection operator graph of Figure 1. The first option is the MSRSense operator, ewma. An operator graph involving ewma is shown in Figure 6. Alternatively, Que provides simple ewma as part of the standard set of data analysis tools, in case MSRSense is not part of the operator graph. Its use is shown in Listing 1.3.

Fig. 6. Operator graph with MSRSense-based EWMA

We ran the latter data cleaning procedure and converted initial results shown in Figure 7(a) to those shown in Figure 7(b). This offered a significant improvement in the usable data values, as evidenced by the reduction in variance. The procedure involved no more than a handful of scripting calls shown in Lemma 1.3. Que is effective at quickly performing data processing

```
1 net = openlocal(opgraph, ...)
2 results = run(net, ...)
3 z = myappconverter(results)
4 # ewma: cleaning
5 ewmaz = ewma(z)
6 plotresults(z,emaz)
```

Listing 1.3. EWMA applied as data processing script

that, once tuned in the scripting environment, can then be applied in a straightforward fashion as a operator on the actual running platform.

7.3 Longevity

Next, we investigate ways to improve the longevity and reliability of our system. While many methods to increase system longevity and reliability are possible, we focused on one in particular: we attempted to increase network reliability by performing application-level data reduction and decreasing cross-traffic. In addition, this reduces the energy spent transmitting messages.

Our approach here is a moving threshold reporting scheme: we convert collection from a periodic event to one in which data is only reported if the measurements are some threshold beyond the previous report. Our main changes to the previous operator graphs was the replacement of the

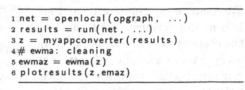

(a) Without EWMA   (b) With EWMA

Fig. 7. A sample time series of data with simple EWMA data cleaning applied

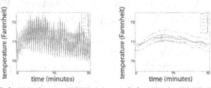

Fig. 8. Operator graph of threshold-triggered reporting

OscM operator by the TrigM operator. This is shown in Figure 8. The corresponding Listing 1.4 is also shown.

When we ran this series of operators, Que immediately produced odd graphs, shown in Figure 9. In this case, Que allowed us to quickly identify an operator that behaved strangely and produced nonsensical results before we deployed into the field.

```
1 net = openlocal(opgraph, ...)
2 results = run(net, ...)
3 z = myappconverter(results)
4 plotresults(z)
```

Listing 1.4. Event trigger script

7.4 Integration

Lastly, we are concerned with the lack of support testing end to end systems with traditional sensor network prototyping systems. In the case of DataCenter.NET, this means that a system controller should function as part of the running simulation in an entirely integrated system.

We explored this area by developing and deploying an open-loop controller alongside our sensor network. This controller assigns jobs to servers in a predetermined fashion, without input from the environment, much like existing controllers used in commercial data centers. At present, this controller is a separate application. As a next step, it is natural to incorporate the controller as a MSRSense microserver operator. In this way, it may be manipulated just like any other operator in Que.

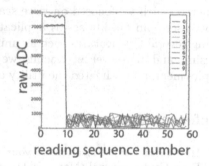

Fig. 9. A bug revealed in trigger program

We have already tested the response of a realistic job load on this controller. Figure 10(a) is a deployed Internet service workload trace representative of one day. We scaled it appropriately to fully load our servers at peak requests.

The temperature fluctuations displayed by our controller are shown in Figure 10. We note several features of this dataset, in particular the high degree

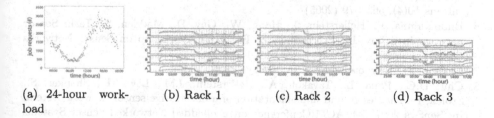

(a) 24-hour workload   (b) Rack 1   (c) Rack 2   (d) Rack 3

Fig. 10. Open-loop controller measurement results over day and half period. Results for part of this time are shown. Notice the large irregularities in local server and rack temperatures as jobs are scheduled without knowledge of environmental conditions.

of fluctuation of the exhaust measurements, and also the uneven degree to which servers are actuated. On several occasions, the fluctuations are on the order of tens of degrees in several minute's time, suggesting that the variance is indeed very great in a very short time span. These results strongly encourage investigation of more informed closed-loop controllers that incorporate temperature feedback. Quick and frequent guidance such as this that Que provides has been very useful for guiding our systems integration rapid prototyping efforts.

8   Conclusion

We have presented Que, an environment in which promising prototypes may be grown into substantial production deployments with relative ease through a simple yet flexible operator wiring and general-purpose scripting. We have argued that a primary ingredient in healthy application maturation is fast diagnoses of areas of concern as they arrise throughout the prototype process. Four areas of concern which we focused on were scale, longevity, data and integration. With Que, users can quickly assess application peformance in these areas. By leveraging several Que features such as unified system assembley, iterative data processing, and high-level interfacing, we have explored our new DataCenter.NET deployment, and validated the utility of Que as a general rapid prototyping tool.

References

1. How to choose the location for your next data center (it's the power stupid). The Data Center Journal (March 2006), http://www.datacenterjournal.com
2. Veriteq humidity and temperature mapping and validation with wireless data loggers (2007), http://www.veriteq.com/validation-data-loggers
3. 109th U.S. Congress. H.r. 5646: To study and promote the use of energy efficient computer servers in the united states (2005–2006)
4. Arumugam, U.: Rapid Prototyping and Quick Deployment of Sensor Networks. PhD thesis, Michigan State University, East Lansing, Michigan, USA (2006)
5. Bhatti, S., Carlson, J., Dai, H., Deng, J., Rose, J., Sheth, A., Shucker, B., Gruenwald, C., Torgerson, A., Han, R.: Mantis os: An embedded multithreaded operating system for wireless micro sensor platforms. Mobile Networks and Applications 10(4), 563–579 (2005)
6. Buonadonna, P., Hellerstein, J., Hong, W., Gay, D., Madden, S.: Task: Sensor network in a box. In: Proceedings of European Workshop on Sensor Networks (2005)
7. Carlson, D.: Keynote address. In: SenSys 2006 (2006)
8. Chu, D.C., Popa, L., Tavakoli, A., Hellerstein, J.M., Levis, P., Shenker, S., Stoica, I.: The design and implementation of a declarative sensor network system. In: SenSys 2007. 5th ACM Conference on Embedded Networked Sensor Systems (to appear, November 2007)
9. Corporation, A.R.: Demo abstract: A new embedded web services experience for wireless sensor networks. In: Proc. of 4th ACM Conference on Embedded Networked Sensor Systems (2006)

10. Elaine Cheong, E.A.L., Zhao, Y.: Viptos: A graphical development and simulation environment for tinyos-based wireless sensor networks. Technical Report UCB/EECS-2006-15, EECS Department, University of California, Berkeley (February 15, 2006)
11. Elson, J., Parker, A.: Tinker: A tool for designing data-centric sensor networks. In: IPSN 2006. Proceedings of the fifth international conference on Information processing in sensor networks, pp. 350–357. ACM Press, New York (2006)
12. Gay, D., Levis, P., von Behren, R., Welsh, M., Brewer, E., Culler, D.: The nesc language: A holistic approach to networked embedded systems. In: ACM SIGPLAN Conference on Programming Language Design and Implementation, 2003 (2003)
13. Girod, L., Elson, J., Cerpa, A., Stathopoulos, T., Ramanathan, N., Estrin, D.: Emstar: A software environment for developing and deploying wireless sensor networks. In: 2004 USENIX Technical Conference, Boston, MA (2004)
14. Gnawali, O., Greenstein, B., Jang, K.-Y., Joki, A., Paek, J., Vieira, M., Estrin, D., Govindan, R., Kohler, E.: The tenet architecture for tiered sensor networks. In: Sensys (2006)
15. Hill, J., Szewczyk, R., Woo, A., Hollar, S., Culler, D.E., Pister, K.S.J.: System architecture directions for networked sensors. In: Architectural Support for Programming Languages and Operating Systems, pp. 93–104 (2000)
16. Hunter, J.D.: Matplotlib (2006), http://matplotlib.sourceforge.net
17. Kohler, E., Morris, R., Chen, B., Jannotti, J., Kaashoek, M.F.: The click modular router. In: The 17th Symposium on Operating Systems Principles (2000)
18. Krause, A., Guestrin, C., Gupta, A., Kleinberg, J.: Near-optimal sensor placements: maximizing information while minimizing communication cost. In: IPSN 2006. Proceedings of the fifth international conference on Information processing in sensor networks, pp. 2–10. ACM Press, New York (2006)
19. Lee, E.A.: Overview of the ptolemy project. Technical Report Technical Memorandum No. UCB/ERL M03/25, EECS Department, University of California, Berkeley (July 2, 2003)
20. Lee, E.A.: The problem with threads. Technical Report UCB/EECS-2006-1, EECS Department, University of California, Berkeley (January 10, 2006)
21. Levis, P., Lee, N., Welsh, M., Culler, D.: Tossim: Accurate and scalable simulation of entire tinyos applications. In: SenSys 2003. Proceedings of the First ACM Conference on Embedded Networked Sensor Systems (2003)
22. Liu, J., Zhao, F.: Towards semantic services for sensor-rich information systems. In: Second IEEE/CreateNet International Workshop on Broadband Advanced Sensor Networks (Basenets) (November 2005)
23. Madden, S., Franklin, M.J., Hellerstein, J.M., Hong, W.: Tinydb: An acquisitional query processing system for sensor networks. In: TODS. Transactions on Database Systems (March 2005)
24. Malmon, D.: Personal correspondence. In: United States Geological Survey (2006)
25. Whitehouse, K., Tolle, G., Taneja, J., Sharp, C., Kim, S., Jeong, J., Hui, J., Dutta, P., Culler, D.: Marionette: Using rpc for interactive development and debugging of wireless embedded networks. In: IPSN 2006. Proceedings of the fifth international conference on Information processing in sensor networks, pp. 416–423. ACM Press, New York (2006)
26. Whitehouse, K., Zhao, F., Liu, J.: Semantic streams: A framework for composable inference over sensor data. In: Römer, K., Karl, H., Mattern, F. (eds.) EWSN 2006. LNCS, vol. 3868, pp. 5–20. Springer, Heidelberg (2006)

Device Driver Abstraction for Multithreaded Sensor Network Operating Systems

Haksoo Choi, Chanmin Yoon, and Hojung Cha

Department of Computer Science, Yonsei University
Shinchon-dong 134, Seodaemun-gu, Seoul 120-749, Korea
{haksoo,cmyoon,hjcha}@cs.yonsei.ac.kr

Abstract. To support the increasing number of sensor devices with various characteristics and requirements, sensor network operating systems should provide an appropriate device driver model that can cover a wide range of device types. Unfortunately, current sensor network operating systems force the user to build complex drivers for even simple devices, provide restricted interfaces, or do not provide any mechanisms. We present a device driver model that is flexible enough to support both simple devices with simple drivers, and complex devices with portable and high-performance device drivers. Users can write a device driver for simple devices with only a few lines of code using the user-mode device driver. Devices that need highly efficient code or portability can be supported by a single-layer or 2-layer kernel-mode device driver. Moreover, shared access and power management can easily be included in the device driver using the device manager. We also provide guidelines for choosing a proper device driver model with concrete examples of real-world devices and support our claims through the evaluation of the device driver model using the RETOS kernel.

Keywords: Multithreaded sensor network operating systems, device driver abstraction.

1 Introduction

Recent research in wireless sensor networks (WSN) technology has made various WSN applications possible, due to advances in sensor hardware and improvements in operating systems for WSN. We have developed RETOS [1], a multi-threaded operating system for WSN. RETOS features a secure operation of the kernel from mal-formed applications, support for multithreaded applications, and easy development of user applications. In order to support this last, RETOS provides various system calls, flexible modules, and an error detection service for user applications. However, it is still hard to guarantee flexibility in supporting various sensor devices through these techniques, and the operating system faces the non-trivial problem of developing hardware device drivers. Unlike in the PC environment, a standard interface for external hardware devices does not exist in WSN, and each sensor device has unique interfaces tailored to the purpose of the device. Therefore, supporting those sensor

R. Verdone (Ed.): EWSN 2008, LNCS 4913, pp. 354–368, 2008.

devices is complicated for sensor network operating systems. We have focused on two aspects of this problem. First, what is a device driver architecture that enables users to easily write their own device driver in support of operating systems? Second, what is a flexible device driver model that can support the various characteristics and needs of sensor devices? Our experience with previous research into RETOS has been highly useful in finding an answer to these problems, and the proposed device driver model exploits the dual-mode operation—user-mode and kernel-mode—of the RETOS kernel.

The proposed device driver model is designed to be flexible enough to meet the various requirements of the sensor hardware and support the diverse characteristics of the devices. Our model has three sub-models from which users can choose to write the most suitable device driver for their own hardware devices. For simple sensor devices that do not require complex operation and high performance, the user-mode device driver model can be used for secure operation and for writing a device driver. The 2-layer kernel-mode device driver model provides better performance and portability, with the separation of hardware-dependent and -independent code. The single-layer kernel-mode device driver has the highest performance of the three and is intended for devices that require high efficiency in device driver code. In addition, our model provides operating system level service for shared access management among multithreads and power management through the device manager.

This paper is structured as follows: In Section 2, we discuss previous research into device driver models and the characteristics of the RETOS kernel. The following section introduces the details of the proposed device driver model with its three sub-models, the device manager, and how to choose the proper device abstraction. In Section 4, we discuss concrete examples of building a device driver using our architecture. We evaluate our device driver model using RETOS in Section 5. Finally, we conclude the paper in Section 6.

2 Related Work

We have analyzed the previously proposed device driver models for several general-purpose, embedded, and WSN operating systems. Linux [2], NetBSD [3] and Windows Mobile [4] are general-purpose operating systems that have mature device driver architectures supporting a wide range of devices. However, their architectures are heavy and generalized for the requirements of WSN, due to the nature of their general-purpose operating systems. TinyOS [5] is a widely used WSN operating system that has a three-tiered device driver architecture [6] for greater portability and flexibility. However, it is hard to build a layered device driver for simple sensors, and our device driver model addresses this issue. SOS [7] and Contiki [8] do not provide any device driver model that enables users to write their own device driver. The device driver model for MOS [9] follows the POSIX model with its interfaces constrained to only four system calls: *dev_read()*, *dev_write()*, *dev_ioctl()*, and *dev_mode()*. This restriction prevents flexibility in the device driver for WSN hardware devices, which have various characteristics and requirements.

The proposed device driver model exploits the dual-mode operation of the RETOS kernel [1]. Dual-mode operation means that the stack for user threads and the kernel are separated so the secure operation of the kernel is guaranteed. Moreover, RETOS is a multi-threaded operating system, so several threads can request access to a device simultaneously, which can possibly lead to a race condition. To address this problem, a device driver model for such operating systems should handle shared access management. TinyOS 2.x [5] includes a dynamic resource management mechanism [10] that arbitrates shared accesses among multiple clients. Because TinyOS is a state-machine-based, event-driven operating system, unlike RETOS, the resource management scheme for TinyOS 2.x is not suitable for multithreaded operating systems. However, our intention for handling the possible race condition and providing proper power management is similar to their work.

3 Flexible Device Driver Model for Dual-Mode Kernel

In our device driver model (Figure 1), there are three different methods for building a driver for a hardware device. These are the user-mode driver, the 2-layer kernel-mode driver, and the single-layer kernel-mode driver. Each method has unique characteristics in terms of performance, portability, and ease of use. The user-mode device driver is simple, easy to build, and provides great portability at the expense of performance. The 2-layer kernel-mode driver has better performance than the user-mode device driver and good portability. The single-layer kernel-mode driver has the best performance but worse portability than the 2-layer kernel-mode driver. Therefore, device driver programmers can select the method that is best for their device. On the other hand, the device manager handles arbitration of shared accesses to specific hardware and performs proper power management based on the information regarding current peripherals in use. In order to achieve shared access management and power management, every device driver should obtain and release the right to use a device through the device manager before it actually uses the device.

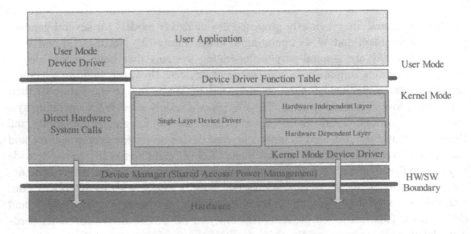

Fig. 1. The proposed device driver model

3.1 User-Mode Device Driver

The user-mode device driver provides the most stable and easy way to access a user's new hardware. It focuses on the fact that most sensor and actuator devices need a very simple interface with the microcontroller of a sensor node. For example, a device driver for a light sensor consists of simple access to the A/D converter (ADC) of the microcontroller, and possibly a little more code to convert the raw ADC readings into physical values. A device driver for the AC power control board controls the general purpose digital I/O (GPIO) of the microcontroller. Controlling the GPIO requires just one line of firmware code. Therefore, the main purpose of the user-mode device driver is to enable a device driver for simple hardware to be easy to design and stable by providing direct hardware system calls and abstraction of operating system level device management.

The user-mode device driver executes in user mode. The kernel therefore provides a set of primitive system calls, so the user-mode device driver can access the hardware. The primitive system calls are direct hardware system calls, which are a kernel-mode service, as shown in Figure 1. A device driver programmer can easily write a device driver for new hardware using the direct hardware system calls.

Because the user-mode device driver resides in user mode, it has several advantages over traditional kernel-mode drivers. First, the kernel is safe from a malfunctioning user-mode driver because the execution flows of the user and the kernel are separated. Second, a device driver programmer does not need to handle shared access and power management for the device. This occurs in kernel mode, and the direct hardware system calls already handle these issues. Moreover, writing code for a user-mode device driver is very simple and easy. Users only need to know how the device is connected to the microcontroller and write code to make the proper direct hardware system calls.

However, user-mode device drivers are not suitable for devices that require a complex interface to the microcontroller. Because the user-mode driver's access to the hardware depends on the direct hardware system calls, it cannot control the hardware in depth. Moreover, the user-mode driver has performance overhead. Because it executes in user mode, every time it requests the direct hardware system calls, kernel/user-mode switching occurs and causes system overhead.

Direct Hardware System Calls. The user-mode device drivers use direct hardware system calls to communicate with hardware devices. This is a set of system calls that provide simple access to the peripherals, such as ADC readings or controlling GPIO. Using these system calls, the user-mode device driver can read the ADC readings or control GPIO and provide device access functions to user applications.

The direct hardware system calls provide all possible interfaces that can be used by the user-mode driver to support a large range of devices. For example, the common microcontroller for the sensor node, MSP430F1611 [12], has several I/O interfaces, such as an analog to digital converter, a digital to analog converter, a general-purpose digital I/O, and a serial communication interface (USART), which can function as an asynchronous UART or synchronous SPI or I^2C interface. New devices can use any of these interfaces, so the direct hardware system calls expose these functionalities to the user-mode device driver.

In addition, the direct hardware system calls handle the operating system-level management of shared access and power. Because shared access and power management is tightly coupled with kernel behavior, the user-mode driver cannot communicate with the device management directly. Moreover, the responsibility of managing shared access and power is too great a burden for the simple user-mode driver; the user-mode driver is not intended for this. Therefore, to write the user-mode device driver easily and simply, the direct hardware system calls handle all the operating system services and let the user-mode device driver be concerned only with accessing its device.

3.2 Kernel-Mode Device Driver

Although the user-mode device driver has several advantages, many devices may still need the kernel-mode device driver due to performance issues or the complexity of the devices. For example, device drivers for radio chips or flash memory that supports a file system are complex and need in-depth hardware control and proper interrupt handling. The user-mode device driver has several drawbacks, such as kernel/user-mode switching overhead and limited ability with regard to controlling hardware. Therefore, the kernel-mode driver is for devices that cannot be handled by the user-mode device driver.

There are two different ways to build the kernel-mode driver to support a wide range of devices, as shown in Figure 1. The 2-layer kernel-mode driver consists of a hardware-dependent layer and a hardware-independent layer to increase portability, whereas the single-layer kernel-mode driver has no separation of hardware-dependent code in order to maximize its performance. Both methods have unique goals; hence, a device driver programmer can choose the model that is suitable for each device.

The device driver function table is necessary for communication between the user application and the kernel-mode driver because the kernel-mode device driver is written as a kernel module so it can be dynamically loaded and unloaded in the kernel. Moreover, the kernel-mode drivers should cooperate with the device manager to manage shared access and power. The behavior of the device manager is discussed in detail in Section 3.3.

2-Layer Kernel-Mode Device Driver. The 2-layer kernel-mode device driver separates the device driver into a hardware-dependent layer (HDL) and a hardware-independent layer (HIL) in order to increase portability. The HDL defines a set of primitive operations that are hardware dependent, and the HIL is implemented in a hardware-independent manner, using the interfaces provided by the HDL. Therefore, a device driver programmer needs to change the HDL part only when a new device driver for different hardware with the same functionality is needed.

The HDL communicates directly with the hardware and creates some level of abstraction to make the HIL part independent of the hardware. For example, the HDL part may include direct access to the memory-mapped I/Os or hardware-specific interrupt handlers. The HDL part then implements the details regarding small, meaningful units of hardware functions and provides them to the HIL part. The HIL part uses interfaces provided by the HDL part, which is an abstraction of the hardware, and implements the actual function of the device driver in a hardware-independent manner. For example, to make a timer device driver that supports virtual timers using one hardware timer, the HIL part implements the virtual timers using the abstraction of the hardware timer provided by the HDL part.

Single-Layer Kernel-Mode Device Driver. Although most devices can be supported by the 2-layer kernel-mode device driver, some devices are highly timing sensitive and require the best possible performance. For example, ultrasound device drivers are timing sensitive, so even 1 ms of error might be a big problem. Flash memory device drivers may need to be implemented in a manner that can reduce their latency as much as possible. To support this type of device, the single-layer device driver model is introduced.

The single-layer kernel-mode driver has no API separating hardware-dependent and - independent code, so it has less code and is more optimized and generally faster than the 2-layer device driver. The single-layer device driver can access the hardware directly at any time to reduce the delay caused by a series of function calls. Moreover, the single-layer driver usually has a smaller code and memory footprint than the identical 2-layer device driver, so it is useful for a resource-constrained sensor node platform.

However, the single-layer kernel driver loses its portability because hardware-independent code is mixed with hardware-dependent code. When performance or timing is more important than portability, however, a device driver programmer might want to write code with better performance. In this case, our device driver model can support the programmer.

3.3 Device Manager

In sensor network operating systems, several simultaneous requests to a device often occur at the same time. For example, one thread is trying to read a certain ADC port and waiting for the ADC to finish reading, and another thread can request access to the same ADC port. Without proper access management, one of the threads will not be able to obtain the result, or both threads might fail to read. Moreover, an even more complicated situation can occur. The widely used sensor node, Tmote Sky, has its radio chipset and external flash memory on the same port [11]. Simultaneous access to the shared port is impossible, and it needs proper shared access management. This kind of hardware implementation detail makes the device manager platform-specific.

Management cannot be handled in each application or each device driver because global information on the device access status is required. Therefore, our model has a device manager (Figure 2). By having a separate device management service, neither the user application nor each device driver needs to handle these issues directly. Instead, each device driver should cooperate with the device manager while it directly accesses its hardware, and the user applications are completely blind to those management services.

Moreover, the device manager can perform proper power management because it has global information on the device access status. The device manager can identify which peripherals are currently used. Therefore, the device manager can turn peripherals on or off properly and change the microcontroller's low power mode. Details regarding each device management scheme are discussed in the following sections.

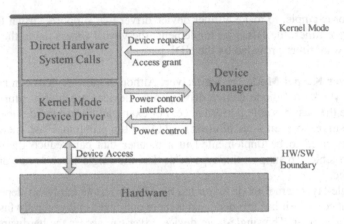

Fig. 2. The device manager

Shared Access Management. Every component of the kernel that accesses hardware devices—the direct hardware system calls and the kernel-mode device driver—cooperate with the device manager. When they need to use a device, they obtain the right to access the device from the device manager. When they have finished using the device, they release the right to use the device. This concept can be considered a binary semaphore. Each device in a sensor node has its own binary semaphore and the shared accesses to the device are managed by requesting and releasing the semaphore.

Several devices connected to the microcontroller on the same port can be managed by the device manager. These devices are accessed when another device on the port is not in use so only one device at a time is used by the device drivers. Because the device manager is aware of the fact that the ports are shared by several devices, each request to one of those devices can be properly granted. This is considered sharing one binary semaphore among several devices on the shared ports.

The following function prototypes comprise the interface for shared access management provided by the device manager. *request_device()* blocks the device driver and waits until the device is available; *request_device_immediate()* does not block and immediately returns with access to the device or error code when the device is not available. *request_device_timeout()* blocks the device driver and waits only for the specified timeout period. *release_device()* is used when the device driver finishes accessing the device.

```
devreq_t request_device(devid_t device);
devreq_t request_device_immediate(devid_t device);
devreq_t request_device_timeout(devid_t device,
                                 time_t timeout);
result_t release_device(devreq_t request_id);
```

Power Management. Because the device manager is aware of which devices are in use through the shared access management, it can determine the best possible low power state of the microcontroller. Moreover, in order to support proper power management, each device driver should provide device-specific power control functions that can be used by the device manager.

The microcontrollers used for the sensor node usually have a set of low power states with different peripherals available. For example, MSP430F1611 [12], used in Tmote Sky [11], has 5 different power modes with different clock sources available in each mode. Therefore, switching to the best possible power mode is necessary to reduce energy consumption, which is very important in an energy-constrained sensor node environment.

In addition to the power management of the microcontroller, device power management is important, as external devices usually consume more energy than the microcontroller. Generally, the devices for small sensor nodes do not have a set of low power modes as in the microcontroller, so the power management scheme is rather simple: just turn it off when it is not in use. However, determining when to turn the devices off or on is not trivial because the operating system should know which devices are currently being used. The device manager in our model tracks the set of currently active and inactive devices because every device driver reports its device use through the shared access management interface. Therefore, the device manager performs power management through the power control interface provided by each device driver.

Below is the data structure used by the device manager for proper power management. Each device driver initializes this data structure when the operating system boots. The *dev_access_ctrl* field shows the status of the device usage. The *power_on* and *power_off* fields are initialized by each device driver to provide power control functions for the device manager.

```
typedef struct
{
    devid_t device_id;
    devctrl_t dev_access_ctrl;
    result_t (*power_on) (void);
    result_t (*power_off) (void);
} device_t;
```

3.4 Choosing Proper Device Abstraction

The proposed device driver model has three different sub-models for writing device drivers—the user-mode, the 2-layer kernel-mode, and the single-layer kernel-mode device driver. Each sub-model has unique characteristics to make our device driver model as flexible as possible. Therefore, choosing a proper sub-model becomes important for exploiting the flexibility of our device driver model. In this section, we provide several metrics that can be used to choose a suitable sub-model.

Complexity. To decide between the user-mode and kernel-mode device drivers, the complexity of the device driver should be considered. The user-mode device driver has limited ability to access the hardware because it uses simple direct hardware system calls. On the other hand, the kernel-mode device drivers can access the hardware directly and obtain full control. Therefore, if the device driver is complex and requires full hardware control, the kernel-mode device driver should be used. If not, the simple and more stable user-mode device driver is sufficient.

Performance. The three device driver sub-models have different performance characteristics. The user-mode device driver has the worst performance among the three, due to the kernel/user-mode switching overhead and indirect access to the device. The single-layer device driver has the best performance among the three because the device driver can be fully optimized to reduce any delay in the code. The performance of the 2-layer device driver is worse than the single-layer but better than the user-mode device driver because no frequent kernel/user-mode switching occurs. Therefore, a device driver programmer should carefully consider the performance needs of the device and choose the device driver model accordingly.

Portability. If the device driver needs to be frequently ported to different hardware, a device driver programmer should consider using the 2-layer device driver model. The single-layer device driver mixes hardware-dependent and -independent code to optimize the code; it is not easy to port it to different hardware. On the other hand, only the HDL part needs to be changed if the 2-layer device driver model is used.

Size. In a resource-constrained sensor node platform, the memory and code size of the device driver is an important issue. Usually, the user-mode device driver takes up the smallest amount of memory and code because most of the hardware control and device management is already implemented in the direct hardware system calls and the user-mode device driver simply calls them. The 2-layer device driver model uses the most memory and code of the three, due to its separation of HIL and HDL parts. The single-layer is usually smaller than the 2-layer but larger than the user-mode device driver because it includes code for direct hardware access and management.

4   Application Examples

In this section, we provide examples and guidelines for building device drivers for various types of devices for a typical WSN platform. By using real-world examples, we demonstrate that our device driver model is flexible enough to satisfy the various capabilities of sensor devices and support a wide range of hardware platforms.

4.1 Analog to Digital Converter and Simple Sensors

The analog to digital converter (ADC) is a common device in a typical sensor node platform. From the viewpoint of a user application, its behavior is quite simple. User applications just need to obtain a digitally converted analog value and convert it into a physical value. This process is completed by requesting a direct hardware system call that accesses the ADC of a microcontroller. Therefore, the user-mode device driver will be sufficient for this type of device.

In addition to obtaining the ADC conversion, the user-mode device driver may want to configure the various properties of the ADC, such as reference voltage and different conversion modes. For example, the MSP430F1611 [12] microcontroller provides such capabilities on its ADC12 module. Therefore, the direct hardware system calls also provide such an interface with the user-mode device driver.

Below is an example interface for the direct hardware system calls that can be used to implement the user-mode device driver with simple sensors based on the ADC.

adc_read() returns a conversion value on the specified ADC channel. *adc_read_seq()* uses a sequence conversion mode that converts the series of the ADC channels. *adc_set_refv()* changes the reference voltage of the specified ADC channel.

```
uint16_t adc_read(uint8_t channel);
result_t adc_read_seq(uint8_t *channels, uint8_t num,
                                  uint16_t *readings);
result_t adc_set_refv(uint8_t channel,
                            adc_refv_t refv);
```

4.2 General Purpose Digital I/O with Simple Actuators

Typical microcontrollers for a sensor node platform have many pins that generate a digital signal. They are called general purpose digital I/O (GPIO). For example, MSP430F1611 [12] has 6 ports with 8 pins on each port, and ATmega128 has 5 ports with 8 pins and 1 port with 5 pins, which can function as GPIO. Usually, controlling GPIO is quite simple because it just requires setting or clearing a pin signal. Therefore, the device driver for hardware based on GPIO can be built using the user-mode device driver model.

A common example device of using GPIO is an AC power control board. It consists of several relays that can connect or disconnect the AC power line, and each relay is controlled by digital signals from the microcontroller's GPIO. Therefore, a user application can control various AC-powered home appliances by controlling GPIO. The device driver for this AC power control board can be implemented with the user-mode device driver model using the direct hardware system calls related to the GPIO functions.

An example interface for the direct hardware system calls related to the GPIO is shown below. *gpio_mode()* changes the pin behavior, input or output. *gpio_set()* makes a high signal and *gpio_clr()* makes a low signal on the specified pin. *gpio_read()* reads the signal on the specified pin.

```
result_t gpio_mode(uint8_t port, uint8_t pin,
                            gpio_mode_t mode);
result_t gpio_set(uint8_t port, uint8_t pin);
result_t gpio_clr(uint8_t port, uint8_t pin);
uint8_t gpio_read(uint8_t port, uint8_t pin);
```

4.3 Serial Communications

Serial communication is a common method for a microcontroller to communicate with various external devices. There are many types of serial communication interfaces, such as UART, SPI, and I^{2}C. These are standard interfaces defining how the microcontroller and the external device should be connected and how they can communicate with each other. Then the actual communication protocol is usually to send commands to and receive data from the device. However, all devices that use a serial interface have their own protocols. Because there is no general communication protocol for these serial interfaces, it is hard to generalize them into the direct hardware system calls. In addition, a device driver for this type of device should communicate with the device frequently to obtain data or configure the device. If the driver is implemented with the user-mode driver model, an excessive amount of kernel/user-mode switching will occur, which is a lot of overhead. Therefore, the kernel-mode device driver is suitable for serial communication devices. Moreover, a simple temperature/humidity sensor does not require high performance and optimization of the device driver code, so using a 2-layer model is acceptable to increase portability.

Let's look at an example. SHT11 [13] is a temperature/humidity sensor from Sensirion Inc., which communicates with a microcontroller via a 2-line serial interface. The actual communication protocol includes sending a command, receiving a measurement, resetting the sensor, and reading and writing the status register. Each communication is initiated by sending a pre-defined code to the serial interface. We can define the hardware independent layer (HIL), which is exposed to user applications, and the hardware dependent layer (HDL), which contains hardware-specific code, as shown below. The HDL contains code for generating a proper clock signal for serial communication and sending and receiving a pre-defined code. In addition, converting the sensor readings into a physical value is completely dependent on the sensor device, so it is included in the HDL. The HIL includes functions for a user to obtain physical values. The HIL part is implemented using the provided HDL functions in a hardware-independent manner. If a new temperature/humidity sensor is introduced, only the HDL part needs to be changed.

```
//HIL interface
uint16_t get_temp();
uint16_t get_humid();

//HDL interface
uint16_t convert_physical_temp(uint16_t reading);
uint16_t convert_physical_humid(uint16_t reading);
uint16_t send_temp_read_cmd();
uint16_t send_humid_read_cmd();
result_t reset_sensor();
```

4.4 External Flash Memory

It is common for a sensor node platform to have an external flash memory for logging sensor readings. To reduce energy consumption, the read/write operation on the external flash memory usually occurs in chunks of bytes. The read/write latency is also significant, and the communication of large chunks of bytes on the communication interface between a microcontroller and an external flash is timing sensitive. Moreover, longer operation time on those energy-consuming devices means a shorter lifetime for a sensor node platform. Therefore, the device driver code must be optimized for high performance and efficiency. Because the energy consumption of the external flash device is not negligible, power-down mechanisms are usually provided by the hardware.

The above characteristics of the external flash memory require that the device driver be highly optimized. Therefore, the single-layer kernel-mode driver model is ideal for such devices. Because the single-layer driver model has no separation of hardware-independent and -dependent code, it can be fully optimized to reduce any possible latency caused by following a layered architecture. Compared to the user-mode driver model, it has less kernel/user-mode switching overhead. In addition, having hardware-specific power control functions enables the device manager to properly manage the energy consumption.

For example, M25P80 [14], from STMicroelectronics Inc., is a 1Mb external flash memory with a high-speed SPI serial interface. The SPI interface supports a clock rate of up to 75MHz so it can operate at very high speed. The read operation occurs in chunks of 1 to infinite bytes with a single instruction, and the write operation can occur in chunks of 1 to 256 bytes. To support the high-speed SPI serial communication and reading and writing chunks of bytes, a fully optimized device driver with high performance is necessary. Moreover, the M25P80 supports a "deep power-down" mode, which typically consumes 1μA current. Therefore, a proper power control interface should be provided by the device driver so the device manager can control the power of the flash memory. An example of the interface to user applications provided by the M25P80 single-layer kernel-mode device driver is as follows:

```
result_t power_on();
result_t power_off();
result_t write_enable();
result_t write_disable();
result_t read_bytes(uint8_t *buf, uint8_t size,
                    uint32_t addr);
result_t read_bytes_fast(uint8_t *buf, uint8_t size,
                         uint32_t addr);
result_t write_bytes(uint8_t *buf, uint8_t size,
                     uint32_t addr);
result_t sector_erase(uint32_t addr);
result_t bulk_erase();
```

5 Evaluation

In this section, we evaluate the proposed device driver model using the RETOS operating system. We focus on two important points. First, we show how the user-mode device driver effectively reduces the amount of code to be written. Second, we compare the performance and portability of a single- and 2-layer device driver for the same device. The device drivers are implemented on a Tmote Sky [11] platform with an MSP430F1611 [12] microcontroller. A user-mode device driver for an acoustic sensor that uses ADC is implemented, and the amount of code is compared to the ADC device driver of the current RETOS kernel. In addition, two UART device drivers are implemented using the single- and 2-layer device driver models for comparison. Table 1 summarizes the devices and the applied model used for the evaluation of the proposed device driver model.

Table 1. The devices chosen for evaluation

Applied model	Device
User-mode device driver	Acoustic sensor
Single- /2-layer kernel-mode device driver	UART

The comparison between the driver in the current RETOS kernel and the new device driver model is as follows. Table 2 shows the code and RAM size comparison for the current RETOS kernel and the new kernel with the proposed device driver model. The measurements include the actual device driver codes mentioned in Table 1. On the MSP430 platform, the new device driver model introduces about 17% of the code size and 50% of the RAM size overhead to the current RETOS kernel. The overheads seem to be relatively big in terms of ratio but the absolute sizes are still small enough for typical sensor node platforms.

Table 2. Code and RAM size comparison

	Current RETOS	New model	Ratio
Code size	20.7 kB	24.3 kB	1.17
RAM size	1.13 kB	1.7 kB	1.50

The following code listing shows the amount of code for the acoustic sensor device driver. We see that only a few lines of code are needed for building a device driver for an acoustic sensor when the user-mode device driver is used. Without the user-mode device driver model, the programmer should know how to control complicated hardware registers to obtain a single ADC reading. However, the direct hardware system call makes writing a user-mode device driver simple and easy.

The current RETOS device driver for ADC

```
uint8_t adc_get(uint8_t owner, uint8_t channel) {
    if (adc_busy == TRUE) return FAIL;
    adc_busy = TRUE;
    adc_owner = owner;
    ADC12CTL0 = ADC12ON | REFON | REF2_5V | SHT0_6;
    ADC12MCTL0 = channel + SREF_1;
    ADC12IE = 0x01;
    ADC12CTL1 = SHP | ADC12SSEL_3;
    ADC12CTL0 |= ENC | ADC12SC; // start the conversion
    return SUCCESS;
}

interrupt(14) __attribute((naked)) adc_intr() {
    ...
    uint16_t data = ADC12MEM0;
    ...
}
```

The user-mode device driver for ADC

```
#define MIC_ADC_CHANNEL     2

uint16_t read_mic() {
    //direct hardware system call
    return adc_read(MIC_ADC_CHANNEL);
}
```

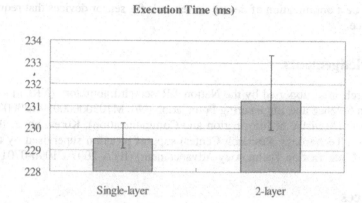

Fig. 3. Comparison of the execution times for UART device drivers

Figure 3 compares the execution time of a single- and 2-layer UART device driver. The total execution time for calling the *serial_send()* system call 1,000 times was measured. The single layer device driver is approximately 1.75 ms faster than the 2-layer device driver. The reason the single-layer device driver is faster is that it does not define an API isolating HIL and HDL, so it has less code and fewer function calls. Therefore, the single-layer device driver model is suitable for devices that need the best performance possible in a given hardware. On the other hand, the 2-layer device driver model has better portability because only the hardware-independent layer (HIL) needs to be changed when, for example, a different UART protocol is needed. A more interesting fact in Figure 3 is that the standard deviation of execution time is quite different between the single- and 2-layer drivers. Clearly, the single-layer device driver has a smaller standard deviation than the 2-layer device driver. It seems that the difference is caused by the fact that the 2-layer device driver uses an API defined by the HDL, so it has more function calls and bottom halves. This means that the 2-layer device driver allows more opportunities for interrupt handlings and bottom halves of other kernel behavior to be invoked because it has shorter critical sections than the single-layer. This indicates that the single-layer device driver should be considered when more stable performance of the device driver is required.

6 Conclusion

The main contribution of this paper is to present a flexible device driver model that can support a wide range of sensor devices that have various characteristics and requirements. Unlike current sensor network device driver models, our solution provides three different approaches from which users can choose the most suitable driver model for their own sensor hardware. Moreover, handling shared access and power management has been made easy with the device manager. The analysis in Section 4 and the evaluation results on a widely used sensor network platform support our device driver model. The user-mode device driver enables a safe and convenient building process for device drivers. The 2-layer kernel-mode device driver provides great portability in device driver code. Lastly, the single-layer kernel-mode device driver allows the best optimization of device driver code for sensor devices that require high performance.

Acknowledgements

This research was supported by the National Research Laboratory (NRL) program of the Korean Science and Engineering Foundation (No. M10500000059-6J0000-05910) and the MIC (Ministry of Information and Communication), Korea, under the ITRC (Information Technology Research Center) support program supervised by the IITA (Institute of Information Technology Advancement) (IITA-2007-C1090-0701-0015).

References

1. Cha, H., Choi, S., Jung, I., Kim, H., Shin, H., Yoo, J., Yoon, C.: RETOS: Resilient, Expandable, and Threaded Operating System for Wireless Sensor Networks. In: IPSN 2007. Proceedings of the Sixth International Conference on Information Processing in Sensor Networks, pp. 148–157 (April 2007)
2. Mochel, P.: The Linux Kernel Device Model. In: Mochel, P. (ed.) OLS 2002. Proceedings of the Ottawa Linux Symposium, pp. 368–375 (June 2002)
3. The NetBSD project, http://www.netbsd.org
4. The Windows Mobile operating system, http://www.microsoft.com/windowsmobile
5. Levis, P., Gay, D., Handziski, V., Hauer, J.-H., Greenstein, B., Turon, M., Hui, J., Klues, K., Sharp, C., Szewczyk, R., Polastre, J., Buonadonna, P., Nachman, L., Tolle, G., Culler, D., Wolisz, A.: T2: A Second Generation OS For Embedded Sensor Networks. Technical Report TKN-05-007, Telecommunication Networks Group, Technische Universität Berlin (November 2005)
6. Handziski, V., Polastre, J., Hauer, J.-H., Sharp, C., Wolisz, A., Culler, D.: Flexible Hardware Abstraction for Wireless Sensor Networks. In: EWSN 2005. Proceedings of the Second European Workshop on Wireless Sensor Networks (January 2005)
7. Han, C.-C., Rengaswamy, R.K., Shea, R., Kohler, E., Srivastava, M.: A Dynamic Operating System for Sensor Nodes. In: Mobisys 2005. Proceedings of the Third International Conference on Mobile Systems, Applications, and Services (June 2005)
8. Dunkels, A., Schmidt, O., Voigt, T., Ali, M.: Protothreads: Simplifying Event-Driven Programming of Memory-Constrained Embedded Systems. In: SenSys 2006. Proceedings of the Fourth ACM Conference on Embedded Networked Sensor Systems (November 2006)
9. Bhatti, S., Carlson, J., Dai, H., Deng, J., Rose, J., Sheth, A., Shucker, B., Gruenwald, C., Torgerson, A., Han, R.: MANTIS OS: An Embedded Multithreaded Operating System for Wireless Micro Sensor Platforms. Ramanathan, P., Govindan, R., Sivalingam, K. (eds.) ACM/Kluwer Mobile Networks & Applications (MONET), Special Issue on Wireless Sensor Networks 10(4), 563–579 (2005)
10. Klues, K., Handziski, V., Culler, D., Gay, D., Levis, P., Lu, C., Wolisz, A.: Dynamic Resource Management in a Static Network Operating System. Technical Report WUCSE-2006-56, Washington University in St. Louis (October, 2006)
11. Tmote Sky sensor node, http://www.moteiv.com
12. MSP430x15x, MSP430x16x, MSP430x161x mixed signal microcontroller, http://www.ti.com
13. SHT11 digital humidity sensor, http://www.sensirion.com
14. M25P80 serial flash memory, http://www.st.com

A Component Framework for Content-Based Publish/Subscribe in Sensor Networks

Jan-Hinrich Hauer, Vlado Handziski, Andreas Köpke,
Andreas Willig, and Adam Wolisz

Telecommunication Networks Group
Technische Universität Berlin, Germany
{hauer,handzisk,koepke,willig,wolisz}@tkn.tu-berlin.de

Abstract. Component-based architectures are the traditional approach to reconcile application specific optimization with reusable abstractions in sensor networks. However, they frequently overwhelm the application designer with the range of choices in component selection and composition. We introduce a component framework that reduces this complexity. It provides a well-defined content-based publish/subscribe service, but allows the application designer to adapt the service by making orthogonal choices about: (1) the communication protocol components for subscription and notification delivery, (2) the supported data attributes and (3) a set of service extension components. We present *TinyCOPS*, our implementation of the framework in TinyOS 2.0, and demonstrate its advantages by showing experimental results for different application configurations on two sensor node platforms in a large-scale indoor testbed.

1 Introduction

The publish/subscribe interaction scheme is a high-level service abstraction that is well adjusted to the needs of large-scale distributed applications [1]. The scalability and robustness of the scheme stem from the indirect and asynchronous type of interaction and make it particularly suitable for creating data-centric sensor network applications. In the content-based publish/subscribe variant, subscribers express their interest in events by injecting subscriptions into the system that contain constraints on the properties of the events. Publishers that generate events post notification messages to the system, and when a notification matches the constraints of a registered subscription, it is delivered to the corresponding subscriber (Fig. 1).

Any design for sensor networks is subject to tight constraints in terms of energy, processing power and memory. These constraints frequently drive developers to pursue vertically integrated solutions that are highly-optimized for specific scenarios but lack flexibility [2,3]. Breaking up the design into fine, self-contained and richly interacting *components*, has proven to be a viable approach for resolving the tension between the need for reusability and the efficiency costs of abstractions [4]. The flexibility provided by the component modularization,

R. Verdone (Ed.): EWSN 2008, LNCS 4913, pp. 369–385, 2008.

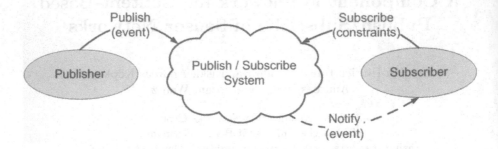

Fig. 1. A content-based publish/subscribe system

however, also carries the risk of overwhelming the application developer with the range of options for component selection and composition.

Component frameworks can reduce this complexity by imposing structure on top of the component model in the form of composability restrictions and by offering well-defined, service-specific interfaces to the rest of the system. Designing a component framework is a fine balancing act of *fixing* the service interface at a level of abstraction that will maximize the gains in productivity, while keeping those parts of the architecture with significant impact on the performance *flexible* enough to be able to benefit from domain-specific optimization [5].

In this paper we present the design, implementation and evaluation of a flexible component framework that provides a well-defined content-based publish/subscribe service, but allows the application designer to adapt the service by making orthogonal choices about the communication components for subscription and notification delivery, the supported data attributes, and a set of service extension components. The framework uses an attribute-based naming scheme augmented with metadata containing soft requirements for the publishers and run-time control information for the service extension components. It supports different addressing schemes and interaction patterns.

In the next section, Sect. 2, we present the general architecture and design rationale behind our concept. Section 3 contains a more in-depth discussion of the implications from the decoupling between the publish/subscribe core and the communication protocols. We evaluate the generality and flexibility of our design in Sect. 4, using experimental results from large-scale deployments of *TinyCOPS*, the implementation of our framework in TinyOS 2.0, on two sensor node platforms, under scenarios involving different types of applications, network protocols and extension components. In Sect. 5 we discuss the related work and Sect. 6 summarizes and concludes the paper.

2   Architecture

In this section we present the main features of the architecture in a top-down fashion, covering the naming scheme and API as well as the internal decomposition and extension facilities of the framework. The discussion on the implications of the decoupling between the publish/subscribe core and the communication protocols is deferred to Sect. 3.

2.1 Naming Scheme and API

To represent subscription and notification content, our framework adopts the attribute-based naming scheme presented in [6]: a subscriber expresses its interest in data through a conjunction of constraints over attribute values. Disjunctive constraints need to be expressed as separate subscriptions. A constraint is a *(attribute, operator, value)* tuple and represents a filter on attribute data, for example (*Temperature*, $\geq$, *30*). Publishers publish data in form of notifications containing *(attribute, value)* tuples, for example (*Temperature, 32*). A notification matches a subscription if every constraint in the subscription is satisfied by a *(attribute, value)* tuple in the notification.

If a subscription consisted only of constraints over attribute values a subscriber would not be able to explicitly influence the properties of the communication or sensing process like, for example, the sampling rate. Such control properties are conceptually different from the data constraints and can usually not be matched by corresponding *(attribute, value)* tuples in the notification. We extended the basic naming scheme by allowing subscribers to include *metadata* in subscriptions. Metadata is either exchanged between publisher/subscriber components or plays a key role in controlling service extensions (Sect. 2.3). It represents control information with soft semantics and is excluded from the matching process.

Metadata is represented by one or more *(attribute,value)* pairs, for example (*SamplingRate, 10*). Conceptually, it represents a notification that the subscriber attaches to the subscription. Metadata is specified per subscription and multiple active subscriptions may have different values for the same metadata attribute. Since metadata is non-binding a publisher may apply local optimization techniques: for example, in order to reduce sampling overhead the publisher may decide to combine two subscriptions that address the same attribute by sampling only once with an average sampling rate when the rates are similar, or using the maximal sampling rate when not.

The modified naming scheme is supported by two extensions of the basic publish/subscribe service: a "listener" service and a "matching" service. The "listener" service can be used to inform the application about newly arrived subscriptions, which it then can inspect to decide whether to start or stop publishing notifications. The "matching" service may be used by the publisher to check whether a set of attributes disqualifies it from matching a registered subscription. If, for example, the first collected attribute violates a constraint, collecting further data is pointless. When used, these primitives may result in a tighter coupling between publishers and subscribers than in the traditional model, but they have the potential to increase the efficiency of the data collection process, resulting in overall application performance gain. Fig. 2 compares our extended API with the basic publish/subscribe service.

Basic Publish/Subscribe API	Extended Publish/Subscribe API
	Subscriber:
Subscribe(C)	Subscribe(C M)
Unsubscribe()	Unsubscribe()
Notify(A)	Notify(A M)
	Publisher:
Publish(A)	Publish(A M , push)
	Listener(C M)
	Matching:
	Matching(C , A)

Fig. 2. The basic publish/subscribe API and the extended version that is provided by our framework. A square represents a set of constraints (C), metadata (M) or attribute-value pairs (A). The extended **Publish** primitive takes an additional **push** parameter which influences the matching point and is explained in Sect. 3.2.

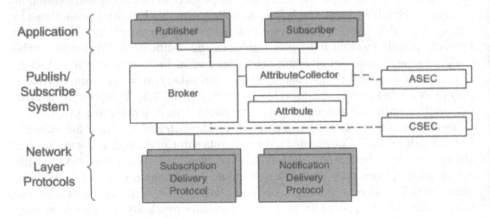

Fig. 3. The high-level decomposition of the framework

2.2 Core Decomposition

Figure 3 shows the decomposition of the framework. The Publish/Subscribe service is distributed and the figure represents an instance of the framework on one sensor node. A publish/subscribe application is divided into a variable number of *Publisher* and *Subscriber* components. A Publisher component can listen for subscriptions, collect data and publish notifications and Subscriber components can issue subscriptions and receive matching notifications. The *Broker* component provides the publish/subscribe service to the application, it manages the subscription table and it can apply the matching algorithm to filter out notifications that do not match a registered subscription.

The data ("events") that subscribers can subscribe to and publishers can publish are encapsulated in *Attribute* components. In addition to a data collection interface, an Attribute component must provide a matching interface that compares two of its data items based on an attribute-specific operator. The motivation is twofold: first, an Attribute component represents functionality that Publisher components should be able to reuse and access independent of the specific attribute properties (data type, metric, etc.). Secondly, matching operators are usually attribute dependent: for example, when sensor readings are affected by hardware-related jitter, the operator "=" should not be interpreted as the exact equality of two values. To increase modularity and keep the core matching algorithm decoupled, this information should be provided by the particular Attribute component.

Within the network, all attributes and operators are represented by integral identifiers. Attribute identifiers are globally unique, while operator identifiers are unique within the scope of a particular attribute. On the edge of the network a translation between identifiers and attribute semantics is performed using XML maps.[1] The *AttributeCollector* component structures access to the attributes: it maps a request based on the attribute/operator identifier to an actual Attribute component that is registered *at compile time* (but could even be added at runtime by dynamic over the air code updates).

2.3 Service Extensions

At the beginning of this section, we introduced the notion of metadata: by including metadata in a subscription a subscriber can influence the communication and sensing process. Often, such control functionality can be isolated in self-contained components for reuse in different applications. For example, a *caching* component could decrease sampling overhead by buffering frequently accessed attribute data when the considered data attribute has high direct sampling costs or is computationally intensive, like feature extraction from acoustic signals. We call such components Service Extension Components (SEC). A SEC represents reusable functionality that can be plugged into the framework without modification of existing code. A SEC can realize an additional service (as in the caching example) or extend the communication path with additional control information (timestamps, message sequence numbers, etc.). A SEC is associated with one or more dedicated metadata attributes, for example the maximum allowed caching duration, and made available by the application designer *at compile time* (it could even be added at runtime by dynamic over the air code updates). A SEC can be activated dynamically by a subscriber on a per-subscription basis by including an appropriate metadata attribute in the subscription.

The framework supports two different types of extension components, *Communication* SEC (CSEC) and *Attribute* SEC (ASEC). A CSEC can intercept incoming packets before (and outbound packets after) they are processed by the Broker in order to scan the included metadata attributes and, if applicable, perform a specific operation. It can, for example, be used to aggregate notification

---

[1] For lack of space we refer the reader to our XML specification made available as part of our implementation described in Sect. 4.

messages in order to reduce overall network traffic. Since CSECs can also be used to add control information (timestamps, etc.) a subscriber can use the CSEC(s) located on the publisher nodes to (conceptually) assemble its own message header by adding appropriate metadata attributes. ASECs are used analogous for attribute access: they can intercept the requests for attribute data and instead return buffered or processed data dependent on the metadata included by the particular subscriber.

In combination, metadata and SECs realize a soft "control path" in parallel to the basic publish/subscribe "data path". Since SECs are self-contained components and can usually be designed agnostic to data attribute semantics they are easily reusable in different applications and on different platforms. However, when multiple SECs are in use, their ordering must be defined by the application designer because it may influence their overall semantics.

3   Communication Decoupling

The classical content-based publish/subscribe systems have tightly integrated filtering, routing and forwarding mechanisms [7,2,8] resulting in more optimized, but less flexible solutions. Our framework departs from this tradition and decouples the communication mechanisms from the publish/subscribe core (Fig. 3). The core broker component has clean interfaces towards the external protocol components, thus *trading some of the optimization potential for increased flexibility* in selecting the subscription and notification protocols.

By exposing the choice of the protocols to the application designer, our framework allows the adaptation of the publish/subscribe service to the specific needs of the application. The type of the communication protocols as well as their energy consumption are likely to have a huge impact on the overall performance, and the application designer should be aware of these implications [9] to make an optimal selection for the particular application. In the following we concentrate on three important aspects of this decoupling and on the architectural features of the framework that address them.

3.1   Different Addressing Models

In contrast to the integrated solutions that rely on a pure content-based routing and forwarding mechanisms, the flexibility of our framework raises the challenge of interfacing with communication protocols that support different dissemination patterns like broadcast, multicast, convergecast, point-to-point, etc., using various addressing models like address-free, id-centric or geographic addressing.

To support this wide range of communication mechanisms we rely on three architectural features. First, the core of the framework is agnostic to the underlying addressing model, and all information relevant for operation of the service is encapsulated in the form of metadata, subscription filters or notification data. Secondly, the interfaces towards the subscription and notification delivery components are kept address-free. Finally, all the addressing information for the communication protocols is provided/consumed by their respective components or wrappers, while the framework provides hooks that facilitate its encapsulation and tunneling when so required. To illustrate this process, we examine the handling of the address information on the subscription and notification path separately.

Subscription Path. On the subscription path, a common delivery pattern is one-to-all (broadcast): a subscriber wants to receive notifications from any publisher with matching data in the network. This pattern is naturally supported by the address-free interface. In the case of one-to-many (multicast), the subscriber application defines the scope of the subscription delivery expressed as metadata attribute (hop-count, geographic scope, etc.) inserted in the subscription. The metadata is transparent to the publish/subscribe core and after registration of the subscription in the subscription table its content is passed onto the respective subscription delivery protocol component. The protocol component (or a thin wrapper) extracts the scoping attributes from the subscription content (via suitable accessor functions provided by the core) so that they can be used or translated into corresponding protocol parameters. Depending on the nature of the scoping parameters, this mechanism might increase the coupling between the subscriber and the subscription delivery protocol, but the publish/subscribe core does not require any adaption. An id-centric, point-to-point subscription delivery, although very atypical communication pattern for a publish/subscribe application, can also be supported with the this mechanism.

Notification Path. On the notification path, the message delivery patterns are potentially more diverse. To abstract from address information and decouple the application from the particular addressing scheme of the notification delivery protocol, we employ the mechanism visualized in Fig. 4: after a subscription has been issued by the application (1), the notification delivery protocol component (on the subscriber node) can use a hook provided by the core to add the local address of the subscriber as metadata information in the subscription, just before it is disseminated in the network (2).

The addressing information may be expressed using any naming/addressing scheme because the metadata value is transparent to the publish/subscribe core. After the subscription has been disseminated (3) and registered in the subscription tables of potential publishers (4), whenever a notification is published (5, 6) the notification delivery protocol instance on the publisher node can extract the particular source address of the subscriber and use it as address parameter (7).

Thus, the core provides two hooks to the notification delivery protocol: one for attaching the local address to a subscription on the subscriber node and one for reading it out on the publisher node. Both hooks are used optionally – if the notification delivery is, for example, based on flooding or uses data-centric addressing, it will neither add nor read any metadata to/from a subscription. In this way, the Broker, Publisher and Subscriber components remain shielded from the addressing models used by the communication substrate. Even more, the addressing on the subscription and the notification path is decoupled so different addressing models can be used with respect to each other.

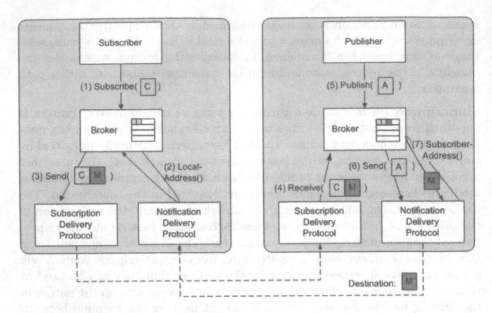

Fig. 4. Enabling different addressing schemes by tunneling address information as metadata between a subscriber and a publisher. Squares represent constraints (C), metadata (M) or attribute-value pairs (A).

At the cost of increased coupling between the core and the communication substrate, the same architecture can even be used to support a "classical" integrated content-based routing protocol. Through single-hop subscription scoping, the core can relinquish complete control over subscription injection and forwarding to the underlying integrated protocol, allowing complex schemes like subscription coverage or merging to be implemented. The resulting duplication of state (subscription table entries, etc.) can be reduced to a certain degree using hooks exported by the core facilitating buffer space sharing. The design of this support is one focus of our future work.

3.2 Control of the Matching Point

The departure from the integrated content-based routing and forwarding approach, brings to the surface the question of the "matching point" in the network, i.e. the point where the published notifications are matched against the content filters in the subscriptions. Since the subscription and the notification messages are delivered by potentially separate protocols that do not explicitly share common state, a conscious decision has to be made about where in the network this information would confluence so that it can be passed to the core for matching.

A misplacement of the matching point with respect to the application requirements and the selected communication protocols can result in significant performance penalties as notifications or subscriptions needlessly consume precious networking resources. In general, the optimal location of the matching point depends on many factors like network topology, ratio of publisher to subscriber nodes, frequency of subscription/unsubscription and publication, selectivity and locality of filters, etc.

Our framework supports two major scenarios by default: the filter matching is either applied on the publisher or on the subscriber nodes. Our decision is motivated by several observations. In many sensor network applications, we are faced with either a "pull" or a "push" interaction pattern, i.e. either a small set of subscribers is interested in notifications generated by a much larger set of publishers, or vice-versa, many subscribers are interested in the notifications from a smaller number of publishers. This means that the optimal approach involves either a network wide subscription dissemination with filter matching performed on the publisher nodes or network wide notification dissemination with matching performed at the subscriber nodes [9].

For the cases in between these two extremes, the framework can be extended with a CSEC that determines the optimal points using an integrated content-based routing and forwarding protocol, or from a dedicated "matchmaker" service [10]. The broker component provides a hook that CSECs can then use to execute the matching algorithm, without introducing tight coupling between the underlying protocols and the publish/subscribe core.

3.3 Protocol Impact on the Service Semantics

The selection of the subscription and notification delivery protocols is also influenced by the non-functional requirements of the particular application. For example, the application designer may be faced with a scenario where subscriptions need to be updated frequently and not reaching exactly all of the available publishers is acceptable. In this case a protocol for probabilistic best-effort subscription dissemination may be sufficient. On the other hand, an application may require more reliable dissemination of subscriptions and is willing to accept continuous control traffic in the background. In this case a reliable dissemination algorithm would be more suitable. If sufficient resources are available, the application designer might even choose multiple subscription or notification protocols in parallel.

Our framework does not impose any limits on the quality of service provided by the underlying communication protocols, effectively treating them as black box components. Whenever a subscription is issued or a notification is published, the framework will eventually convert the subscription/notification content into payload of the selected protocol component. The choice of protocols therefore has direct impact on the delivery semantics of the publish/subscribe messages, and with that on the semantics of the provided service.

The core itself is not influencing the quality guarantees of the underlying protocols, but SECs can be used to this aim, for example, by periodically retransmitting subscription messages, temporarily storing notification messages, etc. We contrast the performance and the semantic effects of different types of subscription dissemination protocols in the evaluation Sect. 4.

4   Evaluation

Assessing the full impact of a component framework is a difficult task. As with any other software architecture, the most reliable feedback ultimately comes from surveying users after extended periods of day-to-day use. The development of a reference implementation and its evaluation, however, can be considered as an important first step towards this goal. A real prototype demonstrates that the general design can be implemented under the specific constraints of the target domain. Furthermore, through careful micro-benchmarking executed in controlled, yet realistic setting of modern sensor network testbeds, it provides an opportunity for gaining deeper insight into the specific feature set and the involved design tradeoffs.

To this end, we have developed a reference implementation of the framework, called *TinyCOPS*, using the TinyOS 2.0 [11] execution environment. TinyOS 2.0 is a second-generation component-based operating system for sensor networks that keeps many of the basic ideas of its predecessor while pushing the design in key areas like portability, robustness and reliability.

For the evaluation, we have opted against head-to-head comparison of *Tiny-COPS* with other monolithic publish/subscribe frameworks because the overall performance of the frameworks is dominated by the underlying protocols and not the architectural features, there is currently no TinyOS 2.0 implementation of a monolithic publish/subscribe framework that would facilitate direct comparison, and even if such an implementation was available, the comparison results would be vulnerable to differences in the invested optimization effort.

Instead, the evaluation scenarios in this section are focused on demonstrating the flexibility and versatility of the design. We present results corroborating our claims that: (1) the framework exports significant performance tradeoffs to the application in an easy-to-use fashion, (2) the framework is general and flexible enough to support different interaction patterns and (3) the code, memory and execution time overhead is acceptable.

The presented data were obtained using TWIST [12], our multi-platform testbed for indoor experimentation with wireless sensor networks. TWIST provides basic services like node configuration, network-wide programming, out-of-band extraction of debug data and gathering of application data. It also allows to control the power supply for individual nodes, a feature we use to introduce node failures in the experiment described in Sect. 4.1. TWIST spans three floors of our office building and is populated with eyesIFX and Tmote Sky nodes in an approximate $3m \times 3m$ grid.

Starting with a simple data collection application scenario we present experimental results which show that the choice of dissemination protocols can exhibit considerable performance tradeoffs (Sect. 4.1). We then gradually increase the complexity of the application. Section 4.2 describes the integration of a send-on-delta service extension component and the effects on application performance and in Sect. 4.3 we show how *TinyCOPS* is used to extend the application with an alarm notification service realizing both "pull" and "push" interaction pattern at the same time. We then report on the code size requirements and processing time overhead in a typical *TinyCOPS* application (Sect. 4.4).

4.1   Tradeoffs in Protocol Selection

To demonstrate the tradeoffs that *TinyCOPS* exposes to the application designer through protocol selection we contrast two subscription delivery protocols: a plain flooding protocol (every node that hears a subscription broadcasts it to all its neighbours once) and an epidemic broadcast protocol. The latter is part of the TinyOS 2.0 core and based on the Trickle algorithm [13]: it lets nodes *continuously* broadcast status information about the subscriptions they have received. Whenever a node hears an older subscription than its own, it broadcasts an update to its neighbours. In contrast to the flooding protocol, which ends its operation after a short time, the epidemic protocol (called "TinyOS 2.0 Dissemination") remains active.

We created a simple *TinyCOPS* application with one subscriber and the rest of the nodes used as publishers. In our first measurement we disseminated the subscription via plain flooding. In the second, we used the TinyOS 2.0 Dissemination protocol. The modification is done by changing a single line of the *TinyCOPS* application configuration. For notification delivery in both measurements we use the TinyOS 2.0 Collection Tree Protocol (CTP) performing best-effort, multihop delivery of notifications to the sink of the tree (subscriber).

Both measurements lasted 90 minutes and were made with 86 Tmote Sky nodes, 85 publisher nodes and one subscriber (used as basestation, bridging to/from a PC). At time t_0 a subscription was injected asking for notifications to be published with a rate of one notification per minute by each publisher. After 30 minutes, at time t_1, one third of the publisher nodes (randomly chosen) were shut down and 30 minutes later, at time t_2, they were powered up again. Nodes that were shut down lost all state including subscription table entries.

Figure 5(a) shows the percentage of active publishers over time. We define active publisher as a node that has registered a subscription and published at least one notification. At time t_1 the number of active publishers decreases by about 30% due to our active power management. The difference between the protocols becomes visible at time t_2 when these nodes are powered up again: the epidemic Dissemination protocol quickly manages to spread the subscription to the recovered nodes, while the flooding protocol cannot (the subscription was injected only once at time t_0).

Figure 5(b) shows the changes in notification goodput perceived by the subscriber. We define notification goodput as the number of distinct notifications that arrive at the subscriber in a fixed time window of one minute. The curves almost match the number of active publishers and indicate a very good delivery ratio of CTP.

We used the serial backchannel of the testbed to let all nodes periodically output status information about the number of different messages they had sent over the wireless channel. This information allowed us to derive the traffic for

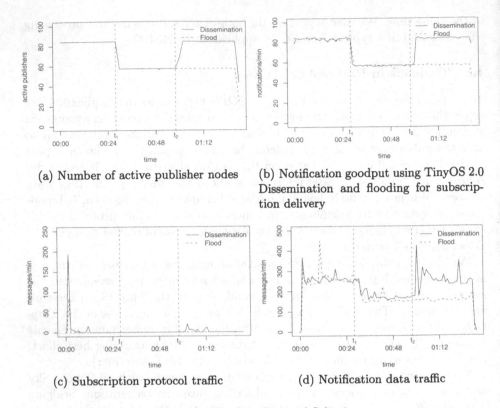

(a) Number of active publisher nodes

(b) Notification goodput using TinyOS 2.0 Dissemination and flooding for subscription delivery

(c) Subscription protocol traffic

(d) Notification data traffic

Fig. 5. Tradeoffs in Protocol Selection

subscription delivery as depicted in Fig. 5(c). The figure visualizes the tradeoff between the protocols: the flooding protocol generates one message for each node in the network at the time the subscription is injected. The Dissemination protocol generates more messages, but is able to update the rebooted publishers at time t_2. Finally, our setup allowed us to determine the number of notification messages sent in the network by all nodes over a time window of one minute (Fig. 5(d)) – on average 3 messages were sent per notification, however our setup did not allow us to differentiate between retransmission and forwarded messages.

4.2   Adding a Service Extension Component

To decrease notification traffic and effective energy consumption, we modified the baseline application described in the previous section to realize a "send-on-delta" approach: notifications should be published only if the attribute values deviate by more than Δ from the previously published notification. Δ is defined by the subscriber and specified as the metadata of the subscription. To make the functionality resuable we implemented it as a CSEC *SendOnDeltaC* that

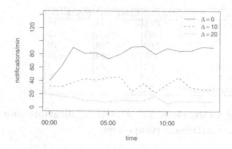

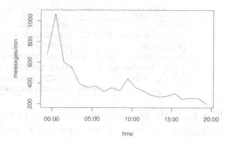

Fig. 6. Effects of a varying delta on notification goodput

Fig. 7. Example of a "pull and push" interaction

intercepts outgoing notifications. It maintains a buffer for the last published notification, calculates the difference between the attribute values and suppresses the publishing if the difference is smaller than specified in the corresponding subscription. It is agnostic to attribute semantics and can be used for an attribute with integral data type.

We performed three measurements with 86 eyesIFX nodes and varying Δ and observed the effects on notification goodput as perceived by the single subscriber. The subscription asked for light sensor data to be published with a rate of one minute by each publisher and Δ was chosen 0, 10 and 20, where 0 means that all notifications are published and 10 and 20 represent the Δ of luminosity in absolute values of the raw eyesIFX light sensor reading. Figure 6 shows the effect on notification goodput: with a higher Δ, more notifications are suppressed by the CSEC, giving to the subscriber application a powerful runtime control over the tradeoff between data resolution and communication overhead.

4.3 Creating a Combined Push and Pull Application

Previous work [9] has shown that the interaction pattern between publishers and subscribers ("pull" vs. "push") can significantly affect application performance and should be carefully aligned with the ratio of publishers to subscribers. We created an application that included two Publisher components, one for periodic temperature data collection and one for generating fire alarm messages. We wanted the fire alarm event to quickly propagate to all rooms of the office building, but periodic measurements to be collected only by a single subscriber. We therefore selected a single node to disseminate a subscription which notifications from the first Publisher component had to match (locally, based on the "pull" model). Fire alarms, however, were "pushed": whenever the second Publisher component detected a fire alarm regardless of any registered subscription, it immediately distributed the notification to all nodes in the network. The first Publisher component was "wiring" the subscription delivery protocol to the core and using CTP for notification delivery. The second Publisher component "wired" the flooding protocol for notification delivery.

Description	Component Name	PSLOC	Flash (B)	RAM (B)
Broker	BrokerImplP	671	2838	19
Send-On-Delta CSEC	SendOnDeltaP	103	1126	12
Publisher	StdPublisherP	180	738	70
Subscriber (+ gateway)	SubscriberGWImplP	138	554	129
AttributeCollector	AttributeCollectorP	87	154	4
CSEC "Glue"	CSECDispatcherImplP	115	98	2
Temperature Attribute	Msp430InternalTemperatureP	20	2	-

Fig. 8. Code Size and memory footprint of an example *TinyCOPS* application: one Publisher, one Subscriber, one CSEC and one Attribute component

Figure 7 shows a trace of the communication rates collected over 20 minutes on 85 Tmote Sky nodes. It represents the total number of packets sent by all nodes for a fixed time window of one minute. One subscription for periodic data collection is issued at the start of the measurement using the TinyOS Dissemination protocol, 10 minutes later we simulate a fire alarm, by sending a serial packet to one of the publisher nodes (randomly chosen). This node the started a flood of notification messages. The increase in traffic is visible by a small spike, however it is almost masked by the high level of CTP "pull" traffic.

4.4 Code Complexity and Execution Time Evaluation

We use the number of "Physical Source Lines Of Code" (PSLOC [21]), as well as the flash and RAM size, to evaluate the relative complexity of the major *TinyCOPS* components. The results in Fig. 8 show that the broker component is by far the most complex one in terms of code size. However, the framework allows composing lean applications, like the *StdPublisherP* component, which is a generic Publisher component included in *TinyCOPS* for convenience. It listens for a subscription and publishes corresponding notifications by querying the AttributeCollector for attribute data. The *Send-On-Delta CSEC* was introduced in Sect. 4.2 and can handle attributes of different integer sizes, a flexibility that is paid in increased flash consumption.

Building a *TinyCOPS* application involves making decisions about the Attribute as well as service extension components, the number of Publisher / Subscriber components and the respective communication protocols. As a result a typical TinyCOPS application configuration (defining the set of components that are linked together) can be composed with about 30 PSLOC – for comparison, the Dissemination protocol wrapper consists of 97 PSLOC.

To get an insight in the processing overhead introduced by *TinyCOPS* we measured the code execution time for the subscribe and publish operations on a Tmote Sky node. We used an application that subscribes to one attribute and measured the time it takes for a subscription/notification message to pass through the *TinyCOPS* core and protocol wrapper components (CTP / Dissemination wrappers). Under this scenario, the main tasks of the core were management of the subscription table and performing the matching algorithm. With a CPU operating frequency of 4 MHz, the subscription send-path took 144 μs and the subscription receive-path 281 μs. For notifications, the execution time for the send-path was 127 μs and 88 μs on the receive-path.[2] While the results are dependent on the time spent for matching an attribute-value pair with a constraint (we used the *TinyCOPS Ping* attribute), there are no additional "deferred" costs involved (for example, posting tasks or setting timers for later execution).

5 Related Work

The problem of providing an effective abstraction representing the sensor network services has been the focus of several prior works. The proposed solutions have ranged from database-like abstractions [3], application-specific virtual machines [14] to mobile agent systems [15] and abstract regions [16].

In [17], the SPIN family of protocols is presented, that use metadata-based negotiation phase to protect the network resources from unnecessary data exchanges. The content filtering capability in our framework has the same goal. In our case, the metadata part of the subscription message is used to convey a set of "non-binding" requirements from subscribers to publishers while the constraints express the imperative filtering. In SPIN, the metadata format is considered to be application dependent. We believe that the attribute-based naming scheme is flexible enough to support the majority of data-driven applications. Having a fixed naming scheme helps in optimization of the matching components and improves the portability of the application code.

Our naming scheme is much closer to the one used in the Directed Diffusion family of protocols [2], but we make clear distinction between the metadata and constraint and support attribute-specific operators. Conceptually, however, more important is the difference in the level of decoupling between the middleware service implementation and the communication protocols. Our framework not only delineates cleanly at this interface, it also allows for individual customization of the subscription and the notification delivery protocols and provides infrastructure for address information tunneling and matching point control.

MiLAN [18] is a flexible sensor networks middleware that continually tracks the application needs and performs run-time optimizations of the network and sensor stacks to balance the application QoS and the energy efficiency. It is positioned as a general framework that can also be used with resource rich wireless technologies like IEEE 802.11 and Bluetooth. Our framework is concentrated on the class of relatively resource limited sensor network hardware [19], where compile-time optimization has comparably large impact, and where the run-time modifications are mostly limited to parameter tuning (like the selection of the concatenation timeout).

Like *TinyCOPS*, the Mires middleware [20] provides a publish/subscribe service, but uses the component architecture of TinyOS 1.x. It uses a topic-based naming scheme that lacks the expressiveness of the content-based filtering. While

---

[2] For comparison: the time between posting a task and executing its first line of code takes 48 μs (assuming an otherwise idle system).

Mires envisions the possibility of introducing new services (like aggregation) using extension components, the choice of the communication protocols is fixed.

6   Conclusion

A major design goal of the presented content-based publish/subscribe framework is to separate out those service sub-tasks which are expected to have large impact on the resource usage. This decomposition strives to give an application designer a simple and flexible means to select protocol components and data attributes according to his needs, and to give him more fine-grained control over the publish/subscribe service through the concept of extension components.

TinyCOPS is the implementation of our component framework aligned with the design philosophy of TinyOS 2.0. The flexibility of *TinyCOPS* to support different sensor node platforms, communication protocols and interaction patterns has been demonstrated experimentally. On the example of a "send-on-delta" service extension component, we have illustrated how the framework can be augmented in order to give the application designers additional control knobs for trading-off different performance objectives. Our experiences with *TinyCOPS* suggest that by careful component decomposition and interface design, it is indeed possible to achieve a good balance between efficient resource usage and reusable software design.

References

1. Eugster, P.T., Felber, P.A., Guerraoui, R., Kermarrec, A.M.: The many faces of publish/subscribe. ACM Comput. Surv. 35(2) (2003)
2. Intanagonwiwat, C., Govindan, R., Estrin, D., Heidemann, J., Silva, F.: Directed diffusion for wireless sensor networking. IEEE/ACM Transactions on Networking (TON) 11(1) (2003)
3. Madden, S.R., Franklin, M.J., Hellerstein, J.M., Hong, W.: Tinydb: An acquisitional query processing system for sensor networks. ACM Trans. Database Syst. 30(1) (2005)
4. Hill, J., Szewczyk, R., Woo, A., Hollar, S., Culler, D., Pister, K.: System architecture directions for networked sensors. In: ASPL 2000. Proc. of the ninth international conference on Architectural support for programming languages and operating systems (2000)
5. Fayad, M., Schmidt, D.C.: Object-oriented application frameworks. Commun. ACM 40(10) (1997)
6. Carzaniga, A., Wolf, A.L.: Forwarding in a content-based network. In: Proc. of ACM SIGCOMM 2003, Karlsruhe, Germany (August 2003)
7. Mühl, G., Fiege, L., Buchmann, A.P.: Filter similarities in content-based publish/subscribe systems. In: Schmeck, H., Ungerer, T., Wolf, L. (eds.) ARCS 2002. LNCS, vol. 2299, Springer, Heidelberg (2002)
8. Hall, C.P., Carzaniga, A., Rose, J., Wolf, A.L.: A content-based networking protocol for sensor networks. Technical Report CU-CS-979-04, Department of Computer Science, University of Colorado (August 2004)

9. Heidemann, J., Silva, F., Estrin, D.: Matching data dissemination algorithms to application requirements. In: SenSys 2003. Proc. of the 1st international conference on Embedded networked sensor systems, New York, USA (2003)

10. Ge, Z., Ji, P., Kurose, J., Towsley, D.: Matchmaker: Signaling for dynamic publish/subscribe applications. In: ICNP 2003. Proc. of the 11th IEEE International Conference on Network Protocols, Washington, DC, USA (2003)

11. Levis, P., Gay, D., Handziski, V., Hauer, J.-H., Greenstein, B., Turon, M., Hui, J., klues, K., Sharp, C., Szewczyk, R., Polastre, J., Buonadonna, P., Nachman, L., Tolle, G., Culler, D., Wolisz, A.: T2: A second generation os for embedded sensor networks. Technical Report TKN-05-007, Telecommunication Networks Group, Technische Universität Berlin (November 2005)

12. Handziski, V., Köpke, A., Willig, A., Wolisz, A.: Twist: A scalable and reconfigurable testbed for wireless indoor experiments with sensor network. In: RealMAN 2006. Proc. of the 2nd Intl. Workshop on Multi-hop Ad Hoc Networks: From Theory to Reality, Florence, Italy (May 2006)

13. Levis, P., Patel, N., Culler, D., Shenker, S.: Trickle: A self-regulating algorithm for code maintenance and propagation in wireless sensor networks. In: NSDI. First USENIX/ACM Symposium on Network Systems Design and Implementation (2004)

14. Levis, P., Gay, D., Culler, D.: Active sensor networks. In: Levis, P., Gay, D., Culler, D. (eds.) NSDI 2005. Proc. of the Second USENIX/ACM Symposium on Networked Systems Design and Implementation (May 2005)

15. Fok, C.L., Roman, G.C., Lu, C.: Mobile agent middleware for sensor networks: An application case study. In: IPSN 2005. Proc. of the 4th Int. Conf. on Information Processing in Sensor Networks, IEEE, Los Alamitos (2005)

16. Welsh, M.: Exposing resource tradeoffs in region-based communication abstractions for sensor networks. SIGCOMM Comput. Commun. Rev. 34(1) (2004)

17. Kulik, J., Heinzelman, W., Balakrishnan, H.: Negotiation-based protocols for disseminating information in wireless sensor networks. Wirel. Netw. 8(2/3) (2002)

18. Heinzelman, W.B., Murphy, A.L., Carvalho, H.S., Perillo, M.A.: Middleware to support sensor network applications. IEEE Network 18(1) (2004)

19. Hill, J., Horton, M., Kling, R., Krishnamurthy, L.: The platforms enabling wireless sensor networks. Commun. ACM 47(6) (2004)

20. Souto, E., Guimares, G., Vasconcelos, G., Vieira, M., Rosa, N., Ferraz, C., Kelner, J.: Mires: A publish/subscribe middleware for sensor networks. Personal Ubiquitous Comput. 10(1) (2005)

21. Wheeler, D.A.: Counting source lines of code (SLOC), http://www.dwheeler.com/sloc

Author Index

Lecture Notes in Computer Science

Sublibrary 5: Computer Communication Networks and Telecommunications

Vol. 4268: G. Parr, D. Malone, M. Ó Foghlú (Eds.), Autonomic Principles of IP Operations and Management. XIII, 237 pages. 2006.

Vol. 4267: A. Helmy, B. Jennings, L. Murphy, T. Pfeifer (Eds.), Autonomic Management of Mobile Multimedia Services. XIII, 257 pages. 2006.

Vol. 4240: S.E. Nikoletseas, J.D.P. Rolim (Eds.), Algorithmic Aspects of Wireless Sensor Networks. X, 217 pages. 2006.

Vol. 4238: Y.-T. Kim, M. Takano (Eds.), Management of Convergence Networks and Services. XVIII, 605 pages. 2006.

Vol. 4235: T. Erlebach (Ed.), Combinatorial and Algorithmic Aspects of Networking. VIII, 135 pages. 2006.

Vol. 4217: P. Cuenca, L. Orozco-Barbosa (Eds.), Personal Wireless Communications. XV, 532 pages. 2006.

Vol. 4195: D. Gaiti, G. Pujolle, E.S. Al-Shaer, K.L. Calvert, S. Dobson, G. Leduc, O. Martikainen (Eds.), Autonomic Networking. IX, 316 pages. 2006.

Vol. 4124: H. de Meer, J.P.G. Sterbenz (Eds.), Self-Organizing Systems. XIV, 261 pages. 2006.

Vol. 4104: T. Kunz, S.S. Ravi (Eds.), Ad-Hoc, Mobile, and Wireless Networks. XII, 474 pages. 2006.

Vol. 4074: M. Burmester, A. Yasinsac (Eds.), Secure Mobile Ad-hoc Networks and Sensors. X, 193 pages. 2006.

Vol. 4033: B. Stiller, P. Reichl, B. Tuffin (Eds.), Performability Has its Price. X, 103 pages. 2006.

Vol. 4026: P.B. Gibbons, T. Abdelzaher, J. Aspnes, R. Rao (Eds.), Distributed Computing in Sensor Systems. XIV, 566 pages. 2006.

Vol. 4003: Y. Koucheryavy, J. Harju, V.B. Iversen (Eds.), Next Generation Teletraffic and Wired/Wireless Advanced Networking. XVI, 582 pages. 2006.

Vol. 3996: A. Keller, J.-P. Martin-Flatin (Eds.), Self-Managed Networks, Systems, and Services. X, 185 pages. 2006.

Vol. 3976: F. Boavida, T. Plagemann, B. Stiller, C. Westphal, E. Monteiro (Eds.), NETWORKING 2006. Networking Technologies, Services, and Protocols; Performance of Computer and Communication Networks; Mobile and Wireless Communications Systems. XXVI, 1276 pages. 2006.

Vol. 3970: T. Braun, G. Carle, S. Fahmy, Y. Koucheryavy (Eds.), Wired/Wireless Internet Communications. XIV, 350 pages. 2006.

Vol. 3964: M.Ü. Uyar, A.Y. Duale, M.A. Fecko (Eds.), Testing of Communicating Systems. XI, 373 pages. 2006.

Vol. 3961: I. Chong, K. Kawahara (Eds.), Information Networking. XV, 998 pages. 2006.

Vol. 3912: G.J. Minden, K.L. Calvert, M. Solarski, M. Yamamoto (Eds.), Active Networks. VIII, 217 pages. 2007.

Vol. 3883: M. Cesana, L. Fratta (Eds.), Wireless Systems and Network Architectures in Next Generation Internet. IX, 281 pages. 2006.

Vol. 3868: K. Römer, H. Karl, F. Mattern (Eds.), Wireless Sensor Networks. XI, 342 pages. 2006.

Vol. 3854: I. Stavrakakis, M. Smirnov (Eds.), Autonomic Communication. XIII, 303 pages. 2006.

Vol. 3813: R. Molva, G. Tsudik, D. Westhoff (Eds.), Security and Privacy in Ad-hoc and Sensor Networks. VIII, 219 pages. 2005.

Vol. 3462: R. Boutaba, K.C. Almeroth, R. Puigjaner, S. Shen, J.P. Black (Eds.), NETWORKING 2005. XXX, 1483 pages. 2005.